BOBBY FISCHER

BOBBY FISCHER

Profile of a Prodigy

BY
Frank Brady

DOVER PUBLICATIONS, INC.
NEW YORK

This Dover edition, first published in 1989, is an unabridged and unaltered republication of the 1973 revised edition of the work first published in 1965 by the David McKay Company, Inc., New York, under the title *Profile of a Prodigy: The Life and Games of Bobby Fischer.*

Library of Congress Cataloging-in-Publication Data

Brady, Frank, 1934–
  Bobby Fischer : profile of a prodigy.

  Reprint. Originally published: Profile of a prodigy. Rev. ed. New York : McKay, 1973.
  Includes index.
  1. Fischer, Bobby, 1943–   . 2. Chess players—United States—Biography. 3. Chess—Collections of games. I. Title.
GV1439.F5B7 1989   794.1′092′4 [B]   88-31001
ISBN 0-486-25925-0

Manufactured in the United States by Courier Corporation
25925010
www.doverpublications.com

To my two fathers

Introduction

Since the publication of the first edition of this book in 1965, I have been haunted by the image of Bobby Fischer. In a sincere attempt to capture his life on paper—he was only twenty-one then—I ran the obvious risk of having him outgrow a number of my conclusions. As he continued his dramatic career by way of a series of turbulent events, his life began to stand in virtual mockery of some of the opinions I had expressed. This is the inevitability of maturation set against the static quality of writing about a subject who is still alive and capable of change.

The first edition ended on a troubled, or certainly a concerned note, since Bobby Fischer was, quite frankly, in much personal difficulty at that time, trying to determine his direction. Now he seems to have found it. This edition looks at Bobby Fischer in a more positive perspective. The cause and effect are evident.

The interested reader is invited to compare the two editions. Where I was wrong in the first, I have admitted it in the second; where time and circumstances have invalidated certain conclusions, I have updated them; where the observations stand as correct, as I see them, I have allowed them to remain as they were.

The art of biography in chess has always been a delicate one, since masters have rarely considered themselves public figures. After Richard Twiss published an account of the life of Philidor in 1787, the great French champion refused ever to talk to him again. Paul Morphy, too, reacted coolly to the glowing tribute penned in 1859 by his obsequious secretary, Frederick M. Edge, and a schism resulted which was never resolved.

Bobby Fischer, however, has altered the literature of the game, the very history of chess, at least as far as he is concerned, by propelling himself into the international limelight and emerging as one of the most widely publicized American celebrities.

During my involvement in chess throughout the late Fifties, the Sixties, and now into the Seventies, in my capacity as referee, writer, and editor, I have continually addressed myself to Fischer and I have made a forthright attempt to understand and interpret his singular career. Fortunately, I've been a privileged witness to a number of behind-the-scenes episodes in Bobby's life. Perhaps most importantly, over the years I have had the opportunity of discussing the Bobby

Fischer mystique with some of the world's foremost chess critics, including many grandmasters intimately involved with his life, and including several former world champions.

One of the occupational hazards of all writing, especially in a biography in which the subject is as mercurial and active as this one, is the possibility of factual error regarding dates, times, and places. The first edition contained such mistakes, and I have diligently corrected them. Should any inaccuracies be discovered in this work, I beg forgiveness for my unscholarly habits and can only assure the reader that the demon of the typewriter or the filing cabinet are to blame, not any wish on my part to distort. My files, notes, cuttings, and tapes, what I like to think is virtually everything of importance ever written about Fischer in English, has become a ganglion of sometimes difficult-to-find research material. Mishaps are bound to occur on occasion.

Some readers might be plagued by the inclusion of material not directly related to Fischer's chess career. I can only refer them to Plutarch, who centuries ago taught that " . . . often some trivial event, a word, a joke, will serve better than great campaigns and battles as a revelation of character."

My selection of Fischer's efforts on the sixty-four squares, sprinkled with light annotations, depended on the depth and interest of the games themselves, win, lose, or draw; and I have committed the unbelievable heresy of including a simultaneous exhibition game—and even a lightning game—simply because I wanted to indicate Fischer's versatility under less than optimum playing conditions. All of the quotes found at the beginning of the chapters are Bobby Fischer's.

In spite of a bias in Bobby's behalf, to which I have always admitted (or else I would not have taken on the complicated task of writing about him), I have tried to remain as detached as possible. All sources at my disposal have been weighed, those of primary origin assuming first preference, of course. Speculation and even intuition have occasionally been used, and though these methods are admittedly not always the best, I hope my work has remained responsible. My motivation has been to look beyond mere facts, to grasp the deeper logic and meaning of Fischer's life.

In conclusion, there are a host of helpful people who deserve my sincere gratitude for assisting me in countless ways. George Wakefield of the Brooklyn Public Library, and Alice Loranth, Head of the John G. White Collection of the Cleveland Public Library, helped me with researching. Robert E. Burger, San Francisco's reincarnation of Sam Loyd, corrected my analysis on a large number of the games and included his own thoroughly imaginative and pungent notes. Guthrie McClain, Editor of the *California Chess Reporter*, allowed me unlimited use of his excellent library and acted as advisor and sounding board during many long, chess-filled luncheons. Annabel Brodie supplied me with ready reference material. Jim Ward of UPI in Copenhagen continually offered me information that I later found invaluable. Finally, I can honestly say that I probably would not have taken on the task of a new edition of this work if it had not been for the support of my wife Maxine: proofreader, grammarian, and friend.

Frank Brady
Reykjavik, Iceland
October, 1972

"A man of genius makes no mistakes.
His errors are volitional and
are the portals of discovery."

—*Ulysses*
JAMES JOYCE

BOBBY FISCHER

CHAPTER I

*"When I was eleven,
I just got good."*

The flag-stop town of Mobile, where Bobby Fischer began his schooling, is located in the Arizona desert about 35 miles southwest of Phoenix, in the shadow of the *Sierra Estrella* mountains. In the late 1940s, the town consisted of a one-room schoolhouse, a small teacher's cottage where the Fischers lived, and not much else. Regina Fischer taught her two children, Bobby and Joan, and seven other students who came from scattered ranches, some of them quite distant. Indians from the nearby Maricopa Reservation would occasionally pass through the junction on their way to the larger village of Gila Bend, twenty-eight miles to the west.

The Fischer children spent most of their time in the desert. In some places, stately stands of *saguaro*, the giant cactus that takes one hundred and fifty years to mature, provided them the only shade from the broiling sun. In other spots, *cholla*, with a spine of silver fuzz, and *ocotillo*, which looked like whips, were spread about in random patches. It was a colorful and vibrant place with living things under every rock. For the first time in their lives, the children had pets; a ground squirrel and an owl, which were captured not far from the house. It was a pleasant time. "It was the first place we were really happy," Joan fondly recalled years later. The peace of the desert, the slow, warm days, and a relatively simple lifestyle afforded the Fischers a respite from the hectic times of travel they had experienced since the end of World War II.

Water was so scarce and difficult to get that they had to devise a relay system for their daily supply, a different child each day bringing a bucket of water from home to school. Those who could afford it had bottled water trucked in from Phoenix, but most had to tote theirs. The indigenous water was so heavily flourided that a peculiar odor accompanied it, and therefore it was used mostly for washing. Soda pop and milk served as the most common drinks; but all of this was just plain fun for the children.

Early one afternoon, young Bobby strayed from the family environs and, after walking awhile, suddenly grew tired. An independent and

1

self-confident child, he sat down right where he was, and began to play. There was only one trouble: in his naïveté the playground he chose was the cinder-supported tracks of the Southern Pacific Railroad. There he sat. The Argonaut, Southern Pacific's New Orleans to Los Angeles run, sped through Mobile eastbound in the morning and westbound in the evening. Fortunately, the train was on schedule that day, or the subject of this book would have long since ceased to exist. He was discovered eventually by a frantic mother, and couldn't quite understand the reason for her excitement. Regina, who had had to be both mother and father to her children after her divorce in 1945, was a concerned and devoted parent.

Robert James Fischer was born in Michael Reese Hospital on the banks of Lake Michigan in Chicago, Illinois. The date was March 9, 1943, and at exactly 2:39 P.M., war time, after nine hours of labor, Regina gave birth to her first son. The young Fischer's sun was in Pisces, his moon was in Aries and his ascendant was on the cusp of Cancer and Leo. Astrologists have indicated a gifted birth since he was also born under the sign of the Grand Trine; many famous people, including Goethe, have this aspect as a part of their astrological story. According to Talmudic law the religion of a child is determined by the faith of the mother. Regina was born Jewish, though she was not particularly devout. Bobby, therefore, was considered a Jew.

His father, Gerard* Fischer, a biophysicist, was born in Berlin, Germany, in 1909. He and his wife Regina Fischer, nee Wender, separated when Bobby was two. Rumors, stories, and second-hand guesses have the father now living in Berlin, Germany; in Santiago, Chile; and even in the suburbs of Chicago. Fischer has never made a public statement concerning him. As his father absented himself from his son's life, so is he now prevented from figuring in any aspect of it, not even in simple acknowledgment.

Bobby's mother, though raised in St. Louis, where her father, Jack Wender, was a dress cutter, was also born abroad, in Switzerland. While on a holiday in the summer of 1938, she met Gerard and they were married soon after. She was about thirty-one when the divorce occurred, and she took charge of her family—Bobby and his sister Joan, who was then seven—with the determination and energy that underlined her whole relationship with her children. In the confused postwar period, with its strikes and swelling unemployment, she found all sorts of jobs to keep food on the table. She had worked as a stenographer, a typist, and even as a shipyard welder in Portland, Oregon, during the war. Moving south to Los Angeles, she found work teaching elementary school and continued doing this in Phoenix and in Mobile, Arizona. But Regina had other plans, and all of them included education. In 1933 she had enrolled in the First Moscow

* On some documents, the name is given in its German form, Gerhardt.

Medical Institute and had spent five years in the Soviet Union working toward a medical degree. Her marriage to Gerard and their subsequent emigration to the United States, with its staggering tuition fees and limited vacancies for women physicians, prevented her from continuing her medical education. But she was a qualified Registered Nurse and wanted to take a Master's Degree at New York University in Nursing Education. Hence, the family moved to Brooklyn. It is there that the story of the world's greatest chess player really begins.

Regina could certainly have found worse environs for the development of Bobby's talent. It is even possible that he would not have become what he is today if he had grown up elsewhere. This is not mere provincialism but a fact of contemporary chess life; in America great players just don't seem to develop outside the New York City area, and if they do, they quickly leave their hometowns. As painters and sculptors flocked to Florence during the Renaissance, and writers learned their craft in Paris during the last two centuries, most young American chess players eager to test their skills against the foremost masters, and possibly make a reputation, eventually find their way to Manhattan. About four-fifths of the leading masters in this country today are New Yorkers either by birth or adoption, and the remnant is widely scattered. Since Bobby Fischer is always the exception, and since his style could barely be discerned as emanating from the United States, let alone New York, perhaps his genius would have flowered anywhere. It's difficult, though, to imagine him blazing quite the rocket trail he has against any but that particular sky.

Brooklyn has an impressive chess tradition of its own. It is the home of the famous old Brooklyn Chess Club, where Frank J. Marshall first won his spurs before going on to take the U.S. Championship, which he held for twenty-seven years. But if Marshall was Brooklyn's chess hero, Hermann Helms was its saint. The undisputed Dean of American Chess, Helms was born in Brooklyn the year after Paul Morphy withdrew from competition. As a boy, he played against Morphy's great contemporary, Steinitz, as well as Marshall and most of the other titans of the game. Although once linked with his friend Harry Nelson Pillsbury as one of the two most promising young players in the country, Helms chose to be Caissa's servant rather than her master. In 1931 and again in 1932 he staged spectacular simultaneous exhibitions at the New York Seventh Regiment Armory where Alekhine and Capablanca each played two hundred opponents and drew record crowds for those bleak and dispirited years.

Long before this, however, Helms's reputation as a great worker for chess was well established. In 1904 he founded the *American Chess Bulletin*. In addition, he was a Life Director of the American Chess Federation (before it merged with the National Chess Federation to form the present United States Chess Federation). For over fifty years he covered chess for *The New York Times*—and, at one period or another, four other New York dailies as well—though his name will always be most lastingly associated with the old *Brooklyn Eagle*. He started his chess column in that paper in 1893, and continued it for sixty-two years, making it one of the most famous and influential in the world.

Up into the late Fifties, Helms could still be seen participating regularly in the weekly rapid transit tourneys at the Manhattan and Marshall Chess Clubs, the spirited octogenarian usually winning prizes and not infrequently capturing games from contemporary U.S. masters. He is easily one of the most beloved figures who ever graced the game, and his life spans the decades from the first great period in this country's chess history to the latest. By a coincidence as appropriate as it is uncanny, his hand was directly to touch the life of Bobby Fischer and help turn him decisively toward the career that made him the greatest force in American chess since Morphy, and perhaps the greatest player of all time. Because Morphy's "chess suicide" deprived Helms of ever seeing an American world champion, his role of minor catalyst in Bobby's life must have seemed an extremely rich source of satisfaction. We know that he rated Bobby's promise as second to none among the many greats he had known. He once told me, after a particularly brilliant performance when Fischer had barely entered his teens, "The boy is well nigh invincible."

Brooklyn is no longer an important center of creative chess. Both Helms and the *Eagle* are gone; so is the "Hawthorne Chess Club"— of which more will be said later. The Brooklyn Chess Club of today cannot in any way be compared in strength with the Marshall and Manhattan Clubs, which draw aspirants from every direction and tend to drain surrounding areas of their best young talent. But in 1949, the Brooklyn Chess Club still had a number of talented players as members.

After the Fischers moved east, Regina Fischer continued teaching for a while and then set herself to studying nursing at Prospect Heights Hospital before entering N.Y.U.

The family first lived in an apartment on Union Street, one block south of Eastern Parkway and within viewing distance of Prospect Park. Later they moved just a short distance to a four room apartment at 560 Lincoln Place, on the corner of Franklin, in a four-story yellow-brick building atop several stores where they could hear the roar of the baseball crowds from nearby Ebbets Field, home of the "Bums," the lovable Brooklyn Dodgers. The colorful neighborhood was middle-class-Jewish where just a few blocks away lived a great chessplayer whom Bobby would ultimately meet—though not as a neighbor—and both secretly admire and clash with many times over the years; the then U.S. Champion, Samuel Reshevsky.

Joan and Bobby were close. The story of how she kept him amused

with games purchased at the candy store over which they lived—
Monopoly, Parcheesi, and finally chess—is famous and has been told
many times. The two children, six and eleven, figured out the moves
from the instructions that went with the set, and for a time considered it as just another diversion. "At first it was just a game like
any other," Bobby recalled later, "only a little more complicated."
Even as a baby, he had been intensely interested in puzzles. "He
would get those Japanese interlocking rings, and things like that, and
take things apart I couldn't figure out at all," Mrs. Fischer remembered.

Chess, like music and mathematics (to which it may be distantly
akin), are the only creative fields known for their child prodigies. Paul
Morphy, Samuel Reshevsky, and José Raul Capablanca were masters
of the board as very young children. Some biographers of Bobby's
early years seem vaguely disappointed that he was not recognized as
a wizard from the moment that he first laid his eyes on a chessboard. The most obvious reply to this is that the age at which any
prodigy discovers his art (unless he has been deliberately reared and
tutored toward this goal) is an accident. And if he happens to discover it before he is fully able to appreciate it or utilize it, the art
may have to wait for the necessary maturity. In a child's development, one or two years can make an immense difference. For example, it was easier for Paul Morphy, who was taught the game at ten,
to start beating his relatives at eleven than it was for Bobby to start
taking on sophisticated players at seven or eight. As a matter of fact,
Bobby *was* doing so at seven and eight, and he began defeating his
elders—including players of practiced strength—by the time he was
twelve, which is just about the age Morphy acquired a reputation for
doing the same thing.

Yet even as a six-year-old, Bobby became increasingly fascinated
with the game and enjoyed enough success in solving its complexities
to avoid discouragement. He found a book of old chess games that
summer while vacationing at Patchogue, Long Island, and he spent
most of his time poring over it so intently that he would not reply
when spoken to. Although he probably played very few actual games
during these first two years, he played enough to whet his appetite.

Bobby claims he became seriously aware of the game when he was
ten years old, but actually he had started studying it at least three
years before that. By his seventh year he was so thoroughly absorbed
that his mother became worried. She decided to use the obsession as
a means of getting Bobby into contact with other children. But not
without difficulty: "Bobby isn't interested in anybody unless they play
chess—and there just aren't many children who like it," she said. She
attempted to place an ad in the *Brooklyn Eagle* inquiring whether
there might be other children of Bobby's age who would come and
play chess with him. Since nobody on the paper knew how to classify

such an ad, the editors solved the problem by rejecting it. However, her postcard, after gathering dust for a while, was finally passed on to Hermann Helms. His reply had better be given in full, not only because it documents the interest in Bobby's incipient career, but because it reveals so much of Helms's personality: the catholicity and sweetness of his old-world courtesy, the unfailing attentiveness to any matter or expression of chess interest from any quarter at any time:

American Chess Bulletin

(ISSUED BI-MONTHLY; $2.00 A YEAR)
ESTABLISHED IN 1904

150 NASSAU STREET

Telephone: BEekman 3-3763

CHESS PARAPHERNALIA
OF EVERY DESCRIPTION

Cable Address: CHESS, New York
Publisher: H. HELMS

New York 7, N. Y.

January 13, 1951

Mrs. R. Fischer,
1059 Union St.,
Brooklyn, N. Y.

Dear Madam:

Your postcard of Nov. 14th, mislaid in The Eagle office, has just reached me.

If you can bring your little chess-playing boy to the Brooklyn Public Library, Grand Army Plaza, next Wednesday evening at eight o'clock, he might find someone there about his own age. If he should care to take a board and play against Mr. Pavey, who is to give an exhibition of simultaneous play at that time, just have him bring along his own set of chessmen with which to play. The boards, I understand, are to be provided.

I will also bring your request to the attention of Mr. Henry Spinner, secretary of the Brooklyn Chess Club, which meets Tuesday, Friday and Saturday evenings on the third floor of the Brooklyn Academy of Music. It is quite possible that Mr. Spinner may know a boy or two of that age.

Yours respectfully,

H. Helms,

Chess Editor.

The late Max Pavey, who gave his simultaneous exhibition that winter evening in 1951, was a topflight master who had been Champion of Scotland. Bobby lasted about fifteen minutes against him. If the crowd expected no more of a seven-year-old, apparently he already did of himself.* He told me, many years later, that he had gone there believing that he would last much longer and do much better than he did. He was routed, of course, Dr. Pavey winning his Queen in about half the time that amateurs average against a master in simultaneous play. Bobby mentioned that the loss did a great deal to motivate him, but since he has been quoted elsewhere as saying that he did not take chess seriously until he was about ten, perhaps he was just reading these sentiments back into his early childhood. Still, for all who know him today, it's easy to believe that he was never an emotional amateur, and that he had a hard time taking a defeat even at seven. Certainly his whole life and character indicate that from the moment he emerged into public chess life he could scarcely imagine himself as less than the best.

Mrs. Fischer's aim of finding Bobby a chess playmate was realized that very evening. Mr. Carmine Nigro, President of the Brooklyn Chess Club, was teaching his son Tommy the game and offered to tutor Bobby also. Tommy was basically uninterested and Nigro, a chess lover all his life, greatly increased his son's allowance on those days that the boy "agreed" to take a chess lesson from his father. Nigro had no such problem with Bobby. He couldn't wait from week to week to take another lesson from Nigro. He became instantly and thoroughly absorbed in the game. He joined the Brooklyn Chess Club, and for the next few years he rarely missed a Friday evening. He played almost as frequently at the Nigro home and in Washington Square Park in Greenwich Village. He was by no means a consistently winning player, but his chess precocity probably helped him obtain a scholarship at a private school, Community-Woodward, when he was in the fourth grade. At any rate, his talent was encouraged there.

In addition to Tommy Nigro and Bobby Fischer, there were a few other children in the same age group, and Nigro mustered them into an unofficial team. Dr. Harold Sussman, a strong Brooklyn master, was teaching his son Raymond and a number of other children from eight to ten years old, and it was arranged for the two teams to meet, thus occasioning Bobby's first formal (though loosely structured) entrance into the world of competitive chess. The teams

---

* In the original manuscript of the first edition of this book, which Bobby read before publication to correct factual errors, I had written that he had expected to win the game. "That's not true," he snapped when he read the passage. "I never thought I could defeat a player of Dr. Pavey's caliber when I was only seven."

played two matches, the first ending in a score of 5–3 for Nigro's protégés; Bobby drew one game and won one game against Raymond Sussman. The score of the second match has been lost or forgotten.

Recollections of Bobby at the age of nine indicate that he was a fairly good player. One master told me that little Bobby would ask him to play constantly, and that even though he didn't win, he kept coming back for more. This same player, who for some unexplained reason asked me not to publish his name, went on to say of the nine-year-old Fischer: "I was impressed with his intuitive sense of the game and his swift thinking. His enthusiasm never flagged and he showed unusual concentration and willpower. He had chess fever early! His main tactic was to challenge me, which showed his strong will and ego view even then (I was rated among the top twenty players in the U.S. at that time). Although amused by the boy's tenacity, I did play him from time to time and while his talent was obvious, I did not realize that I was playing against a future world champion."

Bobby also spent time playing against his grandfather's cousin Jacob Schonberg, who also lived in Brooklyn. Regina would take the boy there almost every day when she was caring for him during his long illness and decline. Bobby would play the old man as he sat in bed. Years later he mentioned the incident to me, and though he was vague on the details, he was affected by the tableau. There was one other relative who played chess. Though he didn't know him, Bobby's great-uncle, Jack Wender's brother, was a strong tournament player in Switzerland.

People who knew Bobby as a small child say that he was fiercely independent and seemed to resent anything his mother told him. She had trouble controlling him and what she called his "chess mania," and felt that her son should be pursuing other interests. Dr. Ariel Mengarini, a New York chess master and a practicing psychiatrist, relates that he received a phone call from Regina Fischer asking him what he could suggest to curb Bobby's chess obsession. After telling her of his own fanaticism for the game, Mengarini said: "I told her I could think of a lot worse things than chess that a person could devote himself to and that she should let him find his own way. . . ." Bobby had no trouble doing that.

Toward the middle Fifties, Fischer was involved in other tournaments at the YMCA and the Brooklyn Chess Club. He didn't win any of these, but he had started winning games. "When I was eleven," he has said, "I just got good." The first tournament Bobby ever played in was the 1953 Brooklyn Chess Club Championship, when he was ten years old. He placed fifth.

In 1954, Nigro took Bobby and some of the other boys from the

Brooklyn Club to the Hotel Roosevelt to see a few of the rounds of the USA-USSR Match. Bobby was wide-eyed with excitement and no doubt dreamed of himself up on the stage competing against the best players in the world.

He began discovering his power through the realization that others did not have it; there were few Dr. Paveys at the Brooklyn Chess Club. Bobby tied for third-to-fifth place in that organization's 1954 annual tournament, just before he was twelve. This was the year that he got his hands on the ropes and started climbing. By May 1955, Bobby was competing in the United States Amateur at Lake Mohegan in New York, persuaded by Nigro, who had to persuade him all over again when the boy lost his nerve and decided that chess could best be enjoyed as a spectator sport. Fischer's wavering confidence may have had some bearing on his minus score. That summer, however, he joined the Manhattan Chess Club, one of the strongest in the world, and all summer long he played game after game, day after day, gaining marvelous experience and a "feel" for the game that has not left him to this day. He often was given the opportunity of playing against the club's finest masters. Reshevsky gave a simultaneous blindfold exhibition in which Bobby competed and he was ecstatic when he defeated the Grandmaster.

Occasionally Bobby would wander into Central Park and play under the open sky at the chess tables near the Wollman skating rink. This was a mixed blessing for his mother. She was delighted to see him get out of the chess club for a while and into the fresh air, but was consumed with anger and worry when he came home one day drenched to the skin from a rain storm. He had been in the middle of a complicated endgame in Central Park when the downpour began, and neither he nor his opponent could be persuaded to cease play. Already, Bobby Fischer was proving that chess meant more to him than anything else in the world.

"For four years I tried everything I knew to discourage him," Mrs. Fischer once said with a sigh, "but it was hopeless." Often it would reach midnight and young Bobby would still be out playing chess, and she would have to take the subway or use the old, often unreliable family car, from Brooklyn into Manhattan and literally drag him out of the Manhattan Chess Club and home to bed. She was certain even then that he would someday be world champion. "The sooner the better," she said. "Then he can get down to some real work."

Bobby won the first match held by the C group at the Manhattan Chess Club, and moved up into group B, where in due time he won their match also. Then he was placed in A reserve, just below the cream of the club's players. Still prodded by Nigro, he entered the U.S. Junior Championship at Lincoln, Nebraska, and despite a heat wave and temperatures of over 100 degrees, won half his games.

Boris Spassky, an eighteen-year-old Leningrad youth, had just won the Junior *World* Championship.

That year in late autumn, Bobby placed fifteenth among the sixty players who entered the Washington Square Park tournament in Greenwich Village. Harry Fajans, a master player at the time, said that when he beat Fischer in that tournament, Bobby walked away in tears. Many who knew him during these years confirm that he often cried when defeated. I asked him once if this were true. "Of course not!" he snapped.

My own first close glimpse of Fischer took place during the Greater New York Open Championship Tournament at the seedy and poorly lit Churchill Chess and Bridge Club in January, 1956. A crowd had gathered around one of the boards, where Bobby—dressed in corduroy trousers, a plaid woolen shirt buttoned at the collar, and black-and-white sneakers—was playing "blitz" chess with a boy slightly older than himself. One elderly kibitzer continually interrupted with advice. Bobby finally spun around and said, *"Please!* This is a *chess game!"* The man, a respected player five times Bobby's age, was silenced. The game of "blitz" continued under the gaze of slightly subdued spectators, now watching with the proper degree of seriousness that the invocation of Caissa and the authority in a twelve-year-old's voice had been able to command.

Bobby, who at that time seemed to me a sort of Tom Sawyer of chess, was being called "Baby *Pfuscher.*" Nevertheless, he made a 5–2 score, tying for fifth with Anthony Saidy, ahead of my plus score of 4–3 but behind McCormick, Feuerstein, Mengarini, and William Lombardy who won.

In the spring or summer of 1956 Bobby began frequenting the "Hawthorne Chess Club," which wasn't a club at all but the home of John W. Collins, a man who contributed at least as much to Bobby's early development as Carmine Nigro and who has been Bobby's friend, colleague, and advisor ever since. Collins held open house two or three nights a week at his residence in Flatbush, and Bobby had dinner there almost as often as in his own home. Jack Collins, a spastic who has been confined to a wheelchair all his life, was New York State Champion in 1952. He has always lived with his sister Ethel, a registered nurse. Both are gentle and friendly people with a deep sense of loyalty and affection for Bobby. It's fortunate, and revealing, that Bobby chose the Collins's as his *alter familia,* indicating a facet of his personality that he rarely shows to the public: that of a genial and soft-spoken member of a household, with a need for lasting and meaningful relationships.

Bobby played literally thousands of speed and off-hand games with Collins and the other regulars of the "Hawthorne," almost all strong masters, or at least lovers of the game, whose enthusiasm for the study of the history, culture, and theory of chess infused Fischer almost automatically. Even though he had been attracted to chess literature from the moment he saw his first chess book, it was not until Bobby started frequenting the Collins household that he began the gigantic reading task that has made him the most educated chess theoretician since the game entered its modern era in 1495. Collins had a substantial library and Fischer devoured everything: it wasn't long after that he began to collect a large number of books himself. I had the opportunity, in May 1972, of spending a few days going through the part of Bobby's chess collection that he was forced to part with because he no longer had room to store it all. It consisted of about 400 books and thousands of magazines and journals; about 90 percent of his total library.

His pencilled-in notes were fascinating. Interspersed with an occasional disparaging comment or punctuation mark pertaining to Alekhine or a reverent one concerning Steinitz, many of the books and periodicals contained corrections of the published texts or Bobby's observations and evaluations regarding positions, openings or endings. One of the most heavily annotated books was *Chess Openings—Ancient and Modern* by Freeborough and Ranken, published in 1893; on conveniently fly-leaved pages, Bobby had included reworked analyses to the Scotch Game, the Giuoco Piano, the Evans Gambit, the King's Bishop Gambit, and the Danish Gambit, among others. I found copies of virtually every modern chess magazine published in almost every language: from *Magyar Sakkelet* of Hungary to *Jaque Mate* of Cuba; from the Russian *"64"* to the *Philippine Chess Bulletin*, in addition to such bound volumes as Steinitz's *International Chess Magazine*, *Fernschach* and *Shakhmatny Byulletin*. A great preponderance of the material was in Russian. A copy of *The Soviet School of Chess* by Kotov and Yudovich, in Russian, appeared to have seen much service, whereas the English edition, also present, did not. Alekhine's *New York International Chess Tournament 1924* looked well used. A relatively obscure ending book, *"Finales de Peones,"* in Spanish, by I. Maizelis, had comments written under almost every diagram, roughly one hundred and fifty to two hundred different pawn endings. A book called *From's Gambit* by Dr. George Deppe was there, as was *Tchigorin's Selected Games* by Romanov, *Selected Games of Boleslavsky*, and even a collection of the games of *The First Inter-Army Tournament of Friendship, 1965*, all in Russian. Bilguer's *Handbüch* in editions of 1858 and 1874, Steinitz's *Modern Chess Instructor*, and *Chess Players' Manual* by Gossip were among some of his older books.

Books on the opening and tournaments comprised the major portion of the collection, with works on endings and games collections next in order of frequency. Tournament books such as *Zinnowitz 1966*,

Oxford 1967, Leipzig 1879, Berlin 1881, AVRO *1938* and *Kemeri 1937* were a part of the collection as well as dozens and dozens of modern master tournaments from every corner of the globe. If a pattern could be discerned as to which group of books looked more "studied" than any other, it would have to be major tournaments that Fischer himself did not play in, such as *Amsterdam 1964,* the *Piatigorsky Cup 1963, Moscow 1967,* and, yes, even *Sousse 1967.* (A complete discussion of the Sousse tournament begins on page 133.) Obviously, Bobby is aware of and probably remembers all the games (or certainly the significant ones) that are played in the tournaments he attends and needs only to study the games from those events where he doesn't compete.

There were a few popular tracts interspersed, such as Fine's *Practical Chess Openings,* Hooper's *A Complete Defense to P–K4, A Study of Petroff's Defense,* and *Theorie des Schacheröffnüngen* by Euwe. There were virtually no books on chess biography, history, or chess sets, with the sole exception (that I remember) of Hannak's biography of Lasker. Curiously, there were a number of checker books and periodicals including the *British Draughts Journal, California Checker Chatter* and *Checker Classic.* Fischer is interested in checkers, but unlike Philidor or Pillsbury, he is not a master of both board games.

Collins not only prompted Bobby into his first great spurt of chess reading, but he was also instrumental in teaching and encouraging some of the country's other young players—Lombardy, Raymond Weinstein, and the Byrne brothers.

A word should be said here about some of these younger American masters if only because they have played such significant roles in making Bobby the great chess player that he is. Actually, we've been living through a Chess Renaissance of sorts for a number of years now. To gauge its dimensions, though, requires a glance at the history of American chess in international competition.

In the Thirties, although producing no world champion, the United States unquestionably led every other nation in chess, winning most of the laurels in all the great contests from Prague in 1931 to Stockholm in 1937. That subtle collision known as the International Team Tournament began to look uncomfortably like an American sweepstakes, though it must be remembered that the Soviet Union did not participate in these events until after World War II. In 1945 the Soviets finally took up an earlier U.S. challenge, and the famous radio match was set for the fall. Most world chess opinion expected that the Americans would win, and so did the Americans. What happened constitutes one of the most abrupt and decisive watersheds in the history of the royal game. The American team—spearheaded by such proven champions as Denker, Reshevsky, Fine—was all but wiped from the boards by a group of relative unknowns, though Botvinnik was already a name to be reckoned with. Since then the seemingly invincible Soviet chess oligarchy—Botvinnik, Smyslov, Tal, Petrosian, Keres, Spassky, Geller, Taimanov, Bronstein, Averbakh, Polugayevsky, Korchnoi, Kholmov (to confine oneself to the better-known of the international grandmasters)—have traded the highest honors of the game almost exclusively among themselves.

While the Soviets were building their chess empire in the late Forties, the game in America seemed to be drifting. There was the usual cultural lag and disruption left by the war. But beyond that many of the most brilliant talents here, like Reuben Fine and Isaac Kashdan, retired from chess much earlier than players of their stature usually do. Economic pressures were to a large extent responsible for this. Although Reshevsky continued to play, off and on, he has been quoted as saying: "Never again will I permit chess to interfere with the more important business of caring for my family." It is possible that the disaster of the radio match was responsible for, or even symptomatic of, a general decline of élan. At the last biennial U.S. Championship tournament in 1948 (the year Soviet Russia captured the world title) many of the country's top players did not even put in an appearance. By 1950 the biennial was dead. The old ranks were breaking up. For them the great days lay behind. It would take the imagination of a new generation to see that comparable triumphs could be scored against the massive strength gathered in the Soviet Union.

These newcomers did not take long making their presence felt. The Chess Renaissance of the Fifties was announced spectacularly by two young New Yorkers, Larry Evans and Arthur Bisguier. In 1951 Evans won the U.S. Championship at eighteen; he also won a championship tournament in which Samuel Reshevsky was competing. Neither of these things had ever happened before, and opinion at the time was divided as to which was the more extraordinary. Bisguier won the international tournament at Southsea in Britain in 1950, then disappeared into the service for a while. He got out in time to enter the U.S. Championship of 1954, sweeping the field without a loss and taking the title from Evans, who had to content himself that year with the U.S. Open Championship. This latter is the second most important tournament in the country, and both Evans and Bisguier won it three times apiece before the decade was over. Both were named International Grandmasters in 1957.

Roughly of the same age group are Brooklyn's Robert and Donald Byrne. Their strong and steady play has made them threats in almost every annual Championship and has buttressed many fine U.S. teams. Late and unexpected American recruits are Pal Benko and

Lubomir Kavalek, who left Hungary and Czechoslovakia, respectively, for political reasons. Both are International Grandmasters. The Reverend William Lombardy has been one of the country's finest players since his teenage years.

Many other names might be mentioned (and probably should be) as among America's relatively better younger players. Anthony Saidy, William Addison, Bernard Zuckerman, and Edmar Mednis are of the slightly older group, and such men as Andrew Soltis and Kenneth Rogoff are of the younger. The important thing is that the Fifties and early Sixties witnessed a resurgence of chess talent of the first magnitude. These players, entirely on their own initiative and always hard-pressed for funds, have re-established the United States as a great power in the game the civilized world takes most seriously. They have shaken the Soviet Union's hold on the laurels, though it is true they have rarely borne them away. Only one young man emerged in America who could do that, and it was sadly uncertain for years that he ever would. As with Morphy, the brilliant stream of Fischer's success ran a swift, short course into the barren sands of renunciation; but unlike the lad from New Orleans, Fischer lifted and embraced the gauntlet. How his career faltered, then succeeded, and how he conquered not only the game but himself, is the story we now have to consider.

CHAPTER II

"All I want to do, ever,
is play chess."

"After the Greater New York Open, Bobby started slaying dragons," a friend once remarked. By his thirteenth birthday he was something of a celebrity, or at least a showpiece. The Log Cabin Chess Club of West Orange, New Jersey, took him on a tour to Cuba, accompanied by his mother, where he gave a twelve-board simultaneous exhibition at Havana's Capablanca Chess Club, winning ten and drawing two. On his return he gave another simultaneous at the Jersey City YMCA, this time playing twenty-one opponents and winning nineteen games.

He tied for first in the A reserve group at the Manhattan Chess Club, and outscored everybody in the New York Metropolitan Chess League series. Late that spring I went to Highland Park in Brooklyn to see the Metropolitan awards presented. My old friend Jack McKenna was to receive the highest B league award and Bobby Fischer was to get the highest A league prize. He had won four games, drawn one, and lost none. Bobby never showed up, and Carmine Nigro accepted for him. I knew Carmine, and asked him what the story was on this Fischer kid. "He's amazing!" Nigro said. "He's master strength."

But Bobby didn't live up to those words that May when he only tied for twelfth at. the U.S. Amateur in Asbury Park, New Jersey. I co-directed the tournament with Kenneth Harkness, and Bobby made little impression on us. But he was being watched by many who expected more than a showing. He did not disappoint them for long. Two months later in Philadelphia at the famous Franklin Mercantile Chess Club, Bobby became the youngest player ever to win the U.S. Junior Championship, taking eight games while losing only to the late Charles Henin and drawing with Arthur Feuerstein. He was awarded a portable typewriter and went off to play against masters at the U.S. Open in Oklahoma City, which was won that year by National Champion Bisguier. Bobby placed fourth through eighth with a score of 8½–3½ and was interviewed on television for the first time.

All this was much more fun than school, and in late summer he

15

descended on the even stronger First Canadian Open where he rippled through a field of eighty-eight, including five international masters, to tie for eighth-twelfth at 7–3. For good measure he gave Montreal a nineteen-board simultaneous exhibition, winning eighteen and drawing one.

Larry Evans met Bobby for the first time in Montreal and later reminisced about it: "He asked if I would drive him back to New York. I had no inkling that my passenger would become the most famous and phenomenal player in the history of chess. On that long drive home he barely glanced at the scenery. All he wanted to do was talk about chess, chess, and more chess. While my eyes were glued to the road he plied me with technical questions and we discussed complicated variations blindfold, calling out the moves without the sight of a board. His total dedication and relentless quest for excellence were apparent even then."

The Lessing J. Rosenwald Trophy Tournament had not yet become the contest that decided the U.S. Championship. But it was already the summit meeting of American chess, limited to the twelve participants considered the best in the country. In the fall of 1956 an invitation was extended to Bobby Fischer. He accepted. The tournament was held at the Manhattan Chess Club on Central Park South, where it was possible to watch the games through the windows of the Club by standing in the street in front.

The tournament was dominated and won by Samuel Reshevsky, the old master powering his way back to the top. The year was his, and he couldn't know that he was not to have another one for an indefinite period. Still, remembering his own famous victories as a child prodigy, it is easy to imagine him watching the adolescent Bobby with just a twinge of subdued jealousy. For it was Bobby who captured the imagination of everyone present. After a sorry start, he beat two of the best, Donald Byrne and Herbert Seidman. His game against Byrne was not only awarded first brilliancy prize but so awed Manhattan Chess Club Director Hans Kmoch that he immediately dubbed it "the game of the century." After weighing Bobby's play against the victory of Paul Morphy—who was also thirteen at the time—over Jacob Lowenthal in 1850, Kmoch decided that Fischer's win could only be compared to the twelve-year-old Capablanca's defeat of Corzo, and he maintained that Bobby's game not only matched this latter in depth of conception but surpassed it in originality. To celebrate, Bobby dined with his mother and a fan in a midtown restaurant that night.

A few weeks later, Bobby gave a simultaneous at the Jamaica Chess Club on Long Island. He won eleven and drew one.

On Thanksgiving Day weekend, Bobby had his traditional turkey dinner in Washington, D.C., in between rounds of the strong Eastern States Open. Berliner came first out of fifty-six players with 6–1 and

Feuerstein, Fischer, Lombardy, and Rossolimo tied for second to fifth at 5½–1½. It was Bobby's best score in a major tournament to date.

Bobby began 1957 by failing to qualify for the Manhattan Club's championship tournament, losing an important game to Max Pavey, the first master he had ever played. Then he made up for it by winning all his games in the Metropolitan League series that spring. He was promptly matched in an exhibition with a former World Champion, the visiting Dutch International Grandmaster, Dr. Max Euwe; Bobby lost creditably with one draw in two games. Fischer then placed a mere seventh in the New Western Open in Milwaukee, the prizes being carried off by Donald Byrne and Larry Evans. Bobby's official rating was now that of Master, the youngest player in the United States to have that title. Some of the wits among his teenage friends now addressed him as "Master Master Fischer."

Stimulated and rankled by these successes and defeats, Bobby flew to San Francisco and plunged into the U.S. Junior Championship tournament. It was held at the Spreckels Dairy Co. and the boys received free ice cream every day. After a week of grueling rounds, Fischer emerged with eight wins and took the title again. And, for good measure, he won first prize in the United States Junior Speed Championship, for which he received a copy of the 1956 Candidates Tournament Book by Euwe and Muhring. Little did he know, but he must have certainly dreamed, that he would be playing in the very next Candidates Tournament for the championship of the world.

As Fischer and the California players, William Addison, Gil Ramirez, and William Rebold drove to Cleveland from San Francisco in chessmaster Guthrie McClain's old car, they played countless games on their pocket sets as they crossed the continent. All were bound for the U.S. Open Championship, and Bobby was eager for another crack at the title. By now, his name was being bandied about all over the world, even in the Soviet Union. *Shakhmatny Byulletin* published his game with Donald Byrne, as did just about every other chess publication in the world. The U.S. Chess Federation received an official invitation for Bobby to visit Russia.

New York City, July 17, 1957

Mr. Ernest Mehwald, Financial Director
The U. S. Open Championship
1374 West 117th Street
Cleveland 7, Ohio

Dear Mr. Mehwald:

The Chess Section of the USSR has expressed interest in having Bobby Fischer visit the Soviet Union on the basis that they would pay his expenses while there but not the transportation to and from the Soviet Union.

Enclosed is a copy of a notice sent yesterday to a number of TV and radio stations as well as to chess columnists and chess clubs.

Public interest in Bobby and in such a trip may make it possible to obtain national TV and radio coverage of the U. S. Open and also for the send-off if the trip materializes. Perhaps Mr. Cyrus Eaton could be interested in assisting financially.

Please let me know your reaction and advise of any possibilities that occur to you or any action you want me to undertake here.

Sincerely yours,

Kenneth Harkness
Business Manager
U. S. Chess Federation.

REPLY

United States Chess Federation
Kenneth Harkness, Business Manager
80 East 11th Street
New York 3, N.Y.

Dear Mr. Harkness:

Received yours in regard to Bobby Fischer. Mrs. Fischer had notified me of his entry in the Open some time ago.

Last week I received a long distance call from Mrs. Fischer, and did not make any rash promises, but investigated the possibilities of financial assistance. After talking to several members of the Finance Committee the consensus of opinion is:

We cannot guarantee any financial assistance at this late date. The Open as a whole comes first, before individual requests. We will use any publicity material submitted by you and try to arouse public interest. We have no way of contacting very rich chess friends.

Every one of us would like to see Bobby go, but we have a hard enough job ahead of us to come up with sufficient funds for the Open.

My personal opinion is that this could have been done easily if there would have been more time, but with visas and preparations and so forth it is very uncertain, if the

financial angle is not solved first. I promised Mrs. Fischer
that I personally would see to it that Bobby is well taken
care of during his stay in Cleveland, but that is all I can do
at this time.

Yours very truly, for Chess,

Ernest Mehwald, Chairman
Finance Committee,
Cleveland Chess Association

The trip failed to materialize in 1957, but Fischer was determined
that one day he would visit the Soviet Union and play some of their
finest masters.

As to the U.S. Open, when the dust had settled, Bobby had drawn
in the last round with Walter Shipman, and found himself tied with
Arthur Bisguier and declared the winner on tie-breaking points.
Bisguier quipped: "Who could have seen in the early stages, by not
winning against Fischer, I created a Frankenstein!" Bobby's prize was
$750, which was considerably more like a Champion's award than
the second portable typewriter he had been given for recapturing the
Junior Championship in San Francisco. The rewards in chess, at least
then, were not those of golf.

Many, however, still chose to live the game, and by now Bobby's
name was being mentioned with such professionals in chess centers
throughout the world. He had already been invited to play in the international Christmas Tournament held each year at Hastings, England, where Harry Nelson Pillsbury had won his greatest victory
more than sixty years before. Meanwhile the Pepsi-Cola Company
sponsored a match with the nineteen-year-old Philippine Junior
Champion, Rodolfo Tan Cardoso, which Bobby won rather easily. He
was awarded a prize of $325. He also picked up the New Jersey
Open Championship: his third title, fourth prize, and fifth major win
in 1957. It had been quite a year, and Fischer paused to survey the
field.

Coming up in midwinter for the first time in four years was the
United States Chess Championship tournament. The U.S. Championship was also the Zonal Tournament, which would qualify the two
top scorers to compete with the winners of other Zonals at the next
Interzonal Tournament. The Zonal-Interzonal-Candidates system is a
complicated arrangement by which the governing body of world
chess, the *Fédération Internationale des Échecs* (FIDE), determines
who is to get the chance to play against the World Champion. Never
one to lower his sights, Bobby forgot about Hastings, and it is my
belief that at this precise moment in his life, at the age of fourteen,
Fischer not only wanted to fight for the World's Championship title
but actually believed he could win it. Although the U.S. Champion-

ship was being held on an annual basis, the forthcoming Interzonal would not occur again for another four years. At fourteen Bobby couldn't afford to wait. Once again he entered the Rosenwald tournament, and to get into playing shape he flew to Milwaukee for the North Central Championship tournament, where he was soundly trounced by Popel and Kalme, ending up in sixth place. If this weakened his nerve, it wasn't apparent. He then played a short training match with Dr. Daniel J. Benninson, a strong Argentine player, who was a scientist with the Committee on the Effects of Atomic Radiation for the U.N. The match was played at the Marshall Chess Club and ended in Bobby's favor 3½–1½.

The U.S. Championship tournament got under way at the Manhattan Chess Club in December. It was to continue at the Marshall and go through fourteen rounds into the new year. International Grandmaster Bisguier was defending champion. World Junior Champion Lombardy was a strong favorite, and International Grandmaster Reshevsky even stronger.

Not that Bobby wasn't widely respected, and even feared. He had won the U.S. Open over Bisguier, and was known as a formidable, if uneven, prodigy who could possibly beat anyone, anytime. With a few years of seasoning he would undoubtedly be great. But as for now—well, after all, Reshevsky had been U.S. Champion four times.

Just before play began, Bisguier said: "Bobby Fischer should finish slightly over the center mark in this tournament. He is quite possibly the most gifted of all players in the tournament; still he has had no experience in tournaments of such consistently even strength."

It was the Centennial Anniversary of the U.S. Chess Championship; the first, in 1857, then called The First American Chess Congress, was won by a young man hardly out of his teens: Paul Morphy.

Bobby, his gaze fixed on the board, solemn-eyed under bangs, was the center of attention at each table where he sat facing the men of solid reputation, the best players in the land. He drew more and more interest as the rounds progressed and scores were posted. Starting with a win over Arthur Feuerstein, he drew with Herbert Seidman, then battled Reshevsky to a standstill in a game of such concentrated will and momentum that it continued after adjournment even though both players had recognized the inevitable draw long before. Round followed round, day after day. Each round brought a new and highly skilled opponent and a fresh set of problems. Bobby played them one at a time—beating Sidney Bernstein, crushing Arthur Bisguier, drawing a confusing game with Hans Berliner. Move by move he developed his openings, tapping the knowledge he had absorbed during the years of poring over diagrams and annotations and analyses. He scored five straight victories, beating James Sherwin, George Kramer, Edmar Mednis, William Lombardy, and Attilo di Camillo. In the final rounds he was a full point

ahead of Reshevsky, who suffered a stunning defeat at the hands of
Lombardy. He tried for a win against ex-Champion Arnold Denker,
settled for a draw, and coasted through a final game he was quite
content to draw with Abe Turner. It was the second week of January,
1958, a few months before his fifteenth birthday, and Bobby Fischer
was Chess Champion of the United States.

American chess will probably never quite get over the wonder and
admiration and envy and excitement of that winter. Larry Evans had
won the Championship as a young man; Bobby was scarcely out of
childhood.

As *Chess Review* neatly phrased it: "Against formidable competition, headed by Reshevsky, he became champion of the United States,
thus making the unique jump from amateur to grandmaster—probably not Grandmaster *de jure*, but certainly *de facto*."

The chess world buzzed with talk of Fischer. Thirteen games
without a loss against the nation's best was certainly convincing; the
boy must be an authentic genius. Yet speculation was mixed with
anxiety. Could he repeat such a performance? How would he do
against the Russians? And what sort of person was the new champion? Some already considered him eccentric and difficult, and there
was no predicting what the impact of fame would do to a child. In
turn, how would it affect his game? The game itself? At this point,
no one could be sure.

A reporter asked Bobby whether he now considered himself the
best chess player in the United States. "No," he said humbly, "one
tournament doesn't mean that much. Maybe," he paused, "maybe
Reshevsky is better!"

Bobby then took a vacation as a guest at Grossinger's Hotel, an
upstate resort, and learned how to ski. When he returned to Brooklyn
he had less use than ever for the Erasmus High School and was forced
to resume his studies while thinking and living almost nothing but
chess. One of his teachers said at the time: "He never seems to be
listening in class. He must always be thinking about chess."

Glancing through his schoolbooks, I found a science assignment on
oxidation, dated October 16, 1956. It had been returned to him by
his teacher with the notation, *"Not Satisfactory,"* accompanied by a
flourishing and censorious checkmark. Not one to be corrected,
Bobby wrote underneath his teacher's remark, with a contemptuous-
ness as humorous as it was rebellious, the single word, *"Tough,"*
accompanied by a checkmark equally as flamboyant.

A fellow classmate related years later: "He was always quiet and
disinterested in the lesson. Occasionally, he would take out his pocket
set and play over some games. Invariably, he would be caught by the
teacher, who would say: 'Fischer, I can't force you to listen to the
lesson and I can't prevent you from playing chess, but for my sake,
please play without the board.' Bobby would courteously put his

pocket set away and sit there in stony silence, and we all knew, including the teacher, that he was playing the games in his mind."

Janice Wolfson Epstein, his geometry teacher, remembered that he was a "poor" student who was also "antisocial." He was a banner scholar, however, in Spanish. The thing he really liked best in school, he recalled years later, was the final bell indicating that classes were over.

Naturally, Bobby would usually do schoolwork in his notebooks, but very often what resulted were sketches of monsters, elaborate doodles, and occasionally the lyrics of original songs he composed himself. In one interview, he professed an interest in astronomy, prehistoric animals, and hypnotism. As are all "red-blooded American teenagers," Bobby was an avid reader of comic books, especially horror types.

His teachers were frustrated with him because they could determine no way to break down the barrier with which he surrounded himself. Bobby was a brilliant child and they knew it, but the overcrowded and understaffed New York City school system made little provision for handling one isolated, exceptional individual. Recently, I spoke to a professor who used to work in the Grade Advisor's Office at Erasmus Hall while Bobby was a student there.

"His I.Q. was in the 180s," he said. "Give or take a point or two. He was definitely a 'high' genius, but with no interest or capacity for schoolwork."

It shouldn't be thought, however, as popular journals would have us believe, that because of a lack of formal schooling, Bobby's education was all that limited. His neighborhood alone, where most Jewish families taught their children to appreciate the finer cultural pursuits of life, was, in a way, an instant *gymnasium* for Bobby. To be sure, he spent little time in the Brooklyn Public Library and the Brooklyn Museum of Art, which were located just walking minutes from his house, but at least he had *some* exposure to these two great institutions. As to his own family, both mother and sister were intellectuals with a number of degrees from various colleges and universities. Regina spoke no less than six languages. In my conversations with her, she showed a high degree of intelligence and erudition. She was supposedly the only person in the history of the New York University Reading Center ever refused admittance since, after testing, it was determined that no improvement could be made. She had a keen interest in art and music and on at least one occasion influenced Bobby to see a performance of *Carmen* at the Metropolitan Opera House. He was, of course, constantly encouraged to read more outside of chess and to become a part of the ongoing cultural life of his family. There were books and prints and musical records in the Fischer household, and it must be remembered that Regina was a teacher by profession, who had formal experience tutoring her own children. Exposure to the intellectual endeavors of both his sister and mother could not have failed to leave a residue with Bobby, and as any casual conversation with him proves, he is now an interested and sympathetic conversationalist on a number of subjects.

Most of Bobby's spare time through the first six months of 1958 was spent preparing (with the help of Jack Collins) a book of his games. He dictated his annotations into a tape recorder and his mother transcribed them. It was a difficult task for Regina Fischer since she didn't play chess, having what Bobby described as an "anti-talent" for the game. Of her chess potential he once said, "She's hopeless."

When the book was finished, Bobby first took it to the World Publishing Co. to see if they would publish it. World eventually declined the manuscript, but Joan often accompanied Bobby when he went there, and she met Russel Targ, the son of the chief editor of the company, whom she later married. Targ is now a physicist and one of the leading experts in the field of laser beams. He has also done extensive research in parapsychology and has invented an extrasensory perception teaching machine.

Kotov writes in his book of reminiscences about receiving a letter from Regina Fischer as early as 1957, which stated in part: "I would like you to publish a collection of my son's games. Bobby would like to have an account in a Russian bank." Kotov was horrified that a fourteen year old boy could be interested in money and pointed to Bobby as a victim of the "sick capitalist system."

But none of these activities could claim Bobby's full attention. He was looking beyond them, beyond this country itself, to a remote spot on the map half a world away—Portoroz, Yugoslavia, where the Interzonal was to be held in August and September. And he was watched carefully. Morphy had gone to Europe at twenty, Pillsbury at twenty-two, and both made their marks for America. Could the fifteen-year-old Fischer do the same? The world wondered; and, perhaps, so did he.

Bobby was determined to go, no matter what the expenses were. "I'll get there even if I have to swim," he said. Somehow the Fischer family got together the round-trip plane fare. A television program, "I've Got a Secret," sponsored a side trip to Moscow, where Bobby and Joan spent two weeks. (Bobby's secret on the TV show was that he was the U.S. Chess Champion.)

Bobby played a number of inventive games against some of the leading players of the Moscow Central Chess Club (fifteen years later he recalled, move by move, a speed game he played against Vasiukov!) but he was disappointed that none of the top Russians agreed to play him. Petrosian was summoned to the club to satisfy both Fischer's wishes and the concern of the directors of the Moscow club—Fischer was beating everyone in sight at blitz. Petrosian finally stopped him, but even against this great player Bobby managed to win a number of games.

The Russian grandmasters wanted Bobby to see their beloved city, go to the museums, possibly visit the Kremlin, be their guest at the Bolshoi. He was introduced to an endless procession of weight lifters, soccer stars, and gymnasts of all kinds. He was bored by it all. Bobby had come to Moscow to play chess . . . and that was all he wanted to do. He left, irritated that he had not met Smyslov, then World Champion, for at least a few encounters. He was Chess Champion of the United States and he felt he had more respect due him. Maybe he was right.

Still contemplating his victories and defeats in Moscow, Fischer traveled to Portoroz to compete in his first Interzonal tournament. Among those awaiting him in Yugoslavia were four Soviet grandmasters. Two of these, Yuri Averbakh and David Bronstein, were seasoned veterans, and each had twice won the Championship of the Soviet Union—the most rigorously contested national title in the world. Tigran Petrosian, the third, was to win it the following year. The youngest, twenty-one-year-old Mikhail Tal, was the current Soviet Champion and the sensation of Soviet chess, having won the title twice in a row. Still in the early stage of a career that was to rival Fischer's own, he was regarded by many as the coming World Champion. These men Bobby faced as play began at Portoroz.

After winning a game and drawing two, he was defeated by Pal Benko, who was there as a result of his 1957 victory at the Dublin Zonal. Fischer remained steady, drawing carefully with Bronstein and Averbakh. He then beat Raul Sanguinetti and the Danish grandmaster, Bent Larsen, drew a short game with Argentina's Oscar Panno, and was once again bested by the brilliant young Fridrik Olafsson of Iceland. It was for Bobby the crisis of the tournament— and his next opponent was Mikhail Tal. Again the boy's amazing nerve and confidence held firm, as he drew with both the Soviet Champion and Tigran Petrosian. He had passed the Russians without a defeat! Now he climbed steadily through the contest, dispatching his compatriot, James T. Sherwin, whose third place in the U.S. Championship had qualified him for the Interzonal when runner-up Reshevsky declined to enter. Bobby won on time against Boris de Greiff, and then drew with four of the most famous grandmasters in Eastern Europe—Laszlo Szabo, Ludek Pachman, Aleksander Matanovic, and Miroslav Filip. He again knocked off his erstwhile Pepsi-Cola opponent, the Filipino Rudolfo Cardoso, who was out to avenge himself. Before the game Cardoso announced to all that he would beat Fischer, and when they sat down at the board, he said: "Would you like to resign now and save time?" Fischer merely laughed and proceeded to win the game.

He then played a neat little 32-move draw with the strongest of the Yugoslavs, Svetozar Gligoric, who had already secured second place and was disposed to be friendly.

Mikhail Tal won the Interzonal, a half-point ahead of Gligoric. Pal Benko was tied with Petrosian for third-to-fourth, and Bobby Fischer was tied with Olafsson for fifth-through-sixth. These standings qualified all of them for the next Candidates (or Challengers) Tournament, which was the final elimination contest deciding who would be matched against World Champion Mikhail Botvinnik. By qualifying, Fischer, Benko, and Olafsson had automatically become International Grandmasters (the other three already were) and became proud holders of that coveted title in use since Nicholas, the Tsar of Russia, first conferred it upon Lasker, Capablanca, Marshall, and Alekhine at the great St. Petersburg tournament of 1914. All of the six winners were young—the oldest, Pal Benko, had just turned thirty—and they would need their stamina. They now formed the essential cast, though there would be a few changes from year to year, in a drama that would be destined to run for many years. While it would have many scenes, there would really be only two acts ever repeating themselves, each culminating in the enthronement and dethronement of a World Champion, a new king. As the players clash again and again in the struggle for the crown, much more than their skills would be tested.

Walter Heidenfeld, writing in the *South African Chessplayer*, said: "Fischer put up an amazing performance, becoming stronger and more sure of himself as the tournament progressed. The days when Bronstein and Szabo were followed by a solid phalanx of five Russians at Stockholm (1948), spread eagled over their Interzonal fields, are decidedly over."

Bobby, being Bobby, was no doubt unhappy over placing fifth, even against the best of the best. But his showing had been anything but disgraceful. At Portoroz he had finished ahead of at least nine international grandmasters, had become by far the youngest ever to have received that title himself, and had qualified for the penultimate contest in world chess. Not surprisingly, he felt that high school had nothing more to give him. He was impatient to quit, but was still too young to drop out and could not obtain permission. These and other factors were rapidly driving him into a smoldering rebellion against restraints that he felt should not be applied to him. He began to turn against all authority—his home, the school, and eventually the chess world itself, for which his respect was rapidly declining.

Adolescent revolt and adolescent scorn are normal enough, but Bobby's capacities for these were enormously inflated by his success. The fact that few could last long against him across a chessboard was generalized into a callow disdain for the abilities of adults *in toto*. Since the game he had mastered requires intelligence of a highly specialized sort, it was all too easy for him to conclude that others were not quite in his mental league. What genuine regard he had for his fellows was limited to the group around Jack Collins and a scattering of peers at the Manhattan Chess Club. He spent the remaining months of 1958 playing with these friends, making reluctant attempts at homework, and preparing seriously for the approaching fifth annual Rosenwald tournament.

He faced a much stronger line-up than he had the previous year. The return of Larry Evans and the Byrne brothers to the contest assured that, but in addition the slate included just about all the most galvanic players in American chess. The defending Champion was of course a favorite, but he was far from being the only one. There was strong support for William Lombardy, and for Pal Benko who had placed third at Portoroz. Conservative opinion still went with Samuel Reshevsky.

It was Larry Evans, however, who quickly took the lead, surprising everyone by defeating Benko in the first round. He topped this with two more successive wins and by round four was still ahead, followed by Reshevsky and Lombardy. How Fischer was doing nobody was quite sure; as late as round three, he was still posted blank on the boards because of adjournments. After round four came the playoffs, and scorers were startled to discover that Fischer had been leading all along. After a long-fought draw with Lombardy, Bobby faced Reshevsky again—and beat him, somehow getting his world-renowned opponent to blunder on the twelfth move.

Meanwhile, Donald Byrne had assumed the spoiler's role by defeating both Evans and Lombardy, and by mid-tournament Bobby was still ahead. Arthur Bisguier was only a half-point behind, though, and Reshevsky rallied through the later rounds to close in again. After Sammy had disposed of Lombardy in round nine, speculation at the Marshall and Manhattan clubs became close to feverish. Reshevsky, one point behind, was past his toughest opponents, whereas Fischer still had to meet Bisguier and Robert Byrne. Then in round ten Reshevsky handily defeated Sherwin while Bobby's adjourned game with Bisguier was clearly running in favor of the older man. The way was now open for one of Reshevsky's famous comebacks, but Bobby was not a competitor to step aside. In the playoff he summoned his resources, turned the game against Bisguier, and won. Both he and Reshevsky then drew the final round, and the new year found Bobby the winner and still United States Champion. He had beaten Kalme, Sherwin, Weinstein, Reshevsky, Mednis, and Bisguier, while drawing with Lombardy, Benko, Evans, and the two Byrnes. Once again he was undefeated, and he also set a precedent by beating Reshevsky personally as well as placing ahead of him. A few had done one or the other in a U.S. Championship before, but nobody had ever done both. *Chess Review* observed, "Each Fischer performance seems to surpass the previous ones!"

Although the Student Council at Erasmus Hall had voted him a gold medal for his accomplishments, Bobby lost no time in shuffling off his academic trammels. Shortly after he was sixteen he left high school, and he has never attended a class since.

Early in 1959 FIDE President Folke Rogard announced the site and the date of the International Candidates Tournament. Again the host country was Yugoslavia, with the rounds scheduled to open that autumn in Bled, continue in Zagreb, and conclude in Belgrade. Bobby apparently already had a following in Yugoslavia, where chess was wildly popular and Russians were not. At least one of that nation's flourishing chess clubs was named after him, and the hope seems to have been widespread that he would eventually take the title away from the Soviet Union.

Bobby was of that opinion also, but there remained the problem of fare and expenses. Now that he was finally free of school, he expected to spend a great deal of his time traveling, and he had accepted invitations to play in widely scattered international tournaments. Although Regina was now a registered nurse, the family income, even supplemented with Bobby's occasional chess prizes, was scarcely adequate to support any such far-ranging activities. Regina decided to seek help, and this occasioned my first formal meeting with the Fischers.

I was working at the United States Chess Federation at the time, and Regina, with Bobby, walked into my office one morning and introduced herself. She was small, dark, and intense, and asked questions so rapidly that I could hardly keep up with her. I liked her. Bobby, a pale, gangling youth, too big for his clothes, stood quiet and awkward, almost outside the situation. I told Mrs. Fischer I'd try to help her. She came back several times, always to inquire about possible financial aid for Bobby. Down the hall from the Federation was the office of Dr. Albrecht Buschke, who specialized in chess literature in all languages. Bobby quickly discovered him, and the bookseller offered to let the boy, since he was U.S. Champion, choose a number of titles free of charge. Most young players would walk off with an armful then and there, but Bobby, Dr. Buschke later told me rather ruefully, took over a year to make his selection, picking nothing but the best.

I ran into them once at the elevator as they were coming back from Buschke's. "Say hello to Mr. Brady," Regina said. Bobby did. She did not seem to see how much her manner and activities embarrassed and irritated him, including possibly this whole business of accosting people for financial assistance; if she did sense his reaction, it deterred her not at all. The money had to be raised, and she pursued her goal with the same inflexible single-mindedness that her famous son devoted to chess. There can of course be no questioning of her motives; she was wholeheartedly devoted to Bobby's "good."

Incidental consequences of this let-the-chips-fall-where-they-may attitude were to be ignored. In many ways the sad ironies in the lives of
both mother and son seem to have common sources.

Bobby was off that spring to the annual international tournament
at Mar del Plata, Argentina, the expenses of this particular trip being
handled by the sponsoring organization. It was his first trip to South
America. He played very unevenly there, committed several crucial
blunders, and ended up tied for third with Yugoslavia's Borislav
Ivkov, behind Ludek Pachman of Czechoslovakia, and Miguel Najdorf
of Argentina. After that tournament, a report appeared in the *Los
Angeles Times* that Bobby had "mysteriously disappeared," but a week
later he "appeared" again, apparently unscathed and ready to play
chess.

He fared even worse at Santiago, Chile, where Pachman shared
first place with Ivkov and Fischer was left behind, tangled in a
three-way tie for fourth, fifth, and sixth. Fischer withdrew from the
tournament for a short while, stating that he had gone there with the
understanding that there was to be $2,000 in cash prizes. It turned
out to be $1,000 in cash and $1,000 in trophies. He was eventually
persuaded to re-enter.

Pachman and Ivkov continued to romp through the continent,
tying each other for first in Lima later in the year, but Bobby had had
enough and flew home. His eyes had been on Europe all along.

Looming in Zurich, Switzerland, was an even more powerful international tournament, which would be a dress rehearsal for the
upcoming Candidates event. Among those grandmasters attending
were four whom Bobby would have to meet on the long road from
Bled to Belgrade—Mikhail Tal, Paul Keres, Svetozar Gligoric, and
Fridrik Olafsson. However disappointingly he had played in South
America, his trip there had been merely spring training for Zurich,
and Bobby was in Switzerland by early summer.

In their New York clubs the men who live chess gathered and
talked and followed the scores via *The New York Times*. The favorite,
Tal, was stopped in the first round by a Swiss player, Edwin Bhend,
but he quickly rallied and took the lead. Then as round followed
round, it became evident that his prime challenger this time was
Bobby Fischer, although Gligoric pressed both leaders hard and neither Bhend nor Keres could ever be discounted. Bobby tied Tal several times and even passed him once, taking the sting out of his
Portoroz loss by beating Olafsson in the process. It was a tiring
tournament for him. His draw against Larsen lasted ninety-two
moves and four sessions and then he played a ninety-five move draw
against Barcza. He remained undefeated until the eleventh round,
but then could not prevail against the strength of Gligoric.

At the Manhattan and Marshall clubs bleak looks were exchanged
when the news came in, because Bobby's next opponent was Paul

Keres—an almost legendary figure in world chess. Their game was played out with almost interminable suspense, adjourned twice from the twelfth round, but the final result showed Bobby the incredible victor. Another legend was taking shape. Meanwhile Gligoric had defeated Tal, and at the end of the thirteenth round Fischer and Tal stood dead even at 10–3 each. Euwe, in an interview in *Swiss Schachzeitung*, said of the teenage Fischer's performance: "His chess technique is nearly a miracle. In their youth, only a few players could handle the endgame so precisely. Only two such players are known to me, Smyslov and Capablanca."

There were two rounds to go. Bobby sat down opposite the Swiss Champion, Dieter Keller, allowed himself to get outplayed, and lost. His game with Tal in the final round was a draw. Gligoric also drew, to end up a half-point behind Tal, just as he had at the Interzonal. Bobby, however, was apparently growing fast; his third-place tie with Keres was far stronger than his Portoroz score.

CHAPTER III

*"If I win a tournament, I win it
by myself. I do the playing.
Nobody helps me."*

Fischer returned from Europe to find his mother engaged in all sorts of activities on his behalf. A tiny ad in *The New York Times* that summer offered "Bobby Fischer Chess Wallets." She had had these made in Argentina, with Bobby's profile and signature stamped in gold. There was also some idea of selling the wallets at the U.S. Open in Omaha that summer. When Bobby found out, he was furious and vetoed the whole venture.

In addition, Mrs. Fischer had written a letter to the *New York Herald Tribune* appealing to chess players and supporters for funds to help finance U.S. participation in overseas tournaments. She asked that contributions be sent to the U.S.C.F. office (without consulting that organization), and the result was surprising. *Sports Illustrated* sent a check for $2,000, and all told about $3,000 was received.

Bobby refused to touch a penny of it. Publicly, his reason was that he didn't want to have anything to do with the Federation. (Bobby's relations with U.S.C.F. officials—or for that matter, with the whole chess community—were either nonexistent or strained.) However, his real reason was that he would not accept money raised by his mother.

It was probably the letter to the *Herald Tribune* with its attendant publicity that was responsible for the incident that took place that summer. I confess I would have had difficulty believing it if I hadn't been an eyewitness. The scene throws more light on the essential character of Bobby Fischer than any anecdote I have to offer. One day at my office I received an anonymous phone call from a lady who said that she was representing someone who was interested in Bobby's career. This person wanted to meet him. Attempting to screen off a possible crackpot, I asked "Why?" Well, this person understood that Bobby was having financial troubles and felt he could possibly help him. I took her number and called up Fischer. "If it's legitimate," Bobby said, "why not?" I phoned the woman and she identified her employer as a businessman who owned a garment factory on Broadway. I'll call him Mr. Blanker. We made an appointment for the next day.

When the two of us arrived at the factory, we were told that Bobby wouldn't be allowed up unless he were wearing the proper kind of shirt and a tie—a way he never dressed in those days. I told the elevator starter that this was the United States Chess Champion, that he had an appointment, and that Mr. Blanker was anxious to meet him. The starter wouldn't be budged, so we walked up many flights of stairs. We passed through a showroom and were admitted to an office with much carpeting and a bar. We took our seats before a large desk. Mr. Blanker turned out to be everybody's image of a garment district tycoon; a bald man in his early fifties, complete with cigar. He started off by asking Bobby all sorts of patronizing questions. What subjects did he like in school? Did he like girls? What did he want to be when he grew up? I was expecting a salty answer from Bobby at any moment, but he remained admirably self-contained and polite. Finally Mr. Blanker got to the point.

"Well, Bobby, I like you very much. I've always had a lot of money in my life, but I've never done anything very philanthropic. I've gambled a lot away, I've spent it on all sorts of things I'm not very proud of. Now I'm getting a little older, I want to change my ways. I admire your chess ability. I like what you stand for. So I'm ready to underwrite your forthcoming trip to Yugoslavia. I'll underwrite the whole thing. Just come to me."

Bobby was wide-eyed, nodding and smiling. It was the movies coming true.

"However, there's just one thing I'd like you to do. If I put up the money to send you to this tournament, and when you win and are interviewed by the press, or anybody, I want you to say: 'I couldn't have won this tournament without the help of Sam Blanker.'"

Bobby was on his feet immediately, seeming to have grown years in a moment. "I can't do that," he said evenly. "If I win a tournament, I win it by myself. I do the playing. Nobody helps me. I win the tournament myself, with my own talent." And after we said our goodbyes we walked out of the office without another word.

We made our way back past staring clerks to the elevator. Bobby didn't say anything. Neither did I. I was proud to be in the same building with him.

In retrospect, it's easy to say that he made the only possible decision. To have carried out the conditions attached to Mr. Blanker's offer would have been demeaning, incompatible with the dignity of a Champion. I think his answer to Mr. Blanker was prompted by many elements—ego, integrity, and jealousy, as well as a fierce pride that insists there can be no names on Bobby's escutcheon but his own. Still I think that the businessman's offer must have touched something even deeper to have triggered a reaction so immediate and final. What emotion it was I shall try to analyze later; for now, it may simply be called a sense of personal autonomy. Its defenses are automatic and inviolable. Bobby Fischer lives alone.

With all this considered, I still can't help looking back at the incident with a kind of awe. How many people could walk out on such an offer without a second thought? And Bobby was just a young man of sixteen who had never known much security, lived only to play chess, was thoroughly acquainted with its starveling wages, and had never demonstrated any indifference to money. Yet he turned down a golden opportunity with no visible qualms. There was no attempt to bargain with his would-be patron, no maneuverings toward compromise, no further consideration of the matter at all. And I doubt there has been any regret.

Shortly before that he had turned down another financial plum, though of not quite the same magnitude. The manufacturers of Fischer pianos had offered him $500 to pose for one photo standing next to one of their instruments, with a chess set on top. He vetoed the idea as demeaning to his title. "It was just a gimmick," he said.

At any rate, wherever his fare may have come from, he was in Yugoslavia by late September. Only eight players gathered at Bled, four of them Soviets. The group was comprised of the Portoroz victors and two Soviet grandmasters "seeded" over from previous qualifying events. Vassily Smyslov had done nothing less than win the World Championship in 1957, although he had lost it back to Botvinnik in a return match a year later. The record of Paul Keres was, if possible, even stronger. Three times Champion of the Soviet Union, he had won the great AVRO tournament of 1938, finishing ahead of Fine, Botvinnik, Alekhine, Euwe, Reshevsky, Capablanca, and Flohr. In that heyday of great international chess he was regarded as the leading challenger. The war had interrupted his career, and perhaps his development, but he had come back to pursue the world title doggedly through the Fifties, placing second in three Candidates Tournaments.

It is no exaggeration to say that he probably would have made it this time, if it had not been for the aggressive giant-killer from Brooklyn. Bobby demonstrated that his Zurich victory owed nothing to chance by defeating Keres in the first round. Despite a second loss to Petrosian, Keres edged into the lead and secured the Bled contest when Petrosian lost to Gligoric in the seventh round. In the second quarter he finally avenged himself on Fischer, took a tenth-round win from Tal, and at the halfway mark held his half-point lead, closely harried by Petrosian, Tal, and Gligoric. At the beginning of the third lap he faced Bobby again, and the determined youngster handed him a second stunning defeat. Thereafter, Mikhail Tal took over, steadily maintaining his lead over Keres, while Gligoric faded and Petrosian continued his drawing ways. Through the last seven rounds Tal gained ground on everyone except Keres, fought off an all-out attack by Fischer in the twenty-seventh round, and in the final game with Benko secured the draw he needed to win. The *Canadian Chess Chat* took a combined boast and swipe at Bobby that overall seemed unfair: "His last game with Tal, in Round 27, was undoubtedly the most exciting of the tournament . . . but he may be destined to play second fiddle to Tal, precisely as the great Pillsbury played to Lasker." It was all over but the dining and speechmaking in Belgrade, and Mikhail Tal had no one but Botvinnik between him and the World Championship. With Smyslov's resurgence in the final quarters, it was a Russian sweepstakes; Keres placed second, Petrosian third, and Smyslov fourth.

Bobby Fischer was again in a frustrated fifth position, but he had achieved it against far stronger opposition than he had met at Portoroz, and in actual play had had minus scores against only two of the seven contesting. He had gained sufficient strength to play Gligoric even throughout the tournament, and had clearly established his superiority over Benko and Olafsson. He had hurt Keres with two defeats, and had inflicted ex-World Champion Smyslov with another one in the final round. Against Petrosian he could draw only two games and win none. Tal, the brilliant Latvian, would not even grant him a half-point, scoring a 4–0 sweep over Fischer. Tal at twenty-two was a man in his prime, as well as one of the most formidable players in the world. He was not to be stopped by a boy, however gifted. And Bobby, as U.S. chess journals were quick to remind themselves, was just a boy.

"Still and all," *Chess Review* speculated, "he has scored impressively at sixteen. What will he do at nineteen? . . ."

Fischer had not the slightest intention of waiting till then. His confidence—already practically messianic—had once again been boosted by the near-tie at Zurich, and there can be no doubt that he had come to Yugoslavia expecting to win. Mikhail Tal later wrote in *Shakhmaty v SSSR:* "Fischer, at the outset, dreamed of being champion of the world. But he would have had better chances in playing, first, for the junior championship. There, without a doubt, he would have won." And in American chess periodicals there were complaints about Bobby's "juvenile optimism."

These observations were completely ignored by Fischer. His image of himself in Caissa's hierarchies, thoroughly crystallized now by his accomplishments, was simple: he is the best player in the world and the strongest of all time. Such a condition is absolute, a given fact, and leaves no room for notions of gradualism, though the possibility of moderation may play about its edges. Defeats and reverses do not affect the image much, stinging as they may be. The kingdom had been prepared for him, and he pressed toward it through a maze of games. He had been the youngest Junior, Open, and U.S. Champion, the youngest International Grandmaster, and one of these days he would be the youngest World Champion.

Where the king can do no wrong, others find they can do nothing right. Bobby held up the 1959 Rosenwald tournament by refusing to participate unless the pairings were publicly drawn. Although these proceedings had always been private, he had found a FIDE rule stating otherwise. The tournament committee conceded his point and agreed that public drawings would be the rule next year. This did not satisfy Fischer, who demanded that the change be instituted forthwith, even though the pairings had already been drawn and published before he had mentioned the issue. The hassle that was making banner headlines in sports sections became increasingly synthetic—a matter of will rather than of principle. The committee named Anthony Saidy as a substitute in the face of the Champion's continued withdrawal and moved to get on with the tournament. After some additional vacillation Bobby decided to play, with the explanation, "I just changed my mind."

Fischer's uncanny skill in manipulating every element of the chess situation to his advantage, particularly his use of the adjournment privilege and the clock, was never more dramatically demonstrated than in this tournament. He adjourned after forty-one moves against Bisguier in the first round, adjourned again in the second when he found himself losing to Robert Byrne, and decided on a third adjournment in a game he later drew with Raymond Weinstein. He didn't secure a win till his fourth-round game against Arnold Denker. In the playoffs that followed, he accomplished a dual swindle, turning a drawn position against Bisguier into a win and converting his losing position against Byrne to a draw. This last was incredible. Byrne clearly and inescapably had Bobby heading for his first defeat in an American tournament since 1957. But Byrne got himself into a time-pressure situation, while Fischer still had plenty of time left on his clock. Forced to move fast, Byrne fell into a triple repetition, which Bobby spotted at once. He notified referee Hans Kmoch, and the game was declared an automatic draw. I remember that even a year later Byrne was still rather bitter about it, especially since he came so close to winning the tournament.

In the fourth round, Herbert Seidman unexpectedly defeated Reshevsky. With this assist, Fischer held to a half-point lead as he ground on through the tournament, beating Junior Champion Robin Ault, tying James T. Sherwin, defeating Seidman, Bernstein, and Mednis. For a time Mednis had threatened the Champion with a loss, but again Bobby's meticulous use of the clock salvaged his game. By round ten he was still a mere half-point ahead and he adjourned an even game against Benko, with Reshevsky his next opponent. Sammy had spent the tenth round defeating Sherwin, though he still had a postponed game to play against Denker. Bobby's several narrow squeaks had suggested a fading Fischer, and as the tournament approached its conclusion the Championship was still very much in doubt.

But Benko sealed a losing move, squirming under time-pressure. Denker, having declined a draw, battled through an ambiguous game and finally won against Reshevsky. Bobby had only to draw his final game to win and relegate Reshevsky to an unheard-of third place. Robert Byrne took second, one point behind Fischer.

Not the least of the tournament's surprises was the fact that Bobby Fischer showed up in a suit, white shirt, and tie (also white). Up until late in 1959 he had dressed atrociously for a champion, appearing at the most august and distinguished national and international events in sweaters and corduroys. A formal photograph taken only a few months before shows him in a ski sweater among the solemnly suited contenders at Bled, incongruous as a hippie at the Plaza. Magazine articles were then portraying a "New Fischer," and the sartorial revolution was usually identified with such an emergence. One writer even implied that the change had something to do with a brush with "romance" that occurred in Buenos Aires a year later. Actually, it was Pal Benko who, on their trip back from Yugoslavia, first encouraged Bobby to dress well. I think that he bought some suits in London, and I know that he had several made for him by Benko's Hungarian tailor in uptown Manhattan. After that, Bobby began buying suits from all over the world, hand-tailored and made to order. I don't believe that the turnabout signified any real change in Bobby's life, though of course certain of his attitudes couldn't help being altered. He became quite clothes-crazy for a while, but later adolescence is a common age for that. As he matured he often slipped out of his overly immaculate ways.

In the spring of 1960 he flew to Argentina's Mar del Plata international tournament, where he and Russia's young Boris Spassky proceeded to bury all other participants in the pampas. They ended up tied for first and second prizes, outscoring their distinguished competitors by the unbelievable margin of 13½–1½. Spassky beat Bobby in a not so classically played classical King's Gambit, but fell into draws with Argentine masters. Both drew with David Bronstein.

Later that spring Mikhail Tal defeated Mikhail Botvinnik in twenty-one games to become the youngest World Champion since Emanuel Lasker. A FIDE announcement meanwhile had begun setting schedules for the long cycle leading to the next match for his title: nine Zonal tournaments in 1960, an Interzonal in 1961, and a Candidates in 1962. If Bobby wanted to achieve the highest honors at a younger age than Tal—and undoubtedly he did—he had obviously only one more chance to do it. He did not have to concern himself with the Zonal, since in the United States, as in the Soviet Union, the winners of the National Championship are automatically qualified. But he still was slated for a full and crucial chess year in 1960. The Chess Olympics were to be held in Leipzig, East Germany. Before that, a great summer contest in Buenos Aires would give Bobby a chance to test himself against the best in international competition. Among scheduled players was Victor Korchnoi, the new Champion of the Soviet Union.

Also scheduled for the approaching summer was the World Student Team Championship, which, unfortunately for the meager resources available to the U.S. Chess Federation, fell only a few months earlier than the Olympiad. It was to be held at Leningrad, and U.S.C.F. felt it absolutely must field a team for it. Both the United States Chess Federation and the American Chess Foundation committed what funds they could, and, with cultural exchange programs receiving attention at high levels, the U.S. State Department for the first time in American chess history offered support. The Federation had formed a committee to try to raise money for the Leipzig event also, but here we ran into difficulties with Washington. Jerry Spann, President of U.S.C.F. and Vice President of FIDE, had been verbally advised by the State Department not to send a team to East Germany. The chairman of our committee, the Reverend Frank Peer Beal, thereupon wrote a letter to President Eisenhower inquiring about the matter, and received a White House reply that endorsed our team's participation and cheerily wished them good luck! U.S.C.F. decided to leave it at that.

Meanwhile the irrepressible Regina Fischer was busy herself. She had not overlooked the American Chess Foundation as a source, but she quickly found it insufficient—if not renegade—in its support of Bobby and the Olympic team generally. She then launched a personal probe of the Foundation's finances, obtaining photostatic copies of its tax reports from the Internal Revenue Service. These demonstrated to her satisfaction that some players and events had received support while others had not. A public accounting was demanded, though the only result was some publicity, largely occasioned by her picketing the Foundation office. In midsummer, I picked up a copy of the New York *Daily News* and found Regina splashed all over the centerfold, this time picketing the White House and State Department, while simultaneously staging a six-day hunger strike, in an attempt to force U.S. Government backing of the Leipzig trip. Contrary to the reports of that incident, she did not chain herself to the White House gate. Nearly every wire service in the country picked up Regina's picture, though, of course, no official action was taken. But she did have an impact upon the chess establishment that can still be felt, and she may even have given our Olympic team a key push toward Leipzig.

A more personal consequence of Regina's activities was to change her whole life. While she had been picketing the American Chess Foundation she had caught the attention of Ammon Hennacy of the *Catholic Worker*, a very well-known figure in radical pacifist circles. He began talking to her, and by fall she had joined the Committee for Non-Violent Action, the most militantly activist of the peace groups. At the time, they were busy organizing the longest peace walk in history, from San Francisco to Moscow. Regina was to leave for the West Coast to join the CNVA group when the march got under way at the beginning of December.

Without wishing to impugn her motives in the slightest, it is still necessary to note that one factor in her decision to get away for a while was almost certainly her deteriorating relations with Bobby. I had a vivid glimpse of just how strained things had become as early as that spring. The Reverend Mr. Beal had suggested a conference on ways and means of promoting and supporting chess, which was attended by about thirty chess officials at the Advertising Club on Park Avenue. When we reached the meeting room we found it had been decorated by Mrs. Fischer with photostatic copies of A.C.F. documents and other literature supporting her various charges and demands. While Harvey Breit and Jean Shepherd were on the dais, Regina stood up in the audience and presented her polemic to the floor. What she said was true enough, I suppose, though nobody knew a solution or wanted to hear more about it, least of all Bobby. He was practically writhing in his seat. His reaction to her various picketing exhibitions later in the year was such that friends were well advised not even to allude to the subject in his presence. Their domestic scene must have become close to impossible. The upshot was that Regina moved out of their Brooklyn apartment and went to live with a girl friend in the Bronx. When she left for California she may have intended only to stay away for the duration of the march and allow the situation to blow over, but it was virtually the end of her life with Bobby. On the walk to Moscow she met a man whom she later married, Cyril Pustan, a college English teacher, and they settled in England. Bobby corresponds with his mother, though they have rarely seen each other since she left their apartment in the fall of 1960.

It is doubtful, however, that family difficulties had anything to do with Bobby's very miserable showing in Argentina that summer, especially since he did so well at other contests during the year. The official group photo taken at Buenos Aires shows Bobby, next to

Evans, in an absolute dream world. Whatever the reason, his performance at Buenos Aires was the worst of his career. (Alekhine
had a more disastrous tournament once, but unlike Fischer, he had
woes with the bottle.) Bobby placed thirteenth for a minus score.
When asked to explain the Buenos Aires debacle, he will still complain that the lighting was poor, and a crusade for proper illumination has been Bobby's theme ever since. Fischer is not the first player
who has complained of the lighting—Botvinnik had to have a special
lamp at his table in Munich 1958 because of poor visibility. Fischer
salvaged draws with Reshevsky, Korchnoi, and Taimanov, but otherwise the less said about this tournament the better.

Fortunately for our side, any traumas for Bobby that had accompanied this tournament were not long lasting. In fact, American
chess was off to its finest year in international competition since the
Soviets had established their iron hegemony in the late Forties.
Reshevsky's tie with the Soviet players sent to Argentina had lifted
morale all around; it reminded us that we had reserves of talent and
even genius that could meet the best in the world on even terms.

The team that left for Leningrad in July was one of the finest the
United States has ever fielded: Bill Lombardy, Ray Weinstein,
Charles Kalme, Edmar Mednis, and Anthony Saidy, with Eliot Hearst
as captain. This was a student team, but all these young undergraduates and graduates were sure and seasoned talents, already
proven masters of the board, and therefore most remarkably like
their Russian opponents. The Americans, though, had done it on
their own, whereas the Russians—as well as many other Eastern
European teams—were at once students and chess professionals,
carefully nourished by their governments. To appreciate fully the
tremendous achievement of the U.S. student team that summer, the
reader must keep in mind the deadly seriousness with which the Iron
Curtain bureaucracies promote their players.

By the end of the tournament, Lombardy had defeated Boris
Spassky and played up to his great promise with a magnificent 12–1
score, with two draws. Kalme did almost as well with 11½–1½, and
Weinstein tallied 7½–2½, losing two. Mednis had two losses also, but
the other three sustained only one apiece. The team defeated the
Russians in their set match and won the tournament with forty-one
victories and eleven defeats to become the first U.S. team to win an
international championship in over two decades. *The New York
Times* delivered an accolade, Mayor Wagner sent a telegram of congratulations to each member of the team, and *Chess Review* began
speaking of "a great national chess renaissance."

It is certain that the long preparation for the Olympiad that fall
was, if possible, intensified. The Soviets brought to Leipzig the full
awesome weight of their grandmaster strength: Tal, Botvinnik,

Smyslov, Keres, Petrosian, and Korchnoi. Each of the first three had won the World Championship; each of the second three were entirely capable of winning it. The game of chess is just about as old as civilization, but it is doubtful whether all its historical luminaries could assemble a team capable of defeating the contemporary Russians at their best. Not that several past giants were not gifted even beyond Botvinnik, but it is almost impossible to imagine their disparate and vagrant styles meshing into the discipline of team play required at the summit of a current international tournament. The United States had only a couple of names that the chess world considered genuine threats to Soviet mastery: Reshevsky and Fischer. The first wasn't participating, and the second was a temperamental seventeen-year-old, years away from his full development. Bill Lombardy was also feared by the Soviets at this time.

The American team was slowly scraped together. Bisguier decided to join, though Evans didn't. Possibly the most valuable member was a non-player, Isaac Kashdan. As team captain, he brought to our players an incomparable knowledge not only of the complications of international tournament chess, but also of the zest and confidence of the Thirties that had seen him front and center in an unbroken succession of American victories. Jerry Spann had been an indispensable behind-the-scenes presence at Leningrad—to an extent that he's never received proper credit for—but it was Kashdan who was active at Leipzig. Coupled with his support was the excellence of the American line-up, which corresponded with the best talent in the country. For once, and for a wonder, Fischer was at the head of a U.S. team, followed by Lombardy, Robert Byrne, Bisguier, and Weinstein. Until practically the eleventh hour of the team's departure, financial and State Department support remained uncertain.

En route to Leipzig, Fischer stopped off in Reykjavik and played in a small tournament there, winning it easily at 3½–½.

The opening rounds of the Olympics weren't promising. Lombardy lost to Drimer of Rumania in the first round and Fischer to Munoz of Ecuador in the second, and both Fischer and Byrne managed mere draws against the Cubans. But the team jelled against Belgium in the fourth round, swept Lebanon 4–0, defeated Spain and West Germany, swept Chile, and was spared the humiliation of not placing first in its section. With these victories behind them, the team settled down; their 3½–½ against Rumania in the first round of the finals was a draw behind the Soviet 4–0 win over Bulgaria. Britain slowed the U.S.A. to an even score, but the team took Bulgaria and won against Yugoslavia by the same margin that the Soviets had managed. Then in round five the two top contending teams met. Fischer played Tal to a dead stop, Lombardy drew with Botvinnik, Byrne tied Korchnoi; but Bisguier lost to Smyslov. Apparently the Soviets were heartened by the close match, for they went on to sweep every one of the eleven remaining, in a display of power that left no doubt about who was in command of international chess. The U.S. team took second, fending off a last-hour Yugoslav uprising. Fischer held down first board all the way—in itself a high feat of stamina—scoring six wins and four draws with one loss (to Gligoric) in the finals. Lombardy at second board won three and drew six, losing once to Dr. Miroslav Filip of Czechoslovakia. Robert Byrne went undefeated, winning five and drawing three, and his claim that he had been lucky convinced no one.

Life Magazine published a highly amusing photograph of both Fischer and Tal at Leipzig, each staring from the very depths of their souls at their respective opponents, with this amusing caption: "Taking a cue from Al Capp's Evil Eye Fleegle, master of the triple whammy, last week demonstrated the use of the Evil Eye at the Olympics in East Germany. Fischer, a less accomplished starer than Tal, put a certain wistful quality into his whammy and lost to Gligoric."

The field at Leipzig included twenty-four International Grandmasters, thirty-seven International Masters, and a hundred and twenty-three masters representing forty nations. At the end of the Olympiad, it was clearly established that the United States was no longer jockeying for position behind this or that East European nation (Yugoslavia had been pre-favored for runner-up honors), but was second only to the Soviet Union.

In an interview at Leipzig with the Spanish master and chess journalist, Roman Toran, Bobby left no doubt that he was off and running. Asked when he thought he might achieve the World Championship, he replied: "Perhaps in 1963."

"So soon?" said Toran. "Yes! Why not?" replied Bobby.

As they talked, Bobby was intently watching the games that Pomar and Korchnoi were playing nearby. He seemed to be searching for the best moves, just as if he were playing himself. His next words were mumbled, spoken almost unconsciously: "Yes, I believe I will soon be World Champion."

CHAPTER IV

*"Don't even mention losing to me.
I can't stand to think of it."*

The 1960 Rosenwald tournament was held in Manhattan that winter. I co-refereed with Hans Kmoch. It was a cliff-hanging contest for Fischer's friends and well-wishers. Bobby barely managed to extricate himself from losing positions against Reshevsky, Kalme, and Saidy. He salvaged narrow wins over Lombardy and Weinstein. But again he was the only one who never lost a game. There was the usual quota of comments on "the Fischer luck," but luck doesn't win games and tournaments against the best, year after year. Bobby simply had more resources, stratagems, variations, cunning, nerve, will to win and talent than his opponents. He won seven and drew four, exactly repeating his score of the previous year, though this time he finished a full two points ahead of his nearest rival, Lombardy. Weinstein took third prize, astonishing even his admirers by defeating Bisguier, Lombardy, Reshevsky, and Robert Byrne. Lombardy contributed the most spectacular game; in a complicated position against Kalme in the final round he made fifteen moves in less than a minute and managed to come out a piece ahead. With Fischer and Weinstein still under twenty, and Lombardy a mere twenty-three, the Championship tournament was more completely dominated by youth than at any time since its inception. Reshevsky was almost outrageously humbled, with a tie for fourth-through-sixth place. Pal Benko and Robert Byrne also hit low points in their championship careers. Only Fischer remained a winner who seemingly could not help winning. For the fourth time his name was inscribed on the Frank J. Marshall Trophy, along with those of all the previous champions dating back to Paul Morphy. He was awarded the $1,000 first prize and secured his right to compete in the next Interzonal tournament.

"I am going to win the World Championship," Bobby told the American journalist Robert Cantwell early in 1961. The interview also quoted him as predicting, with remarkable prescience, "Anyway, Tal hasn't been playing so good and he may not even be World Champion by the time the next match is held." And to a reporter for *Newsweek*, he said, "Give me two years. I'll win it."

41

A few months later, Botvinnik regained the World Championship by defeating Tal convincingly in thirteen out of twenty-one games. He thus became the first to regain the world title twice, and also the last, since a FIDE ruling had earlier eliminated a deposed champion's right to a rematch the year after losing the title. This hurt Tal, who would now have to wait till 1963 for another shot at the title, assuming he survived the Candidates' tournament in 1962. The mills of FIDE grind fine and exceedingly slowly. I know of no other game or sport that sets so many years and so many eliminating contests between a potential champion and the championship.

In the United States that summer, arrangements were progressing for the second most important match of the year, one rivaling the World Championship itself in the interest it stirred throughout the chess world. The American Chess Foundation announced in June that plans had definitely been set for a match between Bobby Fischer and Samuel Reshevsky. It was to consist of sixteen games, the first four to be played in New York, the next eight in Los Angeles, and the final four in New York again. Co-sponsoring with A.C.F. was the new Herman Steiner Chess Club at the posh Beverly Hilton Hotel in Los Angeles, and high on the list of patrons was the name of Mrs. Jacqueline Piatigorsky, wife of the distinguished cellist, Gregor Piatigorsky. *Chess Life* sent out a hasty letter polling the opinion of leading grandmasters throughout the world. "Reshevsky will win with a score of 9½–6½," Tigran Petrosian said. "I think Reshevsky will win—9–7," Paul Keres echoed. Gligoric contributed a flat "Reshevsky will win." All that Bent Larsen said was "Reshevsky."

To the reader who has seen Fischer go undefeated through four U.S. Championship tournaments, while Reshevsky slipped steadily lower in each of these same contests, such predictions may appear puzzling. They were, however, sound and responsible judgments. The man whom Bobby had contracted to play holds one of the most awesome records in the history of chess. He has defeated at least once Lasker, Capablanca, Alekhine, Euwe, Botvinnik, and Smyslov—every World Champion of this century except Spassky or Tal. He has also been victorious in matches against Gligoric, Najdorf, Kashdan, Horowitz, Bisguier, Donald Byrne, Benko, and Lombardy. Fischer himself has been quoted to the effect that a tournament doesn't prove out a player's true strength; only a match does that. It would seem to follow from this statement that Reshevsky had as valid a claim as anyone to being rated the best in the world, since he had at that time never lost a set match in his life. Bobby, on the other hand, had had virtually no match experience since he played his 1957 bout against Cardoso.

There was, needless to say, no love lost between the two grandmasters. Reshevsky, especially, had reasons for enmity. Having earned world respect during a reign of many years, he had been abruptly dethroned, defeated, and all but exiled from the honors by an insurrect youngster with no consistent fear of anybody. Bobby had pulled rank on the displaced sovereign almost immediately after winning the Championship, refusing to participate in the 1958 Olympiad unless he, rather than Reshevsky, played first board. And a scattering of slighting remarks at Reshevsky's expense had been attributed to Bobby in a number of press interviews. Chess journalism frequently uses the word "avenged" when a player defeats an opponent who has previously bested him. So far as Reshevsky was concerned, the match with Fischer offered opportunities in which the term would have connotations well beyond sport.

Reshevsky proved he meant business by defeating Bobby in the first game. The young Champion came right back convincingly to win the second in the most exciting of the New York contests. In the third, Fischer was lucky to escape with a draw. The fourth, summed up by Larry Evans as a "theoretical melee," was also drawn. The players were dead even as the match moved to Los Angeles.

On the Coast, Bobby outplayed Reshevsky and forced him to resign the first time around. After they had drawn game six, Reshevsky seemed to have found his old form and was clearly superior, crushing Fischer in game seven. Bobby's genius for rising to his opponent's strength, however, was demonstrated in the next game, though he somehow missed the win he should have had. By the time the eleventh game had been concluded, five games had been drawn in Los Angeles. The tension grew with every game. A good deal of money was involved, but the real stakes were the contestants' careers and reputations. Each knew that every move he made would be scrutinized and analyzed in this country and throughout the world. They stopped talking to each other. They would not ride in the same car from their hotel to the Steiner Club. Reshevsky wanted air conditioning in the playing room; Fischer thought it was too cold. Both players were accustomed to having their way about playing conditions, both were absolutely determined to win, and neither would concede anything to the other.

There had already been difficulties in scheduling the twelfth game, which fell on Saturday. As an Orthodox Jew, Reshevsky could not play until after sundown—about nine on an August evening in California. Game time was therefore changed from 7:30 to 9:00 P.M. Then it was realized that the playing session probably could not end before two in the morning. Accordingly, the California committee again rescheduled the round to begin at 1:30 Sunday afternoon. However, Mrs. Jacqueline Piatigorsky was planning to go to a concert given by her husband that afternoon, and didn't want to miss the twelfth game. She was a committee member and the principal pa-

troness of the whole series. Couldn't it be set for Sunday morning?
The committee allowed that it could and came up with a fourth
scheduling of 11:00 A.M. The papers were notified, and a mailing
was sent out announcing the new time for the final Los Angeles
game.

Bobby says he was unaware of the change of schedule until
Thursday, August 10th, when he protested immediately. He did
more than that. He informed the referee, in no sweet terms, that he
could not and would not play at such an early hour. According to
Mr. Rivise's later "deposition," a long letter to A.C.F. President
Walter Fried, which was printed in full in *Chess Life*, Fischer then
took up the matter with Mrs. Piatigorsky and Mrs. Grumette (another committee member), whom he ". . . noticed . . . sitting together
in the audience." Mrs. Piatigorsky informed him that it had been
". . . her suggestion that the game be played on Sunday morning instead of Saturday night, since it was certainly more reasonable to all
concerned not to stay up until 2:30 A.M. . . ."

Bobby rejected that reason and repeated that he would not play.

Rivise said: "The next morning arrangements were made for
Mrs. Grumette to go to Fischer's hotel between 9:30 and 10:00 A.M.
to provide transportation and persuade him to play. He refused. As
another precaution we left one of our club members at Fischer's
hotel with a car in the event Fischer later changed his mind.

"At the club the clock was started at 11:00. Shortly thereafter
Jerry Spann called Fischer at his hotel to try and reason with him.
'Bobby, don't you think you ought to come down here and play?' he
asked. Bobby refused.

"One hour and some minutes later I declared the game forfeited
in favor of Reshevsky. . . ."

In view of Fischer's many refusals and known stubbornness, these
"efforts" were largely ceremonial, as everybody involved must have
known.

Fischer's failure to appear set off an uproar that reverberated
throughout the rest of the year. The wire services, radio, television,
and newspapers seized upon the incident and almost universally con-
demned the spoiled brat and prima donna who so unfortunately happened to be U.S. Chess Champion. The "brat" obliged them with
material for further indignant copy by challenging the validity of
the forfeiture and threatening not to proceed with the match if his
claim were not upheld.

The hassle made its way back to New York and fell in the lap of
the president of the American Chess Foundation, Walter Fried. He
insisted that the thirteenth game be played on the scheduled date,
August 15, at the Empire Hotel in New York. Fischer had already
avowed that he would not play, and authority once again coldly

maintained that he *must* play at a certain hour of a certain day, as if the futility of trying to force the Champion to jump on command through any such temporal hoops had not been unmistakably demonstrated. A phone call from the Coast on the afternoon of the 15th acquainted everybody with the fact that Bobby was still in Los Angeles and would not arrive till midnight. The time-squeeze was abruptly relaxed and the game was rescheduled for the 17th of August. Once Fischer was in New York, though, principle was principle. Unfortunately, both sides felt they were equally justified, and the whole thing locked once more into a stiff and irreconcilable contest of wills.

"Upon his arrival in New York late that evening," President Fried writes, "Mr. Fischer telephoned Mr. Kasper and insisted that the next game to be played be the twelfth of the series, in which he was to play the white pieces, an action which would have signified that the referee's decision as to the forfeiture was to be invalidated, and the disputed game played over. . . . Mr. Kasper told him, without passing on the merits of his claim, that the players were expected to proceed with the thirteenth game, and that a decision as to forfeiture or replay of the twelfth game would be made within a few days, after full investigation of the details of all that had taken place in Los Angeles . . . Mr. Fischer again threatened that he would not resume play."

The following day, repeated efforts of A.C.F. officials to reach Bobby by telephone failed. Mr. Fried thereupon sent him a telegram: "We expect your attendance Thursday August 17 5 P.M. . . . as scheduled stop your challenge of twelfth game forfeiture is being reviewed by undersigned whose decision will be made before conclusion of match and is to be binding as per your signed agreement stop your failure to appear . . . will subject you to loss of match and to damage suits for non-compliance with terms of contract." Later in his letter to the A.C.F., Fried quotes Bobby's comment on the telegram, as reported the next morning in *The New York Times*:

"All right, I'll take it into court too. I'm willing to begin play again with the twelfth game, but I won't resume the match at the thirteenth. They are just trying to trap me into continuing the match. They've had all the facts for four days. They could have reached a decision by now."

At about four o'clock, on Thursday, August 17th, Walter Fried received a telegram from Fischer:

"I protest your requirement that I proceed with the thirteenth game prior to a decision on the illegal forfeiture of the twelfth game. The rescheduling of the twelfth game was without my consent and the breach therefore was not on my part. I request that the match continue with the twelfth game, failure of which will cause me to institute action for damages for breach of contract."

Mr. Fried later commented: ". . . Fischer did not appear, and at 5:15 P.M. the clocks were set and at 6:15 P.M. the referee, Mr. Al Horowitz, declared the game forfeited to Mr. Reshevsky. I thereupon gave instructions that the following telegram be sent to Mr. Fischer and we notify the press accordingly:

" 'By reason of your successive failures to appear at scheduled games and your flagrant disregard of your written commitments I have today declared Samuel Reshevsky the winner of the match.' "

It was a case of a maverick versus practically the whole chess establishment, of which the A.C.F. president is a central pillar. To have upheld Fischer would have been to question the reputation of Mr. Irving Rivise, a U.S.C.F. vice president, who was supported by U.S.C.F., FIDE Vice President Spann, and U.S.C.F. National Membership Chairman Lina Grumette, to say nothing of the reputation of Mrs. Jacqueline Piatigorsky, who was perhaps the most promising patron U.S. chess had found since Lessing J. Rosenwald. Bobby, on the other hand, was a notorious troublemaker. In addition, to have decided for Bobby would have made Fried appear to be doing the one thing he had firmly resolved not to do—yield to Fischer's threats.

Eventually, Fischer took the matter into the courts and sued Reshevsky and the American Chess Foundation, lest his ". . . reputation as the most skillful and proficient player in the United States be irreparably damaged and tarnished." After a number of years, the case was dropped.

Another event took place in August 1961 that blemished Bobby's public chess image. Writer-editor Ralph Ginzburg arranged for an interview-in-depth with Fischer, which appeared in *Harper's Magazine* the following January. Mr. Ginzburg succeeded in getting Bobby to open up to an unprecedented extent, and the result was disastrous or pathetic or funny, depending on your point of view. Although not written in malice, the article presents a portrait of the Champion which might not be out of place in a Ring Lardner anthology. Bobby is depicted as a monster of egotism, scornful of everything outside himself and the game, while understanding nothing of what he scorns. As the image is developed, we see a callow *arriviste* who, in attempting to delineate his notions of, and pretensions to "class," convicts himself of an increasingly hopeless vulgarity. The interview was partially tape-recorded and much in it rings true, yet many of us have trouble recognizing the Fischer we knew in this article. An eighteen-year-old doesn't really know who he is yet, and the personality Bobby trotted out for Ginzburg seemed to combine his worst traits, seasoned with *hubris* and sustained by ingenuity. Just how vulnerable he was behind all this swagger was shown by the impact the piece had upon him when the magazine appeared on the stands. It altered his whole life in some ways, particularly by making him more guarded about self-revelations. For a while, he couldn't even stand to hear the name Ginzburg, and when I once brought it up in passing he screamed: "I don't want to talk about it! Don't mention Ginzburg's name to me!"

When he commented on the interview, he claimed emphatically that much in it had been twisted, distorted, and taken out of context. Ginzburg says on the other hand that he toned it down to make Fischer look as good as possible. Both claims may be true, though the latter is less convincing. Ralph Ginzburg is not the type of man to mince words when it comes to sensational copy.

Years later, in an attempt once again to decide for myself in what spirit the questions and answers were made, I asked Ginzburg whether he would let me listen to the tapes of his conversations with Fischer. He claimed that he had disposed of them years earlier.

Some might argue that Bobby had a come-uppance due and that the article might even have helped snap him out of his solipsistic trance. Reading the interview now, over ten years later, I'm sorry that the cruelty of it prevailed. As a writer, I know that it is possible, though not easy, to produce an in-depth profile of someone without hurting him. I wish Ginzburg had managed that.

News of the *Harper's* article was quickly noised about the chess world. "It is incorrect," huffed Soviet International Grandmaster Kotov, "that Mr. Ginzburg should write in such a way about one of the strongest chess players in the world." The case for lese majesty finds unexpected defenders.

CHAPTER V

*"It's just you and your opponent
and the board and you're trying
to prove something."*

American chess that summer was having as many difficulties as
its Champion. At the Helsinki tournament, virtually the same team
that had won the 1960 World Championship—with Lombardy again
at first board—lost it back to the Russians. The United States
placed second, and Raymond Weinstein shared an individual board
performance prize, but the high spirit of the previous year was gone.
There was no more talk of pulling even with the Russians, much less
overtaking them. Considering that the tournament was held in the
midst of the Berlin crisis the fact that the players were friendly at all
was something of an achievement.

The long, slow-burning, potentially eruptive conflict was no doubt
partially responsible for the fact that FIDE was having no luck in its
attempts to find a site for the Interzonal tournament. However, the
year did see a great international tournament in which Bobby participated, and it gave him his first chance in eight months to demonstrate that, however much his adolescence might be showing elsewhere, he had never stopped growing at the board.

Once again the host city was Bled, Yugoslavia; the occasion was
the Alekhine Memorial Tournament, limited to invited grandmasters.
Thirty years previously, Alekhine won the first prize at Bled, ahead
of Bogolyubov and Nimzovich. This time, the Soviet Union was represented by Tal, Keres, Petrosian, and Geller. Arthur Bisguier joined
Bobby as a United States entrant. A generous sampling of other
great grandmasters was also present—Gligoric, Najdorf, Pachman,
Olafsson, Ivkov, Donner, and Parma.

The tournament was well-organized with the venerable Milan
Vidmar as its director. The players were treated to thermal baths at
the Grand Hotel Teplice and attended musical performances by
some of the leading Yugoslavian virtuosos. In addition to paying all
expenses, the organizers allowed each player to bring his wife, and
picked up that tab, also.

Bobby provided the first indication of the way things would go by defeating Mikhail Tal in the second round. Bisguier, in top form, won from Keres in the third. Fischer defeated Olafsson in the fourth, and received a great ovation when he beat Geller in the sixth. After scoring wins against Bisguier in the ninth and Yugoslavia's Bertok in the tenth, Bobby found himself in the lead and remained there through the twelfth. In the fifteenth, Tal pulled even with him and went on to beat Germek in the next round, while Fischer drew with Keres, dropping a half-point behind. Tal gained another half-point by winning against Pachman, Fischer again drawing with Najdorf. In the eighteenth round, Tal quickly drew his own game, expecting Petrosian to make short work of Fischer, but when Bobby defeated the U.S.S.R. Champion, the crowd roared. After this, Ivkov held Fischer to a draw in the final round, and Tal won the game he had to win against Najdorf. The ex-World Champion thus added one more great tournament to his spectacular tally, having lost only the game to Fischer. And Bobby had not only defeated Tal for the first time, but two other Soviet grandmasters in addition. Bisguier had done almost as well against the Russians, beating Geller and Keres, drawing with Petrosian, and losing only to Tal. But he was eclipsed by Fischer's achievement: although Tal won, only Bobby had gone undefeated. It was his first really great success in the arena of world chess competition.

The event stirred the chess world to its depths. In America, of course, excitement was high. "Wonderful!" John Collins exulted. "No other eighteen-year-old player has achieved so much. It puts him on the road to the championship." Arnold Denker called it "the most glowing tribute to youthful talent in the history of chess." "He has shown beyond the shadow of a doubt," Larry Evans said, "that he is a contender for the world title. Fischer has single-handedly broken the Russian iron grip on chess supremacy." Even Samuel Reshevsky forgot the wounds of the previous summer long enough to comment generously: "It was a very excellent showing." World Champion Botvinnik, annotating the Tal-Fischer game, remarked: "There is no doubt that during the next fifteen to twenty years the chess world will witness the struggle of two exceptionally powerful talents—M. Tal and R. Fischer." Svetozar Gligoric put it with unreserved succinctness: "Bobby is going to be world champion."

Winter fell on 1961. In *Chess Life* we ran a light piece on Fall-Out Shelter Chess Clubs. From Stockholm came a message from FIDE President Folke Rogard saying that, for a variety of reasons, it had been found impossible to organize and hold the Interzonal at any of the hoped-for sites. ". . . One thing is clear to me as your president. The international political tension is a sad fact but must not interfere with our non-political work. It seems to me that *just now* it is more important than ever that we chess friends keep together and show that amongst us friendship and confidence are, as always, prevailing." President Rogard made a last-minute appeal to Swedish chess and civic officials and succeeded in getting Stockholm itself to host the Interzonal. A site for the Candidates Tournament had meanwhile been found at Curaçao, a Caribbean island in the Netherlands Antilles near Venezuela, under the auspices of the Royal Dutch Chess League, and the event was already scheduled for May and June of 1962. The two qualifying tournaments were thus telescoped within a few months of each other. The Interzonal was to be held as soon as possible, starting in late January of the new year.

This was probably the primary reason why Bobby did not choose to participate in that winter's Rosenwald tournament, and there might also have been some physical problems he was having at the time. After Bled, Bobby had spent a number of days confined at Hospital Banjaluka in Bosnia, due to an appendicitis attack. He chose not to have the organ removed, and waited out the pain. Eventually it subsided. Bobby thanked the doctors for helping him and not acting too rashly with a scalpel.

Bobby spent Christmas in London and appeared on BBC's outstanding show, "Chess Treasury of the Air." He and Leonard Barden teamed up as White, in a consultation match against Jonathan Penrose and P. H. Clarke. When the show was over, the game had not yet been finished and neither team would agree to the other's analysis of the position. A second session was impossible to arrange, and the game was sent to Dr. Max Euwe for adjudication. Dr. Euwe prepared a five page analysis, proclaiming the game a draw.

For the first ten rounds at Stockholm, Bobby jockeyed for first place with Dr. Filip and Wolfgang Uhlmann of East Germany. One player in the tournament said that when he questioned Bobby about other players' scores, it became evident that he didn't keep track of the points, which would have told him their relative standings and enabled him to determine which games he needed to win and which he could afford to draw. He simply played every game to win.

In the eleventh round he sailed into the lead, and this time he was not to be caught. The Soviet representatives made an all-out attempt to stop him when he met them in rounds sixteen through nineteen, but Bobby survived every assault in masterly style, retaining the plus score he had established against the Russians at Bled by defeating Victor Korchnoi.

Kotov gives us some memorable personal glimpses of Bobby at Stockholm:

"After every game, Bobby took the chessboard and pieces along to the cloakroom . . . the only place available for postmortem analysis. He analyzed his games for many hours, no matter whether his opponent was grandmaster Petrosian or Aaron from India, and often would be still analyzing at midnight when the custodians came to turn out the lights. . . .

"After Geller's defeat by Pomar, Fischer had two points more than his nearest rivals. 'How many points did you score in 1952?' Bobby asked me, as we walked . . . to the hotel. I laughed. 'You are seeking one more rival. I scored 16½ out of 20.' Bobby began to count. 'Then I must have 18½,' he said. 'I shall have!' . . ."

One evening, after the round, Fischer began playing five-minute chess with a few of the Russians. Somehow, he either underestimated or was unaware of Leonid Stein's strength, as he gave him odds in a five-game-five-minute match. According to the 10 *Kroner* wager, Fischer had to score 3 points to win the match, whereas Stein only needed 2 points. Stein quickly won the first two games and, therefore, the match. They played another five game match and Stein won that one, too. All the while, Fischer kept up a humorous banter in English and in Russian, and was pleasing the small crowd around him. "*Seichas ia iego preebiv!*" he would say to the Russians, which roughly translated meant, "Now I'm going to crush you!"

Fischer's difficulties in these offhand games were not reflected in the tournament. By the eighteenth or nineteenth round of the Interzonal, it appeared sure that Fischer would win the tournament, and after he disposed of Bolbochan in the twenty-first round, he had mathematically captured first place. His final score was 17½–4½.

At the end of the final round, he was a full two and a half points ahead of his closest pursuers, Geller and Petrosian, and had won the Interzonal tournament without once having been defeated. *Chess Life* concluded soberly and unequivocally that it was ". . . the finest performance by an American in the history of chess," apparently forgetting Pillsbury's achievement at Hastings, 1895, ahead of Tchigorin, Lasker, Steinitz and Tarrasch.

But it was even more amazing in other ways. "For the first time since the Interzonal and Candidates Tournaments began as eliminating contests for the championship in 1948," wrote British master Leonard Barden, "the Soviet grandmasters failed to capture first prize. Bobby Fischer's winning margin of 2½ points reflects his complete domination of the event. It owed nothing to luck: he never had a clearly lost position.

"This was a victory remarkable not only for its margin, but for the maturity of chess style by which it was achieved. It seemed that Fischer was combining the iron logic of a Botvinnik, the fanatical zeal to win of an Alekhine, and the endgame purity of Capablanca . . ."

Russian International Grandmaster Kotov's observations were similar: ". . . Fischer played the endgame with Barcza in the style of

Capablanca; against Gligoric, he defended in the ending with the wisdom of the most experienced. . . ."

If Bobby was disappointed—and it is possible—nobody else on this side of the Atlantic was. He wasn't greeted with flags and shouts (nor with anything resembling the honors and banquets that met Paul Morphy on his triumphant return from Europe), but *The New York Times* tossed him an editorial bouquet, and the gratification in the clubs was immense.

What Bobby had achieved in going undefeated through the grandmaster tournaments at Bled and Stockholm was the chess equivalent of pitching two no-hitters in All-Star or World Series play, and no less difficult.

On March 8, 1962, the eve of his nineteenth birthday, Fischer was presented first prize in Stockholm at the closing banquet of the Interzonal. "What will he do at nineteen?" *Chess Review* had wondered in 1959. Though Bobby still had a day left before that birthday, the question had been answered in magnificent fashion. After Stockholm, Alexander Kotov, captain of the first Soviet group to lose top honors in an Interzonal, said of Fischer: ". . . his future possibilities are limitless."

Inspired by Fischer's superlative victory, Gideon Stahlberg and Jostein Westberg, two Swedes, issued the first book published about him: *"Bobby Fischer,"* which contained a short biographical sketch and fifty selected games.

Heidenfeld pointed out that ". . . the outcome of the tournament is a significant triumph for Bobby Fischer, who is the first player to have broken through the magic circle of Russian grandmasters to win a major tournament since the end of the War."

CHAPTER VI

"They've almost ruined chess."

PROFILE OF A PRODIGY

Seven other players were qualified for the Candidates Tournament at Curaçao. Pal Benko, the pluckiest and most active of American grandmasters at that time, had managed to stay in the running at Stockholm, nosing out Gligoric and the Russian Leonid Stein. Dr. Miroslav Filip of Czechoslovakia was a seasoned veteran of international tournaments, but not better than half a dozen other grandmasters who might have made the grade. Petrosian, Geller, and Korchnoi had bunched just behind Fischer on the Interzonal scoreboard. Tal and Keres were eligible in a seeded capacity. The Candidates Tournament was to last a full two months, and for the first time since World War II it appeared a solid possibility that a non-Russian (and an American at that!) would win it. The chess world was in a ferment throughout the late winter and early spring of 1962.

"It is absolutely impossible to predict the results!" former World Champion Max Euwe wrote in *FIDE Review*. "Sometimes I have the feeling that Petrosian will win the contest. He is a solid player who picks up his whole and half points in a quiet, unspectacular way. Still, it will be difficult for him to keep pace with hurricanes such as Tal unleashed in the Candidates Tournament of 1959 or Fischer in the . . . Interzonal." But in another place in the same article, he stated: "The big battle will be between the boy hero Bobby Fischer on one side and the five top Russians on the other." Fischer could not have agreed more. It was exactly that "team" effort of the Russians that disturbed him.

In *Chess Life*, U.S. Senior Master Eliot Hearst made a studied and unsurprising choice: ". . . Fischer has scored 6–2 (without a defeat) against Russian opposition (Tal, Petrosian, Geller, Korchnoi, Keres, and Stein) in the last six months and has just secured his greatest triumph by a 2½-point margin in the Interzonal Tournament at Stockholm. Tal has been world champion and has a tremendous desire to make up for his failure against Botvinnik; he is not so much

53

the chess adventurer as he was three or four years ago, but he is still very stubborn about certain variations and favors some lines which almost everyone else thinks are inferior . . . Fischer is only nineteen years old and his critics state that he has not 'the maturity of outlook that the other competitors possess'; but his chess style is almost as mature as Capablanca's. Our choice—of course not influenced by sentimental or nationalistic factors—BOBBY FISCHER! . . ."

From Stockholm, Kotov wrote: "There are still some weaknesses in Fischer's style, because of his youth, and they will not yet permit him to beat all the strongest grandmasters in the world." This was despite the fact that Bobby had done just that.

"The young American grandmaster is absolutely the number one favorite," Paul Keres was quoted as saying in April, "but I do not think it right to exaggerate his chances. Personally, I have faith in the strength of my comrades. . . ."

Two Soviet chess publications, *Sahs* and *Komsomolskaya Pravda,* took readers' polls predicting the outcome; Fischer was second only to Tal.

World Champion Botvinnik, queried at Stockholm about who had the best chance at Curaçao, replied: "In his entire career, Mikhail Tal has won every tournament he had to win."

"One thing seems clear to me," Gligoric concluded, "five Soviet grandmasters cannot be weaker than one Fischer."

When the news started coming back from Curaçao that May, you could hear crystal balls shattering all over the world. Fischer and Tal had both lost in the first and second rounds. Both had been defeated by Pal Benko, who had laughed about his own chances in the tournament. In round three, Fischer finally got a win against Dr. Filip; Tal fell deeper into trouble with still another loss. Fischer and Tal met in round four, and drew. Tal struggled to his first win in round five, and Fischer lost! By mid-May, Victor Korchnoi was leading the contest, with Keres and Petrosian close behind. Tal had lost five games and was practically out of the running. Bobby Fischer was fighting each game with all his famous nerve and spirit, but had fallen to sixth place. All in all, Dr. Eliot Hearst observed in *Chess Life,* the Candidates had furnished ". . . a series of early-round surprises that are probably without parallel in chess history."

In round twelve, Fischer helped knock Korchnoi out of the lead. The Leningrad grandmaster blundered in a superior position and lost the game to Bobby, a defeat that dampened his morale for the rest of the tournament.

Heidenfeld (whom we keep returning to as one of the world's foremost contemporary chess critics) puts it more strongly, first talking of their encounter at Stockholm:

Fischer complained that Korchnoi was very rude to him, and Korchnoi may well feel the same about Fischer— since then their personal encounters have always had psychological undertones. When Bobby lost the first game at Curaçao he was reported as hardly able to control his tears (while he had taken his previous losses to Benko and Geller quite calmly); when Korchnoi blundered and lost to Fischer in the second turn, he was so embittered that he lost to Tal (for the first time in his career!).

At the halfway mark, with fourteen grueling rounds completed, the eight players paused for a five-day rest at St. Maartin. Bobby had climbed to fifth place, and had won more games—five—than anyone else. He had played the Russians dead even at 4½–4½, having beaten Tal and Keres, exchanged a win and a loss with Korchnoi, and dropped one and drawn one with Petrosian. Geller, however, had proved just one Russian too many, and had avenged his Bled loss to Fischer twice over.

At the beginning of the third quarter, Korchnoi's hopes were ruined by consecutive losses to Geller, Petrosian, and Keres, the three who by now easily dominated the tournament. Bobby had scrambled forward into fourth place. Tal, who had recently undergone a serious operation and probably shouldn't have attended the tournament, became ill and had to be hospitalized when the quarter was over. At the end of twenty-three rounds, the three Soviet leaders were a full two points ahead of Fischer, who fought doggedly on, though even he must have seen that he had no chance. Only Petrosian remained undefeated, closely harried by Geller and Keres. In the last two rounds, the fading Benko upset everything by winning a game from Keres he was supposed to lose, and losing against Geller a game anyone else would have drawn.

Tigran Petrosian, still undefeated, won the 1962 Candidates Tournament with a score of 8 wins, 19 draws, and no losses for 17½ points. Geller and Keres tied for second a half-point behind him (Keres later won the playoff for a clear second). Fischer won as many games as anyone, but his seven losses killed him, and his fourth-place score was three full points below the three leaders and only a half-point ahead of Korchnoi. Benko had not so much placed as shown, which was probably all he had wanted to do. Tal was the sad casualty of the race, and Filip never really got started.

Since Curaçao was the turning point in Bobby's career—and neither he nor world chess has been the same since—we shall have to try to see as clearly as possible just what happened there. Before May and June of 1962 he had seemed to be gaining strength with every contest. "Fischer grows from one tournament to the next,"

Mikhail Tal had said. He had surpassed his great achievement at Bled in 1961 with the even more dazzling triumph at Stockholm. He had defeated at least once all of the five Soviet grandmasters he was to meet at Curaçao, and he seemed to be reaching the peak of his powers sooner than anyone (but himself) had expected. His fall to a very laggard fourth place was thus from grandiose heights and even that position was only won by a comeback that is not the most brilliant in Fischer's career.

Some have speculated that Bobby might have been gambling (which is legal in Curaçao). Not one Russian was seen in the Casino gambling during the entire tournament, and that contrast to the conduct of all of the other players may have given vent to the rumor. There were other whisper campaigns about Bobby's behavior during Curaçao, but they are better left unreported.

But the reversal of fortunes was almost shocking. What *did* happen?

In the first place, all expectations had been too giddy. Even after his marvelous showing at the Interzonal, a poll of the grandmasters at Stockholm had revealed widespread doubt that Bobby would win the Candidates this year (though they expected him to place closer to the top than he did), on grounds best summarized by our quotation from Gligoric. The Soviet grandmasters had played Fischer time and again, which had given them ample opportunity to spot and study flaws in his play. Isaac Boleslavsky, a Soviet witness at Curaçao, wrote of Fischer's style there: ". . . certain weaknesses, inevitable for his age, were apparent in almost every game. Having discovered these weaknesses his opponents play carefully against him." And again, Bobby's celebrated stubbornness and will to win—among his greatest assets—here frequently proved liabilities. Another point that could be offered is that the Soviets weren't really trying to win but were just trying to qualify at Stockholm, but at Curaçao they were attempting to capture first place for the Soviet Union. Hence, the comparison in strength with Fischer only *appeared* to be of equal stature between the two tournaments, when all the while the Soviet strength at Curaçao was considerably stronger. It is also possible that the Soviets reserved their best opening lines for Curaçao, and didn't play them at Stockholm because they didn't need them merely to qualify.

And lastly, there is the simple truism that Bobby wasn't at his best, due to psychological intangibles and not to any all-explaining external "reason." "Bobby Fischer is certainly playing below his strength," Boleslavsky wrote during the tournament. All chess masters, including the greatest of all time, can be and have been beaten at ebbtide moments in their careers.

As we have noted before and will again, however, Bobby's conception of himself in relation to his game has little to do with common sense. He is not *like* other players. If his luck and skill run low in the most important tournament of his life, there must be something wrong somewhere, and he is not the man to look for it within himself.

Just prior to the Candidates Tournament, his belief in his unqualified superiority had led to an unpleasant little incident involving Pal Benko. The event occasioned no publicity at all because it was never published. It was told to me by an eyewitness who is in every way reliable and it is relevant to Bobby's Curaçao performance, if only as an illustration of his frame of mind there.

Because the early-spring appeal for funds had had very limited success, the U.S.C.F. and the A.C.F. had decided that they could send only one second to Curaçao with our players. (The second has become practically an indispensable figure in international tournament play, due to the immense complexity of modern chess and the necessity of unflagging, almost constant, analysis. A second may spend a whole night analyzing a game so that the player can get his full rest and still have the necessary information when he wakes up next morning. It is skilled, exhausting work, and the second is well paid for it.)

"The five Russian participants will have plenty of seconds and plenty of backing," Jerry Spann wrote in *Chess Life* for April 1962. "Can we afford to give our players less . . . ?"

The readership apparently thought so, and only the services of Arthur Bisguier were secured. Now, it was more or less tacitly assumed that Bisguier would spend most of his time backing up Fischer, while rendering only incidental assistance to Benko. This was the obvious pragmatic solution, since Bisguier could not do two jobs at once. It also made excellent sense, since Fischer was capable of winning the U.S.A. its first World Championship in this century, while Benko himself admitted that his own chances for winning even the Candidates were almost nil. But it seemed a very undemocratic decision to the Hungarian, who had not emerged from the ordeal of Budapest without certain stubborn notions about equality. Benko let it be known that he was entitled to equal time, which of course legally he was. To Bobby, the idea was preposterous. Here, on the threshold of the World Championship itself, was he to be deprived of the full services of a second? Bisguier writes: "Apparently he [Benko] developed this feeling of righteousness *after* he got off to such a good start. I was willing to give my services to both but Fischer wanted a second all to himself and it was so agreed in advance."

The tension between the two men increased as the tournament wore on. It came to a head in a furious, shouting argument in a hotel room sparked by Fischer's mimicking Benko's accent. They came to blows.

Thereafter, the two American contestants did not speak to each other, and they avoided meeting whenever possible. For some time following Curaçao they remained hostile, to the point that one would shun a tournament if he learned the other was participating. Eventually they established a "speaking terms" arrangement and have since become friends again. The whole thing is all the more regrettable because at that time Benko was one of the few consistent friends that Bobby had among the American grandmasters.

Quite aside from the fight with Benko, Fischer's aloofness, long conspicuous, was so pronounced at Curaçao that it became the talk of the island. He did not eat with the other players in the common dining hall, but had his dinner served to him in his room, usually around midnight after the round had been finished. During the five-day rest at St. Maartin he did not swim, sunbathe, or join the others in any recreation. Moreover, he was hypercritical in the extreme. He had always been a nervous player, objecting to noise and distractions that didn't bother anyone else, but at Curaçao he was constantly complaining about everything—the food, the playing conditions, and above all the behavior of his competitors. However, those who would use such evidence to reduce him to some schizoid stereotype, unable to get outside himself or think of anyone but himself, ignore his complexity. When Mikhail Tal was hospitalized, not one of the other Soviet grandmasters visited him, and Tal was deeply hurt. His only visitor among the tournament participants was Bobby Fischer.

That, so far as I know, is about all that happened at Curaçao. When asked why Fischer hadn't won, Pal Benko replied: "He simply wasn't the best player." That is probably as good an answer as any.

Dr. Euwe's explanation in an article entitled "An Afterlook at the Candidates, 1962" which appeared in the *Canadian Chess Chat*, was well reasoned. He said:

> Fischer was and still is exhausting his forces. In the Stockholm tournament he did his utmost up to the very last move, thus attaining an advance of 2½ points over his nearest rivals, Petrosian and Geller. He could have scored as many as 3½ points less and still have made the Candidates. In view of the short interval of one and one half months between these two important and strenuous tournaments, Fischer must have been tired at the outset of the Candidates . . . Fischer certainly must have underrated his opponents.

The mood Bobby Fischer returned in is perhaps too involved for speculation. What lay in ruins behind him was not just a chance at the Championship that would not be renewed for many years to come. His whole self-image had been shaken. At a certain point in time he had considered it inevitable that he would win the World Championship. His destiny was manifest; everything proclaimed it. In the entire history of the royal game, no other adolescent had been first and finest at the highest levels of national and international chess. Since his record was already exceptional, it must continue being so: he would win the world title at an earlier age than any other player. At Stockholm he seemed to have reached the fullness of his powers, sweeping through the grandmaster ranks with effortless brilliance. He could have had no doubt whatsoever that his hour of triumph was at hand. And then came Curaçao. . . . He had to find an explanation for it; he needed some way to rationalize his losses. He had to place the blame.

As early as 1953—as Bobby was to point out—*Chess Review* had stated that "There has been undeniable collusion by the Russians to freeze out Western competition." *The New York Times*, more cautiously, had editorialized about ". . . possible collusion between Soviet players to help one win a tourney, as against a non-Soviet opponent." And even while the Curaçao tournament itself was in progress, *Sports Illustrated*, June 4, 1962, accused the Russian players of prearranging draws and thus ". . . winning without really trying"—a charge that Dr. Eliot Hearst in *Chess Life* was quick to observe ". . . can be argued endlessly—without any real hope of settling the matter." Dr. Hearst quoted Grandmaster Averbakh, present at Curaçao, to the effect that draws are a matter of style. It was well known that Petrosian played for draws more than any other grandmaster in chess. Paul Keres, hitherto a "romantic" stylist, explained his conservative play at Curaçao by saying: ". . . In the 1959 Challengers tourney, I took chances and it didn't work. Now I'm trying another way!" The Soviet contestant most renowned for a gambling style, Mikhail Tal, met disaster from the beginning. "At present," Dr. Hearst concluded, "the safest comment to make is that Petrosian, Keres, and Geller have played a large number of draws with each other in the past, and therefore the persistent draws at Curaçao give no evidence of anything particularly suspicious. It's true, also, that Fischer's poor start, and the immediate rise of four Russians to the top of the score-table, made it rather convenient for the Soviet stars to continue their point-splitting course. If Bobby had won his first few games, draws among the Russians would have been the worst possible course for them to follow, since that procedure would have placed them further and further behind the American. Bobby could then have used the 'Russian draws' to his own advantage, just as he did at Bled and Stockholm, where over 90% of the encounters between the Russians also ended in draws. . . ."

This rationale did not stop Fischer. In *Sports Illustrated*, August 20, 1962, his *j'accuse*, "The Russians Have Fixed World Chess," burst upon the clubs and cadres that follow the royal game. It was reprinted in German, Dutch, Spanish, Swedish, Icelandic, and (with modifications) Russian. In it Bobby announced that he would never again participate in a Candidates Tournament because the present FIDE system made it impossible for any but a Russian player to win. Direct Soviet control—or sufficient influence—over FIDE itself is clearly implied: "The system set up by the *Fédération Internationale des Échecs* . . . insures that there will always be a Russian world champion. . . . The Russians arranged it that way." Bobby recalled his debut in international chess at Portoroz and his fifth place there behind four Russians, and indicates briefly how he had grown in strength since then sufficiently to have defeated all the Soviet grandmasters competing with him for the title. He stated that during these three years Russian dominance of these events had become a great deal more "open"—presumably in response to the threat of Fischer. It was never more "flagrant" than at Curaçao. Bobby failed to mention that neither he nor anyone else ever proved a threat to the three leading Russians throughout this tournament, so the question of why the stratagems of domination should have been used with such flagrancy here remains unanswered. But Bobby is sure that the Soviet players agreed in advance to draw their games with one another, and that Korchnoi must have agreed to start by losing, through the primary beneficiary of Korchnoi's collapse was Fischer. The constant Russian exchange of draws spared them adjourned games and cut down their work-week, enabling them to spend a good deal of their time in the hotel swimming pool. Even worse, when they didn't go to the pool, they stood around analyzing and commenting upon Bobby's games while they were still in progress. It is easy to imagine how this must have irritated Fischer, who is upset at the slightest distraction while playing, but his repeated protests were ineffectual. In his article Bobby suggests that the other Russians were openly advising his Soviet opponent on occasion, though they must have known that Fischer, not to mention the officials and spectators present, had some command of Russian. At any rate, Bobby reiterated that he was through with the whole present FIDE system of elimination contests, and that his decision was final.

It is true that grandmasters—and not only Russians—"feed" each other moves during tournaments, especially if such a gift will knock out a winner, or a potential one. I have seen this done in tournaments I have refereed, played in, and watched. The "buying" of games, especially to qualify for titles such as International Master and International Grandmaster, is also much more common than is generally imagined and, unfortunately, is becoming even more widespread. I must hasten to add that since the advent of Fischer these shenanigans have, for the most part, ceased to occur in tournaments Fischer himself competes in. He just won't stand for it.

Bobby's circumstantial case was impressive. At Curaçao, Petrosian, Geller, Keres, and, up to the halfway point, Korchnoi, drew all of the games they played with one another, very often in less than twenty moves. "Reports from Curaçao," Eliot Hearst had remarked during the tournament, "indicate that an overwhelming number of the foreign correspondents and local organizers also believed that the Russians were deliberately soft on each other . . . to assure a Soviet victory." Of course, as Dr. Hearst himself has pointed out, half-points don't assure a victory, though they may have some value in protecting a lead already gained. But while three or four Russians, bunched in the lead, were trading draws, a steady winner could have cut right through them.

But to be a consistent winner in game after game in a tournament with the world's best players is almost impossible, even for a Fischer.

Curiously enough, Bobby's attack on this point had been anticipated in a discussion between Leonard Barden and Alexander Kotov at Stockholm. Although the Soviet grandmaster's assertion is scarcely surprising, it is at least buttressed with facts.

"No Soviet player," Kotov said, "has ever thrown a game to another Soviet competitor in an international tournament. On the contrary, I myself defeated Botvinnik when he was fighting it out for first prize with Euwe at Groningen, 1946, and I again won from Smyslov when he and Reshevsky were contesting the lead in the 1953 Candidates. . . .

"Of course, there have been short *draws*, without fight, among Soviet grandmasters in international events: but you can see for yourself that this does not only happen with Russian players, nor indeed only with competitors from the same country. Look, for instance, at the games played in international events between grandmaster Stahlberg and other players with peaceful styles."

Grandmaster Arthur Bisguier, however, disagrees and he was at Curaçao. He stated in an interview in the Fall 1962 issue of *American Chess Quarterly*, "It's my personal belief that they agreed to draws beforehand. . . ." The article went on: "*Question*: All the Russians agreed to draws? *Answer*: No. . . . at least Fischer felt that Keres, Geller, and Petrosian did. Tal and Korchnoi seemed to be outside of this—"

Much later, Paul Keres wrote: "Elementary mathematics shows that a draw can only benefit the score of someone in the lower half of the table." Pal Benko, who has less reason to side with the Russians than any other grandmaster, has been quoted as flatly denying Bobby's indictment against them.

The real reason for Soviet dominance of chess is, of course, their numerical preponderance. The Soviet Union has more first-rate players than any other three nations combined. So long as this is the situation—and with the superb Soviet "farm system" it will almost certainly continue to be—two to three Russians will always survive the Interzonal and enter the Candidates, with one or two more seeded over. In the latter contest, as Larry Evans wrote during the course of Curaçao, "that a Soviet player will win by sheer weight of numbers is almost a foregone conclusion." Like the Las Vegas gambling houses, the Soviets do not *need* to cheat or fix anything; the odds will do it for them. In this sense, there was obvious and verifiable truth in Bobby's charge that no Westerner could hope to win the world title under the present system.

Bobby's polemic shook the very structure of world chess, and not long after Curaçao FIDE made a brave attempt to remedy some of the abuses he had aired. A radical reform of the Candidates' was voted. Instead of following a tournament procedure, it was to consist of a series of matches of ten or twelve games each between the eight individual contestants, with the loser of each match being eliminated. Also, referees and directors were asked to recommence taking seriously the rule barring draws in less than thirty moves successfully in effect at Margate 1936. Thus, possible collusion was made more difficult, and any prearranged draws would take a little longer to play out. This rule has since been abandoned because it was so unenforceable.

FIDE passed yet another major rule change, concerning the World's Championship itself. Beginning with the 1975 Championship match, no draws will count: the title will go to the player who first wins six games.

At the time that Fischer was making all these statements about draws not counting and matches being better than tournaments as true tests of strength, I must admit that I was skeptical. In discussions with Fischer, I told him that I thought his ideas were impractical. I now see, after ten years, the method to his "madness." He has, singlehandedly, cleaned up world chess and transformed it from what was becoming an apathetic and uninteresting pastime with countless draws being produced each year, to an exciting and meaningful struggle, especially in the World Championship cycle, where games are now won or lost in courageous and sometimes brilliant fashion.

If Fischer continues in his insistence that draws should not count in matches,* there is no reason that the transition could not occur in tournaments also, whereby a draw would count as a zero point to be deducted from the scores of *both* players, unless sufficient mating

---

* There is historical precedent, of course, to Fischer's proposed system. In the first unofficial Championship of the World, a match in 1866 between Adolf Anderssen and Wilhelm Steinitz, the first eight wins—draws not counting—decided the winner.

materials are thoroughly depleted. (Or else, players could be forced, as they were in the International Tournament, London, 1872, to replay all drawn games, until a winner emerged.) This would force a duel to the death, as either player would have nothing to gain by a draw. Consequently the entire rules of the game itself, and certainly its strategies and systems, would undergo the first significant change in five hundred years and perhaps the most important change in the rules ever. Bobby Fischer may leave his mark here, also.

CHAPTER VII

*"There are tough players and nice
guys, and I'm a tough player."*

Despite or perhaps because of his world-publicized opinions of
FIDE and the Russians, Bobby was prevailed upon to lead a U.S.
team through an Olympics tournament once again. Behind him was
mustered a great American team: Larry Evans, Pal Benko, the Byrne
brothers, and Edmar Mednis. The Fifteenth Chess Olympiad was to
be held in Varna, a Bulgarian resort town on the Black Sea. A.C.F.
and U.S.C.F., a State Department grant, and a Lamport Foundation
donation helped finance the trip.

Fischer, the Byrnes, Mednis, and team captain Eliot Hearst stopped
over in Warsaw and played the Polish Olympic Team. Though Fischer
beat Sliwa, Poland's strongest player, both Byrne brothers lost, and the
U.S. team barely salvaged a 3–2 victory, which didn't make prospects
at Varna look any better. However, strong second and third board
support was en route to Bulgaria. Evans was driving across the continent from Paris, and Benko was flying in from New York. The latter,
after considering pleas of U.S. relatives not to risk his person deep in
Communist territory, had finally decided to go. As it happened, he
only discovered by alert rechecking that the plane he was to take
from Amsterdam was scheduled to stop over at Budapest. He took a
later flight, which passed directly over his home city, and arrived at
Varna in an emotional state that made it impossible for him to play in
the first-round match. Evans also was unable to play this round, having
spent several sleepless days and nights driving his new Citroën over
what passed for roads in Yugoslavia and Bulgaria.

The U.S. team got through the seven rounds of the preliminaries
with six wins and a draw (with Bulgaria) for a percentage of 86,
which was equaled only by the Soviets in their section. But the Americans had scored clean sweeps only against the four weakest teams.
Fischer, Evans, and Mednis had narrow squeaks; Benko had lost one,
and so had Robert Byrne, who was clearly playing below his best
form. However, the team had qualified for the finals, with the U.S.A.
pitted against East Germany in the first round.

Having been the person most responsible for getting FIDE to insist on the thirty-move draw ruling, Bobby promptly proceeded to become the first major player to break it. In spite of the fact that it had been expressly announced at the start of the Olympiad that the new rules would be in effect, Fischer quickly exchanged Queens with Grandmaster Uhlmann, and the game was drawn in nineteen moves. The referee, Soviet Grandmaster Salo Flohr, wasn't even notified. When he found out, Flohr warned Fischer not to let it happen again. "Those rules," Bobby graciously told him "are for the Communist cheaters, not for me."

In the next round Fischer met Argentina's famed Najdorf, and like Babe Ruth's famed three home run prediction, Bobby made one relative to the Argentinian. He said he would beat him in twenty-five moves; he did it in twenty-four, accounting for Najdorf's only loss of the tournament. The easy win probably made Bobby over-confident, and he could get no better than a draw from Grandmaster Filip in round three. Benko beat the dangerous Pachman, and Donald Byrne crushed Trapl to save a win against Czechoslovakia. The U.S.A. was tied for the lead with Russia and Rumania. Then the Austrian team, the weakest in the finals, took two out of four games, with Benko and Byrne abruptly reversing roles to end up losers. This dropped the U.S.A. a half-point behind the front runners. The ominous trend continued with Fischer's first loss of the tournament to Ciociltea of Rumania. Bobby was suffering from a bad cold, but he insisted on playing that evening against Holland and was handed a second straight loss by Grandmaster Donner. Donald Byrne and Mednis scored solid wins to salvage the match, but the team had now dropped to fourth place. The Americans staved off disaster with a fine rally against West Germany. Fischer, Benko, and Donald Byrne came through with victories over Unzicker, Darga, and Troeger, and Evans escaped from an inferior position by making his game so complicated that his opponent, Schmid, finally had to draw in time-pressure.

In the eighth round against Bulgaria, Fischer again drew before the thirtieth move without consulting Flohr, and then left the room. The referee threatened a forfeit against Bobby unless he returned to the board while a legitimacy decision was made, but of course there was no chance of budging Fischer. Captain Hearst managed to work out a compromise with Flohr and the Bulgarian captain, and the draw was allowed. The next day Evans, after a long night of analysis, drew with Minev, but Robert Byrne won to outscore Bulgaria by a point. The U.S.A. moved into second place. Benko sat out the game against Hungary; Fischer could only draw with Portisch, and though Donald Byrne won, Mednis lost and Robert Byrne drew for an even match. Russia at the same time defeated West Germany, and there was no more hope of an American victory. But their next round was with the Soviet Union, and there was still a chance for glory in defeat.

With spectators crammed into the playing room and wallboards set up outside for the benefit of the overflow crowd, Fischer finally met Mikhail Botvinnik, who was playing first board for the U.S.S.R. Bobby, playing black against the World Champion, moved into a winning position in the middle game, and when he sealed his move, he was sure he had the game won.

At breakfast the next morning, Botvinnik remarked to Leonard Barden that he thought the game was "probably lost." However, Geller had spent the whole night analyzing the adjourned position and had found a drawing line for Botvinnik before resumption. When Bobby saw his win slipping away, he asked U.S. team captain Hearst to make a formal protest that Botvinnik was receiving help from the Soviet team captain, Abramov. Fischer said he had seen Abramov smiling after the Russians had exchanged a few words. "The idea that Botvinnik would even listen to advice from a player so vastly inferior to himself was inconceivable," Hearst wrote much later, "and no protest was lodged. After this incident," he added, "several players on the U.S. team, who had previously been willing to accept Bobby's arguments regarding Russian cheating at Curaçao, expressed skepticism about his claims. It seemed that whenever Bobby suffered a reversal at the hands of a Russian he blamed it on unethical practices." When Fischer conceded the draw the tournament hall was in an uproar. Botvinnik said that drawing the game pleased him even more than regaining the world title from Tal.

Shortly after his game with Botvinnik, Fischer again challenged him to a match for the Championship of the World (first made by Fischer in his article in *Sports Illustrated* published after Curaçao) *with the handicap of two points.* The British newspaper *The People* offered to pay for the expenses of the match if it could be arranged to be played in London. If Fischer was serious, Botvinnik was not. He laughed: "If Fischer wants to spot me two points, I'll accept; and I'll spot him two Pawns in each game!" No serious negotiations ever took place.

In the meantime, at second board, Benko had tested Petrosian's great defensive skill severely before the Russian managed a draw. Evans continued the pattern by carrying the fight to Boris Spassky, but the young Russian grandmaster, current Champion of the Soviet Union and as strong as anyone playing those days, forced him to resign by the twenty-sixth move. Donald Byrne drew with Mikhail Tal, and the U.S.A. lost the match and faced a struggle to retain even third place. Against the powerful Yugoslav, Gligoric, Fischer again developed a seemingly crushing position, but he became overconfident and found the game running the other way. At adjournment he re-

signed for his third loss. When Benko and Evans played out anticli-
mactic draws and Ivkov beat Robert Byrne, the last-round loss
dropped the U.S. team to a sorry fourth behind the Soviet Union,
Yugoslavia, and Argentina.

In a dispatch wired to *Pravda*, Botvinnik wrote that he "was sorry
that the USA had not been second, because they deserved to be . . .
and only Fischer's performance prevented this outcome." This was not
quite fair, for while Bobby's 5½–5½ was a bitterly disappointing come-
down from his 8–3 at the 1960 Leipzig Olympiad, his score in the
preliminaries was good and Larry Evans had won only one game in
the finals, Robert Byrne faring even worse for a minus score of 4–3.
(His brother Donald was the team's high scorer.) The fact remains,
though, that a brilliant or even steady Fischer performance could have
pulled the whole team up—and it was a team of genuinely great
potential. His exhibition off the board, particularly his willingness to
risk a forfeit and so blight his team's chances, was even more
depressing.

In his lengthy description of the month and a half that the U.S.
team spent behind the Iron Curtain (to which this writing is, needless
to say, greatly indebted), Dr. Hearst includes the following bit of
memorabilia: ". . . [At] Blatchik Palace and Roman Gardens, which
a Rumanian queen had built as a gift for a 'friend,' Bobby Fischer
enjoyed having his picture taken as he sat in the throne which faced
the sea. . . ."

This vignette, replete with unintentional ironies, could well have
remained our final image of Bobby's last journey to the East and his
last ambiguous performance in the high halls of international competition. For years it looked like Fischer's relationship to international
chess would only cause him discomfort and sorrow.

CHAPTER VIII

*"Chess demands total
concentration and a love for
the game."*

In 1962 the sponsors and organizers of the Rosenwald tournament doubled the victory prize to $2,000, probably for the express purpose of luring Fischer and Reshevsky back into participation. The event was held at the Henry Hudson Hotel that winter and turned out to be well attended despite the newspaper strike that was then crippling public communication in New York. The slate was quite strong; out of the top ten ratings only Lombardy and Donald Byrne failed to accept invitations. Grandmaster strength was conspicuous, with Fischer, Reshevsky, Benko, Evans, Bisguier, and the long-dormant Nicolas Rossolimo all in attendance.

The beginning of the contest, however, confounded the prognosticators. It was a domestic Curaçao. In the first round, defending Champion Evans was beaten by the low-rated Robert Steinmeyer, and Reshevsky was routed by the California newcomer William Addison. It wasn't until two days later, though, that the most staggering result of that first round became known; for the first time in an American tournament since 1957, Bobby Fischer had been defeated—by Edmar Mednis, of all people. Apparently Bobby just couldn't shake off the overoptimism that had plagued him all year; he persisted in trying to contrive a winning line where no possibility of a win existed. Although Fischer trailed Arthur Bisguier throughout most of the contest, he steadied down to the necessary business of beating the low-ranking Berliner, Addison, Steinmeyer, and Sherwin, and drawing with the high-ranking Benko, Evans, Byrne, and Rossolimo. The crucial margin was provided by his continued domination of Reshevsky and Bisguier, who just never seem to be able to prevail against Bobby in U.S. Championship tournaments. In his fifth-round game with Reshevsky, Fischer made mistakes and still managed to win. Going into the final round Bisguier, still undefeated, was tied with Bobby at 7–3. Through the opening and middle game Bisguier held his own, but on the twenty-third move he made his seemingly inevitable slip-up against Fischer.

Thirteen moves later he resigned, and Bobby was once again United States Chess Champion, equaling Reshevsky's record of five national titles won. A few months later, Reshevsky won playoffs against Evans and Addison to qualify for the next Interzonal tournament.

In April there were renewed negotiations to stage a USA-USSR match to be held in New York in June, but adequate financing could not be found by the U.S. Chess Federation.

That spring Tigran Petrosian defeated Mikhail Botvinnik for the World Championship, an event wildly celebrated in Armenia and almost nowhere else. Since Botvinnik, now in his early fifties, had more than once hinted that he would retire and would be very unlikely to start all over again at the next Candidates Tournament, years hence, his demise seemed to sound the knell of the whole postwar era in chess. Since 1948 he had held the throne (with brief interruptions) as the logical successor to Alekhine, and like Alekhine he played what connoisseurs call "beautiful chess." Petrosian, for all his gifts, has a prudent and shapeless style that even his Soviet colleagues admit gives little logical or esthetic satisfaction.

"Pretty poor chess," was Fischer's unsurprising comment on the match.

Throughout most of 1963 Bobby seemed indecisive, almost adrift, stubbornly sitting out the major tournaments and trying to reorient his career in directions that would still be in keeping with his reputation. In June he turned up as a monthly columnist for *Chess Life* with a page and more of game analysis entitled, with characteristically blunt simplicity, "Fischer Talks Chess." Most of his material was devoted to a running battle with Russian chess pundits who had dared criticize him for having attacked Soviet chess. Bobby met them on the only battlefield he knew—the chessboard—annotating their published games and finding innumerable errors and blunders. He thus sought to hurl their "lack of objectivity" charges back at them, though comparative gamesmanship was not at all what the Soviet critics had in mind. But, for Fischer at this point, irrelevance was apparently unimportant.

His announced boycott of FIDE qualifying tournaments seemed to have spread to international contests in general. This left him universally acknowledged master of only the fifty states, but he showed little interest in indiscriminate plundering of Opens or in cup-collecting. By far the greatest and most glittering event of the year—or of several decades—in the United States was the Piatigorsky Cup Tournament scheduled for July 2 through 28 at the Ambassador Hotel in Los Angeles. It was hailed by FIDE Vice President Spann as "the greatest International All-Grandmaster Chess Tournament ever held in America." The award fund was $10,000, with $3,000 for first prize and $600 even for eighth—an amount calculated to draw grandmasters like flies. Bobby was of course invited and—despite numerous pleas—

declined. He had, perhaps deliberately, asked for a $2,000 appearance fee which was higher than even that posh gala was about to proffer, and he publicly notified one and all of his impending absence. "I lend stature to any tournament I attend," he told me, implying that L.A. had practically ruined their tournament through miserliness. The Piatigorsky Cup roster included only Petrosian (the first World Champion to take part in a U.S. tournament since the Twenties), Keres, Gligoric, Reshevsky, Benko, Najdorf, Olafsson, and Panno. Petrosian and Keres predictably won.

Bobby staged a counter-show to the main event in Los Angeles by abruptly appearing in the Western Open at Bay City, Michigan, that same July, conspicuously boycotting the lush Piatigorsky tournament. For a weekend's "work" he swept up a nice little first prize of $750 out of the $2,500 funded by the Hoffman Houses Corporation and the Milwaukee Chess Foundation. The night before the final round, Fischer played a bout of five-minute chess with Norbert Leopoldi, a Chicago advertising man known as a strong midwest player. Word swept through the tournament hall that Fischer had won $250. The next morning, after playing all night without sleep, the figure had risen to $3,500 with Fischer giving odds of Pawn and move, and Pawn and two moves. Out of hundreds of games played, Leopoldi managed to win three games.

The next morning, Fischer faced Bisguier and though perhaps apocryphal, it has been said that he was so tired he actually fell asleep at the board and had to be awakened. It didn't affect his play, however, as he defeated Bisguier soundly. Fischer was nothing but convivial those three days, signing autographs and offering advice all around; he also noted that the lighting and playing conditions were better than in the big international events. While the September *Chess Life* was still full of the Piatigorsky Cup and the awards banquet at the Beverly Hills Hotel, "Fischer Talks Chess" presented the Western Open as a "model" compared to "foreign ones," and maintained that from five to eight of the games the writer had played there were also models when contrasted to the dreary run of the Los Angeles tournament.

He made one more sortie into a weekend Swiss system tournament that fall. I had remarked to a promotor of the New York State Open at Poughkeepsie that Bobby would probably be willing to appear, and it turned out he was. We travelled upstate via the New York Central railroad, Bobby showing me novel variations on his pocket set, while occasionally gazing at the Hudson River. He swept the field 7–0 ahead of Bisguier and Sherwin on a Labor Day that was not particularly strenuous.

Bobby told me at that time that he was confident that he could defeat Petrosian in a world championship title match and he was interested in securing backing for such an encounter. I attempted to interest a number of chess patrons but could find neither enthusiasm nor money—the closest possibility of backing came from Dr. Harry Bakwin, a member of the Board of Directors of the American Chess Foundation. Dr. Bakwin asked me to list all of the positive and negative aspects of such a match. I sent him the following letter, with Bobby's knowledge:

October 10, 1963

Dear Dr. Bakwin:

To confirm our telephone conversation of this afternoon, Bobby Fischer is interested in throwing out a challenge to Tigran Petrosian, the current champion of the world for a sum of $10,000.00 to comprise a ten-game match with draws aside.

If Petrosian refuses to accept the match, Bobby will then challenge anyone else in the world for the same stakes, the winner of said match to be declared World Champion. If Bobby loses the match, all of the $10,000 will be lost but if he wins, he will retain $5,000 and the backers will get $15,000 in return for their $10,000 investment.

If the match is played in the United States, Bobby would like to play it in cities throughout the United States in auditoriums where admission fees can be charged. Details as to how this can be arranged, etc., have not, as yet, been worked out.

I must warn you, Dr. Bakwin, this this move of Bobby's is going to be very unpopular in many circles. As you know, he is not looked upon kindly by the American Chess Foundation and this rupture with the general procedure in organized chess will not sit favorably with the U.S. Chess Federation either. That is why I asked you not to mention it to anyone at this time, since harmful publicity generated toward Bobby through organized chess circles could upset the possibilities of such a match.

Bobby's action, is, in my opinion, very similar to Paul Morphy's—when Morphy went to Europe to challenge Staunton for the championship of the world and Staunton refused to play. Morphy returned to America and issued a challenge to the world that he would spot anyone a Pawn for a match in the world's championship. No one accepted and Morphy consequently proclaimed himself champion.

Cordially,
Frank R. Brady
Editor and Publisher
Chessworld Magazine

After seriously considering it for a week, Dr. Bakwin ultimately decided not to back the match.

With some idea of getting him into an event worthy of his immense talent, I proposed that he give the most ambitious simultaneous exhibition of all time. The record he would be attempting to break was that set by Swedish Grandmaster Gideon Stahlberg at Buenos Aires in 1941, when the Swede played four hundred opponents for three hundred and sixty-four wins, fourteen draws, and twenty-two losses. I suggested that Bobby try to go beyond this in number of games played and won. Fischer accepted the challenge at once and proposed to give himself the additional handicap of playing half the games with the black pieces rather than having a monopoly of white (as is the custom in most simultaneous exhibitions, including Stahlberg's). The Buenos Aires feat had taken thirty-six hours; Bobby figured that it would take him "five or six hours to complete 75 percent of all the games and a few more hours to knock off those that remain." He was supremely confident, and we were both increasingly excited about the project.

News of the prospective event quickly stirred up even more intense interest than we'd dared hope for. All of the New York newspapers planned to cover it. *Life* and several other magazines expressed interest in doing a picture article on it. Jeremy Bernstein, who was doing a "Talk of the Town" for *The New Yorker*, intended to enter the contest himself for an inside story. ABC-TV's "Wide World of Sports" was prepared to devote a whole Sunday spectacular to the event. We had over one hundred and fifty advance entries, which was better than expected. Fischer was planning to wear a tuxedo for the first time in his life. I had reserved the Grand Ballroom of the Hotel Astor, and the date was set as Thanksgiving Eve, Wednesday, November 27, 1963. I had even sent an invitation to President Kennedy, who was to be in New York at that time.

The terrible news from Dallas on November 22, of course, caused us to postpone the exhibition. Almost exactly a month later, a fire ruined the Astor's Grand Ballroom. There were other possible sites in New York that could hold the crowd we hoped for, but they were prohibitively expensive. Bobby agreed to postpone the event indefinitely. Contrary to rumors noised about, nobody developed cold feet. Those who can imagine Bobby backing out of such a challenge simply don't know Fischer.

The gloom and pathos of the mourning for the President pervaded even our relatively narrow world of chess. The U.S. team at the World Student Championship at Budva, Yugoslavia, that summer—though again led by Lombardy and Weinstein—fell further than ever from the heights of Leningrad to a bedraggled fifth place. The American representative at the World Junior Championship tournament could score no better than a third place in Group C of the finals. The Piatigorsky tournament had a brilliant debut, but none of our players even got within reach of the trophy. Fischer's genius had been wasted throughout the year. What we have called a renaissance seemed to be running out in 1963. For the first time in the decade, our chess had provided no great achievement or thrilling promise. It seemed out of the question that even Bobby would salvage anything from the dead year that could be compared to his previous accomplishments. But he did.

CHAPTER IX

"I give 98 percent of my mental energy to chess. Others give only 2 percent."

The 1963–1964 United States Championship was again set for the Henry Hudson Hotel, with the roster of competitors almost the same as the previous year. William Lombardy was again the only first-grade regular not participating. Donald Byrne had returned to give the slate added strength over 1962. Raymond Weinstein and Anthony Saidy were also back, making this as formidable a field as the Rosenwald had ever drawn. The classic got under way on December 15, with the initial attendance rather sparse. First prize was $2,000.

The first round was as expected; Fischer avenged himself on Mednis in a long game that was once adjourned. In the second round he faced Larry Evans, whom he had never beaten in a tournament game, and surprised the former U.S. Champion with the King's Bishop Gambit. Evans later wrote that he had thought he had the better of the game up till the last five moves, but Fischer's annotations show him aware of Evans's approaching defeat as far back as the seventeenth move (the game went for thirty-six). Later, Evans said that he thought the game had set chess back a hundred years.

After Evans went down, the crowd began to sense that this tournament might produce a remarkable Fischer performance, and they were far from disappointed. Round three brought up Robert Byrne, called the "invincible" because at his best he is almost impossible to defeat. Bobby had never beaten him, and neither had any other U.S. player in the last two years. Playing black, Bobby produced a game that was immediately recognized as an all-time classic. "The culminating combination is of such depth," Byrne wrote in a later analysis, "that, even at the very moment at which I resigned, both grandmasters who were commenting on the play for the spectators in a separate room believed that I had a won game!"

Afterward, Fischer is reported by Stewart Reuben in *Chess* as saying the win was not due to pre-game analysis ". . . but all obvious. Did we seriously think he spent his time analyzing to the death such arid variations for White?"

On Thursday, December 19, as Fischer played round four against Bisguier, *Chess Life* Editor J. F. Reinhardt noted that the Champion "seemed to have aged several generations since Monday." Bisguier succumbed to the Ruy Lopez. The next round brought up Samuel Reshevsky, and a capacity audience watched Fischer mercilessly involve the aging giant in time-trouble and finally present him with a mate. Now Bobby had soundly defeated his most dangerous opposition, though several coming opponents could scarcely be called weak even in a comparative sense. With immaculate timing and an apparently infallible sense for the truth of the board, Fischer dispatched Steinmeyer, Addison, Weinstein, and Donald Byrne. On the last day of 1963 he sank Pal Benko, who had been having a fine tournament; but by now the accumulating tension and the tremendous psychological momentum Fischer had built were affecting everybody, and Benko was flustered in his defensive moves.

That left Anthony Saidy, who in his mid-twenties was a doctor with the Peace Corps in Jamaica. On leave for the Championship tournament, Saidy was in excellent form, having beaten Bisguier, Weinstein, Mednis, Addison, and Donald Byrne. He still had a chance for second place, and in this last match he held the white pieces. He also had a spoiler's opportunity that could make chess history. The hundreds of spectators in the Hudson watched every move on the big demonstration chessboard with all the hushed tension of a Series grandstand watching the final inning of a perfect game—and most of them watched with increasing dismay. It seemed almost impossible that Bobby could win this one; there were just no prospects. Saidy had worked Fischer into an endgame where a breakthrough was all but inconceivable. The two-and-a-half-hour time limit ran out with no finish in sight. It was Saidy's move and he thought for about forty minutes before sealing it. Spectators and experts alike left convinced of an impending draw. But Saidy's sealed move had been an error. A half hour after the adjourned game was resumed, Saidy found himself outplayed in a clever endgame and forced to resign.

"Fantastic, unbelievable," Larry Evans had said of Fischer's performance in an interview during the third week of the tournament. But the incredible was up on the scoreboard for all to see, and the word was being flashed via the wire services and radio, newspapers, and television to every part of the world. *Sports Illustrated* broke precedent to diagram each of the eleven games—"The Amazing Victory Streak of Bobby Fischer"—and interviews were solicited by *Life* and the *Saturday Evening Post*. What Bobby had done was paralleled only by three immortals in chess history, only twice on this continent —by Emanuel Lasker in 1893 and José Capablanca in 1913—and never in a U.S. Championship. It is probably safe to say no other player in the world at that moment in time, could have breezed through that particular U.S. Championship without surrendering at least one half point. Even his tournament competitors recognized that

Fischer was now in a class by himself. The important question was—where would he go from here? "The next step—the only further step possible—" J.F. Reinhardt wrote in *Chess Life*, "is the World Championship."

On New Year's Eve that year, the Collins' household had their traditional chess party. A number of the players from the U.S. Championship attended and though the tournament hadn't ended, it looked as though Fischer was really making history this time. Bobby, Bill Lombardy, William Addison, and many other chess people like Bill and Kathryn Slater, Allen and Sara Kaufman, Joe Reinhardt, Greta Fuchs, Louis Wolff, and my wife and I also attended. At the exact stroke of midnight, I was sitting across the board from Bobby and was beaten soundly in a clock game of ridiculous odds. (I think I had ten minutes and he had two, or perhaps the odds were even greater), and I wondered what 1964 would bring for this gifted young genius. Bobby then played Addison blindfolded, with the odds of Pawn and move, and at five minutes each! It was the first time I had ever seen Bobby play without sight of the board and he conducted himself masterfully. Addison was a formidable master and yet even at the great odds given to him by Fischer, he barely managed to break even. It was a memorable chess experience for all of us to witness.

Bobby's next step was to go on tour. He had announced as early as December that he planned a transcontinental series of appearances, with a fee of $250 for a 50-board simultaneous exhibition and a lecture.

Unfortunately no accurate records of his tour were ever kept. Here are a few scattered results representing much less than half of the exhibitions he actually played:

	Won	Drew	Lost
Chicago, Illinois	49	4	1
Chicago, Illinois	56	1	4
Cleveland, Ohio	51	0	0
Columbus, Ohio	48	0	0
Detroit, Michigan	47	2	2
Little Rock, Arkansas	36	0	0
Los Angeles, California	47	2	1
Montreal, Canada	46	4	5
New Orleans, Louisiana	70	2	3
Ogden, Utah	62	2	1
Rochester, Minnesota	62	5	1
San Francisco, California	38	1	2
Santa Barbara, California	49	1	2
Toledo, Ohio	40	1	3
Washington, D.C.	51	10	4

The exhibition announcement added that the tour would last from February through May. The word "through" was of key significance, since the next Interzonal tournament was now firmly scheduled to begin in Amsterdam on May 20. Apparently Fischer was still stubbornly resolved to boycott the FIDE qualifying contests. The chess world was reluctant to believe it. After all, if he did not compete at Amsterdam he would have to wait a whole half-decade for another chance to try for the world title. And Bobby himself had mentioned the previous December that the $200 first prize for the Interzonal was too small to justify the efforts involved, a statement which seemed to mean that he had shifted from his rigid ideological stand to the much more flexible grounds of economic objection. Many were persuaded that he would change his mind at the last moment. "No one really knows what Bobby Fischer will do next," J.F. Reinhardt stated in January. And in March Vassily Smyslov wrote in the British magazine *Chess* that he thought Fischer would be present at Amsterdam "because he wants to be world champion more than anything else."

I had reason to be a good deal less optimistic. In March I was asked to serve as intermediary between Fischer and a party who asked to remain anonymous. This party was ready to guarantee Bobby a thousand dollars if he would participate in the Interzonal. When Fischer returned to New York for a few days during his tour I told him of the offer. He refused without hearing the amount, and refused again after I specified it. I personally think that he would have refused even $5,000.

It should not be inferred, however, that Bobby had lost interest in the World Championship. In the *Sports Illustrated* manifesto after Curaçao he had expressed a preference for the "old days" (before the present FIDE set-up) when a challenger frequently could get a match with the World Champion simply by putting up enough money. When Bobby's tour took him to Los Angeles that spring, he actually secured through Alexander Bisno, a former American Chess Foundation officer, powerful support in his attempt to renew this practice. He couldn't get past the FIDE machinery to challenge Petrosian directly, but he sent a proposal to the Soviet Chess Federation inviting any one of the top five Soviet grandmasters to play a set match. Half of the games would be held in the United States and half in Moscow, and the amount of the stake was a large one. After waiting almost a year for a reply, the answer was an emphatic "No."

Bobby's thinking probably ran along these lines: If he could convincingly defeat Botvinnik, Keres, Smyslov, Tal, or Spassky, then a challenge issued to Petrosian himself could scarcely be ignored by the World Champion. I personally saw no reason why U.S.C.F. shouldn't have supported a match between Fischer and one of the top Russians. Many, however, thought that this attempt to bypass the whole FIDE apparatus was unreal and merely embarrassed the orderly processes of world chess.

For his twenty-first birthday, Bobby received, significantly, a number of chess books from his mother, including Taimanov's volume on the Nimzo-Indian and the latest *Lehrbüch Des Schachspiels* by Maizelis and Yudovich.

Of course, to make an unforgettable impact on established chess is one of Bobby's sacred missions. In the first issue of *Chessworld* he authored a piece called "The Ten Greatest Masters in History," which included Tal and Spassky and left out Botvinnik and—unpardonable outrage!—Emanuel Lasker, who was named as the greatest ever by Tal, Korchnoi, and Robert Byrne in a poll of the leading players of the day taken sometime after Fischer's list appeared.

A Dutch magazine, *Elsevier*, that summer picked up articles by Botvinnik, Euwe, and Kotov, all denouncing Bobby's omissions. He hadn't included himself among the Greatest Masters, either, but that fooled nobody. When he had previously written that "In a set match . . . [Paul Morphy] would beat anyone alive today," I'd asked him if that included himself. "Oh, no," he replied with an embarrassed smile. "I didn't include myself on the list."

Here are some of his comments on those he selected as the ten greatest masters in history:

PAUL MORPHY—"A popularly held theory about Paul Morphy is that if he returned to the chess world today and played our best contemporary players, he would come out the loser. Nothing is further from the truth. In a set match, Morphy could beat anybody alive today . . . he was the best read player of his time . . . Morphy was perhaps the most accurate player who ever lived. He had complete sight of the board and never blundered, in spite of the fact that he played quite rapidly, rarely taking more than five minutes to decide a move."

HOWARD STAUNTON—"Staunton was the most profound opening analyst of all time . . . Playing over his games, I discover that they are completely modern; where Morphy and Steinitz rejected the *fianchetto*, Staunton embraced it. Staunton's right to be on a list of the ten greatest players of all time is firmly founded in the profundity of his insights, especially in the opening, and the great wealth of book knowledge that was his."

WILHELM STEINITZ—"He is the so-called father of the modern school of chess; before him, the King was considered a weak piece, and players set out to attack the King directly. Steinitz claimed that the King was well able to take care of itself, and ought not to be attacked until one had some other positional advantage . . . He understood more about the use of squares than Morphy and contributed a great deal more to chess theory."

SIEGBERT TARRASCH—"Tarrasch's play was razor-sharp, and in spite of his devotion to this supposedly scientific method of play, his game was often witty and bright. He was a great opening theorist, vastly superior in this respect to Emanuel Lasker, for example, who was a coffee-house player: Lasker knew nothing about openings and didn't understand positional chess."[*]

MIKHAIL TCHIGORIN—"Tchigorin, who was beaten twice by Steinitz, was the finest endgame player of his time . . . Tchigorin had a very aggressive style, and was thus a great attacking player. He was always willing to experiment and as a result was often beaten by weaker players. Tchigorin was the first great Russian chess player, and still is one of the greatest Russians of all time."

ALEXANDER ALEKHINE—"His play was fantastically complicated, more so than any player before or since . . . He played gigantic conceptions, full of outrageous and unprecedented ideas . . . At the chessboard, Alekhine radiated a furious tension that often intimidated his opponents."

JOSÉ RAUL CAPABLANCA—"Capablanca was among the greatest of chess players but not because of his endgame. His trick was to keep his openings simple, and then play with such brilliance in the middle game that the game was decided—even though his opponent didn't always know it—before they arrived at the ending."

BORIS SPASSKY—"His game is marked by super-sharp openings. Spassky sacrifices with complete abandon . . . he rates a place on this list because of his dynamic, individual style."

MIKHAIL TAL—"Tal appears to have no respect for his opponents, and frightens almost every player he opposes."

SAMUEL RESHEVSKY—"For a period of ten years—between 1946 and 1956—Reshevsky was probably the best chess player in the world. I feel sure that had he played a match with Botvinnik during that time, he would have been world champion. He is like a machine calculating every variation. He can see more variations in a shorter period than most players who ever lived."

The question of Fischer's potential military service was an acute one, since as a "1-A" candidate, he was scheduled to undergo his physical examination at the U.S. Army Recruiting Station on Whitehall Street in New York, and at that particular time it was believed that he might play in the Interzonal at Amsterdam. I had a few talks with Fischer on life in the military and related some of my brief experiences. Fischer is as patriotic as anyone I know but at that stage, two years in the army was the last thing he needed.

---

[*] Robert Byrne, an ardent admirer of Lasker, recently stated that Fischer has since changed his mind and that after further study of Lasker's games, he admits to his greatness.

Harold M. Phillips, past president of the U.S. Chess Federation, had been a member of a local draft board for years and I called him to see if he could suggest a way that Bobby could qualify for a temporary deferment until after the Interzonal was completed. He suggested that I contact General George B. Hershey, head of the Selective Service Bureau, and, to my surprise, Hershey was quite cooperative, though not particularly hopeful.

"A *temporary* deferment, on almost any grounds, is usually an easy matter to secure from a local board," Hershey told me "but eventually Fischer will probably be drafted." He suggested I send an appeal to Fischer's local board and then wait until they contacted him.

There was one other way a deferment could be secured: if Bobby entered college. Alfred Landa, then Assistant to the President of the New School for Social Research assured me that Fischer would not only be allowed to matriculate into the college but he would be given a scholarship. When I relayed this to Bobby, he thought long and hard. His experience with schools was still distasteful. He negated the idea.

Eventually, Bobby took his physical examination and was rejected, for reasons that have never been made public. Perhaps the local board decided that this young American would be much more valuable sitting across a chess board in the capitals of the world than he would be toting a bazooka through a Vietnamese jungle. Whatever the reason, Fischer never served in the military.

Up to the eleventh hour, efforts were continued to persuade Bobby to enter the Interzonal. Dr. Hearst refers to a meeting at the U.S.C.F. office during which Fischer remained adamant, arguing that the chances of a non-Russian surviving both Interzonal and Candidates were too slight to justify the time and effort and preparation required. This was true enough, though it wasn't stopping a dozen other aspirant grandmasters who were eagerly flocking to Amsterdam. As the spring wore on, Bobby continued his hugely successful tour and told questioning reporters that its commitments precluded his participation in the Interzonal. "Because this was such a weak reason," Dr. Hearst wrote later, "we all thought he had finally decided to play at Amsterdam!" But when the event opened in late May, Fischer was not present. The U.S. representatives were Reshevsky, Evans, and Benko, who had nosed out Bisguier in a playoff match earlier in the month.

Although there was less right to be surprised than the tone and content of some statements indicated, American and world chess reacted with bitter disappointment. "The furor over Bobby Fischer's failure to play in the Interzonal at Amsterdam," *Chess Review* editorialized, "evoked a loud nation-wide protest . . . Bobby's failure to participate left a real void, one which will not be filled for years to come." *Chess Life* prefaced its coverage of the Interzonal with two paragraphs on Fischer: "There is no doubt that the absence of the sensational young American star . . . has resulted in a tournament sadly deprived of much of its sparkle and suspense. For Fischer, possessed of the most exciting chess talent since Alekhine, is the one player in the world who might reasonably be expected to provide a non-Soviet challenger for World Champion Tigran Petrosian." And from Amsterdam Dr. Max Euwe wrote: "The greatest negative surprise at the beginning of the Interzonal . . . is the absence of Robert J. Fischer. The world press has said some unpleasant things about it and has quoted statements which even for him are on the arrogant side . . . The tournament without him, it can be said, has . . . lost more than half its attractiveness. Because Fischer is the most important non-Russian candidate for the World Championship, he should not have failed to play in Amsterdam."

In a statement released to the press on the eve of the Interzonal, Bobby had returned to his theme of Soviet chicanery, giving this as the real reason why he would not participate at Amsterdam or in any other tournament in which a Soviet team was competing. He had never really modified his more extreme post-Curaçao views, and at times had reiterated them with a strong conviction. "FIDE is a crooked organization, run by the Communists from Moscow," he once told *Holiday* editor Peter Lyons, and in late 1963 he had been set to call it a "Communist front" over the air. At other times his sense of righteousness carried almost biblical overtones. "I'm through with FIDE unless they show some real signs of repentance," he told a friend.

None of our players survived the Amsterdam Interzonal—the first time, significantly enough, that no Americans have qualified for a Candidates since Bobby Fischer began his international career at fifteen. Samuel Reshevsky came closest, tying for sixth place, but in the playoff he was defeated by Lajos Portisch of Hungary. The fact that Sammy had lost a match for the first time in his life didn't help U.S. chess morale. The Danish Grandmaster Bent Larsen, whom Bobby had beaten at Portoroz way back in 1958, emerged tied for first with Tal, Smyslov and Spassky. Botvinnik and Keres, if they cared to avail themselves of their seeded status, would add two more Soviet entries to the Candidates Tournament.

In October, November and December Bobby became a teacher. He gave six lectures designed for players "of all degrees of skill" at the Marshall Chess Club, and they consisted of much erudite and rapid-fire information on King's Pawn, Queen's Pawn and Irregular Openings, in addition to instructive games and endings. One average player who attended told me that though he found watching and listening to Fischer "of interest," he gained little of practical use since Fischer was too fast and too deep. Players of expert strength said they found the lectures of great help. I suggested to Bobby that I tape-record the series for him but he refused, saying that he didn't want to be hampered with microphones and with possibly losing spontaneity worrying about the equipment.

When the U.S.C.F. and the A.C.F. were attempting to round up the strongest possible U.S. team to send to the 16th Chess Olympiad in Tel Aviv, Israel, in the fall of 1964, Fischer responded with a demand for a fee of $5,000. "One must assume that Fischer," *Chess Life* editorialized, "by naming so large a figure and by refusing to compromise on it, realized full well that he was keeping himself off the team as surely as if he had come out with a flat 'No.'" After a reference to "Fischer's Garbo-like behavior," the editorial went on to the usual plea for funds. Bobby hadn't even read the editorial when he dropped by my office several weeks later. I handed him a copy.

"What's he mean by 'Garbo-like'?" Bobby asked. "What was Garbo like?"

She wasn't exactly of my generation, either, but I gave him an answer. "She was aloof, difficult, uncooperative. Almost nobody could reach her or really communicate with her. I think she quit acting around the peak of her career, and went into some kind of retirement. She secluded herself all the time, wore dark glasses and clothes and hats that she thought would protect her from public exposure." Bobby merely smiled.

Thus Fischer entered no tournaments at all in 1964.

CHAPTER X

"Psychologically, you should have confidence in yourself and this confidence should be based on fact."

The U.S. team that went to Israel that year—though it contained such first-rate players as Reshevsky, Benko, Bisguier, Saidy, and Donald Byrne—finished a miserable sixth, which together with our performance at Hamburg in 1930 is the worst we had ever done in a chess Olympiad. There was no 1964–65 Rosenwald tournament and the U.S. Championship—the central and climactic event—did not award any cup for the first time since 1951. The official reason was that the A.C.F. touched bottom financially again, but this hiatus should not have been allowed to come about. It seemed to reflect a general sense of drift and disorientation ominously similar to that of the immediate postwar period. Our chess wheel had traveled full circle.

If this is the situation, then the years we have been describing so far not only cover Bobby Fischer's story but chronicle a whole cycle in American chess. That the period may be considered a chess renaissance we have no doubt. From the appearance of a new and brilliant generation of players in the early and middle Fifties, crowned with the spectacular rise of Fischer himself in the later years of the decade, through the bittersweet near-triumphs of Zurich, Leipzig, and Bled, and the honors of Leningrad and Stockholm, those years have witnessed a chapter in American chess experience that is comparable to the finest in our history. Never had U.S. Championship tournaments been as strong or exciting, never had U.S. teams and individuals scored so proudly against such massively powerful foreign opposition. That decade and a half saw more coronations and depositions, more refinement of analysis and theory, and certainly more upheaval and confusion than any other fifteen years.

At the end of that period both Bobby Fischer and American chess in general seemed to have halted on a curiously troubled note. Although one cannot accurately say that as Fischer goes so goes

American chess, the statement does contain a good deal of truth. For he was at the very beating heart of this renaissance. Whether his fellow masters cared for him personally or not, his mere presence was electrifying and charged the whole field with vitality and aspiration. I have no doubt that his withdrawal after that had a good deal to do with the fall in the level of our general play. A certain apathy inevitably spread in various conscious and unconscious ways. If the greatest American player of the century didn't give a damn, why should any of his former teammates? His boycott of major events automatically cheapened all the prizes—a fact that was felt throughout the whole chess world.

A number of invitations to strong and thoroughly respectable international tournaments were sent to Bobby during the first half of 1965, but none were of quite the eminence he sought, and he steadfastly declined to participate. This included the eighth annual tournament at Sarajevo and a topflight international at Zagreb.

There was speculation that he might play in Belgrade in October, but a request for a $1,000 appearance fee was denied and he consequently declined. The tournament was not a particularly important nor strong one in any event, and had the organizers agreed to Fischer's financial demands, it is my opinion that he ultimately would not have played anyway.

Bobby was certain that he would have won the Amsterdam Interzonal if he had played in it, or at least have qualified into the Candidates cycle, and it was now crucial to his self-image to distinguish himself among the winners of an event that was comparable in strength and stature.

As summer approached, Fischer was ending his third year of renunciation of international tournament competition and it was well over a year and a half since he had played his last official tournament game of any kind. This period of chess abstinence did not receive quite as much press coverage nor engender as much gossip as his second "retirement" in the late Sixties, but a number of chess people and Fischer fans and followers were beginning to doubt whether he would ever enter the international arena again. "He's eating himself up inside," the editor of a prominent American chess journal, and a Fischer intimate, told me at that time. He went on to say that ". . . if Bobby doesn't get back into it soon, like Fine or even worse, Morphy, he'll probably never play serious chess again."

The only public chess that Bobby *did* play during the first half of the year was a simultaneous exhibition in May, at the United Nations. It was part of a promotion sponsored by a New York game manufacturer, that featured their newly designed Mandarin chess set which was used on all boards. Bobby tendered his official endorsement to the set, but it made no serious splash in the chess world or even in the general game market; though attractive, it was much too small for sustained play. It is difficult to imagine the Fischer we know today, with his meticulousness as to the design, size, weighting, and even the degree of glare of the sets that are used in tournaments and matches, becoming enthusiastic about it.

The exhibition was a formal and cordial affair, with opening remarks by the late Maurice Kasper, treasurer of the American Chess Foundation, and who has been described as the "Tex Ricard of Chess." He pointed out to the lucky ones present that they might very well be playing a future world's champion.

Bobby performed well, but he really didn't have his heart in it. He won eighteen games, lost two and drew one. The mere possibility that this activity implied a renewed interest by Fischer in the game started chess circles aflutter and *Chess Review*, with remarkable prescience, featured this relatively minor occurance on the cover of its July issue with the caption "Fischer Returns." Hardly accurate, but close enough, since Bobby obliged not only that chess journal but himself and the whole world by lifting his embargo on international play during the very next month. He accepted an invitation to compete in the great Capablanca Memorial Tournament to be held in Havana, Cuba, from August 25th to September 26th. I know some people who cried with joy when they heard the news.

The tournament list proved to be formidable. Of the twenty-two participants invited, thirteen were Grandmasters and seven International Masters. The Soviet Union was represented by a well-known powerhouse: Geller, Kholmov, and ex-World Champion Smyslov. Fischer realized that his three-year hiatus would mean an uphill struggle every round, but the tournament was exactly what he had been looking for: it was nearly the same size as the 1964 Interzonal and, though not quite up to par with it in strength, it boasted almost as many Grandmasters. A $3,000 appearance fee erased all of his doubts whether to play or not.

Unfortunately, through an ironic twist it soon became unpleasantly apparent that Bobby Fischer wouldn't be playing in Havana after all. Diplomatic relations between the United States and Cuba were still severely strained, though communications were easing at that time and unofficial cultural intercourse was beginning to be considered, and from all indications it seemed, at least at first, that he would have no trouble traveling there. Larry Evans had in fact competed in the 1964 Capablanca Memorial and had had no problems gaining admittance to Cuba, especially when it became known that he was to cover the event journalistically. The U.S. State Department often permitted newsmen and correspondents access to Cuba and other "off limits" countries, while it denied entrance to ordinary citizens. Fischer was a regular contributor to *Chess Life*, he had been an editor of the *American Chess Quarterly*, and he had made special arrangements to do an article on this tournament for the *Saturday Review*. There is no question that his motivations in wanting to go were first, to play in (and win) the tournament, and second, to write about it. But the State Department flatly refused to recognize him as a legitimate columnist and therefore denied him the opportunity to travel to Havana.

The episode was similar to Reshevsky's more serious failure to obtain a visa to Hungary in 1950 to compete in the Candidates Tournament in Budapest. All possibilities had been tried to no avail, and Reshevsky lost his opportunity to become a challenger for the World's Championship.

J. F. Reinhardt opined that ". . . Fischer would have gone to Havana with a prize in mind but it wouldn't have been the Pulitzer. Like any sensible person, Bobby would rather be Superman than Clark Kent." Both the *New York Times* and the *Wall Street Journal* ran editorials on successive days critizing the State Department's action, and an appeal to President Johnson was being talked up.

Fischer accepted the ruling with hardly more than a twitch of possible protest. He had primed himself to play, though, psychologically and emotionally, and his force of will was not to be denied. Fischer rarely takes no for an answer so he came up with one of the most clever and unorthodox concepts of his career—the idea of competing in the tournament via teletype from a room in the Marshall Chess Club in New York. The Cuban officials were not only delighted but they offered to pay for an open telephone line in addition to a teletype machine that would speed up communications between New York and Havana. All the participants in the tournament agreed to the novel arrangements.

It seemed that the Pawns and pieces were all falling into place when the pandemoniacal Fidel Castro forced himself into the act by exploding with a statement that Fischer's teletype maneuver was a ". . . great propaganda victory for Cuba." It made headlines. As soon as the announcement came over the wires to this country and Fischer was called at home and told of it, he shot back a rapid transit reply, via cable, that he was withdrawing unless Castro ceased making any remarks about his participation. Here are the full texts of Bobby's cable and Castro's reply:

TO PRIME MINISTER FIDEL CASTRO, HAVANA
    I PROTEST AGAINST THE ANNOUNCEMENT PUBLISHED TODAY IN THE NEWSPAPER "THE NEW YORK TIMES" IN WHICH MENTION IS MADE OF SOME SORT OF PROPAGANDA VICTORY, AND IN CONNECTION WITH THIS CIRCUMSTANCE I

MUST WITHDRAW FROM PARTICIPATION IN THE
CAPABLANCA MEMORIAL TOURNEY. I WOULD
ONLY BE ABLE TO TAKE PART IN THE TOURNA-
MENT IN THE EVENT THAT YOU IMMEDIATELY
SENT ME A TELEGRAM DECLARING THAT
NEITHER YOU, NOR YOUR GOVERNMENT WILL
ATTEMPT TO MAKE POLITICAL CAPITAL OUT OF
MY PARTICIPATION IN THE TOURNEY, AND THAT
IN THE FUTURE NO POLITICAL COMMENTARIES
ON THIS SCORE WILL BE MADE.

BOBBY FISCHER

TO BOBBY FISCHER, NEW YORK, USA
I HAVE JUST RECEIVED YOUR TELEGRAM. I AM
SURPRISED THAT YOU ASCRIBE TO ME SOME
SORT OF ANNOUNCEMENT TOUCHING ON YOUR
PARTICIPATION IN THE TOURNAMENT. I HAVE
SAID NOT A SINGLE WORD ON THE SUBJECT TO
ANYONE. I KNOW OF THIS ONLY THROUGH
YOUR TELEGRAPHIC COMMUNIQUES FROM THE
NORTH AMERICAN NEWS AGENCIES. OUR LAND
NEEDS NO SUCH "PROPAGANDA VICTORIES." IT
IS YOUR PERSONAL AFFAIR WHETHER YOU WILL
TAKE PART IN THE TOURNAMENT OR NOT.
HENCE YOUR WORDS ARE UNJUST. IF YOU ARE
FRIGHTENED AND REPENT YOUR PREVIOUS
DECISION, THEN IT WOULD BE BETTER TO FIND
ANOTHER EXCUSE OR TO HAVE THE COURAGE
TO REMAIN HONEST.

FIDEL CASTRO

Upon receiving word from Castro, Bobby flatly and without further
dispute confirmed his participation to the chess, cultural, and government officials standing by in Havana. He wanted to play the game
of chess, not sensationalism. This ingenious pastime often journeys
well beyond the sixty-four squares.

The *quid pro quo* of the Fischer-Castro cables and the unique
manner of Bobby's participation produced notice by the media
well beyond that usually generated by a chess tournament. A
number of referees were merry-go-rounded in and out of the tournament and this, too, caused much publicity. At the conclusion of the
first round, Bobby asked if I could be named as the referee, and after
making arrangements to spend a month at the Marshall, I accepted.
The Cuban officials agreed, and I was designated to serve for the
remainder of the tournament.

My reign was short lived. Bobby arbitrarily decided to switch referees for each round: perhaps he wanted to rule out the possibility that people would think that he was receiving help, being all alone in the room but for one referee. He may have felt that if he had a different person each game, it would indicate that he was being scrupulously honest.

Or perhaps there were other, more personal reasons. Whatever the rationale, this too made front page news across the country. A wire service editor from U.P.I. noted that on the very day that I was summarily "dismissed" as the judge for the Capablanca Memorial Tournament, my biography of Bobby, the first edition of this book, appeared in the bookstores. The two incidents were linked as cause-and-effect, in that it was assumed that Bobby did not agree with all the conclusions expressed in the book and did not want to spend a month sitting in a goldfish bowl where I could collect more material for further writings. All of this was patently absurd, of course, since after expending a considerable amount of time and energy writing about Bobby, the last thing I wanted to do was write more; at least at that time. This teapot tempest magnified into front page headlines that proclaimed: "Chess, si—Referee, no!" and generated even more press.

It was difficult not to trip over a reporter or photographer at the Marshall. In the one-hundred-and-fourteen-year history of tournament chess, no individual had ever played in a tournament by teletype. Nimzovich once was forced to play all of his games outside of the actual tournament room because the contest took place in a casino and he, at twenty, was barred as a minor. But he still faced all of his opponents because they, too, had to play outside the main hall. Telegraph team matches have been popular since the city of Washington downed Baltimore in 1844, and cable matches between two players have been fairly common; Tchigorin started that form of chess by defeating Steinitz in a melee and a clash of theories, in 1890.

But the difference and difficulty in Bobby's performance was that he, alone, had to struggle in this cumbersome manner through twenty-one rounds plus adjournments, the majority of which lasted up to eight hours. Some stretched to almost unbearable twelve hour sessions. True, his opponents had to sit through the same punishment—but each of them had to do it just *once* during the month long battle. Bobby had round after round of concentration, anticipation, and prolonged tension, even over positions where he was confident that he had the upper hand.

The situation had to be carefully controlled, to prevent any hint of cheating. Bobby sat confined in a small wood-paneled room at the Marshall, with only his chessboard and the current referee. After deciding on his move, he wrote it down on a slip of paper which was then carried by the referee to a "runner," who brought it quickly to the nearby room where the teletype machine had been set up. Bobby then waited, still alone, as the move was transmitted to Havana, while his opponent considered it and finally answered it, while the answering move was transmitted by wire from Havana back to the Marshall, while the operator turned the reply over to the "runner," and while the move was finally carried back to the silent room where Fischer tensely awaited it.

The English periodical *Chess* stated that this system was an advantage to Bobby, since he became accustomed to the awkward manner of play, whereas his opponents went through the shock only once. I don't agree. An ordeal is an ordeal.

Despite the testiness of the scene, each round presented an almost eerie tableau. As Bobby sat with the referee, not a word was spoken as the afternoons crept very slowly into the summer twilight. A bust of Philidor, perched atop a display case of chess sets, seemed to gaze down upon each game with human intensity. The tick of the chess clock was the only sound.

Outside that room a plethora of players was often not so silently analyzing the current position on the large wall board. With the teletype clacking and the bright television lights glaring in order to transmit Bobby's image when he existentially emerged into the chaos, that hectic scene represented another world from the one in which Fischer sat hour after hour.

A courier would deliver the move from the playing room to the sending room to be punched out by the teletype operator:

HELLO HAVANA THIS IS AMERICA CALLING. WHITE'S FIRST MOVE PAWN TO KING FOUR. TIME THREE THIRTY. STANDING BY FOR CONFIRMATION.

The mechanization of the game went off smoothly, but Fischer must have felt, at least at times, he was competing against that faceless computer, not a living, breathing chessplayer.

"Ask me in a few weeks," was his uneasy comment at the start of the tournament when questioned about what score he thought he would make. Later, the strain very much apparent, he said: "It's a question of how soon I'll crack up."

He started off beautifully, beating Heinz Lehmann of West Germany, and then downing the red-headed Soviet, Smyslov. That game was adjourned on a Thursday evening and the next morning a call came from Havana, confirmed later by teletype, that Smyslov was resigning but wanted to congratulate Bobby over the telephone. A short while later the phone rang. I answered it. "Ha—lo? Bo—bie?" It was Smyslov. The Russian not only congratulated Fischer on his beautiful performance, but the two talked awhile about variations that either could have played. Other players also called during the progress of the event, but the timing was often off and the language barrier on, and not many connected.

Fischer's recent absence from formal competition prevented him from going through the tournament unscathed, and he especially tired toward the middle and end, dropping points to Ivkov, Kholmov, and not for the first nor certainly for the last time in his career, Geller, in addition to drawing with such lesser lights as Wade of England and Jiminez of Cuba. Hans Kmoch, in annotating the Fischer-Kholmov game in *Chess Review*, said that ". . . something went wrong in Fischer's mind. It is impossible to explain what." How about simple fatigue?

Bobby drifted into trouble often, and barely managed a draw against Parma. He looked haggard, almost ill at times, and his clothes hung on him as though they had been bought during more prosperous times. Clearly, this was not the same Fischer who had vacuum-swept the U.S. Championship eighteen months before.

But despite his self-inflicted lapses and the cumbersome handicap of playing by remote control, he fought hard and sometimes almost desperately, and placed second through fourth, just a half-point behind the tournament winner, Smyslov. He had his share of good fortune, too, but as Capablanca was wont to indicate when critics pointed this out in commenting on some of *his* successes, "The good player is always lucky."

Some of Fischer's sterner critics pointed out that when Pillsbury was roughly the same age, he finished ahead of *all* of the world's leading masters at Hastings 1895, and that my claim in the first edition of this book that Fischer was "the most brilliant player of our times" was just so much "high-powered American publicity." (W. Heidenfeld in *Canadian Chess Chat*.)

The young player has had to suffer continuously even into the Seventies when he had already "proven" himself to the chess world beyond all doubt to be "the most brilliant" of contemporary masters. Why? I can only explain it by offering Fischer's image to be in marked contrast to the profile of a great player conjured by most chessplayers. His *sangfroid* has its parallels in that of a long distance runner rather than of a Laskerian intellectual. The chess community demands a stately demeanor for its heroes. The usually conservative *British Chess Magazine*, however, hailed Bobby's accomplishment as ". . . a great achievement . . ." and made allusions to his being the only Western player likely to capture the World's Championship sometime in the near future.

It is my belief that if Fischer had not won, placed, or shown in this comeback, we would not be hearing anything about him today. He had done poorly at Curaçao and disappeared from top-level competition for years. There is reason to believe that this time his disillusionment with himself would have remained. We all know chess is breath to Bobby Fischer, and his way of the game is to win. Though temporary and minor setbacks are permitted, grand defeats cannot be accommodated into his life tempo. The Capablanca tournament was a testing ground for Bobby Fischer, and the solemnity with which he conducted himself throughout the event was a very visible clue as to the seriousness of it in his own mind.

Two setbacks in international tournaments would have been intolerable to him. Bobby Fischer *will* win. Any other attitude is to be discarded.

CHAPTER XI

"I know people who have all the will in the world but can't play good chess."

During the months after the Capablanca Memorial, Bobby annotated a few of his better games from the tournament for *Chess Life* and spent time working on his first primer, *Bobby Fischer Teaches Chess.* The book consisted of programmed instruction, with a question-and-answer method that was quite effective. Donn Mosenfelder, Stuart Margulies, and Leslie Ault, all strong players and coincidentally educational experts, helped him in outlining and editing the work. Basic Systems, the publisher, hired me as their promotional consultant, since they thought his first teaching manual could dominate the chess book market, and they wanted someone to help them who had a knowledge of chess, publishing, and Bobby. The book sold well, as anything written by Fischer has and will continue to do, though it lacked color or even a fleeting glimpse into the real way Bobby's mental processes work. It was not therefore one of the great introductory chess treatises of modern times.

Early in November, Bobby announced his intention to fight for the U.S. Championship title for the seventh time, against the eleven other top-rated players in the country. The event was an important one, especially to him, since it was also the U.S. Zonal Tournament in the FIDE system to determine the challenger for the World's Championship. Though he had not yet decided himself whether he would play in the next Interzonal, to be held almost two years hence, he didn't want once again to bar himself from the possibilities of working his way up to a title shot. Though superficially circuitous at times, Bobby Fischer's *raison d'être*, his *need* to win the World's Championship, never swerved. His eyes were always focused on the very pinnacle of chess. Though it has been accepted theory that "will" or "drive" are the main elements in the makeup of a master, Bobby has repudiated this concept. As a youth he claimed there were three elements that made a great player: "Practice. Study. Talent."[*]

The Henry Hudson Hotel in New York City, then fast becoming the home of U.S. Championships, was the site, and Edgar T. McCormick, one of the most active and cordial players in American chess, was designated as referee. Traditionally, the contest ran through the year-end holidays.

Nicolas Rossolimo joined Grandmasters Benko, Bisguier, Robert Byrne, Evans, and Reshevsky to make the event even stronger than the last Championship, held in 1963–64. Addison, Zuckerman, and Saidy, all of whom were playing winning chess at the time, also participated. Lombardy, due to commitments to his seminary, was again unable to enter, and Raymond Weinstein, who had fought so valiantly the last time he competed, beating Reshevsky, Evans, and Robert Byrne, was kept out by an unfortunate mental illness, which has prevented him from playing tournament chess since. Donald Byrne was the only other first-caliber American player missing from the line-up, but all names considered, it was stronger than most championships of the past. Karl Burger and Duncan Suttles came in next-to-last and last, respectively.

Fischer won the event, to be sure, his seventh U.S. Championship title, together with the $2,000 first prize, but not in quite as convincing a manner as he was accustomed to. He drew against Addison in the first round, thereby breaking the eleven-game winning streak created in his previous title test. In the eighth round, he lost to Byrne by an incredible example of *Amaurosis Schaccistica*—chess blindness —by which he lost the Exchange on the fourteenth move. Bobby temporarily kept his composure, however, and resigned as gracefully as possible under the circumstances, twenty-three moves later. He was inwardly rattled though, for he came back the next night and played passively to lose to Reshevsky, his first defeat at the hands of the old fox since their abortive 1961 collision. Before the game, for the first time in years, Fischer and Reshevsky were cordial to each other. They shook hands, and Sammy actually congratulated Bobby on his Havana triumph. Afterward, no great warmth exuded from either party, and Reshevsky looked as though he was about to swirl into a *Pavan for Ecstatic Master* every now and then during the remainder of the tournament.

Entering the last round, Bobby had clinched at least a tie for first, since he was a point ahead of the pack. While Byrne and Reshevsky,

[*] In 1972 in a joint interview of Colonel Ed Edmondson and Fischer, the former was asked to describe the one trait that made Fischer great. "The will to win," was Edmondson's answer. "I disagree with that," said Bobby, "I know people who have all the will in the world but can't play good chess. You must have talent."

his closest rivals, downed Evans and Suttles, Bobby beat Burger in a tough game and eased himself once again into the Championship a full point in front. International Master Harry Golombek, veteran reporter for the *London Times* and one of the most respected writers in chess, felt that Bobby's performance indicated a general decline in the level of his play. He stated that though Fischer was still clearly the best player in the U.S.A., it was still equally clear that ". . . he has not made the advance one might have expected of a player in his early twenties. Partly, of course, this is due to the fact that he has already attained such great stature as a player; but I think this absence from competitive chess has had an unfavorable effect on his form and that the reality is that he is not so strong a player as he was some two years back."

Similar sentiments were expressed by Svetozar Gligoric who stated in *Chess Review* that Fischer's record, both in Havana and in the U.S. Championship, indicated a ". . . slight decline in his form" and Fischer was "not nearly so impressive as he had proved to be previously."

And Isaac Kashdan reported in the *Los Angeles Times* that ". . . for anyone but Bobby Fischer, the winning margin in the United States Championship Tournament would have been ample and satisfactory. For Fischer, it was one of his poorer results."

There is little to take issue with in these statements, and even Bobby would probably have to agree with them. His play *had* suffered from lack of sharp competition. But he *did* win the championship, though certainly not by such a crowd-pleasing margin as before.

Though admittedly not playing for anywhere near the same stakes of personal danger, Bobby seems to inspire people to react to him in the way they did toward Manolete, who was pushed to the horn less from his own drive than from outward pressures of a taunting crowd. The death-wishing public accustomed to historical tightrope performances always expects more of Bobby. And more, and more. So do the critics. They know he's the Golden Boy of chess, and ignore the fact that his incredible record of forty-five wins, twenty-two draws and *only one loss* in all his previous title attempts will probably never be broken. The two losses in this tournament were somehow unforgivable.

Lamented Bobby: "Sometimes it just doesn't pay to play too well."

CHAPTER XII

*"I like to do what I want to do
and not what other people want or
expect me to do. This is what life
is all about, I think."*

Though he had just emerged from a demanding and strenuous tournament, Bobby was optimistic. He was America's champion again and had qualified to play in the next Interzonal should he elect to do so. It gave him a comfortable sense of psychic security. A number of prestigious chess events were planned for the year and he was beginning to feel his interest, his strength, and his entire verve returning. Though cloaked in drama at times, the events of 1966 would prove to be more energetic and meaningful for him and, also, for chess.

A few weeks after the U.S. Championship, the Borough of Brooklyn held its first open tournament during a bitterly cold New York weekend. Bobby didn't play but he felt chauvinistic enough to root for his old colleague Pal Benko who took first place and added the title "First Brooklyn Open Champion" to the many he had collected over the years.

Bobby appeared at the Greater New York Open Championship held at the beginning of April in the Henry Hudson Hotel, but this time he was neither spectator nor player; he served as the official tournament adjudicator. Fischer was the essence of impartiality and brilliance in analyzing the unfinished games from round to round. He dissected, probed, weighed, re-evaluated and judged the most complicated positions in a matter of minutes—sometimes seconds. However, if a position occurred that was particularly unclear, he would take as much time as needed in coming to a conclusion, and he would not be pushed into making a quick decision. Pensively, he would discern the weaknesses and deterioration of the position shown to him and, like a pathologist, would explain his diagnosis to the two players involved, who would unanimously accept it as Chess Law—though often as not, without really understanding the nuances of his analysis. He was just too rapid and complex for the stock player.

Bobby seemed almost charming that weekend: he signed autographs, freely offered chess wisdom, talked of the forthcoming World's Championship match between Spassky and Petrosian (he favored the former), and speculated on whether either or both would be playing in the all-grandmaster tournament soon to be held in the United States.

In November of 1965, Jacqueline Piatigorsky had sent an invitation to Fischer asking him to play in the second triennial Piatigorsky Cup International Tournament, to be held in Santa Monica, California, from July 17th to August 15th. Early in March Bobby replied, accepting the invitation to play. After having "slighted" the 1963 event with his absence, and because of his somewhat demeaning remarks pertinent to the standard of play in the First Piatigorsky, it was rumored that he was not going to be invited to the 1966 tournament. But Jacqueline and Gregor Piatigorsky proved to be above such pettiness and sincerely urged America's greatest player to take part in what was certainly America's greatest chess tournament held in decades (matched perhaps only by the New York International in 1924).

Actually, the whole fate of the tournament hinged on Bobby's participation, though he didn't know that then. Mrs. Piatigorsky had decided that unless Fischer played, there would be no Cup Tournament that year.

(At the FIDE Congress in Tel Aviv in 1964, a special resolution had been passed designating the Piatigorsky Tournament an event of world-wide significance to the chess community, and member nations were asked not to conduct any tournaments during the period that the "Piatigorsky Cup" was to take place.)

Eight of the world's most renowned grandmasters were invited, including both Spassky and Petrosian who were about to embark on a World's Championship title meet, to take place in Moscow in April of that year. The USSR Chess Federation, influenced by the Kremlin's continuing disapproval of American foreign policy regarding Vietnam, at first declined for the two Soviet players, declaring that none of its top Grandmasters were "available at that date." Only days before the opening, a coincidental (or perhaps not) press conference was held at the Central Chess Club in Moscow in which an official of the USSR Sports and Cultural Section announced that the Soviet Union would not be sending a track team to the United States for the scheduled USA-USSR match at the Los Angeles Coliseum. However, reason and the urging of Petrosian and Spassky, both of whom cherished the concept of a trip to the United States, prevailed and acceptances were cabled to California.

While the Soviet Union was deciding whether Spassky and Petrosian could participate, the tournament committee had invited Wolfgang Unzicker of West Germany and Lajos Portisch of Hungary to play as replacements. They had accepted. The Russians' decision to come raised the roster to ten: in addition to those already mentioned there were Jan Hein Donner of Holland, Borislav Ivkov of Yugoslavia, Bent Larsen of Denmark, Miguel Najdorf of Argentina, and Samuel

Reshevsky of the United States. With the exception of Unzicker and Donner, all the players had, at one time or the other, realistic ambitions in gaining the championship of the world.

The prize fund was increased to $20,000, double that of the 1963 event, the largest amount of money ever offered in a tournament in the history of chess. The Miramar, a well-known resort hotel overlooking the Pacific Ocean, was selected as the playing site and International Grandmaster Isaac Kashdan was named referee for the double round-robin event. Over $75,000 was to be spent before the last King was turned down; virtually no detail was overlooked in making this Grandmaster event really "grand."

For the second time in a generation, a reigning World's Champion would participate in a United States tournament. After his defeat of Spassky by one point, successfully defending his title, Petrosian stated in his first interview that he looked forward to playing a "mature Fischer." Bobby was, apparently, on everybody's mind. D.J. Richard's scholarly work *Soviet Chess* was released at that time, and no less than a full chapter was devoted to "the challenge of Fischer." Bobby was the only non-Soviet player so honored. It indicated, among other things, that even though he had ceased playing in FIDE events, his desire to arrange a match with any leading Soviet player was proof that he had not abandoned his challenge to Soviet supremacy.

Botvinnik stated in another press interview at that same time, that he thought that Fischer was ". . . the strongest player outside the Soviet Union." But when pressured to voice an opinion on what he thought Fischer was thinking of *him*, Botvinnik replied almost wistfully, no doubt conjuring up the vision of the famed Botvinnik-Fischer match that never took place, "I am afraid we have started to forget each other. We have not met for a long time."

The Piatigorskys were busy people that summer. Just a few weeks before the action got underway in Santa Monica, they sponsored yet another event; the first invitational U.S. Junior Championship. The winner was Walter Shawn Browne. Not many people connected the fact that Fischer had won the U.S. Junior Open ten years earlier with the fact that both he and Browne grew up in Brooklyn and had attended Erasmus Hall High School. Browne deserves to be mentioned here because he represents a coterie of young American (though Browne also holds an Australian citizenship) players who have patterned themselves after their champion Bobby Fischer. This hero worship has taken the form of adopting Bobby's lifestyle and even his speech habits and physical mannerisms. These clones not only decline to play the "weak" Queen's Pawn opening but any other non-approved Fischer variation.

Browne's emulation of Bobby, though accused of caricaturing him on occasion, has paid handsome returns: he has since become a powerful Grandmaster in his own right, and could very well enter the hierarchy of world's championship contenders.

Aside from his participation in the two Candidates in 1959 and 1962, the Piatigorsky Cup was undoubtedly the strongest tournament Bobby Fischer had ever competed in. Al Horowitz referred to it, perhaps a bit overenthusiastically, as "the strongest collection of chess players ever convened." The credentials of Petrosian, Spassky, Najdorf, and Reshevsky need not be questioned. *Chess Review* ran an article in June 1966 in which Dr. Petar Trifunovic stated: "The title of 'best player in the Western world' doesn't officially exist, but the press has conferred this honor upon [Bent Larsen] and the chess public confirms it. His colleagues will be jealous, but the results speak for Larsen." Nowhere a mention of Fischer, and even the staunchest of pro-Fischer fans would have to admit that the Dane would have to be considered exactly even with Bobby, if not a shade beyond him at that time.

Gligoric confirmed that Larsen's triumphs ". . . gave some basis to the rumors that—not Fischer—but Larsen was the main danger from the West to the Soviet chess hegemony." And Petrosian, in *Schakhmaty*, was quoted as saying: "Bent Larsen possesses great potential strength. I believe he is no less a dangerous candidate for the chess throne among the Western Grandmasters than Robert Fischer."

Tal, in an interview given to Ivkov and published in a Belgrade news daily, conceded that even though he considered Fischer to be ". . . the greatest genius to have descended from the chessic sky," he felt that Bobby's absence from serious tournament play gave Larsen the "slightest edge."

This conclusion was disputed by Botvinnik and Spassky, both of whom felt that Fischer was the one to watch.

Bobby would soon prove all his critics wrong, but he didn't exactly enter the Piatigorsky Cup as a favorite.

Larsen had just scored a string of successes in international play, including matches with Ivkov and Geller, and came close to winning a match against Tal (he lost 5½–4½), all in the Candidates cycle for the World Championship. He was indeed one of the strongest players in the world. In fact, any player in the tournament was strong enough to best any other player, and no player was too strong not to lose a given game to any other.

As it developed, Spassky, though not playing inspired chess, seemed at times to be practically invincible. Never once did he stray into a position that was even close to being inferior. At his best, sitting rock-like at the board, armed with "stubborn patience," forged with Miltonian "triple steel," Spassky again proved himself to be the most difficult player to defeat in the long history of chess.

The day before the tournament began, the Piatigorskys gave a cocktail party in the garden of their palatial Brentwood home. Almost all the players attended, and Bobby even skittled a few games with Ivkov and Portisch. A news story had just come over the wires that Mikhail Botvinnik won the small but powerful IBM tournament in Amsterdam by a two-point margin. Some of the players wondered how the veteran Grandmaster would fare in Los Angeles, had he been invited, and the consensus was that he would have pulled well ahead of a fifty-percent score.

The Piatigorskys' party was a festive affair and set the tone of the event for the month to come. Everything humanly possible was done to make the tournament pleasant and memorable. The players were treated to a number of excursions: the Art Festival at Laguna Beach, a concert at the Hollywood Bowl where Van Cliburn, much to the delight of the Russians, played Rachmaninoff's Piano Concerto No. 2, and the inevitable trip to Disneyland.

No request by any player, however trivial, was refused. The lighting was perfect, the noise level low, the accommodations spacious, the atmosphere cordial. Mrs. Piatigorsky stated that she intended to provide a "playing environment of good quarters, good food, good manners and good taste." She succeeded.

CHAPTER XIII

*"Genius. It's a word. What does
it really mean? If I win, I'm a
genius. If I don't, I'm not."*

The tournament was officially opened on Sunday, July 17th, by Jerry Spann. Over seven hundred spectators filled the Nautilus Room and when he introduced Jacqueline and Gregor Piatigorsky, a long ovation followed. The world-renowned musician began his greeting by saying: "In the world of music, I am known as a cellist. In the world of chess, I am known as the husband of Mrs. Piatigorsky!" Tournament Director Isaac Kashdan introduced the players, and in moments the clocks were ticking away. All the games were in progress, with the exception of Fischer's. Photographers were permitted the first five minutes to take pictures and Bobby refused to play until the shooting session was over, thereby penalizing himself five minutes on the clock. After the lensmen were cleared from the hall, Bobby made his first move. What followed is chess history.

It had been agreed beforehand that players of the same country would be paired in the first round. Consequently Petrosian, as White, played Spassky; Reshevsky, as White, played Fischer. Assaying a King's Indian, Fischer handled the Black pieces well but could make no headway. Reshevsky wrote later that he "decided to mark time and see what my opponent would do. Fischer advanced his queen-side pawns and embarked on a plan involving the locking-in of his King's Bishop. I was in a position where I could have made progress, but became very short of time. Consequently, I was compelled to simplify by forcing exchanges of pieces, leading to a theoretically drawn position."

Reshevsky, like Schlechter, Flohr, and Petrosian, is a master of the drawn game. If he decides to do nothing, in effect, as he did in this game, it is nearly impossible to beat him.

All the other games, as is often the case in first-round encounters, were also drawn, with the exception of Ivkov-Larsen. The Dane over-reached himself in a clearly advantageous position and threw away the game, thereby becoming the instant tailender at 0–1, while Ivkov, at 1–0, was temporarily crowned leader.

Art Kaye, writing in the *San Francisco Chronicle*, noted that Fischer, dressed in a gray suit, looked "very thin," and a number of eye-witnesses agreed that he looked as though he were in ill health.

I do not mean to imply that frailty is a concomitant of the makeup of a prodigy or genius: Bobby is a strong young man, extremely athletic. Usually his entire physical being operates with the precision of a Swiss timepiece. But in his episode via wireless, and in the early rounds of the Piatigorsky Cup, he appeared to be woefully out of shape.

He had had six months rest since his last tournament but the dark shadows under his eyes and his drawn countenance indicated that either sickness, worry, or insomnia—or a combination of all three—were plaguing him.

Bobby drew his next game, in which he had White against Portisch. Playing his favorite variation of the Ruy Lopez, he constructed a superior position but let the Hungarian slip away in the endgame.

In the third round he finally drew blood, downing Ivkov, who said later that the game was rife with mistakes (his own), the first of which was his deviation from the classical moves of the King's Indian. Explaining his inferior sixth move, Ivkov said that he was trying "to get away from the prepared variations of my young partner." Everybody is fearful of the vast Fischer book knowledge.

Ivkov sealed his forty-second move and the game was adjourned, but he knew that Bobby had more than enough to win it. After a few hours of private analysis, Ivkov announced his resignation.

Bobby didn't care for the chess sets that were used and wanted one slightly smaller and with less glare. A replacement set was brought to him but that, too, was not to his liking. Helen Kashdan, wife of the Grandmaster, was enlisted to conduct an immediate search for a proper set. After driving to all parts of Los Angeles, she returned with several possibilities and Fischer chose the one he preferred. But since this new set was smaller than the rest, all of the other players had to be polled on whether they would agree to play with it. Najdorf was the only objector but he finally consented before playing his game with Fischer.

Fischer's next opponent was Donner, with whom he could only manage to draw. This was particularly upsetting to Bobby because he disdains Donner's playing ability. When Bobby was about to make his 30th move, in a slightly inferior position for Donner, he touched a piece and with a sickening feeling realized it was a mistake. It clinched a draw. As Donner described it: "After touching the Bishop, Fischer sat for seconds with his finger on the piece desperately looking for another move. He had seen the point at the last minute—as usual, there is no other move!" Fischer was no less than furious.

Next came a long and tiring seventy-seven-move draw with Unzicker. Then in the sixth round, Fischer played White against

Larsen, a duel that had been eagerly awaited by the spectators and those who were following the games day by day all over the world.

Since both players' names were being whispered as the "greatest" in the Western world, the two-game match between them from this tournament was a sort of unofficial World's Championship for that hemispheric section of the globe. Fischer and Larsen have always had a more intense rivalry between each other than between either of them and any individual Russian. Fischer, for years, was better than Larsen—but as he repudiated international competition, Larsen couldn't get enough of it. Before he knew it, the Dane had caught up. Many respected chess followers were saying that Larsen was now better.

Fischer played his second Ruy Lopez of the tournament and initiated a classical approach. Larsen felt that Fischer was attempting to avoid the same lines that Geller had tried, unsuccessfully, against the Dane in their recent match. Caution was the untypical hallmark of Fischer's approach in this encounter.

As the position developed into the mid-game with possibilities of developing into overtime, it was at least even: a slight edge for Fischer in that he had two Bishops against Larsen's two Knights. It was a moment laced with tension. The game dominated the tournament hall; most eyes were on it and every chair anywhere near the raised platform where the two players sat was filled.

Larsen wrote after the 20th move: "Perhaps nothing is wrong with the Black position except that it is difficult! I recalled my game against sixteen-year-old Bobby in Zurich of 1959, in which I had to defend a difficult position with two Knights against Bobby's beloved pair of Bishops for about seventy moves to score half a point." It was obvious that Larsen expected a colossal struggle. He was "growing nervous," as he claimed after the game. On the twenty-eighth move, he had just fifteen minutes to complete his time control while Fischer had close to forty minutes.

Fischer hesitated momentarily with his own King-side play and stopped to defend a Pawn that he could have sacrificed. He had overlooked Black's winning line of passed Pawns. Bobby politely offered his damp hand after Larsen made his 30th move. It was all over. The audience burst into a short but enthusiastic ovation that was quickly hushed by Kashdan so as not to disturb the other players.

Larsen seemed almost apologetic about winning the game as he rapidly and astutely analyzed it in the postmortem. The game was not Fischer-like in any way; it appears as though it was played by an automaton version of Bobby. Here's what Hans Kmoch had to say about it:

> Fischer may now and then lose a game, but that he, the model of aggressive chess, loses because of an overdose of

caution, is simply out of character. And so bad is his luck, that this one over-cautious move completely wrecks his position, necessitating almost immediate resignation.

Bobby, at twenty-three the youngest (as usual) player in the tournament, faced the oldest member, Najdorf, fifty-six, in the next round. Once again Fischer overlooked a relatively "simple" move, as Najdorf called it, and lost the game quickly. Kashdan, who as referee had constant contact with Fischer, claimed: "He was morose, fidgety, irritable; he was pressing too hard." The sensation of this round, however, was not Bobby's loss to Najdorf but Larsen's magnificent win over World Champion Petrosian in a game that contained a shimmering Queen sacrifice and has since been hailed as a modern-day "Evergreen Game." Saidy said of it that it would give ". . . endless delight to new generations of chess players as long as books exist."

Though both Fischer and Spassky had been active in high-level chess competition for over ten years at that time, they had met across the board only once. Their Mar Del Plata encounter in 1960, mentioned earlier, in which Bobby had so soundly blitzkreiged the young Russian only to lose to him on a blunder, left an indelibly distasteful impression on him. His classic article in the *American Chess Quarterly*, Summer 1961, titled "A Bust to the King's Gambit" (the opening Spassky had played) was a defense of his performance. He felt psychologically crushed by Spassky and had to justify himself by publishing a theoretical recrimination in which he stated that White (Spassky, in this case) ". . . loses by force," and with credit to Weaver Adams, that if White plays differently, ". . . he merely loses differently." Bobby has since abandoned his rigid stance and has played the King's Gambit himself on occasion.

Bobby was determined to avenge himself when they met in the eighth round. Spassky had White, and Fischer played the Gruenfeld Defense, an opening he uses only for special occasions. He had nearly beaten Botvinnik with it at Varna, in 1962, and had defeated the two Byrne brothers with it in 1956 and 1964, respectively, in games either of which could be called the "Game of the Century."

Andrew Soltis, in his efficiently presented monograph on Spassky* wrote of the 1966 game:

> One can wonder at Fischer's choice of opening. Having lost to Larsen and Najdorf (the latter with his favorite King's Indian) on successive days, Fischer seeks a change of atmosphere and/or luck. But Spassky (before beating Ivkov the day before) had only one win to show for six games. They are both out for blood.

---

* *Best Games of Boris Spassky*, David McKay, 1973.

Gligoric pointed out that Spassky chose to play 1 P–Q4 because he expected Fischer ". . . to be in a wild mood after two successive defeats," and therefore elected to play a closed game.

The game developed along known theoretical lines until the 12th move, when Spassky chose a new variation gaining a valuable tempo. After the exchange of the major pieces, Fischer was left with what looked like a slightly inferior endgame: his Knight and three Pawns against Spassky's Bishop and also three pawns. Minor-piece endings are usually complicated affairs where drawing chances abound. This one might have been a draw, too, but Spassky didn't think so. After the exchanges he felt that the situation spoke for a "clear positional superiority of White." He was partially right. They adjourned on the fortieth move and, as is so often the case in chess, wherein moves preceding the adjournment and the actual sealed move itself can be somewhat inferior due to the release of pressure in making the time control and the "headiness" in knowing that the position can be studied for hours in the privacy of one's room, Fischer played inaccurately and thereby lost all prospects for saving the game. Upon resumption he performed as well as he could under the circumstances, but it was hopeless. He resigned on the fiftieth move.

Never before in his adult career as a Grandmaster did Fischer lose so resoundingly as he did in those three games. It appeared that the fabulous Fischer was losing his prowess.

Something was happening and no one, apparently not even Fischer, knew what it was. When pressed for an explanation, he attributed his losses to rustiness and "poor chess nerves." He was tied for *last* with Ivkov. Both had 3–5.

A memorable glimpse of Fischer, written at that time by Harry Markey, appeared in *Chess Life*. I relate part of it here to indicate the pressure Fischer was experiencing then, and how it manifested itself in his appearance and mannerisms:

> Bobby's longish face is a vertical composition of bony segments, grouped around the exclamation mark of a long, prominent nose and held in submission by a low forehead. The chin is aggressively stubborn. His boyish looks are emphasized by the carelessly combed hair, parted on the side. His features, while highly individualized, still show a striving for fuller maturity. Bobby's sensibilities are exceptionally high-strung. Crouched over the chess table, he seems oblivious of his surroundings, yet reacts with hypersensitiveness to the least distraction. He will shush at some offending whisperer among the audience, and, with evident annoyance, register a complaint with a nearby official. As he rises from his chair, his hand will invariably

disappear in the sidepockets of his trousers. He disdains to walk off his supercharged energies, but repairs with hasty movements to one or another of the chess tables, intently scrutinizing the game in progress; then abruptly, with equal impatience, he returns to his own game. Clearly, here is a man obsessed and possessed by the demon of chess.

Fischer faced World Champion Petrosian in the ninth round two days later, and it was clear from the outset that he would not, paradoxically, allow his spectacular losses to affect his nerve. He immediately constructed an attack against the Armenian and, after exchanging Queens, sacrificed a Pawn. The result was an open, lively game and Petrosian had to summon all of his resources to hang on. Petrosian later claimed that this was his own best game from the tournament.

Fischer won his Pawn back and then won another, but at the expense of an ill-placed Knight. Petrosian played for the draw and after the time control was reached, offered to halve the point with Bobby without further play. Fischer agreed.

Now at the halfway mark, Fischer's results had been disastrous. In nine rounds he had managed to win only once, had lost three times and drawn the rest. He was second from last in the standings. It was certainly the worst result of his career, surpassing his Buenos Aires debacle of 1960. The tournament wasn't over, of course, but the question was not whether Fischer had any chance of working his way to the top, but whether he could avoid coming in last!

The crosstable for the first half of the tournament:

		1	2	3	4	5	6	7	8	9	0	
1	Spassky	x	½	½	½	½	1	½	½	1	1	6
2	Larsen	½	x	½	1	1	½	½	1	1	0	6
3	Reshevsky	½	½	x	½	½	½	1	½	½	½	5
4	Najdorf	½	0	½	x	½	½	½	0	1	1	4½
5	Portisch	½	0	½	½	x	½	½	1	½	½	4½
6	Unzicker	0	½	½	½	½	x	½	½	½	1	4½
7	Donner	½	½	0	½	½	½	x	½	½	½	4
8	Petrosian	½	0	½	1	0	½	½	½	½	½	4
9	Fischer	0	0	½	0	½	½	½	½	x	1	3½
10	Ivkov	0	1	½	0	½	½	½	½	0	x	3

Larsen was probably correct when he pointed out that his game had had "... a depressing effect on Fischer" and that it was at least partially responsible for Fischer's losses to Najdorf and Spassky and his "... mishandling a favorable adjourned game against Unzicker." It is also probably correct that Fischer's draw against Petrosian was the single most important adventure of the tournament in snapping the young American out of his two-week trance. It was a cool plunge on a warm day. Fischer was exuberant after the Petrosian game. Apparently, he had resolved some deeply disturbing problem. Everything will be all right now, he seemed to be saying.

Bobby started steamrolling: he drew with Reshevsky in the tenth round, defeated Portisch in the eleventh, downed Ivkov in the twelfth, crushed Donner in the thirteenth and paused to survey the field while his opponents remained dazed. All of his last four games had been completed before adjournment time, and in barely seven days he had shot from the cellar to the penthouse: he was a clear second, only a point behind Spassky! Larsen, legitimately distressed by the Los Angeles summer heat, had suffered a string of losses since the second half had begun, and Spassky managed to win but one game in that period —against Larsen—and was slowly allowing his lead to be eaten away.

Fischer drew with Unzicker in the fourteenth round and was set to face Larsen in the fifteenth. If he beat the Dane, he could enjoy being a half-point behind Spassky if the latter could be held to a draw by Najdorf. If Fischer lost to Larsen, they'd trade places: Larsen would be second, Fischer third. It was a crucial game. Bobby played well ". . . though not spectacularly" according to Hans Kmoch, and in an ending of Bishops of opposite color, managed to grind out a win. Robert Byrne referred to the game as of "unassuming simplicity" and likened Fischer's play to that of Capablanca in his heyday.

Fischer now faced Najdorf, whom he had lost to in the seventh round, in a game that Larry Evans couldn't stop himself from describing as "Najdorf's night off from the Najdorf." Though he played the Sicilian, Najdorf avoided his own original variation, perhaps because he had lost to Fischer with it at Varna 1962, and also because Fischer is himself a great specialist in it. Najdorf said he thought it would not be "wise" to try it again. In any case, his Pawn formation suffered from mishandling in the opening, and Fischer won a Pawn, then the Exchange, and eventually the game. He had succeeded in pulling even with Spassky!

The two rivals met in the penultimate round on Sunday, August 14th at one o'clock in the afternoon, and the personal struggle, coupled with the overtones of the U.S.A.-U.S.S.R. polarity, aroused immense public interest. Over nine hundred people crammed the Nautilus Room, the largest audience ever to witness a chess tournament in the United States, and hundreds more were turned away because there was no room to accommodate them. It was the first time in the history of American chess that the "gate" was closed because of too many spectators.

The final round pairings favored Spassky. He would have to face Donner who was in last place, while Fischer was to play Petrosian.

Petrosian was expected to hold Fischer to a draw. If he did, and if Spassky drew with Fischer and beat Donner, a likely possibility, then Spassky would emerge the winner. This is exactly what happened.

Fischer permitted Spassky to play the Marshall Attack, a variation of the Ruy Lopez which netted Fischer a Pawn but allowed Spassky the initiative. The game was drawn before adjournment time, on the thirty-seventh move. In the final, almost anti-climactic round, Fischer *was* held to a draw by Petrosian while Spassky downed Donner quite easily, thereby slipping into first place a half-point ahead of the young American. Kashdan said that before the game Petrosian placed great emphasis on drawing with Fischer. Later, Petrosian claimed not too convincingly that even though he had a demonstrable win, he gave Fischer the draw because he wanted Bobby to take second place instead of Larsen, as a reward for his fine comeback. Spassky emerged as the only undefeated player in the tournament and Petrosian achieved what no other World Champion has been able to do in a tournament since Alekhine: he failed to break a fifty-percent score.

Bobby's reaction to the final results was ambivalent. He was overjoyed that he had pulled himself out of the miasmic gloom that had pervaded him in the first half of the tournament. Kashdan said of Fischer's overall performance, in his column in the *Los Angeles Times*, that ". . . a search of the leading chess tournaments of the past did not turn up any result of that caliber in all Grandmaster play."

Fischer's last-half spurt provoked such comments as "sensational" and "phenomenal," and Spassky said: "It was Fischer's tournament. He played better than anyone else, including myself."

Fischer's comeback was certainly one of the most magnificent accomplishments in the history of the game, and yet he was unsatisfied. He was $3,000 richer, had drawn two games with the World Champion, and had proven once again that he was one of the strongest of contemporary players by establishing one of the greatest winning streaks in grandmaster chess. The half-point gap between him and Spassky, the difference between first and second place, however, was a chasm filled with resentment. Though the antagonism hadn't had the time to ferment into bitterness as with the Capablanca-Alekhine feud of the Twenties and Thirties, this rivalry between Fischer and Spassky had all the hallmarks of a monumental clash of personalities. Since Buenos Aires, it had been obvious that the chess world would witness an interesting series of struggles between these two young men. Santa Monica verified it: Spassky had won the tournament by going through it unscathed and came out 1½–½ to the good in their individual encounters. Even though the Piatigorsky yielded Fischer's best result in an all-Grandmaster tournament, he could not and would not tolerate this besting of vanities. How he would cope with it over ensuing years, we will follow step-by-step as he solidified his reputation as the equal—if not the better—of his chess peers.

CHAPTER XIV

"I prepare myself well. I know
what I can do before I go in.
I'm always confident."

Bobby's flight back to Brooklyn coincided nicely with the publication of his book, *Bobby Fischer Teaches Chess*, and after resting awhile he helped to promote it by giving a number of appearances on talk shows. On one such program, the suggestion was made that chess might be better popularized if living games with bikini-clad girls as pieces were used at chess tournaments.

More serious chess conversations were taking place in New York at that time, i.e., whether the United States could and would field a team to compete in the seventeenth Chess Olympiad to be held in Havana, Cuba, from the 25th of October to the 20th of November. There were a number of delicate problems that had to be worked through before American team participation became a reality. Were there sufficient funds? Could the Americans gain clearance by the State Department? Was there a team available worth sending? Could a responsible captain be secured? And finally, and perhaps foremost, would Fischer head the team? The miserable sixth-place showing achieved by the American contingent at Tel Aviv had been a bitter potion to swallow, and chess players were saying that there was no sense sending a team that was only a shadow of our country's true strength. In addition, for almost a year, it had been assumed by the officials of the U.S. Chess Federation that the State Department would not allow an American team to travel to Cuba, especially after having denied Bobby's request to go there for the 1965 Capablanca Memorial; and therefore no concrete arrangements were made for American participation. An inquiry made to the State Department earlier in the year had received a negative reply. As the entry deadline drew near, Caissa scurried: yes, Fischer wanted to play and was willing to go if paid just $2,000, which was immediately spoken for by the American Chess Foundation. Unfortunately, neither Lombardy nor Reshevsky were available, but Robert Byrne, Pal Benko, and Larry Evans could play second, third, and fourth board, respectively, with Addison and Rossolimo serving as alternates. It was perhaps not the strongest possible American team, but it was a vast improvement over the group that had gone to Israel.

The Cuban Chess Federation made an all-out attempt to make their Olympiad the most memorable in chess history. They offered to pay not only all living expenses for each team while in Havana, but round-trip air transportation. Isaac Kashdan was asked to serve as captain but business commitments precluded his going. Donald Byrne, one of America's finest players and a cool judge of both positions and people, was prevailed upon to abandon his teaching duties at Penn State temporarily and take responsibility for the team. The State Department now indicated that it would authorize the trip as long as it could be assured that each team member was a genuine, black-and-white-squared chess player. On Wednesday, October 19th, a dramatic meeting was held in the offices of the U.S. Chess Federation, with FIDE Delegate Fred Cramer, U.S.C.F. Executive Director Ed Edmondson, chess troubleshooter Jerry Spann, and a number of the potential team members, where all the mazelike details were worked out. Edmondson, a retired Lieutenant Colonel of the U.S. Air Force, had been vice president and the president of the U.S.C.F. and had begun to work tirelessly to help Bobby's chess career, especially in pursuit of the World Championship. He spoke to INDER (the Cuban Sports Federation) and received assurances from them that Fischer's religious* observances would be respected. Calls were placed, cables sent, payments made and arrangements verified, and within days, almost magically, the team jetted to Mexico City, then, via Cubana Airlines, across the Yucatan peninsula and into Havana.

Larry Evans in *Chess Review*, January 1967, states that the reason Fischer went to Cuba was because he ". . . felt bored in New York and just wished to play some chess." He failed to explain how after eighteen grueling rounds of some of the most difficult concentration of his life, Fischer could fall victim to ennui in barely two months time. No, the reasons Fischer elected to play in Cuba had nothing to do with his growing restlessness. He realized that his 1964 demand of a $5,000 appearance fee for Tel Aviv was unrealistic. He had wanted to play for his country, but he didn't get the money then and hence, in effect, couldn't play, though he probably would have preferred to.

---

* Since 1962 Fischer has been a follower of the monolithic fundamentalist Christian sect (over two million members), The Worldwide Church of God, which believes in bodily Baptismal immersion, strict interpretation of the Old Testament, Judaic dietary laws, and has a Sabbath that starts on Friday at sundown and lasts until Saturday at sundown. During this period, followers of the religion meditate and have virtually no contact with anyone (no television or other such diversions, and a 24-hour fast is usually practiced during the Sabbath), and for Fischer, this means no chess activity at all.

Now he had his chance to lead another American team and he was determined to do it. He was playing some of the most relevant chess of his career and he wanted to involve himself in more top-level competition. And he was eager to see post-revolutionary Cuba, as he had wanted to in August 1965 when he had been denied access. He fondly remembered his trip there as a child and the enthusiastic response of the Cubans toward him, even then, when he gave a simultaneous at the Capablanca Chess Club in Havana. Finally, this Olympiad had been designated to be one of the most fabulous since London 1927, when it all began. Advanced descriptions indicated that it would even be greater than Leipzig 1960, Varna 1962 and Tel Aviv. Newspapers were referring to it as "the most important sports or recreational event in all Cuban history." Bobby wanted to be a part of it all. He wasn't disappointed.

When the team alighted at José Martí International Airport, they were the first American cultural group to visit Cuba since Castro's takeover in 1959. What they found there was a country that had been transformed into a virtual chessland. Almost every store window in Havana had some sort of chess display; banners hung in the streets; a commemorative chess stamp had been issued by the government; cigarette and cigar packaging bore chess symbols and advertising for the Olympiad; a neon sign, 90 feet high, in downtown Havana, proclaimed the event. Chess dominated the media from full front-page daily coverage in the newspapers to hour-long documentaries and news shows on radio and television every night. The entire month-long operation cost the Cubans in excess of two and a half million dollars. The Cubans chose this opportunity to have the inaugural opening of their luxurious club, *La Casa del Ajedrez*, the House of Chess, containing chess mementos, trophies, and exhibits, most of which concerned Capablanca. Bobby visited the building on at least one occasion and was impressed with the displays.

A record number of fifty-two nations took part: with the monolithic Soviet Union at the top, representing over 3½ million members of their federation, to diminutive Hong Kong with an entire national chess population of just twenty-five. From Indonesia and Iceland, from Monaco and Mongolia, the teams arrived at the luxurious fifteen-storied Havana Libre to do battle.

Chauffeur-driven limousines were assigned to each team and in the case of the United States and the Soviet Union, with their preponderance of super-stars, two cars were always at hand whenever needed. A guide and translator were also available for each country. Nine hundred Cubans were employed to cater to every whim of the players and to officiate at the festivities and in the tournament hall.

After three days of sightseeing, the teams were graciously hosted at an opening candlelight dinner under the stars, in the centuries-old

Plaza de la Catedral of Havana, which was followed by a light operatic variety performance, similar to the Spanish *zarzuela*. Bobby Fischer was brought to Fidel Castro and introduced. Castro congratulated Bobby on his showing in the Havana tournament of the previous year, and thanked him for coming to Cuba to compete in the Olympiad. Fischer, talking acceptable Spanish, spoke to the Premier about Cuba, chess, and Capablanca; it was a convivial evening and not a word was passed between them about their brief but headline-making contretemps of just a year past. Bobby gave Castro an autographed copy of his primer and left with a warm and friendly handshake.

Much wine and hundreds of daiquiris were consumed at the ceremony and poor Tal, who seems to suffer periodically from physically unfortunate events, was attacked by a bottle-wielding drunk and beaten quite soundly. He was injured seriously enough to be treated at V. I. Lenin General Hospital and was kept out of the first five rounds.

The next day brought the official opening ceremonies at the Havana Sports City Coliseum and attracted over fifteen thousand spectators. And what an affair it was! When Castro arrived, the crowd went thoroughly mad for ten minutes until he took his seat in the President's box. Conspicuously absent was Che Guevara, who had been an enthusiastic spectator of chess events in the past, and who was noted as a player of expert strength. It was he who first played with Fidel and spurred the Prime Minister's interest in the game. Castro certainly matches such leaders as Napoleon, Nasser, and Frederick the Great in his enthusiasm for chess.

After introductory speeches, a chess ballet entitled "The Living Game" was presented in which Capablanca's victory over Lasker at Moscow, 1936, was re-enacted on a "board" of 640 square feet. The national orchestra performed, and a chorus of no less than a thousand from the Cubanacion School of Arts sang Cuban compositions—and the FIDE anthem. Never before had a chess event been so glorified by a spectacle of this magnitude. It was a Cecil B. DeMille extravaganza come to life.

Finally, the time to play chess was at hand, and the three hundred players, including forty-seven Grandmasters and forty International Masters, vying for the world's honor, met in the Ambassador Room of the Havana Libre hotel and sat down at their boards.

The Soviets were once again the odds-on favorites, even though they lacked a number of heavyweights from former years: members of the older team, namely, Botvinnik, Smyslov, Bronstein, and Geller were absent. For unexplained reasons (or was it because in their last two encounters he had had a minus score against Fischer?), Petrosian, Champion of the World, was subordinate to Spassky who played first board in many rounds. Petrosian, Korchnoi, and Tal were the regular boards, with Stein and Polugayevsky as first and second alternates. The Yugoslavs fielded a powerful team (Gligoric, Ivkov, Parma, and Matulovic, with Matanovic and Ciric as reserves), and the Hungarians looked equally as proficient. Most critics were predicting the following finishing order: first, U.S.S.R., of course; second, Yugoslavia; third, Hungary; fourth, United States. The West German government refused to send a team due to political pressures and the absence of that group, usually to be counted among the prize winners, altered the finishing line-up.

In one of the first of his many interviews given in Cuba, Fischer said to reporter Orlando Torres: "The Soviet Union's team is the strongest. We should take second place, although we have a chance to win."

Fischer won all of his games in the preliminaries, many in stylish and compelling fashion, but the American team as a whole just barely managed to squeak through into the finals. They drew against Israel and lost to tiny Norway in the final round by the score of 1½–2½. The humiliation of this defeat is more understandable when it is known that three seasoned Grandmasters and one International Master played for the United States, while Norway only mustered one International Master out of four players. They came only just behind the U.S. and thus qualified into the finals for the first time since competing in the Olympics. They edged out Poland, whereupon the captain of that team immediately accused the Americans of "throwing" their match to the Norwegians. Tensions ran high.

The Soviet Union won its section convincingly—by a four-point margin over second-place Spain—but in no way did they equal their Tel Aviv performance of only one drawn game in the whole of the preliminaries.

Before the finals began, the XXXVIIth Congress of FIDE was called to session at the Hotel Nacional, and J. G. Prentice of Canada presided as President Folke Rogard was unable to attend due to illness. The Congress ran from October 27th to the 31st, and fifty nations were represented in this miniature United Nations. For the first time in chess, instant simultaneous translation was used to speed up the meetings. Rules were discussed, titles conferred and bids were made for the upcoming FIDE events. Major Castro was awarded a gold medal for his contribution to the success of the event.

Four offers for the 1967 Interzonal were made to the Assembly by Nicaragua, Puerto Rico, Dutch West Indies, and Tunisia. The last named country won the vote and the Tunisian delegate, Mr. Belkadi, confirmed it. Speculation was running through the Congress, even then, almost a year in advance of the event, as to whether Bobby Fischer would compete.

Fischer, with the assistance of Larry Evans, had prepared a letter addressed to Folke Rogard, outlining his ideas concerning the possible improvement of the Interzonal and Candidates cycle systems, in addition to his long-held opinion that only wins should count in the World Championship itself. Fred Cramer, the U.S. delegate to FIDE, invited Bobby to present and enlarge upon the ideas himself, before the assembled Congress. Bobby thought it over carefully and then declined. All of his proposals were summarily rejected.

The first round of the finals was held on Friday night, November 4th, and Fischer, as arranged, didn't play. On Saturday, November 5th, the U.S. team was scheduled to face the Soviet contingent in the second round at 4 P.M. Fischer's game with Petrosian, however, could not start until six o'clock, the end of the American's sabbath. Though Edmondson had received assurances from INDER that there would be no problems with this matter and every other team had agreed to the arrangement, the Soviets, without notice, became adamant about "giving in" to Fischer. Alexi Serov, manager of the Soviet team and President of the U.S.S.R. Chess Federation, not only flatly refused to postpone the game but tangentially accused Donald Byrne of anti-Soveit sentiments, and then went into a drawn-out and vehement anti-Yankee harangue. That Serov's reasoning was irrelevant to the question at hand, as Fischer had been promised that his Sabbath would be respected and had agreed to play in Havana on that basis, was totally overlooked. Perhaps Serov's problem was one of anti-American mis-identification; news stories at that time were relating tales of the two brash Americans who stole a statue of a Russian bear in Moscow and who were also under arrest for currency violations. The Havana incident bore all the earmarks of an international scandal as wire stories flashed back and forth across the globe.

Byrne telephoned Edmondson in New York and received advice not to bring the American team to the tournament hall until 6 P.M. Serov stated that *his* team would be present when every other nation would be there: at four. He then threw in some disparaging remarks about Fischer's playing ability, just for good measure. Edmondson was apprised of the situation and immediately sent the following cable to Folke Rogard in Stockholm:

> USSR REFUSED PLAY USA MATCH UNDER OR-
> GANIZING COMMITTEE AGREEMENT DELAY
> FISCHER GAME START. YOUR INTERVENTION
> URGENTLY REQUESTED FOR SOVIET COM-
> PLIANCE. IF THEY CONTINUE REFUSAL WE
> CLAIM 4–0 FORFEIT,
>
> > EDMUND B. EDMONDSON,
> > EXECUTIVE DIRECTOR
> > U.S. CHESS FEDERATION

While awaiting Rogard's reply, the U.S. Team appeared at the tournament hall at 6 P.M. to discover that the Czech tournament arbiter, Jaroslav Sajtar, had already impetously taken his own action, regardless of the president of FIDE's response. The U.S.S.R.-U.S.A. match was considered completed and a 4–0 forfeit score was registered in favor of the Soviets! Byrne, of course, lodged an official protest and Edmondson cabled pleas to anyone who he thought could help. In a statement issued to *The New York Times*, Edmondson furiously attacked the forfeit and affirmed that if it were not reversed by Wednesday, November 9th, ". . . we shall tell our team to withdraw."

The *Moscow News* seemed unduly harsh with Bobby: "Robert Fischer, the United States Grandmaster, has been long known for his extravagant fits. In the years past, these fits were explained by adolescence. People hoped that as he grew up, Fischer would learn his manners and consider not only his own interests but also those of his colleagues—other players. But judging by recent events, Fischer is making far less progress in self-restraint than in the field of chess. The United States grossly violated the competition and the FIDE Charter." No mention of Bobby's rights that had been violated.

The very next day brought some relief. Rogard's recommendations arrived in Havana, and he diplomatically asked for "a friendly agreement" to be reached by rescheduling the match. He made two other suggestions if mutual accord could not be obtained; the establishing of an Arbitration Council, and if that were not found appropriate, simply scoring the match as a 2–2 tie.

Serov was unmoved by Rogard's suggestions and stubbornly refused to agree, and hence an Arbitration Council was set up. It's members were Argentina, Austria, Belgium, Canada, Cuba, and Czechoslovakia. This Supreme Court of Chess "urgently requested" the Russians to reconsider. Mysteriously, and quite suddenly, Serov temporarily disappeared and Igor Bondarevsky, captain of the Soviet team, announced that he was now the new Russian spokesman and that before anything could be settled he would have to have a ruling from his homeland. The next day an announcement came from Jesus Betancourt, president of INDER, stating that the Soviets had agreed to reschedule the match on November 14th in order to avoid "international repercussions" and to please the Cuban public. *Granma*, the leading Cuban weekly, referred to the Soviet move as a "noble gesture," while *The New York Times* stated that the Russians had "yielded." The players from both teams, all of whom wanted to play the match and most of whom were just simply embarrassed by the confusion toasted each other with goblets of brandy.

While the U.S.A.-U.S.S.R. brouhaha was in full swing, the two teams had continued competing against other nations, awaiting a final outcome regarding the controversy; and after it was settled, waiting for the newly scheduled match to take place. The American team had downed Denmark 3½–½ in the first round, had their Soviet postponement in the second, swept all four boards against Spain in the third, defeated Iceland 3½–½ in the fourth, and beat East Germany 3–1 in the fifth round, for a total of 14 points. Fischer had defeated Pomar, Olafsson, and Portisch and had drawn with Uhlmann, and it looked as though he might have good chances for the gold medal. His chess was strong and clear, though he sat in a bad position against Uhlmann.

By agreeing to play off the U.S.A. match, the Soviets lost the four points that they had originally claimed by forfeit, and the U.S. moved into first place. Yugoslavia was a narrow second at 13½ and the U.S.S.R. dropped down to third with 13. This standing didn't last very long.

In the sixth round, the U.S. was held even at 2–2 by the Hungarians while the Soviets immediately pulled ahead by defeating Spain 3½–½. And in the seventh round the Russians stayed ahead by beating Iceland 3–1, while the U.S. downed Norway by the same score. Fischer defeated Johannesson in a beautiful game, thus amassing what the *British Chess Magazine* called a "colossal" total, as indeed it was, of 10½ out of 11 points. Pachman and Petrosian were the only other undefeated players on the top boards but Bobby had singularly captured and fired the imagination of the Cuban public. They were rooting for the *yanqui* to keep winning.

Castro often stopped by the tournament hall, and at the half-way mark he gave a private banquet at the Palace of the Revolution for the team members and a few selected friends and government officials. Untypically and somewhat formally garbed, Castro, without his battered cap and olive-drab fatigues, toasted country after country and had only the best to say about chess. Bobby approached Leonid Stein, then Champion of the Soviet Union, and challenged him to a match, to be conducted in Havana either at the conclusion of the Olympiad, or else early in 1967. The winner of the match would be the player who first scored ten wins, draws not counting.

If the Alekhine-Capablanca match of 1927 could be used as a model of that method of conducting a contest (they played twenty-five draws before Alekhine achieved six wins), the proposed Fischer-Stein match could be prolonged to over fifty games and take as long as three months. Fischer felt he had the time, though he had informally committed himself to playing in the forthcoming U.S. Championship. Whether Stein could devote that amount of time was another question.

Perhaps due to the gaiety and spontaneity of the moment, Stein accepted what his country had always refused: a non-FIDE match between a top Soviet and American player. It looked as though Fischer had finally achieved what he had been attempting since 1962. Bobby quickly ushered Stein over to Castro, and he told the Cuban leader of their plans and asked for his approval. Castro, chomping on his ever-present cigar, thoughtfully nodded his assent. At a press conference held immediately afterward, Bobby told reporters: "The Prime Minister said that it was all right with him and that furthermore, he would like to watch the match!" Arrangements were started, Edmondson was cabled in New York, it appeared a *fait accompli* when the very next morning, Stein announced that he never took Fischer's challenge seriously and that he had thought it was a publicity stunt. It was obvious that as soon as word of the impending skirmish reached Moscow, they cabled Stein and the Russian captain, straightaway: "*Nyet!*"

Fischer was aghast. On the following day, in an interview published in *Prensa Latina* he stated:

> I am ready to play against Grandmaster Stein or against any other Soviet master. Yesterday I spoke with Stein about this and he didn't seem to show much interest. He called me a publicity-seeker. I've made a concrete proposal of playing ten games, not counting draws. At first he seemed interested and we told Barreras,* who agreed to it. Later we spoke to the Prime Minister and he said it was all right with him. I eagerly spoke to Stein again the next day and it was then that he accused me of wanting to arrange the match in order to get publicity. This is why I feel that the Soviet master is going back on the match. I, for my part, am perfectly willing to go ahead with it.

Stein didn't take long to answer. In a subsequent interview, he said:

> I, myself, or any other of the Soviet masters, would be willing to play a match with U.S. Champion Roberto Fischer at any time he wished in 1967.

He then went on to say that he was committed to attend other tournaments for the remainder of the year but would be willing to return to Havana sometime in 1967 to play. Fischer is still waiting.

---

* José Luis Barreras, Cuban Vice President of FIDE and Technical Director of the Olympiad.

CHAPTER XV

*". . . If you don't win, it's not a great
tragedy—the worst that happens is
that you lose a game."*

Returning to the Olympiad, the Yugoslavs beat the Americans in
the eighth round with a score of 2½–1½. Fischer played a wild and
lovely game against Gligoric and won in twenty-five moves, but Byrne
was completely off form and lost to Ivkov in a twenty-move French
Defense. The Soviets managed to down the East Germans by 2½–1½
and had amassed 22 points. The Americans had 20½ and now it was
time for these two great teams to meet and settle their differences.

The match was played on November 14th, as scheduled, with
Fischer facing Spassky on board one, Byrne against Tal on board two,
Benko vs. Stein on board three, and Larry Evans opposed to Lev
Polugayevsky on last board. Crowds were turned away from the
tournament hall by the hundreds, but they weren't entirely disappointed. One block away, atop the *Radiocentro* cinema house, was a
32-foot-high electrically illuminated chess board in which all the
moves of the Fischer-Spassky game were displayed. Hundreds of
fans gathered beneath it and across the street to follow and discuss
each maneuver. It was rumored that the board cost 80,000 pesos to
construct.

Fischer, as White, played the Ruy Lopez but Spassky avoided the
Marshall Attack which he had played in their last encounter in Santa
Monica, and assayed the conservative 8 P–Q3. Playing as a part of
a team rather than as an individual, Spassky felt it more important
to attempt to secure a draw in hand than to play speculatively for a
possible spectacular victory. Bobby seized the initiative, and it was
the opinion of all the Grandmasters on the scene that by his thirty-
fifth move he had a superior position; but by adjournment time
(Spassky sealed his fortieth move), the consensus had shifted. Now
it was believed that Fischer was lost. The only player who disagreed
with that judgment was Fischer himself. He was confident that the
game could be drawn.

Meanwhile, Byrne lost to Tal and Benko drew against Stein, all before adjournment. Evans adjourned against Polugayevsky, a Pawn down, and it looked as though both he and Fischer would drop their points to the Soviets, the U.S. team would then only manage to earn one measly half-point. The adjournments were resumed and after much delicate finesse on both their parts, Evans and Fischer salvaged draws. The U.S. had lost 1½–2½, but had managed to avoid the repetition of the disgraceful 0–4 of Tel Aviv. But once again, Fischer was unable to defeat Boris Spassky.

On November 19th, Capablanca's birthday (he was born in 1888), play was suspended at the Olympiad and Castro proclaimed a "World Day of Chess," the first one in history, to my knowledge. A number of shows were given and exhibitions presented but the *pièce de résistance* was the most mammoth simultaneous exhibition ever undertaken: 6,840 boards! It took 380 masters to compete against these numbers and the entire flood-lit *Plaza de la Revolución* was needed to accommodate them. Row upon row of boards set on banquet tables were regimentally and mathematically placed for the most efficient method of coping with the feat. It looked like a Chess Woodstock with pawns, pieces and players stretched over acres of plaza.

Members of the Revolutionary Armed Forces, students, and workers were among the participants. Fischer played a game against Castro and, surprise!—Fischer resigned. Fidel said that he was really getting ready to become a good player, adding that he had already read half of the book that Fischer had given him. He stated that he was also studying Capablanca's games. "But there is no reason to worry," he joked with Bobby. "I will not be among the great masters in the next Olympics!" Petrosian, too, had played against the Caribbean leader and had drawn, after which Castro had said: "There is no doubt that Petrosian, in addition to being a great champion, is a great diplomat." But aside from these chessical jokes, Castro did play an excellent game against Filiberto Terrazas, a member of the Mexican team, and beat him legitimately.

As the fates would have it, this dalliance was destroyed by nature. A rainstorm began as a trickle, then turned into a heavy downpour. By 11 P.M. one hundred and twenty wins and six hundred and thirty-two draws were registered by the Masters, with the remaining games adjourned.

The next day the Olympiad resumed. It was impossible to catch the Soviet team after their American victory. They drew with Hungary but demolished Norway 4–0 and beat Yugoslavia, Argentina, and Bulgaria quite soundly. The U.S. beat Argentina, but could only draw with Bulgaria. They defeated Czechoslovakia, drew with Rumania and downed Cuba in the final round. The Soviets won the XVIIth Olympiad with a score of 39½, five full points ahead of the second place U.S.A. (at 34½), while Hungary and Yugoslavia at 33½ tied for third and fourth.

That the Soviets would win, as mentioned earlier, was a foregone conclusion. We had exactly equaled our score of five points behind the first place Soviets at Varna, 1962, but we were still a far cry from Stockholm, 1937.

Even though it was apparent that the Soviet conquest was a certainty by the tenth or eleventh round, the real drama of the event was captured by Bobby Fischer. By the end of the eleventh round, Fischer had amassed an almost unbelievable tally of 14 points out of fifteen games. "This is like Alekhine in San Remo," said O'Kelly, referring to his thirteen victories and two draws in 1930. It was Fischer's own brand of chess history in a setting that was continually producing superlatives.

Fischer could have elected not to play the last two matches and would have walked away with the gold medal safely tucked in his pocket, since his closest rival for the prize, Petrosian, had 11½ points out of a possible 13 and had not faced the same caliber of opposition. But Bobby was determined to continue to play. Criticism was leveled at Donald Byrne, as team captain, for "allowing" Bobby to jeopardize his chances in the last two rounds, but such attackers probably don't know Fischer: he wants to play chess more than anything else in the world and risks of loss or threats of same will not deter him.

Al Horowitz, in a story in *The New York Times*, produced an almost poetic appraisal of Fischer's performance in Havana:

> He is theoretically equipped. His knowledge of opening lore—key games from key events—and basic endings is encyclopedic. He is imaginative and creative, forcefully aggressive and stubbornly defiant, as circumstances warrant. His positional strategy is sharp and deep. He aims for an early edge, and knows how to convert even a fractional plus to victory. More important, he rebounds from an inferior position with *élan*, and besets his compromised game with perplexing problems. All these attributes, in varying degrees, are those of grandmasters. But Fischer tops the list in nerve and endurance. Emotionally, he is fortified for the kill, quick or long run. That is why he rarely accedes to the draw in an apparently even position. He plays on and on until his opponent, exhausted, breaks under the strain.

To prove that he, too, was human enough to break, Fischer met his Waterloo. Heidenfeld, who was playing for South Africa, wrote later of that encounter that "Fischer, who had been terrorizing his field like a dragon in a fairy tale, was tackled by dragon-killer Gheorghiu—tackled, outplayed, and taken to bits." Larry Evans expressed it more simply and a bit differently: ". . . Bobby, in effect, beat himself . . ." At one point in the game, Gheorghiu offered a draw, which Fischer refused, and at the very opening stages when the Rumanian asked "Are you playing for a win?" Fischer curtly replied "Of course!" Later Gheorghiu stated that when he offered Fischer the draw, he was convinced he actually had a won game but that he wanted Fischer to be awarded the gold medal. It was obvious that Fischer was trying too hard and had tired and over-extended himself. He lost the game decisively. Nevertheless, all of the players and spectators considered Bobby to be the real hero of the most magnificent chess event in history. Who else would have jeopardized his chances for the first-board prize? Larsen might be the only other possibility.

Dimitrije Bjelica interviewed Fischer at Havana, and wrote in *Chess*: ". . . he's changed. He's more polite; answers questions, obliges with his autograph. As always he is the center of attention. I asked him if he would be playing in the World Championship cycle. He replied: 'No, because FIDE will not accept my proposals.' "

The final statistics of the Cuban Olympiad bear almost tragic overtones. Petrosian's percentage was 88.45, against 88.22 percent for Fischer; less than one-quarter of one percent difference. Gligoric stated in *Chess Review* that:

> . . . Fischer had much the harder job to do. He defeated many of the strongest Grandmasters while Petrosian was favored by the special tactics of the captain of the Soviet team, who had in mind the total score for the whole team and so gave Petrosian a lesser number of games (and the consequent rest periods between) and the majority of those with the White side.

Though a heartbreaker to Americans, Bobby Fischer's valiant attempts to do the impossible will be remembered for years, and of the 1,888 games played there, his seventeen were all distinguished and uncompromising fights. He ended by scoring one-third of the points scored by the entire team. Though he might not put it exactly in these terms, Fischer's pursuit is his art, and the manifestation of that art is in the *attempt*. Certainly, first prize is the only one acceptable. But medals and trophies pale against concepts and variations. For Fischer, the play is the thing.

CHAPTER XVI

"It's pretty tough because of all the tension and all the concentration, sitting there hour after hour. It's . . . exhausting."

Fischer remained in Havana for ten days at the conclusion of the Olympiad, as an official guest of INDER, and spent Thanksgiving Day sight-seeing. He then flew back to Mexico City and decided to enjoy a few days in that great land-locked metropolis, relaxing. It was so pleasant that he stayed on for a full week; perhaps he was also trying to confront the questions he had pertinent to the forthcoming U.S. Championship. The tournament committee was frantic. They wanted Bobby to play, of course, but received no official word from him—and time was growing perilously short. Bobby finally called the U.S.C.F. office. He stated his intention to play, but would do so only if the contest were adapted to a larger, or certainly a longer, tournament. Chess players have for many years considered the U.S. Championship as somewhat less than a meaningful chess event because of its relative shortness and hence lack of strength, and Bobby had suffered the jibes of foreign players, especially the Soviets, that his many victories in the American Championship had been, in effect, shallow. Compared to the mammoth U.S.S.R. Championship and to national title events of other countries, the United States had been woefully negligent in recent years in producing a tournament that could be considered a taxing struggle and true test of strength for the best of American players. Organizers have cited: (1) lack of money, and (2) unavailability of most players to spend more than one month competing. How we were able to afford such events in the past (the Sixth American Chess Congress, New York 1889, for example, consisted of a double round-robin between twenty players and stretched over a two month period) and why they have become too expensive in this age of chess opulence, remains unexplained. Also, the days seem to be over when it was impossible for a chessplayer to find necessary time to play in an important event. Such regular U.S.

121

Championship contenders as Reshevsky, Robert Byrne, Larry Evans, Pal Benko, and Fischer himself, have no trouble changing their schedules to play in any tournament they want to compete in. Only those players who are committed to university work are often pressed for time, and then even one month is usually too long, so their participation is not a factor in deciding whether the tourney should be lengthened. Fischer's main contention was that if a player loses just one game in such a short tournament, it is very difficult—if not impossible—to catch up and win the title. In a letter to Kenneth Smith, of *Chess Digest*, he explained it this way:

> In the 1962 U.S. Championship I lost a game to Edmar Mednis in an early round. After losing this game, I had to make a tremendous effort and win game after game to finally draw even with Arthur Bisguier in the last round. I won the last game against Bisguier and the title. After this tournament the idea began to develop in my mind that something was really wrong if a fellow couldn't lose a game in a U.S. Championship without practically being eliminated. This attitude was reinforced after the 1964–65 Championship where I lost two in a row after having won almost all of my earlier games and I found myself in a very close finish taking the title.

Fischer concluded by saying that he was ". . . determined to not play unless the championship was changed."

Theoretically, of course, he was correct but his domination of the U.S. title has been so keenly manifest that there was almost mathematical certainty that it was his to keep, if he so chose, for years to come.

The late Maurice Kasper, perennial chairman of the U.S. Championship Committee and unofficial father-figure to many American master players, called Bobby in Mexico City. He asked Bobby to play "as a special favor" and offered him $500 extra as a participation fee plus his usual hotel and living expenses. First prize, should he win, had been increased to $2,500.

Fischer held out for a longer tournament and said he wouldn't play unless that particular concession was made. Kasper reasoned that there simply was not time to lengthen the tournament (it was literally a few days before the first round was to begin) but that if Bobby would agree to play in the 1966–67 event, he would do everything possible to get the tournament changed for the following year, and that he would back Fischer's proposal at the next player's meeting. Fischer finally consented, and in a few days flew back to New York just before the tournament began. The first round was scheduled to begin on Sunday, December 11th at the Henry Hudson Hotel. The night before, a public drawing was held at the Manhattan Chess Club to determine the pairings and Fischer drew number twelve for the third year in a row. Some of the players jokingly teased him about "rigging" the draw but Fischer made no indication that he heard their taunts.

Chess Review referred to the tournament contenders as an "awesome list." Seven grandmasters played: Fischer, Evans, Benko, Bisguier, R. Byrne, Reshevsky, and Rossolimo. They were joined by Saidy, Zuckerman, Addison, D. Byrne, and Sherwin. The last two mentioned were invited as replacements for Lombardy and Kalme, who could not attend due to school commitments. If there was any skepticism circulating, and there was, about Fischer's ability to monopolize the U.S. Championship, based on his less than divine showing of the previous year, it was dispelled quickly. He had no worries about losing the title.

Commencing by beating Benko, who played his favorite 1 P–KN3 (with which he had defeated Fischer—and Tal—at Curaçao, 1962), Bobby then downed Saidy (with a lovely sacrifice of a piece) and Rossolimo and drew with Robert Byrne in successive rounds. Then he scored a point against Donald Byrne and a crushing win against his friend from Brooklyn, Bernard Zuckerman.

In the seventh and eighth rounds Fischer drew with Evans and Addison respectively and there was absolutely no stopping him after that. He checkmated Sherwin in the next round after one of the longest games of his career, one hundred moves, in an encounter about which Burt Hochberg said: "When Sherwin made his error, Fischer's face lit up like a little boy who was just promised a new bike for his birthday." The Fischer-Reshevsky game, in the tenth round, was played before a capacity crowd, and Reshevsky, though fighting valiantly, went down in forty-three moves. In the final round, Bobby beat Bisguier for the *twelfth successive time*.

He had not lost a game in the tournament. His final score of 9½ was two full points ahead of Evans in second place. The *British Chess Magazine* was so dazzled by his performance that they conceded to call him "almost incredible." I like the "almost."

The date was Thursday, December 29th, 1966. When he left the hotel that night for a celebration dinner, the temperature dropped and snow began to flurry in midtown Manhattan. Bobby Fischer couldn't know then that this, his eighth U.S. Championship attempt and his eighth victory, would be his last for many years to come. He was twenty-three years old.

Early in 1967, the U.S. Chess Federation received an invitation from *Les Amis d'Europe-Échecs*, a group of French chess patrons, for two American players to compete in a small but gamy tournament, the Grand Prix International, to be held in the legendary principality of Monaco from March 24th to April 4th. The request was cordially made that if at all possible, Bobby Fischer should be one of the participants. Prince Rainier would serve as chairman of the tournament committee and lend his financial support. It has also been reported that the Prince wrote personally to Bobby, urging him to play.

Smyslov, Geller, Gligoric, Larsen, and Matanovic were among the grandmasters who had already confirmed their participation, and Forintos from Hungary, and Mazzoni and Bergraser, both of France, were also playing.

Monte Carlo is known for staging four memorable chess events at the beginning of this century, and Americans were always invited to compete. Frank J. Marshall, in his twenties, though not winning his spurs at any of the Monte Carlo tournaments, gained valuable international experience there, and the famed Bostonian, Harry Nelson Pillsbury, played some of the greatest chess of his career under the watchful eyes of Rainier's grandfather, Prince Louis II.

Bobby accepted the invitation as did William Lombardy, who had just finished his seminary tests and was waiting for his ordination. Fischer requested and received an appearance fee of $2,000. It caused an uproar among a number of the players. Matanovic, incensed, wrote in *Politika*:

> The fact that Fischer had demanded and got his extra fee just for coming, while, for example, the ex-World Champion Smyslov was only on a par with all the rest of the participants . . . is an absurdity which could have been even more striking if Petrosian had participated.

Petrosian *had* considered playing but was so enraged when he heard of Fischer's financial demands that he declined.

During the two months prior to the tournament, Bobby spent his time working on the proofs of his forthcoming book, "My 60 Memorable Games" and preparing for Monte Carlo. Dr. Timothy Leary had just announced that he began using chess sets as visual props for preparing classes at Harvard to receive the impact of LSD. "Life is a chess game of experiences we play," he said. And so, conversely, is chess a life-game. Just ask Bobby Fischer.

No sooner had he arrived in the stately *Hall du Centennaire* before the first round than the typical Fischer fireworks started exploding. He wanted the first round to be played at twelve noon; the games on Saturday to be played after 6 P.M.; the sixth round to be played after the first, instead of the second; all the players to start their first round games at noon, also. His conditions seemed endless. He threatened to withdraw immediately and fly back to the United States if they were not met to the letter. The complications were suddenly enormous and not a Pawn had been moved!

The tournament director, Count Alberic O'Kelly, worked things out with the dazed organizers who had little experience coping with a bellicose personality like Fischer. They quietly relented to all his demands, which infuriated many of the players who were already silently burning over Fischer's financial success. Smyslov, veteran of scores of chess tournaments with years of experience facing frustrating situations on and off the board, took it all philosophically: "Like this or like that—it does not really matter . . ." he said gently.

Dragoslav Andric wrote in *Chess* that: "All these procedural matters were eclipsed in interest by Fischer's brilliant start." He won his first five games without even the hint of a draw! Once again, Fischer's beautiful games became the focus of attention. Suddenly, his manipulations of rounds and people didn't matter that much. Matanovic stated that ". . . after this fifth victory a certain amount of uneasiness arose (some might say it was almost panic), among the competitors. Was Fischer going to win the tournament without dropping even a half-point?"

Bobby continued adamant about the scheduling, especially regarding his sabbath. He would not, of course, play from sundown on Friday to sundown on Saturday, but he was miffed that the other games were arranged for that time. He announced he was dropping out but before doing so, he called Edmondson in New York to see if the U.S. Chess Federation could intervene. After a sixty-dollar phone call, Edmondson somehow talked him into remaining in the tournament, and the organizers made yet another change by establishing Saturday as a rest day for all the participants.

Bobby's sixth-round opponent, Smyslov, had to postpone play to have a tooth extracted. Prince Rainier arrived at the tournament hall and was disappointed, since he had expected to see those two greats in action. He talked for a while with Bobby, the photographers recorded the meeting, and the two left chatting amiably and ended up spending the afternoon together. The next evening a concert was given in the *Salle Garnier* in honor of the tournament. His Highness and Princess Grace hosted an informal champagne party for the ten players in the private rooms behind the royal box, and the late Marcel Duchamp, chessplayer, world-renowned cubist painter, and constant spectator at the tournament also attended.

Everyone, including the Prince, wanted to know whether Bobby planned to play in the Interzonal in Tunisia. He let it be known that he probably wouldn't play and cited FIDE's rejection of his proposals as the main reason.

Fischer ultimately drew his game with Smyslov, his only other draw of the tournament being with Matanovic. Going into the last round, Fischer with 7 points had White against Geller, while Smyslov, his closest rival at 6 points, had White against Gligoric. Apparently, Smyslov assumed that Fischer could, at worst, draw against Geller and therefore accepted an almost absurd "Grandmaster draw" of ten moves against his Yugoslavian opponent. Both men appeared very tired. It was undoubtedly a mistake Smyslov still regrets since Geller managed to beat Fischer in the last round, thus robbing Smyslov of his opportunity to share first place with the American.

Thus Fischer's first journey to Europe in five years to compete in an international tournament was a success. He won the contest soundly if not altogether decisively, and picked up a 5,000 Franc first prize, together with a trophy presented to him by the Prince and Princess. Leonard Barden, writing in *The Guardian*, however, was untypically harsh on his friend:

> At Zurich and Bled, 1961, and Stockholm 1962, Fischer had much the better of his individual games against Soviet Grandmasters. Starting with the Candidates' at Curaçao in 1962, where he claimed the Russians cheated during their games with him, he has had only mediocre success. Fischer reappeared in international tournaments at Havana 1965, and from then until Monaco 1967, he had played ten games against Russians, winning only one, with five defeats. It is ominous if a world title claimant can score only 35 percent in a series against his main rivals. Looked at in this light, the most significant game from Monaco is Fischer's loss in the last round when he had already won the tournament.

Though Barden's rationale is well-presented (Fischer at that time had never scored outstandingly against the Soviets), there are some people (I'm one of them) who will argue that his loss to Geller in the last round was a case of super-psychology on the Brooklynite's part. There are others who hold that he found it a psychological hardship playing against his favorite variation. Geller had employed Fischer's pet line of the Sicilian, which he discussed later. "I thought Fischer would be in an amicable mood but I was aware of his love for the one and the same system, and therefore I offered him a chance to fight against his own weapons." Geller would have us believe that it was a noble challenge on his part, as indeed it was, but the psychological element he introduced was enormous.

Smyslov had drawn his game against Gligoric, gratuitously presenting the tournament to Fischer. Even at the risk of losing his game against Geller, Fischer might well have elected to deliberately play an inferior line, rather than to reveal what he had discovered to be the best line against his own preferred opening. His sixth move was one he had never played before in the Sicilian. It's true that it is difficult to imagine Fischer ever compromising himself to such an extent as to actually lose a game on purpose, and to jeopardize half of first prize, to boot, but it is clear from everything that he does—from his demands to his withdrawals, from his statements to his writings, from all of his changes and juggling, his ups and his downs—that Bobby Fischer is continuously playing a "game" of mental manipulation, not necessarily to disarm his opponent but to establish his own psychological credential. Steinitz was the first to express the theory of accumulation of small advantages and he could well have enlarged his ideas to include off-the-board tactics as well. And we mustn't forget that Steinitz is one of Fischer's idols.

CHAPTER XVII

*"When I win, I'll put my title on
the line every year, maybe even
twice. I'll give players a chance
to beat me."*

Fischer returned from Monaco to New York and his suite at the
Tudor Hotel on East 42nd Street, close to the United Nations. He
had given up the family apartment in Brooklyn, mainly because it
had grown too unwieldy for his careless bachelor habits. No neatnik
he, the apartment began to show the wear and clutter of a home
without a housekeeper. He had lived in Brooklyn for more than
seventeen years, grown up there, learned chess there, and after
dazzling five continents with his exploits, would always go back to
his home in Crown Heights. He was used to Brooklyn and in some
ways was sorry to leave it. Also, it was necessary for him to travel
into Manhattan almost daily, mainly by taxicab, so that he could get
to the Manhattan and Marshall Clubs, to those bookstores that
carried the best of chess literature, and to be more readily available
to see his publisher, his friends, and his growing legion of chess
contacts.

He was by now writing a more or less steady chess column for
Boys' Life magazine, which he would continue to do for nearly three
years.

No progress had been made in his own mind as to whether he
would play in the Interzonal at Tunis. In June, Miro Radojcic, a
Yugoslavian journalist, interviewed him briefly. When asked about
his possible participation, Fischer replied: "You know, I haven't made
up my mind. I really can't say one way or the other. Perhaps."
Radojcic interpreted the answer as a "yes" since he felt that Fischer's
negative tone was "unconvincing."

One tournament Bobby *did* want to participate in was the "Inter-
national Tournament to Commemorate the 50th Anniversary of the
Great October Revolution" to be held in Moscow in late May–early
June, with such titans as Spassky, Tal, Smyslov, Petrosian, Stein,

Najdorf, and Gligoric competing. Pal Benko also sought an invitation, but no Americans were asked. Probably the Soviets would have been embarrassed should a Westerner win this highly politicalized event, and they therefore kept the Americans out. Petrosian, in an interview given in *Vjesnik*, stated that the reason Fischer wasn't invited was ". . . because of religious reasons since he doesn't play on Fridays and Saturdays. The U.S.S.R. Chess Federation didn't like to involve religion in a tournament." However, Petrosian failed to offer a rationale for Benko. Stein won the tournament. Najdorf, whom the Russians still consider a Pole, stated in a press interview that he didn't think Fischer was the "greatest player outside of the Soviet Union," but he failed to name who he thought was better.

Bobby accepted an invitation to play in an international tournament in Skopje, Yugoslavia, from August 6th to 30th. The Tunisian Interzonal was scheduled to start on October 15th.

During the Havana Olympiad, Florencio Campomanes, in behalf of the Philippine Chess Federation, had asked Bobby to come to Manila in the summer of 1967 for a series of simultaneous and clock exhibitions. He decided to go, and then continue on to Skopje afterward.

He arrived in the Philippines as a monumental controversy raged throughout the Island on whether to ban or permit women's "hot pants" in public places in downtown Manila. For once Bobby was not the center of a dispute. He toured the Philippines giving a number of simultaneous and single-game exhibitions, visited with his match opponent of 1957, Rodolfo Cardoso, and talked with Renato Naranja, Campomanes, and other top players from the Islands.

At the beginning of August, Fischer flew from Manila to Belgrade, with his jet touching down at Saigon just long enough for him to send some postcards back to the States, and observe an unbelievably hectic scene of thousands of military men arriving by plane and ship.

Though he hadn't committed himself publicly, by the time Bobby arrived in Skopje he had made up his mind to play in the Interzonal at Tunis. It seemed like the entire American chess world was pleading with him to compete. Edmondson, of course, had many talks with Bobby about his possible participation and even offered to meet him in Tunis to act as a buffer should problems arise with scheduling, lighting, or any other details. Kashdan used his chess column in the *Los Angeles Times* to appeal to Bobby's friends to "urge him to play," perhaps overlooking the fact that those who remain as his intimates are the very ones who dare not, under pain of "excommunication," discuss such things with him. And *Chess Review* ran a cover story about the matter based on Soviet rumors that he was not going to play. The magazine pointed out that even though the FIDE system of selecting challengers was far from perfect, so was the old system which permitted the champion to select his own competitors based on the amount of the purse or numerous other factors. "Lasker never got a return match with Capablanca, not even though he won the great New York Tournament of 1924, nor a match with Alekhine," they editorialized. "Capa never got a rematch with Alekhine who took on his 'cousin' Bogolyubov repeatedly, instead." They went on to ask Fischer to "meditate" on how the Soviets ignored Reshevsky's claim to the title, and ended up by urging Bobby to consider the sacrifice of participation for a chance at a title shot. Bobby was, of course, aware of all these factors and had chosen Skopje as his warm-up tournament in preparation for his African debut. His decision not to announce his participation was a waiting game. If the organizers thought he might still play but was busily "making up his mind" they would possibly improve the conditions to meet his eventual (they hoped) approval. He and the other players had everything to gain by his temporarily deferring his affirmation. Meanwhile, it was imperative for him to become involved in some serious practice.

The Yugoslavian tournament was held in the cities of Krusevo, Ochrid, and Skopje, all within short distances of each other. Skopje, the capital of Macedonia, was destroyed by an earthquake in 1963, and had been rebuilt. "The Tournament of Solidarity" was the first chess event held there, and it was conducted to show appreciation to those people of the world who gave aid and brotherly help during the calamity.

Originally planned as a tournament of a dozen grandmasters and several international masters, the starting line-up was not quite that impressive. Four "real" grandmasters, Fischer, Geller, Matulovic, and Kholmov, and two "minor" grandmasters, Damjanovic and Janosevic, played. It was assumed by most that Fischer would have virtually no opposition. And, as usual, whenever it comes to predicting what Bobby Fischer will or won't do, everyone was wrong.

In the first round, almost unbelievably, he drew with Risto Ilijevsky, who was not even a recognized master but a candidate for that title, roughly comparable in strength to an American expert. He then met Geller in the second round, again had the White pieces, against which Geller again employed the Sicilian Defense, and for the second occasion in barely five months, Fischer succumbed—this time in just twenty-three moves. Someone asked Geller why he always won against Fischer. "I don't know," he replied, "maybe it's just luck." His questioner was skeptical: "I don't think it *could* just be chance." Geller laughingly agreed: "Neither do I!"

Fischer then defeated Damjanovic, Dely, Minic, Panov, Maric, Danov, and Bukic in the third to ninth rounds, respectively. He led the tournament with Kholmov at 7½ points. Geller stood at 7.

Just prior to the tenth round in Ochrid, Fischer presented a petition to the tournament committee asking that he be given a chess set in which the difference between the King and Queen would be more distinguishable.* He also asked that in the event of continued noise, spectators be removed from the tournament hall or that he be allowed to play in a separate room. He argued that the tournament room in Ochrid was much smaller than in Skopje and therefore much noisier.

The tournament organizers had no difficulty finding a suitable set for Fischer but they would not give in to his other ultimatums, arguing that a chess tournament—this chess tournament, in any event—was a public exhibition and that all contestants had to abide by the same regulations and play under the same conditions. Fischer stated evenly that he was withdrawing.

Fischer did not appear for his tenth round game against Knezhevic and was promptly forfeited. The next day, however, he surprised everyone by entering the tournament hall to play off an adjourned game. The committee had an emergency meeting to decide what to do, and after much discussion a compromise was reached: the chess set would be replaced and every effort would be made to keep order and silence in the tournament hall. It was Fischer, of course, who had saved the reputation of the event by participating in the first place, and they desperately wanted to keep him playing. Knezhevic agreed to play out his game against Fischer, rather than accept the point, and the committee reversed its forfeit. Even chess stories sometimes have happy endings.

As is often the case with Bobby, his disputations took their toll: he could only draw against Knezhevic and in the eleventh round he drew again, this time to Popov. He then lost to Dragoljub Janosevic, a remarkably inconsistent but dangerous grandmaster who has been able to score victories against such notables as Reshevsky, Larsen, Tal, and Petrosian over the years, and who drew a short two-game match with Bobby in 1958.**

In what *The New York Times* described as "fighting drive," Fischer scored five full points in the remaining five rounds, including wins over Kholmov and Matulovic, who had been slowly creeping on him, and a brilliant miniature against Sofrevsky in the last round. Fischer described his game against Kholmov as "one of the most important tournament games" in his career. It was a harmonious encounter and a decisive victory. First prize was his at 13½

---

* Chess sets in a number of countries, especially Eastern, lack the small cross atop the King which is a feature of the Staunton sets prevalent in the West. It is sometimes very difficult, for people used to playing with Staunton-designed pieces, to distinguish King from Queen.

** At about that time, Fischer also played a four-game match against Matulovic, which he won 2½–1½.

points, ahead of Geller and Matulovic by the smallest possible margin of ½ point. Though his play had been inconstant and he apparently was somewhat off form, he *did* manage to win the tournament. As Radojcic pointed out in *Chess Life*, Bobby did so with the "luxury" of not playing his very best, proving his "enormous strength and qualities as a fighter." He had played in three tournaments in nine months and had collected top honors in all events. He was certain he could win the Interzonal.

Fischer spent over a month in Belgrade waiting for the tournament at Tunis to begin. He analyzed his games from Skopje with an eager, private audience consisting of Gligoric, Trifunovic, and Radojcic, bought as many chess books as he could get his hands on, listened to records at Gligoric's house, looked over the games of the players he knew he would face, and generally prepared himself theoretically and psychologically for the ordeal to come. It was a very hot summer in Belgrade.

CHAPTER XVIII

"I play honestly and I play to win.
If I lose, I take my medicine."

Fischer flew from Yugoslavia to North Africa, arriving in Tunis on October 12th. His hopes and his spirits were realistically buoyant. He had sharpened his play at Skopje, and in his two previous Interzonal attempts he had reached the Candidates easily and would undoubtedly have qualified had he played at Amsterdam in 1964. The possibility of qualification, therefore, was not foremost in his mind during this attempt. He wanted to repeat his achievement of winning the Stockholm Interzonal of 1962, perhaps eclipsing his 2½ point margin there.

A number of writers have indicated that the line-up in Tunisia was stronger than the tournament at Amsterdam, but with the sole exception of Fischer himself, the event in Sousse, Tunisia could not compare to Amsterdam, which had boasted such giants as Smyslov, Spassky, Tal, and Bronstein, all missing in 1967. Amsterdam also consisted of twenty-four players instead of twenty-two. This is not to indicate that Sousse was weak; no Interzonal can be. But in my opinion, it was one of the lesser Interzonals held in recent times. The main contenders were Fischer, Larsen, Geller, Gligoric, Korchnoi, Portisch, Reshevsky, Stein, and Ivkov. The six high scorers were slated to meet Tal and Spassky in the Candidates to determine Petrosian's challenger in 1969.

The city of Sousse, situated on the Mediterranean Sea, is located about eighty miles from the capital of Tunisia. It lies on the site of the ancient *Hadrumetum*, the largest Roman center next to Carthage, and was visited often by Julius Caesar. It is a small but important town of 50,000, the capital of the province in which it is located.

On the day that the tournament started, the announcement was broacast that Che Guevara was killed in La Paz, Bolivia, and the report was confirmed by Castro. Many of the players remembered playing him while the various Havana Tournaments took place.

The Interzonal was held in the modern Sousse-Palace Hotel, in which the players were lodged. They were afforded such unusual options as having the use of the hotel camel, donkey, speed boat, and small yacht. There was also a private beach for guests, where the Russians could be seen almost every morning sunning themselves. Physically it was an ideal location for a chess tournament. Great organizational difficulties, however, plagued the tournament from the very start.

Both Bolbochan and Panno failed to appear in time to play and the relatively weak Tunisian player, Bou Aziz, was placed in the line-up as a reserve. The tournament officials, with the exception of Sajtar of Czechoslovakia, were woefully inexperienced in managing an event of this magnitude, the first FIDE contest to be held on the continent of Africa.

Matanovic wrote in *The South African Chessplayer*:

> During the first half of the tournament, there was not one day that passed without event. The atmosphere was one of continual suspense and uncertainty. There seemed to be a never-ending stream of explanations and announcements by the tournament controllers, while one wondered which competitor would leave the tournament and who would not. In fact, at one stage it was dubious whether the tournament itself would be played to a finish.

It was obvious that the tournament was not the most well-organized of all time, and its unstructured quality was not particularly well-suited for Bobby's chessic fastidiousness.

He didn't care for the lighting; half-hearted attempts were made to improve it. The glittering ballroom chandelier was much too glaring; endeavors were made to subdue it. Photographers were allowed free access; Fischer would not tolerate them.

In the fourth round, playing against Cueller of Colombia, Fischer complained once again about the poor lighting which he felt was ". . . impossible to play under." After making a few moves, he went to the tournament director and told him he could hardly see the board, and the official said a solution would be found. After no action was forthcoming, Fischer himself, together with Cuellar, who had also had difficulties due to the bad lighting, lifted the tournament table and moved it to another spot that afforded them more favorable visibility. Fischer's clock was running throughout the maneuver.

In the sixth round, as he was playing Lubomir Kavalek, then of Czechoslovakia, a photographer began to roam the stage and was about to take a picture of the two players when Fischer stopped his clock, jumped up, and demanded that the photographer be expelled. The tournament director explained to Fischer that the man was the official photographer of the Soviet Embassy of Tunisia and that nothing could be done to make him leave. Fischer's clock was put in motion again while further discussion continued, and after thirty minutes had expired he finally continued the game . . . with the photographer still present. It ended in a draw and expert analysis indicated that Fischer's play had seriously deteriorated starting with the commotion about the use of the camera. It was apparent that no love was lost between Fischer and the officials.

It is important to add here that despite Fischer's problems with the conditions, his form on the board was magnificent. He had scored 6 out of a possible 7 points, beating Barczay, Miagmasuren, Cuellar, Sarapu, and Stein, while drawing with Portisch and Kavalek. Though Larsen was playing winning chess also, it appeared that no one could stop Fischer. Unfortunately, the story muddies.

Due to Fischer's religious observances, his eighth-round game with Korchnoi was postponed. Special requests had been made as early as May 4th, 1967, in a letter from Edmondson to Folke Rogard, for both Fischer and Reshevsky to have days off on their Sabbaths. Presumably this had been granted. But when the official scheduling was issued, it called for Fischer to play six games in a row, without a rest day. In error, his ninth round game against Geller was also postponed.

Fischer had tried communicating with two of the tournament directors, Ahmed Hentati and Paul Diaconescu, but since they spoke no English and he spoke no French, little headway was made. R. Belkadi, another director, did speak English, but Fischer assumed that his command of the language was negligible since he had not acted on a number of details. Fischer therefore put in writing his request that his game with Geller be played at the regular ninth round time. This would have enabled him to have a break instead of playing six games in a row. He received a reply from Hentati: "I acknowledge receipt of your letter dated October 26th, 1967, and would like to inform you that the Organization Committee of the Interzonal Tournament regrets its inability to grant your request." *Why* the Committee could not grant it, or what could be done to accommodate Fischer, perhaps in some compromise position, was not indicated.

On the next day in the hotel dining room, Fischer handed Sajtar a note stating: "I withdraw from the tournament" because his recommendations (regarding lighting, photographers, etc.) were being ignored and because of the hardship being imposed upon him by having to play six games consecutively. His withdrawal was acknowledged formally in writing, and Fischer quit Sousse and left immediately for Tunis, presumably to fly back to the United States.

The tenth round began the next day, and even though Fischer was officially withdrawn from the tournament the directors set up a chessboard, with score sheets and a chess clock, for him and his scheduled tenth-round opponent, Soviet International Master Aivar Gipslis. After one hour they awarded the point to Gipslis.

The next morning, Belkadi drove from Sousse to Tunis and visited Fischer in his hotel room. Bobby had moved from the Tunis Hilton to the Tunisia Palace to the Majestic, all within twenty-four hours, in an attempt to dodge phone calls and inquiring reporters. "Fischer Drops Out of Chess Tourney" was being headlined all over the world.

After hours of discussion, Belkadi convinced Fischer to return to the tournament. He promised Bobby that he could have, as each of the other players had, one or two free days so that he need not play six consecutive games. Fischer wanted the Gipslis forfeit removed straightaway but Belkadi stated that FIDE would have to rule on it and that they would do so as quickly as possible. Assuming that FIDE would judge the forfeit improper and reschedule the game, Fischer returned to Sousse just in time to play his eleventh-round game against Reshevsky.

If the ghost of Morphy had entered the tournament hall, it would not have caused as much of an uproar as Fischer's appearance. Stein, assuming his earned zero against the American would be nullified due to Fischer's withdrawal, visibly paled, played a few moves more against Bou Aziz, blundered into a draw and literally ran from the tournament room.

Fifty minutes had been accumulated on Fischer's clock before he reached Sousse; Reshevsky had completely relaxed, never for a moment expecting his opponent to return. When Fischer was informed that he had only ten minutes to make the one-hour forfeit deadline, he said: "I still have enough time for Reshevsky!" and it was reported that he proceeded to wait five minutes in the lobby of the hotel before entering to play his game.

When Fischer sat down at his board, with barely five minutes to go, Reshevsky was totally shocked and quickly blundered the game away. It was adjourned but he was lost. As soon as he signed his score sheet, he stood up shouting: "Please let me have a French translator. I protest. I will not play with Fischer!" Had he refused to play in the first place, he might have had a basis for a claim; but it was too late then. The next day Reshevsky availed himself of some sweet revenge by not showing up for the adjournment and making Fischer wait an hour till his clock ran out.

Also, in retaliation, Reshevsky organized a number of players and seconds to sign a petition demanding a written apology from Fischer because of his "manners." It is unclear just exactly how Fischer offended the others, but it is significant to note that almost all of the signers had fallen victim to him. Trifunovic pointed out that some people believed that the purpose of the petition was to exert "psychological pressure" on Fischer to provoke him. This explanation rings true.

Before playing any more games, Fischer went to the organizers: "What about my game against Gipslis?" he asked. FIDE had referred the problem back to the Organizing Committee at Sousse and their answer was that the game had been forfeited and that in any event, Gipslis was not prepared to play. "No, that's impossible," replied Fischer. "At the moment when I was supposed to have lost a game by default I had already withdrawn from the tournament. How can a player lose a game when he is not even in the tournament?" Fischer's logic was lucid. He was anxious to resolve the problem since if the committee ruled against him and he then decided to withdraw, he wanted to do so before he had played 50 percent of his games. In that way, according to the rules, his entire score would be voided. After he reached the half-way mark, any forfeits posted would remain, forever in history, as simply lost points. He could not imagine that, let alone tolerate it.

On the evening before his game with Hort, Fischer having a bye during that day, he again put the question of his forfeited game against Gipslis to the Committee. By this time, the entire Soviet contingent let it be known that if the Committee ruled in Fischer's favor and allowed him to play the game with Gipslis, they would withdraw *en masse*. Faced with what appeared to be the demolition of the tournament itself (for how would it be completed if the four Russians dropped out, it was argued), the Committee replied negatively. The forfeit would stand. This time Fischer left the tournament again. "For good," he claimed.

Byrne went to Fischer's hotel room and tried unsuccessfully, for five hours, to talk Bobby into returning to the event. A veritable parade of organizers, journalists, and other such types, including a representative from the American Embassy, used every argument they could muster, but to no avail. When someone used the ploy that he represented the United States and he should play for the interests of his country, he replied: "I represent no one here but myself." Golombek reported that he pointed out to Bobby that he had the ideal opportunity to show the chess world that he could give the Russians a point and still win the tournament. Fischer's answer was: "Why do I need to show it to the chess world?"

Fischer left the hotel the next day. When the clerk presented him a bill for "extras," Fischer ceremoniously tore it up in front of him, threw the bits on the registration desk, and stormed out. He headed for Tunis for the second time.

He did not appear for his game with Hort, naturally, and was forfeited again. Rumors began to spread that Fischer was, yes, considering returning to the tournament and was willing to accept the two forfeits. Was this a dream or a scene from a Fellini movie? Apparently, it was neither. Fischer *did* want to play. The committee announced a decision to all the players that Fischer would be allowed to return to the tournament if he: (1) gave a written promise before his next scheduled game (with Larsen) that he would not again withdraw from the tournament, and (2) would accept his forfeits against Gipslis and Hort.

Reshevsky was furious and demanded immediate and irrevocable exclusion for Fischer. He also stated that *he* would withdraw if Fischer were allowed to re-enter.

Fischer felt he had to have time to consider the committee's requests. They, in turn, took the stand that if Fischer did not appear for his game with Larsen, he would be scratched from the lists permanently (FIDE rules state that expulsion is mandatory if a player forfeits three games). The date was Saturday, November 4th, and Fischer composed the following message and transmitted it from Tunis to the Committee (in Sousse):

> I request to re-enter the 1967 Interzonal Tournament without prejudice to my claim that the forfeited games were decided illegally. I acknowledge that I have been declared forfeit against Gipslis and Hort; if the forfeits are ruled legal and were decided upon according to the rules of FIDE, I shall accept them. I request to play with Mr. Larsen tonight as soon as I can arrive in Sousse, I presume between 9–9:30 P.M.
>
> Signed:
> Robert J. Fischer

The committee received the message at 7:25 P.M. but Fischer's clock had been started against Larsen at 7:00. At 7:40 P.M. the Committee replied to Fischer that it was up to him to make arrangements to be in the tournament hall by 8 P.M. or else he would be forfeited. Since Fischer had no transportation to begin with and was some eighty miles away, it would have taken the proverbial magic carpet to whisk him to Sousse in order to make it on time. When Fischer was not present at 8 P.M., he was declared generally forfeited and was excluded from the most important tournament of his career.

The next day a reporter from U.P.I. tried to interview him at his hotel. Fischer wouldn't even open the door. "Leave me in peace," he shouted. "I have nothing to say." What *could* he say? He left for the United States that same day, stopping off in Rome just long enough to buy a pair of shoes, and then just as briefly in Germany to collect a box of chess books. He was back in New York City on Tuesday,

November 7th, with his vision of the chess championship of the world in fragments.

Shortly after the "Fischer Affair," as it quickly became known, Edmondson stated that "tens of thousands of words have already been written on the elimination of U.S. Champion Robert J. Fischer from the Interzonal Tournament." He may have been grossly underestimating the coverage. Aside from the wire and feature stories traversing the globe, chess columns and magazines had a field day with the controversy, with such ominous-sounding titles as "Drama in Tunisia," "The State of Denmark," and "The Purgatory of Robert J. Fischer." In one issue of *Chess Life* alone, almost ten full pages were devoted to the Interzonal, most of it concerning Fischer's forced withdrawal. Years afterward, articles about it appeared in the chess press and references are still emerging even at this late date.

Looking back on the incident now, it seems all too simple and all too dreadfully a part of human nature.

Fischer, knowing his great capabilities as a chess player, perhaps the greatest of all time, is only interested in "rules and regulations" as far as they can aid him in the realization of his art. His iconoclastic approach to the chess establishment is difficult for many to accept, since what he is saying, in effect, is that *he* and only he knows what conditions are necessary for him to play his finest chess, organizers and directors be damned. The anarchy he creates, certainly in the minds of the organizers, causes conditions antithetical to conducting an orderly competition governed by persons of "established reputation." Did the organizers at Sousse believe that willful perversity motivated Fischer to ask for better lighting? Obviously, they did—or else a lamp or lamps would have been produced immediately. If a chess official cannot provide the very basic needs for playing chess, and certainly proper lighting is of paramount necessity, then he has no business directing a chess tournament in the first place. What difference would it have made if Fischer had one free day (which was acutally his right) in a crowded schedule, as long as the tournament was finished on time and the hotel vacated as promised? The answer is obvious and becomes complicated only when Fischer is viewed not as the greatest chess talent of this generation, but as an adversary to be given no help, no concession, nor even the courtesies one might extend to lesser players.

Much criticism was leveled at Fischer at the time, by responsible chess people. Gligoric said that there was no obstacle to prevent Fischer from wending his way to the world's championship ". . . except Fischer himself." Heidenfeld, in his famous "Letter from Europe," said: "Like the Bourbons, Bobby Fischer has learnt nothing and forgotten nothing. This time he was led to the well, but FIDE was unable to make him drink more than a few drops." Similar sentiments were expressed in other quarters; it was Fischer who was torturing himself, not FIDE. But Al Horowitz in *The New York Times* was openly sympathetic: "We think he is the world's best player. There has never been another to equal him in playing ability and we hope some way can be found to get him back into global competition."

Though FIDE eventually allowed the controversy to suspend itself in limbo, without an official word one way or the other about the actions of the Sousse Committee, we can only assume that Fischer was declared, at least privately, guilty. Without the public statement that should have been issued, FIDE itself and especially its president, Folke Rogard, lost both respect and prestige, especially from pro-Western or pro-Fischer circles. For a time FIDE lapsed into a genuine decline. New stature has been assumed by the world chess organization since naming Dr. Max Euwe as its new president in 1970.

If Fischer is to be faulted, it is in his style rather than his motivations. It is difficult to yield to abruptness. Fischer is not easy to get along with. Once, while I was at the front desk at a U.S. Chess Championship collecting entrance fees from spectators, Fischer tried to tear some tickets out of my hand; and though they were rightfully his—all players were allowed as many free passes as they wished—my instant response was to hold them back in instinctive reaction to his brashness. Genius often disdains diplomacy.

But Bobby has grown immeasurably better in this respect over the years, and there is every reason to believe that he will continue to hone the rough edges of his tact until he has mastered the intricacies of courtesy as completely as he has the art of chess.

The furor caused by the Sousse dispute unsettled and agitated the very foundations of world chess. Among chessplayers, it was a constant source of conversation for months. In Chicago, Robert Byrne lectured on *l'affaire* Sousse in depth, and *Sports Illustrated* ran a feature story on it.

FIDE Vice President Fred Cramer prepared a legalistic brief in Bobby's behalf that would have earned the respect of a Supreme Court Justice. But little was done by FIDE itself in getting him into the Candidates Tournament since, it was argued, he had not finished his Interzonal schedule.

Fischer was enraged. "This all means the destruction of FIDE," he said in an interview published in *Vjesnik*. "I don't wish to play under these conditions. I must have my self-respect." Someone told me that it was at this time that Fischer composed his own version of Beethoven's Heiligenstadt Testament in a long, involved and painful letter stating that he would never play another game of chess. Who the letter was written to (possibly FIDE) or whether its existence is a fact, I leave to future scholars. I never found any evidence of it.

Larsen ended up winning the Interzonal by 1½ points. Geller, Gligoric, Korchnoi, and Portisch were also absolute qualifiers, while Hort, Reshevsky, and Stein tied for sixth place and were compelled to play off for the last seat in the Candidates in Los Angeles. Reshevsky ultimately won the play-off based on Sonneborn-Berger tie-breaking points.

En route back to Moscow after losing his chance to go on to the Candidates, Stein, accompanied by Yuri Averbakh, his second, stopped off in New York and gave a simultaneous exhibition at the Manhattan Chess Club. Bobby appeared briefly as a spectator and it was a strange moment in time as the man who had been the probable winner of the Candidates watched one of the eliminees play chess.

CHAPTER XIX

*"I think my subconscious mind is
working on it all the time. Even
when I'm not playing or studying,
I sit down at the board and I get
a lot of new ideas. Things are
coming to me all the time."*

In the spring of 1968, Bobby gave up his suite at the Tudor Hotel
and moved to Los Angeles, leasing a small house on Ambrose Avenue.
He had been thinking of making the move ever since he had played
in the Piatigorsky tournament in 1966, and was happy when he
finally settled in California. He didn't take all of his possessions
across the continent, however, storing many of his books, records,
and clothes in Manhattan, with Burt Hochberg and Harry Evans
(Larry's father), indicating perhaps that he was not sure he would
stay permanently. "It's better here than New York," he said of his
new home. "The climate is wonderful and it is much more peaceful;
that's what I need."

Fischer's fame was growing in a number of ways and it wasn't
only as a result of his walkout in Tunisia. A novel, *Master Prim*, by
James W. Ellison, was published in early 1968 and its central character, Julian Prim, was based on Bobby Fischer. Edmondson reviewed
the book himself in *Chess Life* and panned it for the most part, especially its manner of handling sexual scenes, but the reviews in
the general press were, though not rave, entirely favorable. Readers
had no difficulty in identifying Bobby Fischer since Ellison took
elaborate pains in building a character who, if not in name, was
certainly the boy from Brooklyn all chess players know.

He used Fischer quotes from interviews, almost without changing
a word, and one wonders why, since the book so closely follows
Fischer's life, the author didn't produce a historical novel similar to
Francis Parkinson Keyes's life of Paul Morphy, *The Chessplayers*.
Ellison interviewed many people in the chess world at length, includ-
ing myself in 1965, to gather his material and he had a few informal

meetings with Fischer himself; I believe he even played Fischer a game or two at the Marshall Chess Club.

Walter Goldwater told me that *Master Prim* was in a collection of books that he bought from Bobby, but that it didn't look as though it had been opened. "Do you want this book?" Bobby had asked him. "It's about me." But Bobby definitely read the book, and so identified it with his own life that he took issue with some of the fictional quotes coming out of the mouth of the fictional Prim: "I never said that!" he would say as he read the lines aloud. A strong master related his opinion to me that he gained more insight into Bobby Fischer from this one book than from following his career for over fifteen years. Though I was not as dazzled as that, I do think it was a highly interesting and valuable profile.

The organizers of the Monte Carlo tournament in 1967 had been very specific in requesting that Bobby Fischer be one of the American participants. In 1968, when organizing a second tournament, however, they were equally insistent that Bobby Fischer *not* be one of the American participants.

Whether this snub was a reaction to Bobby's demands of the previous year, or whether Prince Rainier personally asked the committee to "dis-invite" him is open to speculation, but the event had all the elements of a repetition of chess history.

In 1903, Prince Dadian of Mingrelia, president of the Monte Carlo Tournament Committee, threatened to resign from his post and leave Monaco if Tchigorin, who was among the strongest players in the world at that time, and who was about to begin his first game, was permitted to play. The true origin of the Prince's ire never came to light but the most compelling accounts indicate either that he had been slighted by Tchigorin at a party in the Caucasus or was angered by some of Tchigorin's annotations of the Prince's qualitatively amateurish games. The potentate's demands prevailed and Tchigorin quit Monte Carlo and was compelled to return home to Russia.

Bobby Fischer, however, has never lacked invitations to the world's strongest competitions, nor was he lacking then. Organizers almost automatically invited him to their events since he is the perfect drawing card, both for spectators and for other well-known players who were eager to meet him over the board. His appearance in any tournament guarantees daily international press coverage.

While he worked on finishing *My 60 Memorable Games* in his new Los Angeles home, he received an offer to play a match against Henrique Costa Mecking, the brilliant sixteen-year-old from Brazil who was not only being hailed as a "second Fischer" but was being referred to as *"El Futuro del Ajedrez"* as well. It was arranged for July in Rio de Janeiro, one of Bobby's favorite cities, and the purse, consisting of an attractive $6,000 for the winner and an adequate

$1,000 for the loser, was acceptable to Fischer. The winner of the match was to be the player who first scored five victories; however, the minimum number of games to be played was ten. The match would have helped secure the already growing reputation of the Brazilian prodigy and interest among the South Americans was running high. On April 15, 1968, Luiz Carualho Tavares da Silva, President of the Brazilian Chess Federation and organizer of the match, sent the following letter to E. B. Edmondson:

> I am writing today to inform you that after much effort on my part, I was unable to confirm the Fischer-Mecking match. I found that Mr. Mecking's father was the main difficulty at the moment.
>
> Of course I realize that from his father's point of view it is very important for Mecking to pursue his studies without missing classes. In Brazil, the first semester of the scheduled year runs from March to June and the second from the end of the academic year—in July—and a long vacation from Christmas to the end of February. I beg you to explain to Mr. Fischer that Mr. Mecking's father has finally forbidden his son to play chess during his long vacation.

He concluded by expressing his disappointment and by stating that he would attempt to find another time suitable for both players, but no further negotiations were started and the match was ultimately abandoned.

The 1968 U.S. Championship was scheduled to take place in July in New York City, and Fischer replied negatively to his invitation, again stating that he would play only after the tournament was substantially lengthened, as he had been "promised" when he played in the previous U.S. Championship. At the conclusion of the 1966–67 title test, a player's meeting was held in which Fischer's proposal to lengthen the tournament was voted down 10–1. Here, in Bobby's words, is an account of that meeting:

> All the players were present except Reshevsky. Mr. Kasper opened discussion of my proposal to lengthen the tournament by saying "I'm for it" but that was precisely all the support he gave it. He then did his best to convince the players that the Foundation couldn't possibly put up any more money for prizes—in other words, we play twice the length for the same money just to satisfy Fischer. What chance did the proposal have? Many of the players, to my surprise, actually seemed interested in making it longer.

Benko, for example said "he [Fischer] is right." Of course, I'm always so afraid of losing just one game and being eliminated. But we have to discuss the money and to play twice the length for the same money is ridiculous.

Larry Evans, who to my great surprise, (apparently smelling more money to be had by all) was clearly coming around to a longer championship, said, "Mr. Kasper, you're talking about pies in the sky—how much will you increase the prizes by?" Kasper absolutely refused to discuss increasing the prize money in the proposed lengthened championships by one penny. Anyway, after a very long discussion on the subject—at least one hour, maybe two—Mr. Kasper said we have to take a vote. Benko, Evans, Bisguier, Donald Byrne and others didn't even want to vote on it without discussing the prizes together. Kasper refused—we would vote on the proposal without discussing the money together with the length. This was Kasper's trick—this was the way he had planned it from the beginning. Obviously no one, with the exception of me, would vote for it. This would put me in a very bad situation for getting it changed in the future.

Anyway, the vote was taken, but several players didn't even want to vote on it. For example, Zuckerman abstained—but Mr. Kasper seeing the way the vote was going said "you can't abstain—you have to vote yes or no." Zuckerman, of course, voted no. At least one more player or maybe more wanted to abstain but Kasper wouldn't allow them to. I think Addison also wanted to abstain. Naturally, it's a little vague now. My big mistake was to vote for it. I should have voted against it because it was so ridiculous. But even after the vote was taken Benko and several other players begged Mr. Kasper to take another vote to see if the players were in favor of changing it with increased prizes. Mr. Kasper steadfastly refused to take this vote. Finally, after another half an hour or so of wrangling about this, Mr. Kasper said, "well you can't decide whether you want to change it or not" and finally the meeting broke up. So that is the true story of the 10 to 1 vote against lengthening the U.S. Championship.

Though Fischer seemed to be overly sharp with committee chairman Maurice Kasper, who probably should be forgiven anything in exchange for the meritorious work he has done for American chess so many trying years, it is apparent that the move to lengthen the tournament was glossed over without realistic consideration of Fischer's concerns. At least one grandmaster said the reason that Fischer wished to have the tournament expanded was that he wanted to prove his ultimate superiority by coming in five points ahead of the pack, instead of the usual two. I believe that to be pure poppycock. What Fischer disregarded was the belief of almost all of those present, certainly Kasper, that Fischer could not fail to win *any* American tournament. With the sole exception of the Piatigorsky Cup, Fischer had captured first prize in every tournament he ever competed in on American soil since his victory in the U.S. Junior Championship in San Francisco in 1957, at the age of fourteen. He was alone, somehow, at least in this one instance, in doubting his "invincibility," and no one believed him.

To indicate to the world that he was in no way disillusioned with playing chess, but was rather dissatisfied with tournaments that he felt were improperly organized, Fischer left immediately for Israel to enter a minor international tournament taking place at the same time as the U.S. Championship. Perhaps he felt that this action would slight the U.S. Championship Committee as he was proving his availability and willingness to play anywhere except in the United States. The tournament was held in Netanya, a popular seaside resort town on the Mediterranean, twenty miles north of Tel Aviv. Netanya had been made famous by another Brooklynite, the Hassidic Rabbi S. Klausenberg, who came from the Williamsburg section of Brooklyn and established, together with his followers, a synagogue, numerous homes, and a *yeshiva*, in the small Israeli town.

The event ran from June 17th to July 4th, commemorating the Twentieth Anniversary of Israel. It consisted of fourteen players . . . in addition to Fischer. Dan A. Yanofsky of Canada was the only other grandmaster invited. Fischer won the tournament easily at 11½, 3½ points ahead of Yanofsky in second place. He drew against Yair Kraidman and Yosef Porath of Israel, in addition to Yanofsky, and it was reported that he was dissatisfied with the results, honestly expecting to win every single game.

Trifunovic pointed out that Fischer's success should not be underestimated since even though the tournament was not of major importance, ". . . it is not easy continually to take absolute first in tournaments, even minor ones. That Fischer has done so is one more proof of his ambition, combativeness and skill in constantly maintaining himself in good chess form." Fischer is not "constantly" in good form, but at that period of his life his play was sharp and effortless.

Untypically, Bobby went through the tournament without an incident of any sort. His religious observances gave the Jewish organizers no trouble, of course, since games are never played in Israel from sundown Friday to sundown Saturday; and a number of players and officials still considered Fischer a Jew in any event, despite his well-known conversion to the Worldwide Church of God. During the games, most of the players wore *yarmulkes*, including Yanofsky, but obviously, Fischer declined. They ate traditional Israeli food consisting of pancakes, cheese blintzes, and goulash soup, and Bobby was said to have enjoyed himself immensely; he considered the tournament more of a vacation than the usual tension-riddled struggle that is common in international competitions.

While the cat was away from the U.S. Championship, Larry Evans, described by Burt Hochberg as the "second-best player in the country" walked away with the honors for the third time in his career, admitting, however, that that would not have been the case had Fischer played. Evans wasn't only interested in winning a token first prize though, and insisted that he wanted the reluctant Bobby to compete for a more meaningful tournament. "I tried to get him to play. He was adamant," Evans stated.

Fischer stayed on in sunny Israel for a few weeks and then suddenly appeared in Athens, as a guest of the Greek Chess Federation, which had invited him to undertake a special exhibition against five of the strongest players in the country. The match was played with clocks, as regular tournament games, with one radical difference: each of the Greek players had forty moves to complete in two hours while Fischer had to finish all of his five games in the same time, while also moving from board to board. When asked whether he would take on more than five boards, Fischer declined, stating that he did not want to become "overtired." He regarded the exhibition solemnly and approached it with the same famous determination he is known for in official matches or tournaments. He attempted to win every game, and almost succeeded. He defeated Byzantiadis, Ornitopoulos, Kokkoris, and Anastasopoulos, but he was held to a draw by Trikaliotis, who instantly gained the prominence of a Socrates among his chess friends.

Fischer remained in Athens, one of the most clamorous cities in the world, for seven days and changed hotels four times, always citing "the noise, the noise . . ." as his reason for moving in and out, but probably also wanting a certain degree of privacy from his enthusiastic hosts who took an immediate liking to him.

Before leaving Greece to play in a tournament in Yugoslavia, Bobby visited the ancient island of Delphi and was fascinated by the temple of Apollo and the other famous ruins. He spent a pleasant, sunfilled day touring with Lazarus Byzantiadis and Petar Trifunovic, the latter stating that he put the question "Will Fischer become World Chess Champion" to the great stone of Pythia, which legend describes as emitting an ecstasy-producing vapor, and the answer came back in Greek: "He will change his title!" Trifunovic went on to say that Fischer merely smiled ironically when he heard this.

Vinkovci is a small town in eastern Croatia, situated on the Drava River, and the organizers of the first tournament held there were unhappy they were unable to invite Fischer since they could not afford his usual appearance fee. Bobby came, nevertheless, and the Yugoslavs were frenzied with delight for the month of September, during which the event took place. Reporters and photographers flew from all parts of Yugoslavia to cover Bobby's participation.

The tournament developed into a relatively strong event with such names as Ivkov, Hort, Matanovic, Gheorghiu . . . seven grandmasters in all competing. Most of the players, including Fischer, considered the contest as an ideal warm-up for the forthcoming World Chess Olympiad in Lugano, Switzerland, to be held in October.

It was reported that two Russian grandmasters and one Rumanian player canceled their participation at the very last minute, perhaps after learning that Fischer was going to compete. At the beginning of the tournament, Fischer said: "It will be an interesting battle for second place," and it wasn't mere arrogance that prompted such a remark. Fischer was playing some of the most exciting chess of his career and he knew it, as did everyone else. Still, it was almost unthinkable that he would not walk away with first prize at Vinkovci.

He scored 7½ points in the first eight rounds and continued to blitz his way through the tournament, finishing with a total of 11, two full points ahead of the second-place Hort. He was undefeated and allowed only four draws: with Hort, Gheorghiu, Donald Byrne, and Karl Robatsch. But Bobby's image of his capabilities is more disciplined than his followers', who immediately began lauding his triumph. "I didn't play my last games well," he complained. "I could have won by four points." Disregarding the Interzonal at Sousse, it was Fischer's fifth straight first prize in tournament play.

The Candidates Matches had just ended, Spassky had emerged the winner and challenger for the World's Championship for the second time in succession, having defeated Geller, Larsen and Korchnoi in the quarter-finals, semi-finals and finals, respectively. Bobby was asked whether he was surprised. "I wouldn't have been surprised if Korchnoi had won," he replied. "If he had beaten Spassky, he would have won against Petrosian and become World Champion." When asked who would win in the forthcoming Spassky-Petrosian match, Bobby quickly answered: "Spassky looked bad in their last match. I think Petrosian has the better chances." Yet he still ultimately considered Spassky as the better player.

At the conclusion of the tournament at Vinkovci, instead of traveling across Yugoslavia and Italy directly to Lugano, Bobby chose to journey north to Denmark and enjoy a short vacation in Copenhagen. He had two full weeks to compose himself before play started in the Lugano Olympiad, and he eventually arrived by plane in Switzerland on Wednesday, October 16th. He joined Reshevsky, Evans, Benko, Robert Byrne, and Lombardy as the team. Ed Edmondson and George Koltanowski served the U.S.A. as capable and experienced co-captains. It was a marvelous chess assemblage, the strongest possible American team fielded in modern times, maybe the strongest ever, and pundits were clucking that the United States was going to give the Soviets a bona fide run for their money. This belief was strengthened when it was learned that Tal, due to ill health, was remaining at home in Riga.

Fischer was optimistic about his team's possibilities. "We'll fight with the Russians for first place; Yugoslavia has the best chances for third," he said in an interview.

Everything started off agreeably. Bobby liked his hotel room and appeared to be in good spirits. But on Thursday he asked if he could visit the tournament hall, the *Padiglione Conza*, to inspect the lighting. He didn't approve of the incandescent bulbs and felt that fluorescent lighting should be substituted. The organizers, who were working on one of the tightest budgets of any recent Olympiad, gasped with horror at the expense. They finally compromised with him in agreeing to provide a special fluorescent lamp for his table.

He then reminded them of his incident with the photographer at Sousse and indicated that he would not tolerate any cameras in the tournament hall after play had commenced; the organizers agreed to that also. There were a number of other points that originated in his discussions with the directors, and though they attempted to remain diplomatic, the scene grew antagonistic. Finally, Bobby stated that since the tournament hall was relatively small, he wanted to play his games in a private room so that he would not be bothered by spectators, reporters, and the inevitable noise which always seems to be a problem at tournaments. He said he wanted to give each game his utmost concentration. The officials refused to surrender to this last demand, and Fischer left the tournament hall in a huff.

Later that night, after dinner, Fischer accidentally met the chief arbiter, H. De Graaf, in the street (on Paradiso Boulevard, I believe), and asked whether his request for a private playing room would be granted. De Graaf issued a negative reply that was definite and final. Without further discussion, Fischer returned to his hotel, hurriedly checked out and departed for Milan.

It's imperative to examine Fischer's actions at Lugano closely to determine what might have been the force that compelled him to withdraw. It signaled his total rejection of tournament chess for more than a year and a half, though the fact was naturally not apparent at that time.

Lugano was the first FIDE event that Fischer had considered playing in since his abortive participation at Sousse. His long-standing battle with the world chess organization was reaching a state of crisis because the FIDE Congress had met just prior to the opening of the Lugano Olympiad. The delegates voted upon the U.S. Chess Federation proposal that Fischer be included in the then-current Candidates cycle. Specifically, the motion was introduced that a Spassky-Fischer match be arranged, and the winner of that contest be permitted to challenge Petrosian. This was in line with the American contention that the "irregularities" at Sousse had prevented Fischer, considered not only as a probable winner of that event but almost a certain qualifier into the Candidates, from obtaining the qualification that was rightfully his. The American delegation spent a year building their case. It was impressive, but was voted down after much discussion on the floor. Fischer was both furious and resentful when he was informed.

Though the tournament conditions were far from perfect at Lugano (even mild-mannered Petrosian called the size of the room and the poor illumination "atrocious"), it becomes clear that Fischer's withdrawal was due, at least partly, to what he considered an unjust ruling by FIDE.

What did a team tournament mean to his career? The answer, unfortunately (for the rest of the team), was that it was of no moment to his ambition. Even if he won every game, which he might very well have done, little would have been accomplished for him, personally. It was the World Championship he was set for, nothing less, and he had been cut off from it for another four years.

Thus, Fischer, in frenzied frustration, suffered no remorse at all about withdrawing from Lugano. If FIDE could not learn, he reasoned, that he was the best player in the world and that he was attempting to achieve improvements for professional chess players everywhere, then they would have to operate without his cooperation or participation. In effect he was "punishing" the world chess organization by refusing to produce the games chessplayers all over the world were eager to see. He left Switzerland and was so disgusted with chess organization that the idea of his *ever* competing in another FIDE event seemed almost inconceivable. He stopped off in Germany briefly, to visit his mother who was studying medicine there and then flew back to the United States, still burning with anger.

CHAPTER XX

"Ideas. I never memorize lines."

Returning to Los Angeles, Bobby discovered efforts were being made to induce him to play in the 1968 American Open, to be held in Santa Monica, California, practically in his own back yard, over Thanksgiving Day weekend. He toyed with the idea of entering but ultimately rejected it, since he was still fuming over Sousse, Lugano and FIDE in general. He needed to be away from the board, at least publicly, for awhile.

In the spring of 1969, in Moscow, Boris Spassky defeated Tigran Petrosian to become the tenth official chess champion of the world. Undoubtedly Fischer experienced pangs of resentment, assuming that the title "belonged" to him. There was no question that he still considered himself the greatest player in the world at that time and indeed, he probably would have defeated Petrosian if given the opportunity to play him.

Bobby was induced to play first board for the Manhattan Chess Club in their annual match against their traditional rivals, the Marshall Chess Club. He played only one game, against Saidy, which he won, a game judged by Euwe, Averbakh, Barcza, Filip, Kotov, O'Kelly, and Schmid, as the second best game of the year, the first best-game prize going to Spassky for one of his match games against Petrosian.

Perhaps the most significant incident that occurred in Bobby's career that year happened, coincidentally, away from the sixty-four squares. His long-promised games collection, *My 60 Memorable Games,* was published by Simon & Schuster and it made an immediate and indelible impression on the chess public. Ten years previously, his slender volume *Bobby Fischer's Games of Chess* was looked upon as a novel glimpse of the teenager but was criticized for its sparse annotations. In this new book, his first serious work as an adult, Fischer rectified his youthful approach by producing one of the most painstakingly precise and delightfully presented chess books ever written, rivaling the works of Tarrasch, Alekhine, and Reti. Fischer, like his reflection Morphy, had expended very little energy in writing

151

chess books, and the public greedily awaited each word he produced. He omitted his 1956 "Game of the Century" with Donald Byrne, and included nine draws and three losses, a humble gesture unheard of in the annals of grandmaster literature. His game with Botvinnik at Varna consumes fourteen pages of exhaustive analysis, and Fischer's oft-published statement of priding himself on "never" making a mistake in annotating holds true in this work.

Bobby first chose the Stanislavskian title *My Life in Chess* for the book, then changed his mind, possibly deciding to reserve that title for his future autobiography. It was originally going to include only fifty-two games, but as he continued to make corrections and also to play in more events, he eventually added eight more games. The original manuscript had ended with the Piatigorsky Cup, 1966: the final book included the Interzonal at Sousse, 1967. The title was first changed to *My Memorable Games—60 Tournament Struggles*, and was later changed again to be published as *My 60 Memorable Games*. It took over three years to complete.

Burt Hochberg, in his beautifully written review of the book in *Chess Life*, states that it was a joint effort between Bobby and Larry Evans. It's true that Evans wrote the fine introductions to the games, and he is duly credited. But in my examination of the first and second galley proofs, even though I found Evans's editorial thumb print in a note or two, the book is obviously Bobby's own creation: naturally the games are his, all of the notes and references come from his mind, and also a great many of the "words" are unmistakably Bobby's. The notes are often sprinkled with personal observations of his opponents that Evans could not have invented, e.g. "Petrosian made a wry face" or "Botvinnik visibly relaxed." When asked by a New York friend what role Evans had in helping him write the book, Fischer laughingly understated: "Oh him? He just does the typing!"

When I discussed this with Evans recently, he smiled. He then quickly affirmed that the book was ". . . of course, Bobby's" effort and that he only assisted in an editorial capacity.

Apparently, Simon & Schuster were in a constant state of anxiety over the book since the changes, over the years, seemed almost endless, and at one point, Fischer deleted *all* of the annotations, returned the book to the publisher, and requested a release from his contract! He undoubtedly did not want to reveal all of his lines. They allowed him to buy back the contract and publishing plans were dropped. Two years later, however, he changed his mind. But the editorial changes went on. The Botvinnik game, originally tagged "Noblesse oblige," was changed to "The impetuosity of youth" and finally ended up as "The confrontation." Additions run rampant through the proofs. Evans suggested that Bobby's decision to go ahead with the book was a philsophical one: "He was feeling depressed about the world and thought there was an excellent chance that there would be a nuclear holocaust soon. He felt he should enjoy whatever money he could get before it was too late."

My 60 Memorable Games was an immediate success, and I know of no serious player who has not added it to his library. If Fischer never played another game of chess his reputation would be preserved through it and I'm certain he could still live comfortably for the rest of his life on the royalties that accrue to him from this one monumental effort. Since he experienced such great ambivalance over releasing the work, we might very well be forced to wait for years before we can again benefit from the labors of his pen.

In mid-1969 Fischer received an invitation that he seriously considered: a group of Argentinian promoters proposed an unusual chess event, consisting of three national "teams" of two grandmasters, one player representing the older generation and the other, the younger. Specifically, the three teams, it was proposed, would consist of Fischer and Reshevsky, Botvinnik and Tal, and Najdorf and Panno. The match was to be played in Moscow, New York, and Buenos Aires. Though such a confrontation had a refreshing quality about it, practically none of the players could spare the two months time needed to complete it, and the total of $12,200 in prizes offered as an inducement was spurned by almost all invited. Needless to say, the match never took place.

At about that same time, Fischer did accept an invitation to compete in an international tournament in Ljubljana, Yugoslavia, the Vidmar Memorial, and he requested an appearance fee of $2,000 in addition to his round-trip air fare. The organizers approached some local businessmen who agreed to underwrite the expense, but when the top Yugoslav players were informed of the Tournament Committee's action, they insisted on receiving the same as Fischer. Hence, the committee had to renege on their offer, and Bobby remained in California.

The name of Bobby Fischer appeared in the pages of *Chess Digest* in June, this time as a book reviewer, his first such foray into that form of literary endeavor. Bluntly titled "A Russian Pot Boiler," he reviewed Yudovich's book, *King's Indian Defense*, an opening that is Bobby's specialty, and severely criticized the Russian for undertaking too much in ". . . such a small book," and by his failure to use any references beyond the late Fifties and early Sixties. "There is a bias running through Soviet chess literature in general; they dislike giving credit for opening innovations to foreigners," he said, illustrating his point with the Lombardy-Sherwin game from the U.S. Championship 1958–59 wherein Yudovich and *Shakhmatny Byulletin* failed to give Lombardy credit for his theoretical contribution. "Examples of this glaring lack of integrity are manifold," Bobby concluded, enraging the entire Soviet chess community in the process.

As the spring of 1970 approached, Fischer had gone eighteen months and played only one public game. Stories about his "retirement"—and whether it was permanent—were circulating constantly. I think it's important to indicate here that Fischer's self-removal from tournament chess for an extended period did not necessarily take its effect in any deterioration of his game; as a matter of fact, it could have helped him to increase his strength. Capablanca took almost two years "off" after San Sebastian 1911, and when he returned to chess, he took top place in the first tournament he competed in: New York 1913. And Lasker, at the height of his career, played no tournament chess at all for four years after defeating Janowski in their match in 1910; he came back to capture first prize in the great St. Petersburg tournament of 1914, ahead of Capablanca, Alekhine, Tarrasch and Marshall, among others.

It is often argued that there are many more international tournaments available to compete in now than there were in the age of Lasker, for example, and that that is the reason for any intervals of play of masters of the past; but that really has nothing to do with the question. In Lasker's case, he pursued his other loves, mathematics and philosophy. Fischer never really abandons chess. Bobby studies the game astutely when he is not engaging in tournaments, going over myriad games as they appear, exploring opening innovations, playing over endings, and generally fortifying himself, on the board and psychologically, for the moment when he will compete again. *After his last tournament game in 1968 at the age of twenty-five, Fischer had already played more official tournament and match games than Anderssen, Morphy, Steinitz, Lasker, or Capablanca played in their entire respective careers.*

If anything, it could be reasoned that Bobby Fischer has had too much chess in his lifetime and should consider the possibility of playing in only one match or tournament each year, using his spare time for studying both chess and other subjects, writing, and engaging in activities that would continue to broaden him. And, as top-flight tournament players seem to agree, a break from chess enables them to approach the game, upon their return to it, with a seriousness and purpose that had perhaps been lacking as a result of an overdose of competition. Botvinnik has stated that a player should enter a tournament "revitalized" and too much chess activity is antithetical to an objective view toward oneself or the game.

However, when asked whether he had any weaknesses, Bobby once replied: "Maybe I don't play enough," indicating that he may have begun to believe the press coverage about his "self-imposed exile" and his supposedly deteriorating play.

On October 24th, an invitation to compete in the U.S. Championship and Interzonal Qualifying tournament to be held in New York City in November and December, was sent to Bobby by the U.S. Chess Federation. He replied to it immediately. Here is the full text:

October 29, 1969

Mr. Ed Edmondson
U.S. Chess Federation
479 Broadway
Newburgh, N.Y. 12550

Dear Ed,

Thank you for your inquiry as to my availability to participate in the 1969 U.S.A. Championship. I am not available. Also I would like to take this opportunity to make a correction of fact. It was stated in last year's CHESS LIFE magazine that I never answered my 1968 invitation to the 1968 U.S.A. Championship. This, as you know Ed, is a lie. I answered and declined *in writing* to you well over a month before the championship began. The reason I did not play last year and will not play this year is the same—the tournament is too short. I feel the tournament should be 22 rounds as it is in the Soviet Union, Hungary, Romania, and other East European countries where chess is taken seriously, rather than 11 rounds that the present U.S. Championship is. As you know, Ed, this year's championship is also the Zonal Tournament for the U.S., which is the first step leading to the coveted World Championship. By my not participating in this U.S. Championship, I am not only giving up my chance to regain the U.S. Chess Championship which I have won eight times (every year I participated) but far more importantly I will lose my possibility of becoming official World Chess Champion in 1972, the next time a World Championship Match will be held. So the next opportunity for me to become World Chess Champion won't be until 1975. I want very much to play in the U.S. Championship this year—but not in a tournament where if a player has a bad start and loses a game or two at the beginning, he is practically eliminated from first place. I consider this to be too chancey an affair and it puts an undue burden on the favorite, who does not have enough time to make up for a bad start because the tournament is so short. Our U.S. Championship is the shortest of any major chess country. It is an affront to any professional chess player—such as I am.

In all probability the U.S. will lose its chance to have an
American World Chess Champion for many years as a
result of my not playing. You at the Chess Federation
have an opportunity to see that this does not happen. You
are supposedly dedicated to developing American chess—
here is your chance to prove it, by lengthening the 1969
U.S. Championship scheduled to begin November 30 from
11 to 22 rounds.

Sincerely,
Bobby Fischer
Box 596
New York, N.Y. 10011

Information copies sent
to major news sources

Edmondson was no doubt angered that Fischer sent copies of his
letter to the media, probably because it indicated a breach of the
closeness that was developing between the two. Fischer's rationale
was obvious: he wanted the press to get behind him and bring the
issue into the open to be decided by public opinion and not by an elite
group.

On November 4th, Edmondson replied to Fischer, indicating that
the U.S. Chess Federation could not afford a longer tournament (to
which Fischer remarked that that was ". . . the only logical argument"), and that Bobby would win the tournament anyway, no matter
how many rounds were played. He also asked Fischer why he accepted
the Russian model of the twenty-two round tournament, when in fact
he often accused (the Russians) of collusion.

Unfortunately, as it happened, the letter never reached Bobby because he was traveling, and it was returned, marked "Return to
Sender—Addressee Unknown." Edmondson's arguments were convincing, but when he finally did reach Fischer by telephone (to make
the proposal that the U.S. Championship Committee was willing to
increase the tournament to thirteen or perhaps fourteen players)
Fischer was still adamant in wanting the event to consist of twenty-two
men. The conversation broke down; both men began to shout, and
Fischer later stated that Edmondson made accusations that he was
"afraid" to play. "I finally hung up on him, after saying a very loud
goodbye," Bobby said afterward.

Obviously, Bobby Fischer didn't play . . . and just as obviously he
prevented himself, once again, from a chance to compete for the
world title. It now began to appear that there was virtually no chance
that Bobby could *ever* manage to sit still long enough to go through
the tedious and, to him, odious process of the World's Championship
qualification grind. Spassky, in an interview in *Chess*, said: "He prob-

ably had his reasons for not playing in the U.S. Championship." And then, with what seemed to be sincere regret: "I looked upon him as one of the strongest candidates for a match with me."

The U.S. Championship was won that year by Reshevsky. Addison and Benko came in second and third respectively, and the three men qualified for the Interzonal to be held at Palma de Majorca, a year hence.

CHAPTER XXI

"The ideal has become a reality in tournament chess. FIDE has set standards—indirect lighting, 30-feet minimum distance from spectators, no photographers, and a player's option to accept or reject a schedule."

The Leiden Chess Club in Holland enjoyed its seventy-fifth anniversary in the spring of 1970 and a year in advance had started planning a number of events to celebrate the occasion. Negotiations for a Botvinnik-Fischer match were initiated, and to everyone's surprise both players accepted. Bobby's reaction to it was favorable, and Botvinnik was reported as saying he was "intrigued." Dr. Max Euwe was appointed as match director, and the stakes were healthy for a non-title match: $8,000 for the winner and $5,000 for the loser.

A match of ten or twelve games was proposed; then Bobby started negotiations, that took literally months to resolve, to increase the contest to eighteen games. Eventually he won his point and the organizers agreed to lengthen the contest. No sooner had the contract been drawn up (but not yet signed by Fischer) when he announced that he had had a change of heart . . . or at least of opinion. Renewing his theme of no draws, he stated that he wanted the winner of the match to be the player who scored six clean wins, draws not counting. Leiden wrote to Fischer pointing out the impossibility (to them) of conducting a match of unknown duration, due to the limited availability of the match site, the referee, and other staff members. They implored Fischer to reconsider. His reply was short, and definite: Arrange the match so that the winner of the first six games takes the $8,000 prize, and he'd be happy to play. The organizers refused and the match was immediately canceled. In its place, a tournament consisting of Botvinnik, Spassky, Larsen, and Donner was arranged, with each playing four games against one another. Spassky won it without the loss of a game.

Fischer's determination to play only in those events that he deemed suitable as to: (1) prize fund, (2) number of rounds, and (3) other conditions, was being falsely discerned as a total rejection of the game. Even *Chess Life* was asking: "Will Fischer ever play chess again?" forgetting that Fischer *always* wants to play. But always and only on his own special terms. There is no question, however, that his FIDE-directed anger and his disillusionment with the chess bureaucracy that refused to accommodate any changes in its established routines, was also a meaningful factor in keeping him away from the board. When asked why he had spent the last eighteen months without publicly touching a Pawn, he succinctly replied: "Hangups," failing to state whether he meant such problems existed in himself or in others, but by implication indicating that his withdrawal wasn't merely a temporary vacation. In another interview, he is quoted as giving an additional reason he was playing no chess— ". . . to plot my revenge. I wanted to come back and put all those people in their place."

Negotiations were taking place also at that time for a proposed four-round match in Yugoslavia, sponsored by FIDE, consisting of a team of the ten best Soviet masters to vie with the ten strongest players from other countries in the world. Attempts to secure Fischer to head the "Rest of the World" team started early. His first reaction was negative. He had to know what conditions he was to play under, what the prize fund was, whether a sizeable appearance fee could be guaranteed. The problems were neatly solved, all by transatlantic cable and telephone, and as his objections were met, it appeared that Bobby might play, but only after inspecting the conditions personally. The organizers in Belgrade were so delighted that he might compete that they offered to pay his transportation to and from Yugoslavia just so he could see for himself the tournament hall lighting, visit his accommodations, and discuss the details. Bobby began to soften.

For decades the Soviet Union had dominated world chess, and a team of the most powerful Russian players seemed almost invincible. To cite their line-up is to list almost all the illustrious names in contemporary chess: Boris Spassky, then champion of the world, at board one, followed in respective board sequence by Tigran Petrosian, Victor Korchnoi, Lev Polugayevsky, Yefim Geller, Vassily Smyslov, Mark Taimanov, Mikhail Botvinnik, Mikhail Tal, and Paul Keres, and with no less than Leonid Stein and David Bronstein as alternates.

The world team, selected by Dr. Max Euwe in conjunction with Professor Arpad Elo's famous international rating list, was close to heroic: Bobby Fischer, Bent Larsen, Lajos Portisch, Vlastimil Hort, Svetozar Gligoric, Samuel Reshevsky, Wolfgang Uhlmann, Milan Matulovic, Miguel Najdorf, Borislav Ivkov, and Fridrik Olafsson and Klaus Darga as Reserves. Unfortunately, Euwe made a tactical mistake by announcing his lineup before the Soviets released theirs,

thereby enabling them to make last minute strategical changes. Fischer
was to face Spassky on board one and Larsen would fight Petrosian
on second board. Though no single national team had seriously
threatened the Soviet Union in recent years, it was felt that the best
players of all other nations might make an impression on them, if not
actually end their hegemony. However, a computer programmed with
Elo's ratings for each player predicted a win for the Soviets by a
score of 21½–18½, and a number of usually astute critics were saying
that the Soviets would win easily. Fischer wasn't enthusiastic about
the World's chances and feared, for example, that Botvinnik would win
four straight games from Matulovic.

The event, before it had even begun, was being referred to as "The
Match of the Century" or "The Great Match." It lived up to its
appellations.

On February 20th, in a telephone conversation with Kenneth Smith
of *Chess Digest*, Fischer indicated that he was going to Belgrade:

> *Fischer*: Yes, I've decided to play.
> *Smith*: Vs. Spassky. That will be a good match.
> *Fischer*: Not necessarily. The Russians reserve the right
> to pull him and put in, maybe, Petrosian when they want
> to.
> *Smith*: Surely, they wouldn't do that. They should keep
> their strongest team. I think the World will win, especially
> now that you will play; moving everybody down a notch
> means a lot!
> *Fischer*: If the match is [on] eighteen boards as origi-
> nally proposed then the World side would have a good
> chance. On ten boards, Russia should be the favorite.

I was in Reykjavik at that time, and Olafsson told me he had just
been named as alternate for the World team. I asked him what "our"
chances were. "It all depends on Fischer," he felt. "If he plays, the
World team has a chance to win, and it won't only be because of
Fischer's individual score. He'll raise the standard of play among all
his team-mates. Without Fischer, the World team has slim chances of
winning."

Fischer asked for and received $2,500 as an appearance fee, though
rumors circulated during the match that the figure was $5,000, half
the money provided by the organizers and the other half by an American chess "angel." All of the other players in the match were given
a $500 honorarium. The prize for board one was an Italian-built *Fiat*
automobile, and the board two winner would receive a Russian-built
Moskvich.

Twenty-three conditions were cited and had to be agreed upon
before Fischer consented to compete.

On March 24th, he cabled Belgrade, stating: "I hope you have taken into consideration my request that I play my games in a private room with one Judge." The Serbian Chess Federation cleverly side-stepped the question by answering: "Hall and lighting arranged according to your wishes. We have spent $2,000 on extra lighting."

On March 26th, Fischer flew from Los Angeles to Belgrade, via New York, and telephoned Edmondson from JFK International Airport to say that he was excited about playing in the match and was determined to play the four games even though the playing conditions might not be *totally* to his liking. He arrived at the Hotel Metropol in time for lunch, which he shared with Larry Evans and George Koltanowski, the latter stating that ". . . he told us frankly that he will not make up his mind whether to play or not until after he has seen the playing facilities." Later that day, Fischer ultimately approved the lighting and other conditions of the *Dom Sindikata*, a huge domed theater usually reserved for Trade Union meetings, located on Marx-Engels Square, and repaired back to his hotel. But there was still one difficulty to be faced.

A few weeks before the match started, Bent Larsen had protested Dr. Euwe's decision reserving first board for Fischer. Larsen believed his performance in tournaments in the previous two years had been far superior to anything Fischer had accomplished, and stressed the fact that the American had not played any chess at all for nearly a year and a half. When additional compensation was suggested to him, he replied: "Money isn't an issue. I'm entitled to first place on my record." His reasoning seemed justified, and upon arriving in Belgrade, he informed both the Committee and Dr. Euwe that he would not take part in the event—he said he would be happy to cover it as a journalist for the Danish press—unless Fischer gave up board one. Everyone was sure that Fischer himself would refuse to play if demoted to the second slot. The problem seemed insoluble.

At lunch the next day, Fischer let it be known that he was willing to step down to board two. That night, as a number of players and journalists gathered in Fischer's room to talk chess and play some off-hand games, he announced that he would relinquish his board one position and allow Larsen the top spot on the World team "as a matter of principle." Everyone was astonished; Fischer commented that "Larsen has a point. Besides, to create a better image doesn't require that I do anything dishonorable." He said that even though he considered himself stronger than Larsen, he wanted to cooperate. His only concern was over whether he would still receive the same appearance fee: he was assured by the President of the Organization Committee that he would; the only change was that he was competing for a *Moskvich* rather than a *Fiat*. Larsen was elated.

Fischer's magnanimous gesture instantly produced thousands of new fans. *The New York Times* stated, in untypical, un-*Timesean* language, that the gesture was ". . . a most un-Bobby-like action and it helped to avoid an international incident." However, just before the commencement of the match, he was quoted as saying: "It was a big mistake. I shouldn't have agreed to it," and later, "I must have been mad." Nevertheless, the match proceeded as planned.

Humorously, a huge gong borrowed from the Yugoslavian Boxing Association announced the start of round one; Larsen faced Spassky on first board, Fischer had the White pieces against Petrosian on board two. After fifteen moves, Petrosian had a lost game and resigned on the thirty-ninth move. P.H. Clarke, writing in *British Chess Magazine*, thought that ". . . it was obvious from the limp way he played that he (Petrosian) had not adjusted to meeting Fischer instead of Larsen." Fischer, of course, had prepared to meet Spassky so both players were at an equal disadvantage. Obviously, Fischer found it easier to adapt himself to the new situation.

Spassky-Larsen was drawn; Geller defeated Gligoric quite soundly and Taimanov and Botvinnik both adjourned with slight winning chances. When the tally was finally counted after all games were completed, the score for the first round stood at 5½ for the U.S.S.R. and 4½ for the Rest-of-the-World.

The second round proved sensational. It began by Spassky defeating Larsen in seventeen moves, one of the shortest games of the Dane's career. Meanwhile, Bobby, after winning a Pawn, managed to parlay that advantage into a win and forced Petrosian to capitulate for the second occasion, this time on his sixty-sixth move. The lower boards for the Rest of the World team fared badly and the score at the halfway stage ended with: U.S.S.R. 11½, Rest-of-the-World 8½.

Larsen avenged himself in the third round by defeating Spassky. Petrosian fought stubbornly, and it was Fischer's turn to work. Their game was ultimately drawn. The Rest-of-the-World team made headway in the third round. In addition to Larsen's victory over Spassky, Portisch downed Korchnoi, and Reshevsky beat Symslov, while all other games were drawn. The score, as the players entered the final round, was: U.S.S.R. 15½, Rest-of-the-World 14½.

Larry Evans, in his article on the match in *Sports Illustrated*, wrote that Fischer told him before the start of the last round: "All I need is another half-point to win the *Moskvich*." Evans went on: "I was acting as Fischer's second and his comment told me that the days of trying were over; he was going to play it safe." Of all the players now actively engaged in contemporary chess, Fischer is least likely to "play it safe" under any circumstances. His play for a win against Gheorghiu in the last round of the Havana Olympics of 1966 (when a draw would have guaranteed him the gold medal) is a case in point. There are many other examples of Fischer's disdain for the draw. He inexorably plays to win; damn the consequences.

Fischer's last game *was* drawn, but not because of any timidity on his part. He played well with the Black pieces and selected his special Gruenfeld Defense (which Hans Kmoch says Fischer reserves for all of his attempts at "Games of the Century"). After multiple exchanges, the game developed into a Rook and Bishop ending by adjournment, but Petrosian played better, and created what almost looked like a possible win. He certainly had the advantage. In his hotel room, Fischer carefully analyzed his adjournment. He was disturbed by the noise from adjoining suites and had his room switched. The new room was not quiet enough either and he changed once again. This time he found himself next door to Petrosian. All night long, as Bobby analyzed to find a draw, he could hear the telephone ring in Petrosian's room as the other Russians called to discuss new analyses they had discovered to preserve the win for their compatriot. Fischer worked alone.

At about 4 A.M., he went to Evans's room for a final check of his position. Bobby was worried because it was exactly the type of game that he hates: no chances for any initiative on his part. He had to sit back to see what Petrosian would do.

The next day Bobby appeared at the adjournment, tired and untypically unshaved. He managed to hang on to the draw. Spassky, who was ill in the final round, was replaced by Stein, who promptly lost to Larsen. A number of spectators felt that Spassky was replaced not due to illness but due to his spotty play. In an article in *Newsweek*, the implication of Spassky's possible face-saving move was solidified by Fischer who commented: "He said he was sick but I saw him around." Spassky did subsequently manage to appear on TV and to attend the final banquet.

Other last round encounters resulted in a draw between Portisch and Korchnoi (Fischer claimed Portisch acted ". . . disgracefully" in accepting the draw since he had the better position), and draws between Polugayevsky and Hort, Gligoric and Geller, Botvinnik and Matulovic, and Najdorf and Tal. Smyslov defeated Olafsson (who acted as a reserve for Reshevsky), Taimanov lost to Uhlmann, and Keres defeated Ivkov. The final result was a victory for the Soviet Union, which finished at 20½, just one point ahead of the Rest-of-the-World at 19½.

The Russians were shaken by their near defeat. "It's a catastrophe," said one team member. "At home they don't understand. They think it means there's something wrong with our culture." Players for the Rest-of-the-World team, for the most part, cheered the results, and discussions about a possible return match were instantly initiated. On the top four boards, the Soviets managed to win only *one game* out of a possible sixteen (Spassky's miniature from Larsen). Fischer's 3–1 blitzkreig against Petrosian made him high scorer for his team. It was argued that with a few manipulations of the line-up, and the opportunity, perhaps, of working together as a team beforehand, the Rest-of-the-World might in fact defeat the U.S.S.R. the next time around. It was thought that for this reason the chances of a return match, in this decade in any event, were slim.

At the awards banquet, Rosser Reeves, president of the American Chess Foundation, inspired by Fischer's stellar performance, proposed a non-title match between Spassky and Fischer for a purse of $25,000 in gold, $15,000 to go to the winner and the balance to the loser. Mr. Reeves wanted the match to be played in Moscow, New York, Chicago and Los Angeles. Dr. Max Euwe, who was then slated to be the next president of FIDE in September, gave his consent. Fischer took time out from his fillet of Beef Wellington to agree, and at first Spassky seemed to be in favor of the match. Spassky spoke highly of Fischer's talents and emphasized his own personal desire to play. Ultimately realizing that the match would proclaim the champion of the world even though it was supposedly a non-title contest, he said: "Such external affairs are handled by the World Chess Federation, which sets up a definite system of competition on this account. Besides, it would be unfair to all of my countrymen who have fought so hard for such an opportunity." The match was squelched.

When the official photographs were taken on the stage of the theater, Fischer was nowhere to be found. Najdorf analyzed Bobby's absence astutely: "He prefers to enter chess history alone."

On April 8th, when the fanfare of the Great Match began to abate, a constellation of the world's chess stars were flown to the seaside resort town of Herceg Novi, near Dubrovnik, to compete in a speed tournament. The games consisted of five minutes for each player, and since so many super-caliber masters were competing, the tournament was referred to as the unofficial "Speed Chess Championship of the World." Eleven Grandmasters and one International Master played in the double round-robin event. In the first round, Fischer met Tal—both considered to be the favorites—and Bobby downed the Russian two straight games. From that point, Fischer thoroughly dominated the congregation, losing only one game, drawing four and winning seventeen, for an embarrassingly mammoth total of nineteen points. Tal, in second place, was a woefully distant 4½ points behind.

Bobby's achievement was hailed as nothing less than miraculous. Tal couldn't understand it, pointing out that Fischer ". . . had played some rather weak blitz games" not long before. Actually, Fischer had always been a strong speed player as far back as his capture of first place in the U.S. Junior Speed Championship in 1957. But in the past, in five-minute sessions against the Russians (as Stein learned at Stockholm), Bobby was not then quite equal to them. After the Herceg Novi tourney was completed, Fischer rattled off all his twenty-two games from memory!

"The Tournament of Peace" to be held in Zagreb and Rovinj starting April 12th belied its title and was one of the most trenchant chess
contests of 1970, and though Fischer said he was tired physically, he
was eager to compete. But once again, he would play only after
inspecting and approving the conditions personally. Bobby flew to
Rovinj, a small resort town on the Istrian peninsula. After inspecting
the playing premises and talking to the organizers, Fischer set forty-
one conditions before agreeing to play. Only one request was denied:
he asked that the pairings be drawn in such a manner that the Soviet
grandmasters would have to face each other in the early rounds.
Bobby decided to play anyway. He was in excellent company: Hort,
Gligoric, Smyslov, Korchnoi, Petrosian, Ivkov, and Uhlmann, all of
whom had just finished playing in the Great Match, were competitors,
in addition to a cluster of other international stars. Eleven grandmasters took part.

Fischer began with an impressive drive. He won his first four
games, including a point over Parma. In round five, he met Ivkov,
pressed for a win, but emerged with an inferior position. After three
adjournments, the game was drawn. Fischer then beat Uhlmann and
Ghitescu in subsequent rounds and faced a relatively unknown Yugoslav, Vlado Kovacevic. After adopting a doubtful variation against
Kovacevic's French Defense, Bobby lost time with his Queen and
found himself in a thoroughly lost position. He resigned after thirty
moves, his first tournament loss since his defeat by Geller in Skopje,
1967. In one foreign report of the tournament it stated that Fischer
". . . congratulated his opponent and did not act sadly because of his
loss."

Undaunted, Fischer came back to defeat the second-place Gligoric
in the next round. The standings were Fischer 8, Petrosian, Hort,
Gligoric and Korchnoi, 6½. In the eleventh round, he met Kurajica
and won a Pawn, but at considerable loss of time. The game was
difficult for Fischer but he eventually gained another Pawn, and then
won easily.

Up to this point all the rounds had been played in Rovinj. The
tournament now moved to Zagreb for the remaining six games; round
twelve was played on April 28th. Fischer beat Udovcic, in the thirteenth round he drew with Hort, and in the fourteenth defeated
Bertok. Against Browne, in the fifteenth round, Fischer (the Exchange down) faced definite defeat, but after many hours of play,
Browne tired and blundered on his eighty-eighth move to allow Bobby
to slip away with a draw. Fischer had secured first place, even if he
lost his two remaining games.

The two Russians, Korchnoi and Petrosian, were Bobby's two last
opponents, and it was quite apparent that they were eager to score
at least one win between them from the American. In the penultimate
round, Korchnoi emerged from the opening against Fischer with supe-

riority, and the game developed into an ending of Bishops of opposite color. Both players fought resourcefully and the result was a draw. "In my lifetime, I shall not play such an endgame better," averred Korchnoi proudly.

When Fischer played against Petrosian in the final round, the Armenian secured an opening advantage, but Fischer dominated the Rook ending. Petrosian said later that he remembered Tartakower's statement that "all Rook endgames are drawn," and the thought comforted him. Actually, he had to carefully nurture his position, which finally did end as a draw.

Chess Digest referred to Fischer's result of thirteen points, two above his closest rival Gligoric, as one of his ". . . greatest victories," and players and critics hailed him as now being second only to Spassky, perhaps even the greatest player in the world at that time. Korchnoi's description of what happened at Zagreb was somewhat more sober: "Of course, he plays excellently, but we were somewhat hurt in all the points he gathered in the early rounds with one and the same variation, both with White and Black. Fischer has a healthy knowledge of the Sicilian jungle. Less experienced players try to catch him in prepared lines, but he always deviates and his opponents find themselves in unfamiliar situations. I even tried to convince one or two Yugoslavs not to play the Sicilian against him but to try, for instance, the Marshall attack." Perhaps Korchnoi forgot that Fischer is also expert at playing against the Marshall.

Dr. Trifunovic referred to Fischer's expertise in Yugoslavia as "errorless chess" and went on to say that Fischer declared that he had not been sufficiently prepared but that ". . . taking him at his word, it is hard to visualize what would be left of a tournament after he played in the form which he demands of himself." Fischer received the first prize of $1,000.

Bobby left Zagreb thoroughly exhausted. He had obviously damaged his balance on that fine line that separates too much serious chess activity from too little competition. He flew to Sarajevo to be the guest of the amiable Dimitrije Bjelica and to work on a number of chess projects with him. After resting for a spell, they produced a series of ten television shows, each devoted to a famous master selected and discussed by Fischer and topped off with an illustrative game. Though not naming his video subjects "The Ten Best," it's still interesting to compare his 1970 selections with those he chose (for that honor) in 1964 in his *Chessworld* article:

1964	1970
Alexander Alekhine	Tigran Petrosian
José Raul Capablanca	José Raul Capablanca
Paul Morphy	Paul Morphy

Samuel Reshevsky	Samuel Reshevsky
Boris Spassky	Boris Spassky
Howard Staunton	Mikhail Botvinnik
Wilhelm Steinitz	Wilhelm Steinitz
Mikhail Tal	Mikhail Tal
Seigbert Tarrasch	Bent Larsen
Mikhail Tchigorin	Svetozar Gligoric

Though Fischer's 1970 roster might well have been tailored for Eastern European consumption, it is still significant that he included Botvinnik and Petrosian in the later list to increase the number of contemporary Soviet greats to four. Though a great player, Gligoric must have certainly been included on the urging of Bjelica; it *was* Yugoslavian television. The other sensational changes were the deletion of Alekhine and the inclusion of Larsen, the former decision being as totally eccentric as his omission of Lasker in his 1964 list (he is consistent and omits him in 1970, too), and the latter being a totally fair and logical choice.

Bobby had always loved Yugoslavia and began to seriously explore the idea of living there. He wrote to Bozidar Kazic, a member of the Central Committee of FIDE and one of the organizers of the World Match, asking about his *Moskvich* (which he had originally asked to be sold): "My wish is to buy a house on the Adriatic in Yugoslavia . . . In such a case, I would need a car more than the money since I would be staying in Yugoslavia for some months yearly." The letter arrived too late, however, and the auto had already been sold.

While Bobby was in Sarajevo, an article signed "Bobby Fischer" appeared in the Zagrebian daily paper, *Plavy Vesnik*. It had been placed there by Bjelica and consisted of interviews of Fischer by the Yugoslav, rewritten to appear as though they had been originally penned by Fischer himself. Fischer was indignant with both the approach and the fact that Bjelica was paid for the article though it bore Fischer's name. No compromise over the payment could be agreed upon by the two men, and Fischer left Sarajevo immediately, stopped briefly at Zagreb to engage an attorney to bring action against Bjelica. He then went to Vinkovci, site of his 1968 victory, to stay with a friend, I. Bilusic, and remained there a month.

On Sunday, July 12th, Fischer gave a simultaneous exhibition at Varazdin where the result was 17–3. Bobby began to make preparations to transport his bulky but beautiful trophy, won at Zagreb, back to the United States. Entitled "Rider of Peace," it was a replica of the statue standing before the United Nations in New York and Fischer was greatly honored in receiving it, since only three copies had been made of it. President Dwight D. Eisenhower received one of them.

CHAPTER XXII

"It's like taking a five-hour
final examination."

Bobby had been invited to compete in an international tournament in Buenos Aires that was due to start on July 18th. Smyslov, Reshevsky, Szabo, Bisguier, Najdorf, Panno, Gheorghiu, Mecking, and a carefully selected group of strong South American and European players were slated to compete. On the 16th, Fischer cabled the organizers that he had decided to play and, as originally arranged, he requested a plane ticket to be mailed to him immediately. The ticket arrived on Friday the 17th, but since Bobby doesn't travel on Fridays or Saturdays because of his religious observances, he waited out the weekend and arrived in Argentina on the 20th, only a few hours before the scheduled starting time for round three.

After some preliminary discussions relative to lighting and scheduling, he sat down to play his first game against his Havana spoiler, Gheorghiu. Though the game looked drawish at first, Fischer managed to win a Pawn and was about to win another when the young Rumanian blundered. Gheorghiu resigned when he was forced to give up a piece. Fischer then marched through the next five rounds and all of his opponents, scoring full points against Damjanovic, Schweber, the talented young Russian Tukmakov, Quinteros, and Rossetto. In his game against Tukmakov, Fischer played 1 P–QN3 for the first time in his career, and emerged from the opening in a slightly inferior position; when complications erupted, however, Tukmakov went astray.

In the next round, Fischer faced Najdorf, and the crowds at the *Teatro General San Martin* had to be turned away. Tickets were at a premium and all of the newspapers, which covered the tournament heavily every day, gave special attention to this particular game. Najdorf played the Queen's Gambit Declined, and neither side could make much progress. The game was ultimately drawn on the fortieth move.

Five more victories for Fischer were tallied: against O'Kelly, Panno, Agdamus, Szabo, and Bisguier, before he drew another game, this time against his Brazilian friend, the young prodigy Henrique Mecking. With three rounds to go, he was 3½ points ahead of the field and had easily secured first place. Szabo wrote about his game in "64" that ". . . Fischer had many complicated possibilities open to him and he also had many points! I decided that he might be agreeable to a draw after multiple exchanges. However, when I offered one, Bobby shook his head indignantly."

The next game was another draw against Reshevsky, and there followed a win over Rubinetti. Fischer then drew against Smyslov, in a game which Fischer later claimed was an "easy win," and in the final round won Garcia's Queen and forced his resignation on the thirty-eighth move. Smyslov related that when he offered a draw, Bobby took umbrage: "I don't take draws in under forty moves," perhaps forgetting that he had in fact just taken one on move thirty against Mecking a few days before.

His final score was 15 out of a possible 17, 3½ large points over Tukmakov in second place. Panno was a clear third and Gheorghiu, Najdorf, and Reshevsky tied for fourth through sixth. It was the strongest chess tournament ever held in Argentina.

Arthur Bisguier, writing in *Chess Life*, thought that Fischer ". . . never had a lost position," and that his game against Mecking was the only one in which another player ". . . seemed to enjoy full equality."

It had been two years since Fischer had set foot on South American soil and when he departed after competing in this event, he did so with a lighter heart than after his drastic showing in Buenos Aires in 1960. It was a more than creditable comeback. Now, Bobby had barely three weeks time to get himself to Seigen, Germany, for he had agreed in advance to head the American team at the XIXth Olympiad. The possible Spassky-Fischer confrontation, though only to consist of one game—when the U.S.S.R. faced the U.S.A.—began to produce a stir. Followers of the game from all over Europe had already started to besiege the tiny town. Hotel rooms were at a premium and many players had to find accommodations in obscure parts of town. A record number of sixty teams participated, with over three hundred and sixty masters attending.

The U.S. team was comprised of Fischer, on board one, followed by Reshevsky, Evans, and Benko, and with Lombardy and Mednis as reserves. Ed Edmondson served as team captain, assisted by George Koltanowski. With the exception of Robert Byrne, who was replaced by Mednis, the team was exactly as planned for Lugano before Fischer disappeared. Since Mednis had always fared well in international play, the American chances (it was stressed, mostly by Americans) of capturing first place from the Soviets were, if not excellent, at least plausible. The Soviet team was the same as two years previous in Lugano, i.e., Spassky, Petrosian, Korchnoi, Polugayesky, Smyslov, and Geller, the only changes being a switch of boards for Spassky and Petrosian and Polugayevsky and Geller.

Only one demand was made by Bobby this time. He wanted his board moved three feet further away from the spectators, who were crowded close to him every game; though the *Seigerlandhall* was a huge playing area, the crowds of both players and spectators did not permit much separation between them.

The reasons Fischer had failed to play at Lugano were clear; it is not so simple to determine his motivations for heading the American team at Seigen. He was awarded a respectable honorarium by the American Chess Foundation for his participation at Seigen, but he would have received the same amount had he played at Lugano. That could not have been the influential factor. Most probably he wanted to be present in Germany at the time of the FIDE Congress, since the organization was going to vote whether or not to allow both him and Tal into the Interzonal, even though both had not qualified in their respective Zonals. (Fischer's Zonal, you will recall, was the 1969 U.S. Championship, in which he had refused to play.) He may have thought that his presence might influence the voting body; he was proving that he was finished (at least for the moment) with boycotting FIDE events; he had just competed in the U.S.S.R. vs. the Rest-of-the-World Match and he was now playing in FIDE's most cherished bi-annual contest, the team championship of the world.

The U.S.A. team, though qualifying into Group A of the finals, started off poorly in the preliminaries by managing to come in two full points behind East Germany. It was the first time since Munich, 1958, that the U.S. failed to either capture or tie for first place. Fischer played six out of nine games, won five and drew with Uhlmann. The Soviet Union breezed through its section, as usual, coming in two and a half points ahead of Spain.

A new rule had been introduced at the last Olympiad, which was in effect for the first time at Seigen, i.e., the first round of the finals was scored from the results of the two qualifiers who played each other in the preliminaries, so since the U.S.A. had lost to East Germany 1½-2½, that same score was progressed into the finals as the round one results, even though the two teams didn't actually meet then.

The handicap of an automatic minus score was at least partially overcome in the next few rounds as the U.S. team defeated Rumania and Argentina, Bobby drawing with Gheorghiu and defeating Najdorf. Neither Bobby nor Reshevsky played in the fourth round against Canada, due to their religious observances, and the U.S.A. drew at 2-2. The two players also stayed out of the fifth round against Bulgaria, which the Americans nevertheless succeeded in capturing 3½-½. After five rounds, Hungary and the U.S.A. shared first place at 12½, while almost magically, the U.S.S.R. and Yugoslavia were below at 12 points, tied for third and fourth.

Political acrimony plagued the fourth round when Albania refused to compete against South Africa due to that country's official policies regarding apartheid. Not since the outbreak of World War II, during the 1939 Olympiad at Buenos Aires, had one team refused to play another for political reasons. The violation of the *Gens Una Sumus* spirit theoretically prevalent in FIDE cast an uneasy gloom over the rest of the teams at Seigen. The Albanians were forfeited 4–0.

During this tournament Fischer was spied dashing through the hotel corridor in his pajamas, his face livid and hair disheveled, searching for the source of some unusually loud music that had abruptly awakened him. Although it was noon, it was his custom to sleep at least until two, sometimes much later. As Bobby's friends will attest, there is one inviolable rule that can never be broken if one is to maintain a relationship with him, and that is never to wake him early in the morning. "I'd like to rip all those hotel radios out of the wall," he complained sleepily.

But no lack of sleep was evident in his play. The 1970 summit meeting of chess occurred during the sixth round when not only the two most powerful nations, the U.S.A. and the U.S.S.R., locked horns, but the two men then considered to be the strongest in the world, Boris Spassky and Robert James Fischer, sat down to play each other. Spassky had bettered Fischer in their first two encounters: Mar Del Plata 1960, and the first round of the Piatigorsky Cup 1966. Their last two games before Seigen, however, at the second round of the Piatigorsky Cup and the Havana Olympiad 1966, were both monumental draws. A number of players felt that Fischer had developed immensely in four years, and though Spassky had won the World's Championship, they were looking forward to this encounter to decide who was the better man, ignoring the fact that the result of one single game actually proves nothing except who was the superior player, perhaps, during that isolated encounter. Gligoric said he was overcome with a feeling of ". . . sadness and injustice" that the duel of the year consisted of only one game.

The crowds that came to view the Spassky-Fischer game were enormous. Koltanowski, in his report for *Chess Digest*, described it this way: "Chess fans turned up from all over Europe and the standing-room sign meant nothing. Around the center where the A division teams are playing, the players and captains had problems squeezing their way through. And there were rows, upon rows, and rows of people all around the aisles . . . those that started getting places from 10 A.M. are the lucky ones. Thousands of spectators are watching the U.S.A.-U.S.S.R. four-board match on wall boards outside the playing room and upstairs where the games are shown via cameras."

Both players felt the importance of the game; Fischer desperately wanted to score his first victory over Spassky, and Spassky was so hypertense before the start of the game that he was visibly trembling and chain-smoked one Russian cigarette after the other.

Bobby played his pet Gruenfeld, and the game developed along the same lines as their encounter at Santa Monica which he had lost. Spassky deviated on his twelfth move and, according to O'Kelly, Fischer had achieved theoretical equality after his fifteenth move. O'Kelly went on to say: "During the whole game Spassky remained seated and produced an effort of concentration comparable to that of his matches with Petrosian. Under these circumstances, Spassky adopts a most singular attitude—with his facial expression completely devoid of any external preoccupations."

Though there were several drawing continuations that he could have tried, Fischer elected to play for the win. He overextended himself in the process. An examination of Fischer's own score sheet of the game shows that on about the twentieth move, his handwriting becomes almost illegible as though the concentration he used to find the proper continuations pre-empted all his energy. He consumed over a dozen bottles of *apfel saft* during the five-hour session. Eventually an imbalance in the position was created and though both players stood materially equal, with two Rooks, a Knight, a Queen and four Pawns each, Fischer made a fatal error on his thirtieth move and another on his thirty-second move. About to lose his Queen, Bobby resigned to the Russian on his thirty-ninth move. Fischer's psychic scar as a result of this game must still cause him pain. Spassky said later of Fischer: "He failed to play strong; he failed to find a good plan and to play this plan accurately." Fischer was both resentful and succinct: "Wait till next time. Spassky was lucky."

In the interim, Reshevsky had drawn with Petrosian in eighteen moves, and though both Evans and Lombardy had what looked like winning positions at adjournment time, both could do nothing more than salvage draws. Our final score was 1½–2½, the twentieth year the U.S. was unable to defeat the Soviets in Olympic play.

The U.S. finally placed fourth in the Olympiad at 24½ points, its worst showing at any time with Fischer on the team, and our second worst result of the decade. Breathing on the neck of the Soviet Union, which captured first with 27½, was Hungary, second with 26½, and Yugoslavia, third with 26.

William Lombardy, whose own score was eleven out of fourteen, the best on the team and the highest of the Olympiad on fifth board, tried to explain the failure of the American team in his article in *Chess Life*, entitled "Olympic Letdown."

Bobby Fischer would not be enough to turn the tide of Soviet victories at the chess Olympics. His final percentage of 76.9 was certainly high but nowhere near the heights of his recent tournament successes. What was the problem? Larry Evans, to the astonishment of everyone, could not find his range most of the time, but even when he did find it, the missile would go off in his own face.

At the FIDE Congress, the 41st, heated discussion erupted over the possibilities of allowing Fischer into the Interzonal. The vote was close but negative, with the Soviets especially adamant about making any changes in the existing sequence of the selection of challengers, since the process was already in motion. Signed statements from half-a-dozen grandmasters on the Interzonal roster, who were against the idea, assisted the opposition. There was strong sentiment, however, to allow Fischer to play if one of the three American qualifiers would drop out in his behalf. The USCF received authorization from the Congress to revise its list of Interzonal entrants, and was given until November 8th, about six weeks' time, to report to the FIDE Secretariat if a change was to be made. The Interzonal was to begin in Palma de Majorca, in the Balearic Islands (off the northeast coast of Spain), on November 9th. Isaac Kashdan, who sat in on all of the FIDE meetings, told me that he was convinced that had Fischer not "shown" himself at Seigen, indicating to the Congress members his desire to cooperate, he would never have been permitted to enter the Interzonal.

CHAPTER XXIII

"I really love the dark of the
night. It helps me to concentrate."

Before returning to the United States, Fischer traveled from Seigen to Frankfurt, purchased the latest chess literature, and then flew back to New York. His first meeting with Edmondson in Newburgh, New York, concerned the possibilities of Bobby's participation in the Interzonal. Benko, who always felt friendly toward Fischer despite their Curaçao contretemps, agreed to step out and give Fischer his valuable spot at Palma. When it was suggested to Fischer that Benko was considering the gesture based on a large sum of money to be paid to him, Bobby replied that Benko would not give up his berth for money alone. It was a matter of honor. Lombardy, who was next in line with the right to participate, was queried as to whether he would also step aside. "I would like to play," he answered, "but Fischer should have the chance." Both players longed to play in the Interzonal but they knew that Fischer was the only American player (in the past century) who had any realistic possibilities of being chess champion of the world. It also helped that both men had been long-time colleagues of Fischer's.

Edmondson had received approval from the USCF Policy Board to accompany Fischer to Palma to act in his behalf should any complications arise. The two men had been working together closely, especially at Seigen, where Edmondson had shown an uncanny ability to head off Fischer-directed troubles before they began. I spoke to Edmondson by phone at that time: "Is Bobby *really* going to play in the Interzonal?" I asked. Edmondson said that Bobby was, indeed, but that he was doing so only because he, Edmondson, had agreed to accompany Bobby through the Interzonal, the Candidates cycle (should he qualify), and should Fischer be the sole qualifier, straight through to and including the World's Championship.

Evans went to Bobby as his second, and Kenneth Smith worked for weeks preparing and researching material on every opponent. Smith recounted: "I was up most of the night researching every game, every opening each of the participants had played in the last two years." For once, Fischer seemed to be in favor of a team effort in assisting him through the Interzonal labyrinth.

This tournament was probably the strongest Interzonal ever held since the series began in 1948. Fifteen international grandmasters and nine international masters competed at Palma, and such world renowned players as Polugayevsky, Geller, Ivkov, Uhlmann, Taimanov, Smyslov, Gligoric, Reshevsky, Portisch, and Larsen were there to battle with Bobby for one of the six cherished spots in the Candidates; Korchnoi and Petrosian were automatically seeded, as the first was the finalist from the previous Candidates, and the latter was the deposed World Champion.

In an interview that he gave to Bozidar Kazic, Fischer said: "I have decided to play although I disagree with the system of the world championship competition. I thought, 'what can I lose by playing?' I thought it was important to play for the Candidates, but I also thought, naturally, of the possibility of winning the tournament."

There were some last minute measures taken concerning Fischer's requests that the lighting be to his specifications, but when the drawing of lots took place at 11 A.M. on the beautiful Mediterranean isle on Monday, November 9th, there was no longer any doubt that Fischer would participate in the tournament. Though Fischer and Matulovic did not choose to attend the ceremonies at the *Ayuntamiento*, they were checked into the Hôtel *Jaime I* and were prepared to play when the first round began.

Despite Fischer's affability, the tournament began with a hodgepodge of problems. The early round pairings were supposed to be among players from the same countries, but through some preliminary confusion, no such pairing was made in the first round between the Americans, the Yugoslavs or the Russians. Since the two Czech players, Filip and Hort, *were* paired against one another, and the two Argentinians Panno and Rubinetti were also scheduled to play each other, the quartet claimed they were being discriminated against. Hort actually threatened to withdraw. Taimanov added to the quandary by stating that he thought that FIDE had abolished the rule that players from one country had to meet as early as possible in a tournament. This regulation had always been a sore point among the Russians, since Fischer is the one who promoted it. He wanted it enforced because he claimed it prevented the short grandmaster draws between nationals at the end of a tournament, which if calculatedly manipulated, could easily produce a winner.

Calls were made to the FIDE Bureau in the Hague to clarify the point, and H.J.J. Slavekoorde, secretary of FIDE, confirmed that Taimanov was correct: the rule had been abolished. Finally, Dr. Max Euwe authorized the changing of some rounds, specifically to avoid the last round pairing of Smyslov and Taimanov since Fischer claimed emphatically that he would withdraw unless the switch was made.

Then Larsen sternly objected to having to play Fischer on Friday morning, due to the latter's religious observances. Larsen is almost as notorious a late sleeper as Fischer. The round was switched in Larsen's favor, but had to be switched back when the Russians threatened to withdraw.

To everyone's surprise, the tournament began at 4 P.M., exactly when scheduled.

A naked light bulb distracted Fischer in the first round, and he complained about it, asking that it be covered or removed in future rounds. He had the White pieces against the rising young German star, Robert Hübner, who played the Caro-Kann. This is an opening which is supposed to be difficult for Bobby to handle. Fischer played the conservative 2 P–Q3, a decision which Evans later kidded him about. "This move will spoil your image," Larry said.

Fischer's game developed well. He had the luxury of time on his clock, compared to Hübner, but on the German's thirty-second move Hübner forced the win of a piece. Fischer ultimately netted three Pawns for it, however, and the endgame was a clear draw.

Smyslov played his favorite English Opening in the second round but it lacked luster. Fischer obtained an unequivocally superior position and won. Addison's third-round Center Counter Defense brought a wide smile to Fischer's face. He won that game in twenty-four moves.

For the second time in his career, Fischer played 1 P–QN3, this time against Filip, and aside from winning the game brilliantly, he psychologically undermined his future opponents, many of whom had undoubtedly spent months, perhaps even years, preparing to play against Fischer's beloved but predictable 1 P–K4.

After his defeat of Hort and Reshevsky in the fifth and sixth rounds, Fischer led the tournament with a point-and-a-half advantage at 5½. Larsen, Gligoric, and Uitumen, his closest competitors, trailed at 4 points each. Fischer adjourned against Matulovic, and a draw was agreed upon before resumption of the game. He drew against Naranja, his friend from the Philippines, and on November 20th he met his constant rival, Bent Larsen, in the ninth round. Though Larsen had objected to playing at "the ungodly hour" of 11:30 A.M., he arrived at the tournament hall on time and appeared to be alert enough to play. The Velimirovic Attack of the Sicilian was the order of the day. Larsen was well versed in the opening and consumed less than two minutes on his clock for the first fifteen moves.

Larsen castled early on the Kingside with Fischer quickly castling Queenside, and the predictable result was an attack launched by both men on opposite wings. Fischer, however, went astray, handling his attack without the accuracy to which he and everyone else is accustomed, and Larsen's counterattack netted him a piece for two Pawns. Evans said of this game that ". . . while everyone else is playing it safe to qualify, accepting draws left and right, Fischer goes his own way and plays the only chess he knows—fighting chess." As the game developed, Fischer had much the inferior position and Larsen played the endgame with precision. Bobby resigned after the fifty-second move.

Evans tried to caution Bobby to pace himself. "You don't have to kill everybody. You just have to qualify," he wisely advised. Fischer had dropped in the standings to tie with Geller at 6½, while Panno had worked himself up to 6. Minic and Larsen stood at 5.

Listening only to his own inner directives, Bobby proceeded to try to "crush" Portisch in a Benoni Defense in the next round, and only managed to secure a draw. Against Polugayevsky in the eleventh round, he once again demolished the hopes of his well-prepared opponents, perhaps for all time, by playing the English Opening, 1 P–QB4 for the first time in his professional life. Though Polugayevsky seemed to be under a strain in attempting to determine what hidden tricks, if any, Fischer might have prepared, he defended well. After Queens were exchanged, a traditionally even ending of Bishops of opposite color resulted. The two men agreed to a draw before adjourning.

Entering the twelfth round, Fischer, in second place at 7½ points, was scheduled to meet Geller, who was leading the field with 8 points. Hübner was third at 7.

Geller had not lost a game and had faced a strong schedule. Perhaps more importantly, in their last three encounters Fischer had lost each game. It was believed by many players that Geller was holding the proverbial "Indian Sign" over Fischer's head. He had beaten Bobby in more games than any other living player. Gufeld, Geller's second, explained why the opening 1 N–KB3 was chosen by the Soviet "think tank," stating that his phenomenal run of success with 1 P–K4 against Fischer simply would not continue as a matter of mathematical probability. The real psychological duel began after the game was started. On the seventh move, Geller offered Fischer a draw. Obviously the irritating impact was well-timed since, in effect, Geller was telling Fischer that he would *allow* him to have a draw; but the acceptance of such a ludicrously short draw would have indicated that Fischer was afraid to fight for a win. It was unthinkable that Fischer would have accepted, but the well-calculated insult might well have rebounded in Geller's direction.

Fischer's reaction to the offer was, at first, to laugh. Geller joined in, but then the American retaliated with a statement that no one but Geller quite heard. One bystander reportedly quoted Fischer as saying "Too early!" But Geller's face turned red, and Fischer may well have countered with a much more caustic snipe, probably returning to his theme about short draws being only the property of the Soviet state. Fischer once said that whenever a player attempted to make him "mad," it actually helped him, giving him even more impetus to beat his opponent.

Two moves after this suggested draw, Geller found himself in trouble and took over an hour to make his tenth move; then he blundered away a Pawn. Edmondson protested to the tournament officials that the Soviets were whispering and laughing during the game in Fischer's direct line of vision. They were asked to leave the tournament room but caused a commotion while doing so. When the game reached the forty-first move, Geller was instructed by O'Kelly to seal for adjournment. He was one Pawn down in a Rook-and-Pawn ending, but felt he had drawing opportunities. Upon resumption, both players fought brilliantly, but the game lapsed into a drawn position. The Soviet contingent, on the sidelines, were all convinced that Fischer could make no headway. At the final hour, on the seventy-first move, Geller blundered and awarded Bobby both the point and the lead at 8½ points. It was his first victory over Geller since Curaçao, 1962, and though admittedly a gratuitous win, it helped to strengthen Bobby's drive.

In the thirteenth round, Fischer crushed Ivkov. In the fourteenth he pleased the gallery once again with a (for him) fairly unusual opening: Alekhine's Defense. It was the third time in his career that he had employed it. The first was against Ciociltea, Havana 1965, and he had used it against Browne in Zagreb just six months before Palma. This time Minic was on the White end and lost decisively. Fischer then drew with Jiminez and Uitumen in the fifteenth and sixteenth rounds (against Uitumen he played Alekhine's Defense once again) and scored full points in the seventeenth and eighteenth, against Rubinetti and Uhlmann. With an impressive command of 13½ points, one-and-a-half ahead of Geller, two full points ahead of Huebner and 2½ points ahead of the combined pile-up of Mecking, Taimanov, Portisch, and Larsen, Fischer was almost guaranteed a spot in the Candidates no matter how he concluded his final games. In the same situation, most players ould be content to conserve their energy and maybe some of their preferred lines, and just play for draws. But most players are not like Bobby Fischer. His vigor is the key to his greatness.

In the nineteenth round, Taimanov played the Taimanov Variation against Fischer and developed a slightly superior position at first, but he played poorly just before adjournment. Fischer wanted to continue the game but Taimanov sealed. When they resumed, Fischer sacrificed a Pawn and in a Bishop vs. Knight ending he proved the superiority of his Bishop. Taimanov resigned on the fifty-eighth move.

Indicating that Alekhine's Defense might be a permanent part of his repertory, Fischer played it again and defeated Suttles, but this was accomplished in spite of the opening rather than because of it. Playing well at first, the young Canadian went astray through a miscalculation of timing and Fischer devastated his position.

Against his erstwhile Brazilian match partner Mecking, Fischer played 1 P–QN3 and took his fifth game in a row. He then defeated Gligoric in the twenty-second round and at 17½ points, with one round to go, clinched his first place. He was 2½ points ahead of Hübner in the second slot. Fischer's last-round opponent was Panno and, unfortunately, his performance was tarnished due to the Argentinian's stubbornness.

Panno had announced that he would not play Fischer in the last round at 7 P.M. because all the other games started at four; the special time had been arranged because of Fischer's religious observances. But Panno, almost unbelievably in this age of individualists, said that he couldn't understand why Fischer could not act "normal." Dr. Euwe asked if all the other players would agree to play at seven but the Soviets refused and Panno announced that he would give Fischer the game.

The game was started without Panno (shades of Sousse!) and Fischer played 1 P–QB4, then left the tournament hall and went to Panno's hotel and tried to talk him into playing. He did persuade the Argentinian to return to the tournament hall but was unable to get him to play. After forty-five minutes, Panno announced his resignation, not waiting for the end of the one hour time deadline. The date was December 12th.

Fischer's second Interzonal triumph—18½ points, 3½ ahead of Larsen, Geller, and Huebner who were all tied at 15—was one of the outstanding accomplishments of his career and one of the most remarkable results ever achieved by any player at any time in the long history of the game. Fischer's tally for the entire year of 1970, starting with the Great Match and finishing with the Interzonal, was unparalleled. He had lost only three games while drawing twenty-three and winning fifty against the leading players of the day, establishing what Isaac Kashdan called ". . . the most successful year for any chess player of our time." Uhlmann, who also qualified (together with Taimanov and those mentioned above) had this comment to offer on Fischer's performance: "It's simply unbelievable with what superiority he played in the Interzonal. There is a vitality in his games; the other grandmasters seem to get an inferiority complex. It should be remembered with what ease Gligoric and I lost to him, as if we had been hypnotized."

Najdorf, in a telephone interview with a Moscow newspaper, was asked for his views on Fischer's ability. "He'll have to concede two points start to the rest of the players to make any future tournament in which he competes interesting to all," he said humbly.

Taimanov, however, who was paired with Fischer in the quarter-finals of the Candidates in 1972 (Petrosian would meet Hübner, Korchnoi would face Geller, and Larsen was slated to play Uhlmann) was somewhat more skeptical about Fischer's accomplishments. Even though he looked forward to the quarter-finals match with Bobby and felt that he was ". . . a great danger," nevertheless, he said: "It is inexplicable how Fischer won with a margin like that. He plays well but not that much better than the rest of us. Fischer plays throughout with the same strength, without major oscillations . . . In fact, Fischer makes fewer mistakes than we do."

From these comments and others made by the participants in the Interzonal and some of the other tournaments he played in 1970, it was becoming obvious that Fischer was beginning to establish an unmistakable mystique. Alekhine had it, as did Tal; often their opponents would believe that some mystical force was present at the board. Benko even wore sunglasses once to counter Tal's ". . . hypnotic gaze."

Fischer's force of spirit at the board is unnerving. He rarely leaves the table and when he does, unlike other players, he has virtually no interest in the games around him. His game, his struggle, his creation, consumes him. Like Lasker, who was known for objecting, on occasion, to the clatter of a teaspoon in the tournament hall, Fischer cannot tolerate interruptions and treats any intrusion ruthlessly. To watch him at the board, an artist in his workshop, is a memorable experience; even if the nuances of his strategy are lost to the less sophisticated player, the visual impact of a genius in the throes of creation is unforgettable.

Unlike such vaudevillians as Staunton, in the past, or Mecking, in the present, who histrionically roll their eyes, grimace, stroke their brows, and render audible sighs or comments concerning the agony of their forthcoming creations, Fischer is mysteriously silent, curt and impeccably courteous. The only noticeable tic is a ricochet-like motion of either of his legs that continues for the duration of the game, a peculiarity also displayed by Tchigorin as a young man.

He *empathizes* with the position of the moment with such intensity that one feels that a defect in his game, such as a backward Pawn or an ill-placed Knight, causes him almost physical, and certainly psychical, pain. Fischer would *become* the Pawn if he could, or if it would help his position, marching himself rank-by-rank to the ultimate promotion square. In these moments at the board, Fischer *is* chess. This is the puissance that his opponents sense, unable to label

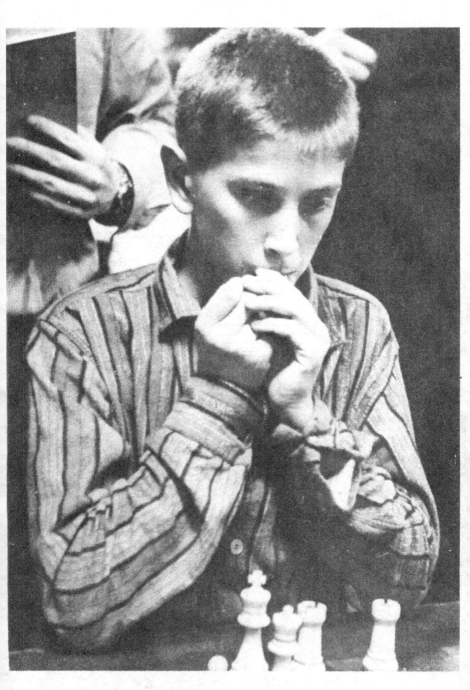

1. During his first invitational masters' event, the Lessing J. Rosenwald tournament of 1956, young Bobby, though extremely tense, played brilliantly.   (Dr. H. Sussman)

2. The original score sheet, in his own handwriting, of Fischer's "Game of the Century" played against Donald Byrne at the Lessing J. Rosenwald tournament of 1956.

3. Even before winning the national title, Fischer's brilliant moves and charisma attracted crowds wherever he played. Here, somewhat self-consciously, he plays an informal game with his friend, James Gore, at the Manhattan Chess Club in 1957.

(R. Echeverria)

4. Fischer's own score sheet of his draw with Lombardy, then World Junior Champion, at the 1957–58 U.S. Championship.

GAME No.
1

MANHATTAN CHESS CLUB
SINCE 1877
America's Oldest - Ever Progressive

Event _U S Ch'ship_ Round _1_ Date _Dec 18-58_
White: Mr. _Lombardy_ Black: Mr. _Fischer_

WHITE	BLACK	WHITE	BLACK	WHITE	BLACK
			31		61
			32		62
			33		63
			34		64
			35		65
			36		66
			37		67
			38		68
			39		69
			40		70
			41		71
			42		72
			43		73
			44		74
			45		75
			46		76
			47		77
			48		78
			49		79
					80
					81
			52		82
			53		83
			54		84
			55		85
			56		86
			57		87
			58		88
			59		89
			60		90

5. In 1958, the newly crowned grandmaster (the youngest in history at 15) confidently returns to the United States from his first trip to Europe, after competing in the Interzonal at Potoroz, Yugoslavia. (U.S.I.S.)

6., 7., 8. Throughout Fischer's career, Reshevsky has been
one of his most dangerous rivals. During the 1957–58 U.S.
Championship, Fischer (No. 6, upper left) (M. Sokoler)
makes the decisive move that brings him his first victory over
the great master. They meet again in 1961 (No. 7, lower left)
(U.S.I.S.), during their abortive match, and Fischer studies
Reshevsky waiting to see what his first move will be. And in
the 1966 Piatigorsky Cup tournament, Fischer waits again for
Reshevsky to make his first move (No. 8, above).

9. During the Candidates' tournament in Yugoslavia in 1959, Fischer listens disinterestedly to the opening speeches while sitting next to his chief competition, Mikhail Tal and Tigran Petrosian.

10. Botvinnik and Fischer struggle in their titanic encounter at the Varna Olympiad in 1962. The game ended in a draw.

11. At Stockholm in 1962, Fischer's first, magnificent international victory, he talks with Soviet grandmaster Alexander Kotov.

12. At the pretournament garden party for the Piatigorsky Cup 1966, Fischer plays a skittles game with Ivkov as (left to right) Najdorf, Portisch, Larsen, and Unzicker watch.

13. Upon arriving at the José Marti International airport in Havana for the 1966 Olympiad, Fischer sips a Cuban daiquiri while relaxing with teammate Pal Benko (at rear) and team captain Donald Byrne, at his left.

14. Fischer poses with the late Maurice Kasper, treasurer of the American Chess Foundation and father-figure to many young masters during the 1966–67 U.S. Championship. Due to organizational disagreements, it was the last U.S. Championship Fischer competed in.

15. After his one-and-one-half year "retirement" ("to plot my revenge") Fischer gives his first press interview at the USSR vs. World match in Belgrade, Yugoslavia in 1970.

16. While photographers scurry behind him, Fischer composes himself prior to the opening game of his match with Petrosian in Buenos Aires, 1970. (U.S.I.S.)

17. A few days after defeating Larsen in their match in 1971, Fischer played in a strong speed tournament at the Manhattan Chess club, which he won quite easily. Here he plays Andrew Soltis as Hans Kmoch at left, Jack Collins (in center with chin on hand), and other club members watch every move.
(U.S.I.S.)

18. Before posing for this publicity shot in 1971 at Grossinger's Hotel, Fischer insisted that the position be set up correctly and that he have the winning side! Larry Evans served as his second for part of the match that Fischer ultimately played with Petrosian.
(U.S.I.S.)

GENS UNA SUMUS

19., 20., 21. The perceptive cartooning of Hálldor Pétursson filled the pages of Iceland's newspapers almost daily during the Fischer-Spassky match of 1972. At upper left (No. 19) Fischer is shown carrying a sack of money cynically labeled "principles" in his quest for the World Championship. Spassky's "castle" is kept up by Geller, assisted by Nei. In the center of the protagonists are arbiters Schmid, Arnlaugsson, and Golombek. Lower left (No. 20), Fischer is depicted as a Knight who would rather fight Chester Fox, owner of the disputed film rights, stationed in the camera tower that Fischer objected to. Above (No. 21) Fischer finally seizes the crown as Dr. Euwe desperately attempts to keep it under FIDE's jurisdiction, perhaps fearful of Fischer's disregard for the world Chess Federation.

22. Fischer emerged from a plane from New York, just hours before forfeiting the game for non-appearance.

23. Arriving at Laugersdalholl for the first game, Fischer is besieged by a barrage of well-wishers and media personnel.

24. After the third game, Fischer's first victory over Spassky in over a decade of trying, he exits from the stadium buoyant with hope, confident of winning the World's Championship.

25. Relaxing between games, Fischer walks with Paalson, his bodyguard, in center, and Lombardy, his second, in front of the Hotel Loftleider. (TIMINN)

26. Just minutes before leaving Iceland after his match with Spassky, Fischer stopped off at the National Museum to inscribe the World's Championship table and board for posterity.

it as the spiritual energy or the super-brilliance of a turbulent, creative master that it is.

The simplistic beauty of his game is the element that confuses those he plays and produces paradoxical comments like Petrosian's ". . . he did not play that well," referring to Fischer's magnificent victory at Palma. The chess world expects the deep and fiery style of a Nimzovich or the sacrificial genre of a Spielmann to be the proper *modus operandi* of their heroes. And that is why the Fischer mystique is even more complex. While his opponents are clamoring for grand schemes and intricate themes, Fischer gives them precision and clarity in an almost mathematical purity.

The beauty of Fischer's style lies in his immense knowledge, his ability to calculate deeply and without error, his immaculate technique, his dependable memory, his effortless and thoroughly rehearsed systems, and, for the major part of his career, even his circumscribed repertoire. Though there is much to be learned from the depths of his iceberg, his chess signature is there for all to see; a study in constant control, each move having its structural justification in a search for the supreme truth of the board.

Bobby Fischer seemed to have come of age at Palma, and though he was still his severest critic ("I am satisfied with the result, but not with my play.") he proved himself to be, without question—fighter, strategist, positionist, innovator, and gentleman—the equal of any master in the annals of chess. Thinking about his previous Interzonal attempt and his fleeing that had become a nightmare to him, he said: "Maybe this was a good thing. I didn't have the maturity to handle it then." He had it at Palma.

CHAPTER XXIV

"Chess is like war on a board."

Fischer remained in Spain as the guest of Roman Toran for almost two months before returning to the United States to prepare himself for his ten-game match with Mark Taimanov.

Fischer had failed in his first Candidates attempt in Yugoslavia in 1959, and in his second in Curaçao in 1962, and an apologist might cite as the underlying reasons his youthful inexperience in the former case and his emotional problems in the latter. But Fischer felt that in both events he was "gang raped" by the Russians, who, with short and premeditated draws, controlled the tournaments. He claimed that they "stole" the championship from him. For years, he had felt that a tournament was an inaccurate test of a player's ability. As a result of his repeated urgings, FIDE had changed its system and eliminated the Candidates Tournament, replacing it with matches among the principals. Fischer still felt the system needed improvement: he wanted only wins to be counted (the winner of the first six or ten games, for example) but at least most of his objections had been removed.

After the quarter-finals, the winner of the Petrosian-Hübner match would play the winner of the Korchnoi-Geller match and, in Bobby's section, the winner of his match against Taimanov would meet the high scorer of the Larsen-Uhlmann fight. Fischer's prognosis was candid: "I believe it will now be the first time that both finalists in the Candidates Matches are not from the Soviet Union. I don't think that Taimanov in our group can defeat both me and Larsen. I hope it will be Larsen or me who plays for the title against Spassky, but it is difficult to make predictions. In short matches, surprises are possible." The quarter and semi-finals consisted of ten games each. The final was to be a twelve-game match.

Though concert pianist Mark Taimanov was considered a dangerous opponent, most serious critics predicted a win, though perhaps a difficult one, for Fischer. The Russian had not played in a Candidates event since 1953 and had only managed to place far down the list even then. In the past year, however, he seemed to be playing some of the best chess of his life, and his performance at Palma was convincing. He was happy that the pairings pitted him against Fischer in the first sequence of the finals because, as he stated, he had nothing to lose and everything to gain, competing with the favorite. "To play with a superb chessplayer like Fischer is highly interesting," he said. Critics pointed to his age, forty-five, as a very possible handicap in a highly charged and world publicized match. Fischer was twenty-eight and in perfect physical shape.

Fischer's ultimate chance of going through the entire Candidates cycle without an incident was in itself highly questionable. Besting each formidable opponent in tension-filled matches spread over six tiring months was a task whose outcome defied unanimous prediction. Larry Evans told people in New York that Fischer's chances of an ultimate shot at Spassky were ". . . one in a million," for a variety of reasons unsubstantiated by elaboration.

Harry Golombek wrote in the London *Times*: "Undoubtedly, the answer from all of those who were watching the Interzonal at Palma (with the exception of a minority blinded by national prejudices) would be Fischer. Such weaknesses as he has (a tendency to underestimate the opposition and a carelessness as regards technical matters in the ending) can obviously be ironed out in the preparation for the matches and in most respects he is superior to the opposition he will have to face this year." Golombek continued with a prediction that Fischer would win the finals of the Candidates, especially if he had to face Korchnoi in the last round. Korchnoi himself thought that Fischer and Petrosian had the best chances and Tal predicted 5½–4½ for Bobby against Taimanov. C.H.O'D. Alexander, who was one of England's finest players, was hardly unsure: "I think Fischer will win the Candidates, he is a clearly stronger player than Larsen, and his other main rivals Petrosian, Korchnoi, and Geller are all past their best—the youngest, Korchnoi, is forty this year." It's almost a cliché to note that Lasker placed high among tournament prize winners even in his late sixties, but it is true that once a player reaches forty, he usually experiences at least some decline in calculating faculty and ability to recall positions, to say nothing of loss of stamina, especially if the match or tournament is a prolonged affair. Fischer had the last word, though, and he appeared unusually unsure: "I am not in the best shape. I feel I am not sufficiently played in. I need more tournaments. Candidates matches require thorough preparations. I have so far played matches only with Cardoso (1956) and Reshevsky (1961)."* In the nine previous months, however, Fischer had played seventy-six tournament games, which had to be some sort of unofficial record for activity for him. Why he felt he had

---

* And Exhibition Matches with Larsen, Euwe, Matulovic, and Janosevic.

to have more competition in order to "play himself in," remains a mystery. He was more than ready, only he didn't know it, or wasn't allowing himself to believe it. This trait of taking nothing for granted is one of the keys to Fischer's success. Trusting nothing or no one, not even himself, he is ready for any eventuality and approaches each chess battle with the solemnity of an examination in which he stakes his entire reputation not only on the final outcome but on every miniscule detail.

All the matches were scheduled to start on the same day, May 13— Korchnoi vs. Geller in Moscow with Mikenas as referee; Larsen vs. Uhlmann at Las Palmas (Canary Islands) with Heinze as referee; Petrosian vs. Hübner at Seville with Golombek as referee; and Fischer vs. Taimanov at Vancouver, British Columbia, with Kazic as referee.

While Fischer was in New York he made arrangements for Evans to be his second once again but Ken Smith, writing in *Chess Digest*, thought that the possibilities of the two working together might be aborted: "If Fischer was easy to get along with, he would not be Fischer. I doubt (but hope so) that Evans will make it all the way as second. There will be problems before Fischer finishes this cycle of world championship matches."

Smith, Evans, and Fischer met in New York on April 20th, to discuss advance preparations and other details pertinent to the match. Smith humorously relates: "Of all the famous restaurants in New York to pick from—Fischer and Evans outvoted me—and we went to a Japanese steak house. My legs were walked off by Fischer and Evans. They never heard of a taxi." Perhaps Smith didn't know that Fischer is a classic, Whitmanesque walker. It's one of his favorite pastimes. Usually, only the energetic and long-legged survive as companions. As a writer for *Life* magazine observed, Fischer ". . . walked with a powerful rambling stride that made him look like Captain Ahab making headway in a high wind . . . he walked for about twenty blocks through the city night at a pace that made me feel like Dopey the Dwarf scrambling to keep up with the big folks."

Fischer set three conditions in determining whether Evans was to be his second. The first was that he did not want Evans to engage in any journalism (Evans had been writing for *Chess Life*, *Chess Digest*, and *Sports Illustrated*, among a number of other publications) while he was at Vancouver. He wanted Evans to concentrate on his games and not on anything else. For that same reason, Bobby objected to Evans's request that his wife accompany him. Too distracting, said Bobby. Finally, Evans told Fischer that he had a project that would take him back to his home in Reno for a few days and that he would meet Bobby in Vancouver. This is where the negotiations foundered though they really could not agree on some of the other points either. Fischer wanted Evans to be in Vancouver on the very day he arrived there, and the two could not come to terms. Hence, Fischer went to British Columbia and played in the most important match of his life to date, without the benefit of a second. He was accompanied by Edmondson, who served as his sounding-board and companion. The match site was the beautiful campus of the University of British Columbia.

Taimanov, on the other hand, arrived with the usual Russian entourage: Vasiukov came as his second, Balashov as an assistant and Kotov as match manager. The U.S.A.-U.S.S.R. confrontation started almost immediately, before the games even began, a tiring charade of inevitable brinksmanship. It's sad and silly that it's often so difficult just to play chess.

On Wednesday, May 12th, the first rumblings of protest came from the Russians who were unhappy over the TV room of the Graduate Centre, where the match was to be played. "I can't breathe in this room," complained Taimanov. It was too small. Fischer also objected to the size of the room but later changed his mind and said he would play there. A frantic search was made by the University officials with Kotov and Edmondson to find a hall that was agreeable to all. The Centre's library was approved by the chess faction but not by the University. Classics Dean Malcolm McGregor vetoed the use of the library on the grounds that he couldn't bar students from one of their most important gathering spots. Kotov and McGregor went at it. "Tell them to stop acting like children," McGregor commanded. He said that the TV room had been accepted for play by the Canadian Chess Federation and the two players should be just "told" that they *must* play there. This produced a vehement rebuttal from Kotov, who threatened to take the four-man "team" home to Russia because of the lack of hospitality. Anyway, he couldn't understand why the match was to be played in Canada: "Spain yes, Belgrade yes. But Canada? No, no, no," he said sarcastically. Of course, Kotov was right. The players had to have proper conditions and if the UBC could not provide them, some other venue would have to be found.

Other problems developed. Fischer wanted to bar spectators from the match. Taimanov, accustomed to crowds from his days as a pianist, wanted to play the match in the University Auditorium. Dr. Max Euwe, who had a premonition that his presence would be needed, was asked to solve the spectator problem. He ruled that each Federation could "nominate" two spectators to be present during every game. The search for a room continued. Each new choice brought new problems. Adequate lighting had to be installed. Furniture had to be removed. Instead of starting on Thursday, as scheduled, the match didn't get under way until Sunday, the 16th, four days later. Euwe ruled that the match would be played in the Student Union Building movie theater and two hundred spectators were ultimately allowed to watch. By this time even Fischer had become disgusted with all the pettiness. "Let's play," he said. "I'm willing to play anywhere!"

Before the first game Fischer played a round of tennis with Robert Byrne, who was at the match site as a reporter, and consequently showed up at the tournament hall ten minutes late. His clock was running but it didn't seem to bother him at all. Taimanov, who is known for his love of 1 P-Q4 as much as Fischer is for his 1 P-K4, had the White pieces and played his favorite move, against which Fischer established a King's Indian Defense. As early as the twelfth move, Taimanov lost a Pawn. Fischer faltered slightly soon after but the Russian failed to take proper advantage. After forty moves and five hours of play the game was adjourned in a hopeless position for Taimanov. He resigned without further play. This was an important win for Bobby since he had the Black pieces and immediately demonstrated his superiority.

Fischer asked Kazic, the referee, to disallow the use of pocket sets by spectators while he played. He stated that during the first game his concentration had been severely marred when someone dropped a traveling set and a commotion ensued. In the second game he arrived late again, though this time only five minutes after the appointed hour. As Black, Taimanov played the Sicilian Defense and Fischer varied his sixth move from the one he had already played with Taimanov at Palma, to a line he had not utilized since his game against Najdorf at the Piatigorsky Cup in 1966.

The game went to eighty-nine moves, took over nine and a half hours to play and was conducted over a three day span. After the second adjournment, Fischer stormed out of the building, following an angry exchange with Kazic. Finding Taimanov's pacing distracting, Fischer had asked for its curtailment while he was thinking, and Kazic had declined to take action on the matter. Before the second game was finished the third was begun and Taimanov quickly found himself in time pressure and was forced to give up his Queen for Fischer's Rook and Bishop. The third game was also adjourned.

The Russians now approached Fischer with the following proposition: Taimanov would resign the third game without resumption if Fischer would agree to a draw in the second, correctly pointing out that the position was a dead draw: Fischer's King, Bishop, and Pawn were pitted against Taimanov's King and Knight and it seemed to be an easy matter to trade Knight for Pawn. Fischer, however, felt he had nothing to gain by accepting the offer. He knew he would win the third game, anyway, and as long as he had a Pawn on the board, as in his second game, there was always a chance of winning, however infinitesimal. He was criticized for this attitude and action. The third game was then played to a conclusion. Fischer won.

In the second game, Taimanov, perhaps plagued by fatigue or irritation, fell victim to an almost unbelievable blunder allowing Fischer to advance the Pawn to the queening square. He resigned in absolute disgust.

Fischer felt that the turning point of the match had already been reached. Out of the remaining seven games, he needed only 2½ points to clinch the victory and it was unthinkable, comparing the caliber of his play to Taimanov's in the current match, that he could not do that with ease.

The Memorial Day weekend was at hand and the match had to be temporarily postponed due to Taimanov's health. He had complained of not feeling well and after a cursory medical examination his symptoms were first described as heart palpitations. Taken to St. Paul's hospital, he was given an electrocardiogram, with negative results. On further examination his illness was diagnosed as high blood pressure, and he was ordered to rest for forty-eight hours before the resumption of the match.

Psychosomatic repercussions notwithstanding, the fourth game began on Tuesday and Taimanov conducted the Taimanov variation of the Sicilian Defense against Fischer's White pieces. Once again he entered an endgame which was hopelessly inferior. He resigned on the seventy-first move, strangled by *zugzwang*. Taimanov was devastated. He saw himself entering chess history possibly unable to win or draw a single game against his famous opponent. As he had long abandoned hopes of winning the match itself, his major concern had become a desperate attempt to garner just one half-point.

Even though they continued to fight, the match, in effect, was all over. In the next game, Taimanov still played strong chess but seemed to wait either for Fischer to produce a brilliant stroke or for himself to blunder. He obliged on his forty-fifth move. In a position that looked as if it might be a draw, he gave away a Rook, the most shocking mistake of his career. Taimanov left the tournament room dazed, almost in tears. Fischer could hardly believe what had happened.

Bobby now needed only a draw to be awarded the match, but he still played the last game as though it were the first when he had everything to struggle for. He played for a win while Taimanov opted for a draw. The result was dynamism on Fischer's part, obtuseness on Taimanov's. The Russian adjourned in a lost position and resigned without continuation. The date: June 2nd; Fischer's score: 6–0.

Bobby Fischer's result was incredible. In the history of the game, perhaps only one other match shutout could surpass it: the 1876 Steinitz 7–0 victory over Blackburne, who was comparable in strength to Taimanov. With the exception of his short four-game contest with Petrosian in the Great Match, Fischer had had difficulties for years in series play against the top Soviets. Though such a resounding defeat of Taimanov indicated that the Russian was terribly off form (and his two mammoth blunders would substantiate that belief), the fantasy of one of the world's leading players being unable to draw *even one game* was almost too surreal to accept. *Obviously*, it was said in chess circles around the world, Taimanov gave Fischer the match because of his poor health. But chess ablibis of that ilk are as old as the game itself. No, Fischer's superlative playing strength won the first few games and then a combination of that ability and his opponent's fear won the remainder. Fischer succeeded in his match against Taimanov because he was a better player. Kotov said after the match: "I expected Fischer to beat Taimanov fairly easily and I expect him to beat Larsen." And Taimanov commented: "Fischer undoubtedly is the best non-Soviet player I have met in my nineteen years of international competition as a grandmaster." It seemed as if his life, or certainly his chess career was over as he sadly commented to Fischer at the conclusion: "Well, I still have my music."

CHAPTER XXV

*"I am the best player in the world
and I am here to prove it."*

The other quarter-final matches were won by Larsen over Uhlmann at 5½–3½, by Petrosian over Hübner by 4–3, and by Korchnoi over Geller by 5½–2½. The semi-final match players were Petrosian and Korchnoi, who played in Moscow, and Larsen and Fischer, who played in Denver. Fischer stayed on in the Pacific Northwest for a few weeks and then flew to New York, remaining there briefly before forging on to Colorado.

A number of cities had been considered and had bid for the Fischer-Larsen match, such as New York, Miami, Los Angeles, and Dallas, but the mile-high city of Denver was finally chosen. Larsen had agreed to play in America (all the other matches were held in neutral countries) since he had enjoyed his many visits here and was highly popular among United States chessplayers. Comparable to Fischer in his utter disdain of the draw, Larsen is known as one of the most forceful scrappers in contemporary chess. Whereas Taimanov was considered to be one of the ten best players in the world at the time of his match with Fischer, Larsen was thought to be one of the best of perhaps four or five supermasters and world's championship contenders. His five consecutive victories in powerful tournaments in the late Sixties had earned him the respect of every player in serious competition. In addition, his optimism and self-confidence seemed even greater than Fischer's. When asked what his chances in the Candidates were, he answered emphatically: "The new World Champion in 1972 will be Bent Larsen!" Fischer had his work cut out for him. The match had all of the drama that a chess duel could muster: the two most successful tournament players of our age, both sworn to an almost *kamikaze* approach to win, competing for a right to a match with the Champion of the world. Their lifetime score consisted of three wins for Fischer, two wins for Larsen and but a single draw.

The match got under way on July 6th at 4 P.M., in the midst of an uncomfortable 100-degree heat wave. Larsen had the Black pieces and played the French Defense against Bobby's then nearly inevitable

1 P–K4. Before the game had begun, Larsen said he had prepared some innovations for Fischer and it appeared he had, since Larsen had not played the French in years. As the game developed, Larsen was prevented from or failed to castle (depending on who's annotating) on the Queenside and ultimately initiated an attack in the center. In a personally ruinous attempt at complication, Larsen allowed Fischer to give up his Queen while retaining a Rook, two Bishops, and two Pawns, while Larsen emerged with a Queen, four Pawns, plenty of positional problems and only ten minutes left to make seven moves. The Dane resigned on his forty-first move. Once again, Fischer started off right, winning the first game and gaining the psychological and mathematical advantage from the onset. Bobby knew what he was doing.

In the second game, Larsen had a draw in hand but pushed himself into a hopeless search for a win, resulting in an easy endgame for Fischer with three passed Pawns. Eyewitnesses have said that after the loss of the second game Larsen began to become demoralized; two days later when he lost the third game in a row, and it looked like another Taimanov fiasco all over again, he became thoroughly morose. Changing strategy in the fourth game, Larsen played for a closed game and got it but he was unable to make any headway against Fischer's defense. Eventually Bobby won the Exchange and Larsen resigned on the thirty-fourth move. The score in favor of Fischer: 4–0.

Like Taimanov, Larsen also fell victim to high blood pressure (which Anthony Saidy, not so humorously, suggests might be an occupational disease of Fischer's opponents) and a four-day rest was ordered by the doctor before resumption of the fifth game. While Larsen tried to recuperate, Fischer played tennis and appeared not to have a worry on his mind.

In the fifth game, Larsen once again played for a win, spurning whatever drawing possibilities did develop (and they were there). He mishandled the game, and resigned before adjournment. And even though he could have had a perpetual check in the final game of the match, Larsen went for the kill, overextended himself and lost. The sixth game ended at 9 P.M. on July 20th. This time Fischer *had* achieved what no one else had ever accomplished in chess: winning two Grandmaster matches without drawing or losing a single game in a gargantuan spurt of mental energy. Counting his seven last games at Palma, his six against Taimanov, and six against Larsen, he had established an unprecedented winning streak of nineteen straight games, surpassing the great Wilhelm Steinitz's record of sixteen straight, in Vienna 1873.

The arguments that Fischer's annihilation of Taimanov was an aberration, a freak accident that had no logical explanation, were themselves annihilated after Fischer's defeat of Larsen. The Dane just didn't have a chance and Fischer verified that he was in a class by himself. International Grandmaster Robert Byrne was astonished: ". . . it is out of the question for me to explain how Bobby, how anyone, could win six games in a row from such a genius of the game as Bent Larsen." A number of American players, though giddy over the most sensational victory ever achieved on these shores, were sorry to see Larsen, in his prime, as humbled as he was. Burt Hochberg, writing in *Chess Life* & *Review*, kindly stated: "However much we share with Fischer the joy and triumph of his Olympian victory, we cannot help feeling a touch of sadness for Larsen's monstrous defeat."

The Russians were, at first blush, elated, since it lessened the stigma of humiliation foisted upon Taimanov, but they were as bewildered as the rest of the chessworld. *Sovietsky Sport* declared that "A miracle has occurred," and television and radio broadcasts were interrupted throughout the Soviet Union to announce the result.

Fischer's victory, to chessplayers, produced more comment, excitement, and pride than America's putting a man on the moon. Most chessplayers always knew Fischer was *good*, but this result proved he was matchless, undoubtedly one of the strongest players in all chess history. Fischer said little about his victory over Larsen, but when pressed, he explained in his typically blunt and honest way: "I played pretty well."

At the conclusion of his match with Larsen, Fischer conferred by telephone with an officer of the Manhattan Chess Club and arranged to participate in an invitational speed tournament on August 8th, to celebrate the official opening of the club's new quarters. Fischer arrived in New York on August 5th and was met at the plane by Rosser Reeves, then president of the Manhattan Chess Club. Reeves recounted: "When we arrived at the Park Sheraton Hotel, where we had reserved a beautiful suite for Fischer with a commanding view of the skyline of New York, he courteously informed us that the quarters weren't to his liking and then proceeded to select a very small and inconspicuous room which had no view at all. When I asked him why he preferred the second room, he said he wanted to be able to study and prepare for his match with Petrosian without benefit of street noises or visual distractions."

Fischer's quest for a modern-day monk's cell is just another indication of his fantastic dedication to chess.

A number of the Club's better players were attending the U.S. Open, and so the field Fischer faced was not the strongest that might have been mustered from the Manhattan Chess Club's illustrious roster. It was a double round robin event with twelve masters and grandmasters competing. After delaying the start of the first few rounds until he could have lox on bagels, with several glasses of milk, Fischer proceeded to trounce almost everyone in sight, uncharacteris-

tically agreeing to playing all of his games at the front of the club to
insure maximum spectator visibility. He had a marvelous time. Walter
Shipman, who drew with him in the last round at Cleveland, 1957,
giving the fourteen-year-old Bobby the U.S. Open Championship, was
the only player who could draw against him that night in the speed
tournament. Bobby's final score was 21½–½. Andrew Soltis and
Robert Byrne were second and third, respectively.

Fischer's World's Championship quest, through the Interzonal and
the quarter and semi-finals of the Candidates, had finally brought him
to the place many of his followers never really believed he would
reach. On September 20, 1971, Bobby was due to play a twelve-game
match against former World Champion Tigran Petrosian. The winner
of the match would play Boris Spassky for the Championship of the
World.

Any prognostication as to the outcome of Fischer's match with
Petrosian depended on your personal opinion. One theory was that
Fischer would emulsify Petrosian. All one needed to do, it was
argued, was compare their respective scores in the Candidates and
then consider Fischer's 3–1 victory over Petrosian in the Great Match.
The opposing point of view offered that the lifetime score of Fischer
and Petrosian was even: three wins each and twelve drawn games,
and that Petrosian had been Champion of the World, had maintained
the throne for six years, and was well known to be one of the most
difficult players in the world to defeat. True, he played a closed,
defensive, almost catatonic game, like a motionless but watchful
snake, ready to strike the moment his opponent makes the slightest
mistake—whereas Bobby's style of relentless aggression shows in
marked contrast. The differences of their philosophies of the game
were used as arguments *for* Petrosian, with his adherents stating that
he was prepared to engage in the most classical waiting-game of his
life, hoping to capitalize on an eventual impetuous move by Fischer.
In his last sixty-two tournament and match games, Petrosian had lost
only two: but both had been to Fischer. Reuben Fine's opinion of the
Armenian was rather low: "Petrosian is probably the weakest player
who has ever held the world's championship." Conversely, it was offered, Fischer was probably the strongest player *never* to have held
the world's championship.

Spassky's view of the Fischer-Petrosian match, though he might be
accused of chauvinism, was revealing: "Fischer can always be counted
on to play a strong game but Petrosian is stronger. Not having en-
countered the strongest opposition throughout his life, the American
grandmaster could not receive the proper training as a chessplayer.
In his match with Petrosian, sooner or later he will meet with an
uncomfortable position and it is not yet known how he will conduct
himself in such a situation."

Larry Evans gained the support of most Americans when he laconically commented in an article in *Time* magazine: "The only way Petrosian can beat Bobby is by boring him to death."

The arguments over where the match would be played had started months before. France, Yugoslavia, Greece, and Argentina were bidding for the contest. Fischer favored Argentina because of the money, and Yugoslavia because of his popularity there. Later, Fischer and Petrosian involved themselves directly in the negotiations. Svetozar Gligoric, acting as translator, arranged a three-way telephone conversation between Fischer in New York, Petrosian in Moscow, and himself in Belgrade. Here are excerpts from the stenographic record of that memorable conversation:

Gligoric: [To Fischer]. Where would you like to play?

Fischer: The biggest prize to the winner is offered in Argentina and besides that, this country is close to the United States, where I live.

Gligoric: [To Fischer]. Don't you think the match could take place in Europe:

Fischer: I am sure that the Russians will decline Argentina, and I suppose they do not care one way or another whether to play in Yugoslavia or Greece. For them, the most important thing is to remain in Europe. There are many reasons for that. They don't accomplish much on the Western Hemisphere. I recall that the match with U.S.A. in 1954 was not an easy one for them, but when the Americans came to the Soviet Union, they lost very quickly. The Russians remember things like this and because of that there will be a fight to determine the location.

Petrosian: Tell him that I will not go to Buenos Aires. Why should I go to his hemisphere to meet him? He is a young man and has already played two matches in America. Let's meet halfway somewhere . . .

Gligoric: Fischer says that the financial conditions are best in Argentina.

Petrosian: I understand. I am not against good conditions but there are other things.

Gligoric: [To Fischer]: Say, Bobby, perhaps there is some other place?

Fischer: Buenos Aires is the best. It's a pretty city and they make excellent steaks there.

Petrosian: For me, climate and general conditions are most important, not financial.

Fischer: Money is not that important to him because his government helps him.

Petrosian: Fischer also has a government. Let it help him. I am not a young man anymore* and it is important to me where I play not only based on financial considerations.

Fischer: The maximum financial offer and the experience that they have had [in staging other chess matches] are to the advantage of Argentina. I think FIDE will speak out for Argentina.

Petrosian [indignantly]: FIDE doesn't have any right to force me. If it tries to do this, Fischer will play someone else, not me.

Petrosian said later that Gligoric translated Fischer's last statement as: "FIDE will decide anyway that play will take place in Argentina," and that this is what irritated him. It all mattered not, however, since shortly afterward, when it became obvious that the two men could not come to agreement on a match site, FIDE chose lots for the host city and Buenos Aires, ironically, won the draw.

Fischer arrived in Buenos Aires a few days before the start of the first round, which had been moved forward to Thursday, September 30th. He was accompanied by Evans (who apparently had solved all of his previous difficulties with Fischer) and the ever-present Edmund B. Edmondson, his manager-representative. Petrosian came with Alexei Suetin and Yuri Averbakh as his seconds, his manager Viktor Baturinsky, and his wife Rona. He also had two bodyguards!

On September 29th, the public drawing for the first round colors was held at the San Martín Theater in the traditional manner. Fischer was given a White and a Black Pawn, and placed his hands behind his back. He complained that the Pawns were too big, since if he brought his hands in front of him Petrosian would be able to discern the colors. He was allowed to keep his hands behind his back, and Petrosian tapped his left arm. Fischer's left hand held the Black Pawn.

After the drawing, but before the first round, the players were received by the Argentinian President, Lieutenant General Alejandro Lanusse, and official photographs were taken. Both Fischer and Petrosian were presented with personal gifts from *El Presidente*, beautiful marble boards with onyx chessmen. Lanusse promised to attend some of the rounds.

Reporters asked Petrosian whether the match would last the full twelve games. "It might be possible that I win it earlier," was his reply. He went on, in what seemed to be a masterpiece of calculation:

* Petrosian was born in 1929.

"Fischer's wins do not impress me. He is a great chess player but no genius. I am glad to face him directly. I do not envy his triumphs and they cannot influence me, because I had many experiences of the same nature. I am not afraid of his aggressiveness. In chess, many factors play their role. Physically, I feel excellent. I have prepared myself conscientiously for this match. I am confident that I will play accurately and well. For me, chess is more than just a sport. It has a relationship to intellectual development and to art."

Fischer would not be flapped. Instead of directing any criticism at his opponent, he made a statement that he felt to be factual, practical, and to the point. In some ways, they are the most important three sentences he's ever uttered: "I am the best player in the world, and I am here to prove it. I have waited ten years for this moment but I was hindered by Russian maneuvers. I shall depart from Buenos Aires before the twelfth game is scheduled."

Captain Francisco Manrique, Minister of Social Welfare, said a few words of greeting, and International Grandmaster Carlos Guimard opened the ceremony by referring to the historic match between Capablanca and Alekhine for the Championship of the World, which took place in Buenos Aires in 1927.

Thousands of chess fans lined up in front of the theater as early as 9 A.M. on the first day of the match, so they would be guaranteed a seat when play began at 5 P.M. Over fifteen hundred followers were not admitted because of lack of space, and were forced to follow the game via the giant wallboard constructed in the lobby. Grandmasters Miguel Najdorf and Herman Pilnik commented on each move for those who couldn't gain admission. International Grandmaster Lothar Schmid was referee.

Originally, it had been arranged to have the games played on the same board and with the same pieces as the famed Capablanca-Alekhine match of 1927, but Carlos Guimard had a better idea: "The Argentine Chess Club offered the Alekhine-Capablanca board and pieces to us but I didn't accept for one simple reason. This event is also one that deserves to go down in history and when it ends we will be able to say as a reminder of the game: 'On this board played Fischer and Petrosian.' "

Petrosian appeared on stage first and, after taking his seat, asked whether he could have a harder chair. A number of chairs were collected from different spots in the auditorium and he picked the hardest, most unornamented one. Soon Fischer appeared, bedecked in a brightly colored tie, perhaps symbolically emblazoned with stars. "It was a last minute whim," he laughed. "I bought it this morning in front of the hotel," no doubt unaware that Capablanca was often "accused" of intimidating his opponents by wearing wildly patterned ties.

The first game was astonishing. It was thought that Petrosian would be on his best conservative behavior and go directly for a draw, in an attempt to break Fischer's winning streak, thereby establishing a degree of psychological equality and stability. Fischer, eager to continue his uninterrupted record, could be counted on to jab incessantly at any of Petrosian's positional weaknesses and to initiate and maintain complications until he could ultimately overpower him. Exactly the opposite occurred.

Petrosian became the unrecognizable aggressor; and Fischer was relegated to defensive tactics, in what must have been a thoroughly distasteful and unfamiliar role. A Sicilian Defense, it followed the same moves as the sixth game of the Fischer-Taimanov match, until Petrosian introduced a "*novinka*" on his eleventh move, an innovation no doubt supplied by the Russian theorists who toil ceaselessly to produce moves of this type, to be launched at just such necessary moments. Petrosian gave up a Pawn and gained the aggression. Fischer was forced to exchange pieces. In what was an apparently even ending, Petrosian began to repeat moves, thereby in effect offering a draw. But Fischer spied an opportunity of obtaining a passed Pawn, and gained it.

Suddenly, the lights went out. Literally. The theater was plunged into darkness. Fischer became alarmed: "What happened? What happened?" he said. He was told that a fuse had blown and that it would take a few minutes to replace. Petrosian left the board; Fischer and the audience of twelve hundred continued to sit in darkened silence. Eventually Petrosian complained that Fischer was still studying the board (in his head? without light?) and that his clock should be started. Fischer agreed, and Schmid started the clock in motion. Fischer continued to evaluate the position without seeing it. Eleven minutes later the lights went back on.

Petrosian soon strayed into time pressure, and instead of trying to blockade the passed Pawn, he foolishly attempted some countermeasures of his own. It was too little and too late. He resigned on the fortieth move, giving Bobby Fischer his twentieth straight win. Both players left the theater immediately, declining statements, interviews, or photographs being sought by the army of assembled media representatives.

A head cold, which was real and apparent enough, plagued Bobby in the second round. He played his Gruenfeld, but was clearly off form. Again, Petrosian attacked; and again Fischer defended, in what could only be described as "unconscious role-reversal." Not only did both players cast off their normal game psychology, but they appeared to switch personalities as well.

Fischer fished for simplification and attempted to manipulate the game into the ending, but Petrosian was relentless. Unable to coordinate his Rooks, and with Petrosian's center Pawns steadily, beadily advancing, Fischer found no adequate defense. He offered a handshake and his resignation. The crowd went wild. Rona Petrosian rushed to her husband's side and embraced him. A victory chant began in the auditorium and spread to the outer lobby and street: *"Tigran un Tigre!—Tigran un Tigre!"* Some players actually rushed the stage and tried, in football star fashion, to shoulder the basking Petrosian, but officials intervened. He had just accomplished what the finest players in the world were thoroughly unable to do on twenty occasions in the previous nine months: he won a game from Bobby Fischer.

"I've been seeing too many people," was all that Fischer said and for the next ten days confined his audiences to the young Argentine player Miguel Quinteros.

In the third game, Petrosian played the French Defense against Bobby's 1 P–K4 and gained an advantage, though not necessarily a clear-cut one. Fischer's sole plus factor was his stock in trade: the clock. After the thirtieth move, he had a full thirty minutes to complete his last ten moves. Petrosian had barely three minutes to do the same. Petrosian began to move rapidly, too rapidly, trying to reach the fortieth move and adjournment without unbalancing his favorable position. He failed to realize that his moves repeated the identical position after Fischer's thirtieth, thirty-second, and thirty-fourth moves, and the game was drawn on Fischer's claim. It was a narrow escape.

The fourth game disappointed the crowds. Whereas the other three encounters, though not perfect displays of chess at its finest, showed a desire to fight on both their parts, number four ended quickly with Petrosian apparently not wanting to initiate anything and Fischer unable to do so. They exchanged Queens early. A few moves later, the Rooks and Knights also came off the board. Fischer offered a draw just as he made his twentieth move and Petrosian accepted immediately.

The fifth game was also drawn. Petrosian played a Petroff Defense, which is rarely seen in contemporary grandmaster play, and Fischer gained the advantage and established a passed Pawn, but was unable to steer the game into a winning position. The point was halved on the thirty-eighth move. The score was 2½–2½. After three successive draws, Petrosian was proving that he was in thorough command of himself and the situation and that unlike the tortured Taimanov, he was going to return to his homeland in an honorable fashion. Some players felt that Fischer might have lost his touch, played himself too hard, too soon, at the beginning of the Candidates cycle, and now, due to poor pacing, was slowing up. Petrosian, on the other hand, was employing the brand of strategy that he had built his career on: draw, draw, and draw again until his opponent experienced the slimmest of inaccuracies, whereupon he would pounce . . . and win. He had just finished doing exactly that with Korchnoi, and was now attempting the same with Fischer.

But now it was the time for Fischer. Despite another incident during the sixth game,* Bobby managed to secure a strong position and after the adjournment had been resumed (it was the first time in the match that a game had gone beyond the five-hour limit) he caught Petrosian in a mating net, forcing the Armenian's resignation after the sixty-sixth move.

In the seventh game, Fischer played imperially, and produced his best game of the match. Petrosian played the Sicilian Defense and had two isolated Pawns upon emerging from the opening. Fischer hammered and chiseled at the two Pawns, increasing his pressure on them and on the entire position until Petrosian was forced thoroughly on the defensive. After an incursion of Fischer's two Rooks to his seventh rank, it was all over. Petrosian played a few more moves and resigned.

Like Taimanov and Larsen before him, Petrosian also fell ill during his match with Fischer. Dr. Carlos Skiliar, the official physician of the Argentine Chess Federation, stated that the forty-eight-year-old Petrosian was suffering from low blood pressure, and he ordered a few days' rest. It was apparent that Petrosian was debilitated from nervous exhaustion. Before the commencement of the eighth game, Fischer was supremely confident, not only of the outcome of the current match, but of his chances in the next one. "I shall dethrone Spassky," he somewhat formally proclaimed.

During the eighth round, the lights went out again. This time there was darkness for only eight minutes. Fischer, as Black, played the Tarrasch Defense, which often terminates in a draw after an early exchange of pieces. An attack on both wings was put into motion by both players and Petrosian sacrificed a Pawn to maintain the initiative. Eventually, however, Fischer countered by gaining a passed Pawn, and since he was a Pawn to the good and began an attack himself, Petrosian resigned. It was Fischer's fourth victory of the match. It was becoming obvious that he could not be stopped.

There were over ten thousand chess fans in the playing hall, the lobby, and in the street in front of the building at the start of the ninth game of the match. Even in Russia, chess crowds of this magnitude were unknown. If Fischer could win the game, he would be the first non-Soviet player in twenty-three years to have had a direct opportunity to play a match for the World's Championship and he would

---

* Unrelated to chess, twenty-two gas bombs were set off in the auditorium, apparently placed there by anti-Peronists (it was a remembrance day for the deposed leader). They had an overwhelming stench, and the hall had to be closed. When Fischer was informed of what happened, he said: "Are the gas bombs poison?" and when told that they were not, he continued his game.

be the first American to do so since Frank J. Marshall played Lasker
in 1907. (Reshevsky played in the World's Championship *tournament*
in 1948 to determine a successor to Alexander Alekhine.)

Fischer was White. Petrosian tried the French again, but played a
different variation from the one he played in the third game. It netted
a doubled Pawn in the center and though to most players such a
minor flaw would not be enough to capitalize upon, Fischer tortured
the weakness unmercifully. Petrosian knew that defensive tactics, in
this game at any rate, would net him nothing, and he began a counterattack. At one point, he constructed a mating net and might have
been able to sacrifice his Rook to force Bobby to resign. Unworried,
Bobby wouldn't let him. At the exact moment to insure victory,
Fischer gave up his Knight for two of Petrosian's Pawns. The final
position consisted of five Pawns and a King for Fischer, and a King,
Knight, and Pawn for Petrosian. There was no way that he could stop
the advance of Fischer's connected passed Pawns. Petrosian resigned
on his forty-sixth move and Fischer was the new challenger for the
World Championship.

The American was given a long, standing ovation. Then Petrosian
was also warmly applauded. Lothar Schmid held up a sign lettered
"*Viva Argentina!*" and the crowd became delirious. There was a small
gathering of officials on the stage; hands were shaken, embraces given,
and congratulations offered. The crowds quickly assembled on the
Avenida Corrientes, at the side entrance of the theater, waiting for
Fischer. When he emerged, a huge roar went up and they practically
mobbed him. He rushed to a taxicab and they pursued. He was
enveloped with arms, legs, and faces as he attempted to enter the
taxi, and with much difficulty succeeded, with the help of Edmondson
and his friend Quinteros. Quickly, the cab drove off.

Fischer, the irresistible force, had conquered Petrosian, the immov-
able object. In light of his shutouts over Larsen and Taimanov, he
must have thought the 6½–2½ victory a minor accomplishment,
though perhaps a much more realistic one. If Fischer had succeeded
in winning *all* of his games against Petrosian, too, the Fischer-Spassky
match would have been too easy to predict. If the tightrope walker
slips just a little, it makes his performance that much more believable;
and though Fischer attempted to win every game against Petrosian,
the fact that he didn't record yet another picket fence actually helped
his career. It also helped to stabilize him for his forthcoming match
with Spassky. He was awarded a prize of $7,500 plus an honorarium
from the U.S. Chess Federation amounting to $3,000.

The commotion generated over Fischer's conquest was unprecedented. In the United States, a genuine chess renaissance occurred
practically overnight, surpassing the chess fever that spread in 1859
upon Morphy's return from Europe. Sales of chess sets shot up over

20 percent. Virtually every major magazine and newspaper in the country ran a story about Fischer. Even the New York *Daily News* reprinted the score of every game played. And *The New York Times*, in addition to doing a cover article in its Sunday Magazine section, published a news story on its front page the day after the match ended. Chess had been so honored rarely before in *Times* history: e.g., when the Soviet team visited the United States in 1954, and when Paul Morphy returned from his triumphant European tour. This time the *Times* went even further, printing a diagram of Fischer's final position against Petrosian, and a picture of Bobby on page one. Fischer was seen on television constantly and his face became so familiar to the general public that he was asked for autographs in the streets of New York City. George Steiner, the noted literary critic, writing in *The New Yorker*, referred to Bobby's "staggering achievements" in etching for himself an instant historical image, accomplished due to his ". . . somnambular certainty of touch and to a peculiar force of the kind marshalled by great or predatory political figures and, in exceptional instances, by performing artists of genius." Bobby Fischer became more than a household name. He inrushed and apprehended the public consciousness as deftly as he exploits an open file. Even if he had accomplished nothing else, he had assuredly roused the interest of the American people in the finest of games and in his own individual odyssey for recognition and artistic appreciation. Bobby Fischer had become a national hero.

CHAPTER XXVI

"Chess depends on you."

Fischer, decked in heroic garb, was still Fischer, however, and his constant companion, controversy, raged about him. Even before his match with Petrosian, he had offered his annual quota of insults to the Russians, and the Battle of Bobby Fischer vs. The Soviet Union continued. "The Russian players are simply employees of the State," he announced to the press. "They have no personalities. They don't think for themselves." And he re-instigated his Curaçao theme. "They try to win every way they can. They have no sense of sportsmanship. They find ways to take advice from their seconds or they arrange the schedule against you as they did to me in the finals of the 1962 World Tournament."

The Russians were on their toes in no time, retaliating. *Sovietsky Sport* reported that Fischer was avidly trying to ". . . stir up an unhealthy hullabaloo . . ." against Soviet players. Taking issue with his recent statements, which also included a remark that over the last ten years he had been the best player in the world, they stated: "He has *not* been the best chess player in the world for the past ten years. He has yet to prove he is now," obviously referring to the existence of the chess champion of the world, who was not, as they hastened to point out, Bobby Fischer. This didn't bother Bobby, however, as he neither forgave nor forgot what he considered the improprieties of Curaçao. "The Russians have held *my* title for ten years and they're going to be in for it when I win the Championship. They're going to have to wait and play under *my* conditions," he said vehemently.

He was also probably disturbed over Spassky's interview in the Yugoslavian journal *VUS* which was wire-serviced all over the world. Talking of Fischer's victory over Petrosian, Spassky said he ". . . was neither impressed nor surprised. Petrosian played a petty game and defeated himself with his own hands." But, perhaps not too conversely, he displayed genuine affection for Fischer when saying: "He's a real fanatic. I feel fond of him." Fischer laughingly countered: "Perhaps I should send Spassky a telegraph saying, 'Congratulations on winning the right to meet me for the world's championship.'"

Bobby's ire continued to mount as he came closer to capturing the world title. The affirmation of his unbounded talent produced a feeling of righteousness that he had, indeed, been the greatest player in the world all along and that only Soviet deception had prevented him from his just position.

He remained in Argentina for over two months, touring the provinces, enjoying the nightlife, and generally unwinding from the effort of the Candidates Matches. His friend Quinteros was often seen with him and Fischer lent him moral support while Quinteros played in the First Pan American Team Tournament in Tucuman. When Fischer arrived there, his very appearance caused as much excitement as the matches and accompanying Congress. He agreed to a simultaneous of twenty boards, winning seventeen, drawing one, and losing two.

A number of other simultaneous exhibitions were arranged for Fischer throughout Argentina at record-breaking fees (up to a reported $500 or more for each appearance) and he played hundreds of games against the South Americans. He caused a minor furor when he overslept before one performance and appeared two hours late: most of the players had left in disgust, but he faced those that remained and they were delighted to get a crack at the famous *norteamericano*.

When he did eventually return to New York, The Westchester Shore Club of Mamaroneck prevailed upon him to give a simultaneous exhibition, and he won against twenty of the club's selected members in less than forty-five minutes. He let it be known that the exhibition was the last he was giving before his championship attack.

Rosser Reeves told me the following story, and though it sounds apocryphal, it is an amusing and significant glimpse into the sense of purpose with which Fischer approached his task as challenger. Shortly after the Westchester exhibition, Fischer was approached by the headmaster of a posh private school on the Upper East Side of Manhattan with an offer to give an exhibition for $1,000 against about a dozen of the school's pre-teenagers. If he could polish off twenty fairly strong club members in three-quarters of an hour, he would probably finish with twelve children in ten or fifteen minutes, reasoned the Headmaster.

Fischer was living only ten minutes away by taxicab from the school so the entire process would have probably taken him less than half an hour from door-to-door. He refused. The fee was raised to $2,000 and Fischer still refused—at any price. He had begun his studying and preparation for the match and he would allow nothing to interfere.

Critics were quick to indicate that simultaneous displays tend both to tire and produce careless play in the exhibitor. They were hardly a valuable, though certainly they were a profitable, way of preparing for a Championship challenge. Botvinnik, for example, noted for his strenuous and carefully regimented preparations for match play, was no doubt appalled at Fischer's cavalier attitude in South America. In any event, the limited number of exhibitions probably didn't affect Fischer adversely, and might have actually served to relax him.

Edmondson and Fischer were in frequent telephone communication about the negotiations for the forthcoming Championship, which in years past had been traditionally held in March or April. Offhandedly, Fischer had stated that he would not play for the Championship unless the stakes were at least $100,000 or better, and after this fact was leaked to the press, countries from all over the world began to bid for the match. Edmondson had told Fischer that there was no real need for him to return to the United States until January 1, 1972, when all of the bids, which were sealed to prevent jockeying and one-upmanship, were to be opened.

According to FIDE regulations in effect at that time, both the Champion's and the Challenger's country, respectively, had the right to organize twelve games each; the first half to be held in the country of the challenger and the last half in the country of the defender. But Fischer wasn't having any of that: "I won't play in Russia, period," he dictated. "They would do everything they could to distract me."

Shortly before Fischer left Buenos Aires, Svetozar Gligoric arranged a transcontinental conference call between Fischer, Spassky, and himself, similar to the one with Petrosian and Fischer before the start of their match. Since Spassky speaks English, no translation was necessary and the result was a lively conversation. The transcript:

> *Gligoric*: When would you like the match to start?
> FIDE's President, Dr. Max Euwe, expressed his wish that the match should not begin later than May 10th.
> *Spassky*: For personal reasons I prefer that the match start only toward the end of June.
> *Fischer*: I think the match should not begin before June 30th, as Spassky has had three years at his disposal to prepare for this encounter, while I had only two months up to now. This might give him a certain advantage.
> *Gligoric*: So, you prefer the end of June?
> *Fischer*: Yes, at the earliest.
> *Gligoric*: Do you both feel the match will go the full twenty-four games?
> *Spassky*: I could not answer that question right now. I think I shall be able to answer all questions concerning the match in more detail some time in April or May.
> *Fischer*: I do not think the match will last all twenty-

four games. However, who knows. . . . I intend to prepare
as well as I can. My responsibility is great; the public expects much from me.

The two men were then informed by Gligoric about details he had
heard from Dr. Euwe regarding the place where the match might be
played. Dr. Euwe thought that the most serious candidates for the
organization of the match were Yugoslavia and Holland. Spassky and
Fischer then voiced their own opinions.

> *Spassky*: I prefer a country with a climate similar to the
> one in my home town, Leningrad. As it cannot, of course,
> be Leningrad, the Scandinavian lands would be my ideal
> second choice.
> *Fischer*: What are the money offers?
> *Gligoric*: According to Dr. Euwe the best offers will be
> at least 50,000 dollars. I have heard that Sarajevo offers
> more, maybe much more. I don't know if this bid will win,
> though. If Sarajevo gets the match, you would play in
> Skenderija Hall, which seats 8,000 spectators. You would
> be isolated behind glass walls, etc.
> *Fischer*: For me the first and most important thing is
> money. The climate comes second. I repeat, money is most
> important.

Spassky then asked Fischer whether he would be ready to play in
one of the European countries, as the preceding Candidates matches
were all played on the other side of the Atlantic. Fischer's answer was
that he would accept it only if the European financial bid were the
best one.

> *Spassky*: What does Fischer think about organizing the
> match in one of the Yugoslav towns?
> *Fischer*: I should agree if the best financial offer would
> be available there.
> *Gligoric*: In case the match should take place in Bel-
> grade, you would play in the Syndicates' Hall, where you
> both played in the World Match. One thing seems to be
> obvious now, namely that there should be no misunder-
> standings as to when the match should be played. But
> there might be disagreements about which principle is the
> more important one: money or climate. That is why Dr.
> Euwe is ready to apply the mathematical principle of the
> best neuter solution, if you two do not reach an agreement
> by yourselves.

Fischer: Dr. Euwe cannot decide this matter. Spassky and I have to decide this matter.

Gligoric: How do you wish to make your decision? Do you intend to send your representatives to FIDE Bureau in Holland soon?

Fischer: I might go myself.

Gligoric: That is best. Do you wish Spassky to go personally, also?

Fischer: I don't know.

Spassky: Should Fischer go to Amsterdam, there is a possibility that I, too, will fly there the same day to talk directly with him and Dr. Euwe.

Gligoric then asked Spassky what he thought about Fischer's play during the last year.

Spassky: Fischer's play has had an impressive effect on me.

Fischer: [asked the same question about Spassky]. I think his results in Göteborg were mediocre. He tied for sixth place in Moscow . . . What could I say?

Gligoric: Do you wish to personally participate in making the choice of the match referee?

Spassky: Of course.

Fischer: I think the referee must not be a Russian, an American, or one of the country where the match is held. That way possible misunderstandings would be avoided.

Gligoric: Who might be your official "seconds"?

Spassky: As before, it should be Grandmaster Bondarevsky.

Fischer: I haven't made up my mind on this matter.

It's remarkable to note that Spassky assumed that the match could not be held in his native land; already, even before all the bids had been received, it had been unofficially but mutually agreed that a neutral country would have to host the event. This was due to a combination of Fischer's protestations over the possibility of playing in Russia and the U.S.S.R. Chess Federation's failure to place a bid. Since previous title events had been played in Moscow for a token fee of $1,400, to offer a championship purse in six-figure sums would have been thoroughly antithetical to the Soviet cultural posture.

"They just saved me the trouble of rejecting them," quipped Fischer.

Fischer arrived in New York City on December 27th and checked into the Park Sheraton Hotel, eagerly awaiting the New Year with the anticipation of the results of the bids. Dr. Euwe made the announcement from Amsterdam that fifteen bids had been received:

Belgrade, Yugoslavia	$152,000
Argentina	$150,000
Iceland	$125,000
Sarajevo, Yugoslavia	$120,000
Chicago	$100,000
Bled, Yugoslavia	$100,000
West Germany	$ 92,000
Brazil	$ 80,000
The Netherlands	$ 80,000
Canada	$ 75,000
Zagreb, Yugoslavia	$ 70,000
Switzerland	$ 60,000
Greece	$ 52,000
France*	$ 50,000
Colombia	$ 40,000

For the first time in the 1,500-year history of the game, chess instantly entered an Age of Opulence. There is every reason to believe that World's Championship chess will never revert to the days of $1,000 purses (as in Lasker-Marshall, 1907), though the magical appeal of a Bobby Fischer and the inherent drama and color of an East-West confrontation as typified in the Fischer-Spassky match may never again quite capture the imagination of the public or affect its pocketbooks precisely as it did in 1972.

For ten years, even longer, Fischer, like another American original, Mohammad Ali, had boasted that he was the "greatest." The whole chess world was eager to see if he could prove his claims, especially against such a formidable player as Spassky, certainly himself one of the greatest by anyone's standards. Fischer's quest for the title went beyond the circumscribed world of chessplayers, however. His charisma, his pure individualism, his almost Horatio Alger-like rise to the summit of his profession seized the interest of even non-players to such an extent that people attracted by his vitality who didn't know the difference between a Pawn and a Ping-Pong ball quickly learned the game, simply to be better able to understand the artistic expression of the young genius from Brooklyn.

But just as intense as the public's fascination with Fischer was Fischer's own fascination with money. His constant arguments that Soviet masters were at an advantage in that they were supported by the State and could devote all their time to the development of their

* The French Chess Federation, opting to hold the match in Deauville or Paris, offered the players an additional 5 percent of all subsidiary gross income from television, souvenirs, books, etc.

game was, of course, entirely correct. Since Fischer was forced to support himself he decided to do it comfortably. Steinitz, Lasker, and Alekhine all lived and died virtually penniless and Fischer was not going to let the same happen to him.

In 1961, I talked to Marcel Duchamp about Bobby's financial difficulties in relationship to those experienced by "fine" artists, and he told me this:

> The plight of the chess master is much more difficult though—much more depressing. An artist knows that maybe someday there'll be recognition and monetary reward, but for the chess master there is little public recognition and absolutely no hope of supporting himself by his endeavors. If Bobby Fischer came to me for advice I certainly would not discourage him—as if anyone could— but I would try to make it positively clear that he will never have any money from chess, will live a monklike existence and will know more rejection than any artist ever has, struggling to be known and accepted.

Fischer faced this monetary and mythic deprivation, as described by Duchamp, all of his life. When he had the opportunity to gain proper remuneration by dint of his formidable talent and the changing, more intellectually liberated values of the American people, which are manifested in restlessness and constant experimentation, who could really blame him for grasping what he could?

It was Dr. Euwe who pointed out that the Russians were, paradoxically, the world's most prosperous chess players: "The best ones have an automobile and a *dacha*. They also have safe, assured incomes so they don't have to worry economically about winning a tournament. And when they retire, the State gives them a pension."

It was within this framework of Capitalism vs. Communism that negotiations to select a venue for the Fischer-Spassky Match began and falteringly progressed. More bids came to light, however, before any serious discussions took place. The Borough President of Brooklyn, Sebastian Leone, aided by Walter Goldwater, President of the Marshall Chess Club, offered $100,000 for the match to be played in the old but lovely Brooklyn Academy of Music. This site would have been an appropriately sentimental selection as it is the home of the old Brooklyn Chess Club, the institution where the young Fischer first got his start. On the other extreme, Caesar's Palace, a brassy Las Vegas nightspot, also made a bid: $175,000.

What did Fischer think of Brooklyn? *Brooklyn!* He was horrified at the thought of something other than a major metropolis. He wanted it in the United States, but ". . . some other city, not Brooklyn." There were many chauvinistic inhabitants of that colorful borough who felt it was a shame that he didn't at least entertain the idea, and were saddened at Fischer's disdain.

Both players were asked by Dr. Euwe to submit a list of the cities they most preferred as possible match sites. According to the rules, only if agreement could not be reached by the two players themselves would FIDE decide. Spassky named Reykjavik, Amsterdam, Dortmund, and Paris, in that order. Fischer's list was comprised of Belgrade, Sarajevo, Buenos Aires, and Montreal. Euwe attempted, by several long distance calls, to negotiate a resolve but was unsuccessful: he thereupon invited both players and their representatives to Holland at the end of January, to try to come to a solution *mano y mano.*

Edmondson, acting in Fischer's behalf, flew not only to Amsterdam but to Belgrade and Sarajevo to inspect the sites, and to Moscow as well, for a closed door meeting with Soviet chess officials, to try to arrange the match in mutually agreed-upon territory.

Fischer flew to Amsterdam but Spassky never appeared there. It was reminiscent of a scene that took place almost fifty years earlier, to the day. Negotiations for another World's Championship match almost totally foundered when Dr. Emanuel Lasker stormed out of a meeting in Amsterdam, claiming that Capablanca was being offensive and insulting. Fifteen years later they still were not speaking to each other.

Meanwhile, in Moscow, Edmondson conducted secret negotiations on February 7th with Soviet chess officials. Though the substance of the talks were not to be released to the press, the Soviets waited a short while and then announced through a Tass bulletin that Edmondson had agreed upon Reykjavik, Iceland, as the site. Edmondson emphatically denies this, and he told me that he felt the reason why the Russians "broke the bond of secrecy" was to embarrass Fischer. Without elaborating on the details of the document, Edmondson offered the following extract to prove his point:

> This tentative agreement will be in effect after approval by Spassky and Fischer . . . The lack of confirmation or attempts to change this agreement will be considered as a refusal of this agreement. Both sides will keep this agreement in secret until confirmation.

The entire to-ings and fro-ings become almost hopelessly confused and entangled in a rat's nest of accusation, counterthreat, and petty bureaucratic shuffling involving television rights, gate receipts, climate, and facilities of competing cities, down to whether sandwiches, coffee, and apple juice could or could not be served to the players during the progress of the actual games. Internecine warfare erupted between the United States and Soviet Chess Federations, and FIDE. Belgrade and Sarajevo were practically at each other's necks. Virtually every edition of every American newspaper carried the latest of either confirmed reports or educated (and sometimes not so) speculation as to who, what, where, or when, and score cards indicating what corner of the world would ultimately get the match would have been entirely appropriate.* Incessant haggling even over the sites of the *meetings* to discuss the match sites took place, and chess has rarely experienced such a display of super-charged egos.

Sovietsky Sport once again got into the act by blasting Fischer's concern over money as the major factor in deciding the match site, and reincarnated Paul Morphy, pointing out that though he is Fischer's "idol," Bobby does not reflect Morphy's attitude toward the prizes he received. "It is common knowledge that the great Morphy regarded the endless financial haggling in chess contests as humiliating and was a model of gentlemanly behavior in this respect," they hissed. But what they didn't point out is that while it is true that the great Morphy indignantly proclaimed that ". . . reputation is the only incentive I recognize" when writing to Staunton in 1858, it is also true that his father had left him an estate of nearly $150,000, making Morphy a virtual millionaire by today's standards. Fischer never knew such beneficence.

Fischer and Edmondson flew to Reykjavik to inspect the conditions there and Bobby remained for about a week. He also paid a visit to the last round of an International Chess Tournament taking place in Iceland at the time. Arni Gunnarsson, News Director of Icelandic State Radio, interviewed the two men:

> *Gunnarsson*: Why did you come to Iceland?
> *Edmondson*: Well, if Iceland didn't have a good chance of being the match site, we wouldn't be here.
> *Fischer*: We came here to look over the conditions and the situation and to talk to the organizers.
> *Gunnarsson*: Where do you want the match to be played? I understand that you prefer Yugoslavia.
> *Fischer*: Well, Belgrade has entered the largest bid.
> *Gunnarsson*: The Russians have accused you of wanting too much money for this match. How do you feel about that?
> *Fischer*: They're always accusing me of something. What can I do about it?
> *Gunnarsson*: How much money do you really want for this match?

* An unexpurgated "White Paper" was published by the Belgrade organizers outlining, in fastidious detail, all of the negotiations. This, combined with an eighteen-page report, dated May 16, 1972, issued by Dr. Euwe in behalf of FIDE, will give the interested reader an almost scholarly rationale of the events.

Fischer: How much do I *really* want? I don't know. That's a trick question.

On February 9th, both the U.S.S.R. and U.S. Chess Federations announced that tacit agreement had been reached by both organizations as to a site, but that it was still subject to the approval of the two contestants. The next day, however, Euwe spoke to Edmondson by telephone and said afterward: "It appears we are in serious trouble." He negated the report of the previous day that agreement had been reached.

On February 11th, the Russians called a press conference in Moscow in which they disclosed the details of Edmondson's visit and the confidential provisional agreement he signed to hold the match in Reykjavik, starting June 25th, for a purse of $125,000, the winner to receive 62.5 percent and the loser 37.5. Spassky, of course, favored the agreement since Reykjavik had been his first choice, but Fischer was appalled, and his negation was adamant. In the first place, Reykjavik's purse was $27,000 lower than Belgrade's, and secondly, he was agitated that Edmondson had made the agreement without his knowledge. "I was betrayed by my Federation," he said later. "I don't know what's behind this. I'm not happy about it. I don't know whether [Edmondson] was doing it for his own ends or whether the U.S. government told him to go easy, give the Russians what they want, just make sure the match comes off so Fischer plays him."

Dr. Euwe, forced to a crisis by the anticipatory organizers breathlessly awaiting a decision, finally made an announcement on February 14th. Since mutual accord could not be reached by Spassky and Fischer, he was allowing Belgrade (Fischer's first choice) to have games one to twelve, and Reykjavik (Spassky's prime preference) games thirteen to twenty-four; or, better phrased, game thirteen to the conclusion of the match. Belgrade's and Reykjavik's bids were averaged to $138,500, divided five-eighths to the winner and three-eighths to the loser. International Grandmaster Lothar Schmid of West Germany, who refereed the Fischer-Petrosian match, would be the Chief Arbiter.

Fischer made no comment at first. A meeting was held in Amsterdam by Dr. Euwe, Edmondson, Messrs. Molerovic and Baseraba representing Yugoslavia, Mrs. Ivushkina and Yefim Geller of the Soviet Union, and Gudmundur G. Thorarinsson representing Iceland. FIDE Deputy President Rabell-Mendez presided. After several days of discussion, ". . . taking more time than one would possibly have expected," as Dr. Euwe described it, two documents were initiated and issued on March 20th and signed by all parties. The first was the "Rules of the Match," and the second was the "Agreement between FIDE and the organizers of the Match."

Two days later, however, Thorarinsson received the following cablegram blast from Fischer:

> I HAVE JUST SPOKEN WITH ED EDMONDSON REGARDING THE FINANCIAL ARRANGEMENTS FOR THE MATCH. UNFORTUNATELY, DUE TO MY PREPARATIONS FOR THE MATCH, I WAS UNABLE TO ATTEND THE MEETING IN EUROPE. MR. ED-MONDSON WAS NOT AUTHORIZED TO MAKE THE FINANCIAL ARRANGEMENTS WITH YOU THAT HE DID. I WILL NOT ABIDE BY THEM UNLESS YOU CAN CONSIDERABLY IMPROVE YOUR OFFER BY A GROUP OF FIDE CONTROLLERS AND AGREE THAT ALL MONEY OVER THE TOTAL EXPENSES FOR THE MATCH GO TO ME AND THE RUSSIANS. I WILL NOT PLAY YOUR MATCH IN ICELAND . . .

FIDE also received the following cable:

> MR. EDMONDSON HAS NOT FOLLOWED MY IN-STRUCTIONS IN THE MATCH NEGOTIATIONS AND HAS MADE A GRIEVANCE IN MY NAME THAT I HAVE NOT AUTHORIZED AND I WILL NOT ABIDE BY THEM. MR. EDMONDSON NOR ANY OTHER USCF REPRESENTATIVE IN THE FUTURE MAY NOT NEGOTIATE OR MAKE ANY AGREE-MENTS IN MY NAME. I PERSONALLY WILL HANDLE ALL FUTURE NEGOTIATIONS AND AGREEMENTS IN REGARD TO THE SPASSKY MATCH. BOBBY FISCHER

Both the Icelandic and Yugoslavian organizers recoiled at Fischer's suggestion because, they argued, they were taking the financial risk in presenting the match, and should there be any income, then it was only fair that they have the right to it. Fischer's reaction was imme-diate. As soon as he learned of the organizers' objections to any changes in the financial arrangements, he shot off another cable to Thorarinsson: "DUE TO UNACCEPTABLE FINANCIAL CONDI-TIONS, I REFUSE TO PLAY ALL OR ANY PART OF THE TITLE MATCH IN ICELAND. BOBBY FISCHER." A similar cable was also sent to Belgrade.

Fischer reasoned that playing in Belgrade and Reykjavik served neither his interests nor those of chess. He felt that, on the one hand, Yugoslavia would not guarantee the players any concrete share in the film and television rights, and on the other hand Iceland was too "primitive" to cope with all the media and organizational details that the match would demand. In the former case, of course, he was justified: an artist, a performer, should garner the financial fruits, or a part of them, from having his art displayed to large numbers of spectators. As far as the latter case is concerned, we will delve later in this narrative into how the Icelandic Chess Federation, a proud and efficient organization, handled Fischer's grievances.

Fischer stopped all communication with Edmondson, refusing to accept even his phone calls, which stoked the situation into even more of a nightmare of confusion. What condition Edmondson's true emotional state was in after hearing that he was, in effect, "fired" by Fischer, is open to conjecture; but it should be fairly evident. He had devoted a large portion of his time and energy in the previous two years to helping Fischer wend his way to the top, by accompanying him to tournaments and matches, acting as his buffer, secretary, adviser, and friend, working him through the Interzonal and Candidates maze, and looking after him in almost fatherly fashion. He had maintained a magnificent balance of diplomatic expertise and intricate psychological finesse in his relationship with Fischer. Edmondson was totally sincere when he said that in the past few years his ". . . major goal in life was to help Bobby Fischer become chess champion of the world." To be so abruptly excluded from Fischer's sphere no doubt had a stinging effect upon the man.

And what were Fischer's motivations in treating Edmondson so ruthlessly? As usual, in any analysis of Fischer's behavior, complexities abound. He was still slowly burning over Edmondson's actions in Moscow. He was furious with what he considered Edmondson's presumptiveness with his personal financial affairs in signing the Amsterdam agreement. It's difficult to suggest how Edmondson could have operated otherwise, however, as he was in Holland as both Executive Director of the U.S. Chess Federation *and* Fischer's representative. One USCF official, who knows both men well and who was in almost daily contact with Edmondson, said: "Fischer is not only angry with him over Amsterdam but he resents that Edmondson is basking in the limelight as a result of his association with Fischer." Edmondson later stated that he thought Fischer *was* angry over the diffusion of publicity and that that factor was at least partially to blame over the rupture. As Fischer is relentlessly unmerciful to his opponent when a mistake appears on the board, so is he when his friends or colleagues make, God forbid, the slightest error in conversation, intention, or action. He divorces them immediately and finally, which forces even some of his closest associates to tiptoe around him lest they utter the wrong word or mention a Fischer-tabooed subject. Tolerance of the idiosyncrasies and flaws of one's friends, one of the foundations of friendship, plays small part in the life of Bobby Fischer.

CHAPTER XXVII

*"Your body has to be in top
condition. Your chess deteriorates
as your body does. You can't
separate body from mind."*

In Australia when he was informed of Fischer's financial objections, Euwe was shocked. He was also told that Belgrade officials were temporarily ceasing any further activity. ". . . Due to the uncertainty still going on . . . it is impossible to carry out all the organizational preparations such a match would require," they stated. Euwe issued Fischer an ultimatum: he must declare his intention to play the match under the original financial conditions, or forfeit his rights as challenger.

If Fischer was refusing to talk to Edmondson, *someone* was not—because Edmondson shot back the following cable in response to FIDE's ultimatum, which was received just moments before Euwe was ready to disqualify the American: "FISCHER READY, WILLING AND EXPECTS TO PLAY AT TIMES AND PLACES AGREED. YOU WILL BE CONTACTED BY OUR FEDERATION REPRESENTATIVE PAUL MARSHALL TO FINALIZE ARRANGEMENTS IN SPIRIT OF FRIENDSHIP."

Marshall, a shrewd attorney for television star David Frost, had begun to handle some of Fischer's business negotiations together with Fischer's regular lawyer, Andrew P. Davis. In order to guarantee Marshall unhindered entrée to the FIDE officialdom, Edmondson appointed him as a temporary USCF representative.

Fischer's latest acceptance was not strong enough for the Belgrade organizers, however. They wanted to be *certain* he didn't change his mind again. The substance of the assurance summoned by Belgrade came in the form of a demand for a $35,000 bond they wanted posted by each player (or his respective Federation), guaranteeing that he would appear and play under the terms of the Amsterdam Agreement. Fischer thought it preposterous. "It's an insult to my manhood," he complained to a friend. The U.S. Chess Federation pleaded poverty as the reason they couldn't produce the bond,

213

but a member of the Manhattan Chess Club claimed he would cover it, if Bobby wanted him to. Fischer flatly refused to post a bond, whether it constituted his money or anyone else's. The Soviet Chess Federation agreed, however, to underwrite Spassky ". . . provided such a step is also taken by the American side, and all Fischer's demands that arose after March 20 are considered annulled."

Belgrade waited a few days, and when no bond was forthcoming to support Fischer, they officially withdrew their participation in the match. They stated that even if the bond *was* posted within a few days, they could no longer accept it since there was not sufficient time to make necessary arrangements.

The date was April 14th. The match was slated to commence on July 2nd, and because the biennial Chess Olympiad was to be held in September, the World Championship Match could not start very much after its allotted date or both events would ultimately collide, something FIDE would not permit.

Then came a round of new bids (or rumors thereof) from potential host cities: San Juan, Puerto Rico; Melbourne, Australia; Mexico City; Edinburgh, Scotland; San Francisco, U.S.A. This last bid, as reported in the *San Francisco Chronicle*, was for $200,000, if the match would be played in its entirety in the Palace of Fine Arts. Cyrus Weiss, an entrepreneur who was promoting the idea, flew to New York to talk to Fischer at Grossinger's Hotel where he was training in scenic seclusion. "He refused to see me," said Weiss. "We passed notes back and forth under the door through the courtesy of a bellboy. It was a weird experience. In principle, though, Fischer was for it." The Russians, of course, would no sooner play in San Francisco than Fischer would in Siberia.

Original bidders were given another opportunity to re-negotiate. But in the case of Sarajevo as in other cities, the money was no longer available. Other cities lost interest or were skeptical about Fischer's intentions. For awhile, it seemed that the entire match would have to be scrapped, at least as far as the large stakes were concerned.

Suddenly, in a dramatic move, the Icelandic Chess Federation made a proposal to host the entire match for their original bid of a $125,000 purse. Though not without further complications, it was accepted by Euwe, the Russians, and by Fischer himself, who on May 6th declared that he would play Spassky ". . . in Reykjavik, Iceland, or anywhere else in the Free World." The formal American communiqué to FIDE was abrupt and to the point: "BOBBY FISCHER AGREES TO PLAY IN ICELAND AS SCHEDULED UNDER PROTEST. EDMONDSON AND MARSHALL." The form this protest was to take would ultimately reverberate throughout the entire world, but for the nonce, the match was on.

Marshall said his client had agreed to the match ". . . in spite of the continued attempts by the Russian Government to defend a title by chicanery instead of skill." *J'adoube!* Apparently, this entirely unexpected *nonsequitur* refers to hidden facts to which only Marshall and Fischer are privy. Perhaps Marshall was referring to the four talks conducted by Spassky and Euwe in Moscow, during which Spassky suggested the match be held in the cities of Bled and Reykjavik, claiming that it was too hot in Belgrade in the summer. There was also a dinner party at the home of Alexander Kotov, during which Spassky and Euwe secluded themselves in a separate room for fifteen minutes. Their discussion concerned whether Spassky still wanted to go through with the match, since the Soviet Chess Federation was on the brink of claiming that Fischer, in not accepting the terms of the contest, should be forfeited. Euwe apparently prevailed upon Spassky to reconsider, as he evidently did, and this had a positive effect on the Russian officials. Both of these incidents sound like anything but chicanery, but depending upon one's attitude toward the Russians, it could conceivably be interpreted that way.

Upon inspection, it was Fischer who broke the Amsterdam Agreement, not the Soviet government. If Fischer did not recognize the Agreement because it was signed by Edmondson, certainly that cannot be blamed on the Russians, FIDE or anyone else. It does seem that the Russians were trying in every possible manner to get the match under way. Though admittedly harsh with Fischer on his financial demands (Anatoly Ivanov, an official of the U.S.S.R. Sports Section, said of him in an article in *Moscow News* that there was ". . . no other Grandmaster more capricious than Robert Fischer"), still, there is every reason to believe that the Soviet Chess Federation, and Spassky in particular, were eager to play. Many chess people of good faith felt Fischer was responsible for the near abort. The Russians, though proud of "their" World Championship title, knew that Spassky had a heavily weighted plus score against Fischer, and both he and they felt he had excellent chances of retaining his championship.

While Spassky ensconced himself in the Caucasus that spring, to train for the forthcoming match, Fischer was deeply entrenched in the Catskills, over seven thousand miles away. Grossinger's, a mammoth hotel complex located in Ferndale, New York, the heart of the "Borscht Belt" where much of the New York City Jewish population have been vacationing for over half a century, served as Fischer's training camp for the four months preceding his match with Spassky. Since Fischer's religion observes the same dietary and many of the Sabbatical laws of the Judaic tradition, Grossinger's was an ideal selection: there was no pork served in the dining room, and from

Friday sundown to Saturday sundown, a Sabbatical decorum might be observed by the devout.

There were also other reasons why Fischer chose Grossinger's as his retreat. It removed him from the pressures of New York City, where he was just a ten-cent telephone call away from anyone (and there were many) who wanted to reach him, and it prevented people from dropping in for a casual visit and disturbing his concentration and study. The hotel was also renowned for catering to famous guests.

Fischer's routine was Spartan. Like Steinitz, who was the first chess champion who trained like an athlete, Fischer too believed that he had to be in superb physical shape in order to play his best. "Your body has to be in top condition," he said. "Your chess deteriorates as your body does. You can't separate body from mind." Waking late in the afternoon, he would leave his room, located in a two-story, Tudor-style cottage, sometime between two and four o'clock and often start the day with a few games of tennis, followed by a strenuous workout in the gym, consisting of anything from weight-lifting to calisthenics to fiercely jabbing a 300-pound punching bag. He would bowl occasionally, dive into the pool for a quick twelve laps, play Ping-Pong, and usually sit in a steam bath every day. Long walks were also a part of his regimen, and he not only benefited from the physical exercise but had the opportunity of thinking things through while alone.

At dinner, which he most frequently took by himself at about 8 P.M. he would unfold his pocket chess board and, in a state of quiet dedication, begin his exhaustive inspection of Spassky's games. This microscopic analysis often continued through the night until the early hours of the morning.

The reference he used most frequently was what journalists were quick to describe as the "Big Red Book," No. 27 of the excellent *Weltgeschichte des Schachs* series containing three hundred and fifty-five games of Spassky's, conveniently typeset with a diagram at every fifth move. In addition, Kenneth Smith dipped into his immense library and resources to produce hundreds of examples of Spassky's pre-1968 endeavors.

Though supremely confident of the eventual outcome—Fischer had said, and would have us believe that he would take Spassky ". . . in thirteen straight"—Bobby was leaving nothing to chance as he dissected every game Spassky had played, comparing and weighing them against the latest theoretical evaluations superimposed with his own experiential and adroit positional judgment.

Two of the three games in which Fischer had been defeated by Spassky in the past had been Queen's Pawn openings, specifically the Gruenfeld Defense, and undoubtedly Fischer devoted much of his pre-match preparations to confronting this technical issue. King Pawn openings, either from the White side '(where he would invariably play the Ruy Lopez if given the opportunity), or from the Black side (where he would offer his standard Sicilian Defense), gave him no difficulties in preparing for Spassky. The problem for Fischer was what to play against Spassky's 1 P–Q4, since as Leonard Barden pointed out in the *Guardian*, it appeared that Fischer's ". . . opening favorites, the King's Indian and Benoni, are not quite solid enough for a world title match." Fischer had to produce more sophisticated options as Black. As White, he had not lost a game against Spassky.

Spassky worked with what was described as a miniature army of helpers, whereas Fischer basically worked alone. The story that a group of "European theoreticians" supplied analyses for Fischer could very well be true, but he did not have the resources available to Spassky—which bothered him not a whit. ". . . I don't think I need them. I'm not worried," he said.

While at Grossinger's, Fischer was visited occasionally by Larry Evans, Svetozar Gligoric, William Lombardy, his friend James Gore, and several other players, and while chess was the discussion of the day, no one really contributed to Fischer's preparatory efforts. Lombardy took issue with the theory that Fischer had achieved his successes all by himself, however: "It's true that he works alone, but he is learning from the games of other players all the time," he said plaintively. "To say that Bobby Fischer developed his talent all by himself is like saying Beethoven or Mozart developed without the benefit of the music throughout history that came before them. If other chess players had never existed for Bobby Fischer to learn from, then there would *be* no Bobby Fischer today."

Fischer took time out to appear on several network television shows that spring, subjected himself to rare personal interviews, and contributed to his growing image as a "super-star." He was invited to fly to Bermuda for lunch, together with an airplane full of other high-level celebrities and "beautiful people," as the guest of David Frost. Fischer accepted, and he spent most of the day in the sun, playing tennis, lounging by the pool, and talking with John Kenneth Galbraith.

On March 9th, his twenty-ninth birthday, news commentator Mike Wallace and a television crew traveled to Grossinger's to do a film segment for the news-feature show, "60 Minutes," and an incident occurred that revealed in poignant fashion Fischer's disdain for the social amenities. At one point in the evening, someone brought out a birthday cake while Fischer was on camera, and the strains of "Happy Birthday" began to lilt through the dining room. Fischer immediately objected.

Fischer: I was worried about this.

Wallace: Why were you worrying about this?

Fischer: I just don't go for it. First of all I don't eat this kind of cake. Second of all, I don't go for these kind of things.

Wallace: All right. Shall we take it away?

Fischer: Please.

Whether Fischer objected to the display of sentimentality or the television crew, who were strangers, is hard to determine. But one thing is certain: He rarely unmasks his private face to the transients who so often enter his life. To all but a select coterie, Bobby Fischer remains a mysterious hermit.

As summer approached, the reality of the match caused such heightened curiosity and fascination that it seemed like Fischer's every remark, his every action, was recorded around the globe. And even at Grossinger's, far removed from the business of Manhattan, he was beseiged by calls, cables, and visits suggesting schemes to make him—and their originators—rich. A "Bobby Fischer Chess Set" was suggested. Endorsements were sought. One Wall Street fagin even tried convincing him to become a "public issue," like the Beatles, so that shares of "Bobby Fischer" could be traded on the New York Stock Exchange. Fischer went merrily on his way, however, agreeing to little and signing nothing.

As Fischer continued his training, every imaginable rumor began to circulate in chess circles. One was that Fischer's games had been programmed into a Russian computer and all the proper continuations had been found. This overlooked the fact that computers are still only capable of playing a rather retarded game of chess.

Another story that surfaced was that the Soviets, upset over Spassky's poor showing in the Alekhine Memorial Tournament (he tied for sixth-seventh) in November, had consequently arranged a secret "training match" for him with the winner of the tournament, twenty-year-old Anatoly Karpov. The contest was said to have comprised twenty-four games, the same number as the World Championship match, and Spassky—it was said—lost resoundingly, with a score of 6–18.*

Further stories included one about Spassky's forthcoming defection, either before, during or after the match, and another that Fischer was going to go to Iceland, wait until the thousands of spectators and hundreds of journalists packed the house for the first game, and then deliver a scathing speech that would denounce the organizers

* While playing in an international tournament in San Antonio, Texas, in November, 1972, Karpov admitted that such a match took place but was reluctant to discuss the details, other than to say: "I didn't lose."

and FIDE, proclaim himself Champion of the World, and leave Iceland without moving a pawn.

Serious discussion among chess players revolved about the ultimate outcome of the Fischer-Spassky duel, which was beginning to be hailed as "The Chess Match of the Century." Spassky's defense of his title became almost a defense of his country. In his well-written article, "The Big Burden Boris Bears" in *Sports Illustrated*, Robert Byrne pointed out that ". . . Spassky is going into battle not as a lone combatant confronting his foremost rival, but as a towering rampart defending Soviet tradition . . . an oppressive psychological burden for anyone." Indeed, Spassky's millstone was a heavy weight to bear, but as his society dispensed the ordeal to him, Fischer, totally aware of the quasi-political and cultural implications of the encounter, gratuitously accepted and perpetuated his own incubus. "I now feel a sense of mission to win the championship," he averred. Asked if the forthcoming bout would be a grudge match, he replied: "In a sense. But not personally between me and between Spassky . . . it's against the Russians. . . ."

The challenger in any contest often has a special advantage in that he's forced to play "up" in order to win; he must prove demonstrably that he is better than the champion. The title holder, however, secure in the knowledge of his superiority, frequently plays on his own "normal" level, falsely assuming that because he *is* the champion, the proven quality of his past play is sufficient for current victory. Chess abounds with such thinly reasoned examples: Steinitz over Anderssen, Lasker over Steinitz, Alekhine over Capablanca; all "underdog" challengers rising above the occasion to demolish their opponents and grasp the title.

One advantage to be savored by the Champion, though, was the fact that he had "draw odds." If he could draw every game, giving him 12 points. Spassky would retain his title. Fischer needed 12½ points to dethrone him.

Professor Arpad Elo's International Rating System, in effect at that time, ranked Fischer at 2760, seventy points higher than Spassky at 2690; and based on a statistical projection of a twenty-four game match, Professor Elo predicted a score of 12½–8½ in favor of Fischer, the contest ending with the twenty-first game.

A sampling of strong American players indicated the following:

REUBEN FINE: Fischer by 12½–7½.
SAMUEL RESHEVSKY: I would give Spassky the better chances.
EDWARD LASKER: Fischer by 12½–10½.
HANS BERLINER: Fischer by 12½–7½ . . . if the match is held!
KENNETH SMITH: Fischer by 13–8.
ANDREW SOLTIS: Spassky by 13–10.

GEORGE SHAINSWIT: Spassky by 13–10.

ROBERT BYRNE: Fischer by 12½–8½.

LUBOMIR KAVALEK: Fischer will win by a wide margin, 12½–6½.

HERBERT SEIDMAN: Fischer by 12½–8½.

KARL BURGER: Spassky by 13–10.

ISAAC KASHDAN: The score should be somewhere between 13–7 and 12½–8½ in favor of Fischer.

GEORGE KANE: Spassky by 12½–10½.

Foreign players were a mite more pro-Spassky in their consensus.

DR. MAX EUWE said he thought the odds should be set at 60–40 in favor of Fischer.

HENRIQUE MECKING predicted 12½–9½ for Fischer.

WALTER BROWNE said Fischer will have no trouble. 12½–7½.

SVETOZAR GLIGORIC thought the match could be very close but that Bobby would win . . . 12½–10½.

OSCAR PANNO predicted a Spassky victory of 12–7.

And both BENT LARSEN and FRIDRIK OLAFSSON went on record backing Spassky as the favorite.

Schach Echo, an authoritative German chess periodical, indicated that only a "miracle" would prevent Fischer from becoming World's Champion now and if he somehow failed this time, his victory in 1975 would be a certainty. Everyone, from the highest of Grandmasters to the lowliest of *patzers*, had an opinion as to who would win and by what score and in what manner. Fischer's overwhelming victories of 1970–71 were weighed against his 1–4 score against Spassky, and yet only one of this three losses had occurred in the previous five years and, once again, there was always Fischer's superior rating.

What did Fischer *really* think of his chances? We can appraise his "13 straight" statement as pure public relations, but just weeks before the commencement in Reykjavik, Fischer, without blinking an eye, stated that he thought ". . . the odds should be 20 to 1"* in his favor. As I. A. Horowitz pointed out in *The New York Times*, commenting on Fischer's remark: "All other things being equal, confidence wins games. Allied to the will to win, it sparks the mental ignition, brings forth ideas, dispels doubts, and promotes clear thinking." And Fischer's supreme self-confidence was almost legendary. He felt he was destined to win the match.

* Ladbroke's, a British bookmaking service, established odds for the match at 6–4 with Fischer as favorite.

CHAPTER XXVIII

*"I now feel a sense of mission to
win the championship."*

Reykjavik, capital and principal city of Iceland, thought primitive
by many skeptics, was actually an ideal location for a World's Championship match. The unprecedented purse of $125,000 represented
fifty cents for every man, woman, and child in the country. The
generosity of the Icelandic people was based on their great love for
chess, steeped in an ancient tradition that dates back to the Norse
kings of the twelfth century. The thirteenth-century sagas, still read
by every Icelandic school child and found in most homes today,
abound in references to chess; and in a book about Iceland published
in 1561, Gories Peerse tells a story concerning the masters of a house,
who lie in bed for weeks during the wintertime, having their servants
and children wait upon them, while they do nothing but play chess.
The lonely isolation of the long, dark, frozen winter evenings helped
chess become the Icelandic farmer's favorite pastime, and today Iceland ranks a close second to the Soviet Union in registered Federation players in proportion to the national population.

Because Iceland is a small country, it was obvious that the holding
of the World's Championship there would dominate the entire island.
Chess did become the sole *raison d'etre* of the Icelanders for over
two months, and they threw their energy, their money, and their
hearts, into making the event memorable.

Downtown Reykjavik took on the characteristics of a Tenniel en-
graving from *"Through the Looking Glass,"* with black-and-white
checked displays backdropping huge papier-mâché chess pieces. Photographic blow-ups of Fischer and Spassky adorned the windows of
virtually every shop in town, and chess, chess, and more chess was
played, talked about, eulogized, front-paged, essayed, and almost
deified, in multitudinous directions. The near-hysterical interest in the
match, combined with all the twists and turns it was to assume, was
unforgettable. But if Reykjavik was a chess wonderland, according
to most Icelanders Bobby Fischer was the Mad Hatter. They liked him,
but considered him not just eccentric but ill-mannered. They disliked

his constant "demands." Most of the residents started out wishing for Fischer's victory in the match; but after the numerous false starts, threats, and general difficulties Bobby caused the Icelandic organizers, sympathy began to swing to the "gentleman," Boris Spassky.

At the beginning of June, Fischer left Grossinger's and traveled to San Diego, California, where he competed in a tournament. It was a tennis competition, sponsored by a large national distiller, featuring sports personalities *other* than tennis stars. Fischer didn't win, but he enjoyed himself and, according to one witness, was treated with awesome respect by the assembled athletes since they were all sports figures, whereas Fischer was someone apart, other-worldly, and outside of their normal reference.

The World Chess Champion, Boris Spassky, arrived in Reykjavik on June 21st, accompanied by his second, International Grandmaster Yefim Geller, who, significantly, had replaced Spassky's ubiquitous mentor, Igor Bondarevsky (". . . we had professional and personal differences . . ."). Also accompanying him were Nicolai Krogius, an International Grandmaster and statistical psychologist, and Ivo Nei, an International Master from Estonia who acted as Spassky's trainer and tennis companion. They all checked into the Hotel Saga, one of Reykjavik's finest. Before leaving Moscow, Spassky had given a press conference at the Journalists' Club in which he had said: "I don't know how it is going to end. Maybe he will win, maybe he will lose. But I am sure of one thing—it will be a highly interesting match in terms of the art of chess."

Fischer was scheduled to arrive in Iceland on June 26th. Journalists and chess lovers began to assemble in increasing numbers in Reykjavik. Feature writers of such renown as Pulitzer-prize winner Harold C. Schonberg, Arthur Koestler, Jeremy Bernstein, George Steiner, David Pryce-Jones, and Clement Freud arrived, while such noted chess writers as Harry Golombek, Heinrich Fraenkel, B. H. Wood, Jens Enevoldson, I. A. Horowitz, Robert Byrne, Larry Evans, Dimitrije Bjelica, Svetozar Gligoric and many others filed daily reports to their respective journals. Over two hundred and fifty journalists eventually made their way to Reykjavik. Though all of their script concerned the dynamics of the match, not all was chess.

Rumblings indicated that Fischer was still not satisfied with the financial arrangements. The winner was to receive $78,125 and the loser $46,875. In addition, each was to be given thirty percent of all television and film rights. Fischer further demanded thirty percent of the gate receipts, arguing that as much as $250,000 might be gained by paid admissions and he felt that he and Spassky should have a share of that money!

The Icelandic chess officials, who were not at all sure how they were going to fill *Laugersdalhöll*, the site of the match, game after game (the stadium could hold about three thousand people) for as many as twenty-four sessions, not counting adjournments, argued that gate receipt income should rightfully belong to them in order to cover the outlay for the stakes and the preparations and arrangements.

Both sides had legitimate, though admittedly subjective, rationales and an impasse was soon reached that quickly began to look like an insurmountable barrier. Communication was strained as officials of the Icelandic Chess Federation in Reykjavik and Fischer's lawyers in New York resorted to trans-Atlantic telephone and cable. Adding to the confusion was the elusiveness of Fischer. After competing in the tennis tournament, he visited friends in Southern California. Then it was reported that he traveled north and stayed awhile with his sister in Palo Alto. If his lawyers were in contact with him after that, no one else was.

Fischer had secretly checked into the Yale Club in midtown New York City as a guest of his lawyer, Andrew Davis.

Davis was a member of the so-called "American delegation" who accompanied Fischer to Iceland. United as a team to jointly help Fischer, this disparate group of highly intelligent men, some almost as controversial as Fischer himself, gave him their untiring assistance— far more than he knew.

Andrew P. Davis, thirty-nine, educated at both Yale and Oxford, is a slightly proportioned, thoroughly accomplished young man who became Fischer's lawyer in the early Sixties. Their relationship has been intermittent and not without its problems. In the mid-Sixties, after an argument, their association was severed and a few years passed with virtually no contact between them. Davis emerged, however, as a staunch supporter of his famous client, and takes a highly personal interest in him that transcends that of the normal attorney-client relationship. Davis has an almost pleasant aggressiveness about him, which is softened with a fine sense of humor. There is only one subject about which he refuses to utter a word: the personal life of Bobby Fischer. ". . . But if *I* ever wrote a book about Bobby, you'd discover facts that would amaze you," he once said, smiling enigmatically.

Davis is unassuming, and by choice is almost invisible in terms of personal publicity, threading his way through a roomful of reporters and photographers without revealing the time of day. He is probably the single most valuable aid for Fischer because of his ability to smoothly negotiate with chess officials and organizers in Bobby's behalf, without causing resentment toward himself or his client.

Paul Marshall, forty-three, is a relative newcomer to the circumscribed world of Bobby Fischer. In the fall of 1971, he began to handle Fischer's rights regarding books, endorsements, films, and appearances. Within six months time he had resigned twice as his attorney. The first time was because of Fischer's position over the Amsterdam Agreement; the second was over Fischer's denial of the agreement Marshall had made in his behalf with the Icelandic Chess Federation, regarding the TV rights. It was Fischer, however, who asked Marshall to represent him during the ensuing troubles that occurred in Reykjavik. "Davis called me and said that Bobby thought I should step in," Marshall told me. "I was amazed, after all the trouble we had, but I guess he had faith in me or else respect in my ability to get the job done. Funny, though. When I called Bobby back, the first thing he said was: 'I'm not apologizing!' "

Marshall is not an easy man to know. He is efficient, tough, and almost ruthless at times, but in a social setting can be warm and friendly. On occasion, he even appears somewhat shy. He met Bobby through another client of his, David Frost, and thought he could help him. "I'm a lousy chessplayer, but I know enough to have respect for the game and Bobby Fischer. I also knew enough of the super-star personality to recognize a budding one in Bobby Fischer." Marshall stated before the championship that he worked for Fischer without payment and flew all over the world for him at his own expense. "I wanted to help him become the first American to do it. I don't regret it," he said.

Fred Cramer, in his late fifties, is a former President of the U.S. Chess Federation and at the time of the Fischer-Spassky match was the Vice President of FIDE of Zone 5 (U.S.A.). He inherited the job as official representative of Fischer at Reykjavik from Ed Edmondson, after the latter's falling out with Fischer, because Cramer was one of the highest ranking members of the American chess fraternity, was friendly toward Fischer, had represented his ideas at FIDE Congresses, knew and loved chess, and was noted for his efficiency and his perfectionist's attention to detail. Often criticized as thick-skinned, Cramer is a curious blend of very high intelligence combined with an obtuse insensitivity as to how he treats others. He is capable of insulting anyone at any time and often does, but maintains the integrity, consistency and strength of a backwoodsman. His position as spokesman for Fischer at Reykjavik was a nightmare at times, where a weaker man would have certainly crumbled. Cramer's main obstacle was most frequently Fischer himself. "I am authorized only to complain, and not to approve," he once remarked ironically.

Reverend William Lombardy, a large, pale and intense Roman Catholic priest, and Fischer's second in the match, was perhaps the chief supporting actor in the drama at Reykjavik. Thirty-five years old, Lombardy is the first chess master of international importance connected with the Catholic church since Ruy Lopez (sixteenth century) and Domenico Ponziani (eighteenth century) made their imprints on the game. He is a childhood friend (and friendly rival) of Fischer's, both being frequent visitors at the Collins household. He was Fischer's second during the latter's adventure at the Portoroz Interzonal in 1958. Lombardy won the World Junior Championship the year before that, and was named an International Grandmaster in 1960. He is one of America's finest players and has enjoyed that distinction for almost fifteen years.

Lombardy is a classic study in ambivalence. On the one hand jovial, compassionate, quick-witted, he can change nearly in mid-breath and show the caustic, introspective, and aloof side of his personality. He's an intriguing character. Occasionally he'll wander off into a reverie, perhaps engaged in a mental analysis of an obscure variation, or listening to the voices of his own inner commands. His eyes will unfocus, he'll become thoroughly oblivious to the conversation about him, and attempts to bring him back will usually be unsuccessful. ("Bill. Bill? Are you there, Bill?" would elicit a decelerated response, if any.) He's his own man, if there ever was one, and for this very reason he was able to cope with Fischer.

As powerful in human relationships as he is over the board, Lombardy generates respect, if not awe, from his peers, and he is very much in command of his emotions and motivations. He was a loyal and competent analyst of adjourned positions for Fischer, and served him well as friend and companion.

Fischer canceled his flight to Iceland at the last minute, on the evening of June 25th. The airline had reserved a full row of seats just for him and had stocked the plane's refrigerator with oranges so that King Fischer could have fresh juice "squeezed in front of him," as the request stated, during the four hour trip across the Atlantic. Marshall said that some detailed "ground rules" had to be settled before Fischer would play, but that he, personally, did not think that this would prevent Fischer's arrival in time for the match.

Meanwhile, talks continued between Marshall, Davis, and the Icelandic Chess Federation, concerning the matter of the gate receipts. Both sides stood firm. During the ensuing week, additional flights were booked and then canceled by Fischer as headlines began to question whether he would appear at all. Icelandic papers were asking *"Hvenaer kemur hinn dularfulli Fischer?"* (When cometh the mysterious Fischer?) When, indeed? A few days after his first flight was changed, Fischer and Davis drove to John F. Kennedy International Airport, apparently to board a Pan American flight. But Fischer unaccountably paused to buy an alarm clock, and was seen by reporters and photographers (there were over a hundred members of the press waiting to interview and photograph him). He fled the airline terminal and missed the flight. Later, he was observed at a nearby Howard Johnson's restaurant, having dinner. Davis was angry.

"Fischer was physically prevented by the press from making his flight," he said. "Before Fischer tries again, we must have media protection for him." Since political leaders, movie stars, and other celebrities make a habit, with the help of airlines officials, of dodging the press at terminals, surreptitiously wending their way through side entrances, and boarding before all other passengers, or being whisked in at the very last moment before take-off, there seems no real reason why the same treatment could not have been afforded to Fischer. Davis's answer was a subterfuge; Fischer had no intention of making the flight until all financial questions were settled, and when Davis intimated that they were not, Fischer played a *zwischenzug*, a waiting move, until the time was exactly right for him to act.

Or was it as simple as all that? A number of chess critics and players in Reykjavik argued that Fischer was simply afraid of Spassky, and that now that he had reached his lifetime goal, the summit of his career, he was traumatized into inaction, frightened that should he play, he might lose. It might be better, like Staunton, to go down in history as the unproven champion. The one crucial difference was, of course, that Staunton *already* had been unofficial champion in that he was the best player of his day (he simply refused to take Morphy on as a challenger); Fischer had yet to prove he could be named as the greatest contemporary player until he could defeat Spassky. After Fischer's second or third airplane cancellation, there was virtually no serious chessplayer in Reykjavik who believed he would come. Larry Evans still had hope, and said: "He's in another world. In Buenos Aires he told me, 'Larry, you can't imagine the pressure I'm under. Every *move* I make is scrutinized the world over. The tension is almost unbearable.' I still think he'll come, though. He's just waging an impressive display of psychological warfare." Robert Byrne was much more succinct: "Perhaps Bobby has lost touch with reality." Whatever the reasons Bobby fled the airport, he was thoroughly expended emotionally. When he finally got to bed that night, he slept for a full 20 hours.

His closer associates were not optimistic. Cramer said: "Why should he show up? From his subjective point of view, he already *is* champion. I don't give it [the match] much of a chance of coming off." And Davis was somber when he said: "I just don't know what Bobby will do."

The fact that even those who were intimately involved in the nuances of the gate receipt negotiatons were themselves unsure of Fischer's participation indicates that money was probably not the only factor motivating Bobby's refusal to appear. And if that is the case, what *were* the other mitigating factors? Evans's explanation that Fischer was attempting to unnerve Spassky by creating a situation permeated with tension and insecurity, is a popularly held theory. If most of the chess world believed as Fischer did ("Anyone who knows anything about chess, knows I've been champion of the world, in every way but name, for the past ten years," he said) that he was indeed "champion," then it could be reasoned that it was incumbent upon Spassky to prove his mettle in a curious case of role reversal where he, as "acting" champion, must behave as the challenger. I believe it is improbable that Fischer was attempting to disturb Spassky in any way. He has never engaged in this type of tactic in the past. His "tantrums" and "walkouts," often grossly exaggerated in the press, have always been directed toward chess *organizers*, never toward an individual player. Other masters boast or hint of their invincibility. Fischer *believes* in his. He doesn't *need*, he reasons, to do anything but play his normal brand of chess, sublime as it is. "I don't believe in psychology. I believe in good moves," he said to reporters when asked why he stayed in the United States, while Spassky fretted in Iceland.

The real reason Fischer stalled, in my opinion, was that he *was* engaging in a classic case of brinksmanship. However, the man on the edge was not Boris V. Spassky but Gudmundur G. Thorarinsson. Thorarinsson had stated, long before Iceland had been slated as the final choice, that he thought Fischer should have forfeited his right as challenger for breaking the Amsterdam Agreement. He was genuinely angry with Fischer over the latter's derogatory remarks about Iceland. ("It's an *awful* choice. It's a hardship place where they give G.I.'s extra pay to serve there," Fischer had said to the press.) And Thorarinsson privately told a number of people that he personally "loathed" Fischer. This prejudice may have made its way across the Atlantic to Fischer. Saidy pointed out in Chess Life & Review that he could "testify" that Fischer ". . . evinced no fear at all of Spassky" but that the Icelandic Chess Federation was his real opponent in the "war of nerves."

Fischer was outraged that Iceland was forced upon him, especially since it was Spassky's first choice. Who was the World's Champion, anyway? If they pressured him to play in Iceland, and threatened to take away his right to play for the title, he'd play there—but they were going to pay for it. He also knew that large expenditures had already been made by the Icelanders and that it was important for them to protect their investment.

Though money was the focal point of the controversy, it was not the actual dollars, or *Kroners*, as the case may be, but the principle of not getting his own way that sent Fischer into a fury. As an editorial in *The New York Times* suggested: "If he plays in Reykjavik and wins—as he has an excellent chance of doing—his prospective earnings would make the amount he is arguing about now seem infinitesimal." Fischer knew that.

The Icelanders stood firm. "We are trying to avoid financial disaster," said Thorarinsson. "We are not budging." Gudmundur Einnarson, another Icelandic organizer, was more direct. "Marshall is guilty of a blatant attempt at extortion in trying to make us give in to all of Fischer's demands. We have calculated what our potential losses might be and if he doesn't appear, we are ready to accept them. If Fischer wants to forfeit his right to play for the World's Championship, that's his business."

In addition to his monetary and psychic manipulations, Fischer's "bead game" included one additional maneuver, created by a facet of his personality of which he himself is probably not consciously aware. Fischer has an innate talent for attracting the press. I know from my twenty years of work in many forms of media that in order to receive the immense coverage that Fischer has stimulated almost all of his life, the subject must generate interest. One journalist who was at JFK airport pointed out that if Fischer, knowing that reporters were hunting him, had not entered the terminal shop to buy an alarm clock, which could have been purchased anywhere, anytime, he would not have been cornered by the press. Hence, he concluded, Fischer had an overwhelming and obvious desire, conscious or unconscious, to be recognized. I believe this to be true. So I further believe that in the final analysis, Fischer would have gone to Reykjavik even if his financial demands had not been met, appearing there perhaps at the very last moment before his ultimate forfeiture, or perhaps even after Spassky had gone home to Moscow.

By the time the opening ceremonies took place at Iceland's National Theater on Saturday evening, July 1st, less than twenty-four hours before the beginning of the scheduled first game, reporters and spectators were making reservations to return home, in the belief that Fischer would not appear. Fischer had moved from the Yale Club to Douglaston, Long Island, the home of his friend Anthony Saidy. As Saidy later related, the house was subjected to an unending media barrage. Fischer was beseiged with calls and cables there, and photographers and journalists staked out the house in hopes of a fleeting glimpse of him. Meanwhile, the constant, by now vicious, bickering between Fischer's and Iceland's representatives continued. Even Davis's reserve was pierced at one point when Fischer was being extraordinarily difficult: "If he's going to be the champion, then he better start acting like one," he said at one of the meetings. The whole situation plummeted out of control, and Fischer-headlines dominated the front pages of newspapers all over the world, crowding off such "secondary" news items as the 1972 United States Presidential nominations.

Saidy suggested that there was an actual plot to keep Fischer from becoming World Champion, and this involved the wire-tapping of his parents' phone. "At one point, when Bobby was talking to Davis who was in Iceland," Saidy told me later, "Bobby made a reference to one of the ICF officials as being 'stupid.' Suddenly, he heard a woman's voice cutting through the line, saying: 'He said "he's stupid." ' The line was obviously tapped."

Anything is possible, of course, and Saidy added that Fischer believed, too, that the line was tapped. Such reasoning depends not only on one's political views or psychological state but on one's philosophical *Weltanschauung*, as well. There was a theory prevalent among a number of Americans that the Icelanders were underhandedly working with the Russians to overthrow Fischer's assault on the Soviet hegemony of chess. Aside from the personal dislike for Fischer that a number of the Icelandic chess officials openly had, I never found, during my entire three month stay in Iceland (and I had constant occasion to peep into much "classified" material), one single instance that they did anything to hinder Fischer's world championship bid. It was just the opposite. Indeed, some of the Icelandic officials were convinced that Spassky was the better player and that he was going to defeat Fischer rather easily. They were privately expecting, hoping, to see Fischer humiliated *on the board*.

CHAPTER XXIX

*"I don't believe in psychology.
I believe in good moves."*

According to World's Championship rules, a player is entitled to a postponement of a game for medical reasons if the illness is attested to in writing by a certified doctor. On July 1st, Davis, meeting with Cramer, Dr. Euwe, Lothar Schmid, and officials of the ICF, asked for a two-day postponement for Fischer, pleading "fatigue." Since everyone knew that the reason Fischer was still in New York was because of his ongoing dispute with the ICF, this excuse was somewhat ludicrous. However, in order to save the match, the officials agreed to the charade—as long as they received confirmation in writing. Cramer insisted that two cables, one from a New York doctor (presumably Saidy) and one from the U.S. Chess Federation, both attesting to Fischer's illness, were sent to Reykjavik. But both cables "mysteriously disappeared." They never did turn up.

Robert Byrne telephoned Fischer to see if he could elicit any information, or perhaps offer assistance. After the call, he commented: "Bobby sounded calm and reasonable. His demands are entirely financial."

That night, the drawing for colors for the first game did not take place during the opening ceremonies, and although the general format of the dignified program was maintained, it didn't develop totally according to schedule. The President of Iceland, Kristján Eldjárn, was there, as was Geir Hallgrimsson, Lord Mayor of Reykjavik, Members of Parliament, representatives from the U.S. and Soviet embassies, and Dr. Max Euwe representing FIDE. Boris Spassky was seated in the first row, elegantly attired in a gray checked vested suit. An empty seat, also in the front row, which Fischer was to occupy, remained conspicuously and desolately vacant. While speeches were made in English, Russian, and Icelandic, the audience fidgeted, craning their necks to the side entrance, half expecting—hoping—that at any moment Fischer would make a grand entrance. It didn't happen.

Most of the speeches had been written, and published, weeks in advance of opening night, and gave no hint of the off-the-board war that was raging in Reykjavik. President Eldjárn, insulted that Fischer had not arrived, did not deliver his talk, but had his remarks read. Mayor Hallgrimsson alluded to the problems when talking of a "living" chess game: ". . . It is obvious that live people do not for long wish to be pawns on a chessboard, even if they are in the hands of geniuses."

Dr. Euwe, speaking very softly, almost somberly, thanked the Icelandic Chess Federation for their efforts in organizing the match, ". . . from the bottom of my heart," and went on to touch on the problems directly. "Mr. Fischer is not an easy man. But we should remember that he has lifted the level of world chess for all players. Even though he is not here, I am personally convinced that he will come tomorrow and the match will begin."

The President hosted a cocktail party after the ceremonies, where Spassky and the other guests gaily sipped champagne. The talk was all of Fischer. Spassky did not act as though he had a care in the world, as if he were assured that there would be no game the next day, or any day for that matter. He told Gligoric that he was looking forward to a two-month vacation, and then he would leisurely return home to Moscow to play Petrosian (who would succeed to the position of Challenger through Fischer's default). He had been prepared to play Fischer, but now began to allow his psychological mainspring to loosen, if not unwind.

The next day, Spassky met Dr. Euwe and the Icelandic officials at the Hotel Loftleider and discussed what to do. Euwe left the decision in the hands of Spassky himself, and though it's not generally known, he offered to disqualify Fischer right then and there. Spassky would retain his championship until another match could be arranged. The alternative was to allow Fischer a two day postponement. Though technically breaking the rules, since no medical certificate had been received, Euwe wanted to try everything possible to keep the match alive. He, like Spassky, showed the utmost of sportsmanship. Fred Cramer himself commented that ". . . The Russians don't want to win the championship on a technicality. They want a real chess match."

Later, Euwe related what had occurred in the meeting: "The Russians were more or less neutral on the possibilities of a postponement. Spassky said, 'Well, I've waited here for more than a week. Fischer has never said anything personally. I don't know whether I should consent to a further delay. I don't disagree with it, but I don't agree either.'"

Immediately afterward, Euwe announced at a press conference— the beginning of a series of epic and understandably obscure conferences—that he was considering a postponement. He was not particularly happy when he said: "The situation is extremely difficult.

Fischer did not show up, and there is not the least sign that he would show up tomorrow, the day after tomorrow, or even in a week. It would be the easiest way, and perhaps the right way, to say, 'Well, Fischer is not here, he hasn't given any sign; he is disqualified and he loses his right to play for the World's Championship.' " The consequences were obvious. Aside from the potential loss of the estimated $75,000 already invested by the Icelanders, there was the ruination of Fischer's career.

Euwe chose to allow Fischer the postponement. "But if he does not show up by Tuesday at twelve noon, at the drawing of lots, he loses all of his rights as challenger."

At the end of the conference I asked Euwe who he thought would win the match. "No one," he replied. "I think there will be no play at all."

Fischer remained apparently unmoved. People not only began to leave Iceland, but the ICF received hundreds of cancellations for tickets and reservations. "A charter group in England had reserved a hundred seats for an entire week, but they just cancelled," said the depressed Freistein Johannson, the ICF Press Secretary. "They don't believe there will be a match." Hundreds of people who had come from all over Iceland to see the first game, and who had not heard that it had been cancelled, were sadly turned away from the hall. Thorarinsson thought that phone contact between Spassky and Fischer might ease the situation and he asked the Russian if he would call New York. Spassky considered it overnight and then refused, saying he thought he could add nothing: "I don't really understand why Fischer is doing this. It would be senseless for me to reason with him," he told Thorarinsson.

The Soviet Chess Federation lodged a biting protest with FIDE against the forty-eight-hour postponement, stating that Fischer actually warranted "unconditional disqualification." Charging Dr. Euwe as the responsible agent, they warned him that they would consider the match "wrecked" if Fischer did not appear in Reykjavik by noon on July 4th, Euwe's final deadline. Poor Euwe, who was under criticism from all sides for not conceding to their demands, finally received relief by way of a phone call from British chess expert Leonard Barden. The call saved the match.

Barden said that British financier James Derrick Slater, a chess devotee and investment banker, was willing to donate $125,000 to double the existing prize fund—if Fischer would agree to play. Slater, a millionaire, stated: "The money is mine. I like chess and have played it for years. Many want to see this match and everything was arranged. If Fischer does not go to Iceland, many will be disappointed. I want to remove the problem of money from Fischer and see if he has any other problems."

Fischer's first reaction was immensely positive. "It's stupendous," he said. "I have to accept it." Later, he told a newsman that though he hadn't studied the offer in detail, he had decided to play the match because ". . . there's an awful lot of prestige of the country at stake."

After a six-hour scan of the position, it was official. Fischer asked Saidy to call in the press, so that he could announce it himself. When the newsmen arrived at the Saidy home, Fischer was nervous. "We've had these problems with the organizations," he said. "They've been very petty, but it doesn't pay to be petty like they are." He wouldn't comment on whether the U.S. government had prodded him to accept, but said that he actually would have preferred an "all-or-nothing" prize to the winner of the first ten games. Later, it was learned that Henry Kissinger, Nixon's presidential adviser, had called Fischer and appealed to him to play to avoid insulting the Icelandic nation. Marshall added, privately, that ". . . Fischer thought that Slater's offer was incredible, generous, and brave. It was couched in a way he couldn't refuse. It said: 'If he isn't afraid of Spassky, then I, Jim Slater, have removed the element of money.' So Bobby felt he had to accept . . . he couldn't go down as a coward."

After months of disenchanting negotiations, Slater, backed by an assist from Kissinger, had accomplished the impossible. He had found, and sparked, the one element that set fire to the heart of Fischer: pride.

After being smuggled onto a *Loftleider* airlines flight to avoid reporters and public recognition, Fischer made the overnight trip with the Reverend Lombardy, whom he had announced as his official second that same day. The question of who was going to serve as Fischer's second had become sticky. A number of masters wanted the job, and Cramer at one point compiled a list of almost fifty candidates. Fischer had studied the list but selected no one. He felt, as he had not in his recent Candidates matches, that he would need the services of a second in his bid for the world title. He needed companionship and reconnaissance, if nothing else. There would also be complicated adjourned games occasionally, which two men could analyze better than one; Fischer wanted to be prepared for them.

Quinteros was mentioned as a possibility, but Fischer thought only grandmasters should be considered. Gligoric was a possibility, but it didn't work out. He recalled what happened in New York: "Bobby said three yesses and three noes. Fortunately I left the States before he had a chance to say yes again. I would have been embarrassed to have been named his second, as it would have created an impossible situation. I'm a good friend of both Fischer and Spassky."

Evans stated that overtures had been made, not by Fischer but by his associates. "I realized I could make much more money writing about the match than by taking an active part in it, so I declined," he said.

Lombardy had written Fischer a letter telling him that he was available for the summer, but had not received a reply as late as a few days before the match began. He was bitter about Fischer's cavalier attitude toward his offer. "I've lost interest," he said, "and I've made plans to host a television show on the match. I don't think I can get out of it."

On the very morning Fischer was to depart, he called Lombardy on the phone. "Well, are you coming?" he inquired of the priest. Lombardy told him he wasn't sure he could release himself from his television commitments. "Without me, there won't be a television show!" he informed Bobby. "That's O.K.," countered Bobby, "without me, there won't be a match!" When Fischer's plane touched down at Keflavik Airport in Iceland, a mere five hours before the forfeiture deadline, Lombardy, dressed in his clericals, was by his side.

Fischer was quartered in a spanking new, $60,000 villa located in Wodaland, on the outskirts of Reykjavik and had the use of the 3-room Presidential Suite at the Hotel Loftleider. A twenty-four-hour police guard was stationed outside of the house to keep away photographers and curiosity seekers. Fischer moved into the house on his first day in Iceland, refused to talk to the organizers or the press, drew the heavily lined drapes against the perpetual Icelandic summer daylight, and went into a deep and presumably restful sleep. When he awoke, some twelve hours later, it was past midnight. Cautiously, he leaned out a window and called to the policeman stationed there: "Any journalists around?" "No, sir," answered the officer, whereupon Fischer emerged from the house, walked to the police jeep, and asked "Which direction towards the town?" Then, characteristically, he set off alone, striding down the empty, slightly darkening streets.

Perplexed, the officer radioed his station for instructions; he was ordered to follow Fischer. He drove up alongside the gamboling American and, showing his professional training, asked whether Fischer knew his Icelandic address for the return home. "No idea," was the answer, "but I'm cold so please take me back to get a sweater."

Emerging again from the villa, Fischer surprisingly accepted the policeman's half-joking offer of a ride. He got into the passenger seat, and off they went, beginning a journey of many hours into the countryside of Iceland.

The policeman was Saemunder Paalsson, and shortly after that night, at Fischer's request, he was assigned to permanent guard duty for Bobby Fischer. "Sammy" accompanied Fischer everywhere, drove him to and from nearly every game of the match, accompanied Fischer when he went bowling at the military base as Keflavik, played Ping-Pong, played tennis at the indoor court, and even when he swam at the Loftleider hotel. In time, Fischer began having dinner occasionally at Sammy's home, and spent hours playing with the five children, even volunteering on at least one occasion to babysit with them.

The friendship continued after the match ended. When Fischer left Iceland, Sammy and his wife went with him to New York. For a while, there was speculation that Sammy would stay with Fischer in America, as his combination companion-chauffeur-bodyguard. But after a few weeks in the U.S., Sammy returned to Iceland with his wife, concerned about raising their children anywhere else.

While Fischer slept that day away, the general business of the match continued. The Drawing of Lots, scheduled for noon at the Hotel Esja, attracted hundreds of journalists; officials of the ICF and the American and the Russian sides were also present.

When Spassky arrived, he was told that Fischer was still sleeping and had sent Lombardy to draw for him. Obviously unnerved, Spassky refused to draw and left the hotel in a huff. At lunch, shortly afterward, he told a newsman that he was ". . . not abandoning the match," but that he thought Fischer had acted improperly. "I still want to play," he said, "but *I* will decide when." He then issued the following statement:

> By his refusal to come to the opening ceremony of the match, Fischer has violated the rules of the match. Thus he has insulted myself personally and the country I'm representing.
>
> Soviet public opinion and I, personally, are full with indignation at Fischer's behavior. According to concepts common to all people, he has completely disqualified himself.
>
> Therefore he has, in my opinion, called in doubt his moral rights to play the match.
>
> If there now is to be any hope for conducting the match, Fischer must be subjected to just penalty. Only after that I can return to the question whether it is possible to conduct the match.
>
> Boris Spassky
> World Champion

The penalty, mentioned by *Tass*, was the forfeit of the first game.

Confusion continued to grow. Speaking to newsmen after the Russians left the Esja, Euwe replied "certainly" when asked whether the walkout threatened to wreck the match.

"The Russians gave no indication what action, if any, would satisfy them," he said. "Perhaps they want an apology." Lombardy and Marshall left immediately for the Hotel Saga to meet with the Russians, to determine what could be done. In an open and honest discussion, the Russians suggested that an apology *might* reduce the tension. Later, in another press conference, Lombardy made the requested *mea culpa*:

> This statement I am about to make is not of my own origins. It is that of Bobby Fischer, who has authorized me to make the following remarks: "We are sorry that the World's Championship was delayed. The problem causing the delays were not with World Champion Spassky, whom I respect and admire as a man and a player. If Grandmaster Spassky or the Soviet people were inconvenienced or discomforted, I am indeed unhappy, for I had not the slightest intention of this occurring." I know that Fischer is anxious to get the match going, and he is really further unhappy about the delay and further unhappy about Spassky's feelings about the matter.

The apology was unacceptable to Spassky since it was neither signed by Fischer nor delivered personally by him. It had been rumored that it was written by Marshall and delivered by Lombardy, without Fischer's knowledge, simply to give the Russians a token excuse in order to preserve the match. It had lacked the human touch, and since Spassky felt justifiably hurt by Fischer's inaction, he wanted an unqualified and sincere apology.

Geller, Krogius, and Nei gave their own press conference the next day, in which they stated that the match would take place only if the following conditions were met:

1. Robert Fischer must apologize.
2. The President of FIDE has to condemn the behavior of the challenger.
3. The President of FIDE has to admit that this two-day postponement violated FIDE rules.

Euwe, again rising to the occasion, said, in a touching display of humility, that since two of the conditions concerned him, he would be happy to compose a statement right there, admitting that he had broken the rules, and condemning Fischer ". . . not only in the last two days but all through the negotiations." After working on his statement for about ten minutes, while the audience of Russians, Americans, FIDE officials and reporters sat in uncomfortable sympathy for him, Euwe read his confession aloud, signed it, and handed it to Geller. It stated: "1. The FIDE condemns the behavior of the challenger in not arriving on time, thus leaving the entire delegation and others in doubt about the realization of the match, and causing many troubles. 2. The President of FIDE admits that we had to post-pone the match for two days; we violated the FIDE rules. I think it's for special reasons, and on the basis of some presumptions which proved to be wrong afterward. I declare that the FIDE rules and match agreements approved by FIDE shall be strictly observed in future."

Lothar Schmid said that Euwe's statement was ". . . a great gesture by a great man, and it saved the match. I was filled with emotion while he was reading his remarks." Spassky had come to Reykjavik to defend his title, but neither he nor the Soviet Union would tolerate any slurs upon him. Fischer's behavior and the "improprieties" of Euwe's actions had to be addressed, they argued. According to the rules, the Soviets felt that Fischer should have technically lost the match when he did not appear on opening day, and only through their benevolence was the match continuing. It was now up to Fischer to make the next move, and it had better be the right one.

It was. That night, Fischer, with the aid of Marshall, composed an elegant apology to Spassky, which served as what Richard Roberts of *The New York Times* described as ". . . the sword that finally sliced through the Gordian knot."

One writer contended that in the first draft of the letter, Fischer had renounced any share in the prize money, and had said he was willing to play the match for nothing but the love of chess. Though I can imagine Bobby, on the spur of the moment, proclaiming: "I'll prove to the world that I love chess more than the Russians!" it's difficult to understand why he wouldn't have chosen a less self-damaging method of proving his devotion to Caissa. I tried a number of times to get a glimpse at a copy of the original draft but was unsuccessful.

I asked Marshall about the draft, and though he claimed it existed, complete with Bobby's offer to give up the money, he could not or would not allow me to read it. "There are other things in that letter that are damaging to Bobby," he said, "and show him in a bad light. I'm sorry." So history will simply have to accept as a matter of faith, that Bobby Fischer offered to play for the world's title for no money at all.

In any event, a second letter was composed, and it was this version that was finally presented to Spassky. Fischer and Marshall drove to the Hotel Saga early on the morning of July 6th and accompanied the bellboy to Spassky's room to watch him slide the apology, ad-dressed to Spassky, under the door. The text:

Dear Boris:
Please accept my sincerest apology for my disrespectful behavior in not attending the opening ceremony. I simply became carried away by my petty dispute over money

with the Icelandic chess organizers. I have offended you and your country, the Soviet Union, where chess has a prestigious position. Also, I would like to apologize to Dr. Max Euwe, President of FIDE, to the Match Organizers in Iceland, to the thousands of chess fans around the world and especially to the millions of fans and the many friends I have in the United States.

After I did not show up for the first game, Dr. Euwe announced that the first game would be postponed without prejudice to me. At that time you made no protest. Now I am informed that the Russian chess federation is demanding that the first game be forfeited to you. The timing of this demand seems to place in doubt the motives for your federation's not insisting at the first for a forfeit of the first game.

If this forfeit demand were respected, it would place me at a tremendous handicap. Even without this handicap, you will have an advantage to begin with of needing twelve points out of twenty four to retain your title whereas I will need twelve and a half to win the title. If this demand were granted, you would need only eleven points out of twenty three but I would still need twelve and a half out of my twenty three. In other words I must win *three!* games without losses, just to obtain the position you would have at the beginning of the match and I don't believe that the world's champion desires such an advantage in order to play me.

I know you to be a sportsman and a gentleman, and I am looking forward to some exciting chess games with you.

> Sincerely,
> Bobby Fischer

Reykjavik, July 6, 1972

One further obstacle remained and that was the Soviet Union itself. A Russian Minister, Sergei Pavlov, head of the State Sports Committee, had cabled Spassky furiously insisting that he return home to Moscow, mentioning that Fischer's numerous "tantrums" were an insult to the World Champion, who had every legal and moral right to refuse to meet Fischer. Normally, such a "recommendation" has the force of a ukase, but Spassky refused, as politely and diplomatically as possible. He replied to Pavlov that he could not debase his own standards of sportsmanship and would see the match through ". . . despite Fischer's outrageous" conduct. It was a courageous act, and one that called for much finesse and force of will on

Spassky's part. He called Schmid immediately, in strict confidence, to enlist his help. Spassky reasoned that if he initiated a "face-saving" measure of postponing the match himself, Pavlov would be more sympathetic to him in believing that the honor of the Soviet Union had been preserved. The situation was extremely delicate. Fischer now wanted to start the match immediately; Spassky asked Schmid to attempt to get Fischer to agree to postpone the match until Tuesday, July 11th. Schmid called a secret meeting with Marshall and a number of Americans who are close to Fischer, and asked them to prevail upon him to accept the delay. The Drawing of Colors had been arranged for that evening on the stage of *Laugersdalhöll*. Schmid related that ". . . until just a few minutes before the ceremonies began, I was not at all sure the match was a reality. Such pressure!"

Someone, presumably Marshall or Lombardy, appealed to Fischer just moments before he left for the stadium . . . and received his unhappy but conditional approval. But first he wanted to talk to Spassky face-to-face.

Fischer arrived twenty minutes late, and he and Spassky met backstage. After shaking hands, Spassky humorously tested Fischer's biceps, as though they were two boxers at a "weighing in." They then sequestered themselves for a few minutes to discuss the problems. Cramer said later that Fischer agreed to postpone the start of the match if Spassky would drop the demand for a forfeit. They came to terms, and a moment later they both walked out onto the stage, applauded by the journalists and well-wishers who had been waiting patiently at the closed ceremony. Fischer, spying the chess table, galumphed to the center of the stage and immediately lifted the White Queen, testing its weight. Then, one hand in his pocket, he tested all the other White pieces and sat down, stretching his long legs under the Scandinavian-designed mahogany table. Spassky also sat down.

After introducing both challenger and champion, and their respective seconds and aides, FIDE representative Harry Golombek, an International Master, announced that Geller wanted to make a statement before the drawing of lots took place. Speaking in Russian, Geller said:

> The challenger apologized in writing and the President of FIDE has declared that the match rules of FIDE will be strictly observed in the future. Taking into consideration the efforts made by the Icelandic organizers of the match, and the desire of millions of chess admirers all over the world to see the match, the World Champion has decided to play with Robert Fischer.

Though the statement was mild enough, I sensed a growing irritation in Fischer as it neared the end, and a real but inhibited flush of indignation by the time it was completed. Though I'm not sure the Russians or anyone else was aware of it, Fischer was mortified. For one very brief second, I believe he considered walking off the stage and out of the match forever. He felt he had complied with the wishes of the Russians by making the apology to Spassky, writing it by hand, and personally delivering it, and he had just agreed to go along with Spassky's postponement. The Geller statement was soiling the first official ceremony of the match for him. The Russians were censuring his behavior in front of his friends and the world press. Somehow, Bobby maintained his composure. Fortunately, the drawing of colors quickly followed before there was any opportunity to reflect further on this latest incident.

Lothar Schmid handed each man a blank envelope, and Spassky chose the one that indicated that he would hold the pieces. Spassky concealed a black Pawn and a white Pawn behind his back in the time-honored fashion, then brought his closed hands forward across the board. Fischer, without hesitation, tapped Spassky's right hand—and Spassky opened it to reveal the black pawn. Fischer did not change his expression.

When the ceremony ended, the two men shook hands and Spassky said: "Good luck." Fischer quickly left the stadium and went bowling with Lombardy at Keflavik Airfield. The NATO base there has the only bowling alley in Iceland.

Fischer moved from his villa because of construction noises nearby and the lack of restaurants in the vicinity. He was offered the services of a house cook but declined. Thereafter he permanently occupied the Loftleider suite. Aside from a few forays to dine out and occupation of the hotel's swimming pool every night he stayed sequestered in his quarters, studying and waiting for the first game to begin.

Fischer sneaked into the hall during the early hours of the morning before the match, to check out the conditions at his leisure. After an eighty-minute inspection, Bobby had a number of complaints: he thought the lighting should be brighter; the pieces of the chess set were too small for the squares of the custom-built board; the board itself was not quite right—it was made of stone—and he thought a wooden board would be better. Finally, he thought that the two cameras hidden in burlap-covered towers might be distracting when he began to play, and the towers themselves, looming over the stage like medieval battering rams, were disconcerting. The organizers started working on the problems immediately. They wanted everything perfect before the first Pawn was moved on opening day. "These things are troublesome but not critical," said Cramer.

CHAPTER XXX

*"You have to have the fighting
spirit . . . You have to force moves
and take chances."*

When Fischer awoke on the afternoon of the first game, July 11,
1972, and it slowly began to permeate his consciousness that he
was actually in Iceland playing for the championship of the world, he
was nervous. After years and years of tribulation and controversy, and
the recent brouhaha about the match, Fischer had arrived at the
threshold of his lifelong goal. *Laugersdalhöll* was to be his universe
for the next two months.

All details had been checked and double-checked in the playing hall
to ensure maximum comfort for the players. *Laugersdalhöll* is a
cavernous, dome-shaped stadium (someone described it as a large
Icelandic mushroom), with huge, white-covered sound baffles on the
ceiling that resemble mammoth albino bats. The entire first floor was
covered with carpeting to muffle the sound of entering and exiting
spectators, and the folding seats were replaced with upholstered and
consequently "soundless" chairs. The two film towers were pushed
back, on Fischer's request, and the lighting intensity on stage was
increased. A handsome, Eames-designed executive swivel chair, an
exact duplicate of the one he sat in while playing Petrosian in Buenos
Aires, was flown in from the U.S.

Bobby was driven to the stadium by Lombardy, and due to heavy
traffic they arrived shortly after five o'clock, the scheduled starting
time. Fischer rushed through the backstage corridor on to the horticul-
tured stage, and was greeted by the polite applause of an audience of
2,300 spectators. Spassky had made his first move precisely at five—it
was 1 P–Q4—and Schmid had started Fischer's clock. Fischer, dressed
in a white shirt and blue conservative business suit, sped to the table;
the two men shook hands while Fischer kept his eyes on the board.
Then he sat down in his black leather chair, considered his move for
ninety-five seconds, and played his Knight to his King Bishop's third
square.

Lombardy stood on the sidelines and watched. Later, he said:

"When I finally saw Bobby up there on the stage and he was actually playing for the Championship of the World, I was filled with emotion. Tears almost came to my eyes." Many American players and spectators felt the same way. One of their finest players, after a decade of hope, had finally come into his own: the first American ever to seriously challenge the Soviet hegemony of nearly a half century.

It was a unique moment in the life of a dynamic prodigy in that he had somehow overcome the irrationality of his character to arrive where he was. Everyone knew it, not only in *Laugersdalhöll*, but all over the world. As Isaac Kashdan said: "It was the single most important chess event in the history of the game."

Fischer had been known for his predilection in recent years for the Gruenfeld Defense and the King's Indian, so it was somewhat surprising that he played the Nimzo-Indian, his first attempt with it in over two years. The first game developed along uninspired lines.

Fischer left the stage twice during the game (pre-adjournment), once complaining that the orange juice left in his dressing room backstage was not cold enough. Ice cubes were provided. He also asked for a bottle of cold water and a dish of *skyr*, an Icelandic yogurt-type dessert. This last request caused quite some confusion in the stadium's cafeteria, as they were unable to supply the *skyr* themselves. Fortunately, a local restaurant could.

As moves were made on the board, they were simultaneously shown on forty closed-circuit television monitors in all points of the stadium. In the cafeteria, where spectators wolfed down the local variety of lamb-based hot-dogs and gurgled bottles of two-percent Icelandic beer, the action on the stage was discussed vociferously. In the basement, Icelandic masters more quietly explained and analyzed the moves on a large demonstration board, while in the press rooms, a condescension of grandmasters surveyed the television screens and analyzed in their heads, to the confusion and awe of most of the journalists. In the playing hall itself, decorum and quiet reigned. But when it did not, Lothar Schmid or the Assistant Arbiter, Gudmundur Arnlaugsson, would activate a large white electrical sign that insisted, in both English and Icelandic, upon immediate attention: Silence! *Thögn!*

As the first game progressed, most experts were beginning to predict a draw. And then, on the twenty-ninth move, with the position equal, Fischer engaged in one of the most dangerous gambles of his career. Without consuming much time on his clock (he had equalized on the seventeenth move and was now ahead of Spassky on time) Fischer sacrificed his Bishop for two Pawns in a move that thoroughly electrified the audience, and literally sent Spassky's eyebrows arching.

At first impression, it appeared that Fischer, overly eager to gain the psychological momentum of winning the first game, had overextended himself and simply blundered. But on closer inspection, the game still looked like a draw. Next, Fischer complained to Schmid that the camera poking through a hole in the blue-and-white FIDE sign located at the back of the stage, was disturbing him. No change was made, however, in the camera's position.

On his forty-first move, Spassky, to take advantage of overnight analysis, decided to adjourn the game. Since five hours, the official adjournment time, had not yet been reached, he took a loss of thirty-five minutes on his clock. Spassky had a Bishop and three Pawns against Fischer's five Pawns. He sealed his move and handed the large brown envelope to Schmid.

As the crowds began to file out, Fischer drove back to the Loftleider to analyze the position with Lombardy, discussing it in the car without sight of the board. Byrne said: "Fischer is playing desperately for a draw." Larry Evans felt Fischer had drawing chances, "perhaps." Gligoric thought Fischer's chances were "slim." But Krogius said it was ". . . probably a draw."

Fischer analyzed the position through the night and appeared for the adjournment, looking tired and worried, just two minutes before Schmid opened the sealed-move envelope.

Schmid made Spassky's move for him on the board, showed Fischer the score sheet so he could check that the correct move had been made, and activated his clock. Fischer responded within seconds, and a few moves were exchanged.

Fischer then pointed to the camera aperture that he had complained about the day before, and quickly left the stage with his clock running. Backstage, he vehemently complained about the camera, and said he wanted it dismantled before he continued play. ICF officials quickly conferred with Chester Fox, owner of the film and television rights, who agreed to remove the camera. All of this took time, and Fischer's clock continued running while the dismantling went on. Schmid finally went back to Fischer's dressing room and knocked at his door. "Bobby, the cameras have been removed," he called. "You're a liar," Fischer snapped. Schmid, furious, went back to the stage. Eventually, Saemunder Paalsson, the policeman who had been acting as Fischer's unofficial bodyguard, assured Bobby that he had personally checked that the camera was no longer in operation. When Fischer returned to the stage, thirty-five minutes had elapsed on his clock.

Fischer began fighting for a draw, but Spassky's moves were a study in precision and his position became stronger as they played on. Eventually, it became clear that Spassky could queen a Pawn. Instead of making his fifty-sixth move, Fischer stopped the clock and offered his hand in resignation. He wasn't smiling. Spassky did not look him in the eye as they shook, but continued to study the position. Fischer signed his score sheet, made a helpless gesture as if to say "What am I supposed to do now?" and left the stage. It is not difficult to guess his emotional state.

Though there have been a number of world's championship matches where the loser of the first game went on to win the match, including Spassky-Petrosian, 1969 (and Euwe-Alekhine, 1935, Petrosian-Botvinnik, 1963 and Stenitz-Tchigorin, 1892), there is no question that Fischer considered the loss of the first game almost tantamount to losing the match itself. Not only had he lost, but he had been unable to prove to himself and to the public that he could win a single game from Spassky. Their lifetime score stood at four wins for Spassky, two draws, and no wins for Fischer. Bobby undoubtedly descended into a rage of self-doubt and uncertainty. Since an inner-directed revenge was unthinkable, the cameras were to blame for his loss, not Spassky's superior—or his own inferior—play.

The next morning, Thursday, July 13th, the American delegation announced that Fischer would not play the second game unless *all* cameras were removed from the hall. "I can't think," he said. "It's a distraction." Since the film rights for Fischer, Spassky, and the Icelandic Chess Federation were integrally and intricately woven into the financial arrangements of the match, the problem seemed insoluble. Chester Fox claimed that he had already made binding commitments to deliver a "first quality product" to various film outlets, and that the cameras *must* remain. Lothar Schmid cited Rule 21 of the "Rules of the Match for the Men's World's Championship 1972"* as his guideline for retaining the cameras. Since Rule 21 states that the official cameras will be "neither visible nor audible to the players," it is difficult to understand how Fischer's demand that they be either removed or, by implication, be made soundless and invisible, should *not* have prevailed. But because measures were made to decrease the noise and visibility of the cameras and to relocate them, the organizers, and consequently Schmid, felt the conditions were acceptable. Fischer, on the other hand, claimed—and rightly so—that only he could say what disturbed him. But he refused to go to the hall to inspect the new conditions personally, and to decide whether they had been sufficiently improved.

Schmid declared that the second game would start at 5 P.M., and if

* "All taking of still photographs and any disturbance of the players during play is forbidden without the express permission of both players. The only filming, video taping, or televizing allowed will be that which is exclusively and officially arranged by the organizers. Therefore, unless prior permission has been given by both players, no cameras will be allowed in the playing room except those required for the official uses described in the preceding sentence. The organizers guarantee that these official cameras will be neither visible nor audible to the players and they will not be disturbed in any way, such as by flash, extra lights, or extra personnel in the playing area."

Fischer did not appear after one hour of official play had elapsed, he would be forfeited. To complicate matters even further, Krogius leaked to the press that if Fischer failed to come for the second game, Spassky would probably return to Moscow.

Spassky appeared on stage at two minutes to five, to a round of applause. At precisely 5 P.M., Schmid started Fischer's clock, since Bobby was to play the White pieces. Back at the Loftleider, Cramer and Lombardy futilely appealed to Fischer to go to the hall. A police car, with its motor running, was stationed outside the hotel to whisk Fischer down Suderlansbrut Blvd. to the hall, should he change his mind. At 5:30 P.M., with Fischer's clock still running, Richard C. Stein, Fox's lawyer in Reykjavik, agreed to Davis's suggestion that the cameras be removed just for the one game, pending further discussion. When this solution was relayed to Fischer, he demanded that his clock be set back to its original time. Schmid would not agree. As the Arbiter put it, "There must be some limits."

The spectators continued to gaze hypnotically at the two empty chairs (Spassky had repaired to his dressing room backstage) and a chessboard of thirty-two pieces, none of which had been moved. The only motion was the minute-hand and the agitated, red star-shaped time indicator on Fischer's clock.

When Fridrik Olafsson, Iceland's only grandmaster and an old friend of Fischer's, arrived at the hall, I suggested that he drive over to the Loftleider to reason with Fischer. A few minutes later, he and Gudmundur Einnarsson sped away. When Olafsson reached Fischer's room, he was "allowed" in, but Fischer said: "Talk to me about everything but the match. I lost interest in it six months ago." Fischer told Olafsson he would consider playing the game only if his clock was set back. Olafsson relayed this to the hall, but Schmid had already made his decision. When Olafsson left the room, he lamented: "Fischer was not very coherent. He was quite upset and he said he thought that there was a conspiracy against him by the Icelandic Chess Federation which he believed was a communist front. There was no opportunity of reasoning with him."

At exactly 6 P.M., Schmid stopped the clock and walked to the front of the stage, and announced the first forfeiture in world's championship history. "Ladies and gentlemen, according to Rule 5 of the Amsterdam regulations, Robert Fischer has lost the game. He has not turned up within the stipulated hour of time."

Spassky was given a standing ovation. He said to Schmid, "It's a pity," while someone from the audience yelled, "Send him back to the United States!" Harry Golombek added, "It's an insult to the World Champion and the chess world in general. He seems to have spoiled what had the makings of the greatest match in chess history. But you never know with that man. He has such extraordinary capabilities that it is perfectly possible for him to turn up on Sunday, recover from his defeat, and go on to win the series."

Davis flew from New York to Reykjavik immediately. He was incensed, threatening to sue in Fischer's behalf, to have the forfeiture removed. "The noise from the television was noticeable to Bobby," he complained. "It's obvious he is very sensitive to noise and distractions." Within six hours after the forfeiture, Fischer, assisted by Cramer, lodged a formal protest. The complaint is a unique document, outlining Fischer's position and giving a rare glimpse into the workings of his mind. Here are excerpts:

July 13, 1972

Mr. Lothar Schmid
Chief Arbiter
World's Championship Match Committee
Reykjavik, Iceland
Dear Sir:

I must most vigorously protest your action today in starting my clock when playing conditions were grossly below the minimum standards set by the official rules . . . and your subsequent action in forfeiting me.

For the past four years of my tournament career I have not permitted any filming or picture-taking while play was in progress. In all events I have participated in, the organizers have agreed in writing to my letter of conditions which I send out as a matter of course to all prospective organizers of chess events who would like my participation. Some months ago I was asked about the possibilities of televising this match and of taking films, still photos and using closed-circuit television, and so on. I was skeptical because the noise, commotion, and distraction surrounding such things . . . had always proved to be an unbearable annoyance to me in the past.

However, I was assured by all parties concerned that modern technology had progressed to such an extent that they could photograph me without the least disturbance, using telephoto lenses in fixed positions behind plate-glass panels, all equipment and supporting structures and personnel and their cameras to be completely out of sight. . . .

Tentatively, I agreed, without signing any contracts, that if and when I saw and approved such equipment in operation at the match site, that I would allow TV and the other devices mentioned provided they were under my control at all times.

The organizers knew how strict I have always been on the

matter of playing conditions. In fact, though from time to time I have compromised on money matters, I have never compromised on anything affecting playing conditions of the game itself, which is my art and my profession. It seemed to me that the organizers deliberately tried to upset and provoke me by the way they coddled and kow-towed to that [film] crew.

You had been repeatedly warned by my representative after the adjourned game and again this morning that conditions must be corrected. It can therefore have been no surprise to you that I did not appear at game time. Yet suddenly, half an hour after game time and only half an hour before the moment when I would risk a forfeit, I was informed that the cameras were being removed at last. I then had a choice of going to the hall and starting play immediately and at a considerable disadvantage in time, a condition for which I bore no fault, not to mention the fact that I could have no assurance on such short notice that there would be no problems in future games with camera equipment, and for that matter even during to-day's game; or of going to the hall and facing the necessity of arguing with the arbiter for the return of the clock to its starting position and obtaining a written agreement that there would be no further trouble with the cameras, all this while thousands of people waited uncomfortably in the hall for play to begin. I decided in favor of a third course, which was to allow my time to run out, to be' for-feited, even though the forfeit was contrary to the rules under these circumstances, and then to protest the forfeit in writing to you and the committee, as I now do.

As you know, I have been very anxious for people in my own country, the United States, to see this event. It was for this reason that I was willing for the first time to try filming. My personal representative, Mr. Paul Marshall, was assured that the process of filming would not be evi-dent to the players. While I wanted TV, and while it could mean a great deal of money to me personally, it is more important that the world chess championship be played under full professional conditions than that I make a personal monetary gain. The rules were designed so that the contestants could play the finest chess of which they are capable. They protect the players from interference with their concentration. My concentration has been dis-turbed by an evasion of these rules. I only ask what I have always asked, that the rules providing for proper championship chess conditions be observed. Therefore I request that today's ruling be reversed. When that happens, and when all camera equipment and supporting equipment has been removed from the hall, I will be at the chessboard. I am keen to play this match, and I hope Game Two will be scheduled for Sunday, July 16 at five in the afternoon.

Sincerely,

Bobby Fischer

Reykjavik, Iceland

The match committee overruled Fischer's protest on the grounds that he had failed to appear at the game. By FIDE regulations, a contestant must make his protest of a given game within six hours after that game has ended. The committee upheld the forfeiture, but not without some trepidation and soul-searching. Everyone knew, of course, that Fischer would not accept it lightly. And he did not. His instant reaction was to make a reservation to fly home immediately. He was dissuaded by Lombardy, but it seemed very likely that he would refuse to continue the match unless the forfeit was removed. Schmid himself voiced his sincere concern over the danger to Fischer's own career if he walked out of the match: "What will happen to Bobby? What city would ever host a match for him?"

Notified of the decision and realizing its implications, Dr. Euwe, who had returned to the Netherlands, cabled his own decision to Schmid in case Fischer refused to appear at the next game:

IN CASE OF NON-APPEARANCE OF FISCHER IN THIRD GAME, PRESIDENT OF FIDE DECLARES IF FISCHER NOT IN THE FOURTH GAME, MATCH WILL BE CONCLUDED AND SPASSKY WILL BE PROCLAIMED WORLD CHAMPION.

Euwe's precedent for this is the FIDE ruling that, in a tournament, a player who forfeits three consecutive games by non-appearance, forfeits the whole tournament.

Fischer began receiving letters and cables—thousands according to Cramer—urging him to continue the match, and presidential adviser Henry Kissinger called him from Washington to appeal to his patriotic interests in playing for the United States. *The New York Times* even issued an open plea urging Fischer to continue his challenge. In an editorial entitled "Bobby Fischer's Tragedy," they wrote: ". . . the possibility seems strong that his temper tantrums will turn the present world championship match into a non-event in which Spassky will retain his crown because of Fischer's refusal to play."

"The tragedy in all this is particularly great because for nearly a decade, there has been strong reason to suppose that Fischer could demonstrate his supremacy convincingly if only given the opportunity to do so. . . .

"Is it too much to hope that even at this late state he will regain his balance and fulfill his obligation to the chess world by trying to play Spassky without histrionics? Consequential as is the two-game lead the Soviet champion now enjoys, the board is still set for a duel that could rank among the most brilliant in this ancient game's annals."

In an effort to ease the situation and encourage Fischer to continue the match, Schmid announced that according to the rules, he had the right to move the match from the stage of the hall to a back-stage room, ". . . at least temporarily to give Fischer a chance to calm down." To get the third game underway, Schmid then appealed to Spassky ". . . as a sportsman" to agree to play in a room backstage, out of sight of cameras and audience, in an attempt to normalize the situation. Spassky was willing ". . . but just for this one game." Fischer had made reservations on all three flights going back to New York on the day of the game, but ninety minutes before the start of play he said he would be willing to give it a trial, if he was assured complete privacy and no cameras.

A few minutes before the game started, I asked Davis what had convinced Bobby to play. "Your guess is as good or maybe better than mine. I have no real idea," he replied vaguely.

Why *did* Fischer continue to play? Probably a combination of genuine nationalism, faith in his ability to overcome the odds of a two-point deficit, a desire to secure the money (even if he lost the match, he would have received $91,875 in prize money, in addition to an estimated $30,000 from television and movie rights), and an overwhelming need to do what he said he was going to almost from the day he first moved a Pawn: prove that he was the most gifted chess player on earth.

Together with the swagger of his self-assurance and the stride of his devotion to chess, Bobby Fischer must have experienced an overwhelmingly phobic dread, almost a stark terror, when he decided to sit down and play the third game. In that he confronted and conquered this existential uncertainty, Fischer emerges as his own hero, true to himself and his destiny.

The temporary playing room, located on the second floor of the stadium, above and to the rear of the stage, was a large, breezy, green-carpeted affair, used normally for table-tennis tournaments. Police guards were placed at the stairways to prevent anyone from reaching the room and disturbing the players. One unmanned, noiseless closed-circuit television camera, looking not unlike a spindly robot, was positioned about ten feet from the board.

During the game, I was in a small room about twenty feet away from the players, doing a remote broadcast for ABC's "Wide World of Sports," following the action on a soundless closed-circuit monitor and using an open telephone line to New York. Spassky appeared on time; at first sat in Fischer's chair, and, perhaps unaware that he was on camera, smiled and swivelled around several times as a child might do. Then he moved to his own chair, and waited. Fischer arrived eight minutes late ("Hamlet sauntering back," as Steiner described it), looking very pale, and the two men shook hands. Spassky, as White, played 1 P–Q4, and Fischer replied . . .N–KB3. Suddenly, Fischer began pointing to the camera and shouting. I could plainly hear his voice through the closed door, as I watched his image on the TV screen.

"What is this?" he demanded, worrying the on-off switch of the camera.

"Will you please be quiet, Bobby?" said Schmid. "The game has started."

Fischer whipped around. "Shut up!" he yelled at Schmid, who blanched in disbelief.

"What did you say? I'm sorry," Schmid replied evenly and then made a comment that indicated he would not "allow" such language to be used.

Spassky was now on his feet. "I am leaving!" he announced curtly but with the bearing of a Russian count, informing the two men that he was going to the stage to play the game there.

Schmid recalled later that ". . . for a second, I didn't know what to do. Then I stopped Spassky's clock, breaking the rules. But somehow I had to get that incredible situation under control."

The voices continued, but became somewhat subdued. Schmid put his arms around Spassky's shoulders, saying: "Boris, you promised me you would play this game here. Are you breaking that promise?" Then turning to Fischer, Schmid said: "Bobby, please be kind."

Spassky gaped for about ten seconds, thinking about what to do, and finally sat down. Fischer apologized for his hasty words, and both men finally got down to business. They played one of the best games of the match. After Fischer's seventh move (fifteen minutes had elapsed on his clock to Spassky's five), he left the room and I had an opportunity to see his face closely, without his seeing me. He appeared intensely grave. "He looked like death," said Schmid. Yes, and also incensed, indignant and thoroughly, almost maniacally, determined.

Playing the Benoni Defense, Fischer made an unorthodox eleventh move, which caused Spassky to ponder for over thirty minutes. Eventually, Fischer seized the attack, won a Pawn and, when they adjourned on the forty-first move, his position was irresistible. The game was resumed the next day, again on the stage. Spassky took one fleeting glimpse at Fischer's sealed move, which won by force, and stopped his clock, signaling his resignation.

Tardy as usual, Fischer dashed on to the stage fifteen minutes late, out of breath. Spassky was already en route back to his hotel. "What happened?" he asked, and Schmid said: "Mr. Spassky has resigned." Fischer signed his score sheet and left the stage without another word. By the time he reached the backstage exit, he could no longer resist a smile for the well-wishers waiting there. It was undoubtedly one of the happiest moments of his life.

Though it seems ludicrous to suggest that the outcome of the Fischer-Spassky match was predictable after only two games had been completed, one point going to each player, the conclusion is quite sound. Fischer's first win over Spassky was more than a narrowing of the gap. It was the creation of his "set," the gestalt he needed to prove to himself that he was capable of dominance. A drawn game would have had no significance. He had demonstrated in the past that he could, though admittedly infrequently, draw with Spassky. An actual win was the needle that extracted the first drop of blood. The drop soon turned into torrents of energy streaming from Spassky's psyche.

In the fourth game, after a tiring and tension-filled five hour session, a Sicilian Defense that resulted in a Bishops of opposite color ending, Spassky and Fischer looked up at each other almost simultaneously, catching each other's eyes, and without exchanging a word agreed to a draw. Fischer offered his hand and Spassky shook it. They had played forty-five moves, and it was a brilliant game, worthy of a World's Championship duel.

That night, Fischer dined with his friend Lina Grumette, and at one point, thinking about the game, he said almost wistfully "Maybe I should have adjourned that game. What am I going to do with myself tomorrow?"

After committing what was perhaps the worst blunder of his career, Spassky resigned on the twenty-ninth move of the fifth game, one of the shortest decisive encounters in World's Championship history. Fischer had just won a Pawn and threatened to immediately win more material with the threat of mate. The match score now stood even at 2½–2½. Olafsson said: "Spassky is worried, although he doesn't show it."

Playing White in the sixth game, Fischer chose the Queen's Gambit Declined, playing it for the first time in his career! There is a possibility that he had been saving this very opening for over a decade, just waiting for the right time to unleash it on his unwary opponent. Miguel Najdorf, seated on the sidelines, likened the game to a symphony by Mozart. Fischer built a crushing attack and enveloped Spassky in a mating net, forcing his capitulation on the forty-first move. Fischer has since implied that this was his favorite game of the match.

Lombardy was ecstatic: "Bobby has played a steady, fluent game, and just watched Spassky make horrendous mistakes. Spassky has not met a player of Bobby's genius and caliber before, who fights for every piece on the board; he doesn't give in and agree to draws like the Russian grandmasters. This is a shock to Spassky."

The seventh game, a Sicilian Defense, was adjourned after Spassky pondered his forty-first move for forty-five nerve-wracking minutes. Geller conferred by phone with Mikhail Tal in Latvia and Tigran Petrosian in Armenia and received their appraisals that the position was drawn. When Spassky and Fischer resumed the next day, they played several more moves, and in an even endgame, agreed to a draw on the forty-eighth move. Fischer's sister Joan Targ and her husband Russell and their three children appeared in Reykjavik in time for this game, and remained for several days. "I would like to spend more time with my niece and nephews," Uncle Bobby said to a friend, "but I must keep to my training."

Again, altering his repertoire, Fischer next played the English Opening, for the second time in his career. Spassky floundered, falling behind in time and consuming almost an hour on his eleventh move when Fischer varied from known theoretical lines. Fischer won a Pawn on the nineteenth move, and at one point later on in the game appeared to be making a series of pointless moves, as if he were toying with Spassky. Gligoric said: "I think he's giving him the Chinese water torture. If Spassky won't resign, Fischer is going to make him suffer . . . and prolong the game." Spassky resigned on the thirty-seventh move.

Only the first game and part of the second had been filmed, due to Fischer's insistence that the cameras disturbed him. ABC-TV, nervous that their own agreement with Chester Fox might be worthless if Fischer continued to object to the current film arrangements, sent producer Loren Hassan to negotiate a new deal. Fischer listened at length, then told Hassan to take the matter up with Paul Marshall.

Marshall and ABC came to terms, which everyone, including Marshall, assumed Fischer would agree to. The cameras were brought into the playing hall once again to film the eighth game, but this time they were discreetly positioned in the very back of the hall, up in the balcony, where it was believed they could not possibly disturb either player.

Taking a rare bit of time off, Fischer decided to have a leisurely dinner with his sister. But a news report came over the radio, and from it Fischer learned that the game had been filmed. He went into a rage and demanded apologies from virtually everyone, cutting short all plans to continue making a filmed record of the historic match. No further games were filmed, despite negotiations which continued until the very last day of play.

Trailing 5–3 and watching his title slip away, Spassky asked for a postponement of the ninth game due to a head cold. It was assumed that he was suffering from stress and fatigue and was attempting to get himself back into a stronger psychological frame of mind. Fischer began telling friends that he thought the match would be over in his favor in two weeks time. He was becoming convivial and even made attempts at dry, almost British, humor. At the beginning of August, while gazing out of the picture window of his hotel room at the northern void during a gray, uninviting and wetly cold day, he quipped: "Iceland is a nice place. I must come back here in the summertime."

When the ninth game was eventually played, it ended in twenty-nine dull moves, a draw being agreed upon. After the round, Fischer played Ping-Pong with friends at the Loftleider and then went bowling at Keflavik.

Fischer won the tenth game, a splendidly played Ruy Lopez, in fifty-six moves, and moved ahead of Spassky in their lifetime results; Fischer now led 5–4. In the World's Championship match, he led by a full three points. The score stood at 6½–3½. To relax, he went sailing on Vitheyjar Sound that night.

In the eleventh game, Spassky fiercely retaliated, capturing Fischer's Queen on the twenty-fourth move. His Russian seconds, Krogius and Geller, were smiling for the first time since July 11th, the day of the first game. The crowd was on tenterhooks! Rankled, since he was playing his favorite variation of the Sicilian Defense—the Najdorf—Fischer played on for a few more moves. Schmid observed that ". . . perhaps he did not want the books to record such a quick triumph for Spassky. He could have resigned straight away." When Fischer finally did relent, Spassky was pacing up and down the backstage corridor. Fischer stopped his clock and left the stage before his opponent returned. Spassky was greeted with a tremendous ovation when he came out on stage again, but he lifted both hands pleading for the crowd to stop.

Fischer was emotionally crushed; as his car drove away from the playing hall, he was staring dejectedly downward, unable to utter a word, his chin resting on his chest, his probable illusion that he would never lose another game to Spassky for the rest of his life, smashed.

The twelfth game was drawn, another Bishops of opposite color ending. Toward the end of the game, Fischer kept flickering glances at Spassky, no doubt waiting for him to offer a draw. When he did, after the fifty-fifth move, Fischer immediately accepted. "Fischer's *too* relaxed. It's a problem. I'm worried," said Cramer.

The next morning at about five o'clock, Fischer and Lombardy had breakfast at the Loftleider Hotel cafeteria. They sat at their table for over two hours, analyzing the twelfth game.

Alekhine's Defense had not been played in a World's Championship match since Euwe bravely tried it against Alekhine himself in their match in 1935 (they drew), until Fischer played it in the thirteenth game. Spassky was standing at the board when he played 1 P–K4. In many ways, "unlucky thirteen" was the pivotal game of their entire encounter. It was a nine-and-a-half hour marathon in which Fischer, even though a pawn ahead, had a difficult position right up to adjournment. He could find no improvement with overnight analysis and upon resumption he had to continue to try to keep what looked like a draw. Spassky had both drawing and winning chances.

On the sixty-ninth move, obviously exhausted, Spassky blundered. When he realized his mistake, he could barely look at the board, turning his head away several times in humiliation and frustration. Fischer sat back in his chair, grimly, staring at Spassky—studying him. For a long, long moment, he did not take his eyes off the Russian. There was just a bit of compassion in Fischer's eyes which turned the episode into a true Aristotelian tragedy: Spassky's terror combined with Fischer's pity. Spassky finally moved, but resigned on the seventy-fourth move.

Fischer was up and out of *Laugarsdolhöll* in no time, instantly revitalized, a man secure in his knowledge of impending victory. That evening, Spassky took a long walk in the rain through the Seltjarnanes section of Reykjavik with his wife Larissa, who had arrived in Iceland the previous day. Discussing that night some time afterward, he said he spent most of that walk "pitying" himself. So did many of those who had witnessed the game, even Fischer sympathizers.

A series of drawn games followed, unparalleled in modern World Championship history. The points of seven games—fourteen to twenty —were halved, and though many were dynamic encounters (either player was often lost but managed to evade defeat), one must go back to the Capablanca-Alekhine match, Buenos Aires, 1927, to surpass this number of consecutively indecisive skirmishes. Fischer seemed to be content with draws for the first time in his career, perhaps reasoning that, with a three point margin, half-points were tantamount to wins. After the match Fischer stated that though he was not playing for drawn games after he had established his three point margin, he *had* ceased taking chances. He kept getting closer and closer to the title with each game, since Spassky had to win to reduce Fischer's lead. "It's not the Bobby we know and love," said Gligoric, "but who can blame him? He wants the championship more than anything in the world."

After twenty games, the score stood at 11½–8½ in favor of Fischer. He needed just two draws out of the remaining four games to wrest the title from the Russian. Fischer's future was manifest.

Though perhaps not the "match of the century" in the quality of games played, nor in the degree of resistance offered by Spassky, the contest did cause more furor and attention, more *awareness* of the game by the general public, than any other chess event in history.

Off-the-board maneuvers screamed for publicity. During the course of the match, Fischer was sued for $1,750,000 by Chester Fox. Fox's lawyer, Barry Fredericks, flew to Iceland to attempt to negotiate. "But we won't serve any papers on Fischer until after the match is over," he told me sincerely. "We realize that this is a championship match, and we don't want to do anything that will disturb Fischer." Shortly afterward, Fischer *was* served—before the match was over. Perhaps Fox was more straightforward than his lawyer when he said: "All I want to do is grab his [Fischer's] money and get out of here."

Since chess is one of the few arts where composition takes place simultaneously with performance, the amount of concentration necessary is overwhelming. Disturbances cannot be tolerated. But Fox was a motion picture producer and not a chess devotee, and was attempting to protect his investment. Whether or not Fischer lost the match because he was being rattled by cameras didn't interest Fox. He never understood that Fischer was not a movie star, but a chess player.

A barrage of discourteous memos from Cramer, and sometimes from Fischer himself, were sent to Lothar Schmid almost daily for the duration of the match, complaining about everything from the closeness of spectators to the stage, to the noise of crinkling candy wrappers. Almost all the memos complained about noise in the playing hall. It was surprising that the American delegation, with the possible exception of Lombardy, did not realize, or did not care, that the rudely written, vicious attacks on Schmid were causing more problems than they were solving. The Arbiter accomplished a superlative and herculean task in helping to obtain and maintain the best possible playing conditions for both players. Unswervingly fair and objective, Schmid must have found it difficult to act on all of Fischer's demands when they were posed in a way that made it necessary for him to defend himself. A kind remark or genteel gesture from Fischer or his representatives would have made it easier for Schmid to cooperate in a spirit of friendship. "The hall is as quiet as I can make it," he insisted (and he was right). "What do they want me to do, shoot the spectators? That's it! I will shoot the spectators to make them happy!" But Schmid was often more bitter: "In my twenty-three years of international tournament play, I have never met anyone like Cramer," he remarked. "I feel sorry for the United States."

The United States, however, was busy feeling affectionate toward Fischer, and gave no thought to criticism of its hero or his confederates. President Nixon indicated that he wanted Bobby Fischer to visit him after the match, "win or lose," adding that he admired the young chess player because "he is a fighter."

Shortly before the concluding week of the match, the Soviet delegation, by way of a long and preposterous statement issued by Geller but probably initiated by a petty bureaucrat in the Kremlin, made an accusation that Fischer might be "influencing" the World Champion's behavior by "chemical substances or electronic means." Straight out of *1984*, a serious investigation was launched by what could have been the Ministry of Truth under the direction of Big Brother but what was actually the Reykjavik Police Department and some Icelandic scientists. They field-stripped Spassky's chair, X-rayed it, took scrapings of all the surroundings and even examined the air on the stage. One object was found in Spassky's chair that was not in Fischer's otherwise identical chair! But the "secret weapon" turned out to be a blob of wood filler, placed there by the manufacturer. Fischer guffawed when he heard of it and said he had been expecting rougher tactics from the Russians. The case was embarrassingly closed. Harry Golombek summed up the world's first chess circus in humorous, though poignant, fashion: "It started out as a farce by Beckett—*Waiting for Godot*. Then it turned into a Kafka tragedy. Now it's beyond Kafka. Perhaps Strindberg could do it justice."

The twenty-first game commenced on August 31st and Fischer, playing Black, elected the Sicilian Defense; after a few moves the game transposed into the Scotch Game. On his nineteenth move, Spassky sacrificed the Exchange but emerged with two passed Pawns on the Queenside. But Fischer played the endgame in stellar fashion, and at adjournment it looked as though he could win the game.

The next day, a Scotsman, Harry Benson, a photographer for *Time-Life*, met Spassky at the Hotel Saga. "There's a new champion," Spassky said. "I'm not sad. It's a sporting event and I lost. Bobby's the new champion. Now I must take a walk and get some fresh air."

Benson immediately drove to the Hotel Loftleider and called Bobby on the house phone. "Are you sure it's official?" Fischer asked. When told that it was, he said: "Well, thanks."

At 2:47 P.M., Fischer appeared on stage at *Laugarsdalhöll* to sign his score sheet. Schmid made the official announcement: "Ladies and gentlemen, Mr. Spassky has resigned by telephone at 12:50. This is a traditional and legal way of resignation. Mr. Fischer has won this game, number twenty-one, and he is the winner of the match."

The spectators went wild. Fischer smiled when Schmid shook his hand, nodded awkwardly at the audience, looked uncomfortable, and started to go. Just before leaving, he paused ever so briefly and looked out into the crowd, as though he might be about to say something or perhaps wave, then he quickly disappeared backstage and left the building. A mob swarmed around his car, which was driven by Paalsson. Television and radio reporters poked microphones and cameras at the closed windows. Lombardy sat in the back seat, and the three men drove off. Only after they were under way did Fischer allow himself to break into a big, boyish grin. He was the Chess Champion of the World.

THE WORLD'S CHAMPIONSHIP MATCH, 1972
ROBERT J. FISCHER VS. BORIS SPASSKY

Game No.	Opening	Fischer	Spassky	No. of Moves
1	Nimzo-Indian Defense	0	1	56
2	(Forfeit by Fischer)	0	1	—
3	Benoni Defense	1	0	41
4	Sicilian Defense	½	½	45
5	Nimzo-Indian Defense	1	0	27
6	Queen's Gambit Declined	1	0	41
7	Sicilian Defense	½	½	49
8	English Opening	1	0	37
9	Tarrasch Defense	½	½	29
10	Ruy Lopez	1	0	56
11	Sicilian Defense	0	1	31
12	Queen's Gambit Declined	½	½	55
13	Alekhine's Defense	1	0	74
14	Queen's Gambit Declined	½	½	40
15	Sicilian Defense	½	½	43
16	Ruy Lopez	½	½	60
17	Pirc Defense	½	½	45
18	Sicilian Defense	½	½	47
19	Alekhine Defense	½	½	40
20	Sicilian Defense	½	½	54
21	Sicilian Defense	1	0	40
		12½	8½	45 (Average)

Fischer had White in all even numbered games.

CHAPTER XXXI

"Chess is life."

Any attempt to understand the life of Bobby Fischer must be, by definition, wracked with frustration. The pursuit of his illustrious career is counterbalanced by his bizarre and bombastic behaviour. If he is the rainbow, he is also the storm.

Aloof, uncooperative, elusive, evasive, Fischer emerges as one of the most ephemeral and enigmatic characters of contemporary society. At the precise moment when the examiner believes he has discovered a truth about him, Fischer dissolves it, or at least transforms it. It is for this very reason that efforts like this one, to comprehend him or at least interpret his development, will continue to be made.

Though psychological assessments of Fischer are inevitable, the Freudian interpretation of his relationship to chess really gives us little insight. All psychologists agree that chess provides an outlet for hostile impulses in a non-retaliatory situation, and for this reason the therapeutic value of the game is enormous. There is no question that Fischer has substituted the chessboard for the couch, and has been both calmed and stimulated by this therapy all his life.

Fully aware of the risks and inadequacies of trying to understand him, I would guess the essential story of Bobby Fischer's development is something like this:

Without a father, and in the early years of his life without a settled home, the young Bobby found emotional security—to an extraordinary degree—in a game. The inanimate wooden pieces almost came to life and became the friends in whom he could be assured of total consistency. Upon this checkered field he could be as good as any; better than most. As many gifted and solitary children turn away from reality into a world of books, so Bobby buried himself in chess. And soon, like the young Mozart demanding to play in string quartets at the age of four, Bobby was insisting on the opportunity to improve his art through constant practice. He fell into immediate conflict since the world at large considers chess a sport of kings, perhaps, an eminent struggle and a noble pastime at best, but hardly an *art*.

If he had elected to lift the violin or test his hand at the brush, the encouragement from his mother, his friends, and his teachers would undoubtedly have been immediate. But *chess?* It was a mere game!

Fascinated by a field for which others cared little, Bobby slowly discovered his great talent. And soon he ignored everything else. The fact that illiterates find no pleasure in Shakespeare, and that to people totally unschooled in classical music, Stravinsky is just so much noise, was probably never considered analagous by those who had no knowledge of chess and who were associated with Bobby. George Bernard Shaw's cynical view that chessplayers are people who ". . . believe they are doing something very clever when they are only wasting their time," was prevalent for years. It is rarely held today even among those who do not know how to play.

The process of Bobby's evolution went even beyond obsession. An actual fusion between his deepest needs and a mastery of the game seems to have occurred. He pursued chess with a religious fervor. The game became his one discipline, direction, and power. He no longer needed a father to show him the way to manhood. With these carved pieces, each charged with potency, he could march against the world. When he emerged from his solitary apprenticeship, he had his sword and shield, but any chink in this armor left him naked.

At the risk of stressing the obvious, three interrelated aspects of his early experience with chess should be emphasized here. First, the process was *exclusive*: all other concerns were ignored. Second, it was *solitary*: despite being taught by his sister, and receiving assists from Nigro and Collins, Bobby essentially learned chess by himself and owes his mastery to nobody but himself. Third, his interest became the determining ingredient in his developing self-image.

I have singled out these three points with the hope that a closer look at each will make Fischer's life more comprehensible. To start, his immense capacity for private study was never turned to any area outside chess. His compulsive need to prove himself was invested in this discipline alone, and the result was an early perfection of his craft, which separated him from any broad cultural base. Such is the price of creativity. Van Gogh knew very little other than how to create masterpieces on canvas. But for Bobby his craftsmanship resulted in a radical split between special capability and general knowledge. Though somewhat influenced by his mother's and sister's love for learning, basically he was not aware, secure in his special excellence, that the larger world of general culture had anything to teach or even tell him. In defensive moments, he has been contemptuously anti-intellectual and anti-academic. More often his sense of immunity became so acute that he was simply beyond the reach of criticism. Inevitably the fortress becomes a prison. Intellectually, Bobby was isolated in a single dimension. Psychologically, he was trapped by his own temperament, unable to realize that a sensitivity to the rights and interests of others is a condition of social being. He backed himself into such a small cultural corner that his ideational mobility suffered every time it was tried. For years his lack of sophistication hampered him everywhere he turned.

Indeed, Fischer was scarcely able, for the major part of his life, to communicate with the world of larger interests except through the medium of the chessboard. Mikhail Tal once said that Bobby should read more outside of chess or his game would eventually suffer from the thinness of his education. Bobby replied by slighting his critic's chess ability and adding a series of sneers at intellectual pretensions on the part of certain chess masters. Botvinnik, in a speech in Leningrad in 1971, said Fischer ". . . had not the necessary intellect to become World Champion," no doubt meaning he showed no love of intellect, or lacked education.

That Botvinnik was proven wrong indicates the depth and complexity of Fischer. He became chess champion of the world not in *spite* of his cultural deficiency, but *because* of it. But I must insist that Fischer is no phrenological *sport*, no *idiot savant*, who is incapable of superiority in other fields. Fischer is an artist who *selected* chess as his medium of expression; if others do not consider chess a high form of creative endeavor he cannot assume the blame. Fischer has *made* his chess an art. While others were studying Dostoevsky and attending ballet, Fischer was learning the nuances of the Nimzo-Indian or determining *why* Steinitz played 12 N–N1 against Anderssen in Vienna, 1873. Fischer knows more about chess theory than any other player in history.

I once asked Fischer if he would give me chess instruction, and he agreed. "For the first lesson, I want you to play over every column of *Modern Chess Openings*, including footnotes," he said, smiling but totally serious; "And for the next lesson, I want you to do it again."

In many ways, the crossroad of Bobby's life came when he dropped out of Erasmus Hall at sixteen. Though I sympathize with his feeling that high school had no more to offer him, the event symbolized his formal rejection of general culture. More recently he's been interested in learning, and not too long ago said: "After I win the title, then I can think of developing myself in other areas." He is sincere.

The second point we want to look at is that Bobby developed his genius almost entirely alone. It was his total absorption in the game that caused his mother to place the ad in the *Brooklyn Eagle* that led to his introduction to Carmine Nigro. "Mr. Nigro was possibly not the best player in the world, but he was a very good teacher," Bobby wrote in the introduction to his *Games of Chess* in 1958. Nigro and Jack Collins are probably among the very few teachers Fischer has ever respected, but it is clear from this quotation that even as a child he regarded himself as their equal.

Many children recoil from the emotional discomfort of their lives and through transference make themselves masters of the situation through games or pretence. Bobby's intensity was legend. From the beginning, he believed chess was a game in which you sat alone and achieved everything from within yourself. Its mastery held the promise of almost complete autonomy. As soon as he realized his powers, Bobby focused upon this goal. He all but single-handedly worked his way to the top; he owed his success to nobody but himself. Such persons are frequently natural anarchists, with little sense of outside obligation or duty. They have an abundant store of righteousness. They are quick to see themselves as victimized, or about to be victimized, by those who envy their gifts and fear their ambitions. This suspiciousness is reinforced by the anxiety of the loner, who keeps his few friends and relatives at a distance, and has no one but himself to fall back upon in times of trouble.

Bobby's claim to autonomy goes deeper. Almost every man of genius is beset with people who want to include themselves within his sphere. Bobby reacts ruthlessly to such intrusions. This is an often overlooked factor, behind his frequent and apparently deliberate alienation of well-meaning colleagues. Others must not try to walk on his level. Ed Edmondson suddenly and sadly discovered Fischer's ruthlessness when he attempted to act *for* him in Amsterdam, assuming the prerogative Fischer never grants. Those who would claim closeness to a king court the fate of Falstaff.

"I don't have to report to anybody," Bobby told me years ago. After Regina Fischer left their home in 1960, he realized his much hoped-for autonomy. From then on he was accountable, as he boasted, to no one. His studies and efforts begin and end in solitude. Bobby Fischer lives alone.

The third significant factor in Bobby's development was also evident from his childhood. For the young male, the vision of having matchless power over others is practically irresistible. Social and parental pressures keep most young men from acting out the fantasy, and those who try quickly discover reality. With Bobby, however, the dream and the reality merged to such an extent that for a long time, he had trouble telling them apart.

At fourteen, he had conquered the best a whole continent could muster against him, and long before that he must have felt himself invincible. Every artist tends to exaggerate his talent, especially when young. The modestly gifted assume a large talent, the more richly gifted assume genius. And it is not without precedent for men of genius to assume unto themselves what can only be called divinity. It was noticed fairly early that Bobby's conception of himself had mythic

overtones. As far back as 1960, *Shakhmaty* stated: "Fischer is undoubtedly a talented player . . . but he thinks himself absolutely the
strongest player in the world . . ."

Bobby could not question this personal myth, and others could
validly do so only across the board. Certainly this Olympian faith
stimulated his drive for perfection, and in its irrationality served to
propel him to greatness. "Every game is a challenge that I must
meet," he told the Spanish journalist Toran. Defeats and inexcusable
setbacks have no more effect upon his convictions than they would
upon those of any true believer. When things go wrong he seeks the
reason outside himself rather than within. When Toran asked him
if he had ever doubted himself, he replied, "Never." He *knows* that
he is Caissa's Chosen.

Without this personal belief, Bobby probably would not have kept
going. But his collision with reality had to come sooner or later. After
his magnificent victory at Stockholm he seemed on the threshold of
the World Championship, an honor he desperately needed to secure
his self-image. He could have had no doubt that his hour of triumph
had come. Older and wiser opinion was skeptical, but agreed with
remarkable unanimity that he would almost certainly win the world
title sometime in the future. Kotov's Stockholm dictum on Fischer—
"His future possibilities are limitless"—has become famous. After that
tournament, ex-World Champion Max Euwe wrote: "I have asked
several experts their opinion on Fischer's chances [at Curaçao]. The
general consensus was that should Fischer not succeed this time, he
is bound to become the winner of the Candidates' . . . Fischer's
progress, especially this past year, is so overwhelming and impressive
that in a few years he will be irresistible. In other words, according
to the prophecy cited, Fischer will be World Champion in 1966 . . ."
Euwe also predicted Fischer's victory in 1969.

The period of crisis began at Stockholm and continued through
Curaçao, though the issue wasn't finally or publicly resolved till he
refused to compete at Amsterdam, and then dropped out of Sousse.
Sousse could be considered Fischer's greatest tragedy. Not only would
he have qualified easily, but his magnificent chess would have no
doubt helped him to surpass his Stockholm performance.

But Bobby wasn't reading any "prophecy cited" except his own.
He believed he must succeed at Curaçao. He knew he would at
Sousse. But if he did not succeed in the first event, he would lose his
chance to be the youngest World Champion of all time; he has since
referred to his loss in exactly those terms.

Fischer's subsequent bitter and overwhelming reaction to the chess
world was not just disappointment or heartbreak. Even the most
gifted sportsmen learn to take defeat, accept it, and start over again.
But Bobby Fischer *cannot* accept defeat. The personal myth must

be proven at the precise hour marked for its demonstration; and since his basic faith could not be doubted, something had to be wrong with the surrounding externals.

It is this conflict with the exoteric, the constant, almost endless contretemps concerning lighting, seating, prizes, schedules, organizers, referees, and any of a myriad of other complaints, that serve as Fischer's outlet for the pent-up energy and hostilities that he cannot sate over the board. His rage for combat is immense, almost classically primal in its ferocity and raw anger, constantly honed for the attack. He assumes the personality of Lasker's creature, the *Macheïde*,* the son of battle, whose senses have been so sharpened by millions of years of reincarnated struggle throughout the ages that it *always* chooses, automatically, the best and most efficient way of perpetuating itself; hence, as a chessplayer, the *Macheïde* would select the perfect, most devastating move, at each opportunity.

No lucid impression of Bobby Fischer's life can be experienced without an appraisal of his relationship to his art, and to other great players. Is Fischer the greatest contemporary player in the world? Is he the greatest player ever?

Two compelling facts are that Fischer *is* World's Champion and that in accomplishing this deed he lost only five games (one of them by forfeit) out of sixty-five, from Palma to Reykjavik, playing against the world's chess élite (a record I will gladly wager will go unequalled in this century). It should also be noted that on the Elo scale, a thoroughly reliable device, Fischer has achieved the highest rating of *any* player in history. Thus responsible critics will invariably select Fischer as the strongest chess player in the world at this moment in time.

But Bobby is much more than that. For decades chess has acknowledged champions who were, as Botvinnik perhaps too humbly once described himself, *primus inter pares*—first among equals. Our generation had not produced an authentic genius. The last supermaster was Alekhine. Preceding him, in reverse order, were Capablanca, Lasker, and Steinitz, all World Champions who comprised a magic circle of greatness. Players like Tal and Spassky have touched the perimeters of the circle and even entered it on occasion, but were never card-carrying members. Bobby is.

Perhaps only the young Alekhine of the mid-1920's and early 30's had sufficient power to equal the Fischer of the early 1970's. But whereas Alekhine had reached his peak at that time, Fischer is apparently still in the throes of development and will undoubtedly, like Lasker and Steinitz, enjoy a reign of decades as World Champion.

---

* To be found in *Das Begreifen Der Welt* (The Comprehension of the Universe), 1913, by Dr. Emanuel Lasker.

Fischer, though still a young man, has already played more tournament and match games than virtually any other great grandmaster, living or dead. He is about to enter his twentieth year of formal competition against the finest players of the world. During most of his life, he has been a member of one of the strongest chess clubs in the world. He has studied and remembers more complete games, positions and variations than any other in history. Of all the tournaments and matches he has played in and completed since 1966, he has captured first prize in every one. In game after game, trial after trial, he demonstrates his superiority over his opponents by out-thinking, out-sitting, out-witting and out-playing them in every phase of chess, from the mazelike complications of modern opening theory, struggling through the terrible tension of the middle game, and into the experiential precision of the ending, where the loneliness of logic prevails. Bobby is the complete player.

Fischer has said that the best summary of his life and career can be found in his games. Perhaps so. It has been noted that Alekhine embodied the theoretical history of the game in his style, and though it is correct that he was multifaceted, it is Fischer who emerges as the true focal point of chess, the fusion of centuries of technique and theory.

The games of Steinitz taught Fischer how to disturb the equilibrium of a position, how to accumulate small advantages, how to discern adequate motivation for attack and, perhaps most important of all, how to discover the best move in any given position: not the best move relatively or the best move for the occasion, but the *absolute* best move. From Lasker, Fischer learned resourcefulness: how to bypass a difficult situation and develop alternate routes to establish what Nimzovich called the "heroic defense." Alekhine's recognition of the dynamically eccentric qualities of a position where normal relationships no longer apply, sparked in Fischer a familiarity with such events so that his scholarship was absorbed just as surely as it was experienced. Fischer has learned from all the great masters. But in many ways it is Capablanca whom we can recognize stylistically as his Karmic forbear.

Reti pointed out that for Capablanca, chess was "a mother tongue" due to his learning the game at the age of four. But Fischer has been playing steadily since he was six, with much more intensity and activity than his Cuban counterpart, so that he responds naturally, often instinctively, to positions and variations that appear complex to others. Unlike Anderssen and Rubinstein who started their chess careers at a much later age, Fischer has the ability merely to glance at a position and thereby grasp its nuances and difficulties. That is why, like Capablanca (and Morphy), he has one of the fastest total sights of the board in the history of the game. In Fischer the machinery of thought from mind to board transmits itself so quickly it often appears as the same process.

Fischer was impressed very early with the total *accuracy* of Capablanca's play, his thorough understanding of a position, his logical approach to chess, which assumes—on first impression—the appearance of almost effortless style. But it has been Fischer who pointed out that Capablanca's simplicity was a myth. "His almost complete lack of book knowledge forced him to push harder to try to squeeze the utmost out of every position. Every move he made had to be supersharp so as to make something out of nothing."

Fischer's style, like Capablanca's, has its crystalline aspects: sharp, clean, thoroughly devoid of the brooding murkiness of Alekhine. The similarity between Capablanca and Fischer cannot be pressed too far, however. Though both are classicists, Fischer does allow an element of risk to enter his play. As Capablanca would never enter complications he had not had time to work out, Fischer says in a hint of possible abandon: "Concentrate on material gains. Whatever your opponent gives you, take, unless you see a good reason not to." The implication is that it is safe to capture material even if the ultimate conclusion is unclear, as long as it cannot be refuted or the outlook is not *demonstrably* unfavorable. There are many other differences between the two, from Fischer's profound knowledge of the openings to his deep love of the game, as compared to Capablanca's opening ignorance and his professed, or assumed, lack of genuine interest in chess. Where Capablanca's laziness forced him to an agony of materialism, Fischer's regimen has led him to a pursuit of uncorrupted dialectics.

Fischer's whole approach to the game, and consequently his style, is a study in pragmatic conscientiousness. "I give 98 percent of my mental energy to chess." he observed. And he once described his own system as eclectic, resorting to the romantics, the classicists, and even the hypermoderns when necessary. A number of his recent games, especially in his match against Spassky, bore distinctive modernistic traces.

Overall, it is Fischer's Bach-like purity in a deep but simultaneously unhidden display of forceful tactics, that characterizes his game. Classical principles are inculcated into his every move. Following the fundamentals, he is rewarded with superior positions. He is tenacious and patient. When at a disadvantage, he can play for hours, even days, waiting for his opponent to weaken. As Kashdan has pointed out, in Fischer's hands a slight theoretical advantage is as good as being a Queen ahead.

His ideas are generated by a disciplined imagination. He knows what he's doing at every turn, and never makes a move until he thoroughly understands the position. Scientifically, Fischer places every move under his mental microscope. What is true, is true and is ravenously absorbed. What is false, is false and is ruthlessly discarded. He has said ". . . the objective move will stand up a hundred years from now." He is consistently meticulous, and has more *sitzfleisch* than any other player since Steinitz.

Bobby Fischer's style on the board, and his lifestyle in approaching chess, are an assault on genius; for genius implies pure inspiration. Fischer's concepts, for the most part, are a result of his ceaseless and lifelong research. He is a drone, a Zen monk striving, waiting for enlightenment, an archer whose existence is concerned solely and exclusively with the problem of getting each arrow to the mark each and every time. He is thoroughly in love with chess, and this dedication produces an energy that is almost impossible to resist.

Because this power at the board is so overwhelming, a number of observers have discussed the so-called Fischer "aura," implying that, in effect, like Lasker, Tal and Alekhine before him, he virtually hypnotizes his opponents by striking fear into their hearts, thus making them play below their usual standards. Fischer's reaction is sarcastic: "People have been playing against me below their strength for fifteen years!" It's obvious that most chessplayers, certainly world masters not known for their modesty, are outraged to be so humbled by Fischer. They resort to the "magnetic force" theory in explaining their losses. What they find too painful to admit is that Fischer is in a class by himself, light years away from any opposition. He is virtually opponentless. Andrew Soltis, a promising American International Master, should be lauded for his honesty in describing his feelings about playing Fischer: "You know you're going to lose," he said. "Even when I was ahead I knew I was going to lose."

Fischer has been accused of psychic murder. Harold Schonberg attests in *The New York Times*: ". . . the Fischer aura is the will to dominate, to humiliate, to take over an opponent's mind. A player losing to any other player shrugs and walks away. He lost and all chess players lose at one time or another, and there will be another day, another game. But a loss to Fischer somehow diminishes a player." Fischer's enormous appetite to win sometimes assumes Dracularian proportions, but it is difficult to imagine him *consciously* attempting to obliterate his opponent's mind. After a lifetime of besting the world, Fischer does realize his own prowess. Only people who feel inferior themselves have a need to humiliate others. Fischer is more human and more humane, despite his often quoted statement of wanting to see his opponents' egos crumble (Fischer is sometimes an actor). What his opponents *do* feel in Fischer is what Alekhine said is the trait necessary to being a great player: the desire to embrace danger. This flirtation with the potentially destructive unknown produces a lucidity that is irresistible at moments and resembles the cunning of the insane or the flash of strategic brilliance of the infantryman faced with unavoidable capture or annihilation. As Fischer totters on the abyss himself, he lures his opponents to join him, and the result is often a Homeric journey fraught with peril, culminating most often with the opponents' destruction on the board. He also has what Emanuel Lasker once said a champion must have: "The passion that whips the blood when great stakes can be gained by resolute and self-confident daring."

It is difficult to discern Fischer's weaknesses. Spassky, after losing the title, stated that Fischer's simplistic style was almost childlike and that unless he developed more "sensitive alternatives," this would remain a defect. However, he quickly indicated that Fischer's straight-forwardness was also one of his greatest strengths.

Aside from the Jungian bromide that Fischer is potentially his own worst enemy, it is a remark of Euwe's which leads us to the possibility of a flaw in Fischer:

"Fischer thinks in systems, not moves. With him, it's not good enough to say a player has made a good move. You must know the system he is playing and what fits into the system."

The implication we can extract from Euwe is that it is useless to refine any particular *line*, or combination of moves resulting from that line, in preparing for Fischer. Since he is thoroughly versed to counter the most well-reasoned and sophisticated debut, *because he understands the basic motivating methodology*, all attempts at a prepared surprise attack in any known opening will fall short; and since, by virtue of his superior abilities of calculation, he is capable of finding his way through the middle and end game, a thoroughly new approach must be attempted in order to realize consistent victory over him: a grand system, virtually a new school of chess, or certainly a new opening. The Grandmaster who can emerge from the chess laboratory with such an approach might well find himself a dangerous threat to Fischer's hegemony.

What lies in store for Bobby Fischer? And for chess? As Fischer's cultural base continues to broaden on his own initiative and as he accepts opportunities to meet some of the finest minds of our generation, as he is wining and dining with heads of state, Fischer will no doubt soften in his nationalistic prejudice toward the Soviet Union. He will come to realize that most of the Russian attacks against him have been, in effect, counterattacks; defensive measures, taken only in desperation to preserve self-respect and to protect themselves from *his* aggressions. What he could not realize during this past decade of strife was that the Russians have deep respect for his talent and great admiration for his accomplishments and that in many ways he owes his own mature identity to the Soviet Union. The Soviets have followed every move of Bobby Fischer's ascent from his first tournament. Their respect for the game, and for those who master it, is obvious.

Should Fischer, in a noble gesture, visit the Soviet Union and, like Lasker, remain for a few years, imparting his theoretical knowledge and practical advice, he might also gain some valuable insights of his own. More importantly, he would simultaneously elevate the art while helping to demolish the cold war politics of chess, all at once.

The $250,000 purse for the Fischer-Spassky match, directly attributable to the Fischer charisma, has altered the game and those who play it in so many ways that chess will never be the same. Devoted parents, who in the past might have discouraged their children from taking chess too seriously, believing that the game was fit only for neurasthenic gray men sitting in the back of smoke-filled cafés, now encourage their progeny to pattern themselves after Bobby Fischer. Suddenly, one of the ways to secure wealth and fame in America is to become a great chess player. The new legion of young hopefuls, fired by a chess fervor heretofore unknown in America, should begin a fierce competition for top honors that will result in a level of excellence previously known only in the Soviet Union, where, incidentally, Fischer's impact has already been felt. Within the next two decades, Fischer will be pitted against players, now unknown, who will test his genius in ways that he can now hardly imagine; and ironically, *he* may be the inspiration for his ultimate defeat. But for the moment, Fischer will remain supreme, as he is now, in a class by himself, perhaps for many years, before a new player can mature beyond his scope. The only flaw that might blemish Bobby's future is his sublime *obsession* to be the very best player the world has ever known. This subjective involvement in his own will for power, together with a precarious manipulation of objective detachment, projecting himself above the wiliness of his opponents in the truth of the board, is the tableau his invincibility will continue to enact over the years. This conflict is all beyond intellect or psychology. It's Bobby Fischer's search for his soul. Can he discover it on a plain of sixty-four squares?

Goethe said that chess is ". . . the touchstone of the intellect," in effect, a paradigm of the cognitive processes of the human mind. Others believe that its essence lies in a psychological duel to the death between two supercharged egos. It may be both. For Bobby Fischer, however, chess must also be a lifelong fulfillment of the spirit.

An Analysis of Ninety of
Bobby Fischer's Games

GAME 1

Outplaying a wily tournament veteran of di Camillo's ability was not an easy task for a teenager. This game represents one of Bobby's finest early efforts; it was played when he was only thirteen years old.

EASTERN STATES OPEN 1956

Washington, D.C.

RUY LOPEZ

Robert J. Fischer	Attilio di Camillo
WHITE	BLACK
1 P-K4	P-K4
2 N-KB3	N-QB3
3 B-N5	P-QR3
4 B-R4	N-B3
5 O-O	P-QN4
6 B-N3	P-Q3
7 P-B3	...

7 N-N5 achieves nothing after 7 ... P-Q4 8 PxP N-Q5.

7 ...	B-N5

The pin has no point if White has not played P-Q4.

8 P-KR3?	...

Very risky. Since Black has not castled, he has the option of playing for a Kingside breakthrough.

8 ...	B-R4
9 P-Q3	B-K2
10 QN-Q2	O-O?

10 ... Q-Q2, intending 11 ... P-N4, was Black's best course of action.

11 R-K1	Q-Q2
12 N-B1	N-R4
13 B-B2	P-R3
14 P-KN4!	...

Obtaining a positional advantage. Black cannot play 14 ... NxNP 15 PxN QxPch 16 N-N3 QxN 17 NxB.

14 ...	B-N3
15 N-N3	N-R2
16 N-B5	N-N2
17 P-Q4	PxP
18 PxP	N-Q1
19 NxBch	...

White wants to restrict Black's Knight with 20 P-Q5 without allowing 20 ... B-B3.

19 ...	QxN
20 P-Q5	P-QB4

If 20 ... N-N2 21 N-Q4!

21 B-B4	N-N2
22 B-KN3	KR-K1
23 P-QR4	Q-B3
24 PxP	PxP
25 K-N2	N-N4

25 ... QxP 26 R-QN1.

26 NxN	PxN
27 RxR	RxR
28 P-K5	...

Forcing a powerful passed Pawn.

28 ...	BxB
29 QxB	PxP
30 BxP	Q-Q1
31 P-Q6!	...

Passed Pawns must be pushed!

31 ...	P-B5

White wins after 31 ... NxP by 32 R-Q1 or 32 QxP.

32 Q-K4	N-B4

Black's position is not without counterplay.

33 Q-B6	N-Q6
34 R-K3	R-B1
35 Q-N7	R-N1
36 Q-Q5	N-N5
37 Q-B5	N-Q6
38 Q-Q4	R-N3
39 P-Q7	R-N2

40 B-B7!   . . .

The beautiful point of White's 39th move. It wins on the spot.

40 ...	N-B5ch
41 K-B1	Resigns

GAME 2

This game so impressed noted analyst Hans Kmoch that he called it "the game of the century." The first indication that it is an unusual game is the totally unexpected eleventh move, which superficially seems to give away a piece. But it is a sound sacrifice and leads to a complicated position in which Bobby's main advantage is Donald Byrne's inability to castle. Then comes a thunderbolt—a Queen sacrifice which wins by force. This 17th move will be talked about for centuries to come. By playing it, Bobby Fischer established his place among the great prodigies of all time.

LESSING J. ROSENWALD TOURNAMENT 1956

New York, N.Y.

GRUENFELD DEFENSE

Donald Byrne
WHITE

Robert J. Fischer
BLACK

The first of Fischer's many famous efforts with the Gruenfeld.

1 N-KB3	N-KB3	6 Q-N3	PxP
2 P-B4	P-KN3	7 QxBP	P-B3
3 N-B3	B-N2	8 P-K4	QN-Q2
4 P-Q4	O-O	9 R-Q1	N-N3
5 B-B4	P-Q4	10 Q-B5	. . .

Unnecessarily courting danger. 10
Q-N3 was best.

| 10 ... | B-N5 |
| 11 B-KN5? | ... |

A violation of principle. White
neglects development in moving a
piece for the second time.

| 11 ... | N-R5! |

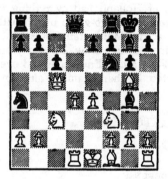

A brilliantly original way to refute
White's weak position.

| 12 Q-R3 | ... |

White does not dare take the
Knight. If 12 NxN NxP 13 Q-N4
(13 QxKP QxQ 14 BxQ KR-K1)
NxB 14 NxN BxR 15 KxB BxP with
a winning game.

| 12 ... | NxN |
| 13 PxN | NxP! |

Launching a sacrificial attack.

| 14 BxP | Q-N3 |
| 15 B-B4 | ... |

If 15 BxR BxB 16 Q moves,
NxQBP.

15 ...	NxQBP
16 B-B5	KR-K1ch
17 K-B1	B-K3!

An unexpected Queen sacrifice that
wins in all variations.

| 18 BxQ | ... |

White had nothing better. Alternatives were 18 BxB Q-N4ch or 18
QxN QxB or 18 B-K2 N-N4.

18 ...	BxBch
19 K-N1	N-K7ch
20 K-B1	NxPch
21 K-N1	...

Black wins easily after 21 R-Q3
PxB.

21 ...	N-K7ch
22 K-B1	N-B6ch
23 K-N1	PxB
24 Q-N4	R-R5

Gaining a decisive material advantage, since if 25 Q-Q6 NxR 26 QxN
RxP, and White has no defense to
27 ... R-R8.

25 QxP	NxR
26 P-KR3	RxP
27 K-R2	NxP
28 R-K1	RxR
29 Q-Q8ch	B-B1
30 NxR	B-Q4
31 N-B3	N-K5
32 Q-N8	P-QN4
33 P-R4	P-R4
34 N-K5	K-N2

Freeing the Black Bishop. White is helpless against the combined action of Black's minor pieces.

| 35 | K-N1 | B-B4ch |
| 36 | K-B1 | N-N6ch |

Mating by force.

37	K-K1	B-N5ch
38	K-Q1	B-N6ch
39	K-B1	N-K7ch
40	K-N1	N-B6ch
41	K-B1	R-B7 mate

GAME 3

Former world champion Max Euwe of Holland had everything to lose and very little to gain, but he agreed to a two-game match with the 14-year-old Bobby. It was played at the Manhattan Chess Club. The veteran Dutchman scored one win and one draw. Fifteen years later, as President of the World Chess Federation, Euwe presided over the championship matches which pitted Fischer against Taimanov, Larsen, Petrosian and Spassky.

EUWE-FISCHER MATCH 1957

New York, N.Y.

NIMZO-INDIAN DEFENSE

Dr. Max Euwe   *Robert J. Fischer*

WHITE	BLACK
1 P-Q4	N-KB3
2 P-QB4	P-K3
3 N-QB3	P-Q4
4 PxP	PxP
5 B-N5	B-QN5

Transposing from the Exchange Variation of the Queen's Gambit to the Nimzo-Indian.

6 P-K3	P-KR3
7 B-R4	P-B4
8 B-Q3	N-B3
9 N-K2	PxP
10 PxP	O-O
11 O-O	B-K3

An error. 11 . . . B-K2 or BxN was better.

| 12 B-B2 | . . . |

White plays simply but powerfully.

| 12 . . . | B-K2 |
| 13 N-B4 | Q-N3? |

Black was already in dire straits. 13 . . . P-KN4 was his best chance.

| 14 BxN | BxB |
| 15 Q-Q3 | KR-Q1 |

The only move. If 15 . . . P-N3 16 NxNP.

| 16 QR-K1 | . . . |

Threatening 17 Q-R7ch K-B1 18 N(3)xP.

| 16 . . . | N-N5 |

If 16 . . . P-N3 17 RxB!

| 17 Q-R7ch | K-B1 |

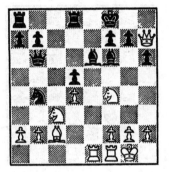

18 P-QR3!   . . .

A quiet move that wins by force.

18 . . .	NxB
19 QNxP	RxN
20 NxR	Resigns

GAME 4

Probably still smarting from his loss to Fischer in the 1956 Rosenwald, Byrne plays a delicate and clever game, almost establishing a winning position. He goes astray, however, and Fischer discovers the razorsharp continuation.

U.S. OPEN CHAMPIONSHIP 1957

Cleveland, Ohio

ENGLISH OPENING

Donald Byrne	Robert J. Fischer
WHITE	BLACK
1 N-KB3	N-KB3
2 P-B4	P-KN3
3 P-QN3	B-N2
4 B-N2	O-O
5 P-K3	P-Q3
6 B-K2	P-K4
7 O-O	. . .

White doesn't mind 7 . . . P-K5. The whole opening is rather unusual.

7 . . .	QN-Q2
8 N-B3	R-K1
9 R-B1	P-K5

Now this advance is more reasonable.

10 N-K1	N-K4
11 P-Q3	B-B4
12 PxP	NxKP
13 NxN	BxN
14 B-QB3	P-KB4

Preventing 15 P-B3 and 16 P-K4.

15 P-QN4	P-N3
16 Q-N3	Q-K2
17 P-B5ch	K-R1
18 P-B6!	. . .

A surprising move. The Pawn is immune and White threatens to win a piece with 19 P-B3.

18 . . .	Q-K3
19 Q-N2	. . .

Now the threat is 20 P-B4.

| 19 ... | Q-B2 |
| 20 P-N5 | P-N4 |

Black gains space on the Kingside.

21 P-QR4	P-B5
22 P-B3	B-B4
23 P-K4	B-K3
24 N-B2	Q-N3
25 N-Q4	R-KB1

Black is massing his men for a Kingside assault.

| 26 P-R5 | ... |

White plans action on the Queen Rook file.

26 ...	QR-K1
27 PxP	RPxP
28 R-R1	P-N5
29 PxP	QxKP

A risky capture. 29 . . . BxP was Black's best.

30 QR-K1	Q-Q4
31 P-R3	R-R1
32 NxB	QxN
33 Q-N4	...

Now Black cannot defend his King Bishop Pawn. If 33 . . . Q-R3 34 B-Q2 or 33 . . . B-R3 34 P-R4.

| 33 ... | Q-Q4!? |
| 34 K-R1? | ... |

A serious error. White should have captured the Pawn.

| 34 ... | P-B6 |

Now Black has fine chances.

| 35 PxP | NxKBP |
| 36 R-Q1? | ... |

A blunder in time-pressure. Correct was 36 BxBch and 37 BxN.

| 36 ... | N-Q5ch! |

White is defenseless.

| 37 R-B3 | RxR |
| 38 RxN | RxPch |

38 . . . R-B8ch! forces mate.

39 K-N1	Q-R8ch
40 K-B2	R-B1ch
41 R-B4	Q-R7ch
Resigns	

GAME 5

While in San Francisco to compete in the U.S. Junior Championship just a few months prior to this game, Fischer and Addison played literally hundreds of speed games together. But Bobby was careful not to reveal all of his lines. For this tournament, he comes up with a strong and startling move in the opening by playing 7 Q–K2ch!

U.S. OPEN CHAMPIONSHIP 1957

Cleveland, Ohio

CARO-KANN DEFENSE

Robert J. Fischer   *William Addison*

WHITE	BLACK
1 P-K4	P-QB3
2 N-QB3	P-Q4
3 N-B3	PxP
4 NxP	N-B3

Black concedes White the better Pawn structure.

5 NxNch	KPxN
6 B-B4	B-Q3
7 Q-K2ch	...

White has the better ending because of his Queenside majority.

7 ...	Q-K2
8 QxQch	KxQ
9 P-Q4	B-KB4
10 B-N3	R-K1
11 B-K3	K-B1
12 O-O-O	N-Q2
13 P-B4!	...

The Pawns start advancing.

13 ...	QR-Q1
14 B-B2	BxB
15 KxB	P-KB4
16 KR-K1	P-B5
17 B-Q2	N-B3
18 N-K5	...

The Knight takes up a dominating post.

18 ...	P-KN4
19 P-B3	N-R4
20 N-N4	K-N2
21 B-B3	...

Preparing a decisive advance on the Queenside.

21 ...	K-N3
22 RxR	RxR
23 P-B5	B-N1
24 P-Q5	PxP
25 RxP	P-B4
26 N-K5ch	BxN
27 RxB	N-B3
28 RxR	NxR
29 B-K5	...

Trapping the Knight. Black is helpless since he cannot make a passed Pawn to counteract White's majority.

29 . . .	K-R4
30 K-Q3	P-N5
31 P-N4	P-QR3
32 P-QR4	PxP
33 PxP	K-R5
34 P-N5	PxP
35 P-R5	. . .

Assuring a new Queen.

35 . . .	K-R6
36 P-B6	Resigns

GAME 6

By drawing this game, Fischer won his most important tournament to that date, edging out Bisguier on tie-breaking points. Shipman was one of the ten highest-rated chess players in the United States at the time.

U.S. OPEN CHAMPIONSHIP 1957

Cleveland, Ohio

RUY LOPEZ

Robert J. Fischer   Walter Shipman

WHITE	BLACK
1 P-K4	P-K4
2 N-KB3	N-QB3
3 B-N5	P-QR3
4 B-R4	N-B3
5 O-O	B-K2
6 R-K1	P-QN4
7 B-N3	O-O
8 P-B3	P-Q3

Shipman sometimes plays the Marshall Gambit (8 . . . P-Q4).

9 P-KR3	P-QR4

A rarely seen defense. Usual is 9 . . . N-QR4, etc.

10 P-Q4	PxP
11 NxP	. . .

Considered best.

11 . . .	NxN
12 PxN	B-N2
13 N-B3	. . .

Good alternatives are 13 B-B2 and 13 Q-Q3.

13 . . .	P-N5
14 N-Q5	NxN
15 BxN	BxB
16 PxB	B-N4
17 Q-N4!	B-B3!

White would have pressure after 17 . . . BxB 18 QRxB. The text gives Black a satifactory position.

18 B-K3	Drawn

This draw won the U.S. Open for Fischer.

GAME 7

Carlos P. Romulo, Ambassador from the Philippines and Secretary-General of the United Nations, made the first move of this plucky game for his young countryman. Bobby's strength as compared to other teen-aged players becomes clearly evident in this battle as he outplays and outclasses his opponent.

CARDOSO-FISCHER MATCH 1957

New York, N.Y.

SICILIAN DEFENSE

Robert J. Fischer   Rodolfo Cardoso

WHITE	BLACK
1 P-K4	P-QB4
2 N-KB3	P-Q3
3 P-Q4	PxP
4 NxP	N-KB3
5 N-QB3	P-QR3
6 B-QB4	...

This move has become very popular because of Fischer's results with it.

6 ...	P-K3
7 O-O	B-K2

Black wisely decides not to win a Pawn with 7 . . . P-QN4 8 B-N3 P-N5 9 N-R4 NxP because of 10 Q-B3 with a strong attack.

8 B-K3	O-O
9 B-N3	N-B3
10 P-B4	N-QR4
11 Q-B3	Q-B2
12 P-N4!?	NxB

A mistake; correct was 12 . . . N-B5 with counterchances.

13 RPxN	R-N1
14 P-N5	N-Q2
15 P-B5	...

White has a dangerous attack rolling.

15 ...	N-K4
16 Q-N3	K-R1
17 N-B3	...

Exchanging Black's best piece.

17 ...	NxNch
18 RxN	P-N4
19 Q-R4	PxP

Forced. White was threatening 20 R-R3 P-R3 21 P-B6.

20 PxP	Q-B3
21 QR-KB1	B-N2
22 B-Q4!	P-N5

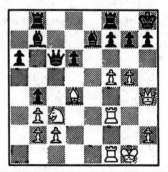

23 BxPch!?   ...

Brilliant but not quite sound. 23 Q-R5! was the move. If then 23 . . . PxN 24 P-N6.

23 . . .	KxB
24 Q-R6ch	K-R1
25 P-N6	Q-B4ch?

A losing check. Black had a brilliant
defense with 25 . . . PxP 26 PxP
R-B2! 27 PxR R-KB1 after which
White would have to give back some
material.

| 26 R(1)-B2 | PxP |
| 27 PxP | Q-N4ch |

Black was defenseless.

28 QxQ	BxQ
29 RxRch	RxR
30 RxRch	K-N2
31 PxP!	Resigns

GAME 8

Fischer introduces a powerful and restrictive move (14 P–B4!)
which permits him to infiltrate Feuerstein's Kingside. Halfway through
this game, Feuerstein began to smile as if recognizing that he was lost
and philosophically accepting the fact.

U.S. CHAMPIONSHIP 1957–1958

New York, N.Y.

SICILIAN DEFENSE

Robert J. Fischer	Arthur Feuerstein
WHITE	BLACK
1 P-K4	P-QB4
2 N-KB3	P-K3
3 P-KN3	. . .

Psychological warfare! Fischer
adopts one of Feuerstein's own
favorites, the King's Indian Reversed.

3 . . .	N-KB3
4 P-Q3	P-Q4
5 QN-Q2	B-K2
6 B-N2	O-O
7 O-O	N-B3
8 R-K1	Q-B2
9 Q-K2	R-Q1

Better was 9 . . . B-Q2, leaving the
Rook on KB1. Then if 10 P-K5 N-K1
11 P-B3 P-B3, attacking White's
center.

| 10 P-K5 | N-K1 |
| 11 P-B3 | P-QN4 |

12 N-B1	P-N5
13 B-B4	Q-R4?
14 P-B4!	. . .

Locking the Queenside so as to pursue a Kingside attack with P-KR4-
5-6.

14 . . .	N-B2
15 P-KR4	Q-N3
16 P-R5	P-N6
17 P-R3	PxP
18 PxP	B-R3

If 18 . . . P-KR3, Black would have
to beware of sacrifices on KR3 and
a White breakthrough with P-
KN4-5.

19 N(1)-R2	QR-B1
20 P-R6	P-N3
21 B-N5	N-Q5

Trading Black Bishops helps weaken
Black's King position.

| 22 Q-K3 | . . . |

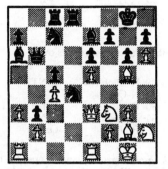

22 ...	BxB
23 QxB	N-K1
24 N-N4	N-B4
25 QR-B1	Q-B2
26 N-Q2	R-Q5
27 NxP	RxP
28 QR-Q1	R-R5
29 R-K4!	B-N4

Forced. After 29 . . . RxR 30 BxR, Black's Knight on B4 would be removed, and with it his chances for defense.

| 30 R-QB1 | Q-N3 |

| 31 N-Q2 | RxR |
| 32 NxR | B-Q6 |

This loses a piece. 32 . . . Q-Q1 was best but Black would have a lost endgame.

| 33 N(N4)-B6ch | K-R1 |
| 34 P-KN4 | . . . |

Winning the piece. The Knight cannot move because of 35 NxN, followed by Q-B6ch and mate.

34 ...	BxN
35 BxB	N-Q5
36 NxN	Q-Q1
37 QxQ	RxQ
38 N-Q6	. . .

White's final point. He remains a piece ahead.

38 ...	N-K7ch
39 K-B1	NxR
40 NxPch	K-N1
41 NxR	N-N6
42 K-K2	N-Q5ch
43 K-Q3	K-B1
44 N-B6	Resigns

GAME 9

Sometimes it seems that one player so understands the psychology of another's play that he can virtually predict his opponent's moves. This game is one of the first of a series of many losses by former U.S. Champion Bisguier to Fischer, establishing one of the strangest "Indian sign" relationships in chess history.

U.S. CHAMPIONSHIP 1957–1958

New York, N.Y.

FRENCH DEFENSE

Robert J. Fischer   *Arthur Bisguier*

WHITE	BLACK
1 P-K4	P-K3
2 P-Q4	P-Q4

| 3 N-QB3 | B-N5 |
| 4 P-K5 | P-QN3 |

An old Nimzovich favorite.

| 5 P-QR3 | BxNch |
| 6 PxB | Q-Q2 |

Anticipating 7 Q-N4. 5 Q-N4 would have been answered by B-B1.

7	Q-N4	P-KB4
8	Q-N3	B-R3
9	BxB	NxB
10	N-K2	O-O-O
11	P-QR4	...

Taking advantage of Black's poorly placed Knight on R3, White starts attacking.

11	...	K-N2
12	O-O	Q-B2
13	P-QB4	...

White dissolves his doubled pawn and gains more room for Queenside operations.

13	...	N-K2
14	B-N5	PxP
15	Q-B3	N-Q4
16	QxP	R-R1
17	B-Q2	...

Black was threatening 17 ... P-B5, after which White's Bishop would be stranded.

17	...	P-B5
18	R-R3	P-KN4
19	P-R5	P-B3
20	PxP	PxP
21	Q-N3	...

Preparing P-B4, decentralizing Black's Knight. 21 KR-R1 would have been answered by N(3)-B2.

21	...	N(3)-B2
22	P-QB4	RxR
23	QxR	R-R1
24	Q-QN3	N-K2
25	N-B3	...

The White Knight heads for Q6.

25	...	Q-B4
26	Q-N4	N-B1
27	N-R4	P-B6

Black has threats of his own.

28	N-B5ch	K-N1
29	N-Q7ch	K-N2
30	Q-N3	Q-N5
31	N-B5ch	K-N1
32	P-N3	QxP?

A grave error giving scope to the White Bishop. Black's best chance was R-R7! (33 QxR? Q-R6).

33	B-K3	Q-R8
34	R-N1	R-R6

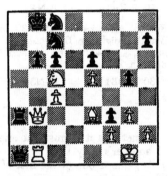

35	N-Q7ch	K-N2
36	Q-Q1!	...

Decisive. White wins the Black KBP, stopping all counterplay and launching the final attack.

36	...	Q-R7
37	NxP	NxN
38	RxNch	K-B1
39	QxP	QxP
40	Q-B8ch	K-Q2
41	QxR	Resigns

GAME 10

This first game with the young Danish grandmaster who later became one of the two greatest players outside the Soviet Union helped to establish Bobby's international reputation. He takes apart the Dragon Variation.

INTERZONAL CHAMPIONSHIP 1958

Portoroz, Yugoslavia

SICILIAN DEFENSE

Robert J. Fischer	Bent Larsen
WHITE	BLACK
1 P-K4	P-QB4
2 N-KB3	P-Q3
3 P-Q4	PxP
4 NxP	N-KB3
5 N-QB3	P-KN3
6 B-K3	B-N2
7 P-B3	O-O
8 Q-Q2	N-B3
9 B-QB4	...

With this move White has set up the most aggressive formation against the Dragon Variation. The line is one of Fischer's favorites.

9 ...	NxN
10 BxN	B-K3
11 B-N3	Q-R4
12 O-O-O	P-QN4
13 K-N1	...

Safeguarding the King and at the same time threatening to win a Pawn with 14 N-Q5.

13 ...	P-N5
14 N-Q5	BxN
15 BxB	QR-B1
16 B-N3	R-B2
17 P-KR4	Q-QN4
18 P-R5!	...

The key move in White's plan of attack. Black cannot play 18 . . .

NxP because of 19 BxB, followed by Q-R6 and P-KN4 with a forced win.

18 ...	KR-B1
19 PxP	PxP
20 P-N4	P-R4
21 P-N5	N-R4

Any other Knight move is answered by 22 Q-R2, threatening 23 Q-R8ch.

22 RxN!	...

Smashing Black's King position.

22 ...	PxR
23 P-N6!	P-K4
24 PxPch	K-B1
25 B-K3	P-Q4
26 PxP	RxKBP
27 P-Q6	R-KB3
28 B-N5	Q-N2

Black could not move his attacked	29 BxR	BxB
Rook because of 29 B-K7ch K-K1	30 P-Q7	R-Q1
30 P-Q7ch.	31 Q-Q6ch	Resigns

GAME 11

When Reshevsky played 8 . . . N–QR4 the whispers in the tournament room at the Manhattan Chess Club grew to a barely suppressed uproar. The move had been analyzed just a few weeks earlier in *Shakhmatny Byulletin* and many of the stronger players in the club were thoroughly familiar with it. Reshevsky might have resigned after the twelfth move, but either pride or anger forced him to continue until it was absolutely hopeless.

U.S. CHAMPIONSHIP 1958–1959

New York, N.Y.

SICILIAN DEFENSE

Robert J. Fischer *Samuel Reshevsky*

WHITE	BLACK
1 P-K4	P-QB4
2 N-KB3	N-QB3
3 P-Q4	PxP
4 NxP	P-KN3
5 N-QB3	B-N2
6 B-K3	N-B3
7 B-QB4	O-O
8 B-N3	. . .

The best. Fischer played 8 P-B3 against Panno, in Portoroz, 1958, allowing 8 . . . Q-N3! In this position Black can now play 8 . . . P-Q3, leading to a regular line of the Dragon Variation.

8 . . .   N-QR4?

An amazing blunder. Black must now lose material.

9 P-K5!   N-K1?

Unaware of what is to follow, Black retreats his Knight. Relatively best was 9 . . . NxB 10 KPxN NxR 11 PxB NxPch 12 QxN, after which White should win with correct play.

10 BxPch!   . . .

The crushing point! If 10 . . . RxB or 10 . . . K-R1, 11 N-K6! wins Black's Queen.

10 . . .   KxB
11 N-K6!   . . .

Winning the Queen. Black cannot play 11 KxN because of 12 Q-Q5ch K-B4 13 P-N4ch KxP 14 R-N1ch with a forced mate.

11 ...	PxN

Black surrenders his Queen and continues in a hopeless cause.

12 QxQ	N-QB3
13 Q-Q2	BxP
14 O-O	N-Q3
15 B-B4	N-B5
16 Q-K2	BxB
17 QxN	K-N2
18 N-K4	B-B2
19 N-B5	R-B3

Black keeps defending himself, but his position is too cramped for counterplay.

20 P-QB3	P-K4
21 QR-Q1	N-Q1
22 N-Q7	R-B3
23 Q-KR4	R-K3

24 N-B5	R-KB3
25 N-K4	R-B5
26 QxKPch	R-B2
27 Q-R3	N-B3
28 N-Q6	...

Forcing more simplification.

28 ...	BxN
29 RxB	B-B4
30 P-QN4	R(2)-B1
31 P-N5	N-Q1
32 R-Q5	N-B2
33 R-B5	P-QR3
34 P-N6	B-K5
35 R-K1	B-B3
36 RxB!	...

Removing Black's best piece.

36 ...	PxR
37 P-N7	QR-N1
38 QxP	N-Q1
39 R-N1	R-B2
40 P-KR3	R(2)xNP
41 RxRch	RxR
42 Q-R8	Resigns

GAME 12

An absolutely amazing draw and the first between these two great masters. After this game was completed, Tal predicted that Fischer would become World Champion. It was barely a year later that he himself defeated Botvinnik and was crowned Champion of the World.

INTERNATIONAL TOURNAMENT 1959

Zurich, Switzerland

SICILIAN DEFENSE

Mikhail Tal	Robert J. Fischer
WHITE	BLACK
1 P-K4	P-QB4
2 N-KB3	P-Q3
3 P-Q4	PxP
4 NxP	N-KB3
5 N-QB3	P-QR3
6 B-N5	...

Tal prefers this move to the more positional 6 B-K2.

6 ...	P-K3
7 P-B4	B-K2

Black refrains from 7 ... Q-N3 which, after 8 Q-Q2, would lead to the kind of complications Tal likes.

8	Q-B3	Q-B2
9	O-O-O	QN-Q2
10	Q-N3	P-R3

Beginning a positional plan of gaming control of his own K4.

11	B-R4	R-KN1
12	B-K2	P-KN4
13	PxP	N-K4!
14	P-N6	...

White makes sure that his Bishop will not be trapped.

14	...	NxNP
15	KR-B1	NxB
16	QxN	R-N3

Black now has a positional advantage, which is counter-balanced by White's superior development.

| 17 | B-Q3 | N-N5 |
| 18 | Q-R5 | N-K4 |

Black decides not to go in for the complications which would follow on 18 ... N-K6 19 P-K5.

19	N-B3	Q-R4
20	NxN	QxN(4)
21	QxQ	PxQ
22	P-KN3	B-Q2
23	B-K2	B-QB3
24	B-R5	R-B3

Not 24 ... R-N2? 25 RxP! RxR 26 R-B1, winning a Pawn.

| 25 | P-QR3 | R-Q1 |
| 26 | RxRch | BxR |

27	RxR	BxR
28	K-Q2	B-N4ch
29	K-Q3	B-B8
30	N-Q1	B-N4ch
31	P-B4	B-R5
32	N-B3	B-B3

32 ... B-N6 would be answered by 33 B-Q1!

| 33 | N-Q1 | K-B1? |

| 34 | P-KR4 | ... |

Cutting off the retreat of Black's Bishop and threatening to trap it with 35 K-B2.

| 34 | ... | B-R5 |

The only move to save the piece.

| 35 | N-B3 | Drawn |

Forcing the draw by 35 ... B-B3 36 N-Q1, etc. Not 35 ... B-N6? 36 B-Q1! and White wins.

GAME 13

Fischer rarely has trouble with Benko (though he has lost to him on occasion) except when he overextends himself. In this game, he counters all of Benko's good ideas with ones that are just a shade stronger.

CHALLENGERS' TOURNAMENT 1959

Bled-Belgrade-Zagreb, Yugoslavia

SICILIAN DEFENSE

Robert J. Fischer   *Pal Benko*

WHITE	BLACK
1 P-K4	P-QB4
2 N-KB3	N-QB3
3 P-Q4	PxP
4 NxP	N-B3
5 N-QB3	P-Q3
6 B-QB4	Q-N3

This unorthodox move is a favorite of Denker's. Its main strength lies in its surprise value.

7 KN-K2	P-K3
8 O-O	B-K2
9 B-N3	O-O
10 K-R1	N-QR4
11 B-N5	...

White develops his Bishop to its most aggressive post.

11 ...	Q-B4
12 P-B4	P-N4
13 N-N3	...

White threatens 14 P-K5, followed by 15 BxN and 16 QN-K4 with a decisive attack.

13 ...	P-N5
14 P-K5	PxP
15 BxN	PxB
16 QN-K4	...

White has a winning attack.

16 ...	Q-Q5
17 Q-R5	NxB
18 Q-R6	...

There is no good defense to 19 N-R5. Black is forced to give up his Queen.

18 ...	PxP
19 N-R5	P-B4
20 QR-Q1!	...

White saves his Rook and still wins the Queen. If 20 . . . QxP 21 P-B3!

20 ...	Q-K4
21 QN-B6ch	BxN
22 NxBch	QxN
23 QxQ	N-B4

| 24 Q-N5ch | K-R1 | 25 ... | B-R3 |
| 25 Q-K7 | | 26 QxN | BxR |

Winning more material.

| 27 RxB | Resigns |

GAME 14

Fischer would have liked to defeat Gligoric in each of their four individual games in this tournament, and he went to Yugoslavia with that determination. Each won one game, and two were drawn. Following is Bobby's snappy win in their unexplained and unpublicized "blood match."

CHALLENGERS' TOURNAMENT 1959

Bled-Belgrade-Zagreb, Yugoslavia

SICILIAN DEFENSE

Robert J. Fischer	*Svetozar Gligoric*
WHITE	BLACK
1 P-K4	P-QB4
2 N-KB3	N-QB3
3 P-Q4	PxP
4 NxP	N-B3
5 N-QB3	P-Q3
6 B-QB4	B-Q2

Preparing 7 . . . P-KN3 with a switch to the Dragon Variation. 6 . . . P-KN3 is inferior because of 7 NxN PxN 8 P-K5! with a strong attack.

7 B-N3	P-KN3
8 P-B3	N-QR4
9 B-N5	B-N2
10 Q-Q2	P-KR3
11 B-K3	R-QB1
12 O-O-O	N-B5
13 Q-K2	. . .

White decides to part with his Queen's Bishop instead of his King's, planning action in the center if Black continues to postpone castling.

| 13 . . . | NxB |
| 14 QxN | O-O |

Black is almost forced to castle in view of the threat of 15 P-B4 and 16 P-K5.

| 15 P-KN4 | . . . |

With the Black Pawn on KR3, White obtains a strong attack even without his dark-squared Bishop.

| 15 . . . | Q-R4 |
| 16 P-KR4 | P-K3 |

Black prevents a future N-Q5, but weakens his Queen Pawn.

17 KN-K2	R-B3
18 P-N5	PxP
19 PxP	N-R4
20 P-B4	KR-B1
21 K-N1	Q-N3
22 Q-B3	. . .

White threatens a breakthrough with 23 P-B5.

| 22 . . . | R-B4 |
| 23 Q-Q3 | . . . |

A strong move, allowing Black to win the KBP.

| 23 . . . | BxN |

24 NxB	NxP
25 Q-B3	N-R4

If 25 ... P-K4, White gets a mating attack with 26 N-Q5.

26 RxN   ...

Smashing open the Black King's fortress.

26 ...	PxR
27 QxP	B-K1
28 Q-R6	...

Preventing the King's escape via KB1.

28 ...	RxN
29 PxR	RxP

Planning to counter 30 R-R1 with Q-Q5.

30 P-N6!   ...

White forces open the King Bishop file and forces mate.

30 ...	PxP
31 R-R1	Q-Q5
32 Q-R7ch	Resigns

GAME 15

If there were any lingering doubts that Bobby had elevated himself to the highest ranks of the world's best players, they were dispelled by his two spectacular wins over Keres in this tournament. Keres, a seasoned and positively brilliant player, blunders after struggling to achieve a strong and sound game.

CHALLENGERS' TOURNAMENT 1959

Bled-Belgrade-Zagreb, Yugoslavia

KING'S INDIAN DEFENSE

Paul Keres	*Robert J. Fischer*
WHITE	BLACK

1 P-Q4	N-KB3
2 N-KB3	P-KN3
3 B-B4	...

An old move seldom seen in modern tournament play.

3 ...	B-N2
4 QN-Q2	P-B4

5 P-B3	PxP
6 PxP	P-Q4

Preventing 7 P-K4 with advantage to White. The move is actually a Pawn sacrifice, which White accepts.

7 BxN	RxB
8 Q-R4ch	B-Q2
9 QxP	N-K5
10 P-K3	NxN
11 NxN	P-K4!

Opening lines for the attack.

12	N-N3	O-O
13	Q-B5	R-B1
14	Q-N4	...

After 14 QxP B-K3 15 QxQ KRxQ, Black would have excellent attacking chances despite the exchange of Queens.

14	...	R-K1
15	B-K2	PxP
16	NxP	Q-R5!

Threatening 17 ... BxN and 17 ... RxP. White cannot castle because he would lose a piece after 17 ... BxN.

| 17 | QxP! | ... |

A counter-attack which should hold the game for White. Not 17 Q-Q2 BxN! 18 PxB B-N4 and Black wins.

17	...	BxN
18	QxB	BxNP
19	R-Q1	B-B6ch
20	K-B1	P-Q5
21	PxP	Q-K5
22	Q-N4	Q-B7
23	P-N3	QxP

The storm is just about over, and a draw should be the result. White ought to play 24 B-B3.

| 24 | B-N5? | ... |

An awful blunder, losing a piece and the game.

24	...	Q-Q4
25	BxR	QxRch
26	K-K2	RxBch
27	K-Q3	B-K8
Resigns		

GAME 16

It's apparent that Bernstein expended a great deal of midnight oil in preparation of this opening in order to catch Bobby unaware. The result is exciting chess, pervaded with ideas.

U.S. CHAMPIONSHIP 1959–1960

New York, N.Y.

RUY LOPEZ

Robert J. Fischer	_Sidney Bernstein_	3 B-N5	P-QR3
		4 B-R4	N-B3
WHITE	BLACK	5 O-O	B-K2
		6 R-K1	P-QN4
1 P-K4	P-K4	7 B-N3	O-O
2 N-KB3	N-QB3	8 P-B3	P-Q4?!

The Marshall attack is a natural for a speculative player like Bernstein.

9 PxP	P-K5!?

This has the merit of being less well known than the usual 9 . . . NxP.

10 PxN	PxN
11 QxP	B-KN5
12 Q-N3	B-Q3
13 Q-R4	. . .

White diverges from the recommended move, 13 P-KB4.

13 . . .	R-K1
14 P-B3	B-KB4

Black threatens a bind with 15 . . . B-Q6.

15 P-Q4	BxPch!

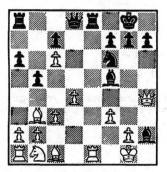

A sharp sacrifice which White must accept.

16 KxB	N-N5ch
17 K-N3	QxQch

The immediate 17 . . . RxR would save a tempo since 18 QxQch is forced, but in that case White has the option of sacrificing the Exchange with 18 . . . RxQ 19 B-Q2!

18 KxQ	RxR
19 PxN	RxB
20 PxB	R-Q1!

The best chance to keep the White pieces locked in.

21 P-R4	P-N5
22 P-Q5	R-N1?

The losing move, allowing White to free his position. The best line for Black was 22 . . . PxP 23 PxP P-QR4.

23 P-Q6	. . .

Leading to the establishment of a strong passed Pawn.

23 . . .	PxQP
24 B-B4	R-QB1

There is no good defense. White was threatening 25 BxP and 26 P-B7.

25 BxP	R(1)xP
26 B-N5	R-N3
27 P-B4	. . .

Now the passed Rook Pawn becomes decisive.

27 . . .	P-Q4
28 P-R5	P-N4ch

Black hopes to exploit the exposed position of White's King.

29 KxP	P-R3ch
30 K-N4	R-N1
31 P-R6	PxP
32 P-R7	R-R1
33 B-B6	P-R4ch
34 K-N5	RxN
35 RxR	RxP
36 R-QB1	R-R7
37 RxP	RxP
38 P-B6!	Resigns

GAME 17

Fischer said after this game ". . . while I was trying to figure out what was going on in his head, I blundered and lost the game." It was one of the few times in his tournament career that Bobby answered 1 . . . P-K4 to White's 1 P-K4, and the result was a serious loss. A short while later, after much analysis of the King's Gambit, Bobby published an article in the *American Chess Quarterly* entitled "A Bust to the King's Gambit," proving, at least to *his* satisfaction, that the opening was unsound. He has since reverted, however.

INTERNATIONAL TOURNAMENT 1960

Mar del Plata, Argentina

KING'S GAMBIT

Boris Spassky	*Robert J. Fischer*
WHITE	BLACK
1 P-K4	P-K4

Fischer departs from his usual Sicilian.

2 P-KB4	. . .

The King's Gambit is a personal favorite with Spassky, and it has scored many an impressive victory for him.

| 2 . . . | PxP |
| 3 N-KB3 | P-KN4 |

A double-edged move. In the article in 1961, Fischer recommended the defense with 3 . . . P-Q3 as leading to Black's advantage.

| 4 P-KR4 | P-N5 |
| 5 N-K5 | . . . |

White chooses the Kieseritzky Gambit. 5 N-N5 is the Allgaier Gambit.

5 . . .	N-KB3
6 P-Q4	P-Q3
7 N-Q3	NxP
8 BxP	B-N2

A suggestion of Keres's. The usual defense is 8 . . . Q-K2.

| 9 N-B3 | NxN |
| 10 PxN | P-QB4 |

Striking at the White center.

| 11 B-K2 | . . . |

White continues in true gambit style, offering Pawns for the sake of development.

| 11 . . . | PxP |
| 12 O-O | N-B3 |

Black refrains from any Pawn-grabbing and concentrates on activating his pieces.

13 BxNP	O-O
14 BxB	RxB
15 Q-N4	P-B4
16 Q-N3	PxP
17 QR-K1	. . .

Taking the Queen Pawn would be dangerous on account of 17 . . . R-B3.

| 17 . . . | K-R1 |
| 18 K-R1 | R-KN1 |

Black threatens 19 . . . B-K4, with
a strong initiative. Now White is
forced to play 19 BxP, freeing
Black's pieces.

19 BxP	B-B1!
20 B-K5ch	NxB
21 QxNch	R-N2
22 RxP	QxPch
23 K-N1	. . .

White now has good chances, due
to the superior coordination of his
pieces.

| 23 . . . | Q-N5? |

Fischer does not realize the danger.
Correct was 23 . . . Q-N6, after
which Spassky would have a very
difficult ending to defend.

| 24 R-B2 | B-K2 |
| 25 R-K4 | Q-N4 |

Fischer should have taken a draw
by repetition with 25 . . . Q-Q8ch
26 R-K1 Q-N5 27 R-K4 Q-Q8ch,
etc.

| 26 Q-Q4 | R-B1? |

The correct move was 26 . . . B-B1
27 QxRP B-Q3.

| 27 R-K5! | . . . |

Winning a piece, as the Black
Queen cannot defend the Bishop.

27 . . .	R-Q1
28 Q-K4	Q-R5
29 R-B4	Resigns

GAME 18

Another fierce battle between the two young rivals. In jeopardy,
Black forces a perpetual check and extricates himself from a precarious position.

WORLD TEAM OLYMPICS 1960

Leipzig, East Germany

FRENCH DEFENSE

Robert J. Fischer   *Mikhail Tal*

WHITE   BLACK

1 P-K4	P-K3
2 P-Q4	P-Q4
3 N-QB3	B-N5
4 P-K5	P-QB4
5 P-QR3	B-R4

More often seen is 5 . . . BxNch
6 PxB N-K2 or Q-B2.

| 6 P-QN4! | PxQP |

If 6 . . . PxNP 7 N-N5 with good
attacking chances.

| 7 Q-N4 | N-K2 |

8 PxB	PxN
9 QxNP	R-N1
10 QxP	QN-B3

Black concentrates on developing his pieces for action in the center. White has the better long-range prospects because of his passed KRP.

11 N-B3	Q-B2
12 B-QN5	B-Q2
13 O-O	O-O-O
14 B-N5	NxKP!

Leading to a long series of simplifying exchanges.

15 NxN	BxB
16 NxP	BxR
17 NxR	RxB
18 NxKP	RxPch
19 K-R1!	. . .

If 19 KxB RxP!, and Black wins.

19 . . .	Q-K4
20 RxB	QxN
21 KxR	Drawn

Black has a perpetual check with 21 . . . Q-N5ch 22 K-R1 Q-B6ch, etc.

GAME 19

Though Szabo was considered a strong candidate for the World's Championship at one time, Fischer here ties him up in a few moves. Szabo's experience indicated that resignation was not premature.

WORLD TEAM OLYMPICS 1960

Leipzig, East Germany

KING'S INDIAN DEFENSE

Laszlo Szabo   *Robert J. Fischer*

WHITE	BLACK
1 P-Q4	N-KB3
2 P-QB4	P-KN3
3 N-QB3	B-N2
4 P-K4	O-O
5 B-N5	. . .

In an earlier round of this event, Letelier tried 5 P-K5, but soon got the worst of it. 5 N-B3 or 5 P-B3 are usual and good.

5 . . .	P-Q3
6 Q-Q2	P-B4
7 P-Q5	P-K3

| 8 B-Q3 | PxP |
| 9 NxP | ... |

Looks good, but actually makes Black's development easier. Recapturing with either Pawn was better.

9 ...	B-K3
10 N-K2	BxN
11 KPxB	QN-Q2
12 O-O	N-K4
13 P-B4?	...

Hoping to play P-B5 later, but N-B3 was better.

| 13 ... | NxB |
| 14 QxN | P-KR3 |

Black prevents White from starting an attack with P-B5, since he will be able to answer that move with P-KN4.

| 15 B-R4 | R-K1 |
| 16 QR-K1? | ... |

16 N-B3 was best.

| 16 ... | Q-N3! |
| 17 BxN | ... |

Now this exchange becomes necessary to prevent 17 ... N-K5.

17 ...	BxB
18 P-B5	P-N4
19 P-QN3	Q-R4!

Preventing 20 N-B3. White is almost in zugzwang. If now 20 P-QR4 B-Q5ch, followed by R-K6 and QR-K1.

| 20 R-QB1 | QxP |
| 21 R-B2 | R-K6! |

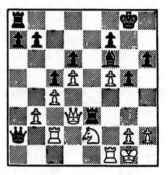

Adding greatly to Black's advantage.

22 QxR	QxR
23 K-R1	P-QR4
24 P-R4	P-R5

Leading to the win of several Pawns. White now makes a time-saving decision.

Resigns

GAME 20

The two Brooklyn youths engage in quite a slugging match in this game. Weinstein defends expertly but is the victim of a slip caused by the clock. Fischer played this entire game in a very short period of time.

U.S. CHAMPIONSHIP 1960–1961

New York, N.Y.

FRENCH DEFENSE

Robt. J. Fischer   Raymond Weinstein

WHITE	BLACK
1 P-K4	P-K3
2 P-Q4	P-Q4
3 N-QB3	B-N5
4 P-K5	N-K2
5 P-QR3	BxNch
6 PxB	P-QB4
7 P-QR4	. . .

White prepares to post his Bishop on the QR3 diagonal. The text also prevents Black from establishing a Queenside bind with 7 . . . Q-R4 and 8 . . . Q-R5.

7 . . .	QN-B3
8 N-B3	Q-R4
9 Q-Q2	B-Q2
10 B-Q3	P-B5

Black must play this move sooner or later, but it deprives him of counterplay on the Queenside. The ending after 10 . . . PxP 11 PxP QxQch 12 BxQ favors White.

11 B-K2	O-O-O
12 B-R3	P-B3
13 O-O	N-B4

13 . . . N-N3 was played against Fischer by Sherwin later in this tournament.

14 KR-K1	B-K1
15 P-N4	. . .

White weakens his Kingside in order to decentralize Black's Knight and also prevent 15 . . . B-R4.

15 . . .	N(4)-K2
16 B-KB1	B-Q2

Black has clearly lost several tempi.

17 B-R3	P-KR3

Black prevents 18 P-N5.

18 B-Q6	QR-B1
19 QR-N1	R-B2

Obviously Black could not take the QRP without losing his Queen.

20 PxP	PxP
21 B-N3	N-N3
22 R-N5	Q-R3

22 . . . QxP gives White good attacking chances after 23 R(5)-N1.

23 R(1)-N1	P-N3
24 Q-B1	QxP

Now Black takes the Pawn in order to prevent 25 Q-R3 and 26 Q-Q6.

25 R(5)-N2	Q-R6
26 Q-K3	K-N2
27 N-R4	NxN
28 BxN	P-K4?

| 29 PxP | PxP |
| 30 RxPch! | . . . |

Smashing Black's position to bits. If 30 . . . PxR, it's mate in two.

30 . . .	K-R1
31 R(6)-N5	B-K3
32 B-N3	P-K5?

32 . . . Q-Q3 was Black's only hope.

| 33 QxKRP! | Resigns |

After defending very well in a difficult position, Black blunders in time-pressure. 28 . . . P-KR4 or 28 . . . Q-B1 were good continuations.

Black cannot take the Queen because of 34 R-N8ch and mate, nor can he save both of his attacked pieces (33 . . . R-K1 34 QxB!).

GAME 21

Fischer roamed the tournament hall during this game, while Berliner struggled. Though Black plays an excellently prepared game, White either "out-prepared" his opponent or found the answers over the board in rapid order. All problems are solved with machine-like precision.

U.S. CHAMPIONSHIP 1960–1961

New York, N.Y.

ALEKHINE'S DEFENSE

Robert J. Fischer	*Hans Berliner*
WHITE	BLACK
1 P-K4	N-KB3
2 P-K5	N-Q4
3 P-Q4	P-Q3
4 P-QB4	. . .

Fischer prefers this sharp line to the "modern" line 4 N-KB3, or the Four Pawn Attack.

4 . . .	N-N3
5 PxP	BPxP
6 N-QB3	P-N3
7 B-Q3	B-N2

8 KN-K2	N-B3
9 B-K3	O-O
10 O-O	P-K4

Black's best chance in this variation is to start a Pawn advance on the Kingside.

| 11 P-Q5 | N-K2 |
| 12 P-QN3 | N-Q2? |

An unnecessary maneuver. The natural 12 . . . P-B4 is Black's best try.

| 13 N-K4 | . . . |

Gaining a tempo by attacking the Queen Pawn.

13 ...   N-KB4

Black is forced to block his King Bishop Pawn in order to defend himself.

14 B-N5!   ...

Inducing Black to block off his own pieces.

14 ...   P-B3
15 B-Q2   N-B4

Giving White a passed Pawn. Black was already at a loss for constructive moves.

16 NxN   PxN
17 BxN   ...

Before the Knight could go to Q5.

17 ...   BxB
18 P-B4   ...

Gaining more scope for his pieces.

18 ...   PxP
19 NxP   Q-Q3

20 N-R5!   ...

Sharp tactics. White clears KB4 for his Bishop.

20 ...   QR-K1
21 NxB   KxN
22 B-B4   Q-Q2
23 Q-Q2   R-B2
24 B-R6ch   K-N1
25 QR-K1   R(2)-K2
26 RxR   QxR
27 P-KR3   ...

White's strategy now centers around playing P-KN4 at the right moment.

27 ...   Q-K5
28 Q-KB2   Q-K2
29 P-KN4   B-Q6
30 R-Q1   B-K5
31 P-Q6   ...

At last the passed Pawn is rolling.

31 ...   Q-K4
32 B-B4   Q-B6
33 P-Q7   R-Q1
34 Q-K2   Q-B6
35 QxQ   BxQ
36 B-B7!   Resigns

White gets a new Queen.

GAME 22

At the time this game was played, Herbert Seidman could be considered one of the most imaginative players in American chess. This encounter bristles with ideas, most of them Seidman's. Fischer defends like a champion, however, and builds a steamroller attack.

U.S. CHAMPIONSHIP 1960–1961

New York, N.Y.

RUY LOPEZ

Robert J. Fischer	*Herbert Seidman*
WHITE	BLACK
1 P-K4	P-K4
2 N-KB3	N-QB3
3 B-N5	P-QR3
4 B-R4	N-B3
5 O-O	B-K2
6 R-K1	P-QN4
7 B-N3	O-O
8 P-B3	P-Q4?!

The enterprising Marshall attack is well suited to Seidman's style.

9 PxP	P-K5

This is the same line that Bernstein tried against Fischer the year before. More often seen is 9 . . . NxP 10 NxP NxN 11 RxN P-QB3.

10 PxN	PxN
11 QxP	B-KN5
12 Q-N3	B-Q3
13 P-KB4	P-N4

A violent attempt. Usual is 13 . . . R-K1.

14 P-Q4	K-R1

Black intends 15 . . . R-KN1.

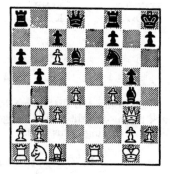

15 R-K5!	. . .

A strong move, leading to a sacrifice of the Exchange but breaking up Black's attack.

15 . . .	PxP
16 QBxP	N-R4
17 RxN!	. . .

The point of White's play. He gets two Pawns for the exchange and a free position. If 17 QxB NxB 18 QxN P-B3.

17 . . .	BxR
18 N-Q2	R-K1
19 R-KB1	R-K7

A rash excursion. The Rook is needed for defense.

20 B-Q1	RxN
21 BxB(5)	P-B3

White was threatening 22 B-K5ch.

| 22 R-K1 | BxB |

Black had no good move. Now he is forced to give up his Queen.

23 QxB	RxP
24 R-K8ch	QxR
25 BxQ	RxB
26 P-KR3	...

There is no hurry to grab the KBP. Black cannot well protect it.

26 ...	P-N5
27 PxP	RxNP
28 QxPch	K-N1

29 Q-N5ch	K-R1
30 Q-B4	R-R5
31 Q-B7	...

Decisive. White wins the Black QBP, at the same time guarding his own QP indirectly.

31 ...	R-KN1
32 QxP	RxRP
33 Q-K5ch	R-N2
34 P-N4	P-R3
35 Q-N8ch	R-N1
36 P-B7	Resigns

After 36 . . . R-QB7, the White Queen Pawn marches on.

GAME 23

After losing the first game in their ill-fated match, Fischer comes back the next night with a vengeance. All Black's defenses crumble to White's handling of his pieces.

FISCHER-RESHEVSKY MATCH 1961

Game 2

New York, N.Y.

SICILIAN DEFENSE

Robert J. Fischer	Samuel Reshevsky
WHITE	BLACK
1 P-K4	P-QB4
2 N-KB3	N-QB3
3 P-Q4	PxP
4 NxP	P-KN3

Reshevsky is one of the few leading grandmasters who ever play the Dragon Variation consistently. He obviously doesn't fear the Maroczy Bind, 5 P-QB4, either.

5 N-QB3	B-N2
6 B-K3	N-B3
7 B-K2	...

Psychological warfare here. Fischer plays something completely different from his usual 7 B-QB4.

7 ...	O-O
8 P-B4	P-Q3
9 N-N3	B-K3
10 P-KN4	...

White chooses the sharp Alekhine attack, first played by Levenfish against Botvinnik, Moscow, 1936.

| 10 ... | P-Q4 |
| 11 P-B5 | ... |

If 11 P-K5 P-Q5 12 NxP NxN 13 BxN NxP, with equal chances.

11 ...	B-B1
12 PxQP	N-N5
13 B-B3	...

13 P-Q6 was played in Alekhine-Botvinnik, at Nottingham, 1936. The game was quickly drawn.

13 ...	PxP
14 P-QR3	PxP
15 B-N2!	...

15 PxN PxB 16 QxP gives White some advantage, but Fischer prefers to sacrifice a Pawn in order to attack.

15 ...	N-R3
16 Q-Q3	...

A stronger move than the book recommendations 16 Q-Q2 or 16 Q-K2.

16 ...	P-K3
17 O-O-O	NxP
18 P-R3	P-N6

Black must try to keep the Rook file closed.

19 KR-N1	Q-Q3
20 BxN	PxB
21 NxP	K-R1
22 B-B4	Q-KN3
23 Q-Q2	...

White is playing to win and so is not satisfied with recovering his Pawn and trading Queens.

23 ...	BxP
24 RxP	B-N5
25 R-R1	KR-K1
26 N-K3	Q-K5

26 ... P-B4 was the best. Black is too anxious to simplify.

27 Q-R2	B-K3

The strain of defending a difficult position finally tells on Black. 27 ... B-B4 was the only chance.

28 RxB!	...

Decisive, leading to a win of the Queen.

28 ...	KxR
29 Q-R6ch	K-N1

Forced. If 29 ... K-R1 30 B-K5ch and mate.

30 R-N1ch	Q-N3
31 RxQch	BPxR
32 N-Q4	QR-Q1
33 B-K5	R-Q2
34 NxB	RxN
35 N-N4	R-KB2
36 Q-N5	R-B8ch
37 K-Q2	P-R4
38 Q-Q8ch	Resigns

White wins everything.

GAME 24

Meeting his constant rival once again, Bobby tries everything in the book to displace him. The result is a draw.

ALEKHINE MEMORIAL 1961

Bled, Yugoslavia

KING'S INDIAN DEFENSE

Svetozar Gligoric	Robert J. Fischer
WHITE	BLACK
1 P-Q4	N-KB3
2 P-QB4	P-KN3
3 N-QB3	B-N2
4 P-K4	P-Q3
5 N-B3	O-O
6 B-K2	P-K4
7 O-O	N-B3
8 P-Q5	N-K2
9 N-K1	N-Q2
10 N-Q3	P-KB4
11 PxP	NxBP

Recapturing with the Pawn is not bad, either.

12 P-B3	N-B3
13 N-B2	N-Q5
14 N(2)-K4	N-R4
15 B-N5	Q-Q2

A strange-looking move, but it has its points, as will soon be seen.

16 P-KN3	P-KR3
17 B-K3	P-B4
18 BxN	KPxB
19 N-QN5	P-R3

The beginning of a series of combinations on both sides.

20 N(5)xP(6)	P-Q6!
21 QxP	B-Q5ch
22 K-N2	NxP!

Black's point is that after 23 NxN (23 PxN??, Q-R6 mate) 23 . . . QxN, he will get a strong attack on White's weakened Kingside.

23 NxB! . . .

White refuses to cooperate. Instead he sacrifices the Exchange for strong counterplay.

23 . . .	NxR
24 N-N6	Q-QB2!
25 RxN	. . .

Forced. 25 NxR?? QxPch and mates.

| 25 . . . | QxN |
| 26 P-N4! | . . . |

White forces open the Queen Knight file for his Rook and obtains a strong attack.

26 . . . QxP

After 26 . . . PxP 27 P-B5! BxP 28 NxB QxN 29 QxPch, White has at least a draw.

| 27 R-QN1 | Q-R4 |
| 28 NxP | . . . |

This sharp sacrifice leads to a forced draw by repetition.

28 . . .	QxN
29 QxPch	B-N2
30 RxP	Q-Q5
31 B-Q3!	. . .

White's point. Now Black must move his Rook to prevent mate.

| 31 . . . | R-B5 |

31 . . . KR-K1 32 Q-B7ch K-R1 33 Q-N6 would also lead to a draw.

| 32 Q-K6ch | K-R1 |

Not 32 . . . K-B1?? 33 B-R7!, and Black gets mated.

| 33 Q-N6 | Drawn |

Black is forced to repeat moves.

GAME 25

In six previous encounters, Fischer could not win a game from Tal. Here is his first victory. Dr. Mikhail Botvinnik, writing about this game at the conclusion of the tournament, said: "Tal did not guess the artful and cunning scheme of his youthful partner in the opening and could not save the game. Fischer played with inventiveness and with great technical perfection."

ALEKHINE MEMORIAL 1961

Bled, Yugoslavia

SICILIAN DEFENSE

Robert J. Fischer	*Mikhail Tal*
WHITE	BLACK
1 P-K4	P-QB4
2 N-KB3	N-QB3
3 P-Q4	PxP
4 NxP	P-K3
5 N-QB3	Q-B2
6 P-KN3	. . .

White combines the possibilities of a fianchetto and B-KB4.

| 6 . . . | N-B3? |

Black continues in a very risky manner. 6 . . . P-QR3 was indicated.

| 7 N(4)-N5! | Q-N1 |
| 8 B-KB4 | N-K4 |

After 8 . . . P-K4 9 B-N5!, White would have the advantage through his control of Q5.

| 9 B-K2! | . . . |

Much stronger than the natural 9 B-N2. The text move limits the scope of the Black Knights.

| 9 . . . | B-B4 |

Black was already in serious trouble. 9 . . . P-QR3 would have been answered by 10 Q-Q4 P-Q3 11 R-Q1 PxN 12 BxN.

| 10 BxN! | . . . |

This simple move ruins Black's position completely.

10 . . .	QxB
11 P-B4	Q-N1
12 P-K5	P-QR3

12 . . . N-N1 13 N-K4 would leave
Black in dire straits.

13 PxN	PxN
14 PxP	R-N1
15 N-K4	B-K2
16 Q-Q4	. . .

Forcing the exchange of Black's better Bishop for White's Knight.

16 . . .	R-R5

According to Botvinnik 16 . . . Q-
B2 was the best.

17 N-B6ch	BxN
18 QxB	Q-B2

Parrying the threat of 19 B-R5
which could now be answered by
19 . . . P-Q4.

19 O-O-O!	. . .

White's Rook Pawn means nothing.
He threatens 20 B-Q3. If 19 . . .
Q-Q1 20 Q-R6.

19 . . .	RxRP
20 K-N1	R-R3
21 BxP	R-N3
22 B-Q3	P-K4

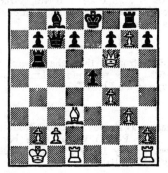

23 PxP!	. . .

A surprise combination which
greatly increases White's advantage.

Black would still have some faint
hope after 23 QxKPch QxQ 24 PxQ
RxP.

23 . . .	RxQ
24 PxR	Q-B4!

If 24 . . . Q-N3 25 KR-B1!, and
Black is defenseless.

25 BxP	Q-KN4
26 BxR	. . .

If 26 KR-B1 RxP.

26 . . .	QxBP
27 KR-B1	QxP
28 BxPch	K-Q1

All of Black's moves have been
forced since White sacrificed his
Queen. White now has both material advantage and a strong attack
on Black's King.

29 B-K6	. . .

Threatening 30 R-B7.

29 . . .	Q-R3
30 BxP	BxB
31 R-B7	QxP
32 R(1)xBch	K-K1
33 R(Q)-K7ch	K-Q1
34 R-Q7ch	K-B1
35 R-B7ch	K-Q1
36 R(KB)-Q7ch	K-K1
37 R-Q1	. . .

White guards his first rank. The rest
is technique.

37 . . .	P-N4
38 R-QN7	Q-R4

If 38 . . . QxP 39 R-R1 Q-K4 40
R-R8ch!

39 P-KN4	Q-R6
40 P-N5	Q-KB6
41 R-K1ch	K-B1
42 RxP	K-N2
43 R-N6	Q-KN6
44 R-Q1	Q-B2
45 R(1)-Q6	Q-B1
46 P-N3	K-R2
47 R-R6	Resigns

GAME 26

In a combinational melee, Bobby gives his Queen away for two Rooks against the Icelandic grandmaster and emerges with a winning attack.

ALEKHINE MEMORIAL 1961

Bled, Yugoslavia

SICILIAN DEFENSE

Robert J. Fischer *Fridrik Olafsson*

WHITE	BLACK
1 P-K4	P-QB4
2 N-KB3	P-KN3
3 P-Q4	PxP
4 NxP	B-N2
5 N-QB3	N-QB3
6 B-K3	N-B3
7 B-QB4	Q-R4

By an unusual order of moves, a position in the Accelerated Fianchetto Variation of the Dragon has been reached. Black's last move is trappy. If now 8 P-B3? Q-N5! 9 B-N3 NxP!

8 O-O	P-Q3
9 N-N3	Q-B2
10 B-K2	O-O

The game has transposed into a normal line of the Dragon but with Black's Queen on a poor square.

11 P-B4	P-QR4

Gaining a post for his Knight at QN5, but permanently giving up control of his QN4.

12 P-QR4	. . .

Stopping 12 . . . P-R5-R6.

12 . . .	N-QN5
13 R-B2	. . .

Planning to bring the Rook over to the Queen file.

13 . . .	P-K4
14 B-B3	B-Q2
15 R-Q2	KR-Q1
16 K-R1	. . .

Safeguarding the King and clearing N1 for the Queen. If 16 RxP, Black could play 16 . . . BxP.

16 . . .	B-B3
17 Q-KN1	N-Q2

Black parries the threat of 18 B-N6.

18 P-B5	P-N3
19 QR-Q1	N-B4
20 N-N5	. . .

Initiating a favorable series of exchanges. If Black plays 20 . . . BxN 21 PxB, his Knight on QN5 would soon be trapped.

20 . . .	Q-K2
21 NxQP	NxBP
22 NxN	NxB
23 QxN	PxN
24 B-K2!	. . .

The beginning of a long combination. White disdains the defensive 24 P-QN3.

24 . . .	BxRP
25 P-QN3	B-K1

Anticipating White's attack on his KB2.

26 B-B4	P-R5
27 B-Q5	RxN

Black decides to sacrifice the Exchange for counterplay.

28 BxR	R-Q5
29 PxNP	KRPxP
30 PxP	BxP
31 R-R1	Q-B1!

What is White to do now? Black threatens his Bishop and also 32 . . . B-R3, winning a Rook.

| 32 B-Q5! | B-R3 |
| 33 RxR! | . . . |

The point of White's play. He gets two Rooks for his Queen and a winning attack on Black's weak KB2.

33 . . .	BxQ
34 R(4)xB	Q-R3
35 R-KB1	B-B5
36 P-N3!	Q-R6

If 36 . . . BxP 37 R-R8ch wins the Queen.

| 37 R(4)-R1 | BxP |
| 38 R-R8ch | Resigns |

GAME 27

Geller has been one of the leading Soviet players for years and won the Soviet Championship in 1955. This "crush" by Fischer was one of the biggest upsets in Geller's career.

ALEKHINE MEMORIAL 1961

Bled, Yugoslavia

RUY LOPEZ

Robert J. Fischer	Yefim Geller
WHITE	BLACK
1 P-K4	P-K4
2 N-KB3	N-QB3
3 B-N5	P-QR3
4 B-R4	P-Q3
5 O-O	. . .

5 P-B3 is almost always played.

| 5 . . . | B-N5 |
| 6 P-KR3 | B-R4 |

Black tries something unusual. 6 . . . P-KR4 used to be played here,

but latest opinion is that White can get the advantage.

| 7 P-B3 | Q-B3 |

A questionable move. 7 . . . N-B3 was indicated.

| 8 P-KN4 | B-N3 |
| 9 P-Q4! | . . . |

Sacrificing the King Pawn, White soon obtains an overwhelming position.

| 9 . . . | BxP |

Black has nothing better. He must meet the threats of 10 P-Q5 and 10 B-N5.

10	QN-Q2	B-N3
11	BxNch	PxB
12	PxP	PxP
13	NxP	. . .

White has won back his Pawn and has a big advantage in development.

| 13 | . . . | B-Q3 |

Black hopes for 14 NxQBP P-KR4.

| 14 | NxB | QxN |
| 15 | R-K1ch | K-B1 |

If 15 . . . N-K2 16 N-B4 and Black still cannot castle.

| 16 | N-B4 | P-KR4 |

Black vainly tries to counterattack.

| 17 | NxB | PxN |
| 18 | B-B4 | P-Q4 |

| 19 | Q-N3 | . . . |

The crusher. White threatens both 20 Q-R3ch and 20 Q-N7.

| 19 | . . . | PxP |

Black is defenseless. 19 . . . N-K2 fails against 20 RxN KxR 21 Q-N7ch.

| 20 | Q-N7! | . . . |

Winning two pieces.

| 20 | . . . | PxPch |
| 21 | B-N3 | R-Q1 |

If 21 . . . R-K1 22 RxRch KxR 23 R-K1ch and mates.

| 22 | Q-N4ch | Resigns |

GAME 28

Outplaying and outwitting a Soviet ace of Korchnoi's caliber is a newsmaking, almost historic, event. When Korchnoi resigned to Bobby in this game, there was thunderous applause for the American star.

INTERZONAL CHAMPIONSHIP 1962

Stockholm, Sweden

RUY LOPEZ

Robert J. Fischer	Victor Korchnoi
WHITE	BLACK
1 P-K4	P-K4
2 N-KB3	N-QB3
3 B-N5	P-QR3
4 B-R4	N-B3
5 O-O	B-K2
6 R-K1	P-QN4
7 B-N3	O-O
8 P-B3	P-Q3
9 P-Q4	. . .

White chooses a continuation less known than the usual 9 P-KR3. The text move is best known from the game Capablanca-Bogolyubov, London 1922.

9 . . .	B-N5
10 B-K3	PxP
11 PxP	N-QR4
12 B-B2	N-B5
13 B-B1	P-B4
14 P-QN3	N-QR4

14 . . . N-N3 is Black's best move.

15 P-Q5!	. . .

This is Fischer's improvement on the above-mentioned game where 15 B-N2 was played.

15 . . .	N-Q2
16 QN-Q2	B-B3
17 R-N1	P-B5

17 . . . N-K4 was better. Now Black is forced to exchange his Bishop.

18 P-KR3	. . .

The best. If 18 P-N4 P-B6! Now if 18 . . . B-R4 19 P-KN4, followed by 20 PxP, with a big advantage.

18 . . .	BxN
19 NxB	PxP
20 PxP	Q-B2
21 B-K3	B-B6
22 R-K2	P-N5
23 N-Q4	KR-K1
24 N-B5	N-N2
25 B-Q4	. . .

White is working up a promising Kingside attack.

25 . . .	P-N3
26 N-R6ch	K-B1
27 R-B1!	. . .

Operating on the Queenside, too.

27 . . .	QR-B1
28 B-Q3	. . .

28 R-K3!, threatening 29 BxB and 30 Q-Q4, was strongest.

28 . . .	Q-R4
29 R(2)-B2	N-K4
30 B-B1	N-B4

Black sacrifices a Pawn to activate his pieces.

31 BxB	PxB
32 RxP	K-N2
33 N-N4	NxN
34 QxN	R-QN1
35 R-B3	. . .

White abandons his extra Pawn and concentrates on Black's King.

35 ...   NxKP

The only playable capture. If either Rook takes a Pawn, then 36 RxN! or 35 ... NxNP 36 Q-Q7!

36 Q-B4   P-B4

36 ... R-N2 was a better defense.

37 R-K3   R-K4
38 R-B6   QR-K1

Black overlooks the threat. He should have played 38 ... P-N4.

39 RxQP!   Q-R8?

Another error. 39 ... P-N4 was still best.

40 RxP   Q-Q5
41 R-Q3   Q-N7
42 P-Q6   ...

Black is defenseless against the advance of this Pawn.

42 ...   P-N4
43 Q-K3   P-B5
44 Q-R7ch   Resigns

GAME 29

Bolbochan, an experienced grandmaster, allows himself to be outplayed in the opening. Fischer follows with a series of star moves. A great performance.

INTERZONAL CHAMPIONSHIP 1962

Stockholm, Sweden

SICILIAN DEFENSE

Robert J. Fischer	Julio Bolbochan
WHITE	BLACK
1 P-K4	P-QB4
2 N-KB3	P-Q3
3 P-Q4	PxP
4 NxP	N-KB3
5 N-QB3	P-QR3
6 P-KR3	...

A surprise. Fischer chooses a little-known continuation. The text was a favorite of the late U.S. master and analyst Weaver W. Adams.

6 ...   N-B3
7 P-KN4   ...

The point behind White's last move.

7 ...	NxN
8 QxN	P-K4
9 Q-Q3	B-K2

9 . . . B-K3 would have given Black better chances for smooth development. Now he loses time.

| 10 P-N5 | N-Q2 |
| 11 B-K3 | ... |

If now 11 . . . BxP 12 BxB QxB 13 QxP.

11 ...	N-B4
12 Q-Q2	B-K3
13 O-O-O	O-O
14 P-B3	R-B1
15 K-N1	N-Q2

Black's Knight on B4 was only in his own way.

| 16 P-KR4 | P-N4 |
| 17 B-R3 | ... |

Trading Black's Queen Bishop gives White a positional advantage, since he can get control of Q5.

17 ...	BxB
18 RxB	N-N3
19 BxN	QxB
20 N-Q5	...

White has achieved the ideal position in this opening. It is amazing how Fischer gets these positions against experienced opponents, seemingly with such ease.

20 ...	Q-Q1
21 P-KB4	PxP
22 QxP	Q-Q2
23 Q-B5	QR-Q1

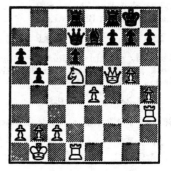

The only move that doesn't lose by force! Among other things, Black had to beware of 24 N-B6ch.

| 24 R-R3! | ... |

White maneuvers to get control of the Queen Bishop file.

| 24 ... | Q-R2 |
| 25 R-QB3 | ... |

Threatening both 26 R-B7 and 26 N-B6ch.

| 25 ... | P-N3 |
| 26 Q-N4 | Q-Q2 |

If 26 . . . R-Q2 27 P-R5 is strong.

27 Q-B3	Q-K3
28 R-B7	QR-K1
29 N-B4	Q-K4
30 R-Q5	Q-R1
31 P-R3	...

Black is in near zugzwang.

| 31 ... | P-R3 |
| 32 PxP | QxP |

| 33 P-R5 | B-N4 |
| 34 PxP! | PxP |

If 34 . . . BxN 35 PxPch RxP 36
RxR KxR 37 R-R5 and wins.

| 35 Q-QN3 | RxN |

If 35 . . . K-R1 36 NxPch! QxN 37
RxB QxR 38 Q-R3ch and mate.

| 36 R-K5ch | K-B1 |
| 37 RxRch | Resigns |

Mate is forced after 37 . . . KxR 38
Q-K6ch.

GAME 30

With his defeat of Dr. Max Euwe registered on the cross table of
the 1960 Olympics at Leipzig, Aaron plays confidently but errs in a
difficult position. One mistake is all Fischer needs, and he capitalizes
on it in inventive style.

INTERZONAL CHAMPIONSHIP 1962

Stockholm, Sweden

KING'S INDIAN DEFENSE

Manuel Aaron	*Robert J. Fischer*
WHITE	BLACK
1 P-Q4	N-KB3
2 P-QB4	P-KN3
3 N-QB3	B-N2
4 P-K4	P-Q3
5 P-B3	O-O
6 B-K3	QN-Q2

6 . . . P-K4 is most often played
here.

| 7 Q-Q2 | P-B4 |
| 8 KN-K2 | P-QR3 |

Black prepares for Queenside action.

| 9 N-N3 | . . . |

The Knight turns out to be not well
placed here.

9 . . .	PxP!
10 BxP	N-K4
11 B-K2	B-K3

Black already has the sounder development.

| 12 N-Q5 | P-QN4 |

Undermining White's advanced
Knight. The text gives White two
passed Pawns on the Queenside, but
Black gets the advantage in the
center.

| 13 PxP | PxP |
| 14 BxP | . . . |

If first 14 NxNch, White would lose
his Queen Rook Pawn.

14 . . .	NxN
15 PxN	BxP
16 P-QR4	P-K3
17 O-O	Q-R5

Threatening 18 . . . NxPch.

| 18 N-K2 | KR-B1 |
| 19 B-K3 | N-B5 |

Gaining the two Bishops.

20 BxN	QxB
21 KR-B1	Q-R3
22 RxRch	RxR
23 N-B3	B-B5
24 P-B4	P-Q4
25 B-Q4	. . .

White is eager to swap off Black's powerful Bishop, but his position is not improved thereby.

25 ...   BxBch
26 QxB   Q-N2

Black has pressure on the backward QNP.

27 Q-B2   B-R3
28 R-Q1   R-B5

Black is angling to get in an eventual P-Q5. White's passed Pawns have little future.

29 R-Q2?   ...

White blunders in a difficult position. Relatively best was 29 P-R3.

29 ...   RxN!
Resigns

GAME 31

In his element with 6 B–QB4 in the Sicilian, Fischer sometimes appears unbeatable. Fischer simplifies in this game and Olafsson is helpless against his Rooks and Pawns.

INTERZONAL CHAMPIONSHIP 1962
Stockholm, Sweden

SICILIAN DEFENSE

Robert J. Fischer   *Fridrik Olafsson*

WHITE   BLACK

1 P-K4   P-QB4
2 N-KB3   P-Q3
3 P-Q4   PxP
4 NxP   N-KB3
5 N-QB3   N-B3
6 B-QB4   ...

A Fischer favorite, with which he has scored many an impressive victory.

6 ...   P-K3
7 B-N3   B-K2
8 P-B4   O-O

The sharpest continuation.

9 B-K3   NxN
10 BxN   P-QN4

A good try. If 11 NxP NxP.

11 P-K5   PxP
12 PxP   N-Q2
13 O-O   ...

If 13 NxP Q-R4ch 14 N-B3 NxP.

13 ...   P-N5

13 . . . B-B4, played by Geller against Fischer, is Black's best.

14 N-K4   B-N2
15 N-Q6!   ...

Leading to the establishment of a powerful passed Pawn.

15 ...	BxN
16 PxB	Q-N4
17 Q-K2	B-Q4
18 QR-Q1	BxB
19 RPxB	P-K4
20 Q-N5!	...

Forcing a favorable exchange.

20 ...	P-QR3
21 QxN	PxB
22 Q-B5!	QxQ

Black would have done better to avoid the exchange of Queens, but he loses a Pawn in any event.

23 RxQ	KR-Q1
24 RxQP	QR-B1
25 R-B2	P-QR4
26 R(2)-Q2	...

Now the other Rook is free to move, preparing the advance of the QBP.

26 ...	P-B3
27 R-QB4	K-B2
28 R-B7ch	...

Greatly increasing White's advantage.

28 ...	K-N3
29 R-K7	P-R4
30 P-Q7	R-B2
31 P-B4!	K-R2
32 P-R4	K-N3
33 R-Q5	Resigns

Black is helpless. He can do nothing about the decisive advance of White's King.

GAME 32

Playing the "Benko" attack, Benko instigates a cramped position for Black. Fischer took this defeat very hard, and an unpleasant rivalry ensued throughout the remainder of the tournament.

CHALLENGERS' TOURNAMENT 1962

Curaçao, Dutch West Indies

IRREGULAR OPENING

Pal Benko	Robert J. Fischer
WHITE	BLACK
1 P-KN3	...

Benko's secret weapon, with which he defeated both Fischer and Tal in this tournament.

1 ...	N-KB3
2 B-N2	P-KN3

3 P-K4	P-Q3
4 P-Q4	B-N2
5 N-K2	O-O
6 O-O	P-K4

Black is playing a King's Indian, which turns out not to be satisfactory without White's Pawn on Queen Bishop Four.

7 QN-B3	P-B3

8 P-QR4	QN-Q2
9 P-R5	...

White gains space on the Queen-side. He prevents P-QR4 by Black.

9 ...	PxP
10 NxP	N-B4
11 P-R3	R-K1
12 R-K1	KN-Q2
13 B-K3	Q-B2
14 P-B4	R-N1
15 Q-Q2	P-QN4

A violent attempt to break out of a cramped position.

16 PxP e.p.	PxP
17 P-QN4	...

White strikes to force a weakness in Black's Queenside.

17 ...	N-K3
18 P-N5	NxN
19 BxN	BxBch
20 QxB	P-QB4
21 Q-Q2	...

White has a big advantage in the position. Black's best line of resistance is 21 ... N-B3.

21 ...	B-N2
22 QR-Q1	R-K3
23 P-K5	...

Winning the weak Queen Pawn with a decisive advantage.

23 ...	BxB
24 KxB	Q-N2ch
25 K-B2	R-Q1
26 PxP	N-B3
27 RxR	PxR
28 Q-K2	K-B2
29 Q-B3	Q-N1
30 N-K4	...

White simplifies into an ending where his passed Pawn renders Black helpless.

30 ...	NxN
31 QxN	R-Q2

Black could not have played 31 ... RxP because of 32 Q-K5! R-Q1 33 R-Q7ch! or 32 ... K-K2 33 Q-N7ch.

32 Q-B6!	Q-Q1
33 K-B3	K-N2
34 P-N4	P-K4

Black tries to open some lines to White's King.

35 PxP	R-B2ch
36 K-N2	Q-R5
37 R-KB1	...

Simplifying to a clear win.

37 ...	RxR
38 KxR	QxPch
39 Q-N2	Q-K6
40 Q-K2	Resigns

Black did not continue after adjournment.

GAME 33

Still in his teens at the time of this game Fischer nevertheless refuses to be nettled and consequently displays a wisdom beyond his years. He plays a game of cat and mouse which favors the cat (himself) in a won ending.

CHALLENGERS' TOURNAMENT 1962

Curaçao, Dutch West Indies

RUY LOPEZ

Robert J. Fischer WHITE	Paul Keres BLACK
1 P-K4	P-K4
2 N-KB3	N-QB3
3 B-N5	P-QR3
4 B-R4	N-B3
5 O-O	B-K2
6 R-K1	P-QN4
7 B-N3	P-Q3
8 P-B3	O-O
9 P-KR3	N-QR4
10 B-B2	P-B4
11 P-Q4	N-Q2

This sharp move leads to liquidation of the center and gives White good attacking prospects.

This move proved quite popular at Curaçao. Usually Black proceeds here with 11 . . . Q-B2.

12 PxBP	. . .

The exchange attack, a promising line. The main alternative is 12 QN-Q2.

12 . . .	PxP
13 QN-Q2	Q-B2
14 N-B1	N-N3
15 N-K3	R-Q1
16 Q-K2	B-K3
17 N-Q5!	. . .

17 . . .	NxN
18 PxN	BxP
19 NxP	R-R2
20 B-B4	Q-N3
21 QR-Q1!	. . .

Threatening 22 RxB and 23 Q-K4. If 21 . . . BxRP, White obtains a winning attack starting with 22 RxRch and 23 P-QN4.

21 . . .	P-N3
22 N-N4	N-B5

Parrying the threat of 23 Q-K5.

23 B-R6	B-K3
24 B-N3	Q-N1
25 RxRch	BxR

26 BxN	PxB
27 QxP	...

White has won a Pawn and threatens 28 RxB.

27 ...	Q-Q3
28 Q-R4	Q-K2
29 N-B6ch	...

White keeps on taking advantage of the weakness of Black's first rank.

29 ...	K-R1
30 N-Q5	Q-Q2
31 Q-K4!	...

Threatening 32 Q-K5ch and mate. Obviously Black cannot capture the Knight either way.

31 ...	Q-Q3
32 N-B4	R-K2
33 B-N5	R-K1

34 BxB	RxB
35 NxB	QxN
36 QxQ	PxQ
37 RxP	...

White has simplified into an easily won ending.

37 ...	R-Q8ch
38 K-R2	R-Q7
39 R-N6	...

White keeps his Pawns connected.

39 ...	RxBP
40 R-N7!	...

Trapping Black's King.

40 ...	R-B3
41 K-N3	Resigns

Black did not continue after adjournment.

GAME 34

In order to avoid Fischer's virtuosity in the Ruy Lopez or the Sicilian, players often consider less than popular—and in some cases less than sound—opening lines against him. In this game, such strategy results in another sparkling Fischer miniature.

WORLD TEAM OLYMPICS 1966

Varna, Bulgaria

CENTER COUNTER DEFENSE

Robert J. Fischer	*Karl Robatsch*
WHITE	BLACK
1 P-K4	P-Q4
2 PxP	QxP
3 N-QB3	Q-Q1

3 ... Q-QR4 is usually played here. Black's last is a clear loss of time. But the move is not as bad as it looks. The idea is to entice White to become overextended in the center.

4 P-Q4	P-KN3

5 B-KB4	B-N2
6 Q-Q2!	...

A surprising point! White need not spend time defending his Queen Pawn, and after 7 O-O-O, he will have a fine development with good attacking chances.

6 ...	N-KB3

Black dared not take the Pawn. If 6 ... BxP 7 O-O-O P-QB4 8 N-N5 and wins. Or 6 ... QxP 7 QxQ BxQ

8 N-N5 B-N3 9 BxP, with a great
advantage.

| 7 O-O-O | P-B3 |
| 8 B-KR6 | ... |

Preparing the advance of his King
Rook Pawn by fixing Black's.

8 ...	O-O
9 P-KR4	Q-R4
10 P-R5!	...

White threatens to get his Queen to
KR6 with decisive effect after 11
PxP. If 10 . . . NxP, then 11 B-K2,
with an overwhelming attack.

10 ...	PxP
11 B-Q3	QN-Q2
12 KN-K2	R-Q1

| 13 P-KN4! | ... |

A crusher, leading to the opening of
the Knight file. If 13 . . . NxP 14
QR-N1 wins.

13 ...	N-B1
14 PxP	N-K3
15 QR-N1	K-R1
16 BxBch	NxB
17 Q-R6	R-KN1
18 R-N5	Q-Q1
19 R(1)-N1	...

Black has no good move. After 19
. . . Q-B1, White would continue
with 20 P-Q5 and Black would soon
lose material.

| 19 ... | N-B4 |
| 20 BxN | Resigns |

GAME 35

Fischer takes his opponent just a few steps further than the book, and wins the game convincingly. An impressive montage of meticulous preparation combined with blazing originality.

WORLD TEAM OLYMPICS 1962

Varna, Bulgaria

SICILIAN DEFENSE

Wolfgang Unzicker	Robt. J. Fischer
WHITE	BLACK
1 P-K4	P-QB4
2 N-KB3	P-Q3
3 P-Q4	PxP
4 NxP	N-KB3
5 N-QB3	P-QR3
6 B-K2	P-K4
7 N-N3	B-K3

Better than the routine 7 . . . B-K2. Black develops his Queenside first.

8 O-O	QN-Q2
9 P-B4	Q-B2

Black keeps control of his QB5.

10 P-B5	B-B5
11 P-QR4	B-K2
12 B-K3	O-O
13 P-R5	P-QN4

Avoiding any possibility of getting into a Queenside bind.

14 PxP e.p.	NxNP
15 BxN	QxBch
16 K-R1	B-N4!

Much better than 16 . . . BxN or BxB.

17 BxB	PxB
18 N-Q5	NxN
19 QxN	R-R5!

Black has enough play on the Queenside to compensate for his bad Bishop.

20 P-B3	Q-R3

Not 20 . . . KR-R1? 21 QxRch!

21 P-R3	. . .

This position arose in a Tal-Fischer game, Curaçao 1962, where 21 QR-Q1 was played.

21 . . .	R-B1
22 KR-K1	P-R3
23 K-R2	. . .

A pointless move.

23 . . .	B-N4

Black takes the opportunity to get his Bishop into the game.

24 P-N3?	. . .

A serious weakening of the 2nd rank.

24 . . .	Q-R2!
25 K-N2	. . .

White must parry 25 . . . Q-B7ch, but 25 R-KN1 or 25 P-R4 were better ways to do it.

25 ...   R-R7

Already a decisive stroke. White has no good defense to the double threats of 26 . . . RxPch and 26 . . . RxP.

26 K-B1   . . .

26 ...   RxP!
Resigns

GAME 36

When Fischer and Botvinnik sat down to play this game, their heads almost collided. Fischer made only one remark: "Sorry." The tournament hall was filled to capacity, with spectators in the high balconies, in the lounges, and in the streets outside the hall. Botvinnik received tremendous applause when he drew what appeared to be a lost game.

WORLD TEAM OLYMPICS 1962

Varna, Bulgaria

GRUENFELD DEFENSE

Mikhail Botvinnik	*Robert J. Fischer*
WHITE	BLACK
1 P-QB4	P-KN3
2 P-Q4	N-KB3
3 N-QB3	P-Q4

Fischer seems to save this defense for important occasions.

4 N-B3	B-N2
5 Q-N3	PxP
6 QxBP	O-O
7 P-K4	B-N5

Smyslov's variation.

8 B-K3	KN-Q2
9 B-K2	N-QB3
10 R-Q1	N-N3
11 Q-B5	Q-Q3!
12 P-KR3	BxN
13 PxB	. . .

If 13 BxB QxQ 14 PxQ, N-B5.

13 ...   KR-Q1

13 . . . P-K3 was a good alternative.

14 P-Q5	N-K4
15 N-N5	Q-KB3
16 P-B4	N(4)-Q2
17 P-K5	QxBP!

A surprise move that White overlooked. Black wins a Pawn, but White is not without compensation.

18	BxQ	NxQ
19	NxBP	QR-B1
20	P-Q6	PxP
21	PxP	BxP
22	O-O	...

White has the two Bishops and a strong passed Pawn.

| 22 | ... | N(3)-Q2 |

According to Botvinnik, Black should have proceeded with 22 ... N(4)-Q2, followed by 23 ... B-K4.

| 23 | R-Q5 | P-N3 |
| 24 | B-B3 | ... |

Better was 24 B-B4!, threatening to bring a Rook to K7.

| 24 | ... | N-K3! |

Forcing a favorable exchange.

25	NxN	PxN
26	R-Q3	N-B4
27	R-K3	P-K4

Eliminating White's passed Pawn.

28	BxP	BxB
29	RxB	RxP
30	R-K7	R-Q2
31	RxR	NxR

Now Black has a clear advantage.

| 32 | B-N4 | R-B2 |
| 33 | R-K1 | ... |

The Rook ending after 33 BxN would be lost for White.

33	...	K-B2
34	K-N2	N-B4
35	R-K3	R-K2
36	R-B3ch	K-N2
37	R-B3	R-K5
38	B-Q1	R-Q5
39	B-B2	K-B3
40	K-B3	K-N4

Forcing White into a Rook and Pawn ending, since he cannot allow 41 ... K-R5.

41	K-N3	N-K5ch
42	BxN	RxB
43	R-R3	...

If 43 R-B7 R-QR5.

| 43 | ... | R-K2 |

Better was 43 ... P-QR4 44 R-N3 R-N5!

| 44 | R-KB3 | R-QB2 |
| 45 | P-R4 | ... |

Now White threatens to obtain a draw by exchanging a pair of Queenside Pawns. Black could have prevented this by playing 44 ... P-N4!

| 45 | ... | R-B4 |

The sealed move.

| 46 | R-B7 | ... |

White decided to try for active counterplay. The position which now arises could have resulted if White had played R-B7 on his 43rd move.

| 46 | ... | R-R4 |
| 47 | RxKRP | RxP |

Even with two connected passed Pawns, Black has difficulties because of his poor King position.

48	P-R4ch	K-B4
49	R-B7ch	K-K4
50	R-KN7	R-R8
51	K-B3	P-QN4?

Black plans to give up his KNP in order to advance his passed Pawns, but he tries to do so with his King on the wrong square.

Best was 51 . . . K-Q5 52 RxP P-N4 53 P-R5, etc., after which Black queens first with a won game.

52	P-R5!	. . .

A surprising tactical point.

52	. . .	R-R6ch
53	K-N2	PxP
54	R-N5ch	K-Q3
55	RxNP	. . .

White has forced a book draw. The rest follows without comment.

55	. . .	P-R5
56	P-B4	K-B3
57	R-N8	P-R6ch
58	K-R2	P-R4
59	P-B5	K-B2
60	R-N5	K-Q3
61	P-B6	K-K3
62	R-N6ch	K-B2
63	R-R6	K-N3
64	R-B6	P-R5
65	R-R6	K-B2
66	R-B6	R-QN6
67	R-R6	P-R6
68	K-N1	Drawn

GAME 37

Najdorf has been considered one of the most dangerous players in the world for years. It was, therefore, an historic occasion for him to lose to a 19-year-old in 24 moves (and to have had a lost game from as early as the 14th move). Fischer plays magnificently.

WORLD TEAM OLYMPICS 1962

Varna, Bulgaria

SICILIAN DEFENSE

Robert J. Fischer	*Miguel Najdorf*
WHITE	BLACK
1 P-K4	P-QB4
2 N-KB3	P-Q3
3 P-Q4	PxP
4 NxP	N-KB3
5 N-QB3	P-QR3
6 P-KR3	. . .

Fischer decided to use this little-known move against Najdorf, who is an expert on all the more regular lines.

6	. . .	P-QN4
7	N-Q5!?	B-N2?

Black's best was 7 . . . NxP 8 Q-B3 N-B4 9 P-QN4 P-K3 10 PxN PxN 11 QxP R-R2 with equality.

8 NxNch	NPxN
9 P-QB4!	. . .

An enterprising move. White sacrifices a Pawn to open up lines toward the Black King.

9 . . .	PxP
10 BxP	BxP

Black has nothing better.

11 O-O	P-Q4
12 R-K1!	. . .

White keeps right on developing.

12 . . .	P-K4
13 Q-R4ch	N-Q2

14 RxB!	. . .

A powerful sacrifice. White eliminates the only piece that could defend the white squares.

14 . . .	PxR
15 N-B5	B-B4
16 N-N7ch	K-K2
17 N-B5ch	K-K1
18 B-K3	. . .

Having stopped Black from castling, White brings new forces into play.

18 . . .	BxB
19 PxB	Q-N3
20 R-Q1	R-R2
21 R-Q6	Q-Q1

Black is hopelessly tied down. All of White's pieces are ideally posted for the final onslaught.

22 Q-N3	. . .

The crusher. Black cannot play 22 . . . R-B1, because of 23 N-N7ch K-K2 24 Q-R3, and wins.

22 . . .	Q-B2
23 BxPch	K-Q1
24 B-K6	Resigns

For if 24 . . . Q-B1 25 Q-N6ch R-B2 26 RxNch.

GAME 38

Greenwald is a deceptively strong player who is noted for playing "over his head." He's beaten Lombardy and Bisguier on occasion, and has lost to veritable duffers. In this game, he plays strongly but buckles under Fischer's class.

NEW YORK STATE OPEN 1963

Poughkeepsie, N.Y.

GRUENFELD DEFENSE

Ben Greenwald	Robert J. Fischer
WHITE	BLACK
1 P-Q4	N-KB3
2 P-QB4	P-KN3
3 N-QB3	P-Q4

4 PxP	NxP
5 P-K4	NxN
6 PxN	B-N2
7 B-QB4	N-B3
8 P-QR4	. . .

White wants to free the squares QR2 and QR3 for occupation by his Bishops.

8 ...	N-R4
9 B-R2	P-QB4
10 N-K2	PxP

Fischer says that 10 . . . P-N3 was best.

11 PxP	P-N3
12 Q-Q3	O-O
13 B-Q2	...

White eyes the Knight on the rim. Consistent and better was 13 O-O, followed by 14 B-K3.

13 ...	B-N2
14 O-O	P-K3
15 KR-Q1	Q-Q2
16 BxN	...

This exchange helps Black, who soon takes charge of the Queenside.

16 ...	PxB
17 B-B4	QR-N1
18 R-R2?	...

Obviously 18 B-N5 should be played.

18 ...	B-QB3
19 N-B3	R-N5!

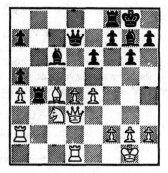

White is now in near zugzwang.

20 P-Q5	B-N2!

Now 21 PxP loses a piece after 21 . . . QxQ. White should play 21 R-B2.

21 B-N5	Q-Q3
22 N-K2?	...

22 R-B2 was still relatively best. Now White loses material because of the weakness of his first rank. If 22 R(2)-Q2, Black cements the Knight's position by . . . R-N6.

22 ...	PxP
23 PxP	QxP
24 QxQ	BxQ
25 RxB	R-N8ch
26 N-B1	RxNch
27 B-B1	R-K1
28 P-B4	R(1)-K8
29 R-KB2	B-B1!
Resigns	

There is no good defense to 30 . . . B-B4.

GAME 39

Bisguier told me that Fischer's 9th move did not come as a shock to him—he had seen it in Russian analysis shortly before the game. Fischer's influence on the chess fraternity is overwhelming; ever since the game was played, at least a dozen master games have been attempted with the same variation and the same unorthodox 9th move.

NEW YORK STATE OPEN 1963
Poughkeepsie, N.Y.

TWO KNIGHTS DEFENSE

Robert J. Fischer *Arthur Bisguier*

WHITE	BLACK
1 P-K4	P-K4
2 N-KB3	N-QB3
3 B-B4	...

Fischer has a tactical struggle in mind. Against 3 . . . B-B4, he may well have played the Evans Gambit.

3 ...	N-B3
4 N-N5	P-Q4
5 PxP	N-QR4

If 5 . . . NxP? 6 P-Q4!, known as Rio's Variation, leaves Black in dire straits.

6 B-N5ch	P-B3
7 PxP	PxP
8 B-K2	P-KR3
9 N-KR3!?	...

An odd move that was first recommended by Steinitz. It seems to be as good as the usual 9 N-KB3.

9 ...	B-QB4
10 O-O	O-O
11 P-Q3	BxN
12 PxB	Q-Q2
13 B-B3	...

A possibility here was 13 B-N4 NxB 14 PxN P-B4 15 P-N5. White decides to return the extra Pawn, keeping the two Bishops and sounder Pawn structure.

13 ...	QxRP
14 N-Q2	QR-Q1
15 B-N2	Q-B4
16 Q-K1	...

16 Q-B3 was a good alternative.

16 ...	KR-K1
17 N-K4	B-N3
18 NxNch	QxN
19 K-R1	P-B4?

Best was 19 . . . P-N4, stopping White's break with P-KB4.

20 Q-B3!   ...

Now Black's Bishop is blocked, and he cannot prevent 21 P-B4 (20 . . . P-N4 21 P-B4!).

20 ...	N-B3
21 P-B4	N-Q5
22 Q-B4	Q-N3

23 P-B3	N-B4
24 PxP	RxKP
25 B-B4	R-K7
26 B-K4	...

Black is now in difficulty because of the pin on his Knight. He should play 26 . . . Q-K3, or still better 26 . . . R-K1, threatening 27 . . . R(1)xB. Best for White would then be 27 B-B3 RxP 28 QR-K1, with good chances.

26 ...	RxNP?

At the crucial point Black blunders, losing a piece.

27 B-K5!	R-K1
28 RxN	RxB
29 RxR	Resigns

GAME 40

A few days after this spectacular game was played, Evans said: ". . . I was one of the few people who had a halfway decent position against him and for most of the game I thought I had the better of it. It was only in the last five moves that disaster fell. Up to that point I had the better of it and I think he thought so too." Whether Bobby did or not we'll probably never know. We do know that this is one of the most exciting games he has ever produced.

U.S. CHAMPIONSHIP 1963–1964

New York, N.Y.

KING'S GAMBIT

Robert J. Fischer	Larry Evans
WHITE	BLACK
1 P-K4	P-K4
2 P-KB4	...

Surprise!

2 ...	PxP
3 B-B4	...

Fischer prefers this to 3 N-KB3, which he says is refuted by 3 . . . P-Q3.

3 ...	Q-R5ch

A very old-fashioned move. Modern and better is 3 . . . N-KB3 4 N-QB3 P-B3.

4 K-B1	P-Q3

Another old move, as is 4 . . . P-KN4. 4 . . . P-Q4 is usually played now.

5 N-QB3	...

The natural 5 N-KB3 is best.

5 ...	B-K3

A strong defensive move.

6 Q-K2	P-QB3
7 N-B3	Q-K2
8 P-Q4	BxB
9 QxB	P-KN4

Black has his Pawn, but White leads in development.

10 P-K5!	...

A sharp move that keeps Black from developing his Kingside normally. If 10 . . . PxP, White could play 11 NxP or 11 B-Q2.

| 10 . . . | P-Q4 |
| 11 Q-Q3 | N-QR3 |

If 11 . . . P-KR3 12 P-KR4!

| 12 N-K2 | N-N5 |
| 13 Q-Q1 | O-O-O |

Here 13 . . . P-B3 has been recommended as Black's best try.

| 14 P-B3 | N-QR3 |
| 15 P-KR4 | . . . |

Smashing Black's Pawns. Now White has a clear edge.

15 . . .	P-N5
16 N-R2	P-KR4
17 NxBP	QxRP?

A serious error.

| 18 K-N1 | . . . |

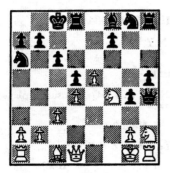

Threatening both 19 NxNP and 19 N-B1.

18 . . .	N-R3
19 N-B1	Q-K2
20 NxRP	R-N1
21 N(1)-N3	. . .

White's pieces have gained devastating activity.

21 . . .	R-N3
22 N-B4	R-N4
23 B-K3	N-B2
24 Q-Q2	. . .

Threatening 25 NxP. Black has no good defense.

| 24 . . . | R-N1 |
| 25 N(4)-K2 | . . . |

Winning a piece.

25 . . .	P-B3
26 PxP	QxP
27 BxN	B-Q3
28 R-KB1	Q-K3
29 B-B4	QR-K1
30 R-R6	. . .

Forcing simplification.

30 . . .	BxB
31 QxB	Q-K2
32 R-B6	N-K3
33 Q-K5	N-N4
34 QxQ	RxQ
35 R-B8ch	RxR
36 RxRch	Resigns

GAME 41

This is the game that was so complicated that no one in the tournament hall (including a prominent grandmaster) except the two players involved, realized that Fischer had a winning position. It was his first win against Byrne, and one of the most excellently played miniatures in all of chess history.

U.S. CHAMPIONSHIP 1963–1964

New York, N.Y.

GRUENFELD DEFENSE

Robert Byrne	Robert J. Fischer
WHITE	BLACK
1 P-Q4	N-KB3
2 P-QB4	P-KN3
3 P-KN3	P-B3
4 B-N2	. . .

Most dynamic is 4 P-Q5. White proceeds conservatively.

4 . . .	P-Q4
5 PxP	PxP
6 N-QB3	B-N2
7 P-K3	O-O
8 KN-K2	. . .

White breaks the symmetry.

8 . . .	N-B3
9 O-O	P-N3
10 P-N3	B-QR3
11 B-QR3	R-K1
12 Q-Q2	. . .

12 P-KB4 was an interesting try.

12 . . .	P-K4!

Black decides to get more play for his pieces at the cost of accepting an isolated Pawn.

13 PxP	NxP
14 KR-Q1	. . .

14 BxP? N-B6ch.

14 . . .	N-Q6!

Black already has a dominating position.

15 Q-B2	. . .

An error, but other moves also lose.

15 . . .	NxP!

A powerful sacrifice which tears through the White position.

16 KxN	N-N5ch
17 K-N1	NxKP
18 Q-Q2	NxB!

Black's main point. White must have expected 18 . . . NxR.

19 KxN	P-Q5!

Opening the diagonal for the Queen Bishop with decisive effect.

| 20 NxP | B-N2ch |
| 21 K-B1 | ... |

No other move is any better. If 21 K-N1 BxNch 22 QxB R-K8ch!

| 21 ... | Q-Q2! |

Leaving White defenseless. If now 22 Q-KB2 Q-R6ch 23 K-N1 R-K8ch! 24 RxR BxN.

Resigns

GAME 42

A crippling smash by Fischer—over so fast that hardly any time accumulated on his clock.

U.S. CHAMPIONSHIP 1963–1964

New York, N.Y.

CARO-KANN DEFENSE·

Robert J. Fischer   Robert Steinmeyer

WHITE	BLACK
1 P-K4	P-QB3
2 P-Q4	P-Q4
3 N-QB3	PxP
4 NxP	B-B4
5 N-N3	B-N3
6 N-B3	N-B3

6 ... N-Q2 is usually played.

7 P-KR4	P-KR3
8 B-Q3	BxB
9 QxB	P-K3
10 B-Q2	QN-Q2
11 O-O-O	Q-B2
12 P-B4	...

Recommended by theory as best.

| 12 ... | O-O-O |

Most accurate is 12 ... B-Q3, and if 13 N-K4 B-B5.

| 13 B-B3 | Q-B5ch |

Black starts an unsound counteraction. 13 ... B-Q3 is a regular line with a slight advantage for White.

| 14 K-N1 | N-B4 |
| 15 Q-B2 | N(4)-K5 |

| 16 N-K5! | ... |

The winning move. Black lacks a satisfactory reply.

| 16 ... | NxP |
| 17 QR-KB1 | Resigns |

For if 17 ... QxN(6) 18 RxN, threatening both 19 NxP and 19 R-R3.

GAME 43

At the post-tournament celebration held in honor of Bobby's sensational clean sweep in the 1963–1964 U.S. Championship, a replica of a chessboard (complete with pieces) was made out of cake and icing. The position used was from the Fischer-Benko game showing move 19 R–B6!! A beautiful game.

U.S. CHAMPIONSHIP 1963–1964

New York, N.Y.

PIRC DEFENSE

Robert J. Fischer	Pal Benko
WHITE	BLACK
1 P-K4	P-KN3
2 P-Q4	B-N2
3 N-QB3	P-Q3
4 P-B4	N-KB3
5 N-B3	O-O
6 B-Q3	...

Nowadays considered best.

6 ...	B-N5

Preparing to give up a Bishop for a Knight. Better was 6 . . . QN-Q2, followed by 7 . . . P-K4.

7 P-KR3	BxN
8 QxB	N-B3
9 B-K3	P-K4
10 QPxP	PxP
11 P-B5	...

Threatening a Kingside Pawn storm with 12 P-KN4.

11 ...	PxP

The best chance. If now 12 PxP P-K5!?, with counterchances.

12 QxP	N-Q5
13 Q-B2	...

Fischer says he considered 13 QxP N-N5 14 QxBch!? KxQ 15 PxN, as quite promising for White.

13 ...	N-K1
14 O-O	N-Q3

Intending 15 . . . P-KB4.

15 Q-N3	K-R1

If 15 . . . P-KB4 16 B-R6 would be strong.

16 Q-N4	...

Stopping 16 . . . P-KB4.

16 ...	P-QB3

Much better was 16 . . . P-QB4.

17 Q-R5!	...

Threatening 18 BxN PxB 19 P-K5.

17 ...	Q-K1?

The defense slips. 17 . . . N-K3 was necessary.

18 BxN	PxB

Now 19 P-K5 is answered by 19 . . . P-KB4.

19 R-B6!!   . . .

A bolt from the blue! With his KBP blocked. Black is defenseless against 20 P-K5.

19 . . .   K-N1

If 19 . . . PxN 20 P-K5 P-KR3 21 RxPch K-N1 22 R-R8ch BxR 28 Q-R7 mate.

| 20 P-K5 | P-KR3 |
| 21 N-K2! | Resigns |

GAME 44

Competing in this tournament by teletype, Fischer was under the severe handicap of having to play most of his games in grueling eight-hour sessions. Here he defeats the tournament winner, former World Champion Smyslov, in the endgame, a phase of chess in which both are noted for their expertise.

CAPABLANCA MEMORIAL 1965

Havana, Cuba

RUY LOPEZ

Robert J. Fischer	*Vassily Smyslov*
WHITE	BLACK
1 P-K4	P-K4
2 N-KB3	N-QB3
3 B-N5	P-QR3
4 B-R4	N-B3
5 P-Q3	. . .

This antiquated move, a favorite of Steinitz, came as no surprise to Smyslov. He had played it himself and won in his first meeting with Euwe (Groningen, 1946).

5 . . .	P-Q3
6 P-B3	B-K2.
7 QN-Q2	O-O
8 N-B1	. . .

The point of this Nimzovichian type of move is to defer castling, implying a possible threat of a Kingside Pawn attack, simultaneously allowing the Knight to move to K3.

8 . . .	P-QN4
9 B-N3	P-Q4
10 Q-K2	PxP
11 PxP	B-K3

In his analysis of this game in *My 60 Memorable Games*, Bobby says after this move: "I was surprised that Smyslov was prepared to saddle himself with doubled King pawns, but surmised that it must be all right since he doesn't do such things lightly."

12 BxB	PxB
13 N-N3	Q-Q2
14 O-O	QR-Q1
15 P-QR4	Q-Q6

Smyslov assumes that his doubled pawns should cause him little trouble in the ensuing endgame.

| 16 QxQ | RxQ |
| 17 PxP | PxP |

| 18 R-R6 | R-Q3 |
| 19 K-R1 | ... |

To prevent 19 . . . N-Q5 followed by NxNch, weakening White's pawns.

19 ...	N-Q2
20 B-K3	R-Q1
21 P-R3	P-R3
22 KR-R1	N(2)-N1

| 23 R-R8 | R-Q8ch |
| 24 K-R2 | RxR |

At this point Smyslov offered Fischer a draw which was rejected.

| 25 RxR | N-Q2 |
| 26 P-N4 | K-B2 |

27 N-B1	B-Q3
28 P-N3	N-B3
29 N(1)-Q2	K-K2
30 R-R6	N-QN1

Black likes that square. Tension results after 30 . . . K-Q2 31 N-K1 N-QN1 32 R-R5 K-B3.

31 R-R5	P-B3
32 K-N2	N(1)-Q2
33 K-B1	R-QB1

33 . . . N-K1 immediately is a stronger alternative.

34 N-K1	N-K1
35 N-Q3	N-B2
36 P-QB4	PxP
37 NxBP	N-N4
38 R-R6	K-B3
39 B-B1	...

Off to N2!

39 ...	B-N1
40 B-N2	P-B4
41 N-N6!	NxN
42 RxN	P-B5
43 N-B5	...

Winning a piece, because of the threat of N-Q7ch.

| 43 ... | P-B6 |
| 44 B-B1 | Resigns |

GAME 45

Three small tactical finesses—winning a Pawn, giving it back favorably, and opening up the center—totally frustrate White to the extent that he plays on, several Pawns down, until all pieces are exchanged.

U.S. CHAMPIONSHIP 1965-1966

New York, N.Y.

NIMZO-INDIAN DEFENSE

Larry Evans	*Robert J. Fischer*	3 N-QB3	B-N5
		4 P-K3	P-QN3
WHITE	BLACK	5 N-K2	B-R3
		6 P-QR3	BxNch
1 P-Q4	N-KB3	7 NxB	P-Q4
2 P-QB4	P-K3	8 P-QN3	...

Here White can obtain a winning Kingside attack with 8 Q-B3.

8 . . .	N-B3
9 B-K2	O-O
10 P-QR4	PxP
11 B-R3	R-K1
12 P-QN4	N-K2
13 O-O	N(2)-Q4
14 R-B1	P-B3
15 B-B3	. . .

White must now play a gambit, since there is no way to stop P-QN4 without loss of a Pawn.

15 . . .	P-QN4
16 P-R5	Q-B2
17 Q-B2	QR-Q1
18 KR-Q1	B-N2
19 R-Q2	NxN
20 QxN	P-B4!

By returning the Pawn Black avoids a blocked position and disrupts the White Kingside—a bargain.

21 QPxP	BxB
22 PxB	RxR
23 QxR	R-Q1
24 Q-K1	R-Q6
25 B-N2	N-Q4
26 B-B3	P-B3
27 B-R1	P-K4
28 K-N2	Q-Q2
29 R-B2	. . .

29 . . .	P-K5!

Winning. The Pawn cannot be taken because of Q-N5ch winning the Queen.

30 R-B1	PxPch
31 K-R1	. . .

The White Kingside cannot be defended—for if KxP, then Q-R6ch and NxKP. The only wonder is that Black plays on at all.

31 . . .	NxNP
32 Q-N1	K-B2
33 B-Q4	N-B3
34 Q-N3	NxB
35 PxN	RxP
36 R-KN1	P-N4
37 P-B6	QxP
38 Q-N8	R-Q2
39 P-R3	Q-K3
40 R-N3	P-B6
41 Q-KR8	Q-B4
42 K-R2	R-Q7
43 RxBP	RxPch
44 RxR	QxRch
45 K-R1	Q-B6ch
46 K-R2	Q-B5ch
47 K-N1	Q-K6ch
48 K-B1	QxPch
49 K-K2	P-KN5
50 P-R6	Q-B6ch
51 K-K1	Q-K6ch
52 K-B1	Q-Q6ch
53 K-B2	P-N6ch
54 K-N2	Q-K5ch
55 KxP	Q-N3ch
Resigns	

GAME 46

It might seem that the French Defense is least effective against Fischer's attacking game. Nevertheless, he has had several close calls and a few upsets due to his risky King position. Here he again takes chances and in a fighting game gets to his opponent first.

U.S. CHAMPIONSHIP 1965–1966

New York, N.Y.

FRENCH DEFENSE

Robert J. Fischer   *Nicolas Rossolimo*

WHITE	BLACK
1 P-K4	P-K3
2 P-Q4	P-Q4
3 N-QB3	N-KB3
4 B-N5	B-N5
5 P-K5	P-KR3
6 B-Q2	BxN
7 PxB	N-K5
8 Q-N4	P-KN3
9 B-Q3	NxB
10 KxN	P-QB4
11 N-B3	N-B3
12 Q-B4	Q-B2
13 P-KR4	. . .

22 P-R5	Q-B6ch
23 K-K2	N-B3
24 PxPch	K-N2
25 QR-Q1	. . .

Allowing Black to establish a good defensive alignment. 13 Q-B6 first was called for.

The White Rooks will finally reach solid defensive positions, allowing White to force exchanges and secure a won ending.

13 . . .	P-B4
14 P-N4	PxQP
15 PxQP	N-K2
16 PxP	KPxP
17 B-N5ch	K-B1

25 . . .	NxPch
26 K-B1	KR-K1
27 R-N3	N-B3
28 Q-KR4	NxP
29 N-B4	N-N5
30 NxBch	RxN
31 BxP	Q-B5ch
32 K-N1	Resigns

The wrong way! Black will be safer on the Queenside, as the following Knight maneuver indicates.

18 B-Q3	B-K3
19 N-N1	K-B2
20 N-R3	QR-QB1
21 KR-KN1	P-N3

GAME 47

Fischer introduced the Nimzo-Indian into his repertoire in this tournament, winning twice and losing to Reshevsky. As this game shows, his success was less a matter of opening choice than of his combinative resourcefulness.

U.S. CHAMPIONSHIP 1965–1966

New York, N.Y.

NIMZO-INDIAN DEFENSE

Anthony Saidy   *Robert J. Fischer*

WHITE	BLACK
1 P-QB4	N-KB3
2 N-QB3	P-K3
3 P-Q4	B-N5
4 P-K3	P-QN3
5 KN-K2	B-R3

First seriously tested in Botvinnik-Bronstein, 1951.

6 N-N3	BxNch
7 PxB	P-Q4
8 Q-B3	. . .

Here Saidy abandons the continuation he played against Maršalek at the Student's World Championship, Reykjavik, 1957: 8 PxP BxB 9 NxB QxP 10 P-B3 P-B4 11 N-N3 O-O with a position that slightly favors Black because of his gain of time.

8 . . .	O-O
9 P-K4!	PxBP
10 B-N5	P-R3
11 B-Q2	. . .

Saidy writes: "As soon as the game ended, a flock of masters swooped down, exclaiming, 'Why didn't you play 11 P-KR4! How does Black escape?' Indeed why not? Fischer declined to say how he would have met it." After 11 P-KR4 PxB 12 PxP R-K1 13 PxN QxBP 14 Q-R5

P-N3 15 P-K5 White maintains the attack.

11 . . .	QN-Q2
12 P-K5	N-Q4
13 N-B5!	PxN

Otherwise, 14 NxPch with a winning attack.

| 14 QxN | R-K1 |
| 15 KBxP | . . . |

15 B-K2 is a dire necessity (Black will have difficulty holding both of his weak pawns).

| 15 . . . | NxP! |
| 16 QxQ | NxBch! |

The surprising point of 15 . . . NxP. The sacrifice of the Exchange reduces White to a helpless state, with the King caught on the back rank between two Rooks.

17	QxRch	RxQch
18	K-Q1	NxB
19	KxN	R-K7ch
20	K-B1	RxBP
21	P-N3	B-N2
22	R-K1	B-K5
23	R-K3	RxKRP
24	P-R4	P-KR4
25	R-R3	P-KN4
26	R-N3	P-KB3
27	P-R5	P-R5
28	RPxP	QRPxP
29	PxP	. . .

White is merely going through the motions in preparation for resigning.

29	. . .	RxP
30	R-QR3	R-R2
31	R-R7	R-K2
32	P-Q5	K-B2
33	K-Q2	P-B5

The Pawns are unstoppable.

34	R-K1	P-KB4
35	P-B4	P-N5
36	R-N7	P-N6
37	P-Q6	PxP
38	RxP	P-B6
Resigns		

GAME 48

Fischer lost to Larsen in the first half of this tournament and now attempts to avenge himself, in the second half. He succeeds. Although the Gruenfeld is Fischer's most successful defense to P–Q4, he is also at home in the straight King's Indian, as this game demonstrates.

PIATIGORSKY CUP TOURNAMENT 1966

Santa Monica, California

KING'S INDIAN DEFENSE

Bent Larsen	*Robert J. Fischer*
WHITE	**BLACK**
1 P-Q4	N-KB3
2 P-QB4	P-KN3
3 N-QB3	B-N2
4 P-K4	P-Q3
5 B-K2	O-O
6 B-N5	. . .

Played to obstruct the advance of Black's King Pawn—6 . . . P-K4? 7 PxP PxP 8 QxQ RxQ 9 N-Q5 wins a Pawn.

6 . . .	P-B4
7 P-Q5	P-K3

The speculative 7 . . . P-N4 8 PxP P-QR3 9 PxP BxP is popular nowadays.

8	N-B3	P-KR3
9	B-R4	PxP
10	BPxP	P-KN4
11	B-N3	N-R4

Opening his Kingside a bit for a valuable Bishop.

12	N-Q2	NxB
13	RPxN	N-Q2
14	N-B4	Q-K2

Black's defense is now a Benoni.

15	N-K3	N-B3
16	Q-B2	R-K1
17	B-N5	R-Q1
18	B-K2	R-K1

Willing to repeat moves at least once more.

19 P-B3	N-R2
20 P-KN4	N-B1

With a future of N-N3-B5.

21 P-R4	N-N3
22 K-B1	...

Stronger than O-O, when White's Kingside is full of holes.

22 ...	R-N1
23 B-N5	R-Q1
24 N-B5	BxN
25 KPxB?	...

Opening up a direct route to the King.

25 ...	N-K4
26 N-K4	P-R3
27 B-K2	N-Q2

In order to stop 27 P-B6 BxP 28 RxP with some possibilities for White's attack.

28 R-K1	N-B3
29 N-B3	Q-Q2
30 P-R5	R-K1
31 K-B2	Q-B2

Forcing White to decentralize his already ineffectual Rooks.

32 R-R1	P-B5
33 K-N3	R-K6
34 Q-Q2	QR-K1
35 KR-K1	P-R4
36 B-B1	NxNP!

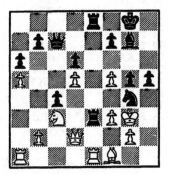

Finally Fischer has the position he wants, and the combination begins.

37 RxR	RxR
38 K-R3	Q-K2
39 P-KN3	BxN
40 PxB	RxKBP
41 R-K1	R-K6
42 RxR	QxR
43 QxQ and Resigns	

GAME 49

A typical Fischer game, except for the opening. When White piles up on the Kingside, even delaying tactics fail for Black.

PIATIGORSKY CUP 1966

Santa Monica, California

SICILIAN DEFENSE

Robert J. Fischer   *Borislav Ivkov*   Fischer had not played this move for ten years (U.S. Championship 1957).

WHITE   **BLACK**

1 P-K4	P-QB4
2 N-KB3	P-K3
3 P-Q3	...

3 ...	N-QB3
4 P-KN3	P-Q4
5 QN-Q2	B-Q3

5 . . . N-B3 is considered more effective.

6	B-N2	KN-K2
7	O-O	O-O
8	N-R4	P-QN3
9	P-KB4	PxP

This gives White a post for his
Knight on K4, but Black seeks immediate counterplay.

10	PxP	B-R3
11	R-K1	P-B5
12	P-B3	N-R4
13	P-K5	B-B4ch
14	K-R1	N-Q4
15	N-K4	B-N2
16	Q-R5	N-K2

| 17 | P-KN4 | . . . |

Threatening to break the game open
with P-B5.

17	. . .	BxN
18	BxB	P-N3
19	Q-R6	. . .

P-B5 remains the unstoppable
threat.

19	. . .	N-Q4
20	P-B5	R-K1
21	PxNP	BPxP
22	NxP	Q-Q2

Black hopes to hold the game by
conceding this Pawn, as he already
decided with 17 . . . BxN.

23	N-B4	QR-Q1
24	N-R5	K-R1
25	N-B6	NxN
26	PxN	R-KN1
27	B-B4	RxP
28	QR-Q1	QR-KN1
29	P-B7!	Resigns

An easy answer to a cheap shot.

GAME 50

This game typifies the Fischer approach to the openings: a willingness to resurrect ancient lines with a new-found energy.

WORLD TEAM OLYMPICS 1966

Havana, Cuba

RUY LOPEZ

Robert J. Fischer	Lajos Portisch
WHITE	BLACK
1 P-K4	P-K4
2 N-KB3	N-QB3
3 B-N5	P-QR3
4 BxN!	. . .

The beginning of a series of novel
moves—as surprising as Lasker's last
round make-or-break game with
Capablanca, St. Petersburg, 1914,
the most famous previous instance
of this opening.

4 ...	QPxB
5 O-O	...

Fischer's slight improvement over the immediate P-Q4. Black must commit himself to a defense of the KP.

5 ...	P-B3
6 P-Q4	PxP
7 NxP	P-QB4
8 N-N3	QxQ
9 RxQ	B-Q3
10 N-R5	...

Better than 10 B-K3 (Ciocîltea-Gligoric, Hamburg, 1965). The threat here is 11 N-B4, and Black loses more ground.

10 ...	P-QN4
11 P-QB4	N-K2
12 B-K3	P-B4

To relieve the pressure on his own B4 and to open up the position.

13 N-B3	P-B5
14 P-K5!	BxP
15 BxQBP	...

Threatening R-K1.

15 ...	BxN
16 PxB	N-N3
17 N-B6	B-K3
18 PxP	PxP
19 N-R7	...

And the Pawn belongs to White.

19 ...	R-QN1
20 KR-N1	K-B2

If 20 ... B-Q2 21 P-QR4.

21 NxP	KR-Q1
22 R-N4	BxP
23 NxP	R(N)-B1
24 P-R4	R-Q7

If 24 ... RxN 25 B-N6 wins the Exchange.

25 B-N6	P-B6
26 B-K3	...

Dispersing Black's pieces and simplifying.

26 ...	R-K7
27 N-N5	R-QR1
28 P-R5	N-K4
29 R-B4ch	K-K2
30 R-Q1	...

Threatening mate beginning with B-B5ch.

30 ...	R-QB1
31 R-K4	K-B3
32 R-Q6ch	K-B4
33 R-B4ch	K-N4
34 RxPch	Resigns

GAME 51

As hard as he tries, Fischer is caught with too little and too late against an aggressive opening line. This loss cost him the Olympic Gold Medal.

WORLD TEAM OLYMPICS 1966

Havana, Cuba

NIMZO-INDIAN DEFENSE

Florin Gheorghiu   *Robert J. Fischer*

WHITE	BLACK
1 P-Q4	N-KB3
2 P-QB4	P-K3
3 N-QB3	B-N5
4 P-B3	P-Q4
5 P-QR3	BxNch
6 PxB	O-O
7 PxP	PxP
8 P-K3	N-R4

The attempt to take advantage of White's temporary weakness at KN3 fails.

9 Q-B2	R-K1
10 P-N4	...

This, however, is hardly called for, since White can develop adequately with 10 B-Q3.

10 ...	N-B5
11 P-KR4	P-QB4
12 K-B2	N-N3
13 B-Q3	N-B3
14 N-K2	B-K3
15 P-N5	R-QB1
16 P-R5	N-B1

17 P-N6   . . .

White's energetic play pays off, and he now defends against Black's only threat on the Queenside (PxP), keeping his pawns intact.

17 ...	KBPxP
18 RPxP	P-KR3
19 Q-N1	N-R4
20 N-B4	P-B5
21 B-B2	R-B3
22 R-QR2	N-Q2
23 P-R4	N-B3
24 B-R3	Q-Q2
25 R-N2	P-N3
26 R-N5	N-N2
27 P-K4	...

With every piece forcefully placed, White opens up the game to his advantage.

27	...	PxP
28	BxP	R(3)-B1
29	R-K5	B-N5

The Bishop is trapped, but this clever escape is just as cleverly answered. Fischer wriggles, but cannot get off the hook.

30	N-Q5	RxR
31	NxNch	PxN
32	PxR	N-B4
33	BxN	Q-Q7ch

34	K-N3	BxP
35	BxB	RxB
36	Q-QB1	QxQ
37	RxQ	RxP
38	K-B4	K-N2
39	B-K4	P-KR4
40	R-Q1	R-K2
41	R-Q5	K-R3
42	R-Q6	K-N2
43	R-B6	P-R5
44	RxQBP	P-R6
45	K-N3	K-R3
46	B-N1	R-K6ch
47	K-R2	R-K8
48	B-Q3	R-K6
49	R-R4ch	K-N4
50	P-N7	Resigns

GAME 52

Hans Kmoch dubbed the end of this game a defeat that occurred after "a long illness." Reshevsky goes astray as early as the 6th move and Fischer "books" him to death.

U.S. CHAMPIONSHIP 1966–1967

New York, N.Y.

SICILIAN DEFENSE

Robert J. Fischer	Samuel Reshevsky
WHITE	BLACK
1 P-K4	P-QB4
2 N-KB3	P-Q3
3 P-Q4	PxP
4 NxP	N-KB3
5 N-QB3	P-K3
6 P-KN4	...

Fischer has played this move of Keres' before.

| 6 ... | P-Q4 |

Originally suggested by Euwe, this response has fallen into disrepute. Better is 6 . . . P-KR3 7 B-N2 P-R3 8 P-KR4 P-KN3 9 P-N5 PxP 10 PxP RxRch 11 BxR N-R2 12 Q-N4 B-N2

as in O'Kelly-Stahlberg, Mar del Plata, 1948, with excellent counterchances for Black.

7 PxP	NxP
8 B-N5ch	B-Q2
9 NxN	PxN
10 Q-K2ch	Q-K2
11 B-K3	P-KN3
12 BxBch	NxB
13 N-N5	N-K4
14 O-O-O	B-N2

Black must concede a Pawn to finish his development.

| 15 RxP | O-O |
| 16 R(1)-Q1 | P-QR3 |

Reshevsky acts as Fischer's Sancho Panza.

17 N-Q6	Q-R5
18 P-KB3	P-QN4
19 B-Q4	N-B5
20 BxB	KxB
21 NxN	PxN
22 QxP	QxRP
23 R-Q7	QR-B1

24 RxPch	RxR
25 QxR	Q-B5ch
26 K-N1	QxBP

Reshevsky holds on grimly, knowing well the difficulties of Q+R endings.

| 27 R-QB1 | P-N4 |
| 28 P-N3 | Q-K7 |

| 29 Q-B3ch | K-N3 |
| 30 Q-R3 | . . . |

Preparing a mating net starting with Q-R5ch.

30 . . .	P-R3
31 R-R1	R-KR2
32 P-R3	R-R1
33 P-R4	R-R2

"Show me how," insists Black.

34 R-R2	Q-K8ch
35 K-R2	Q-K5
36 Q-R5ch	. . .

Black's Queen no longer controls central scope-squares for the White Rook.

36 . . .	K-N2
37 R-Q2	Q-K2
38 Q-R3	K-N1
39 Q-KB3	. . .

Threatening 40 Q-R8ch, followed by R-Q8.

39 . . .	R-B2
40 Q-R8ch	K-N2
41 QxP	Q-K5
42 Q-K2	Q-KB5
43 R-Q5	Resigns

GAME 53

A game worthy of inclusion as an example of Fischer's objective treatment of the Sicilian. In true iconoclastic fashion, he uses every tactical opportunity to gain a material advantage, even in the face of risk to his position.

U.S. CHAMPIONSHIP 1966

New York, N.Y.

SICILIAN DEFENSE

Robt. J. Fischer	Bernard Zuckerman
WHITE	BLACK
1 P-K4	P-QB4
2 N-KB3	N-QB3
3 N-B3	P-KN3
4 P-Q4	PxP
5 NxP	B-N2
6 B-K3	N-B3
7 B-QB4	P-Q3
8 P-B3	B-Q2
9 Q-Q2	R-QB1
10 B-N3	N-K4
11 O-O-O	. . .

Fischer's demolition of the Dragon is now so well known that it needs no comment. The simple but forcing idea is P-R4, P-R5, with an exchange sacrifice, if necessary, at R5.

11 . . .	N-B5
12 BxN	RxB
13 N-N3	Q-B2
14 B-Q4	B-K3
15 P-K5	. . .

See Fischer-Camara, Siegen, 1970 (game 64).

15 . . .	PxP
16 BxKP	Q-B1
17 N-R5	R-B2

The Rook is out of good squares—17 . . . R-QN5 18 N-K4 or 17 . . . R-B4 18 BxN BxB 19 N-K4 R-KB4 20 NxBch RxN 21 NxP. With the Exchange sacrifice Black hopes to get counterplay from his Bishop pair.

18 BxR	QxB
19 N-N5	Q-N3
20 N-Q4	B-Q2
21 KR-K1	O-O
22 RxP	Q-Q3
23 R(7)-K1	QxP
24 K-N1	Q-B2
25 N(5)-N3	R-B1
26 P-N4	P-N3
27 R-K7	Q-Q3
28 R-K2	N-Q4
29 P-B3	P-QR4
30 N-B2	. . .

30 . . .	P-R5

A last attempt at complications.

31 QxN	QxQ
32 RxQ	B-K3
33 R-QN5	PxN
34 PxP	R-B3
35 R-Q2	B-B3
36 N-N4	Resigns

GAME 54

Fischer's bad luck with Geller continues, this time in the "poisoned Pawn" line which Fischer usually plays for both sides and with more than average success. Geller, however, outplays his opponent in a wild and deadly brawl.

INTERNATIONAL TOURNAMENT

Monaco 1967

SICILIAN DEFENSE

Robert J. Fischer	Yefim Geller
WHITE	BLACK
1 P-K4	P-QB4
2 N-KB3	P-Q3
3 P-Q4	PxP
4 NxP	N-KB3
5 N-QB3	P-QR3
6 B-N5	P-K3
7 P-B4	Q-N3
8 Q-Q2	QxP
9 R-QN1	Q-R6
10 P-B5	N-B3
11 PxP	PxP
12 NxN	PxN

13 P-K5	. . .

This move involves the sacrifice of a second Pawn to maintain the initiative.

13 . . .	N-Q4
14 NxN	BPxN
15 B-K2	PxP
16 O-O	B-B4ch
17 K-R1	R-B1
18 P-B4	RxRch
19 RxR	B-N2
20 B-N4	. . .

Overlooking Black's threat to exchange Queens. A better chance was 20 Q-B2 P-N3 21 B-R5?! Now White runs out of gas as the Black pieces swarm all over the board.

20 . . .	PxP
21 BxP	Q-Q6
22 Q-K1	B-K5
23 B-N4	R-N1
24 B-Q1	K-Q2
25 R-B7ch	K-K3
Resigns	

GAME 55

Fischer "mixes it" in an unbalanced variation in which his opponent is at home. The American is just able to handle each crisis with dynamic counter-threats.

INTERNATIONAL TOURNAMENT 1967

Skopje, Yugoslavia

GRUENFELD DEFENSE

Robert J. Fischer	Milan Matulovic
WHITE	BLACK

| 1 | P-K4 | P-QB4 |
| 2 | N-QB3 | ... |

A minor surprise. Fischer seldom plays this slower line, which tends to resemble a King's Indian Reversed.

2 ...	N-QB3
3 KN-K2	P-K3
4 P-Q4	...

The normal line after all! But the awkward position of the KN suggests a more dynamic reply.

4 ...	PxP
5 NxP	Q-B2
6 P-B4	P-QR3
7 B-K3	B-N5
8 NxN	QxN
9 Q-Q4	BxNch

White's doubled pawns will be only apparently weak, since he will have time to advance them, inhibiting P-Q4.

10 PxB	N-B3
11 B-Q3	P-QN4
12 P-QR4	B-N2
13 R-QN1!	...

The key to White's defense of K4—attack. After 13 . . . PxP 14 R-N6 Q-B2, 15 Q-N4 is a crusher.

13 ...	O-O
14 R-N4	P-Q4
15 RPxP	RPxP

| 16 | BxP | Q-B2 |
| 17 | O-O | ... |

Black's active defense has maintained the balance.

17 ...	NxP
18 B-Q3	B-R3
19 P-B4	...

The orphan has his day.

19 ...	N-B3
20 P-QB5	N-N5
21 P-R3	NxB
22 QxN	KR-B1
23 R-R1	...

Just in time.

23 . . .	BxB
24 RxR	RxR
25 PxB	P-R4
26 R-N6	R-R8ch
27 K-R2	P-Q5!

The best chance—counterattack.

28 QxQP	R-QB8
29 R-N5	Q-B3
30 R-R5	R-B7
31 Q-Q8ch	K-R2
32 Q-N5	Q-Q4

33 QxQ	PxQ
34 P-B5!	. . .

The ending will be won because Black's King is shut out.

34 . . .	K-R3
35 P-R4	P-Q5
36 K-N3	R-B6
37 K-B4	RxQP
38 K-K4	R-Q8
39 R-R3	P-N4
40 PxP e.p.	KxP
41 R-Q3	R-QB8 and
	Resigns

GAME 56

A combinational treat, as Fischer pursues the logic of the Ruy Lopez to its conclusion: center breakthrough (17 P–K5!), Kingside sacrifice (29 BxP) and an accurate major-piece, minor-piece ending. This multifarious game is in the pure Fischer style.

INTERZONAL TOURNAMENT 1967

Sousse, Tunisia

RUY LOPEZ

Robert J. Fischer	*Leonid Stein*
WHITE	BLACK
1 P-K4	P-K4

Stein's choice of the Ruy in effect underlines one of Fischer's weaknesses—his reluctance to vary his openings with White. Fischer had expected the Sicilian.

2 N-KB3	N-QB3
3 B-N5	P-QR3
4 B-R4	N-B3
5 O-O	B-K2
6 R-K1	P-QN4
7 B-N3	P-Q3

For the Marshall (7 . . . O-O 8 P-B3 P-Q4) see Game 72, against Spassky. Fischer has great respect for a Pawn advantage.

8 P-B3	O-O
9 P-KR3	B-N2
10 P-Q4	N-QR4
11 B-B2	N-B5
12 P-QN3	N-N3
13 QN-Q2	N(N)-Q2
14 P-QN4	. . .

White grabs space on the Queenside, intending B-N2 and P-B4. Black therefore simplifies.

14 . . .	PxP
15 PxP	P-QR4
16 PxP	P-B4
17 P-K5!	. . .

This spatial gain allows White to build up a menacing array of pieces aimed at the enemy King.

17 . . .	QPxP
18 PxKP	N-Q4
19 N-K4	N-N5
20 B-N1	RxP
21 Q-K2	N-N3

But here Black throws everything into counterplay on the Queenside when 21 . . . R-K1 and N-B1 were called for.

22 N(3)-N5	QBxN
23 QxB	P-N3
24 Q-R4	P-R4
25 Q-N3	N-B5
26 N-B3	. . .

Here the impending P-K6 was more accurate since 26 . . . P-B4 is almost forced. In this case Black does not have the defense B-B3, which becomes possible later.

26 . . .	K-N2
27 Q-B4	R-KR1
28 P-K6	P-B4
29 BxP	Q-KB1

If 29 . . . PxB 30 N-K5!

30 B-K4	. . .

Here 30 N-R4! could have won easily, for if the Knight is exchanged, the KP becomes active. One of the weaknesses of the Black position is underlined here: the back two ranks are protected only by the Queen.

30 . . .	QxQ
31 BxQ	R-K1

In time pressure Black misses 31 . . . RxP. Now he loses the Exchange and White's pieces remain active.

32 QR-Q1	R-R3
33 R-Q7	RxKP
34 N-N5	R-KB3
35 B-B3	RxB
36 N-K6ch	K-B3
37 NxR	N-K4
38 R-N7	B-Q3
39 K-B1	N-B7
40 R-K4	N-Q5
41 R-N6	R-Q1
42 N-Q5ch	K-B4
43 N-K3ch	K-K3
44 B-K2	K-Q2
45 BxPch	NxB
46 R(6)xN	K-B3
47 P-QR4	B-B2
48 K-K2	P-N4
49 P-N3	R-QR1
50 R-N2	R-KB1
51 P-B4	PxP
52 PxP	N-B2
53 R-K6ch	N-Q3
54 P-B5	R-QR1
55 R-Q2	RxP
56 P-B6	Resigns

GAME 57

The young Dutchman is the victim of yet another Fischer revival of an ancient line, 11 P–B4. A simplifying combination leads to a simple ending, all in 25 moves.

INTERNATIONAL TOURNAMENT 1968

Netanya, Israel

RUY LOPEZ

Robert J. Fischer   *Hans Ree*

WHITE	BLACK
1 P-K4	P-K4
2 N-KB3	N-QB3
3 B-N5	P-QR3
4 B-R4	N-B3
5 O-O	NxP
6 P-Q4	P-QN4
7 B-N3	P-Q4
8 PxP	B-K3
9 Q-K2	B-K2
10 R-Q1	O-O
11 P-B4	NPxP
12 BxP	Q-Q2
13 N-B3	. . .

This and the following series of moves show that White has the slight advantage of mobility that can easily translate into the win of material.

13 . . .	NxN
14 PxN	P-B3
15 PxP	BxP

16 B-KN5	. . .

Now there is no defense against the following exchange, for if 16 . . . QR-K1 17 BxB RxB 18 N-N5 B-B2 19 Q-Q3.

16 . . .	N-R4
17 QxBch	QxQ
18 BxQP	QxB
19 RxQ	BxP
20 R-QB1	B-N5
21 RxP	QR-B1
22 R-R7	R-B7
23 R(5)-Q7	B-B6
24 R(R)-B7	P-R3
25 B-K3	Resigns

The Bishop is trapped, as well as the Knight.

GAME 58

The King's Gambit, once "busted" by Fischer, is here played by him to avoid the well trod paths of the Ruy. The result is a penetrating miniature.

INTERNATIONAL TOURNAMENT 1968

Vinkovci, Yugoslavia

KING'S GAMBIT

Robert J. Fischer	Dragoljub Minic
WHITE	BLACK
1 P-K4	P-K4
2 P-KB4	PxP
3 B-B4	N-K2
4 N-QB3	P-QB3
5 N-B3	P-Q4
6 B-N3	PxP
7 NxP	N-Q4
8 Q-K2	B-K2
9 P-B4	N-B2
10 P-Q4	...

White has achieved everything one would want from a gambit without the slightest risk or waste of energy.

10 ...	O-O
11 BxP	N-K3
12 B-K3	B-N5ch

13 K-B2	...

White keeps his minor pieces in their threatening positions, even at the cost of castling "by hand."

13 ...	N-Q2
14 P-B5	N-B3
15 NxNch	QxN
16 KR-KB1	N-B5
17 BxN	QxB
18 P-N3	Q-R3
19 K-N1	B-KR6
20 N-K5!	...

The delightful point.

20 ...	BxR
21 RxB	B-Q7
22 R-B3	QR-Q1
23 NxKBP	RxN
24 Q-K7	Resigns

GAME 59

The three-time champion of Greece engaged Fischer in a simultaneous with clocks (as one of five players). Fischer took the exhibition quite seriously, going all out to prove that his "patented" Exchange Variation of the Ruy Lopez should win.

CLOCK SIMULTANEOUS 1958

Athens, Greece

RUY LOPEZ

Robert J. Fischer	*Anastasopoulos*
WHITE	BLACK
1 P-K4	P-K4
2 N-KB3	N-QB3
3 B-N5	P-QR3
4 BxN	QPxB
5 O-O	P-B3
6 P-Q4	PxP
7 NxP	P-QB4

Early simplification gives White a pull, instead of which 7 . . . N-K2 is equal.

8 N-N3	QxQ
9 RxQ	B-Q2
10 P-QR4	O-O-O
11 B-K3	P-QN3
12 N-B3	B-Q3
13 P-R5	P-B5!

After 14 N-Q4 P-QN4 the Black position is solid. Fischer wants a full point.

14 PxP?!	PxN
15 RxP	N-K2!
16 R-R8ch	K-N2
17 R-R7ch	K-N1
18 N-Q5	NxN
19 PxN	B-QB1?!

A delightful trap. After 20 PxPch BxP 21 R-Q3 PxP! 22 R-N3ch B-N3 White must retreat R-R1.

20 PxPch	BxP
21 P-QB4!	. . .

Fischer now finishes with elan. Black is about equal as the game stands, but he is playing a determined man.

21 . . .	B-N2
22 R-Q3	R-Q2
23 RxP	B-Q3
24 R-R5	K-B1
25 R(5)-N5	B-N1
26 P-N3	R-K1
27 P-B5	B-R2
28 P-B6	BxP
29 PxB	R-QB2
30 R-N7!	Resigns

GAME 60

Fischer's one-and-a-half year retirement from the chess arena did not seem to affect his play adversely, if this game is any indication. In his first game he faced both an opponent and a defense which had been his nemeses in the past.

USSR VS. THE WORLD 1970

Belgrade, Yugoslavia

CARO-KANN DEFENSE

Robert J. Fischer	Tigran Petrosian
WHITE	BLACK
1 P-K4	P-QB3
2 P-Q4	P-Q4
3 PxP	PxP
4 B-Q3	...

The ancient Exchange Variation which often leads to an early draw. Fischer was once convinced that the Panov-Botvinnik attack, 4 P-QB4 N-KB3 5 N-QB3 N-B3 6 N-B3, etc., was the best continuation for White. In his last encounter with the Caro-Kann, against Hort at Vinkovci, 1968, Fischer was only able to draw in the line 4 N-KB3 N-KB3 5 P-B3 B-B4 6 B-N5ch.

4 ...	N-QB3
5 P-QB3	N-B3
6 B-KB4	B-N5
7 Q-N3	N-QR4
8 Q-R4ch	B-Q2
9 Q-B2	P-K3

Less committal than Capablanca's old suggestion of 9 . . . Q-N3 first, but the result is the same.

10 N-B3	Q-N3
11 P-QR4	...

Preventing the exchange of his King's Bishop by 11 . . . B-N4.

11 ...	R-B1
12 QN-Q2	N-B3

13 Q-N1	...

Again preventing the exchange of his King's Bishop—awkward but essential. White's remote pressure on the Kingside induces Black to try the following dubious maneuver.

13 ...	N-KR4
14 B-K3	P-KR3

Kholmov points out that if 14 . . . B-Q3 15 P-B4 N-N5 16 P-B5 Q-R4, White cannot play 17 PxB because of 17 . . . R-B8ch 18 QxR NxBch, winning the Queen.

15 N-K5	N-B3

After 15 . . . NxN 16 PxN B-B4 17 P-R5 Q-B2 18 P-KN4 the Knight is trapped.

16 P-R3	B-Q3
17 O-O	K-B1?

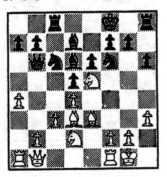

Petrosian, cautious to a fault, creates more problems than he solves by failing to castle. But he had reason to fear such possibilities as 17 . . . O-O 18 N-N4 B-K2 19 NxPch PxN 20 BxP KR-Q1 21 N-B3.

18	P-KB4	B-K1
19	B-KB2	Q-B2
20	B-R4	N-KN1
21	P-B5	...

Here it comes.

| 21 | ... | NxN |
| 22 | PxN | BxKP |

22 B-B4ch followed by 23 . . . QxKP hastens the downfall.

23	PxP	B-KB3
24	PxP	BxKBP
25	N-B3	BxB
26	NxB	N-B3

| 27 | N-N6ch | BxN |
| 28 | BxB | K-K2 |

Black attempts to free the Rook with this desperate plan of bringing the King across the board.

| 29 | Q-B5 | K-Q1 |
| 30 | QR-K1 | Q-B4ch |

Hoping to be able to play K-B2 and K-N1.

31	K-R1	R-B1
32	Q-K5	R-QB2
33	P-QN4	...

Winning the Rook if 33 . . . QxBP.

33	...	Q-B3
34	P-B4!	PxP
35	B-B5	R(1)-B2
36	R-Q1ch	R(KB)-Q2
37	BxR	RxB
38	Q-N8ch	K-K2
39	QR-K1ch	Resigns

GAME 61

Speed games are rarely included in games collections since they are probably indicative only of technique and natural ability. But these qualities are amply evident in this well-rounded five-minute duel, making it a classic of its kind.

BLITZ TOURNEY 1970

Herceg Novi, Yugoslavia

SICILIAN DEFENSE

| *David Bronstein* | *Robert J. Fischer* |
| WHITE | BLACK |

1	P-K4	P-QB4
2	P-QB3	N-KB3
3	P-K5	N-Q4
4	P-Q4	PxP
5	QxP	P-K3
6	N-B3	N-QB3
7	Q-K4	P-Q3

The "declined" Morra Gambit by transposition? Q-B2 here or next is probably most forcing.

8	QN-Q2	B-K2
9	B-Q3	PxP
10	NxP	NxN
11	QxN/K5	O-O
12	B-B2	B-Q3
13	Q-R5	P-B4
14	N-B3	N-B5
15	BxN	BxB

16 O-O	P-KN3
17 Q-R3	. . .

Rather embarrassing, but Black cannot unleash his QB.

17 . . .	Q-B3
18 QR-Q1	P-N3
19 KR-K1	K-R1
20 P-KN3	B-B2
21 Q-R6	Q-N2
22 QxQch	KxQ
23 B-N3	R-K1
24 N-Q4	K-B3
25 P-KB4	. . .

Black has escaped middle game complications, but appears to have endgame problems.

25 . . .	P-QR3
26 N-B3	R-K2
27 P-KR4	P-R3
28 K-B2	B-N2
29 N-K5	QR-K1
30 P-R4	P-KN4
31 RPxPch	PxP
32 PxPch	KxP
33 R-Q4	R-R2

Also P-N4 opens up deadly Bishop lines.

34 N-B3ch	K-B3
35 R-R4	RxR
36 PxR	P-K4
37 P-KR5	P-K5
38 N-Q4	P-B5
39 R-KN1	P-K6ch
40 K-K2	B-K5

When in doubt, centralize. White now misses his way.

41 B-B2	P-B6ch
42 KxP	BxBch
43 KxP	B-K5ch
44 K-B2	B-R2
45 P-R6	R-K2
46 R-N4	B-N3
Resigns	

GAME 62

Fischer plays for and against the Sicilian—always able to ". . . float like a butterfly, sting like a bee." This game shows why it is the player and not the variation that counts.

TOURNAMENT OF PEACE 1970

Zagreb, Yugoslavia

SICILIAN DEFENSE

Dragoljub Minic	*Robert J. Fischer*
WHITE	BLACK

1 P-K4	P-QB4
2 N-KB3	P-Q3

3 P-Q4	PxP
4 NxP	N-KB3
5 N-QB3	P-QR3
6 B-N5	P-K3
7 P-B4	B-K2

Fischer also plays the well-known Q-N3.

8 Q-B3	Q-B2
9 O-O-O	QN-Q2
10 P-KN4	P-N4
11 BxN	NxB
12 P-N5	...

White's steamroller has not as much steam as it appears.

12 ...	N-Q2
13 P-QR3	...

Temporarily stopping the advance of Black's NP.

13 ...	R-QN1
14 P-KR4	P-N5
15 PxP	RxP
16 B-R3	O-O

If 16 . . . N-B4, White retaliates with an immediate 17 P-B5.

17 N-B5	N-B4

17 . . . PxN? 18 N-Q5 Q-R4 19 NxBch K-R1 20 N-B6 wins.

18 NxBch	QxN
19 P-R5	B-N2
20 P-R6	...

20 KR-K1 loses to 20 . . . P-B4 21 PxP e.p. QxP 22 P-B5 NxP 23 NxN QxPch.

20 ...	BxP
21 NxB	NxN
22 PxN	...

Forcing the Black Rook to the square he really longs to occupy.

22 ...	R-B1
23 R-R2	R-R5
24 K-N1	...

Else mate.

24 ...	P-Q4
25 P-B4	R(5)xP
26 B-B1	...

Hoping for a tempo and making room for the White Queen to occupy the King Rook file.

26 ...	R-N5

27 Q-KR3	...

A calculated risk—who comes first? The pressure is on Black, who has no defense except attack.

27 ...	N-B6ch
28 K-B1	N-R5ch
29 K-N1	RxPch!
30 RxR	N-B6ch!
31 K-B1	Q-R6

Threatening 32 . . . NxRch 33 KxN QxR, or else 32 . . . Q-R8ch.

32 B-Q3	Q-R8ch
33 K-Q2	QxR(7)ch
34 K-K1	N-K5
Resigns	

GAME 63

Fischer gains two passed pawns in this game but can make no progress. Korchnoi's defense is perfect. "In my lifetime, I shall not play such an endgame better," he said to Fischer.

INTERNATIONAL TOURNAMENT 1970

Zagreb, Yugoslavia

SICILIAN DEFENSE

Robert J. Fischer	Victor Korchnoi
WHITE	**BLACK**
1 P-K4	P-QB4
2 N-KB3	P-K3
3 P-Q4	PxP
4 NxP	N-QB3
5 N-QB3	P-Q3
6 B-QB4	N-B3
7 B-N3	B-K2
8 B-K3	O-O
9 O-O	NxN
10 BxN	P-QN4

This little twist really doesn't change the normal course of the Sicilian, unless White, as here, tries for something extra. 11 P-QR3 is good.

11 NxP	B-R3
12 P-QB4	BxN
13 PxB	NxP
14 Q-N4	N-B3
15 Q-K2	N-Q2
16 Q-K3	B-B3
17 BxRP	Q-R4
18 P-N6	B-Q1
19 QR-Q1	NxP
20 BxN	BxB
21 Q-Q2	P-Q4
22 QxQ	RxQ
23 R-QB1	. . .

A most difficult ending now ensues, in which White's pawns become targets.

23 . . .	B-Q5
24 R-B2	P-N4

25 R-Q1	B-K4
26 R-K1	B-Q3
27 R-B6	R-Q1
28 KR-QB1	B-K4
29 R(1)-B2	R-N1
30 P-N3	R(4)-N4
31 K-B1	R(4)-N3
32 R(6)-B5	K-N2
33 R-K2	K-B3
34 R(5)-B2	P-R4
35 R-K3	P-R5
36 R(2)-K2	B-Q3
37 R-B3ch	K-N2
38 R-B3	R-N5
39 K-N2	R(1)-N2
40 R-B6	R(5)-N3
41 RxR	RxR
42 B-Q1	K-B3
43 R-Q2	B-K4
44 P-N3	. . .

At last! The stage is now set for an instructive finish.

44 ...	K-K2
45 P-KN4	K-Q3
46 R-B2	R-N1
47 P-KR3	B-Q5
48 B-K2	B-B4
49 R-B3	B-N5
50 R-B2	B-R4
51 K-B1	R-N5
52 R-B8	B-N3
53 R-B3	R-KB5
54 R-B3	RxR
55 BxR	K-B4
56 B-Q1	K-Q5

57 B-B2	B-B4
58 K-K2	B-R6
59 B-R7	K-B6
60 B-N1	...

White must not allow the advance of the QP, even with the gain of the KBP, for then the Black King can penetrate to the Kingside.

60 ...	B-B4
61 B-R7	P-K4
62 P-B3	Drawn

GAME 64

Fischer "remembered" his game with Zuckerman, New York, 1966; this is almost a carbon copy of that game, up to move 18. Black failed to castle in both cases, allowing the back-rank mate threat and the center advance P–K5.

WORLD TEAM OLYMPICS 1970

Siegen, Germany

SICILIAN DEFENSE

Robert J. Fischer	Ronald Camara
WHITE	BLACK
1 P-K4	P-QB4
2 N-KB3	P-Q3
3 P-Q4	N-KB3
4 N-B3	PxP
5 NxP	P-KN3
6 B-K3	B-N2
7 P-B3	N-B3
8 Q-Q2	B-Q2
9 B-QB4	R-QB1
10 B-N3	Q-R4

Less aggressive than 10 . . . Q-B2, which saves a tempo. The position is one which Fischer loves to "milk," either with a Kingside attack beginning P-R4-R5, or with middle game tactics in the center.

11 O-O-O	N-K4
12 P-KR4	N-B5
13 BxN	RxB
14 N-N3	Q-B2

15 B-Q4	B-B3
16 P-K5	PxP
17 BxKP	Q-B1
18 Q-K2	B-Q2

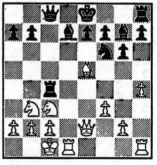

19 RxB!	KxR
20 N-N5	Q-B3
21 R-Q1ch	K-K1
22 N-B7ch	QxN
23 BxQ	RxB
24 Q-N5ch	Resigns

GAME 65

The classic idea of the Exchange Variation of the Ruy—to gain a Pawn majority on the Kingside, which is almost like having an extra Pawn—is demonstrated here against a dogged, but not inspired defense.

WORLD TEAM OLYMPICS 1970

Siegen, Germany

RUY LOPEZ

Robt. J. Fischer	Wolfgang Unzicker
WHITE	BLACK
1 P-K4	P-K4
2 N-KB3	N-QB3
3 B-N5	P-QR3
4 BxN	QPxB
5 O-O	P-B3
6 P-Q4	PxP
7 NxP	N-K2
8 B-K3	N-N3
9 N-Q2	B-Q3
10 N-B4	O-O
11 Q-Q3	N-K4
12 NxN	BxN
13 P-KB4	B-Q3
14 P-B5	. . .

As in Lasker-Capablanca, St. Petersburg, 1914, the gain of space in this type of position can compensate for the hole at K5.

14 . . .	Q-K2
15 B-B4	BxB
16 RxB	B-Q2
17 R-K1	Q-B4
18 P-B3	QR-K1
19 P-KN4	. . .

White's position becomes rather loose, but he maintains control.

19 . . .	Q-Q3
20 Q-N3	R-K2
21 N-B3	P-B4
22 P-K5	PxP
23 R(4)-K4	B-B3
24 RxP	R(1)-K1

25 RxR	RxR
26 N-K5	P-R3
27 P-KR4	B-Q2?

"Saving" the Bishop turns out badly, since the Knight proves to be far stronger in the endgame. Instead, a Queen ending after 27 . . . Q-Q4 28 NxB RxRch, etc. was defensible.

28 Q-B4	Q-KB3
29 R-K2	B-B1
30 Q-B4ch	K-R2
31 N-N6	RxR
32 QxR	B-Q2
33 Q-K7	QxQ
34 NxQ	P-KN4
35 PxP	PxP
36 N-Q5	B-B3
37 NxP	B-B6
38 N-K8	K-R3
39 N-B6	K-N2

40 K-B2	. . .

Various Knight forks protect the Knight Pawn, as well as the thematic "extra" Pawn.

| 40 ... | B-Q8 |
| 41 N-Q7 | P-B5 |

BxP is prevented by the neat combination 42 P-B6ch and P-B7. Another fork!

| 42 K-N3 | Resigns |

GAME 66

Fischer has his first chance at the World Champion, having lost twice and drawn twice with him in tournament play when Spassky was just "another" Soviet Grandmaster. The result does not dishonor either player, but indicates an eagerness on Fischer's part which is both his weakness and his strength as a player. Spassky offers a draw at a critical juncture; Fischer declines, oversteps himself, and loses to a fine counterattack. O'Kelly, who refereed, reports that Spassky remained seated throughout the game.

WORLD TEAM OLYMPICS 1970

Siegen, Germany

GRUENFELD DEFENSE

Boris Spassky	Robert J. Fischer
WHITE	BLACK
1 P-Q4	N-KB3
2 P-QB4	P-KN3
3 N-QB3	P-Q4

The Gruenfeld has been Fischer's favorite weapon in many critical games. Here he follows his game with Spassky at Santa Monica, 1966, to move 11.

4 PxP	NxP
5 P-K4	NxN
6 PxN	B-N2
7 B-QB4	P-QB4
8 N-K2	N-B3
9 B-K3	O-O
10 O-O	Q-B2
11 R-B1	R-Q1
12 P-KR3	...

Instead of Q-K1 or P-B4, which Spassky has favored. Meanwhile, on an adjoining table, Gligoric was making the same move against Hort.

12 ...	P-N3
13 P-B4	P-K3
14 Q-K1	N-R4
15 B-Q3	P-B4!
16 P-N4!	...

The position is still quite similar to the Santa Monica game—but here Spassky makes his break. His King position looks loose, but all his pieces are well placed for attack.

16 ...	PxKP
17 BxP	B-N2
18 N-N3	N-B5
19 BxB	QxB
20 B-B2	Q-B3
21 Q-K2	PxP
22 PxP	P-QN4
23 N-K4	BxP

Fischer takes the Pawn, even though his Kingside (and KP in particular) are weakened. Yet not to grasp the initiative now would be to agree to Spassky's draw offer.

24	N-N5	BxBch
25	RxB	R-Q3
26	R-K1	Q-N3
27	N-K4	R-Q5
28	N-B6ch	K-R1
29	QxP	R-Q3

White has no win yet, but Black must play accurately to maintain the

balance. Fischer has been forced to give back the Pawn, and he seeks to complicate when he should try to keep equality.

30 Q-K4	R-KB1?

Perhaps the first step downhill. QR-Q1 offers the defense R-Q6 and checks along the sixth rank.

31	P-N5	R-Q7
32	R(1)-KB1	Q-B2?

Black is now lost. Exchanging Rooks and Queens (RxR followed by Q-K6) offered some chances.

33	RxR	NxR
34	Q-Q4	R-Q1
35	N-Q5ch	K-N1
36	R-B2	N-B5
37	R-K2	R-Q3
38	R-K8ch	K-B2
39	R-B8ch!	Resigns

GAME 67

A number of players adopt the English against Fischer, hoping for a positional rather than a combinative struggle. But Fischer's element is any type of game, as he demonstrates masterfully here.

INTERNATIONAL TOURNAMENT 1970

Buenos Aires, Argentina

ENGLISH OPENING

M. A. Quinteros	Robert J. Fischer
WHITE	BLACK

1	P-QB4	P-KN3
2	N-KB3	B-N2
3	N-B3	P-QB4
4	P-Q4	PxP
5	NxP	N-QB3
6	N-B2	BxNch

Black decides early to play for the endgame advantage of a superior Pawn formation.

7 PxB	N-B3
8 P-B3	...

8 B-R6 N-KN5 9 B-N7 R-KN1 10 B-Q4 and Black remains with a superior game.

8 ...	P-Q3

Now allowing B-R6 for several moves.

9 P-K4?	B-K3

9 . . . P-N3 is to be considered, though it reduces the mobility of the Queen.

| 10 B-K2 | R-QB1 |

Adding some indirect pressure to White's QB4, indirectly preventing B-R6.

11 N-K3	Q-R4
12 B-Q2	N-K4
13 Q-N3	N(3)-Q2
14 P-B4	N-B4
15 Q-B2	N-B3
16 O-O	Q-R5
17 Q-N1	...

Avoiding what would probably result in a won ending for Black.

| 17 ... | N-R4 |
| 18 P-K5 | ... |

Hoping for 18 . . . NxP 19 NxN BxN 20 BxB QxB 21 PxP PxP 22 R-K1ch with a nice open line to the King's heart.

18 ...	PxP!
19 PxP	O-O
20 R-B4	...

Temporarily defending the Pawn and preparing for a Kingside attack.

20 ...	N-Q2
21 N-Q5	KR-K1
22 Q-K4	P-QN4!
23 RxP!?	...

23 PxP QxQ costs White a piece.

23 ...	KxR
24 Q-R4	K-N2
25 NxP	Q-B7
26 Q-R6ch	K-R1
27 R-QB1	QxRch!
28 BxQ	RxN

Emerging with a material advantage and a won game.

| 29 PxP | N-B5 |
| 30 Q-R4 | R-KB2 |

Grabbing the open file and preparing for QR-KB1 at the right moment.

31 Q-Q4	K-N1
32 B-B4	R-QB4
33 B-B3	RxNP
34 P-KR3	N(5)xP

35 B-R8	R-B1
36 BxN	NxB
37 QxP	B-Q4
38 BxBch	...

Without supportive material the Queen is hard pressed to initiate any counter-offense.

38 ...	RxB
39 Q-K3	R-R4
40 Q-K2	R(1)-R1
41 P-QR4	N-B2
42 P-R4	RxP
Resigns	

GAME 68

Fischer gets off to a nice start in this tournament, accelerating powerfully with his third win, this one particularly sweet because it redeemed a loss to Gheorghiu at the Olympiad. His play is direct and forceful against a particularly innocuous defensive line.

SECOND INTERNATIONAL TOURNAMENT 1970

Buenos Aires, Argentina

PETROFF DEFENSE

Robert J. Fischer   Florin Gheorghiu

WHITE	BLACK
1 P-K4	P-K4
2 N-KB3	N-KB3
3 NxP	P-Q3
4 N-KB3	NxP
5 P-Q4	B-K2
6 B-Q3	N-KB3
7 P-KR3	. . .

An improvement over 7 O-O first.

7 . . .	O-O
8 O-O	R-K1
9 P-B4	N-B3
10 N-B3	P-KR3
11 R-K1	B-B1
12 RxR	QxR
13 B-B4	B-Q2
14 Q-Q2	Q-B1
15 P-Q5	N-QN5
16 N-K4	. . .

The first break. The threat of NxNch gains space.

16 . . .	NxN
17 BxN	N-R3
18 N-Q4	N-B4
19 B-B2	P-QR4
20 R-K1	Q-Q1
21 R-K3	P-QN3
22 R-KN3	K-R1
23 N-B3	. . .

Black cannot stop White from taking over the long diagonal (Q-B3 24 B-K3).

23 . . .	Q-K2
24 Q-Q4	Q-B3
25 QxQ	PxQ
26 N-Q4	R-K1
27 R-K3	R-N1
28 P-QN3	P-N4
29 PxP	BxNP
30 N-B5	B-Q2
31 NxRP	R-N5

This small trap backfires, and it is Black who loses a piece.

32 R-N3	BxN
33 BxB	N-K5
34 B-N7ch	K-R2
35 P-B3	Resigns

GAME 69

Fischer plays no favorites in tournaments: almost assured of first place, he gives his full attention to the final games with admirable objectivity. The opening gambol is one of the handful of games to that date wherein he did not start 1 P–K4.

INTERZONAL TOURNAMENT 1970

Palma de Majorca, Spain

NIMZO-LARSEN DEFENSE

Robert J. Fischer   Henrique Mecking

WHITE	BLACK
1 P-QN3	P-Q4
2 B-N2	P-QB4
3 N-KB3	N-QB3
4 P-K3	N-B3
5 B-N5	B-Q2
6 O-O	P-K3
7 P-Q3	B-K2
8 KBxN	...

So we really have a Nimzo-Indian with colors reversed. The extra move allows for an early Kingside Pawn advance.

8 ...	BxB
9 N-K5	R-QB1
10 N-Q2	O-O
11 P-KB4	N-Q2
12 Q-N4!	NxN
13 BxN	B-B3
14 R-B3	Q-K2
15 QR-KB1	P-QR4
16 R-N3	BxB
17 PxB	P-B4
18 PxP e.p.	RxP

19 QxNPch!   ...

A simplifying combination, which Capablanca could well have played. A small advantage tends to grow.

19 ...	QxQ
20 RxR	QxR
21 PxQ	R-K1
22 P-KN4	P-R5
23 N-B3	PxP
24 RPxP	K-N2
25 P-N5	P-K4
26 N-R4	B-Q2
27 R-Q6	B-K3
28 K-B2	K-B2
29 R-QN6	R-K2
30 P-K4	PxP
31 PxP	P-B5
32 P-QN4	B-N5
33 K-K3	R-Q2
34 P-N6ch	K-B1
35 PxP	RxP
36 N-N6ch	K-K1

37 NxP	B-B1	40 K-B2	K-B2
38 NxP	K-Q1	41 NxB	KxN
39 N-Q6	R-N2	42 R-Q6	Resigns

GAME 70

At their last meeting in Buenos Aires three months previous to this encounter, Smyslov, the former World Champion, transposed from the Reti into the English and the result was a difficult but drawing continuation. Here Smyslov changes his tactics in the opening but falls victim to Fischer's genius to capitalize on the slightest mistake.

INTERZONAL TOURNAMENT 1970

Palma de Majorca, Spain

ENGLISH OPENING

Vassily Smyslov	*Robert J. Fischer*
WHITE	BLACK
1 P-QB4	P-KN3
2 N-QB3	B-N2
3 P-KN3	P-QB4
4 B-N2	N-QB3
5 P-N3	. . .

5 P-K3, in preparation for advancing the Queen Pawn and establishing a Pawn center, is worth considering. In Buenos Aires, Smyslov tried 5 N-B3 P-K3 6 P-N3 KN-K2 7 B-N2 O-O 8 N-QR4, but 8 . . . P-K4! secures the initiative for Black and if 9 NxP? P-K5 wins.

5 . . .	P-K3
6 B-N2	KN-K2
7 N-R4	BxB
8 NxB	O-O
9 P-K3	P-Q4
10 PxP	NxP

With an eye on what is becoming White's progressively weak Q3 square.

11 N-K2	P-N3
12 P-Q4	. . .

After 12 O-O B-R3 White's position is cramped, though the text is hardly an improvement. Smyslov's failure to castle contributes to his weakening position.

12 . . .	B-R3
13 PxP	Q-B3

Fischer's opportunity—and he seizes it.

14 N-QB4	N-B6

Continuing the pressure and opening the Queen's file for the Rook.

15 NxN	. . .

15 Q-B1 fails after NxN 16 KxN QR-B1 followed by 17 PxP? N-K4 18 P-N7 RxN 19 PxR BxPch with an easy win.

15 . . .	QxNch
16 K-B1	. . .

Where else? If 16 N-Q2, Black wins with 16 . . . N-N5!

16 . . .	KR-Q1!

Winning the Pawns can come later. Fischer holds on to the initiative.

17	Q-B1	BxNch
18	PxB	Q-Q6ch
19	K-N1	QR-B1
20	PxP	PxP
21	Q-N2	...

Looking for some counterplay. Evans suggests the possibility of a draw after 21 BxN RxB 22 K-N2 Q-K5ch 23 P-B3 QxBP 24 QxQ R-Q7ch 25 K-R3 RxQ, but it is a game without hope for White.

21	...	N-R4
22	P-KR4	...

Correct. For if 22 QxP then 22 ... NxP 23 Q-N3 Black's Rooks invade the 7th and defeat is even swifter.

22	...	NxP
23	Q-B6	...

Threatening P-R5.

23	...	Q-B4

Holding everything and forcing the beginning of a won ending.

24	QxQ	NPxQ
25	P-R5	...

25 P-K4 is also hopeless since 25 ... PxP 26 BxP R-Q7 and White stands with no prospects.

25	...	R-Q7

Even if White had played 25 K-R2, the Rook still would have come down.

26	R-QB1	R-B4
27	R-R4	N-K4!

28	RxR	PxR
29	R-R4	P-QB5
30	P-R6	...

Obvious.

30	...	K-B1
31	R-R8ch	K-K2
32	R-QB8	...

32 R-KR8 is much too slow to stop the advance of Black's passed Pawn.

32	...	RxRP

White should resign.

33	B-B1	R-B7
34	K-N2	N-N5
35	K-N1	RxP
36	BxP	R-B6
37	K-N2	RxP
38	R-KR8	NxP
39	RxP	N-N5
40	B-N5	R-N6
41	B-B6	R-N7ch
42	K-N1	N-K4
43	B-R8	R-N1
Resigns		

GAME 71

For the first time in his tournament career, Fischer plays the English! These little surprises are casually reserved for the Russians (e.g. vs. Tukmakov, Buenos Aires 1970). In this encounter, a sharply contested middle game produces an equal ending.

INTERZONAL TOURNAMENT 1970

Palma de Majorca, Spain

ENGLISH OPENING

Robert J. Fischer   *Lev Polugayevsky*

WHITE	BLACK
1 P-QB4	N-KB3
2 P-KN3	P-B3
3 B-N2	P-Q4
4 N-KB3	B-B4
5 Q-N3	Q-N3
6 PxP	QxQ
7 PxQ	PxP
8 N-B3	N-B3
9 P-Q3	P-K3
10 O-O	B-K2
11 B-K3	N-KN5
12 B-B4	O-O
13 P-K4	PxP
14 PxP	B-N3
15 P-K5	B-Q6
16 KR-Q1	B-B7
17 KR-QB1	BxP
18 P-R3	P-KN4

The saving move. White should now simply regain the Pawn with 19 PxN and 20 PxP, but he strives for more.

19 PxN	PxB
20 N-Q2	P-B6

Another finesse, yet White maintains a slight pressure.

21 BxP	NxP
22 B-N2	B-Q4
23 NxB	PxN
24 R-B7	B-Q1
25 RxNP	B-N3
26 BxP	QR-Q1
27 N-K4	NxP
28 R-Q1	K-N2
29 R-Q2	N-B3
30 NxN	KxN
31 R-Q3	K-N2
32 K-N2	R-QN1
33 R-Q7	QR-Q1
34 B-B4	RxR
35 RxR	K-N3
36 P-KN4	R-Q1

The reduction of material now precludes any winning chances.

37 BxPch	K-N4
38 RxR	BxR
Drawn	

GAME 72

A much played variation of the Modern Benoni results in a Fischer "blitzstorm" as he takes full advantage of an opening lapse by his famous East German opponent.

INTERZONAL TOURNAMENT 1970

Palma de Majorca, Spain

Wolfgang Uhlmann   *Robt. J. Fischer*

WHITE	BLACK
1 P-Q4	N-KB3
2 P-QB4	P-B4
3 P-Q5	P-K3
4 N-QB3	PxP
5 PxP	P-Q3
6 P-K4	P-KN3
7 B-KB4	P-QR3
8 P-QR4	B-N2
9 N-B3	O-O
10 B-K2	B-N5
11 O-O	R-K1
12 P-R3?	NxKP!

This had occurred as long ago as Vladimirov-Yudovich, Gorky 1954, when 13 PxB BxN 14 PxB NxQBP followed by NxBch also leaves Black a Pawn to the good. Had 7 . . . P-QR3 8 P-QR4 not been played, White would maintain dynamic chances with B-QN5 after Black's BxN (Korchnoi-Lutikov, Tallinn, 1959).

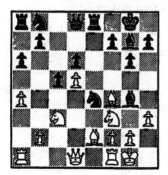

13 NxN	RxN
14 B-KN5	Q-K1
15 B-Q3	BxN
16 QxB	R-QN5
17 QR-K1	B-K4
18 Q-Q1	QxP
19 QxQ	RxQ
20 P-B4	B-Q5ch
21 K-R1	. . .

After this further inaccuracy (K-R2!) Black cleans up with dispatch.

21 . . .	N-Q2
22 R-K7	N-B3
23 RxNP	N-R4!
24 K-R2	B-K6
25 B-K2	BxPch
26 BxB	RxB
27 R-N6	RxR
28 BxR	R-Q1
29 RxRP	K-N2
30 B-N5	K-B3
31 B-B6	K-K4
32 R-R7	R-KB1
33 R-K7ch	K-Q5
34 R-Q7	N-B3
Resigns	

GAME 73

Fischer elected to "prepare" for this first game of one of the most important confrontations of his career by playing a round of tennis just prior to the start of the match. He entered the Student Union Building 10 minutes late, with his clock ticking away. In a complicated game, Taimanov failed to make the most of his chances—but Fischer did, down to the final mating net.

CANDIDATES MATCH 1971

Vancouver, B.C.

TAIMANOV-FISCHER

Game 1

KING'S INDIAN DEFENSE

Mark Taimanov	Robert J. Fischer
WHITE	BLACK
1 P-Q4	N-KB3
2 P-QB4	P-KN3
3 N-QB3	B-N2

This and the Gruenfeld (3 . . . P-Q4) are Fischer's favorites.

| 4 P-K4 | . . . |

Preventing the Gruenfeld. After 4 B-N5 P-Q3 5 P-K3 P-B4 6 N-B3 P-KR3 7 B-R4 P-KN4 8 B-N3 N-R4 9 PxP NxB 10 RPxN PxP 11 QxQch KxQ 12 O-O-Och there are equal chances, as in Benko-Fischer, Bled 1959.

| 4 . . . | P-Q3 |
| 5 N-B3 | . . . |

Robert Byrne pointed out that Fischer, in deciding on the King's Indian, "could be fairly certain of facing the classical system initiated by Taimanov's last move, since the Russian Grandmaster is one of the presiding geniuses of the variation. So, Bobby had surely decided that Black cannot be subjected to any-

thing worse than the normal White initiative."

5 . . .	O-O
6 B-K2	P-K4
7 O-O	N-B3
8 P-Q5	N-K2
9 B-Q2	. . .

Not new—only differing from P-QN4 or N-K1.

9 . . .	N-K1
10 R-B1	P-KB4
11 PxP	PxP

11 . . . NxP allows the White Knight a strong post on K4.

12 N-KN5	P-KR3
13 N-K6	BxN
14 PxB	Q-B1
15 Q-N3	P-B3

Threatening to win Black's King Pawn outright by playing 16 . . . R-N1.

16 B-R5	QxP
17 QxP	N-B3
18 B-K2	KR-N1
19 Q-R6	RxP

Black wins a Pawn, but his position
is precarious for the next few moves.

20 KR-Q1	P-K5

21 Q-R3	R-N2
22 B-B4	P-Q4
23 PxP	PxP
24 N-N5	N-N3

A great show of bravado. Fischer
defends against N-B7 with a long-
range combination: 25 N-B7 Q-Q2
26 NxR NxB 27 B-R6 N-K1! and
Black has at least 3 pieces for 2
Rooks.

25 N-Q4	Q-Q2
26 Q-K3	. . .

Q-KN3 was more forcing. The indirect threat is more lasting than the
direct.

26 . . .	K-R2
27 P-KR3	R-KB1
28 B-R6	R-N3
29 R-B7	Q-R5
30 RxBch	. . .

Tempting, as he wins two Pawns for
the Exchange and keeps the Bishop
pair. 30 BxP fails to QxRch 31 K-R2
P-B5.

30 . . .	KxR
31 BxPch	K-B2
32 B-K2	R(1)-QN1
33 NxP	R-N8
34 RxR	RxRch
35 K-R2	Q-Q2
36 N-Q4	Q-Q3ch

It turns out that White's King is
more vulnerable.

37 P-N3	Q-N5

Threatening . . . Q-K8 with mate to
follow.

38 N-B6	Q-N3
39 NxP	QxQ
40 BxQ	R-K8

White sealed 41 B-N4 but before
play resumed, he resigned. After 41
B-N5 he would have avoided the
mating net (41 . . . N-K4 was the
threat) with 42 P-R4, but then
comes N-N5ch and NxB.

GAME 74

There are no false steps in this relentless game as Fischer outplays his opponent from the opening to the final Pawn advance. As Golombek has observed, Fischer plays sounder chess when he does not have to "prove" himself.

CANDIDATES MATCH 1971

Vancouver, B.C.

FISCHER-TAIMANOV

Game 4

SICILIAN DEFENSE

| *Robert J. Fischer* | *Mark Taimanov* |
| WHITE | BLACK |

1	P-K4	P-QB4
2	N-KB3	N-QB3
3	P-Q4	PxP
4	NxP	Q-B2

An old line which has come back into vogue, avoiding the uncertainties of the second game.

5 N-QB3 ...

5 N-N5 leads to no demonstrable advantage. 5 P-QB4 loses a Pawn to ... Q-K4 6 N-KB3 QxPch 7 B-K2 P-Q3 8 N-B3 Q-B4 9 O-O N-B3 10 N-Q5 Q-Q2 where Black remains with a thoroughly respectable position (Matanovic-Benko, Portoroz, 1958).

5	...	P-K3
6	P-KN3	P-QR3
7	B-N2	N-B3
8	O-O	NxN
9	QxN	B-B4
10	B-B4	P-Q3
11	Q-Q2	P-R3
12	QR-Q1	P-K4
13	B-K3	B-KN5
14	BxB	PxB

| 15 | P-B3 | B-K3 |
| 16 | P-B4 | R-Q1 |

17 N-Q5 ...

The strength of Q5 is White's slim advantage.

| 17 | ... | BxN |
| 18 | PxB | P-K5 |

This is desperation already. But 18 ... O-O 19 P-Q6 Q-N3 20 PxP N-N5 21 Q-B3 KR-K1 22 KR-K1 offers little solace.

| 19 | KR-K1 | RxP |
| 20 | RxPch | K-Q1 |

Or K-B1 21 R-K8ch.

21	Q-K2	RxRch
22	QxRch	Q-Q2
23	QxQch	KxQ

24 R-K5   . . .

The seemingly dry endgame offers Fischer his best weapons: a minor piece/major piece ending with a bind on the position.

| 24 | . . . | P-QN3 |
| 25 | B-B1 | P-QR4 |

Black has now allowed nearly full scope for the Bishop.

26	B-B4	R-KB1
27	K-N2	K-Q3
28	K-B3	N-Q2
29	R-K3	N-N1
30	R-Q3ch	K-B2
31	P-B3	. . .

Robbing the Knight of its Q5 and QN5 squares.

31	. . .	N-B3
32	R-K3	K-Q3
33	P-QR4	N-K2
34	P-R3	N-B3
35	P-R4	P-R4

To prevent P-KN4 and further advances.

36	R-Q3ch	K-B2
37	R-Q5	P-B4
38	R-Q2	R-B3

39	R-K2	K-Q2
40	R-K3	P-N3
41	B-N5	R-Q3
42	K-K2	K-Q1
43	R-Q3	. . .

The point. Without Rooks, Black's Kingside Pawns posted on White squares are all succulent targets for the Bishop.

43	. . .	K-B2
44	RxR	KxR
45	K-Q3	N-K2
46	B-K8	K-Q4
47	B-B7ch	K-Q3
48	K-B4	K-B3
49	B-K8ch	K-N2
50	K-N5	N-B1
51	B-B6ch	K-B2
52	B-Q5	N-K2
53	B-B7	K-N2
54	B-N3	K-R2
55	B-Q1	K-N2
56	B-B3ch	K-B2
57	K-R6	N-N1
58	B-Q5	N-K2

58 . . . N-B3 loses to 59 B-B7 N-K5 60 BxP NxNP 61 K-N5 N-K7 62 BxRP NxP 63 B-B7 and the Rook Pawn advances.

59	B-B4	K-B3
60	B-B7	K-B2
61	B-K8	K-Q1
62	BxP!	. . .

Stunning. After White picks off Black's Queenside Pawns, he steamrolls over the Knight. There is no way to make progress otherwise.

62	. . .	NxB
63	KxP	K-Q2
64	KxBP	N-K2
65	P-QN4	PxP
66	PxP	N-B1
67	P-R5	N-Q3
68	P-N5	N-K5ch
69	K-N6	K-B1
70	K-B6	K-N1
71	P-N6	Resigns

A beautiful ending.

GAME 75

Taimanov, broken in spirit, tries desperately to at least draw this game to avoid the devastation of a shutout. Fischer plays flawlessly and after gaining a Pawn, wins easily.

CANDIDATES MATCH 1971

Vancouver, B.C.

FISCHER-TAIMANOV

Game 6

SICILIAN DEFENSE

Robert J. Fischer	Mark Taimanov
WHITE	BLACK
1 P-K4	P-QB4
2 N-KB3	N-QB3
3 P-Q4	PxP
4 NxP	P-K3

Abandoning his 4 . . . Q-B2 attempt which gained Taimanov nothing in Game Four, but going back to the variation he used in the second game.

5 N-N5	P-Q3
6 B-KB4	P-K4
7 B-K3	N-B3
8 B-N5	B-K3

Varying from 8 . . . Q-R4ch which was still probably best.

9 QN-B3	P-QR3
10 BxN	PxB
11 N-R3	N-Q5
12 N-B4	P-B4
13 PxP	NxP
14 B-Q3	R-B1
15 BxN	RxN

Otherwise, White's Knights will control Q5.

16 BxB	PxB
17 Q-K2	. . .

Q-R5ch was superficial, since the Black King must stay in the center or Queenside.

17 . . .	R-Q5
18 O-O	Q-N4
19 QR-Q1	Q-B4
20 RxR	PxR
21 N-K4	B-K2
22 R-Q1	Q-K4

If 22 . . . P-K4, Black loses quickly on 23 RxP!

23 Q-Q3	R-B1
24 QxQP	QxQ
25 RxQ	P-Q4
26 N-B3	B-B4
27 R-Q2	R-B5
28 P-KN3	R-B5
29 N-K2	R-QR5
30 P-QR3	K-Q2
31 K-N2	P-N4
32 P-QB3	P-QR4
33 N-Q4	P-N5
34 N-N3	. . .

With this sidestep, White avoids any danger on the Queenside and presses home his advantage.

34 . . .	B-N3
35 RPxP	PxP
36 P-QB4	K-B3

37	P-B5!	B-B2
38	N-Q4ch	K-Q2
39	P-B4	P-K4
40	P-B6ch	K-B1
41	N-N5	...

The transformation of the Knight and Pawn into an attacking combination quickly decides the game.

41	...	R-R7
42	P-B5	B-Q1
43	RxP	...

Taimanov adjourned here and eventually came back with the only verdict: Resigns.

GAME 76

Larsen rarely plays the French Defense but rehearsed some innovations preparing for this match, before which he stated that he would spring "several surprises." Fischer quickly distorts Larsen's plans, and produces a classic attacking game, the final combination being particularly sharp.

CANDIDATES MATCH 1971

Denver, Colorado

FISCHER-LARSEN

Game 1

FRENCH DEFENSE

Robert J. Fischer	Bent Larsen
WHITE	BLACK

1	P-K4	P-K3
2	P-Q4	P-Q4
3	N-QB3	B-N5
4	P-K5	N-K2
5	P-QR3	BxNch
6	PxB	P-QB4
7	P-QR4	QN-B3

8	N-B3	B-Q2
9	B-Q3	Q-B2
10	O-O	P-B5

Black is forced to close the center in order to castle—but then he declines castling and tries to undermine the center.

11	B-K2	P-B3
12	R-K1	N-N3

A dangerous Pawn grab, as the following shows.

13 B-R3	PxP
14 PxP	QNxP
15 NxN	NxN
16 Q-Q4	...

To inhibit O-O-O.

| 16 ... | N-N3 |
| 17 B-R5 | ... |

White plays for increased pressure rather than Pawns.

| 17 ... | K-B2 |
| 18 P-B4 | ... |

The typical breakthrough, right on time (compare Fischer-Petrosian, U.S.S.R.-World Match 1970).

18 ...	KR-K1
19 P-B5	PxP
20 QxQPch	K-B3
21 B-B3	...

Subtle regrouping, but 21 B-B5 was also forcing. Now Black plays out a desperate combination.

21 ...	N-K4?!
22 Q-Q4	K-N3
23 RxN	QxR
24 QxB	QR-Q1
25 QxP	...

Finely calculated.

| 25 ... | Q-K6ch |
| 26 K-B1 | R-Q7 |

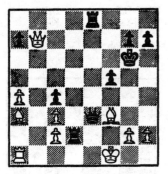

| 27 Q-B6ch | R-K3 |

Now, both the Queen and mate on the move are threatened.

| 28 B-B5! | ... |

The neat point—Bishop, not Queen, challenges the threatened mate.

28 ...	R-B7ch
29 K-N1	RxNPch
30 KxR	Q-Q7ch
31 K-R1	RxQ
32 BxR	QxP(6)

Perhaps saving the QRP would have held out longer.

| 33 R-N1ch | K-B3 |
| 34 BxP | ... |

White's two happy-go-lucky Bishops will chaperone his Rook's Pawn to the queening square.

34 ...	P-B5
35 B-N6	QxP
36 P-R5	Q-N7
37 B-Q8ch	K-K3
38 P-R6	Q-R6
39 B-N7	Q-B4
40 R-N1	P-QB6
41 B-N6	Resigns

A complete game of chess!

GAME 77

Fischer, like Morphy and Capablanca, is an incredibly fast chess-player and is often way ahead of his opponent on the clock. Even though he achieves a most promising position, Larsen stumbles in time pressure while Fischer calmly turns defense into attack. Larsen plays enough good moves to win three games—but he makes one big mistake.

CANDIDATES MATCH 1971

Denver, Colorado

LARSEN-FISCHER

Game 2

ENGLISH OPENING

Bent Larsen   *Robert J. Fischer*

WHITE	BLACK
1 P-QB4	P-QB4
2 N-KB3	P-KN3
3 P-Q4	PxP
4 NxP	N-QB3
5 P-K4	N-B3
6 N-QB3	P-Q3

So we have a Sicilian, in effect, with the "Maroczy Bind."

7 B-K2	NxN
8 QxN	B-N2
9 B-N5	P-KR3
10 B-K3	O-O
11 Q-Q2	K-R2
12 O-O	B-K3
13 P-B4	R-B1
14 P-QN3	Q-R4
15 P-QR3	P-R3
16 P-KB5	B-Q2

Black loses his Queen if he plays 16 . . . PxP 17 PxP BxKBP 18 RxB QxR 19 B-Q3.

17 P-QN4   . . .

The precarious position of the Queen is largely psychological. If it can't be attacked, it is strong; if it can, it is hopeless. Here Fischer has his favorite play of "in-between" moves to keep the Queen alive. B-B4 or B-Q4 are answered by NxP!

17 . . .   Q-K4

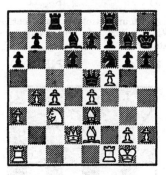

18 QR-K1   B-B3

A brilliant retort, maintaining threats against the White Queen.

19 B-B4	NxP
20 NxN	QxN
21 B-Q3	Q-Q5ch
22 K-R1	QR-K1
23 B-K3	. . .

Instead of this regaining of the Pawn, 23 R-K3 offered longer-lasting attacking advantages, preventing Q-B6 and threatening R-N3.

23 . . .	Q-B6
24 BxP	QxQ
25 BxQ	B-K4
26 B-B4	BxB
27 RxB	PxP
28 RxBP	K-N2

White keeps a slight advantage in being aggressively developed.

29 R-N5ch	K-R3
30 P-KR4	P-K3
31 R-KB1	P-B4
32 R-K1	R-B2
33 P-N5	PxP
34 PxP	B-Q2
35 P-N4	. . .

White chooses to press his initiative, whereas the simple 35 P-R4 would have solidified his Pawn position and threatened P-R5, to gain another passed Pawn.

| 35 . . . | R-QR1 |

The counterstroke that catches White short of time and over-extended.

| 36 PxP | PxP |

37 B-B4?   . . .

Although aggressive looking, Black has prepared a sufficient "in-between" move, the *leitmotif* of this game. Hard to figure under the circumstances, but quite playable, was 37 QR-KN1 R-R5 38 QR-N2! RxPch 39 K-N1 when White's bind is hard to break. For example, the simple 39 . . . R-KN5 40 QRxR PxR 41 R-N6ch K-R4 42 RxQP B-B4? 43 R-Q5 K-N3 44 RxB! RxR 45 P-R4! and White wins by a tempo.

| 37 . . . | R-R5 |

A great shot!

38 R-QB1   . . .

Compounding the previous error. BxR at once at least doesn't lose a move.

38 . . .	BxP
39 BxR	RxPch
40 K-N2	KxR
41 B-Q5	B-R3
42 R-Q1	R-R5

Sealing it, since a supine defense of the QRP is hopeless.

43 B-B3	RxP
44 RxP	R-R7ch
45 K-N1	K-B5
46 B-N2	R-N7
47 R-Q7	P-N3
48 R-Q8	B-K7
49 B-R3	B-N5
50 B-B1	B-B6
51 R-QN8	B-K5
52 B-R6	K-K6
53 R-QB8	R-N8ch
54 K-R2	K-B5
Resigns	

GAME 78

Fischer returns to the King's Indian after the unhappy opening result of the second game. Again, the counter-punch is the decisive blow. Fischer's game is unobjectionable, though not brilliant.

CANDIDATES MATCH 1971

Denver, Colorado

LARSEN-FISCHER

Game 4

KING'S INDIAN DEFENSE

Bent Larsen   *Robert J. Fischer*

WHITE	BLACK
1 P-QB4	P-KN3
2 N-KB3	B-N2
3 P-Q4	N-KB3
4 N-B3	O-O
5 P-K4	P-Q3
6 B-K2	P-K4
7 O-O	N-B3
8 P-Q5	N-K2
9 N-Q2	...

Up to now the same as Taimanov-Fischer, first and third games, where 9 B-Q2 was tried with success as far as the opening was concerned. Also possible is 9 N-K1 N-Q2 10 N-Q3 P-KB4 11 PxP NxBP 12 P-B3 as in Reshevsky-Fischer, 11th match game, Los Angeles, 1961, leading to an equal game.

9 ...	P-B4
10 R-N1	N-K1
11 P-QN4	P-N3
12 P-QR4	P-B4
13 P-R5	N-KB3
14 Q-R4	B-Q2
15 Q-R3	B-R3

Larsen is leaning all over the board, but Black reserves his options.

16 B-Q3	Q-B2
17 NPxP	NPxBP
18 PxP	PxP
19 B-B2	P-R3
20 N(2)-K4	...

The exchange of two minor pieces leads to nothing for White. But already it is apparent that Black has the dynamic position.

20 ...	BxB
21 NxNch	RxN
22 KRxB	QR-KB1
23 R-N6	...

Q-N3-N6 is probably wiser.

| 23 . . . | B-B1 | 26 . . . | Q-KN2 |
| 24 N-K2 | P-B5! | 27 R-N1 | N-R5 |

Black gains space on the Kingside at an alarming rate.

The White squares simply are underprotected.

| 25 B-K4 | N-B4 |
| 26 R-B6 | . . . |

28 Q-Q3	B-B4
29 K-R1	P-B6!
30 N-N3	PxPch
31 K-N1	BxB
32 QxB	N-B6ch
33 KxP	N-Q7
Resigns	

Larsen obviously underestimates Fischer's Kingside attacking possibilities.

GAME 79

Perhaps the finest game of the preliminary matches. Though the score is hopeless, leaving Larsen little room for maneuvering in drawn positions, he plays this one to the hilt. Only Fischer's aggressive defense turns the game around.

CANDIDATES MATCH 1971

Denver, Colorado

LARSEN-FISCHER

Game 6

BIRD'S OPENING

Bent Larsen	*Robert J. Fischer*
WHITE	BLACK
1 P-KB4	. . .

An important part of Larsen's repertoire; he and Tartakower are the only masters in modern times who have played Bird's Opening with any consistency.

1 . . .	P-QB4
2 N-KB3	P-KN3
3 P-K4	B-N2
4 B-K2	N-QB3
5 O-O	P-Q3

So a Sicilian-type game results, with the White King Bishop and King

Knight reversed.

6 P-Q3	P-K3
7 N-R3	KN-K2
8 P-B3	O-O
9 B-K3	P-QR3
10 P-Q4	PxP
11 NxP	P-QN4
12 NxN	NxN
13 Q-Q2	Q-B2
14 QR-Q1	R-Q1
15 N-B2	R-N1
16 P-QR3	N-R4
17 P-K5	B-B1
18 P-QN4	. . .

Provoking 18 . . . N-B5 and then 19 BxN QxB 20 B-Q4 followed by 21 N-K3, etc., and some interesting attacking chances.

18 . . .	N-B3
19 N-Q4	PxP
20 PxP	NxKP
21 B-N5	R-Q4
22 Q-B4	R-N2
23 P-KR4	B-N2
24 B-B6	BxB
25 QxB	QxP

Proving too much. White now gets attacking chances that the simple 25 . . . Q-K2 would have avoided.

26 P-R5	PxP

P-R6 was a threat.

27 K-R1	. . .

For several moves hereabouts, White can take a perpetual check, starting with NxKP. But there is no reason why he should settle for a half-point.

27 . . .	N-N5
28 BxN	PxB
29 Q-R6	B-Q2
30 R-B4	P-B4

31 Q-B6	. . .

Incredible! As so often in this match, Larsen (as before him, Taimanov) draws back from the final stroke that justifies his previous play. The obvious 31 Q-N5ch wins, e.g. 31 . . . K-R1 32 Q-Q8ch K-N2 33 NxBPch, etc., or 31 . . . K-B1 32 Q-B6ch, or 31 . . . K-B2, 32 QR-KB1 with interesting mating lines in all three cases.

31 . . .	B-B1
32 R(4)-B1	R-KB2
33 Q-R6	B-N2
34 NxKP	Q-KB3
35 Q-K3	R-K2
36 QR-K1	R-Q3
37 Q-N5ch	. . .

The only way to hold the piece.

37 . . .	QxQ
38 NxQ	RxR
39 RxR	B-Q4
40 R-K8ch	K-N2
Resigns	

GAME 80

Petrosian's style favors the Caro-Kann Defense, but as the further progress of the match was to make clear, the ex-World Champion was determined to avoid the expected. He no doubt felt that he could not match Fischer's encyclopedic knowledge of the openings; he would rely instead on over-the-board analysis.

With the Caro-Kann, Petrosian had been able to hold only a half point in two games against Fischer in their most recent encounters (U.S.S.R.-World Match, 1970). In the twelve years since their first encounter in this semi-closed game (Candidates Tournament, 1959), Fischer had become not only stronger but wiser. As Petrosian challenged Fischer's favorite line against the Sicilian, with which he had demolished Taimanov in the first round of the candidates matches, Fischer may have instinctively sensed the danger.

The innovation came. Yet at the very moment when the attack might have been vigorously pursued, Petrosian drew back. Missing several promising lines, he settled for an "equal" ending, which in time pressure he was unequal to handling. Fischer had then won 20 straight games on the road to the World Championship.

Fischer "should have lost," said the critics. Yet careful analysis fails to bear out this conclusion. And Petrosian did not repeat the variation.

CANDIDATES MATCH 1971

Buenos Aires, Argentina

FISCHER-PETROSIAN

Game 1

SICILIAN DEFENSE

Robert J. Fischer	*Tigran Petrosian*
WHITE	BLACK
1 P-K4	P-QB4
2 N-KB3	P-K3
3 P-Q4	PxP
4 NxP	N-QB3
5 N-N5	P-Q3

Fischer moves inexorably into a line he has been known to favor since his game against Najdorf at Los Angeles, 1966, and with which he won two games in the Taimanov match. It was later disclosed that Petro-

sian's second, Suetin, had discovered a dramatic sacrificial improvement in this line at move 11, which accounts for its adoption by Petrosian in this crucial first game.

6 B-KB4	P-K4
7 B-K3	N-B3
8 B-N5	B-K3

For . . . Q-R4ch see second game, Fischer-Taimanov. White plays to weaken the White squares at the cost of a move or two. Logically, Black could afford 7 . . . P-KR3, since White has wasted time merely to dominate Q5.

9 QN-B3	P-QR3
10 BxN	PxB
11 N-R3	P-Q4

For 11 . . . N-Q5, see Fischer-Taimanov, sixth game. The "prepared innovation" gives rise to a tense position in which White holds a nominal Pawn advantage in exchange for a lag in development. The tension around White's square Q5 is extremely subtle: White can hold the Pawn only by keeping it pinned for some time, while Black can threaten the Pawn only by keeping two pieces forked by it.

12 PxP	BxN
13 NPxB	Q-R4
14 Q-Q2	O-O-O
15 B-B4	...

Reuben Fine suggests B-Q3 as a drawing line after multiple exchanges. This is hard to understand in view of the fact that Black ends up with a Pawn and a superior Pawn formation, e.g. 15 B-Q3 BxP 16 NxB QxN 17 B-B5ch (a recurring theme) K-B2 18 QxQ RxQ 19 B-K4 R-R4 20 BxN KxB 21 O-O-O RxP 21 K-N2 R-R5 22 R-Q3 R-KN1.

| 15 ... | KR-N1 |
| 16 R-Q1! | ... |

Fine still insists that B-Q3 is better, and so gives R-Q1 a question mark. But the real point of R-Q1 is not over-protection of Q5 (for which the move received an exclamation point in several commentaries!) but the protection of Q2 and the eventual threat of B-Q3, as we shall see. For, if 16 B-Q3 BxP 17 NxB Black does not play either QxN or RxN (as Fine suggests) but QxQch. Then 18 KxQ RxN 19 K-K3, R-R4 gives Black a fine endgame.

| 16 ... | B-B4 |

The first move in the game on which Petrosian spent any time at all (35 minutes) has been roundly criticized. The Russian analysts wonder why 16 . . . RxNP shouldn't win, giving elaborate variations for 17 Q-K3 or 17 N-K4. But then the real point of 17 B-Q3! becomes apparent (and we assume it had occurred to Fischer). Black cannot take the QP because of 17 . . . BxP 18 NxB RxN 19 K-B1! when B-B5ch will win the Exchange. He can gamble with 17 . . . B-N5 18 PxN BxR 19 PxPch K-N1 20 KxB when White has nothing to fear. Likewise 16 . . . B-N5 is answered by B-K2 (not P-KB3), so that the KNP is indirectly protected by the threat to trap the Rook (17 B-K2 BxB 18 NxB RxNP 19 QxQ NxQ 20 N-N3, etc.).

| 17 B-Q3 | BxB |

Strangely enough, the commentators who criticized 16 . . . B-B4 now show that 17 . . . P-K5 would win, even though 17 B-Q3 was "forced." Certainly after 17 . . . P-K5 the Pawn cannot be taken because of the pin on the King file, but White is not without other resources. Steinitzian is 18 B-B1 B-N5 19 R-QN1 N-K4 20 R-N3, favorable to Black but distinctly unclear.

18 QxB	N-Q5
19 O-O	K-N1
20 K-R1	...

To prevent QxN.

20 . . .	QxRP

Now Black has not only equalized material, but has all the open lines. Petrosian's play cannot yet be faulted.

21 P-B4(?)	. . .

So natural, so necessary as an active defense, but 21 N-K4 at once was more solid. Black now has almost a forced win.

21 . . .	R-QB1
22 N-K4	QxQ?

Fine shows that 22 . . . QxP leads to a nice King hunt after 23 NxP KRxP! 24 KxR RxPch, etc. If this game has a turning point, this is it.

23 PxQ	R-B7
24 R-Q2	RxR
25 NxR	P-B4

Quite logical. The KB file must be held, and the Knight is secure because of White's weak first rank. The endgame is drawn, but Fischer manages to squeeze an advantage out of the weak Black Kingside Pawns—and Petrosian's lack of time.

26 PxP	R-K1
27 R-K1	N-B7
28 R-K2	N-Q5

29 R-K3	N-B7
30 R-R3	RxP
31 N-B3	RxP
32 RxP	RxP
33 P-KR4	N-K6

Simplest was N-Q5, but it is difficult to find the right square in an open board with the clock ticking.

34 RxP	R-Q8ch
35 K-R2	R-QR8

Too slow. P-QN4 is the right counter, as White cannot easily advance the KRP because of the possibilities of Rook and Knight checks.

36 P-R5	P-B5

Fine contends that this is the "decisive blunder," instead of which 36 . . . RxP "draws." But after 37 R-N7 P-B5 38 R-N5 R-B7 39 N-Q4 R-B1 40 K-R3 White will support his passed Pawns with his King, whereas Black will be in constant danger of losing his or opening a disastrous check by the White Rook, e.g. 40 . . . R-R2 41 K-R4, P-N4 42 R-N6 and P-R6.

37 RxP	RxP
38 R-K4!	NxP
39 K-N3!	R-R4
40 N-K5	Resigns

A memorable game, for players and analysts alike.

GAME 81

"Tigre, Tigre—Tigran un Tigre!" was the chant that filled the San Martin Theater when Fischer resigned this game, his first loss in over a year and the end of his 20–game winning streak. Petrosian plays masterful chess in this, his only win of the match. The game was replayed in Moscow on that evening's television and radio news program.

CANDIDATES MATCH 1971

Buenos Aires, Argentina

FISCHER-PETROSIAN

Game 2

SICILIAN DEFENSE

Tigran Petrosian	Robert J. Fischer
WHITE	BLACK
1 P-Q4	N-KB3
2 P-QB4	P-KN3
3 N-QB3	P-Q4

Fischer retains the Gruenfeld for special encounters but his results with it might be considered inconclusive, e.g., four historical games: his monumental draw against Botvinnik (Varna 1962), his spectacular loss against Spassky (Siegen 1970), his brilliant miniature against R. Byrne (N.Y. 1963), and his "Game of the Century" against D. Byrne (N.Y. 1956).

4 B-B4	. . .

Spassky adopted the sharper 4 PxP NxP 5 P-K4 with initiative.

4 . . .	B-N2

If 4 . . . N-R4? 5 B-K5 P-KB3 6 B-N3 NxB 7 RPxN P-B3 8 P-K3 B-N2 9 B-Q3 with a winning position for White as in Euwe-Alekhine, 14th match game, 1935.

5 P-K3	P-B4

Not really a gambit, as the sequel shows.

6 PxBP	Q-R4
7 R-B1	N-K5
8 PxP	NxN
9 Q-Q2	QxRP
10 PxN	Q-R4

The whole line must depend on the sacrificial 10 RxN BxR 11 QxB P-B3 12 N-B3 Q-N8ch, since Black now gets an excellent game. 10 . . . QxQch is quite playable, since Black has time to recapture the QBP.

11 B-B4	N-Q2
12 N-K2	N-K4

An attempt to milk something out of a level position. QxP(4) here or on the previous or next move gives Black a safe game with long-term advantages in the Queenside pawn majority.

13 B-R2	B-B4
14 BxN	BxB
15 N-Q4	QxP(4)

White now threatens to hold the "gambit" with N-N3, and so forces a favorable Exchange.

16 NxB   PxN

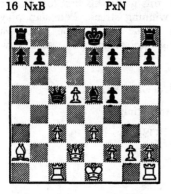

17 O-O   Q-R4?

A critical juncture. Black is desperately weak on White squares, making it difficult to castle on either wing. Fischer now begins to "swim," but perhaps he could mix it better with 17 KR-N1 or P-B5 at once.

18 Q-B2   P-B5
19 P-B4!   . . .

The winning idea—open the central lines.

19 . . .   PxP
20 P-B5   . . .

Not allowing Black to correct his mistake with 20 PxP Q-B4.

20 . . .   Q-Q7

On 20 . . . PxPch 21 QxP O-O 22 B-N1 White has the attack, but Black can still defend with P-B4. The text is played almost to justify his last sequence of moves.

21 Q-R4ch   K-B1
22 QR-Q1   Q-K7

If 22 . . . P-K7 23 RxQ BxPch 24 KxB PxR(Q) 25 P-Q6 wins.

23 P-Q6   Q-R4

Winning the Exchange and losing the game. R-KN1 is natural, and if 24 PxPch K-N2 with fighting chances.

24 P-B4!   P-K7
25 PxB   PxQR(Q)
26 RxQ   QxP
27 R-KB1   P-B3

The tempting 27 . . . QxBPch loses to 28 K-R1 and after 28 . . . P-K3 29 Q-Q7 is an easy win. Nevertheless, it is interesting to speculate as to why Black, with ample time, plays into a simple, forced loss. The miracle does not come.

28 Q-N3   K-N2
29 Q-B7ch   K-R3
30 PxP   P-B4
31 RxP   Q-Q5ch
32 K-R1   Resigns

GAME 82

The decisive game of the match. At this critical juncture, a dead-even match with the openings all in Petrosian's favor, he chooses a wait-and-see opening with White. It was with this opening that he won the only game of the previous match with Korchnoi. Does he hope to lock Bobby in the same grip of tedium with which he exhausted his previous opponents in the candidates matches? Fischer refuses to be drawn out. He counters methodically, sits on the position until he obtains the decisive endgame breakthrough. Overlooking a finesse that could have forced early resignation, he is extended through a doubtful ending in which Petrosian finally falters.

CANDIDATES MATCH 1971

Buenos Aires, Argentina

PETROSIAN-FISCHER

Game 6

NIMZOVICH OPENING

Tigran Petrosian   *Robert J. Fischer*

WHITE	BLACK
1 N-KB3	P-QB4
2 P-QN3	P-Q4
3 B-N2	. . .

Petrosian's choice of different openings and defenses in every game has the advantage of testing Fischer's repertoire, but this is an elemental mistake, as Korchnoi himself indicates. The man after whom the opening is named said in the 1930's that White must always maintain a pawn at Q4 *potentially*. Thus 3 P-K3 is necessary.

3 . . .	P-B3!

Fine chastises Bobby for lackadaisical play. But his suggested 3 . . . N-QB3 actually allows White to redeem himself with 4 P-K3, when 5 P-Q4 is unstoppable. It is remarkable that after three moves by both sides modern opening theory is still so open to discussion.

4 P-B4	P-Q5
5 P-Q3	P-K4
6 P-K3	N-K2

Refusing to be baited, Black simply finds the right positions for his pieces on the Queenside. Fine's 6 . . . N-KR3 merely telegraphs a plan of playing on both wings.

7 B-K2	KN-B3

As Byrne points out, Black leaves himself the option of N-Q2 and N-QB4 if White exchanges Pawns in the center. Najdorf and Fine think N-B4 more "in Fischer's style," but Fischer's style here is simplicity itself.

8 QN-Q2	B-K2
9 O-O	O-O
10 P-K4	. . .

White in effect cedes the advantage of the first move. But after the often suggested 10 PxP BPxP! 11 N-K4 P-B4 followed by N-Q2, Black has all he needs (another reason, by the way, that Fine's 8 . . . B-Q3 is not "more aggressive").

10 . . .	P-QR3
11 N-K1	P-QN4
12 B-N4	BxB
13 QxB	Q-B1!

Psychologically perfect. Black says, "I am content to maintain endgame pressure—without risks." White draws back.

| 14 Q-K2 | N-Q2 |

Byrne alone among the annotators shows the hopelessness of White's game after exchanging Queens. Black simply has too much space on the Queenside.

15 N-B2	R-N1
16 KR-B1	Q-K1
17 B-R3	. . .

Just playing around. After this further waste of time, Black takes over to make room for the Queen at K2 if needed. Fischer seeks no complications.

| 17 . . . | B-Q3 |
| 18 N-K1 | P-N3 |

In the mood! Black says, "Commit yourself"—and he *does*.

19 PxP	PxP
20 B-N2	N-N3
21 N(1)-B3	. . .

White appears to be doing a soft-shoe shuffle, without much progress afoot.

21 . . .	R-R1
22 P-QR3	N-R4
23 Q-Q1	Q-B2
24 P-QR4	PxP
25 PxP	P-B5

Fine and Byrne heartily approve— the Russians disagree, suggesting 25 . . . KR-B1 first contains more punch. As the game goes, however, 25 . . . P-B5 is a winner.

26 PxP	N(R)xP
27 NxN	NxN
28 Q-K2	NxB
29 QxN	KR-N1
30 Q-R2	B-N5

Eyeing B6 as an outpost.

31 QxQch	KxQ
32 R-B7ch	K-K3!
33 P-N4	. . .

| 33 . . . | B-B6 |

The key to the endgame. A Pawn means little against active pieces.

| 34 R-R2 | . . . |

| 34 . . . | R-QB1? |

Fine says "!" but the ending is probably drawn after this, when actually 34 . . . R-N8ch 35 K-N2 R-QB8! 36 R-B6ch K-K2 37 R-B7ch K-K1 38 RxP R-R4 39 R-QB7 P-Q6 wins a piece. Pinning his own Rook to make P-Q6-7 possible is a rare combination, which all of the commentators have overlooked. Najdorf and

Suetin now criticize 35 RxR, but overlook the point of 34 ... R-QB1, namely 35 RxP P-Q6! 36 R-QN7 B-R4, etc. Now after the agonizing win of the QRP Black still must play "another game" to win.

35	RxR	RxR
36	P-R5	R-QR1
37	P-R6	R-R2
38	K-B1	P-N4

Preventing White's P-N5.

39	K-K2	K-Q3
40	K-Q3	K-B4
41	N-N1	K-N4

The position was adjourned here, with Petrosian sealing. The Russians were to analyze all night—in vain.

42	N-K2	B-R4
43	R-N2ch	KxP
44	R-N1	R-QB2

Temporarily chaining the Knight to a defense of White's QB3.

45	R-N2	B-K8
46	P-B3	K-R4
47	R-B2	R-QN2
48	R-R2ch	K-N4
49	R-N2ch	B-N5

Retaining the Rook is imperative.

50	R-R2	R-QB2
51	R-R1	R-B1
52	R-R7?	B-R4

Fine correctly analyzes the waiting 57 R-R2 as a draw. Now the Rook is shut out.

53	R-Q7	B-N3

All Fischer's subtle maneuverings are calculated to get his Rook behind White's pawns eventually.

54	R-Q5ch	B-B4
55	N-B1	K-R5
56	R-Q7	B-N5
57	N-K2	K-N6
58	R-QN7	R-QR1
59	RxP	R-R8

The beginning of the end.

60	NxPch	. . .

Useless.

60	. . .	PxN
61	KxP	R-Q8ch
62	K-K3	B-B4ch
63	K-K2	R-KR8
64	P-R4	K-B5
65	P-R5	R-R7ch
66	K-K1	K-Q6
Resigns		

GAME 83

Fischer demonstrates in superlative style his ability to extract the most from minor piece/major piece endings. With his first really solid game of the match, he begins another rout.

CANDIDATES MATCH 1971

Buenos Aires, Argentina

FISCHER-PETROSIAN

Game 7

SICILIAN DEFENSE

Robert J. Fischer	Tigran Petrosian
WHITE	**BLACK**
1 P-K4	P-QB4
2 N-KB3	P-K3
3 P-Q4	PxP
4 NxP	P-QR3

Petrosian persists in refusing to repeat an opening, even though the burden would have been on Bobby to answer the innovation of the first game.

5 B-Q3	N-QB3
6 NxN	. . .

This variation against the Sicilian, introduced by Paul Morphy more than a century ago, got Spassky nowhere in his 1969 World Championship match with Petrosian.

6 . . .	NPxN
7 O-O	P-Q4
8 P-QB4	. . .

8 N-Q2, as played by Smyslov against Tal in the Candidates Tournament, Yugoslavia 1959, as well as by Spassky, is not as directly aggressive as the text.

8 . . .	N-B3
9 BPxP	BPxP
10 PxP	PxP

"An isolated Pawn spreads gloom all over the chessboard." (Tartakower.) Yet 10 . . . NxP or 10 . . . QxP leaves Black seriously behind in development as White brings his pieces to bear on his Q5.

11 N-B3	B-K2
12 Q-R4ch	. . .

The idea is to centralize the Queen after 12 . . . B-Q2 13 Q-Q4, which Black decides to avoid.

12 . . .	Q-Q2
13 R-K1	. . .

White can win the Exchange by 13 B-QN5 PxB 14 QxR and probably hold everything with patient defense, but he prefers to take a small advantage into the endgame, without risks.

13 . . .	QxQ
14 NxQ	B-K3
15 B-K3	O-O

16 B-B5   . . .

Fischer distinguishes himself in this game by refusing to be distracted by the lure of material gain. Byrne has shown that 17 N-N6 QR-N1 18 BxP N-N5 gives ample counterchances.

16 . . .	KR-K1
17 BxB	RxB
18 P-QN4	. . .

Fixing the second target, the QRP.

18 . . .	K-B1
19 N-B5	B-B1
20 P-B3	R(2)-R2

As Byrne suggests, Black should exchange Rooks and try to guard the black squares with N-K1, N-B2, N-K3. Otherwise, the White King simply marches to Q4. Noteworthy in the position are the contortions Black must go through to defend himself against direct threats.

21 R-K5   B-Q2

If Black is permitted B-N4, his position improves rapidly.

22 NxBch   . . .

Polugayevsky points out in "64" that this move "is characteristic of Fischer's practice. He often tries to transform one advantage into another. He easily exchanges the strong Knight in order to get Bishop vs. Knight. Stronger for White was the natural 22 P-QR4." Byrne calls 22 P-QR4 "incomparably weaker" because the text is relatively clearcut.

| 22 . . . | RxN |
| 23 R-QB1 | R-Q3 |

Black cannot defend both the sixth and seventh ranks.

24 R-B7   N-Q2

24 . . . R-K1 is met by 25 RxRch KxR 26 R-R7.

25 R-K2	P-N3
26 K-B2	P-KR4
27 P-B4	P-R5

White has a stranglehold on the position, which allows him to actively provoke further Pawn weaknesses.

| 28 K-B3 | P-B4 |
| 29 K-K3 | P-Q5ch |

Attempting to keep White's King out of the fray for as long as possible. But now White has three active pieces to Black's one, the Knight.

30 K-Q2	N-N3
31 R(2)-K7	N-Q4
32 R-B7ch	K-K1
33 R-QN7	NxNP
34 B-B4	Resigns

There is no defense to R-KR7.

GAME 84

By winning this game Fischer finally qualified for the right to play a match for the World's Championship. But it was something of an anti-climax. Petrosian plays one of the weakest games of his career, per-haps because he had never before been in the situation of having to overcome a two-point deficit against a better player.

CANDIDATES MATCH 1971

Buenos Aires, Argentina

FISCHER-PETROSIAN

Game 9

FRENCH DEFENSE

Robert J. Fischer	Tigran Petrosian
WHITE	BLACK
1 P-K4	P-K3
2 P-Q4	P-Q4
3 N-QB3	N-QB3

Kholmov suggests that the reason Petrosian had selected such seldom played variations against Fischer is that he felt less theoretically pre-pared. Fine derides this as a duffer's move—but it only seems so.

4 N-B3	N-B3
5 PxP	PxP
6 B-QN5	B-KN5

As a matter of fact, Black has more options here than in the Petroff.

7 P-KR3	BxN
8 QxB	B-K2
9 B-N5	P-QR3

Difficult to explain. O-O apparently saves a tempo, but White would then have the option of O-O-O. This at least is forcing.

10 BxNch	PxB
11 O-O	O-O
12 KR-K1	P-R3
13 B-R4	Q-Q2

14 R-K2	P-QR4
15 QR-K1	B-Q1
16 P-QN3	R-N1
17 N-R4	N-K5

So in this simple, drawish position, Black is forced to make the first break.

18 BxB	QRxB!

One is immediately tempted to say "wrong Rook" but on 18 . . . KRxB White plays 19 N-B5, and if N-N4 20 NxQ NxQch 21 PxN RxN 22 R-K8ch RxR 23 RxRch K-R2 24 R-QR8 R-K2 25 K-B1 Black is lost.

19 Q-B4	. . .

Threatening to dislodge the Knight with P-KB3. Black cannot afford to sit and wait.

19 . . .	Q-Q3
20 QxQ	PxQ

NxQ is the only safe line, but hardly promising. White could play a pleasant endgame simply by con-centrating on the weak Queenside Pawns.

21 P-QB4	N-B3
22 R-QB1	R-N1

Why?

23 PxP	PxP

And that beautiful Queen's Bishop's file now has White's name engraved on it.

24 P-B3	N-R4
25 R-B6	N-B5
26 R-Q2	KR-K1
27 RxP	R-K8ch

Black erroneously feels he has enough initiative to sacrifice a few Pawns. As will be seen, he is wrong.

28 K-B2	R-KR8
29 K-N3	N-R4ch
30 K-R4	P-N3
31 RxP	R-K1

Reporters at the scene tried to glamorize this game as a last desperate counterattack by Petrosian (Bastogne?) but the reality is that it is a cheap shot and he should resign.

32 RxP	R(1)-K8
33 N-B3	N-B5
34 K-N4	N-K3

35 R-K5	P-B4ch
36 K-N3	P-B5ch
37 K-R4	K-R2
38 N-K4	P-N4ch
39 K-N4	N-N2
40 NxPch	. . .

Thematic simplification.

40 . . .	PxN
41 RxR	RxR
42 KxP	. . .

Has Petrosian ever tried to stop 6 Pawns with a Knight? He tries. . . .

42 . . .	N-K3ch
43 K-B5	R-K7
44 RxR	NxPch
45 K-K5	NxR
46 P-QR4	Resigns

The final position, as published on the front page of *The New York Times*. Next stop, Spassky.

GAME 85

Fischer began the first game of his "Match of the Century" by arriving seven minutes late at the board, and then playing his moves in rapid-fire succession. After an early exchange of Queens and then of minor and major pieces, the game appeared to be drifting into a draw. On his 29th move, however, Fischer—perhaps through stress—miscalculated and tallied his fourth lifetime loss against Spassky.

WORLD'S CHAMPIONSHIP MATCH 1972

Reykjavik, Iceland

Game 1

NIMZO-INDIAN DEFENSE

Boris Spassky	*Robert J. Fischer*
WHITE	BLACK
1 P-Q4	...

Spassky's last two triumphs over Fischer, Seigen 1970 and Santa Monica 1966, had been Queen's Pawn openings. He initiates the formula once again.

1 ...	N-KB3
2 P-QB4	P-K3

Saving the Gruenfeld, perhaps, for a future attempt.

3 N-KB3	P-Q4
4 N-B3	B-N5

4 ... O-O is followed by 5 Q-N3 P-B4 6 PxBP N-R3 7 B-Q2 with good chances for White.

| 5 P-K3 | ... |

According to Pachman, 5 Q-R4ch is strong.

5 ...	O-O
6 B-Q3	P-B4
7 O-O	N-B3
8 P-QR3	B-R4
9 N-K2	...

Or 9 BPxP KPxP 10 PxP BxN 11 PxB with opportunities and weaknesses for both sides.

9 ...	QPxP
10 BxP	B-N3
11 PxP	...

Avoiding the *isolani* but allowing Black to enter an even endgame.

11 ...	QxQ
12 RxQ	BxP
13 P-QN4	B-K2
14 B-N2	B-Q2

Preparing for more active and immediate use of his Rooks.

15 QR-B1	KR-Q1
16 N(2)-Q4	NxN
17 NxN	...

17 BxN is met with ... B-R5 and White's target square, Q1, becomes weak.

17 ...	B-R5
18 B-N3	BxB
19 NxB	RxRch
20 RxR	R-QB1

Attempting to prove the superiority of the QB file over White's domination of the Q file.

21 K-B1	K-B1
22 K-K2	N-K5
23 R-QB1	RxR
24 BxR	...

White keeps his Knight closer to the center of action with the threat of N-R5.

24 ...	P-B3
25 N-R5	N-Q3
26 K-Q3	B-Q1
27 N-B4	B-B2
28 NxN	BxN
29 P-N5	...

Placing his pawns on white squares to avoid the eventual attack of the black-squared Bishop.

| 29 ... | BxKRP? |

An incredible blunder caused by Fischer's overenthusiastic attempt to win an obviously drawn game. He overlooked that after 30 P-N3 P-KR4 31 K-K2 P-R5 32 K-B3 P-R6 33 K-N4 B-N8 34 KxP BxP White cuts off the escape of Black's Bishop by playing 35 B-Q2.

30 P-N3	P-KR4
31 K-K2	P-R5
32 K-B3	K-K2

Black attempts to speed his King to the Queenside. Another possibility is this line: 32 ... P-N4 33 K-N2 P-N5 34 KxB P-R6 35 P-K4 K-K2 36 P-B3 P-B4 37 PxBP PxBP 38

PxP PxP 39 B-K3 P-N3 40 K-N1 K-Q3 41 K-B1 K-Q4 42 B-N1 K-B5 43 K-K2 KxP 44 K-K3 K-R5 45 K-B4 KxP 46 KxP P-R7 47 BxP P-N4 48 K-B5 P-N5 49 P-N4 P-N6 50 B-K5 P-N7 51 BxPch KxB 52 P-N5 P-R4 53 P-N6 P-R5 54 P-N7 P-R6 55 P-N8(Q) P-R7 draw.

33 K-N2	PxP
34 PxP	BxP
35 KxB	K-Q3
36 P-R4	...

If 36 P-K4 K-B4 37 B-K3ch KxP 38 BxP K-B5 and Black has drawing chances.

36 ...	K-Q4
37 B-R3	K-K5
38 B-B5	P-R3

38 ... P-N3 loses to 39 BxP followed by 40 P-R5.

| 39 P-N6 | P-B4 |
| 40 K-R4 | P-B5 |

Petrosian suggests 40 ... K-Q4 41 B-Q4 P-K4 42 B-B3 P-B5 43 PxP PxP 44 K-N4 K-B4, and after 45 P-R5, Black journeys to QR1, via B1, allowing White to win his two Kingside Pawns and establishing a drawn position.

| 41 PxP | ... |

White had sealed his 41st move assuming 35 minutes on his clock, since five hours of play had not been completed at that moment.

| 41 ... | KxP |
| 42 K-R5 | K-B4 |

Black tries to maintain the opposition to prevent White from approaching the Queenside.

43 B-K3	K-K5
44 B-B2	K-B4
45 B-R4	...

Black is almost in zugzwang.

| 45 ... | P-K4 |

| 46 | B-N5 | P-K5 |
| 47 | B-K3 | K-B3 |

There is no other move.

48	K-N4	K-K4
49	K-N5	K-Q4
50	K-B5	P-R4
51	B-B2	P-N4

52	KxP	K-B5
53	K-B5	K-N5
54	KxP	KxP
55	K-Q5	K-N4
56	K-Q6	...

Heading for QB7 and the win.

| 56 | ... | Resigns |

GAME 86

Fischer continued his camera protest in this game, and play commenced in a private room out of view of the audience. The result was the best-played game of the match. After 12 years, since first meeting Spassky over the board, Fischer finally scores his first victory, in superb fashion.

WORLD'S CHAMPIONSHIP MATCH 1972

Reykjavik, Iceland

Game 3

BENONI DEFENSE

Boris Spassky	Robert J. Fischer
WHITE	BLACK
1 P-Q4	N-KB3
2 P-QB4	P-K3
3 N-KB3	P-B4

Fischer had adopted the Benoni on only 9 previous occasions throughout his tournament career.

4 P-Q5	PxP
5 PxP	P-Q3
6 N-B3	P-KN3

Nimzovich suggested 6 . . . B-N5 here to exchange Black's Queen Bishop for White's Knight, to reduce the White Knight's energetic influence on K5.

| 7 N-Q2 | ... |

7 P-K4 is more frequently played.

| 7 ... | QN-Q2 |

Avoiding the continuation 7 . . . B-N2 8 N-B4 O-O 9 B-B4 N-K1 with difficulties for Black, as in Van den Berg-Korchnoi, Wijk aan Zee 1971.

| 8 P-K4 | ... |

On 8 P-KN3, there follows . . . B-N2 9 B-N2 O-O 10 O-O Q-K2 11 P-KR3 P-N3 12 P-QR4 B-QR3 13 R-K1, with an even game as in Donner-Petrosian, Göteborg 1955.

8 ...	B-N2
9 B-K2	O-O
10 O-O	R-K1
11 Q-B2	...

Tal suggests 11 P-KB4, followed by 12 B-KB3.

| 11 ... | N-R4 |

Unorthodox but sharp in taking advantage of White's Queen off the Q1-R5 diagonal, and to trade

White's Bishop, removing his control over the white squares. Spassky studied this move for 30 minutes before replying.

12 BxN   PxB
13 N-B4   . . .

If 13 P-B4 B-Q5ch 14 K-R1 N-B3, etc.

13 . . .   N-K4
14 N-K3   . . .

With an eye on KB5. 14 NxN may have been better.

14 . . .   Q-R5
15 B-Q2   N-N5

On 15 . . . N-B6ch 16 PxN B-K4 17 KR-B1.

16 NxN   PxN
17 B-B4   Q-B3
18 P-KN3   B-Q2
19 P-QR4   P-N3

Black solidifies his Pawn structure on his Queenside while he makes plans to initiate a Kingside attack.

20 KR-K1   P-QR3
21 R-K2   P-N4
22 QR-K1   . . .

On 22 PxP PxP 23 RxR RxR 24 P-K5 R-R8ch becomes difficult to meet.

22 . . .   Q-N3
23 P-N3   R-K2

Beginning to mount pressure on White's KP.

24 Q-Q3   R-N1
25 PxP   PxP
26 P-N4   . . .

A lovely defense in blockading Black's Pawns.

26 . . .   P-B5

If 26 . . . PxP, there follows 27 N-R2 R-QB1 28 NxP R-B5 29 N-B6

with a slightly favorable position for White.

27 Q-Q2   R(1)-K1
28 R-K3   P-R4

If 28 . . . BxN 29 QxB RxP 30 RxR RxR 31 RxR QxR 32 Q-B6 and Black has problems.

29 R(3)-K2   K-R2
30 R-K3   K-N1
31 R(3)-K2   . . .

White would be satisfied with a draw. He forces Black to show his hand and speculate on a breakthrough.

31 . . .   BxN

32 QxB   RxP
33 RxR   RxR
34 RxR   QxR
35 B-R6   . . .

35 BxP? is met with . . . QxP followed by Q-Q8ch and B-B3ch.

35 . . .   Q-N3
36 B-B1   Q-N8
37 K-B1   . . .

Trying to extricate himself from future mating threats.

37 . . .   B-B4
38 K-K2   Q-K5ch
39 Q-K3   Q-B7ch

If 39 ... QxP 40 Q-N5ch.

40 Q-Q2	Q-N6
41 Q-Q4	...

The game was adjourned at this point with Fischer sealing. When they returned the next day, Spassky looked at the sealed move and re-

signed without making a further move.

41 ...	B-Q6ch!

Resigns

If 42 K-K3 Q-Q8 quickly leads to mate.

GAME 87

Fischer is a specialist in the vagaries of the Sicilian—on either the White or Black side—Spassky plays it somewhat less often. Here is their first joint experience, resulting in a lively and complex draw, worthy of a Championship battle.

WORLD'S CHAMPIONSHIP MATCH 1972

Reykjavik, Iceland

Game 4

SICILIAN DEFENSE

Robert J. Fischer   *Boris Spassky*

WHITE	BLACK
1 P-K4	P-QB4
2 N-KB3	P-Q3
3 P-Q4	PxP
4 NxP	N-KB3
5 N-B3	N-B3
6 B-QB4	...

The Sozin, Fischer's favorite variation against the Sicilian. He has played and won with this move many times over the years.

| 6 ... | P-K3 |
| 7 B-N3 | ... |

To prevent the simplifying 7 ... NxP 8 NxN P-Q4.

7 ...	B-K2
8 B-K3	O-O
9 O-O	...

9 Q-K2 P-QR3 10 O-O-O Q-B2 11

P-N4 N-Q2 12 P-KR4, tried by Fischer against Larsen, Palma de Majorca 1970, deteriorated into a weak position for White.

9 ...	P-QR3
10 P-B4	NxN
11 BxN	P-QN4
12 P-QR3	B-N2
13 Q-Q3	P-QR4

An obviously prepared and aggressive move, sacrificing a Pawn for open lines. Fischer accepts the challenge but not without first improving his position slightly.

| 14 P-K5 | ... |

14 QR-K1 may have been steadier.

14 ...	PxP
15 PxP	N-Q2
16 NxP	N-B4
17 BxN	...

Allowing Black to dominate two

major diagonals, Fischer keeps his white-squared Bishop for the defense of his Queenside Pawns. 17 Q-K3 was to be considered.

17 ...	BxBch
18 K-R1	Q-N4

The exchange of Queens favors White in the endgame.

18 Q-K2	...

Holding the Pawn, protecting against the mate, and preparing for QR-Q1.

19 ...	QR-Q1
20 QR-Q1	RxR
21 RxR	P-R4!

Initiating a Kingside attack is Black's most logical plan.

22 N-Q6	B-R1
23 B-B4	...

Trying to get his Bishop centralized.

23 ...	P-KR5
24 P-R3	B-K6
25 Q-N4	...

25 ... Q-N6 had to be prevented.

25 ...	QxP
26 QxRP	P-N4!

Undaunted, Black continues with his assault.

27 Q-N4	B-B4

If 27 ... R-Q1 28 NxP RxRch 29 QxR KxN 30 Q-Q7ch with a perpetual check.

28 N-N5	K-N2
29 N-Q4	R-R1?

In heavy time trouble, Spassky plays an inferior continuation. 29 ... R-Q1 is to the point. If 30 N-B5ch K-B3!

30 N-B3	BxN
31 QxB	B-Q3
32 Q-B3	QxQ
33 PxQ	B-K4
34 R-Q7	K-B3
35 K-N1	BxP

If 35 ... R-QB1 36 B-K2 threatening 37 B-R5.

36 B-K2	B-K4
37 K-B1	R-QB1
38 B-R5	R-B2
39 RxR	BxR

Except in rare cases, and this is not one, a win is not possible with Bishops of opposite color and even material.

40 P-QR4	K-K2
41 K-K2	P-B4
42 K-Q3	B-K4
43 P-B4	K-Q3
44 B-B7	B-N6
45 P-B5ch	Drawn

GAME 88

To play an opening for the first time in one's life during a match for the World's Championship takes self-confidence and courage. In this game, Fischer avoids his beloved King's Pawn opening and wanders into Spassky's milieu. The result is total defeat for the Russian.

WORLD'S CHAMPIONSHIP MATCH 1972

Reykjavik, Iceland

Game 6

QUEEN'S GAMBIT DECLINED

Robert J. Fischer	Boris Spassky
WHITE	BLACK
1 P-QB4	P-K3
2 N-KB3	P-Q4
3 P-Q4	. . .

The surprise value alone of this move is not to be underestimated.

3 . . .	N-KB3
4 N-B3	B-K2

An early 4 . . . P-B4, the Tarrasch Defense, has been a favorite of Spassky's in the past.

5 B-N5	O-O
6 P-K3	P-KR3
7 B-R4	. . .

7 BxN BxB 8 Q-Q2 P-QN3 9 PxP PxP 10 P-QN4 B-N2 11 R-QN1 P-B3 12 B-Q3 gives White a solid position as in Petrosian-Spassky, 20th match game, Moscow 1969.

7 . . .	P-QN3
8 PxP	NxP
9 BxB	QxB
10 NxN	. . .

10 R-B1 B-N2 11 NxN BxN avoids weakening Black's Pawn structure and is not as favorable as the text.

10 . . .	PxN
11 R-B1	B-K3
12 Q-R4	P-QB4
13 Q-R3	R-B1
14 B-N5	. . .

Not 14 B-K2 as . . . N-Q2 allows Black defensive outlets. The text, Furman-Geller, USSR 1970, attempts to exchange White's Bishop for the Black Knight, with a view toward undermining Black's Pawn structure.

14 . . .	P-QR3
15 PxP	PxP

If 15 . . . RxP 16 O-O, White gains a valuable tempo.

16 O-O	R-R2
17 B-K2	N-Q2
18 N-Q4	Q-B1

Correct, since the more natural 18 . . . N-B3 is countered with 19 N-N3 and Black must defend both QB and QR Pawns.

19 NxB	PxN
20 P-K4!	. . .

An energetic assault on Black's Pawn mass.

20 ...	P-Q5
21 P-B4	Q-K2
22 P-K5	...

Cementing Black's backward King Pawn to its weak square.

| 22 ... | R-N1 |
| 23 B-B4 | ... |

If Black hits the Bishop with 23 ... N-N3, White retaliates with the sharp Q-N3!

| 23 ... | K-R1 |
| 24 Q-R3 | N-B1 |

Black cannot play 24 ... RxP as after 25 BxP, White's attack is irresistible.

25 P-QN3	P-QR4
26 P-B5	PxP
27 RxP	N-R2
28 R(1)-B1	...

If 28 R-B7, Black counters with ... N-N4.

28 ...	Q-Q1
29 Q-N3	R-K2
30 P-KR4	...

Preparing for R-B7 by keeping Black's Knight from KN4.

30 ...	R(1)-N2
31 P-K6	R(N)-B2
32 Q-K5	Q-K1

If 32 ... P-Q6 33 R(5)-B3 not only stops the Pawn but wins the game.

33 P-R4	Q-Q1
34 R(1)-B2	Q-K1
35 R(2)-B3	Q-Q1
36 B-Q3	Q-K1

36 ... R-B3 is impossible because of 37 Q-K4.

37 Q-K4	N-B3
38 RxN!	PxR
39 RxP	K-N1
40 B-B4	...

Preparing for 41 R-B7.

| 40 ... | K-R1 |
| 41 Q-B4 | Resigns |

If, e.g., 41 ... K-N1   42 Q-N3ch.

GAME 89

Unplayed in World's Championship matches since Euwe adopted it in his 29th match game against Alekhine in 1935, Alekhine's Defense had only been played by Fischer on five previous occasions. Here we see a potpourri of talents forcefully exhibited by both players: cunning, technique, drive and patience. The loss of this marathon contest produced a psychological shock from which Spassky never really recovered.

WORLD'S CHAMPIONSHIP MATCH 1972

Reykjavik, Iceland

Game 13

ALEKHINE'S DEFENSE

Boris Spassky	*Robert J. Fischer*
WHITE	BLACK
1 P-K4	N-KB3
2 P-K5	N-Q4
3 P-Q4	P-Q3
4 N-KB3	. . .

Spassky has tried the bolder 4 P-QB4 N-N3 5 P-B4, e.g., Spassky-Kopylov, USSR 1959, with success. On 4 B-QB4 N-N3 5 B-N3 PxP 6 Q-B3 P-K3 7 PxP P-QR4!

4 . . .	P-KN3
5 B-QB4	. . .

In his near-loss against Browne (Rovinj-Zagreb, 1970), Fischer faced 5 B-K2 and replied . . . B-N2 6 P-B4 N-N3 7 PxP BPxP 8 N-B3 O-O 9 O-O N-B3 10 B-K3 B-N5 11 P-QN3 P-Q4 with a good game.

5 . . .	N-N3
6 B-N3	B-N2
7 QN-Q2	O-O
8 P-KR3	. . .

Somewhat slow.

8 . . .	P-QR4
9 P-QR4	. . .

To meet the threat of 9 . . . P-R5, Reshevsky suggested 9 P-QR3 which also allows a flight square for the Bishop at QR2.

9 . . .	PxP
10 PxP	N-R3
11 O-O	N-B4
12 Q-K2	Q-K1!

White's Queen Rook Pawn cannot be saved.

13 N-K4	N(3)xP
14 BxN	NxB
15 R-K1	. . .

If 15 Q-B4, Black plays . . . B-Q2 16 QxP B-QB3! with superiority.

15 . . .	N-N3
16 B-Q2	P-R5

Black is now a full Pawn ahead with barely recognizable compensation for White.

17 B-N5	P-R3
18 B-R4	B-B4
19 P-KN4	. . .

White must attempt some counterplay. This is a beginning.

19 ...	B-K3
20 N-Q4	B-B5
21 Q-Q2	Q-Q2
22 QR-Q1	KR-K1
23 P-B4	...

The Pawn storm is courageous.

23 ...	B-Q4
24 N-QB5	Q-B1
25 Q-B3	...

25 P-K6 is met with ... N-B5 followed by 26 ... N-Q3 or P-R6.

25 ...	P-K3
26 K-R2	N-Q2
27 N-Q3	...

27 N-N5 was more aggressive.

| 27 ... | P-QB4 |

| 28 N-N5 | Q-B3 |
| 29 N-Q6 | QxN! |

Establishing an excellent, if not won, endgame.

| 30 PxQ | BxQ |
| 31 PxB | P-B3 |

Perhaps over–ambitious. 31 ... P-R6 was sounder.

32 P-N5	RPxP
33 PxP	P-B4
34 B-N3	K-B2
35 N-K5ch	NxN
36 BxN	...

With a Pawn advantage, Black has excellent chances despite Bishops of opposite colors.

| 36 ... | P-N4 |
| 37 R-KB1 | ... |

Threatening R-B4-R4 and the check on R-R7 is difficult to meet.

| 37 ... | R-R1! |
| 38 B-B6! | ... |

If 38 BxR RxB and Black disposes of White's passed Queen Pawn and secures an easy win.

38 ...	P-R6
39 R-B4	P-R7
40 P-B4	...

40 R-QR1 hints at drawing chances. The text is inferior.

| 40 ... | BxP |
| 41 P-Q7 | B-Q4 |

Spassky sealed at this point and came up with the only continuation.

| 42 K-N3! | ... |

Threatening 43 R-KR4 and if 43 ... RxR 44 KxR and Black must give up the other Rook to capture the queening Pawn. Moving the Rook for Black gains at least a perpetual check for White with R-R7ch, etc.

| 42 ... | R-R6ch |

The only continuation that continues the fight.

43 P-B3	R(1)-R1
44 R-KR4	P-K4!
45 R-R7ch	K-K3
46 R-K7ch	K-Q3
47 RxP	RxPch
48 K-B2	R-B7ch
49 K-K1	...

White plays all forced but best moves.

49 ...	KxP
50 R(5)xBch	K-B3
51 R-Q6ch	K-N2
52 R-Q7ch	K-R3

Avoiding White's B-Q8ch, Black races to the aid of his three passed Pawns.

53 R(7)-Q2	RxR
54 KxR	P-N5
55 P-R4!	K-N4
56 P-R5	P-QB5
57 R-QR1	...

To counterbalance 58 . . . P-B6ch and P-R8(Q).

57 ...	PxP
58 P-N6	P-R5

Working both wings.

59 P-N7	P-R6
60 B-K7	...

White intends to enter KB8 with his Bishop.

60 ...	R-KN1
61 B-B8	P-R7
62 K-B2	K-B3

Black flees to the other side of the board to initiate further threats.

63 R-Q1	P-N6ch
64 K-B3	P-KR8(Q)

To allow the Black King to cross over his own Queen's file.

65 RxQ	K-Q4
66 K-N2	P-B5
67 R-Q1ch	K-K5
68 R-QB1	K-Q6
69 R-Q1ch??	...

Spassky not only ruined any chances he had in this particular game, but he wrecked all hopes of retaining his title after making this one colossal blunder. The drawing continuation is as follows: 69 R-B3ch K-Q5 70 R-B3 P-B6ch 71 K-R1 P-B7 72 RxPch K-B6 73 B-N4ch K-Q6 74 B-R3 RxP 75 R-B3ch K-B5 76 R-B4ch K-Q4 77 R-B1 K-K5 78 B-B1! R-Q2 79 K-N2 R-Q8 80 R-B4ch K-Q6 81 R-QR4 RxB 82 KxR K-B6 83 RxP and draw.

69 ...	K-K7!
70 R-QB1	P-KB6
71 B-B5	RxP
72 RxP	R-Q2

Threatening R-Q7ch.

73 R-K4ch	K-B1
74 B-Q4	P-B7
Resigns	

GAME 90

With the score 11½–8½ in favor of Fischer, Spassky was compelled to play for a win in this final game of the World's Championship. Fischer needed two draws or a win to take the title. The result is a fighting, sacrificial game, where Spassky errs in the final hour.

WORLD'S CHAMPIONSHIP MATCH 1972

Reykjavik, Iceland

Game 21

SICILIAN DEFENSE

Boris Spassky	*Robert J. Fischer*
WHITE	BLACK
1 P-K4	P-QB4
2 N-KB3	P-K3

Once again in this match, Fischer varies from his preferred lines, in this case 2 . . . P-Q3.

| 3 P-Q4 | PxP |
| 4 NxP | . . . |

The Paulsen variation.

| 4 . . . | P-QR3 |
| 5 N-QB3 | . . . |

5 B-Q3 is more fluid but Spassky prefers the text.

| 5 . . . | N-QB3 |
| 6 B-K3 | . . . |

More popular is 6 P-KN3 KN-K2 7 N(4)-K2 N-N3 8 B-N2 B-B4 9 O-O P-N4 10 N-B4 B-N2 as in Kapengut-Taimanov, Leningrad, 1971, with good chances for Black.

6 . . .	N-B3
7 B-Q3	P-Q4
8 PxP	PxP

8 . . . NxP avoids the isolated Pawn but 9 N(4)xN PxN 10 B-Q4, White has the advantage.

| 9 O-O | B-Q3 |

| 10 NxN | PxN |
| 11 B-Q4 | O-O |

If 11 . . . P-B4? 12 BxN and the Black Queen Pawn falls.

| 12 Q-B3 | B-K3 |

Discarded by Fischer is the risky but plucky 12 . . . N-N5, which Gligoric states is premature. There follows 13 P-KR3 Q-R5 14 KR-K1 N-R7 with complications.

13 KR-K1	P-B4
14 BxN	QxB
15 QxQ	PxQ
16 QR-Q1	KR-Q1

Meeting the threats of 17 B-B4 or 17 B-K4.

| 17 B-K2 | QR-N1 |
| 18 P-QN3 | . . . |

The tempting 18 NxP proves to be a blunder, e.g., . . . BxN 19 RxB BxPch winning the Exchange.

| 18 . . . | P-B5 |
| 19 NxP! | . . . |

Now White sacrifices rather than loses the Exchange.

19 . . .	BxN
20 RxB	BxPch
21 KxB	RxR
22 BxP	R-Q7

| 23 | BxP | RxQBP |
| 24 | R-K2 | ... |

Forced to avoid loss of material.

| 24 | ... | RxR |
| 25 | BxR | R-Q1 |

With the threat of R-Q7.

| 26 | P-QR4 | R-Q7 |
| 27 | B-B4 | R-R7 |

A loss quickly follows 27 . . . RxP because of 28 P-R5 R-R7 29 P-R6 K-B1 30 P-N4 R-R5 31 P-N5 RxB 32 P-R7 R-R5 33 P-N6, etc.

28	K-N3	K-B1
29	K-B3	K-K2
30	P-KN4	P-B4
31	PxP	P-B3

Establishing a potentially dangerous passed Pawn.

32	B-N8	P-R3
33	K-N3	K-Q3
34	K-B3	R-R8
35	K-N2 ·	...

Responding to the threat of 35 . . . R-KN8 to isolate the White King from the Black passed Pawn.

35	...	K-K4
36	B-K6	K-B5
37	B-Q7	R-N8
38	B-K6	R-N7

Establishing a zugzwang.

39	B-B4	R-R7
40	B-K6	P-R4
	Resigns	

Spassky sealed 41 B-Q7. If his move had been 41 K-R3, there would have been drawing chances. The World's Championship was awarded to Bobby Fischer.

BOBBY FISCHER

TOURNAMENT AND MATCH RECORD

1955	Result
Brooklyn Chess Club Championship	3rd–5th
U.S. Amateur Championship, New Jersey	minus score
U.S. Junior Championship, Nebraska	10th–20th

1956

Greater New York City Championship	5th–7th
Manhattan Chess Club, "A" Reserve	1st
U.S. Amateur Championship, New Jersey	21st
U.S. Junior Championship, Philadelphia	1st
U.S. Open Championship, Oklahoma	4th–8th
Canadian Open Championship, Montreal	8th–12th
Eastern States Championship, Washington	2nd

1956–1957

Rosenwald Trophy Tournament, New York	8th

1957

Log Cabin Open Championship, New Jersey	6th
Western Open Championship, Milwaukee	7th
U.S. Junior Championship, San Francisco	1st
U.S. Open Championship, Cleveland	1st
Eight-game match with Cardoso, New York	Won 6–2
New Jersey Open Championship	1st
North Central Championship, Milwaukee	6th

1957–1958

U.S. Championship, New York	1st

1958

Interzonal, Portoroz	5th–6th
Four-game match with Matulovic, Belgrade	Won 2½–1½

1958–1959

U.S. Championship, New York	1st

1959

Mar del Plata, Argentina	3rd–4th
Santiago, Chile	4th–7th
Zurich, Switzerland	3rd–4th
Candidates Tournament, Yugoslavia	5th–6th

1959–1960

U.S. Championship, New York	1st

1960

Mar del Plata, Argentina	1st
Buenos Aires	13th
Reykjavik, Iceland	1st
Olympic Team Tournament, Leipzig (First Board)	High-scorer, finals

1960–1961

U.S. Championship, New York	1st

1961

Sixteen-game match with Reshevsky, New York and Los Angeles (uncompleted)	5½–5½
Bled, Yugoslavia	2nd

1962

Interzonal, Stockholm	1st
Candidates Tournament, Curaçao	4th
Olympic Team Tournament, Varna (First Board)	High-scorer, preliminaries

1962–1963

U.S. Championship, New York	1st

1963

Western Open, Michigan	1st
New York State Open Tournament	1st

1963–1964

U.S. Championship, New York	1st

1965

Capablanca Memorial, Havana, Cuba	2nd–4th

1965–1966

U.S. Championship, New York	1st

1966

Piatigorsky Cup, Los Angeles	2nd
Olympic Team Tournament, Havana (First Board)	2nd-High-scorer

1966–1967

U.S. Championship, New York	1st

1967

Monaco	1st
Skopje, Yugoslavia	1st
Interzonal, Sousse	withdrew

1968

Netanya, Israel	1st
Vinkovci, Yugoslavia	1st

1970

U.S.S.R. vs. Rest of the World (Second Board)	3–1
Rovinj-Zagreb	1st
Buenos Aires	1st
Olympic Team Tournament, Seigen (First Board)	2nd
Interzonal, Palma de Majorca	1st

1971

Six-game match with Taimanov, Vancouver	Won 6–0
Six-game match with Larsen, Denver	Won 6–0
Nine-game match with Petrosian, Buenos Aires	Won 6½–2½

1972

World's Championship: Twenty-one-game match with Spassky, Reykjavík	Won 12½–8½

INDEX OF PLAYERS

CROSSTABLES OF MAJOR TOURNAMENTS

OF

BOBBY FISCHER

THIRD LESSING J. ROSENWALD 1956

New York, N.Y.

		1	2	3	4	5	6	7	8	9	0	1	2	
1	Reshevsky	x	1	½	1	1	0	1	1	½	1	1	1	**9**
2	Bisguier	0	x	½	½	0	½	1	1	1	½	1	1	**7**
3	Feuerstein	½	½	x	0	1	0	0	½	1	1	1	1	**6½**
4	Mednis	0	½	1	x	1	1	1	½	½	0*	½	½	**6½**
5	Bernstein	0	1	0	0	x	1	0	½	1	½	1	½	**5½**
6	D Byrne	1	½	1	0	0	x	1	0	0	1	0	1	**5½**
7	Turner	0	0	1	0	1	0	x	1	0	1	1	½	**5½**
8	Fischer	0	0	½	½	½	1	0	x	1	0	½	½	**4½**
9	Seidman	½	0	0	½	0	1	1	0	x	0	½	1	**4½**
10	Hearst	0	½	0	0*	½	0	0	1	1	x	0	1	**4**
11	Pavey	0	0	0	½	0	1	0	½	½	1	x	½	**4**
12	Shainswit	0	0	0	½	½	0	½	½	0	0	½	x	**2½**

MANHATTAN CHESS CLUB CHAMPIONSHIP 1956–1957
(SEMI-FINALS)

New York, N.Y.

		1	2	3	4	5	6	
1	Pavey	x	½	½	1	1	1	**4**
2	Turner	½	x	½	1	1	½	**3½**
3	Vine	½	½	x	½	1	1	**3½**
4	Fischer	0	0	½	x	1	1	**2½**
5	Tamargo	0	0	0	0	x	1	**1**
6	Baron	0	½	0	0	0	x	**½**

U.S. CHAMPIONSHIP 1957–1958
New York, N.Y.

		1	2	3	4	5	6	7	8	9	0	1	2	3	4	
1	Fischer	x	½	1	1	½	½	1	1	½	1	1	1	½	1	**10½**
2	Reshevsky	½	x	0	0	1	1	1	½	1	½	1	1	1	1	**9½**
3	Sherwin	0	1	x	½	½	1	0	½	½	1	1	1	1	1	**9**
4	Lombardy	0	1	½	x	½	½	½	½	0	1	0	1	1	1	**7½**
5	Berliner	½	0	½	½	x	0	0	½	½	1	1	1	½	1	**7**
6	Denker	½	0	0	½	1	x	0	1	½	0	1	0	1	1	**6½**
7	Feuerstein	0	0	1	½	1	1	x	½	1	0	0	½	½	½	**6½**
8	Mednis	0	½	½	½	½	0	½	x	0	1	½	½	1	1	**6½**
9	Seidman	½	0	½	1	½	½	0	1	x	0	1	0	1	0	**6**
10	Bernstein	0	½	0	0	0	1	1	0	1	x	0	1	½	0	**5**
11	Bisguier	0	0	0	1	0	0	1	½	0	1	x	½	0	1	**5**
12	Di Camillo	0	0	0	0	0	1	½	½	1	0	½	x	0	1	**4½**
13	Turner	½	0	0	0	½	0	½	0	0	½	1	1	x	½	**4½**
14	Kramer	0	0	0	0	0	0	½	0	1	1	0	0	½	x	**3**

INTERZONAL TOURNAMENT 1958
Potoroz, Yugoslavia

		1	2	3	4	5	6	7	8	9	0	1	2	3	4	5	6	7	8	9	0	1	
1	Tal	x	½	1	½	½	½	½	½	0	½	1	1	1	½	½	1	½	1	½	1	1	**13½**
2	Gligoric	½	x	½	½	½	0	½	½	½	1	½	½	1	½	1	1	0	1	1	1	1	**13**
3	Benko	0	½	x	½	1	½	1	½	1	½	½	½	0	1	½	½	½	½	1	1	1	**12½**
4	Petrosian	½	½	½	x	½	½	½	½	1	1	½	½	½	½	½	0	1	1	1	½	1	**12½**
5	Fischer	½	½	0	½	x	0	½	½	½	½	½	½	½	1	½	1	1	½	1	1	1	**12**
6	Olafsson	½	1	½	½	1	x	1	0	½	½	1	½	½	½	0	1	0	0	1	1	1	**12**
7	Averback	½	½	0	½	½	0	x	½	1	½	0	½	½	1	1	1	½	1	½	½	1	**11½**
8	Bronstein	½	½	½	½	½	1	½	x	½	1	½	½	½	½	½	½	1	½	0	½	1	**11½**
9	Matanovic	1	½	0	0	½	½	0	½	x	½	1	½	½	½	½	1	1	½	1	½	1	**11½**
10	Pachman	½	0	½	0	½	½	½	0	½	x	½	½	½	½	1	1	1	½	1	1	1	**11½**
11	Szabo	0	½	½	½	½	0	1	½	0	½	x	1	½	½	0	½	1	1	1	1	1	**11½**
12	Filip	0	½	½	½	½	½	½	½	½	½	0	x	½	½	1	½	½	½	1	1	1	**11**
13	Panno	0	0	1	½	½	½	½	½	½	½	½	½	x	1	½	½	1	½	1	½	½	**11**
14	Sanguinetti	½	½	0	½	0	½	0	½	½	½	½	½	0	x	1	½	1	1	½	1	½	**10**
15	Neikirch	½	0	½	½	½	1	0	½	½	0	1	0	½	0	x	0	½	1	½	1	1	**9½**
16	Larsen	0	0	½	1	0	0	0	½	0	0	½	½	½	½	1	x	1	1	½	0	1	**8½**
17	Sherwin	½	1	½	0	0	1	½	0	0	0	0	½	0	0	½	0	x	1	0	1	1	**7½**
18	Rossetto	0	0	½	0	½	1	0	½	½	½	0	½	½	0	0	0	0	x	1	½	1	**7**
19	Cardoso	½	0	0	0	0	0	½	1	0	0	0	0	0	½	0	½	1	0	x	1	1	**6**
20	de Greiff	0	0	0	½	0	0	½	½	½	0	0	0	½	0	½	1	0	½	0	x	0	**4½**
21	Fuster	0	0	0	0	0	0	0	0	0	0	0	0	½	½	0	0	0	0	0	1	x	**2**

U.S. CHAMPIONSHIP 1958–1959
New York, N.Y.

		1	2	3	4	5	6	7	8	9	0	1	2	
1	Fischer	x	1	1	1	½	½	½	½	½	1	1	1	**8½**
2	Reshevsky	0	x	1	½	½	1	1	½	½	1	½	1	**7½**
3	Sherwin	0	0	x	½	1	1	½	1	1	½	½	½	**6½**
4	Bisguier	0	½	½	x	1	0	½	½	½	1	1	½	**6**
5	D Byrne	½	½	0	0	x	1	1	½	1	½	½	½	**6**
6	Evans	½	0	0	1	0	x	0	1	1	½	1	1	**6**
7	Lombardy	½	0	½	½	0	1	x	1	½	½	½	1	**6**
8	Benko	½	½	0	½	½	0	0	x	1	½	1	1	**5½**
9	R Byrne	½	½	0	½	0	0	½	0	x	½	1	½	**4**
10	Kalme	0	0	½	0	½	½	½	½	½	x	½	½	**4**
11	Mednis	0	½	½	0	½	0	½	0	0	½	x	½	**3**
12	Weinstein	0	0	½	½	½	0	0	0	½	½	½	x	**3**

INTERNATIONAL TOURNAMENT 1959
Santiago, Chile

		1	2	3	4	5	6	7	8	9	0	1	2	3	
1	Ivkov	x	½	1	1	1	1	½	½	0	1	½	1	1	**9**
2	Pachman	½	x	½	1	1	0	1	1	1	½	1	½	1	**9**
3	Pilnik	0	½	x	0	½	½	1	1	1	1	1	1	½	**8**
4	Fischer	0	0	1	x	0	1	½	0	1	1	1	1	1	**7½**
5	Sanguinetti	0	0	½	1	x	½	½	½	½	1	1	1	1	**7½**
6	Sanchez	0	1	½	0	½	x	½	1	½	1	½	1	1	**7½**
7	Flores	½	0	0	½	½	½	x	1	1	0	½	1	½	**6**
8	Jauregui	½	0	0	1	½	0	0	x	1	1	1	0	1	**6**
9	Letelier	1	0	0	0	½	½	0	0	x	½	½	½	½	**4**
10	Romo	0	½	0	0	0	0	1	0	½	x	1	0	1	**4**
11	Ader	½	0	0	0	0	½	½	0	½	0	x	½	1	**3½**
12	Stekel	0	½	0	0	0	0	0	1	½	1	½	x	0	**3½**
13	Souza Mendes	0	0	½	0	0	0	½	0	½	0	0	1	x	**2½**

INTERNATIONAL TOURNAMENT 1959
Mar del Plata, Argentina

		1	2	3	4	5	6	7	8	9	0	1	2	3	4	5	
1	Najdorf	x	½	½	1	½	1	½	1	1	½	1	1	½	1	½	10½
2	Pachman	½	x	1	½	1	½	½	½	1	0	1	1	1	1	1	10½
3	Fischer	½	0	x	½	0	1	1	½	1	½	1	1	1	1	1	10
4	Ivkov	0	½	½	x	1	½	1	1	½	1	½	1	1	½	1	10
5	Letelier·	½	0	1	0	x	1	½	½	0	1	1	1	½	1	1	9
6	Rossetto	0	½	0	½	0	x	½	½	½	1	½	1	1	1	1	8
7	Wexler	½	½	0	0	½	½	x	½	½	½	½	1	½	1	1	7½
8	Sanchez	0	½	½	0	½	½	½	x	1	½	½	½	1	1	0	7
9	Sanguinetti	0	0	0	½	1	½	½	0	x	1	½	½	1	½	1	7
10	Emma	½	1	½	0	0	0	½	½	0	x	1	0	1	0	½	5½
11	Bolbochan	0	0	0	½	0	½	½	½	½	0	x	½	½	1	0	4½
12	Pilnik	0	0	0	0	0	0	0	½	½	1	½	x	0	1	1	4½
13	Shocron	½	0	0	0	½	0	½	0	0	0	½	1	x	0	1	4
14	Souza Mendes	0	0	0	½	0	0	0	0	½	1	0	0	1	x	1	4
15	Redolfi	½	0	0	0	0	0	0	1	0	½	1	0	0	0	x	3

INTERZONAL TOURNAMENT 1959
Zurich, Switzerland

		1	2	3	4	5	6	7	8	9	0	1	2	3	4	5	6	
1	Tal	x	0	½	½	1	1	½	1	1	0	1	1	1	1	1	1	11½
2	Gligoric	1	x	1	0	1	½	0	1	½	1	½	1	1	½	1	1	11
3	Fischer	½	0	x	1	½	1	½	1	1	1	1	0	1	½	½	1	10½
4	Keres	½	1	0	x	½	1	½	½	1	½	1	1	½	1	1	½	10½
5	Larsen	0	0	½	½	x	½	0	1	½	½	1	1	1	1	1	1	9½
6	Unzicker	0	½	0	0	½	x	½	½	1	1	1	½	1	1	1	1	9½
7	Barcza	½	1	½	½	1	½	x	0	0	0	½	1	0	1	1	1	8½
8	Olafsson	0	0	0	½	0	½	1	x	0	1	½	1	1	½	1	1	8
9	Kupper	0	½	0	0	½	0	1	1	x	½	0	½	½	1	½	1	7
10	Bhend	1	0	0	½	½	0	1	0	½	x	1	1	0	0	½	½	6½
11	Donner	0	½	0	0	0	0	½	½	1	0	x	0	1	1	1	1	6½
12	Keller	0	0	1	0	0	½	0	0	½	0	1	x	1	1	1	0	6
13	Duckstein	0	0	0	½	0	0	1	0	½	1	0	0	x	0	1	1	5
14	Walther	0	½	½	0	0	0	0	½	0	1	0	0	1	x	½	1	5
15	Blau	0	0	½	0	0	0	0	0	½	½	0	0	0	½	x	½	2½
16	Nievergelt	0	0	0	½	0	0	0	0	0	½	0	1	0	0	½	x	2½

CANDIDATES TOURNAMENT 1959

Bled-Zagreb-Belgrad, Yugoslavia

		1	2	3	4	5	6	7	8	
1	Tal	xxxx	0010	½½½½	01½1	1111	1½11	111½	111½	**20**
2	Keres	1101	xxxx	0½½½	1½½0	0101	½½11	1110	1111	**18½**
3	Petrosian	½½½½	1½½½	xxxx	½½0½	11½½	0½½1	100½	½11½	**15½**
4	Smyslov	10½0	0½½1	½½1½	xxxx	½½10	0½10	½1½1	½011	**15**
5	Fischer	0000	1010	00½½	½½01	xxxx	10½½	01½1	½1½1	**12½**
6	Gligoric	0½00	½½00	1½½0	1½01	01½½	xxxx	½½10	½1½½	**12½**
7	Olafsson	000½	0001	011½	½0½0	10½0	½½01	xxxx	00½1	**10**
8	Benko	000½	0000	½00½	½100	½0½0	½0½½	11½0	xxxx	**8**

U.S. CHAMPIONSHIP 1959–1960

New York, N.Y.

		1	2	3	4	5	6	7	8	9	0	1	2	
1	Fischer	x	½	½	1	1	½	1	½	1	1	1	1	**9**
2	R Byrne	½	x	½	1	½	1	½	½	1	½	1	1	**8**
3	Reshevsky	½	½	x	½	1	1	0	1	1	1	0	1	**7½**
4	Benko	0	0	½	x	½	1	1	½	½	1	1	1	**7**
5	Bisguier	0	½	0	½	x	½	½	1	½	1	1	1	**6½**
6	Weinstein	½	0	0	0	½	x	1	0	1	1	1	1	**6**
7	Seidman	0	½	1	0	½	0	x	½	1	0	1	1	**5½**
8	Sherwin	½	½	0	½	0	1	½	x	½	0	½	1	**5**
9	Mednis	0	0	0	½	½	0	0	½	x	1	1	1	**4½**
10	Bernstein	0	½	0	0	0	0	1	1	0	x	½	1	**4**
11	Denker	0	0	1	0	0	0	0	½	0	½	x	1	**3**
12	Ault	0	0	0	0	0	0	0	0	0	0	0	x	**0**

INTERNATIONAL TOURNAMENT 1960
Buenos Aires, Argentina

		1	2	3	4	5	6	7	8	9	0	1	2	3	4	5	6	7	8	9	0	
1	Korchnoi	x	½	½	½	1	0	½	½	1	1	½	1	1	½	1	1	½	1	0	1	**13**
2	Reshevsky	½	x	½	0	1	1	½	½	½	½	½	1	½	½	1	1	½	1	1	1	**13**
3	Szabó	½	½	x	1	0	1	1	½	½	½	0	½	½	½	1	½	½	1	1	1	**12**
4	Evans	½	1	0	x	0	1	½	½	½	1	1	½	½	½	0	½	½	1	½	1	**11**
5	Guimard	0	0	1	1	x	0	1	0	½	1	1	1	1	0	1	½	½	0	½	1	**11**
6	Rossetto	1	0	0	0	1	x	½	½	0	½	1	1	1	0	½	1	½	1	½	1	**11**
7	Taimanov	½	½	0	½	0	½	x	½	1	½	1	0	½	½	½	½	1	1	1	1	**11**
8	Unzicker	½	½	½	½	1	½	½	x	½	½	½	½	½	1	0	0	½	1	1	½	**10½**
9	Olafsson	0	½	½	½	½	1	0	½	x	½	1	1	½	½	½	½	½	1	1	0	**10½**
10	Gligoric	0	½	½	0	0	½	½	½	½	x	0	½	½	½	1	1	1	½	1	1	**10**
11	Uhlmann	½	½	1	0	0	0	0	½	0	1	x	0	½	1	½	1	½	0	1	1	**9**
12	Benko	0	0	½	½	0	0	1	½	0	½	1	x	½	1	½	0	1	1	0	1	**9**
13	Ivkov	0	½	½	½	0	0	½	½	½	½	½	½	x	½	1	½	½	½	½	½	**8½**
14	Fischer	½	½	½	½	1	1	½	0	½	½	0	0	½	x	0	½	0	½	1	½	**8½**
15	Wexler	0	0	0	1	0	½	½	1	½	0	½	½	0	1	x	0	1	½	1	½	**8½**
16	Pachman	0	0	½	½	½	0	½	1	½	0	0	1	½	½	1	x	½	0	1	½	**8½**
17	Eliskases	½	½	½	½	½	½	0	½	½	0	½	0	½	1	0	½	x	1	½	0	**8**
18	Bazán	0	0	0	0	1	0	0	0	0	½	1	0	½	½	½	1	0	x	1	0	**6**
19	Wade	1	0	0	½	½	½	0	0	0	0	0	1	½	0	0	0	½	0	x	1	**5½**
20	Foguelman	0	0	0	0	0	0	0	½	1	0	0	0	½	½	½	½	1	1	0	x	**5½**

INTERNATIONAL TOURNAMENT 1960
Mar del Plata, Argentina

		1	2	3	4	5	6	7	8	9	0	1	2	3	4	5	6	
1	Fischer	x	0	½	1	1	1	1	1	1	1	1	1	1	1	1	1	**13½**
2	Spassky	1	x	½	1	1	½	1	1	1	1	1	1	1	1	½	1	**13½**
3	Bronstein	½	½	x	½	1	1	½	1	½	½	½	1	1	1	1	1	**11½**
4	Olafsson	0	0	½	x	1	1	0	1	1	½	½	1	1	1	1	1	**10½**
5	Bazan	0	0	0	0	x	1	½	½	½	1	1	½	1	1	1	1	**9**
6	Wexler	0	½	0	0	0	x	1	½	½	½	1	1	½	1	1	1	**8½**
7	Letelier	0	0	½	1	½	0	x	0	½	1	1	1	0	½	1	1	**8**
8	Foguelman	0	0	0	0	½	½	1	x	0	1	0	0	1	1	1	½	**6½**
9	Incutto	0	0	½	0	½	½	½	1	x	0	½	½	1	½	½	½	**6½**
10	Redolfi	0	0	½	½	0	½	0	0	1	x	1	½	1	0	½	1	**6½**
11	Bielicki	0	0	½	½	0	0	0	1	½	0	x	½	½	1	½	1	**6**
12	Eliskases	0	0	0	0	½	0	0	1	½	½	½	x	½	1	½	1	**6**
13	Alvarez	0	0	0	0	0	½	1	0	0	0	½	½	x	0	½	1	**4**
14	Gadia	0	0	0	0	0	0	½	0	½	1	0	0	1	x	1	0	**4**
15	Marini	0	½	0	0	0	0	0	0	½	½	½	½	½	0	x	1	**4**
16	Saadi	0	0	0	0	0	0	0	½	½	0	0	0	0	1	0	x	**2**

INTERNATIONAL TOURNAMENT 1960
Reykjavik, Iceland

		1	2	3	4	5	
1	Fischer	x	1	1	1	½	3½
2	Johannsson	0	x	½	1	1	2½
3	Olafsson	0	½	x	1	½	2
4	Gudmundsson	0	0	0	x	1	1
5	Thorbergsson	½	0	½	0	x	1

U.S. CHAMPIONSHIP 1960–1961
New York, N.Y.

		1	2	3	4	5	6	7	8	9	0	1	2	
1	Fischer	x	1	1	1	½	1	½	½	1	½	1	1	9
2	Lombardy	0	x	0	½	½	½	1	½	1	1	1	1	7
3	Weinstein	0	1	x	1	1	½	0	½	½	1	½	½	6½
4	Bisguier	0	½	0	x	½	½	1	1	0	1	1	½	6
5	Reshevsky	½	½	0	½	x	½	½	½	1	½	1	½	6
6	Sherwin	0	½	½	½	½	x	½	1	1	0	½	1	6
7	Kalme	½	0	1	0	½	½	x	1	½	0	½	½	5
8	Benko	½	½	½	0	½	0	0	x	½	1	0	1	4½
9	Berliner	0	0	½	1	0	0	½	½	x	0	1	1	4½
10	R. Byrne	½	0	0	0	½	1	1	0	1	x	0	½	4½
11	Saidy	0	0	½	0	0	½	½	1	0	1	x	1	4½
12	Seidman	0	0	½	½	½	0	½	0	0	½	0	x	2½

INTERNATIONAL TOURNAMENT 1961
Bled, Yugoslavia

		1	2	3	4	5	6	7	8	9	0	1	2	3	4	5	6	7	8	9	0	
1	Tal	x	0	½	½	½	½	½	1	1	1	½	1	1	1	½	1	1	1	1	1	14½
2	Fischer	1	x	1	½	½	1	1	½	1	½	½	½	½	1	1	½	½	1	½	½	13½
3	Petrosian	½	0	x	½	1	½	½	1	½	½	½	½	1	1	0	½	1	1	1	1	12½
4	Keres	½	½	½	x	½	½	½	½	0	½	½	1	½	1	1	1	1	½	1	1	12½
5	Gligoric	½	½	0	½	x	½	½	½	1	1	½	½	½	½	½	1	1	1	1	1	12½
6	Geller	½	0	½	½	½	x	½	1	0	½	½	½	½	0	1	1	½	1	1	½	10½
7	Trifunovic	½	0	½	½	½	½	x	½	½	½	½	½	½	½	½	½	1	½	1	1	10½
8	Parma	0	½	0	½	½	0	½	x	½	½	½	½	½	1	½	1	½	½	1	1	10
9	Bisguier	0	0	½	1	0	1	½	½	x	0	½	0	1	0	½	1	½	½	1	1	9½
10	Matanovic	0	½	½	½	0	½	½	½	1	x	½	½	0	1	½	½	0	1	1	½	9½
11	Darga	½	½	½	½	½	½	½	½	½	½	x	½	½	0	½	0	½	1	0	1	9
12	Donner	0	½	½	0	½	½	½	½	1	½	½	x	1	0	½	1	½	0	0	1	9
13	Najdorf	0	½	0	½	½	½	½	½	0	1	½	0	x	1	½	0	½	1	1	½	9
14	Olafsson	0	0	0	0	½	1	½	0	1	0	1	1	0	x	1	½	½	½	½	½	8½
15	Portisch	½	0	1	0	½	0	½	½	½	½	½	½	½	0	x	0	½	½	½	1	8
16	Ivkov	0	½	½	0	0	0	½	0	0	½	1	0	1	½	1	x	1	½	½	½	8
17	Pachman	0	½	0	0	0	½	0	½	½	1	½	½	½	½	½	0	x	½	½	½	7
18	Bertok	0	0	0	½	0	0	½	½	½	0	0	1	0	½	½	½	½	x	½	1	6½
19	Germek	0	½	0	0	0	0	0	0	0	0	1	1	0	½	½	½	½	½	x	½	5½
20	Udovcic	0	½	0	0	0	½	0	0	0	½	0	0	½	½	0	½	½	0	½	x	4

INTERZONAL TOURNAMENT 1962
Stockholm, Sweden

		1	2	3	4	5	6	7	8	9	0	1	2	3	4	5	6	7	8	9	0	1	2	3	
1	Fischer	x	½	½	1	½	½	½	½	1	½	1	½	1	1	1	1	1	1	1	1	½	1	1	**17½**
2	Geller	½	x	½	½	½	1	½	1	1	1	½	0	1	½	1	1	½	1	½	½	1	0	1	**15**
3	Petrosian	½	½	x	½	½	½	½	½	½	½	1	1	½	½	1	½	1	½	1	1	1	½	1	**15**
4	Korchnoi	0	½	½	x	1	½	½	½	0	½	1	1	½	1	1	½	1	½	½	1	1	0	1	**14**
5	Filip	½	½	½	0	x	½	½	1	½	0	½	½	1	1	½	½	½	1	1	½	1	1	1	**14**
6	Benko	½	0	½	½	½	x	½	½	½	1	0	½	½	½	1	1	1	0	1	1	½	1	1	**13½**
7	Gligoric	½	½	½	½	½	½	x	0	½	½	1	½	½	1	0	1	½	1	½	1	½	1	1	**13½**
8	Stein	½	0	½	½	0	½	1	x	1	0	0	½	1	½	½	1	½	1	½	1	1	1	1	**13½**
9	Portisch	0	0	½	1	½	½	½	0	x	1	½	½	½	½	½	1	1	1	0	1	1	1	0	**12½**
10	Uhlmann	½	0	½	½	1	0	½	1	0	x	1	1	½	0	1	1	1	0	1	1	0	1	0	**12½**
11	Olafsson	0	½	0	0	½	1	0	1	½	0	x	½	½	0	½	½	1	½	1	1	1	1	1	**12**
12	Pomar	½	1	0	0	½	½	½	½	½	0	½	x	0	0	1	½	½	1	1	½	1	1	1	**12**
13	Bolbochan	0	0	½	½	0	½	½	0	½	½	½	1	x	½	½	½	½	1	1	½	½	1	1	**11½**
14	Barcza	0	½	½	0	0	½	0	½	½	1	1	1	½	x	½	½	½	½	½	½	1	0	1	**11**
15	Bilek	0	0	0	0	½	0	1	½	½	0	½	0	½	½	x	½	½	1	1	1	1	1	1	**11**
16	Bisguier	0	0	½	½	½	0	0	0	0	0	½	½	½	½	½	x	½	½	1	½	1	1	1	**9½**
17	Bertok	0	½	0	0	½	0	½	½	0	0	0	½	½	½	½	½	x	½	½	0	½	1	½	**7½**
18	Yanofsky	0	0	½	½	0	1	0	0	0	1	½	0	0	½	0	½	½	x	1	½	½	0	½	**7½**
19	German	0	½	0	½	0	0	½	½	1	0	0	0	0	½	0	0	½	0	x	½	½	1	1	**7**
20	Schweber	0	½	0	0	½	0	0	0	0	0	0	½	½	½	0	½	1	½	½	x	1	½	½	**7**
21	Teschner	½	0	0	0	0	½	½	0	0	1	0	0	½	0	0	0	½	½	½	0	x	1	1	**6½**
22	Cuellar	0	1	½	1	0	0	0	0	0	0	0	0	0	1	0	0	0	1	0	½	0	x	½	**5½**
23	Aaron	0	0	0	0	0	0	0	0	1	1	0	0	0	0	0	0	½	½	0	½	0	½	x	**4**

CANDIDATES TOURNAMENT 1962
Curaçao, Dutch West Indies

		1	2	3	4	5	6	7	8	
1	Petrosian	xxxx	½½½½	½½½½	½1½½	½½11	½½1½	11½–	½11½	**17½**
2	Keres	½½½½	xxxx	½½½½	0½1½	½½1½	1110	1½1–	½11½	**17**
3	Geller	½½½½	½½½½	xxxx	11½0	½½1½	½½½1	½11–	½11½	**17**
4	Fischer	½0½½	1½0½	00½1	xxxx	010½	01½1	½1½–	1½1½	**14**
5	Korchnoi	½½00	½½0½	½½0½	101½	xxxx	½½½0	10½–	1111	**13½**
6	Benko	½½0½	0001	½½½0	10½0	½½½1	xxxx	10½–	011½	**12**
7	Tal	00½–	0½0–	½00–	½0½–	01½–	01½–	xxxx	10½–	**7**
8	Filip	½00½	½00½	½00½	0½0½	0000	100½	01½–	xxxx	**7**

U.S. CHAMPIONSHIP 1962–1963
New York, N.Y.

		1	2	3	4	5	6	7	8	9	0	1	2	
1	Fischer	x	1	1	½	1	½	1	0	½	½	1	1	8
2	Bisguier	0	x	1	½	½	½	½	1	½	1	½	1	7
3	Addison	0	0	x	½	1	½	1	1	½	½	1	½	6½
4	Evans	½	½	½	x	½	½	1	½	1	½	0	1	6½
5	Reshevsky	0	½	0	½	x	½	1	1	1	½	1	½	6½
6	R Byrne	½	½	½	½	½	x	½	½	½	1	½	½	6
7	Berliner	0	½	0	0	0	½	x	1	½	½	1	1	5
8	Mednis	1	0	0	½	0	½	0	x	½	1	½	1	5
9	Benko	½	½	½	0	0	½	½	½	x	0	1	½	4½
10	Rossolimo	½	0	½	½	½	0	½	0	1	x	½	½	4½
11	Steinmeyer	0	½	0	1	0	½	0	½	0	½	x	1	4
12	Sherwin	0	0	½	0	½	½	0	0	½	½	0	x	2½

U.S. CHAMPIONSHIP 1963–1964
New York, N.Y.

		1	2	3	4	5	6	7	8	9	0	1	2	
1	Fischer	x	1	1	1	1	1	1	1	1	1	1	1	11
2	Evans	0	x	1	½	½	½	0	1	1	1	1	1	7½
3	Benko	0	0	x	1	½	1	1	1	½	1	½	½	7
4	Saidy	0	½	0	x	0	½	1	1	1	1	½	1	6½
5	Reshevsky	0	½	½	1	x	½	0	½	1	1	1	½	6½
6	R Byrne	0	½	0	½	½	x	0	½	1	1	1	½	5½
7	Weinstein	0	1	0	0	1	1	x	0	0	0	1	1	5
8	Bisguier	0	0	0	0	½	½	1	x	1	0	½	1	4½
9	Addison	0	0	½	0	0	0	1	0	x	½	½	1	3½
10	Mednis	0	0	0	0	0	0	1	1	½	x	½	½	3½
11	Steinmeyer	0	0	½	½	0	0	0	½	½	½	x	½	3
12	D Byrne	0	0	½	0	½	½	0	0	0	½	½	x	2½

INTERNATIONAL TOURNAMENT 1965
Havana, Cuba*

		1	2	3	4	5	6	7	8	9	0	1	2	3	4	5	6	7	8	9	0	1	2	
1	Smyslov	x	0	½	0	½	½	1	½	1	½	1	1	1	1	0	1	1	1	1	1	1	1	**15½**
2	Fischer	1	x	0	0	0	½	1	1	1	½	1	1	½	1	½	½	1	1	½	1	1	1	**15**
3	Geller	½	1	x	½	½	½	½	½	1	1	½	½	½	½	1	½	1	1	½	1	1	1	**15**
4	Ivkov	1	1	½	x	0	½	1	0	1	½	½	½	1	1	1	½	1	1	1	1	0	1	**15**
5	Kholmov	½	1	½	1	x	½	½	½	½	½	½	½	½	1	1	1	½	½	½	1	1	1	**14½**
6	Pachman	½	½	½	½	½	x	1	0	½	½	½	½	½	½	½	½	1	½	1	1	1	1	**13**
7	Donner	0	0	½	0	½	0	x	1	1	½	1	1	1	½	1	½	½	½	½	½	1	1	**12½**
8	Robatsch	½	0	½	1	½	1	0	x	½	½	0	1	½	½	½	½	½	½	½	1	1	1	**12**
9	Bilek	0	0	0	0	½	½	0	½	x	½	½	½	½	½	½	1	1	1	1	1	1	1	**11½**
10	Parma	½	½	0	½	½	½	½	½	½	x	1	0	½	½	1	½	½	½	1	½	½	½	**11**
11	Pietzsch	0	0	½	½	½	½	0	1	½	0	x	0	½	1	½	½	½	½	½	1	1	1	**10½**
12	Szabo	0	0	½	½	½	½	0	0	½	1	1	x	½	½	½	1	0	½	1	1	1	0	**10½**
13	O'Kelly	0	½	½	0	½	½	0	½	½	½	½	½	x	½	½	0	1	½	½	½	1	1	**10**
14	Tringov	0	0	½	0	0	½	½	½	½	½	0	½	½	x	0	½	1	1	1	1	1	½	**10**
15	Jimenez	1	½	0	0	0	½	0	½	½	0	½	½	½	1	x	½	½	½	½	½	1	½	**9½**
16	Ciocaltea	0	½	½	½	0	½	½	½	0	½	½	0	1	½	½	x	½	0	1	0	1	½	**9**
17	Doda	0	0	0	0	½	0	½	½	0	½	½	1	0	0	½	½	x	1	0	1	1	½	**8**
18	Lehmann	0	0	0	0	½	½	½	½	0	½	½	½	½	0	½	1	0	x	1	½	0	½	**7½**
19	Wade	0	½	½	0	½	0	½	½	0	0	½	0	½	0	½	0	1	0	x	½	1	1	**7½**
20	Cobo	0	0	0	0	0	0	½	0	0	½	0	0	½	0	½	1	0	½	½	x	½	1	**5½**
21	G Garcia	0	0	0	1	0	0	0	0	0	½	0	0	0	0	0	0	0	1	0	½	x	1	**4**
22	Perez	0	0	0	0	0	0	0	0	0	½	0	1	0	½	½	½	½	½	0	0	0	x	**4**

* Fischer played in this tournament, via teletype, from the Marshall Chess Club in New York City.

U.S. CHAMPIONSHIP 1965–1966
New York, N.Y.

		1	2	3	4	5	6	7	8	9	0	1	2	
1	Fischer	x	0	0	½	1	1	1	1	1	1	1	1	**8½**
2	R Byrne	1	x	½	½	½	1	0	1	1	½	½	1	**7½**
3	Reshevsky	1	½	x	1	½	½	½	1	0	1	½	1	**7½**
4	Addison	½	½	0	x	½	½	½	1	1	1	1	0	**6½**
5	Zuckerman	0	½	½	½	x	½	1	½	1	½	½	1	**6½**
6	Rossolimo	0	0	½	½	½	x	1	1	0	1	1	½	**6**
7	Benko	0	1	½	½	0	0	x	½	0	½	1	1	**5**
8	Evans	0	0	0	0	½	0	½	x	1	1	1	1	**5**
9	Saidy	0	0	1	0	0	1	1	0	x	½	1	½	**5**
10	Bisguier	0	½	0	0	½	0	½	0	½	x	½	½	**3**
11	Burger	0	½	½	0	½	0	0	0	0	½	x	1	**3**
12	Suttles	0	0	0	1	0	½	0	0	½	½	0	x	**2½**

INTERNATIONAL TOURNAMENT 1966
Santa Monica, Calif.

		1	2	3	4	5	6	7	8	9	10	
1	Spassky	xx	1½	½1	½½	1½	½½	½½	½½	1½	½1	11½
2	Fischer	0½	xx	01	½1	½½	½½	½1	01	11	½1	11
3	Larsen	½0	10	xx	1½	½0	11	½1	1½	01	½0	10
4	Portisch	½½	½0	0½	xx	½½	1½	½½	½½	½1	½1	9½
5	Unzicker	0½	½½	½1	½½	xx	½½	½½	½½	1½	½½	9½
6	Petrosian	½½	½½	00	0½	½½	xx	½½	11	½½	½1	9
7	Reshevsky	½½	½0	½0	½½	½½	½½	xx	½1	½½	1½	9
8	Najdorf	½½	10	0½	½½	½½	00	½0	xx	1½	½1	8
9	Ivkov	0½	00	10	½0	0½	½½	½½	0½	xx	½1	6½
10	Donner	½0	½0	½1	½0	½½	½0	0½	½0	½0	xx	6

U.S. CHAMPIONSHIP 1966–1967
New York, N.Y.

		1	2	3	4	5	6	7	8	9	0	1	2	
1	Fischer	x	½	1	1	1	½	1	½	1	1	1	1	9½
2	Evans	½	x	½	½	1	1	½	½	1	1	0	1	7½
3	Benko	0	½	x	0	1	0	½	1	½	1	1	½	6
4	Sherwin	0	½	1	x	½	1	1	½	½	0	1	0	6
5	Bisguier	0	0	0	½	x	½	1	0	½	1	1	1	5½
6	Addison	½	0	1	0	½	x	1	0	1	½	½	0	5
7	Saidy	0	½	½	0	0	0	x	1	1	½	1	½	5
8	R Byrne	½	½	0	½	1	1	0	x	1	1	0	0	4½
9	Reshevsky	0	0	½	½	½	0	0	½	x	½	1	1	4½
10	Rossolimo	0	0	0	1	0	½	½	½	½	x	½	1	4½
11	D Byrne	0	1	0	0	0	½	0	1	0	½	x	1	4
12	Zuckerman	0	0	½	1	0	1	½	1	0	0	0	x	4

INTERNATIONAL TOURNAMENT 1967
Monte Carlo, Monaco

		1	2	3	4	5	6	7	8	9	0	
1	Fischer	x	½	0	1	½	1	1	1	1	1	**7**
2	Smyslov	½	x	½	½	1	½	½	1	1	1	**6½**
3	Geller	1	½	x	0	½	½	1	½	1	1	**6**
4	Larsen	0	½	1	x	0	1	1	½	1	1	**6**
5	Matanovic	½	0	½	1	x	½	½	½	½	1	**5**
6	Gligoric	0	½	½	0	½	x	½	½	1	1	**4½**
7	Lombardy	0	½	0	0	½	½	x	1	1	1	**4½**
8	Forintos	0	0	½	½	½	½	0	x	1	1	**4**
9	Mazzoni	0	0	0	0	½	0	0	0	x	½	**1**
10	Bergraser	0	0	0	0	0	0	0	0	½	x	**½**

INTERNATIONAL TOURNAMENT 1967
Skopje, Yugoslavia

		1	2	3	4	5	6	7	8	9	0	1	2	3	4	5	6	7	8	
1	Fischer	x	0	1	1	1	1	1	1	½	½	1	1	1	0	1	½	1	1	**13½**
2	Geller	1	x	1	½	1	1	½	1	½	½	½	1	½	½	½	1	1	1	**13**
3	Matulovic	0	0	x	½	1	1	1	1	1	½	½	1	1	1	½	1	1	1	**13**
4	Kholmov	0	½	½	x	½	½	½	½	1	1	1	½	½	½	1	1	1	1	**11½**
5	Bukic	0	0	0	½	x	½	½	1	½	½	½	1	½	1	1	½	½	1	**9½**
6	Maric	0	0	0	½	½	x	½	½	½	½	½	½	½	1	1	½	1	1	**9**
7	Minic	0	½	0	½	½	½	x	½	½	½	½	½	1	0	½	½	1	1	**8½**
8	Damjanovic	0	0	0	½	0	½	½	x	½	1	½	½	0	1	½	1	1	1	**8½**
9	Popov	½	½	0	0	½	½	½	½	x	½	½	0	½	1	1	½	1	½	**8½**
10	Knezevic	½	½	½	0	½	½	½	0	½	x	½	0	½	1	½	1	½	1	**8½**
11	Sofrevski	0	½	½	0	½	½	½	½	½	½	x	1	½	½	½	½	1	0	**8**
12	Dely	0	0	0	½	0	½	½	½	1	1	0	x	1	0	1	1	0	1	**8**
13	Soos	0	½	0	½	½	½	0	1	½	½	½	0	x	1	0	0	1	1	**7½**
14	Janosevic	1	½	0	½	0	0	1	0	0	0	½	1	0	x	1	1	0	1	**7½**
15	Nicevski	0	½	½	0	0	0	½	½	0	½	½	0	1	0	x	½	½	1	**6**
16	Ilievski	½	0	0	0	½	½	½	0	½	0	½	0	1	0	½	x	½	1	**6**
17	Panov	0	0	0	0	½	0	0	0	0	½	0	1	0	1	½	½	x	0	**4**
18	Danov	0	0	0	0	0	0	0	½	0	0	1	0	0	0	0	0	1	x	**2½**

INTERNATIONAL TOURNAMENT 1968
Netanya, Israel

		1	2	3	4	5	6	7	8	9	0	1	2	3	4	
1	Fischer	x	½	1	1	1	1	½	1	1	½	1	1	1	1	**11½**
2	Yanofsky	½	x	½	0	1	½	1	½	½	1	1	½	½	½	**8**
3	Czerniak	0	½	x	1	1	½	½	0	½	½	½	1	1	1	**8**
4	Hamann	0	1	0	x	0	1	0	½	1	1	½	0	1	1	**7**
5	Kagan	0	0	0	1	x	½	½	½	½	1	1	1	0	1	**7**
6	Ciocaltea	0	½	½	0	½	x	1	½	½	½	½	0	1	1	**6½**
7	Kraidman	½	0	½	1	½	0	x	½	1	½	0	0	½	1	**6**
8	Aloni	0	½	1	½	½	½	½	x	0	½	0	1	1	0	**6**
9	Domnitz	0	½	½	0	½	½	0	1	x	½	½	1	0	1	**6**
10	Porath	½	0	½	0	0	½	½	½	½	x	½	1	1	½	**6**
11	Troianescu	0	0	½	½	0	½	1	1	½	½	x	0	0	1	**5½**
12	U Geller	0	½	0	1	0	1	1	0	0	0	1	x	½	0	**5**
13	Ree	0	½	0	0	1	0	½	0	1	0	1	½	x	½	**5**
14	Bernstein	0	½	0	0	0	0	0	1	0	½	0	1	½	x	**3½**

INTERNATIONAL TOURNAMENT 1968
Vinkovci, Yugoslavia

		1	2	3	4	5	6	7	8	9	0	1	2	3	4	
1	Fischer	x	½	1	½	1	½	1	1	½	1	1	1	1	1	**11**
2	Hort	½	x	½	½	½	1	½	1	½	½	½	1	1	1	**9**
3	Matulovic	0	½	x	½	½	1	1	½	1	1	½	1	½	1	**9**
4	Gheorghiu	½	½	½	x	½	½	½	½	½	½	1	1	1	1	**8½**
5	Ivkov	0	½	½	½	x	½	½	½	1	½	1	1	1	1	**8½**
6	D Byrne	½	0	0	½	½	x	0	1	½	1	1	1	1	1	**8**
7	Matanovic	0	½	0	½	½	1	x	½	½	½	1	1	1	½	**7½**
8	Bertok	0	0	½	½	½	0	½	x	½	½	½	1	1	1	**6½**
9	Robatsch	½	½	0	½	0	½	½	½	x	½	½	½	1	1	**6½**
10	Minic	0	½	0	½	½	0	½	½	½	x	½	½	1	1	**6**
11	Wade	0	½	½	0	0	0	0	½	½	½	x	½	1	1	**5**
12	Nikolic	0	0	0	0	0	0	0	0	½	½	½	x	1	1	**3½**
13	Jovanovic	0	0	½	0	0	0	0	0	0	0	0	0	x	1	**1½**
14	Matov	0	0	0	0	0	0	½	0	0	0	0	0	0	x	**½**

INTERNATIONAL TOURNAMENT 1970

Rovinj-Zagreb, Yugoslavia

		1	2	3	4	5	6	7	8	9	0	1	2	3	4	5	6	7	8	
1	Fischer	x	½	1	½	½	½	1	½	1	0	1	½	1	1	1	1	1	1	**13**
2	Hort	½	x	½	½	½	½	½	1	½	1	½	1	½	½	½	½	1	1	**11**
3	Gligoric	0	½	x	1	½	1	½	½	½	½	½	½	1	½	½	1	1	1	**11**
4	Smyslov	½	½	0	x	½	½	½	1	½	½	1	1	½	1	½	1	½	1	**11**
5	Korchnoi	½	½	½	½	x	½	0	1	0	1	½	1	½	1	1	½	1	1	**11**
6	Petrosian	½	½	0	½	½	x	½	½	½	1	½	1	½	½	1	½	1	1	**10½**
7	Minic	0	½	½	½	1	½	x	½	½	½	1	½	½	½	½	0	½	1	**9**
8	Ivkov	½	0	½	0	0	½	½	x	½	½	½	1	½	½	1	½	1	1	**9**
9	Bertok	0	½	½	½	1	½	½	½	x	0	½	½	½	½	½	½	½	1	**8½**
10	Kovacevic	1	0	½	½	0	0	½	½	1	x	1	0	½	½	½	½	1	½	**8½**
11	Uhlmann	0	½	½	0	½	½	0	½	½	0	x	1	1	1	½	1	1	0	**8½**
12	Browne	½	0	½	0	0	0	½	0	½	1	0	x	½	½	½	1	1	1	**7½**
13	Ghitescu	0	½	0	½	½	½	½	½	½	½	0	½	x	½	½	½	0	½	**6½**
14	Kurajica	0	½	½	0	0	½	½	½	½	½	0	½	½	x	½	½	½	½	**6½**
15	Parma	0	½	½	½	0	0	½	0	½	½	½	½	½	½	x	½	½	½	**6½**
16	Marovic	0	½	0	0	½	½	1	½	½	½	0	0	½	½	½	x	0	½	**6**
17	Udovcic	0	0	0	½	0	0	½	0	½	0	0	0	1	½	½	1	x	1	**5½**
18	Nicevski	0	0	0	0	0	0	0	0	0	½	1	0	½	½	½	½	0	x	**3½**

INTERNATIONAL TOURNAMENT 1970

Buenos Aires, Argentina

		1	2	3	4	5	6	7	8	9	0	1	2	3	4	5	6	7	8	
1	Fischer	x	1	1	1	½	½	½	½	1	1	1	1	1	1	1	1	1	1	**15**
2	Tukmakov	0	x	1	½	½	½	½	½	1	1	½	½	1	½	½	1	1	1	**11½**
3	Panno	0	0	x	½	½	½	½	1	½	1	1	½	1	1	½	1	1	½	**11**
4	Gheorghiu	0	½	½	x	½	½	½	½	½	1	½	1	½	1	1	½	½	1	**10½**
5	Najdorf	½	½	½	½	x	½	½	½	0	1	½	1	1	1	1	½	0	1	**10½**
6	Reshevsky	½	½	½	½	½	x	½	½	½	½	½	1	1	1	½	½	½	1	**10½**
7	Smyslov	½	½	½	½	½	½	x	½	½	½	½	½	1	½	½	½	½	½	**9**
8	Mecking	½	½	0	½	½	½	½	x	½	½	½	½	0	½	½	½	1	1	**8½**
9	Quinteros	0	0	½	½	1	½	½	½	x	0	½	1	0	½	½	½	1	1	**8½**
10	Damjanovic	0	0	0	0	0	½	½	½	1	x	½	½	½	½	1	1	½	1	**8**
11	O'Kelly	0	½	0	½	½	½	½	½	½	½	x	0	½	½	½	½	1	1	**8**
12	Bisguier	0	½	½	0	0	0	½	½	0	½	1	x	1	½	0	½	1	1	**7½**
13	Szabo	0	0	0	½	0	0	0	1	1	½	½	0	x	½	1	½	1	1	**7½**
14	Garcia	0	½	0	0	0	0	½	½	½	½	½	½	½	x	1	1	0	1	**7**
15	Rubinetti	0	½	½	0	0	½	½	½	½	0	½	1	0	0	x	½	½	1	**6½**
16	Rossetto	0	0	0	½	½	½	½	½	½	0	½	½	½	0	½	x	0	½	**5½**
17	Schweber	0	0	0	½	1	½	½	0	0	½	0	0	0	1	½	1	x	0	**5½**
18	Agdamus	0	0	½	0	0	0	½	0	0	0	0	0	0	0	0	½	1	x	**2½**

INTERZONAL TOURNAMENT 1970
Palma de Majorca, Spain

		1	2	3	4	5	6	7	8	9	0	1	2	3	4	5	6	7	8	9	0	1	2	3	4	
1	Fischer	x	0	1	½	1	1	½	1	½	1	1	1	1	1	1	1	1	½	1	1	½	½	1	½	**18½**
2	Larsen	1	x	½	½	0	1	½	½	½	½	1	1	0	½	½	1	½	1	½	1	1	½	1	½	**15**
3	Geller	0	½	x	1	½	1	½	1	½	½	½	1	½	½	1	½	1	½	½	½	1	1	½	½	**15**
4	Hübner	½	½	0	x	½	1	½	0	½	½	0	½	½	1	½	1	1	1	1	½	1	1	1	1	**15**
5	Taimanov	0	1	½	½	x	½	½	½	½	½	½	0	½	0	1	1	½	1	½	1	½	1	1	1	**14**
6	Uhlmann	0	0	0	0	½	x	1	½	½	1	½	½	1	½	0	1	½	1	1	½	1	1	1	1	**14**
7	Portisch	½	½	½	½	½	0	x	½	0	1	½	1	1	½	½	½	1	½	½	1	½	1	1	0	**13½**
8	Smyslov	0	½	0	1	½	½	½	x	1	½	½	0	½	½	½	½	½	½	1	1	½	1	1	1	**13½**
9	Polugayevsky	½	½	½	½	½	½	1	0	x	½	1	½	½	½	½	1	0	½	1	1	½	½	½	½	**13**
10	Gligoric	0	½	½	½	½	0	0	½	½	x	1	½	1	½	1	½	½	1	0	½	1	½	1	1	**13**
11	Panno	0	0	½	1	½	½	½	½	0	0	x	½	½	½	1	1	½	½	½	½	1	1	½	1	**12½**
12	Mecking	0	0	0	½	1	½	0	1	½	½	½	x	1	½	½	½	½	0	½	½	1	1	1	1	**12½**
13	Hort	0	1	½	½	½	0	0	½	½	0	½	0	x	1	½	1	½	½	½	½	1	½	1	½	**11½**
14	Ivkov	0	½	½	0	1	½	½	½	½	½	½	½	0	x	½	½	0	½	½	½	½	1	½	½	**10½**
15	Suttles	0	½	0	½	0	1	½	½	½	0	0	½	½	½	x	0	½	½	1	½	0	1	½	1	**10**
16	Minic	0	0	½	0	0	0	½	½	0	½	0	½	0	½	1	x	1	½	½	½	1	½	1	1	**10**
17	Reshevsky	0	½	0	0	½	½	0	½	1	½	½	½	½	1	½	0	x	½	½	½	0	0	½	1	**9½**
18	Matulovic	½	0	½	0	0	0	½	½	½	0	½	1	½	½	½	½	½	x	½	½	0	0	½	1	**9**
19	Addison	0	½	½	0	½	0	½	0	0	1	½	½	½	½	0	½	½	½	x	½	0	0	1	1	**9**
20	Filip	0	0	½	½	0	½	0	0	0	½	½	½	½	½	½	½	½	½	½	x	½	1	½	0	**8½**
21	Naranja	½	0	0	0	½	0	½	½	½	0	0	0	0	½	1	0	1	1	1	½	x	0	0	1	**8½**
22	Uitumen	½	½	0	0	0	0	0	0	½	½	0	0	½	0	0	½	1	1	1	0	1	x	1	½	**8½**
23	Rubinetti	0	0	½	0	0	0	0	0	½	0	½	0	0	½	½	0	½	½	0	½	1	0	x	1	**6**
24	Jimenez	½	½	½	0	0	0	1	0	½	0	0	0	½	½	0	0	0	0	0	1	0	½	0	x	**5½**

GENERAL INDEX

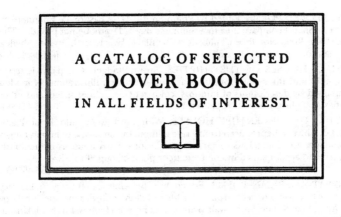

A CATALOG OF SELECTED
DOVER BOOKS
IN ALL FIELDS OF INTEREST

A CATALOG OF SELECTED DOVER BOOKS IN ALL FIELDS OF INTEREST

100 BEST-LOVED POEMS, Edited by Philip Smith. "The Passionate Shepherd to His Love," "Shall I compare thee to a summer's day?" "Death, be not proud," "The Raven," "The Road Not Taken," plus works by Blake, Wordsworth, Byron, Shelley, Keats, many others. 96pp. 5 3/16 x 8 1/4. 0-486-28553-7

100 SMALL HOUSES OF THE THIRTIES, Brown-Blodgett Company. Exterior photographs and floor plans for 100 charming structures. Illustrations of models accompanied by descriptions of interiors, color schemes, closet space, and other amenities. 200 illustrations. 112pp. 8 3/8 x 11. 0-486-44131-8

1000 TURN-OF-THE-CENTURY HOUSES: With Illustrations and Floor Plans, Herbert C. Chivers. Reproduced from a rare edition, this showcase of homes ranges from cottages and bungalows to sprawling mansions. Each house is meticulously illustrated and accompanied by complete floor plans. 256pp. 9 3/8 x 12 1/4. 0-486-45596-3

101 GREAT AMERICAN POEMS, Edited by The American Poetry & Literacy Project. Rich treasury of verse from the 19th and 20th centuries includes works by Edgar Allan Poe, Robert Frost, Walt Whitman, Langston Hughes, Emily Dickinson, T. S. Eliot, other notables. 96pp. 5 3/16 x 8 1/4. 0-486-40158-8

101 GREAT SAMURAI PRINTS, Utagawa Kuniyoshi. Kuniyoshi was a master of the warrior woodblock print — and these 18th-century illustrations represent the pinnacle of his craft. Full-color portraits of renowned Japanese samurais pulse with movement, passion, and remarkably fine detail. 112pp. 8 3/8 x 11. 0-486-46523-3

ABC OF BALLET, Janet Grosser. Clearly worded, abundantly illustrated little guide defines basic ballet-related terms: arabesque, battement, pas de chat, relevé, sissonne, many others. Pronunciation guide included. Excellent primer. 48pp. 4 3/16 x 5 3/4. 0-486-40871-X

ACCESSORIES OF DRESS: An Illustrated Encyclopedia, Katherine Lester and Bess Viola Oerke. Illustrations of hats, veils, wigs, cravats, shawls, shoes, gloves, and other accessories enhance an engaging commentary that reveals the humor and charm of the many-sided story of accessorized apparel. 644 figures and 59 plates. 608pp. 6 1/8 x 9 1/4. 0-486-43378-1

ADVENTURES OF HUCKLEBERRY FINN, Mark Twain. Join Huck and Jim as their boyhood adventures along the Mississippi River lead them into a world of excitement, danger, and self-discovery. Humorous narrative, lyrical descriptions of the Mississippi valley, and memorable characters. 224pp. 5 3/16 x 8 1/4. 0-486-28061-6

ALICE STARMORE'S BOOK OF FAIR ISLE KNITTING, Alice Starmore. A noted designer from the region of Scotland's Fair Isle explores the history and techniques of this distinctive, stranded-color knitting style and provides copious illustrated instructions for 14 original knitwear designs. 208pp. 8 3/8 x 10 7/8. 0-486-47218-3

Browse over 9,000 books at www.doverpublications.com

ALICE'S ADVENTURES IN WONDERLAND, Lewis Carroll. Beloved classic about a little girl lost in a topsy-turvy land and her encounters with the White Rabbit, March Hare, Mad Hatter, Cheshire Cat, and other delightfully improbable characters. 42 illustrations by Sir John Tenniel. 96pp. $5\frac{3}{16} \times 8\frac{1}{4}$. 0-486-27543-4

AMERICA'S LIGHTHOUSES: An Illustrated History, Francis Ross Holland. Profusely illustrated fact-filled survey of American lighthouses since 1716. Over 200 stations — East, Gulf, and West coasts, Great Lakes, Hawaii, Alaska, Puerto Rico, the Virgin Islands, and the Mississippi and St. Lawrence Rivers. 240pp. $8 \times 10\frac{3}{4}$. 0-486-25576-X

AN ENCYCLOPEDIA OF THE VIOLIN, Alberto Bachmann. Translated by Frederick H. Martens. Introduction by Eugene Ysaye. First published in 1925, this renowned reference remains unsurpassed as a source of essential information, from construction and evolution to repertoire and technique. Includes a glossary and 73 illustrations. 496pp. $6\frac{1}{8} \times 9\frac{1}{4}$. 0-486-46618-3

ANIMALS: 1,419 Copyright-Free Illustrations of Mammals, Birds, Fish, Insects, etc., Selected by Jim Harter. Selected for its visual impact and ease of use, this outstanding collection of wood engravings presents over 1,000 species of animals in extremely lifelike poses. Includes mammals, birds, reptiles, amphibians, fish, insects, and other invertebrates. 284pp. 9 x 12. 0-486-23766-4

THE ANNALS, Tacitus. Translated by Alfred John Church and William Jackson Brodribb. This vital chronicle of Imperial Rome, written by the era's great historian, spans A.D. 14-68 and paints incisive psychological portraits of major figures, from Tiberius to Nero. 416pp. $5\frac{3}{16} \times 8\frac{1}{4}$. 0-486-45236-0

ANTIGONE, Sophocles. Filled with passionate speeches and sensitive probing of moral and philosophical issues, this powerful and often-performed Greek drama reveals the grim fate that befalls the children of Oedipus. Footnotes. 64pp. $5\frac{3}{16} \times 8\frac{1}{4}$. 0-486-27804-2

ART DECO DECORATIVE PATTERNS IN FULL COLOR, Christian Stoll. Reprinted from a rare 1910 portfolio, 160 sensuous and exotic images depict a breathtaking array of florals, geometrics, and abstracts — all elegant in their stark simplicity. 64pp. $8\frac{3}{8} \times 11$. 0-486-44862-2

THE ARTHUR RACKHAM TREASURY: 86 Full-Color Illustrations, Arthur Rackham. Selected and Edited by Jeff A. Menges. A stunning treasury of 86 full-page plates span the famed English artist's career, from *Rip Van Winkle* (1905) to masterworks such as *Undine, A Midsummer Night's Dream,* and *Wind in the Willows* (1939). 96pp. $8\frac{3}{8} \times 11$. 0-486-44685-9

THE AUTHENTIC GILBERT & SULLIVAN SONGBOOK, W. S. Gilbert and A. S. Sullivan. The most comprehensive collection available, this songbook includes selections from every one of Gilbert and Sullivan's light operas. Ninety-two numbers are presented uncut and unedited, and in their original keys. 410pp. 9 x 12. 0-486-23482-7

THE AWAKENING, Kate Chopin. First published in 1899, this controversial novel of a New Orleans wife's search for love outside a stifling marriage shocked readers. Today, it remains a first-rate narrative with superb characterization. New introductory Note. 128pp. $5\frac{3}{16} \times 8\frac{1}{4}$. 0-486-27786-0

BASIC DRAWING, Louis Priscilla. Beginning with perspective, this commonsense manual progresses to the figure in movement, light and shade, anatomy, drapery, composition, trees and landscape, and outdoor sketching. Black-and-white illustrations throughout. 128pp. $8\frac{3}{8} \times 11$. 0-486-45815-6

THE BATTLES THAT CHANGED HISTORY, Fletcher Pratt. Historian profiles 16 crucial conflicts, ancient to modern, that changed the course of Western civilization. Gripping accounts of battles led by Alexander the Great, Joan of Arc, Ulysses S. Grant, other commanders. 27 maps. 352pp. 5⅜ x 8½. 0-486-41129-X

BEETHOVEN'S LETTERS, Ludwig van Beethoven. Edited by Dr. A. C. Kalischer. Features 457 letters to fellow musicians, friends, greats, patrons, and literary men. Reveals musical thoughts, quirks of personality, insights, and daily events. Includes 15 plates. 410pp. 5⅜ x 8½. 0-486-22769-3

BERNICE BOBS HER HAIR AND OTHER STORIES, F. Scott Fitzgerald. This brilliant anthology includes 6 of Fitzgerald's most popular stories: "The Diamond as Big as the Ritz," the title tale, "The Offshore Pirate," "The Ice Palace," "The Jelly Bean," and "May Day." 176pp. 5⅜ x 8½. 0-486-47049-0

BESLER'S BOOK OF FLOWERS AND PLANTS: 73 Full-Color Plates from Hortus Eystettensis, 1613, Basilius Besler. Here is a selection of magnificent plates from the *Hortus Eystettensis,* which vividly illustrated and identified the plants, flowers, and trees that thrived in the legendary German garden at Eichstätt. 80pp. 8⅜ x 11. 0-486-46005-3

THE BOOK OF KELLS, Edited by Blanche Cirker. Painstakingly reproduced from a rare facsimile edition, this volume contains full-page decorations, portraits, illustrations, plus a sampling of textual leaves with exquisite calligraphy and ornamentation. 32 full-color illustrations. 32pp. 9⅜ x 12¼. 0-486-24345-1

THE BOOK OF THE CROSSBOW: With an Additional Section on Catapults and Other Siege Engines, Ralph Payne-Gallwey. Fascinating study traces history and use of crossbow as military and sporting weapon, from Middle Ages to modern times. Also covers related weapons: balistas, catapults, Turkish bows, more. Over 240 illustrations. 400pp. 7¼ x 10⅛. 0-486-28720-3

THE BUNGALOW BOOK: Floor Plans and Photos of 112 Houses, 1910, Henry L. Wilson. Here are 112 of the most popular and economic blueprints of the early 20th century — plus an illustration or photograph of each completed house. A wonderful time capsule that still offers a wealth of valuable insights. 160pp. 8⅜ x 11. 0-486-45104-6

THE CALL OF THE WILD, Jack London. A classic novel of adventure, drawn from London's own experiences as a Klondike adventurer, relating the story of a heroic dog caught in the brutal life of the Alaska Gold Rush. Note. 64pp. 5³⁄₁₆ x 8¼. 0-486-26472-6

CANDIDE, Voltaire. Edited by Francois-Marie Arouet. One of the world's great satires since its first publication in 1759. Witty, caustic skewering of romance, science, philosophy, religion, government — nearly all human ideals and institutions. 112pp. 5³⁄₁₆ x 8¼. 0-486-26689-3

CELEBRATED IN THEIR TIME: Photographic Portraits from the George Grantham Bain Collection, Edited by Amy Pastan. With an Introduction by Michael Carlebach. Remarkable portrait gallery features 112 rare images of Albert Einstein, Charlie Chaplin, the Wright Brothers, Henry Ford, and other luminaries from the worlds of politics, art, entertainment, and industry. 128pp. 8⅜ x 11. 0-486-46754-6

CHARIOTS FOR APOLLO: The NASA History of Manned Lunar Spacecraft to 1969, Courtney G. Brooks, James M. Grimwood, and Loyd S. Swenson, Jr. This illustrated history by a trio of experts is the definitive reference on the Apollo spacecraft and lunar modules. It traces the vehicles' design, development, and operation in space. More than 100 photographs and illustrations. 576pp. 6¾ x 9¼. 0-486-46756-2

Browse over 9,000 books at www.doverpublications.com

A CHRISTMAS CAROL, Charles Dickens. This engrossing tale relates Ebenezer Scrooge's ghostly journeys through Christmases past, present, and future and his ultimate transformation from a harsh and grasping old miser to a charitable and compassionate human being. 80pp. 5³⁄₁₆ x 8¼.   0-486-26865-9

COMMON SENSE, Thomas Paine. First published in January of 1776, this highly influential landmark document clearly and persuasively argued for American separation from Great Britain and paved the way for the Declaration of Independence. 64pp. 5³⁄₁₆ x 8¼.   0-486-29602-4

THE COMPLETE SHORT STORIES OF OSCAR WILDE, Oscar Wilde. Complete texts of "The Happy Prince and Other Tales," "A House of Pomegranates," "Lord Arthur Savile's Crime and Other Stories," "Poems in Prose," and "The Portrait of Mr. W. H." 208pp. 5³⁄₁₆ x 8¼.   0-486-45216-6

COMPLETE SONNETS, William Shakespeare. Over 150 exquisite poems deal with love, friendship, the tyranny of time, beauty's evanescence, death, and other themes in language of remarkable power, precision, and beauty. Glossary of archaic terms. 80pp. 5³⁄₁₆ x 8¼.   0-486-26686-9

THE COUNT OF MONTE CRISTO: Abridged Edition, Alexandre Dumas. Falsely accused of treason, Edmond Dantès is imprisoned in the bleak Chateau d'If. After a hair-raising escape, he launches an elaborate plot to extract a bitter revenge against those who betrayed him. 448pp. 5³⁄₁₆ x 8¼.   0-486-45643-9

CRAFTSMAN BUNGALOWS: Designs from the Pacific Northwest, Yoho & Merritt. This reprint of a rare catalog, showcasing the charming simplicity and cozy style of Craftsman bungalows, is filled with photos of completed homes, plus floor plans and estimated costs. An indispensable resource for architects, historians, and illustrators. 112pp. 10 x 7.   0-486-46875-5

CRAFTSMAN BUNGALOWS: 59 Homes from "The Craftsman," Edited by Gustav Stickley. Best and most attractive designs from Arts and Crafts Movement publication — 1903–1916 — includes sketches, photographs of homes, floor plans, descriptive text. 128pp. 8¼ x 11.   0-486-25829-7

CRIME AND PUNISHMENT, Fyodor Dostoyevsky. Translated by Constance Garnett. Supreme masterpiece tells the story of Raskolnikov, a student tormented by his own thoughts after he murders an old woman. Overwhelmed by guilt and terror, he confesses and goes to prison. 480pp. 5³⁄₁₆ x 8¼.   0-486-41587-2

THE DECLARATION OF INDEPENDENCE AND OTHER GREAT DOCUMENTS OF AMERICAN HISTORY: 1775-1865, Edited by John Grafton. Thirteen compelling and influential documents: Henry's "Give Me Liberty or Give Me Death," Declaration of Independence, The Constitution, Washington's First Inaugural Address, The Monroe Doctrine, The Emancipation Proclamation, Gettysburg Address, more. 64pp. 5³⁄₁₆ x 8¼.   0-486-41124-9

THE DESERT AND THE SOWN: Travels in Palestine and Syria, Gertrude Bell. "The female Lawrence of Arabia," Gertrude Bell wrote captivating, perceptive accounts of her travels in the Middle East. This intriguing narrative, accompanied by 160 photos, traces her 1905 sojourn in Lebanon, Syria, and Palestine. 368pp. 5⅜ x 8½.   0-486-46876-3

A DOLL'S HOUSE, Henrik Ibsen. Ibsen's best-known play displays his genius for realistic prose drama. An expression of women's rights, the play climaxes when the central character, Nora, rejects a smothering marriage and life in "a doll's house." 80pp. 5³⁄₁₆ x 8¼.   0-486-27062-9

Browse over 9,000 books at www.doverpublications.com

THE BATTLES THAT CHANGED HISTORY, Fletcher Pratt. Historian profiles 16 crucial conflicts, ancient to modern, that changed the course of Western civilization. Gripping accounts of battles led by Alexander the Great, Joan of Arc, Ulysses S. Grant, other commanders. 27 maps. 352pp. 5⅜ x 8½. 0-486-41129-X

BEETHOVEN'S LETTERS, Ludwig van Beethoven. Edited by Dr. A. C. Kalischer. Features 457 letters to fellow musicians, friends, greats, patrons, and literary men. Reveals musical thoughts, quirks of personality, insights, and daily events. Includes 15 plates. 410pp. 5⅜ x 8½. 0-486-22769-3

BERNICE BOBS HER HAIR AND OTHER STORIES, F. Scott Fitzgerald. This brilliant anthology includes 6 of Fitzgerald's most popular stories: "The Diamond as Big as the Ritz," the title tale, "The Offshore Pirate," "The Ice Palace," "The Jelly Bean," and "May Day." 176pp. 5⅜ x 8½. 0-486-47049-0

BESLER'S BOOK OF FLOWERS AND PLANTS: 73 Full-Color Plates from Hortus Eystettensis, 1613, Basilius Besler. Here is a selection of magnificent plates from the *Hortus Eystettensis,* which vividly illustrated and identified the plants, flowers, and trees that thrived in the legendary German garden at Eichstätt. 80pp. 8⅜ x 11.
0-486-46005-3

THE BOOK OF KELLS, Edited by Blanche Cirker. Painstakingly reproduced from a rare facsimile edition, this volume contains full-page decorations, portraits, illustrations, plus a sampling of textual leaves with exquisite calligraphy and ornamentation. 32 full-color illustrations. 32pp. 9⅜ x 12¼. 0-486-24345-1

THE BOOK OF THE CROSSBOW: With an Additional Section on Catapults and Other Siege Engines, Ralph Payne-Gallwey. Fascinating study traces history and use of crossbow as military and sporting weapon, from Middle Ages to modern times. Also covers related weapons: balistas, catapults, Turkish bows, more. Over 240 illustrations. 400pp. 7¼ x 10⅛. 0-486-28720-3

THE BUNGALOW BOOK: Floor Plans and Photos of 112 Houses, 1910, Henry L. Wilson. Here are 112 of the most popular and economic blueprints of the early 20th century — plus an illustration or photograph of each completed house. A wonderful time capsule that still offers a wealth of valuable insights. 160pp. 8⅜ x 11.
0-486-45104-6

THE CALL OF THE WILD, Jack London. A classic novel of adventure, drawn from London's own experiences as a Klondike adventurer, relating the story of a heroic dog caught in the brutal life of the Alaska Gold Rush. Note. 64pp. 5³⁄₁₆ x 8¼.
0-486-26472-6

CANDIDE, Voltaire. Edited by Francois-Marie Arouet. One of the world's great satires since its first publication in 1759. Witty, caustic skewering of romance, science, philosophy, religion, government — nearly all human ideals and institutions. 112pp. 5³⁄₁₆ x 8¼. 0-486-26689-3

CELEBRATED IN THEIR TIME: Photographic Portraits from the George Grantham Bain Collection, Edited by Amy Pastan. With an Introduction by Michael Carlebach. Remarkable portrait gallery features 112 rare images of Albert Einstein, Charlie Chaplin, the Wright Brothers, Henry Ford, and other luminaries from the worlds of politics, art, entertainment, and industry. 128pp. 8⅜ x 11. 0-486-46754-6

CHARIOTS FOR APOLLO: The NASA History of Manned Lunar Spacecraft to 1969, Courtney G. Brooks, James M. Grimwood, and Loyd S. Swenson, Jr. This illustrated history by a trio of experts is the definitive reference on the Apollo spacecraft and lunar modules. It traces the vehicles' design, development, and operation in space. More than 100 photographs and illustrations. 576pp. 6¾ x 9¼. 0-486-46756-2

AN ENCYCLOPEDIA OF BATTLES: Accounts of Over 1,560 Battles from 1479 B.C. to the Present, David Eggenberger. Essential details of every major battle in recorded history from the first battle of Megiddo in 1479 B.C. to Grenada in 1984. List of battle maps. 99 illustrations. 544pp. 6½ x 9¼. 0-486-24913-1

ENCYCLOPEDIA OF EMBROIDERY STITCHES, INCLUDING CREWEL, Marion Nichols. Precise explanations and instructions, clearly illustrated, on how to work chain, back, cross, knotted, woven stitches, and many more — 178 in all, including Cable Outline, Whipped Satin, and Eyelet Buttonhole. Over 1400 illustrations. 219pp. 8⅝ x 11¼. 0-486-22929-7

ENTER JEEVES: 15 Early Stories, P. G. Wodehouse. Splendid collection contains first 8 stories featuring Bertie Wooster, the deliciously dim aristocrat and Jeeves, his brainy, imperturbable manservant. Also, the complete Reggie Pepper (Bertie's prototype) series. 288pp. 5⅜ x 8½. 0-486-29717-9

ERIC SLOANE'S AMERICA: Paintings in Oil, Michael Wigley. With a Foreword by Mimi Sloane. Eric Sloane's evocative oils of America's landscape and material culture shimmer with immense historical and nostalgic appeal. This original hardcover collection gathers nearly a hundred of his finest paintings, with subjects ranging from New England to the American Southwest. 128pp. 10⅝ x 9. 0-486-46525-X

ETHAN FROME, Edith Wharton. Classic story of wasted lives, set against a bleak New England background. Superbly delineated characters in a hauntingly grim tale of thwarted love. Considered by many to be Wharton's masterpiece. 96pp. 5³⁄₁₆ x 8 ¼. 0-486-26690-7

THE EVERLASTING MAN, G. K. Chesterton. Chesterton's view of Christianity — as a blend of philosophy and mythology, satisfying intellect and spirit — applies to his brilliant book, which appeals to readers' heads as well as their hearts. 288pp. 5⅜ x 8½. 0-486-46036-3

THE FIELD AND FOREST HANDY BOOK, Daniel Beard. Written by a co-founder of the Boy Scouts, this appealing guide offers illustrated instructions for building kites, birdhouses, boats, igloos, and other fun projects, plus numerous helpful tips for campers. 448pp. 5³⁄₁₆ x 8¼. 0-486-46191-2

FINDING YOUR WAY WITHOUT MAP OR COMPASS, Harold Gatty. Useful, instructive manual shows would-be explorers, hikers, bikers, scouts, sailors, and survivalists how to find their way outdoors by observing animals, weather patterns, shifting sands, and other elements of nature. 288pp. 5⅜ x 8½. 0-486-40613-X

FIRST FRENCH READER: A Beginner's Dual-Language Book, Edited and Translated by Stanley Appelbaum. This anthology introduces 50 legendary writers — Voltaire, Balzac, Baudelaire, Proust, more — through passages from *The Red and the Black, Les Misérables, Madame Bovary,* and other classics. Original French text plus English translation on facing pages. 240pp. 5⅜ x 8½. 0-486-46178-5

FIRST GERMAN READER: A Beginner's Dual-Language Book, Edited by Harry Steinhauer. Specially chosen for their power to evoke German life and culture, these short, simple readings include poems, stories, essays, and anecdotes by Goethe, Hesse, Heine, Schiller, and others. 224pp. 5⅜ x 8½. 0-486-46179-3

FIRST SPANISH READER: A Beginner's Dual-Language Book, Angel Flores. Delightful stories, other material based on works of Don Juan Manuel, Luis Taboada, Ricardo Palma, other noted writers. Complete faithful English translations on facing pages. Exercises. 176pp. 5⅜ x 8½. 0-486-25810-6

Browse over 9,000 books at www.doverpublications.com

FIVE ACRES AND INDEPENDENCE, Maurice G. Kains. Great back-to-the-land classic explains basics of self-sufficient farming. The one book to get. 95 illustrations. 397pp. 5⅜ x 8½. 0-486-20974-1

FLAGG'S SMALL HOUSES: Their Economic Design and Construction, 1922, Ernest Flagg. Although most famous for his skyscrapers, Flagg was also a proponent of the well-designed single-family dwelling. His classic treatise features innovations that save space, materials, and cost. 526 illustrations. 160pp. 9⅜ x 12¼.
0-486-45197-6

FLATLAND: A Romance of Many Dimensions, Edwin A. Abbott. Classic of science (and mathematical) fiction — charmingly illustrated by the author — describes the adventures of A. Square, a resident of Flatland, in Spaceland (three dimensions), Lineland (one dimension), and Pointland (no dimensions). 96pp. 5³⁄₁₆ x 8¼.
0-486-27263-X

FRANKENSTEIN, Mary Shelley. The story of Victor Frankenstein's monstrous creation and the havoc it caused has enthralled generations of readers and inspired countless writers of horror and suspense. With the author's own 1831 introduction. 176pp. 5³⁄₁₆ x 8¼. 0-486-28211-2

THE GARGOYLE BOOK: 572 Examples from Gothic Architecture, Lester Burbank Bridaham. Dispelling the conventional wisdom that French Gothic architectural flourishes were born of despair or gloom, Bridaham reveals the whimsical nature of these creations and the ingenious artisans who made them. 572 illustrations. 224pp. 8⅜ x 11. 0-486-44754-5

THE GIFT OF THE MAGI AND OTHER SHORT STORIES, O. Henry. Sixteen captivating stories by one of America's most popular storytellers. Included are such classics as "The Gift of the Magi," "The Last Leaf," and "The Ransom of Red Chief." Publisher's Note. 96pp. 5³⁄₁₆ x 8¼. 0-486-27061-0

THE GOETHE TREASURY: Selected Prose and Poetry, Johann Wolfgang von Goethe. Edited, Selected, and with an Introduction by Thomas Mann. In addition to his lyric poetry, Goethe wrote travel sketches, autobiographical studies, essays, letters, and proverbs in rhyme and prose. This collection presents outstanding examples from each genre. 368pp. 5⅜ x 8½. 0-486-44780-4

GREAT EXPECTATIONS, Charles Dickens. Orphaned Pip is apprenticed to the dirty work of the forge but dreams of becoming a gentleman — and one day finds himself in possession of "great expectations." Dickens' finest novel. 400pp. 5³⁄₁₆ x 8¼.
0-486-41586-4

GREAT WRITERS ON THE ART OF FICTION: From Mark Twain to Joyce Carol Oates, Edited by James Daley. An indispensable source of advice and inspiration, this anthology features essays by Henry James, Kate Chopin, Willa Cather, Sinclair Lewis, Jack London, Raymond Chandler, Raymond Carver, Eudora Welty, and Kurt Vonnegut, Jr. 192pp. 5⅜ x 8½. 0-486-45128-3

HAMLET, William Shakespeare. The quintessential Shakespearean tragedy, whose highly charged confrontations and anguished soliloquies probe depths of human feeling rarely sounded in any art. Reprinted from an authoritative British edition complete with illuminating footnotes. 128pp. 5³⁄₁₆ x 8¼. 0-486-27278-8

THE HAUNTED HOUSE, Charles Dickens. A Yuletide gathering in an eerie country retreat provides the backdrop for Dickens and his friends — including Elizabeth Gaskell and Wilkie Collins — who take turns spinning supernatural yarns. 144pp. 5⅜ x 8½. 0-486-46309-5

Browse over 9,000 books at www.doverpublications.com

HEART OF DARKNESS, Joseph Conrad. Dark allegory of a journey up the Congo River and the narrator's encounter with the mysterious Mr. Kurtz. Masterly blend of adventure, character study, psychological penetration. For many, Conrad's finest, most enigmatic story. 80pp. 5³⁄₁₆ x 8¼.　　　　　0-486-26464-5

HENSON AT THE NORTH POLE, Matthew A. Henson. This thrilling memoir by the heroic African-American who was Peary's companion through two decades of Arctic exploration recounts a tale of danger, courage, and determination. "Fascinating and exciting." — *Commonweal.* 128pp. 5⅜ x 8½.　　　　　0-486-45472-X

HISTORIC COSTUMES AND HOW TO MAKE THEM, Mary Fernald and E. Shenton. Practical, informative guidebook shows how to create everything from short tunics worn by Saxon men in the fifth century to a lady's bustle dress of the late 1800s. 81 illustrations. 176pp. 5⅜ x 8½.　　　　　0-486-44906-8

THE HOUND OF THE BASKERVILLES, Arthur Conan Doyle. A deadly curse in the form of a legendary ferocious beast continues to claim its victims from the Baskerville family until Holmes and Watson intervene. Often called the best detective story ever written. 128pp. 5³⁄₁₆ x 8¼.　　　　　0-486-28214-7

THE HOUSE BEHIND THE CEDARS, Charles W. Chesnutt. Originally published in 1900, this groundbreaking novel by a distinguished African-American author recounts the drama of a brother and sister who "pass for white" during the dangerous days of Reconstruction. 208pp. 5⅜ x 8½.　　　　　0-486-46144-0

THE HUMAN FIGURE IN MOTION, Eadweard Muybridge. The 4,789 photographs in this definitive selection show the human figure — models almost all undraped — engaged in over 160 different types of action: running, climbing stairs, etc. 390pp. 7⅞ x 10⅝.　　　　　0-486-20204-6

THE IMPORTANCE OF BEING EARNEST, Oscar Wilde. Wilde's witty and buoyant comedy of manners, filled with some of literature's most famous epigrams, reprinted from an authoritative British edition. Considered Wilde's most perfect work. 64pp. 5³⁄₁₆ x 8¼.　　　　　0-486-26478-5

THE INFERNO, Dante Alighieri. Translated and with notes by Henry Wadsworth Longfellow. The first stop on Dante's famous journey from Hell to Purgatory to Paradise, this 14th-century allegorical poem blends vivid and shocking imagery with graceful lyricism. Translated by the beloved 19th-century poet, Henry Wadsworth Longfellow. 256pp. 5³⁄₁₆ x 8¼.　　　　　0-486-44288-8

JANE EYRE, Charlotte Brontë. Written in 1847, *Jane Eyre* tells the tale of an orphan girl's progress from the custody of cruel relatives to an oppressive boarding school and its culmination in a troubled career as a governess. 448pp. 5³⁄₁₆ x 8¼.

0-486-42449-9

JAPANESE WOODBLOCK FLOWER PRINTS, Tanigami Kônan. Extraordinary collection of Japanese woodblock prints by a well-known artist features 120 plates in brilliant color. Realistic images from a rare edition include daffodils, tulips, and other familiar and unusual flowers. 128pp. 11 x 8¼.　　　　　0-486-46442-3

JEWELRY MAKING AND DESIGN, Augustus F. Rose and Antonio Cirino. Professional secrets of jewelry making are revealed in a thorough, practical guide. Over 200 illustrations. 306pp. 5⅜ x 8½.　　　　　0-486-21750-7

JULIUS CAESAR, William Shakespeare. Great tragedy based on Plutarch's account of the lives of Brutus, Julius Caesar and Mark Antony. Evil plotting, ringing oratory, high tragedy with Shakespeare's incomparable insight, dramatic power. Explanatory footnotes. 96pp. 5³⁄₁₆ x 8¼.　　　　　0-486-26876-4

THE JUNGLE, Upton Sinclair. 1906 bestseller shockingly reveals intolerable labor practices and working conditions in the Chicago stockyards as it tells the grim story of a Slavic family that emigrates to America full of optimism but soon faces despair. 320pp. 5³⁄₁₆ x 8¼. 0-486-41923-1

THE KINGDOM OF GOD IS WITHIN YOU, Leo Tolstoy. The soul-searching book that inspired Gandhi to embrace the concept of passive resistance, Tolstoy's 1894 polemic clearly outlines a radical, well-reasoned revision of traditional Christian thinking. 352pp. 5³⁄₁₆ x 8¼. 0-486-45138-0

THE LADY OR THE TIGER?: and Other Logic Puzzles, Raymond M. Smullyan. Created by a renowned puzzle master, these whimsically themed challenges involve paradoxes about probability, time, and change; metapuzzles; and self-referentiality. Nineteen chapters advance in difficulty from relatively simple to highly complex. 1982 edition. 240pp. 5⅜ x 8½. 0-486-47027-X

LEAVES OF GRASS: The Original 1855 Edition, Walt Whitman. Whitman's immortal collection includes some of the greatest poems of modern times, including his masterpiece, "Song of Myself." Shattering standard conventions, it stands as an unabashed celebration of body and nature. 128pp. 5³⁄₁₆ x 8¼. 0-486-45676-5

LES MISÉRABLES, Victor Hugo. Translated by Charles E. Wilbour. Abridged by James K. Robinson. A convict's heroic struggle for justice and redemption plays out against a fiery backdrop of the Napoleonic wars. This edition features the excellent original translation and a sensitive abridgment. 304pp. 6⅛ x 9¼.
0-486-45789-3

LILITH: A Romance, George MacDonald. In this novel by the father of fantasy literature, a man travels through time to meet Adam and Eve and to explore humanity's fall from grace and ultimate redemption. 240pp. 5⅜ x 8½.
0-486-46818-6

THE LOST LANGUAGE OF SYMBOLISM, Harold Bayley. This remarkable book reveals the hidden meaning behind familiar images and words, from the origins of Santa Claus to the fleur-de-lys, drawing from mythology, folklore, religious texts, and fairy tales. 1,418 illustrations. 784pp. 5⅜ x 8½. 0-486-44787-1

MACBETH, William Shakespeare. A Scottish nobleman murders the king in order to succeed to the throne. Tortured by his conscience and fearful of discovery, he becomes tangled in a web of treachery and deceit that ultimately spells his doom. 96pp. 5³⁄₁₆ x 8¼. 0-486-27802-6

MAKING AUTHENTIC CRAFTSMAN FURNITURE: Instructions and Plans for 62 Projects, Gustav Stickley. Make authentic reproductions of handsome, functional, durable furniture: tables, chairs, wall cabinets, desks, a hall tree, and more. Construction plans with drawings, schematics, dimensions, and lumber specs reprinted from 1900s The Craftsman magazine. 128pp. 8⅛ x 11. 0-486-25000-8

MATHEMATICS FOR THE NONMATHEMATICIAN, Morris Kline. Erudite and entertaining overview follows development of mathematics from ancient Greeks to present. Topics include logic and mathematics, the fundamental concept, differential calculus, probability theory, much more. Exercises and problems. 641pp. 5⅜ x 8½. 0-486-24823-2

MEMOIRS OF AN ARABIAN PRINCESS FROM ZANZIBAR, Emily Ruete. This 19th-century autobiography offers a rare inside look at the society surrounding a sultan's palace. A real-life princess in exile recalls her vanished world of harems, slave trading, and court intrigues. 288pp. 5⅜ x 8½. 0-486-47121-7

Browse over 9,000 books at www.doverpublications.com

THE METAMORPHOSIS AND OTHER STORIES, Franz Kafka. Excellent new English translations of title story (considered by many critics Kafka's most perfect work), plus "The Judgment," "In the Penal Colony," "A Country Doctor," and "A Report to an Academy." Note. 96pp. 5³⁄₁₆ x 8¼. 0-486-29030-1

MICROSCOPIC ART FORMS FROM THE PLANT WORLD, R. Anheisser. From undulating curves to complex geometrics, a world of fascinating images abound in this classic, illustrated survey of microscopic plants. Features 400 detailed illustrations of nature's minute but magnificent handiwork. The accompanying CD-ROM includes all of the images in the book. 128pp. 9 x 9. 0-486-46013-4

A MIDSUMMER NIGHT'S DREAM, William Shakespeare. Among the most popular of Shakespeare's comedies, this enchanting play humorously celebrates the vagaries of love as it focuses upon the intertwined romances of several pairs of lovers. Explanatory footnotes. 80pp. 5³⁄₁₆ x 8¼. 0-486-27067-X

THE MONEY CHANGERS, Upton Sinclair. Originally published in 1908, this cautionary novel from the author of *The Jungle* explores corruption within the American system as a group of power brokers joins forces for personal gain, triggering a crash on Wall Street. 192pp. 5⅜ x 8½. 0-486-46917-4

THE MOST POPULAR HOMES OF THE TWENTIES, William A. Radford. With a New Introduction by Daniel D. Reiff. Based on a rare 1925 catalog, this architectural showcase features floor plans, construction details, and photos of 26 homes, plus articles on entrances, porches, garages, and more. 250 illustrations, 21 color plates. 176pp. 8⅜ x 11. 0-486-47028-8

MY 66 YEARS IN THE BIG LEAGUES, Connie Mack. With a New Introduction by Rich Westcott. A Founding Father of modern baseball, Mack holds the record for most wins — and losses — by a major league manager. Enhanced by 70 photographs, his warmhearted autobiography is populated by many legends of the game. 288pp. 5⅜ x 8½. 0-486-47184-5

NARRATIVE OF THE LIFE OF FREDERICK DOUGLASS, Frederick Douglass. Douglass's graphic depictions of slavery, harrowing escape to freedom, and life as a newspaper editor, eloquent orator, and impassioned abolitionist. 96pp. 5³⁄₁₆ x 8¼. 0-486-28499-9

THE NIGHTLESS CITY: Geisha and Courtesan Life in Old Tokyo, J. E. de Becker. This unsurpassed study from 100 years ago ventured into Tokyo's red-light district to survey geisha and courtesan life and offer meticulous descriptions of training, dress, social hierarchy, and erotic practices. 49 black-and-white illustrations; 2 maps. 496pp. 5⅜ x 8½. 0-486-45563-7

THE ODYSSEY, Homer. Excellent prose translation of ancient epic recounts adventures of the homeward-bound Odysseus. Fantastic cast of gods, giants, cannibals, sirens, other supernatural creatures — true classic of Western literature. 256pp. 5³⁄₁₆ x 8¼. 0-486-40654-7

OEDIPUS REX, Sophocles. Landmark of Western drama concerns the catastrophe that ensues when King Oedipus discovers he has inadvertently killed his father and married his mother. Masterly construction, dramatic irony. Explanatory footnotes. 64pp. 5³⁄₁₆ x 8¼. 0-486-26877-2

ONCE UPON A TIME: The Way America Was, Eric Sloane. Nostalgic text and drawings brim with gentle philosophies and descriptions of how we used to live — self-sufficiently — on the land, in homes, and among the things built by hand. 44 line illustrations. 64pp. 8⅜ x 11. 0-486-44411-2

Browse over 9,000 books at www.doverpublications.com